# Business Research Methods

## Second European Edition

# Boris Blumberg, Donald R. Cooper and Pamela S. Schindler

**McGraw-Hill**
**Higher Education**

**London**  Boston  Burr Ridge, IL  Dubuque, IA  Madison, WI  New York  San Francisco
St. Louis  Bangkok  Bogotá  Caracas  Kuala Lumpur  Lisbon  Madrid  Mexico City
Milan  Montreal  New Delhi  Santiago  Seoul  Singapore  Sydney  Taipei  Toronto

*Business Research Methods, second European edition*
Boris Blumberg, Donald R. Cooper and Pamela S. Schindler
ISBN-13 978–0-07–711745–0
ISBN-10 0–07–711745-X

# McGraw-Hill
# Higher Education

Published by McGraw-Hill Education
Shoppenhangers Road
Maidenhead
Berkshire
SL6 2QL
Telephone: 44 (0) 1628 502 500
Fax: 44 (0) 1628 770 224
Website: www.mcgraw-hill.co.uk

**British Library Cataloguing in Publication Data**
A catalogue record for this book is available from the British Library

**Library of Congress Cataloguing in Publication Data**
The Library of Congress data for this book has been applied for from the Library of Congress

New Editions Editor: Catriona Watson
Development Editor: Karen Harlow
Marketing Manager: Mark Barratt
Senior Production Editor: James Bishop

Cover design by ego creative
Printed and bound in Singapore by Markono Print Media Pte Ltd

First Edition published in 2005 by McGraw-Hill Education

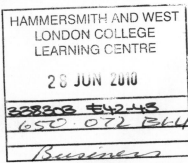

The *McGraw-Hill* Companies

**Dedicated to my two daughters Antonie and Hermine**

Because both keep asking 'why' questions

# Brief table of contents

\* Free with every copy of *Business Research Methods*

# Detailed table of contents

The first European edition of this book was very well received and this second edition has been designed to build on its successes. It keeps the successful features of the first edition, such as:

**A good balance of quantitative and qualitative methods** acknowledging that both approaches help us to better understand business phenomena.

**A student-focused pedagogic approach** examining student and academic research and helping students to design and conduct research for assignments and theses.

The usage of **European and international examples**, which are most relevant to real-life experience.

**An accompanying CD-ROM containing five complete chapters on data analysis**. This acknowledges that research and analysis methods are highly interwoven and allows the book to be used on both courses that focus on research methods and courses that combine both.

**The inclusion of different types of questions** at the end of each chapter. There are questions to support the student in checking whether they have grasped the knowledge presented, questions which ask the students to apply their knowledge and questions which address the trade-offs that many research decisions involve.

**An accompanying website that offers additional resources for students and instructors** including:

- **NEW** EZTest – an online testbank containing hundreds of questions, in both multiple choice and short answer format, enabling lecturers to easily create the perfect tests for their courses.
- **NEW** Student Skills Centre – contains bonus resources, including an interactive research guide, to help get students started with a research project.

Based on my and my students' experience with the first edition as well as useful comments by other users of the book and reviewers, the following changes were made:

- A running case study, Research Methods in Practice, that continues from chapter to chapter to show how the issues discussed in each chapter play a role in a real research project.
- A new chapter covering case study research and qualitative, semi-structured interviews.
- The chapter on research proposals now contains an example of a well-written proposal.
- The former chapter on observation and action research has been extended with sub-sections on content analysis and narrative analysis.
- The chapters on literature review, sampling, and survey research discuss the use of the Internet to conduct research more deeply, reflecting recent developments.
- The chapter on writing up and presenting research outcomes now gives practical guidelines on how to motivate a piece of research, how to integrate literature in the theory section and how to present limitations.

- The order of the chapters has been changed to fit better with the structure of many courses.
- Boxes have been updated to include more recent examples.

## Pedagogical features

Each chapter starts with clear **learning objectives** and concludes with a **summary** which highlights the important aspects of each chapter. All chapters are complemented by many real-life examples that show students how research methods may be applied in practice. These examples enable students to see how each of the research methods topics applies to business situations.

The **running case study, Research Methods in Practice**, which features in each chapter shows how issues discussed in the chapters play a role in a real research project.

The **end of chapter questions** will help students gauge their understanding of the core chapter concepts. These questions are pitched at different levels, both for individual study and class discussion.

The book also features a separate 'Cases' section that presents six diverse case studies, along with questions suitable for individual or group work. These cases offer a more detailed example of research methods relating directly to business scenarios that complement the examples given in the chapters.

A CD-ROM containing additional chapters on data analysis and the data files referred to in the text accompanies the book. These supplementary chapters can be used by students for additional study or by those students taking courses where a more quantitative approach is taken.

The book and CD-ROM are also supported by an Online Learning Centre featuring supplementary material that includes a selection of cases, and both tutor and student downloads. For more details see page xiv.

# Guided tour

## Learning objectives

Each chapter opens with a set of Learning Objectives, introducing the reader to the topics they should come to understand after having worked through each chapter.

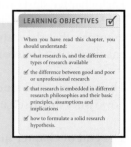

LEARNING OBJECTIVES ☑

When you have read this chapter, you should understand:

☑ what research is, and the different types of research available

☑ the difference between good and poor or unprofessional research

☑ that research is embedded in different research philosophies and their basic principles, assumptions and implications

☑ how to formulate a solid research hypothesis.

## Key terms

These are highlighted in bold throughout each chapter and defined in a glossary which can be found on the Online Learning Centre associated with this book.
*www.mcgraw-hill.co.uk/textbooks/blumberg*

models that demonstrate how to conduct
The study of research methods will p
solve the problems and meet the challeng
ness research may be defined as a systema
tion that will allow managerial problems
students preparing to manage business,
tional areas – need training in a discipli
solve a research or management dilem
management decision). Three factors hav
decision-making:

1 the need for more and better informa
2 the availability of improved techniqu
3 the resulting information overload if

The past two decades have seen dramatic
what is, historically, an economic role, th

## Snapshots

Each chapter features these varied and pertinent snapshots of research, to offer succinct illustrations of different kinds of research work.

Snapshot

**Research and the val responsibility**

Consumer magazines, such as *Wh* Netherlands, have a significant im panies whose products have receive these products from the market. Li used in advertising to emphasize t independent consumer organizatio into different categories, such as tec

Since 2002, consumer organi responsibility as an additional research director of Stiftung War decision to include ethical criteri these social and environmental i Stiftung Warentest addresses them

Most consumer magazines st consumers. Rob Harrison, the ed

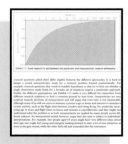

Exhibit 1.1 Good research in and between the positivist and interpretivistic research philosophy.

## Exhibits

A number of exhibits are provided in each chapter to help the reader visualise the various research models, and to illustrate and summarise important concepts.

## Summary

Positioned at the end of each chapter, the Summaries briefly review and reinforce the main topics covered in each chapter to ensure readers have acquired a solid understanding of the key topics covered.

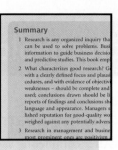

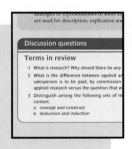

## Discussion questions

Each chapter includes four categories of discussion questions, each of which encourages readers to review and apply the knowledge acquired from each chapter. The four categories cover the main types of learning used in the book. **Key Terms in Review, Making Research Decisions, From Concept to Practice** and **Classroom Discussion**.

## Research Methods in Practice

This running case study featured in each chapter maps the progress of a research project as it develops, putting the relevant concepts into a real life context.

## Spotlight on research

This feature offers readers more in-depth insights into more specialised topics of research designed to broaden understanding.

## CD-ROM

Each text comes with a free CD-ROM which includes five chapters on statistical research. Fully paginated and indexed, with the same features as the rest of the chapters, this CD-ROM can be used in conjunction with the remaining text for teaching and personal study.

# Technology to enhance learning and teaching

## Online Learning Centre (OLC)

After completing each chapter, log on to the supporting Online Learning Centre website. Take advantage of the study tools offered to reinforce the material you have read in the text, and to develop your knowledge in a fun and effective way.

**Resources for students include:**

- *New Research Skills Centre, including **interactive guide** on how to write a research project and **bonus chapters** to aid studying*
- *Case studies*
- *Dataset exercises*
- *PowerPoint Tutorial*
- *Web Links*
- *Learning Objectives*
- *Glossary*
- *Self-test questions*

**Also available for lecturers:**

- *EZ Test testbank*
- *Power Points*
- *Lecture Outlines*
- *Artwork*

## Visit **www.mcgraw-hill.co.uk/textbooks/blumberg** today

# Test Bank available in McGraw-Hill EZ Test Online

A test bank of hundreds of questions is available to lecturers adopting this book for their module. A range of questions is provided for each chapter including multiple choice, true or false, and short answer or essay questions. The questions are identified by type, difficulty, and topic to help you to select questions that best suit your needs and are accessible through an easy-to-use online testing tool, **McGraw-Hill EZ Test Online.**

**McGraw-Hill EZ Test Online** is accessible to busy academics virtually anywhere – in their office, at home or while travelling – and eliminates the need for software installation. Lecturers can chose from question banks associated with their adopted textbook or easily create their own questions. They also have access to hundreds of banks and thousands of questions created for other McGraw-Hill titles. Multiple versions of tests can be saved for delivery on paper or online through WebCT, Blackboard and other course management systems. When created and delivered though EZ Test Online, students' tests can be immediately marked, saving lecturers time and providing prompt results to students.

To register for this FREE resource, visit *www.eztestonline.com*

# Custom Publishing Solutions: Let us help make our **content** your **solution**

At McGraw-Hill Education our aim is to help the lecturer find the most suitable content for their needs and the most appropriate way to deliver the content their students Our **custom publishing solutions** offer the ideal combination of content delivered in the way which suits lecturer and students the best.

The idea behind our custom publishing programme is that via a database of over two million pages called Primis, *www.primisonline.com* the lecturer can select just the material they wish to deliver to their students:

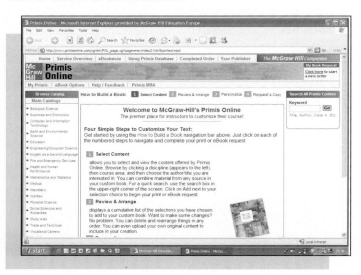

Lecturers can select chapters from:

- textbooks
- professional books
- case books – *Harvard Articles, Insead, Ivey, Darden, Thunderbird* and *BusinessWeek*
- Taking Sides – debate materials

Across the following imprints:

- McGraw-Hill Education
- Open University Press
- Harvard Business School Press
- US and European material

There is also the option to include material authored by lecturers in the custom product – this does not necessarily have to be in English.

We will take care of everything from start to finish in the process of developing and delivering a custom product to ensure that lecturers and students receive exactly the material needed in the most suitable way.

With a Custom Publishing Solution, students enjoy the best selection of material deemed to be the most suitable for learning everything they need for their courses – something of real value to support their learning. Teachers are able to use exactly the material they want, in the way they want, to support their teaching on the course.

Please contact your local McGraw-Hill representative with any questions or alternatively contact Warren Eels at: *warren_eels@mcgraw-hill.com*.

## Study Skills and Research Methods Resources

We publish guides to help you study, research, pass exams and write essays, all the way through your university studies. Visit *www.openup.co.uk/ss* to see the full selection and get 30% discount by entering promotional code **getahead** when buying online! In addition, we also have a number of resources specific to research methods and SPSS software to assist you with your course visit *www.mcgraw-hill.co.uk/research* to see the full selection.

## Computing Skills

If you'd like to brush up on your computing skills, we have a range of titles covering MS Office applications such as Word, Excel, PowerPoint, Access and more.

Get £2 off these titles by entering the promotional code **app** when ordering online at
*www.mcgraw-hill.co.uk/app*

Visit our Study Skills website to read helpful hints about essays, exams, dissertations and much more.
*www.openup.co.uk/studyskills*

# Acknowledgements

## Publisher's acknowledgements

Our thanks go to the following reviewers for their comments at various stages in this textbook's development:

Raphaël Akamavi – University of Hull
Andy Armitage – Anglia Ruskin University
Stephen Barr – Glasgow Caledonian University
Jan Broeckmans – University Hasselt, Belgium
Mary Deuchar – University of Hertfordshire
Rami Djebarni – University of Glamorgan
David Douglas – Staffordshire University
Katrin Muehlfeld – University of Groningen
Peter Nicholls – University of the West of England
Rene Olie – Erasmus University
Nandish Patel – Brunel University
Marius Rietdijk – Free University, Amsterdam
Jennifer Tomlinson – University of Leeds
Frits Wijbenga – Durham University
Hong Woo – Middlesex University
Stephen Woods – Leeds Metropolitan University
Ying Xie – University of Greenwich

## Authors' acknowledgements

The response to the first European edition of the book under my authorship was flattering and I am very happy that it was so well received. My overriding motivation for being a researcher is the curiosity to understand by asking why? I understand that answering the 'why' question often asks for a sound descriptive account of 'what', but if we want to improve situations we describe, we need to understand why things are as they are, thus we need to go beyond the what. It is only if we have understood the 'why' that we can have ideas about how to change.

Having said this, I would like to thank the many people who encouraged me to love research and answering 'why' questions:

Martin Abraham, Richard Arum, Ronald Batenburg, Pascal Beckers, Peter Berends, Katinka Bijlsma-Frankema, Richard Blundel, Christoph Boone, Malte Brettel, Josef Brüderl, Gerard Bunt, Vincent Buskens, Martin Carree, Stewart Clegg, Bas van Diepen, Stuart Dixon, Thomas

Dohmen, Tom Elfring, Henk Flap, Hans Frankfort, Anita van Gils, Ursula Glunk, Hans Georg Gmünden, Paul de Graaf, Dietmar Grichnik, Peter Groenewegen, John Hagedoorn, Mariëlle Heijltjes, Walter Hendriks, Ad van Iterson, Matthijs Kalmijn, Daniela Kirchberg, Heinz Klandt, Lambert Koch, Jasper Kok, Hans van Kranenburg, Ben Kriechel, Mindel van de Laar, Ed Lauman, Emmanuel Lazega, Wilko Letterie, Jia Li, Elke Messenholt, Aad van Mourik, Josef Mugler, Christoph Müller, Walter Müller, David Obstfeld, Woody van Olffen, René Olie, Jose Peiro, Jacqueline Pennings, Marc Peterson, Gerard Pfann, Jonathan Raelin, Anneloes Raes, Werner Raub, Robert Roe, Gerrit Rooks, Sarah Safay, Patrick Sassmannshausen, Albert Schram, Chris Snijders, Omar Solinger, Uli Staber, Frans Stokman, Yvette Taminiau, Frits Tazelaar, Robert Vandenberg, Beste Völker, Mary Wallers, Jeroen Weesie, Marc van Wegberg, Reinhard Wippler, Hans van der Zouden and all my students.

The dedication of the McGraw-Hill team to this 2nd edition has been wonderful. My thanks go to Mark Barratt, James Bishop, Rachel Crookes, Rachel Gear, Karen Harlow, Caroline Prodger and Catriona Watson. My thanks also extend to the copy editor Mandy Gentle and proofreader Michael Monaghan as well as the people from Shift Media who designed the accompanying website, namely Ian Large and Cheryl Luzet. Throughout the revision of the first edition I could count on valuable comments from different reviewers (listed at the top of this section) who read parts of, or even the whole book. Thank you very much.

Finally, a personal hearty thanks to Monika Anna Hofmann, my spouse.

Boris F. Blumberg

# PART 1

# Essentials of research

## Part contents

## Chapter 1

# The nature of business and management research

## Chapter contents

## LEARNING OBJECTIVES

When you have read this chapter, you should understand:

☑ what research is, and the different types of research available

☑ the difference between good and poor or unprofessional research

☑ that research is embedded in different research philosophies and their basic principles, assumptions and implications

☑ how to formulate a solid research hypothesis.

## 1.1 Why study research?

Assume for the moment that you are the new head of the South European office of a Swedish machinery manufacturer. Your appointment makes you the fourth person to hold this post in just three years. Some of the sales and service staff, who have worked for the company for more than 10 years, have packed in their jobs, and complaints from customers regarding poor after-sales service are on the increase. What will you do? How do you begin to think about how to solve this problem?

Here's another decision-making scenario. You are talking with the head of the academic department of the subject you are studying. She chairs the committee that is responsible for selecting the textbook for the research methodology course. How should she begin to evaluate the committee's options? Finally, the production of a thesis marks the end of your business studies course. A thesis requires more from you than just a comprehensive overview of the current literature related to your research topic. Theses that offer at least a small new contribution to our understanding of the issues investigated usually receive a better assessment. However, how do you set up a research project – that is, how do you come to a problem statement? And once you have a research problem and research questions, how will you come to answers to these research questions? Research methods provide you with ideas, instruments and models that demonstrate how to conduct sound research.

The study of research methods will provide you with the knowledge and skills you need to solve the problems and meet the challenges of a fast-paced decision-making environment. **Business research** may be defined as a systematic inquiry whose objective is to provide the information that will allow managerial problems to be solved. Business research courses recognize that students preparing to manage business, not-for-profit and public organizations – in all functional areas – need training in a disciplined process that will enable them to investigate and solve a research or **management dilemma** (i.e. any problem or opportunity that requires a management decision). Three factors have stimulated an interest in this scientific approach to decision-making:

1  the need for more and better information as decisions become more complex
2  the availability of improved techniques and tools to meet this need
3  the resulting information overload if discipline is not employed in the process.

The past two decades have seen dramatic changes in the business environment. Emerging from what is, historically, an economic role, the business organization has evolved in response to the social and political mandates of national public policy, explosive technology growth and continuing innovations in global communications. These changes have created new knowledge needs for the manager and new publics that should be considered when evaluating any decision. Other knowledge demands have arisen as a result of problems with mergers, trade policies, protected markets, technology transfers and macroeconomic savings–investment issues.

The current trend towards complexity has increased the risks associated with making business decisions, meaning that it is more important than ever to have a sound information base. Likewise, the complexity of the phenomena that scientists are investigating impedes our understanding of what is really happening. Rather than concluding that 'all depends on almost everything' we must strive for meaningful explanations. Below is a list of factors that characterize the complex business decision-making environment; each demands that managers and scientists have more and better information on which to base their decisions.

- There are more variables to consider in every decision.
- More knowledge exists in every field of management.
- Global and domestic competition is more vigorous, with many businesses downsizing in order to refocus on primary competences, reduce costs and make competitive gains.
- The quality of theories and models available to explain tactical and strategic results is improving.
- Government is continuing to show concern for all aspects of society, becoming increasingly aggressive in protecting these various publics.
- The explosive growth of company websites on the World Wide Web, e-commerce, and the availability of company publications via desktop and electronic publishing, have heralded the presence of extensive new arrays of information. Its quality, however, is not always impeccable.
- Workers, shareholders, customers and the general public are demanding to be included in company decision-making; they are better informed and more sensitive to their own interests than ever before.

To succeed in such an environment, we need to know how to identify high-quality information and how to recognize the solid, reliable research on which high-risk decisions can be based. Luckily, while the decision-making environment has become more complicated, business research tools have at the same time become more sophisticated and improvements in information technology have served to streamline the research process. Each of the factors listed below demonstrates how recent developments have affected the business research process.

- Organizations are increasingly practising data-mining – learning to extract meaningful knowledge from volumes of data contained within internal databases.
- Advances in computing technology have allowed businesses to create the architecture required for data warehousing – electronic storehouses where vast arrays of collected, integrated data are kept, ready for mining.
- The power and user-friendliness of today's computers means that data may easily be analysed and used to deal with complex managerial problems.
- Quantitative analysis techniques take advantage of increasingly powerful computing capabilities.
- The communication and measurement techniques used in research have been enhanced.

As a researcher, you will need to know how to conduct such research. If you are to develop the skills required in this area, you will need to understand the scientific method as it applies to the managerial decision-making environment. That's why this book addresses your needs as an information processor. Throughout the text we give a slight emphasis to the perspective of an academic researcher or student, as we believe that most users of the text currently belong to these two groups. However, business decisions and research are also often conducted, or at least

Snapshot

## Research and the valuation of corporate social responsibility

Consumer magazines, such as *Which?* in the UK, *Test* in Germany and *Consumentengids* in the Netherlands, have a significant impact on consumers' buying behaviour. It is common for companies whose products have received unsatisfactory marks in a consumer magazine test to withdraw these products from the market. Likewise, positive assessments of consumer organizations are often used in advertising to emphasize the superior quality of products. The classical tests conducted by independent consumer organizations evaluated the quality of products, and were often subdivided into different categories, such as technical performance, durability, ease of use, safety and price.

Since 2002, consumer organizations have increasingly been introducing corporate social responsibility as an additional criterion to assess consumer products. Holger Brackeman, research director of Stiftung Warentest, the German consumer organization, comments on its decision to include ethical criteria in its test: 'Our initiative has created either hope or fear that these social and environmental issues will gain extra weight in society if as major a player as Stiftung Warentest addresses them in a more concerted way.'

Most consumer magazines started to include ethical criteria as a response to requests from consumers. Rob Harrison, the editor of the UK's *ethical consumer* magazine, states that there is a general trend among consumers to request information regarding ethical issues. A common problem for all organizations testing consumer products is how to establish procedures for assessing corporate social responsibility. Some industry representatives seriously question the usefulness of such ethical information because of the methodological difficulties involved. Even consumer magazines acknowledge these methodological problems. Ms O'Brian of *Which?* mentions three. First, which products should one focus on: popular ones with high volumes (e.g. mobile phones), or those where it is well known that ethical issues are hardly considered (e.g. many textiles)? Second, how can we be sure that the information collected on products is reliable and verifiable, as many companies have not implemented procedures to collect information on corporate social responsibility. Third, how can consumer magazines balance the two objectives of providing simple and understandable guidance for their readers and providing a differentiated and detailed picture of the issues at hand.

## References and further reading

'Product tests highlight ethics', *Financial Times*, 1 July 2004, p. 12.
www.stiftung-warentest.de
www.consumentenbond.nl
www.which.uk

requested, by managers. By and large, academic researchers, students and managers encounter the same methodological problems while conducting business or management research, although the former often emphasize aspects other than the latter. As many of our users are currently students who will become managers in the near future, we will also address issues that pertain to research in a commercial rather than an academic setting.

## 1.2  What is research?

Having seen *why* research is a vital part of the business decision-making process, it's time to look at just what research *is*. We'll begin with a few examples of management problems that involve decision-making based on information-gathering. When you have read through each of these, you will be able to abstract the essence of research. How is it carried out? What can it do? What should it not be expected to do? As you read the four cases below, bear in mind the possible range of situations available for conducting business research, and think about how you might answer the following questions.

1  What is the decision-making dilemma facing the researcher or manager?

2  What must the researcher accomplish?

## Cases
### Air Swiss

You work for Air Swiss, an aviation company that is searching for new international partners. The senior vice president for development asks you to head a task force to investigate six companies that are potential candidates. You assemble a team composed of representatives from the relevant functional areas. Pertinent data are collected from public sources because of the sensitive nature of the project. You examine all of the following: company annual reports; articles in business journals, trade magazines and newspapers; financial analysts' assessments; and company advertisements. Your team members then develop summary profiles of the candidate firms based on the characteristics gleaned from these sources. The final report highlights the opportunities and problems that acquisition of the target firm would bring to all areas of the business.

### Akademiska Sjukhuset

You are the commercial manager of Akademiska Sjukhuset, a major academic hospital in Sweden. A prominent manufacturer of medical equipment has contacted you to ask whether you would be willing to purchase a new-generation MRI scanner, which uses magnetism, radio waves and a computer to produce images of body structure.

The doctors' committee at the hospital, to which you will need to make a recommendation, will have to decide on this question. If they choose to purchase the new scanner, they will also agree to test new applications for it and report back to the manufacturer on their experiences. In exchange for this they will get access to the latest technology at a significantly reduced price, and become a member of the manufacturer's network of preferred hospital partners.

You begin your investigation by mining data from patient files to learn how your current MRI scanner is used and what kind of diagnoses it can be used for. You then consult other Swedish hospitals to find out how well equipped they are with MRI technology, and how many patients might, potentially, be treated in your hospital if you invest in the technology. You attempt to confirm your data with information from professional and association journals. Based on this information, you develop a profile that details the number of patients that could be treated and the overheads and potential revenue that would be realized as a result of purchasing the new scanner.

## ColorSplash

ColorSplash, a paint manufacturer, is having trouble maintaining profits. The owner believes inventory management is a weak area of the company's operations. In this industry, the many paint colours, types of paint and container sizes make it easy for a firm to accumulate large inventories and still be unable to fulfil customer orders.

The owner asks you to make some recommendations. You look into the company's present warehousing and shipping operations, and find excessive sales losses and delivery delays because of out-of-stock conditions. An informal poll of customers confirms your impression. You suspect that the present inventory database and reporting system do not provide the prompt, usable information that is needed to allow appropriate production decisions to be made.

Based on this supposition, you familiarize yourself with the latest inventory management techniques in a local college library. You ask the warehouse manager to take an accurate inventory and you review the incoming orders for the last year. In addition, the owner shows you the production runs for the last year and the method he uses to assess the need for a particular colour or paint type.

Modelling the last year of business using production, order and inventory management techniques, you select the method that, in theory, will provide the greatest profit. You run a pilot line using the new control methodology. After two months, the data show a much lower inventory and a higher order fulfilment rate. You recommend that the owner adopt the new method.

## York College

You work for York College's alumni association. It is eager to develop closer ties with its ageing alumni in order to encourage increased donation levels and to persuade older, non-traditional students to return to education and thus supplement enrolment numbers. The president's office is considering the construction of a retirement community that is geared towards university alumni and asks your firm to assess the attractiveness of the proposal from an alumni viewpoint. Your director asks you to divide the study into four parts as follows.

Phase 1    First, you are to report on the number of alumni in the appropriate age bracket, the rate of new entries per year and the actuarial statistics for the group. This information will allow your director to assess whether the project is worth pursuing.

Phase 2    Your early results reveal that there are sufficient alumni to make the project feasible. The next step in the study is to describe the social and economic characteristics of the target alumni group. You review gift statistics, analyse job titles, and assess home locations and values. In addition, you review files from the last five years to see how alumni responded when they were asked about their income bracket. When you have finished, you are able to describe the alumni group for your director.

Phase 3    It is evident that the target alumni can easily afford to join a retirement community as proposed. The third phase of the study is to explain the characteristics of the alumni who would be interested in a university-related retirement community. For this phase, you engage the National Pensioners Convention (NPC) and a retirement community developer. In addition, you search for information on senior citizens from federal government sources.

From the developer you learn what characteristics of retirement community planning and construction are most attractive to retirees. From the NPC you learn about the main services and features that potential retirees look for in a retirement community. From government publications you become familiar with existing regulations and recommendations for operating retirement communities, and uncover a full range of descriptive information on the typical retirement community dweller.

You make an extensive report to both the alumni director and the university president. It covers the number of eligible alumni, their social and economic standing, and the characteristics of those who would be attracted by the retirement community.

Phase 4    The report excites the college president. She asks for one additional phase to be completed. She needs to predict the number of alumni who would be attracted to the project so that she can adequately plan the size of the community. At this point, you call on the college business school's research methods class for help in designing a questionnaire for the alumni. By providing telephones and funding, you arrange for the class to conduct a survey among a random sample of the eligible alumni population. In addition, you have the class devise a second questionnaire for alumni who will become eligible in the next 10 years.

Using the data collected, you can predict initial demand for the community and estimate growth in demand over the next 10 years. You submit your final report to the director and the president.

## What is the dilemma facing the researcher or manager?

The researcher's/manager's predicament is fairly well defined in the four cases described above. Let's see how carefully you read and understood them.

- In the Air Swiss case, the senior vice president for development must make a proposal to the president, or possibly the board of directors, about which is the preferred international partner with which to join forces.
- In the Akademiska Sjukhuset case, the doctors in the group must decide whether to purchase the new-generation MRI scanner.
- In the ColorSplash case, the owner of the paint manufacturer must decide whether to implement a new inventory management system.
- At York College, the president must propose to the board of directors whether to fund the development of a retirement community.

How did you do? If you didn't come to the same conclusions, reread the cases before proceeding to find out what you missed. Make sure that you have a strong grasp of the process before you read on.

In real life, management dilemmas are not always so clearly defined. In the ColorSplash case, rather than pinpointing the problem as a simple one of inventory management, the paint manufacturer's owner could have faced several, possibly intertwining, problems:

- a strike by employees that had an adverse effect on inventory delivery to retail and whole-sale customers
- the development of a new paint formula that offers superior coverage but requires a hard-to-source ingredient in its manufacture, thereby affecting production rates
- a fire that destroyed the primary loading dock of the main shipping warehouse in Belgium
- the simultaneous occurrence of all three of these events.

As the research process begins with the manager's decision-making task, it is of paramount importance to have an accurate definition of the dilemma; this, however, can often prove difficult. We address this issue in Chapter 2.

### What must the researcher accomplish?

The different types of study represented by the four cases can be classified as reporting, descriptive, explanatory or predictive. We look at these in more detail below.

### Reporting

At the most elementary level, a **reporting study** may be produced simply to provide an account or summation of some data, or to generate some statistics. The task may be quite simple and the data readily available. At other times, the information may be difficult to find. A reporting study calls for knowledge and skill in using information sources and dealing with their gate-keepers. Such a study usually calls for little in the way of inference or conclusion drawing.

In the Air Swiss case, the researcher needs to know what information should be assessed in order to value the company. In the study of management, this knowledge would primarily be acquired in courses on financial management, accounting and marketing.

Knowing the type of information needed, the researcher in the Air Swiss case identifies possible sources, like trade press articles and annual reports. Because of the possible effects of the evaluation of potential partners on the company's stock prices, only public sources are used. Other reporting studies of a less sensitive nature might have the researcher interviewing source gatekeepers. In the York College case, for example, interviewing the director of a local retirement facility might have revealed other sources that could be included in the research. Such an expert is considered a gatekeeper.

Purists claim that reporting studies do not qualify as research, although data that are gathered carefully can have great value. Others argue that at least one form, investigative reporting, has a great deal in common with widely accepted qualitative and clinical research.[1] A research design does not have to be complex, or require the use of inference, for a project to be labelled research.

### Descriptive

A **descriptive study** tries to discover answers to the questions who, what, when, where and, sometimes, how. The researcher attempts to describe, or define, a subject, often by creating a profile of a group of problems, people or events. Such studies may involve the collection of data and an examination of the distribution and number of times the researcher observes a single event or characteristic (this is known as a **research variable**). They may also involve an assessment of the interaction of two or more variables.

In the Akademiska Sjukhuset case, the researcher must present data that reveal who is affiliated with the insurer, who uses managed healthcare programmes (both doctors and patients), general trends in the use of imaging technology in diagnosing illness or the severity of injury, and the relationship of patient characteristics, doctor referrals and technology use patterns.

Descriptive studies may or may not have the potential for drawing powerful inferences. Organizations that maintain databases of their employees, customers and suppliers (internal information) already have significant data that can be used to conduct descriptive studies. Yet many firms that have such data files do not mine them regularly in order to take advantage of the decision-making insight they might provide.

A major deficiency of descriptive studies based on existing data sources, however, is that they cannot explain why an event has occurred or why the variables interact in the way they do.

The descriptive study is popular in business research because of its versatility across disciplines. In not-for-profit corporations and other organizations, descriptive investigations have broad appeal to administrators and policy analysts for planning, monitoring and evaluating. In such contexts, 'how' questions address issues such as those related to quantity, cost, efficiency, effectiveness and adequacy.[2]

## *Explanatory*

Academics have debated the relationship between the next two types of study – explanatory and predictive – in terms of which one should precede the other. Both types of research are grounded in theory, and theory is created to answer 'why' and 'how' questions. For our purposes, an **explanatory study** goes beyond description and attempts to explain the reasons for the phenomenon that the descriptive study has only observed.

Research that studies the relationship between two or more variables is also referred to as a correlational study. In an explanatory study, the researcher uses theories, or at least hypotheses, to account for the forces that caused a certain phenomenon to occur.

In the ColorSplash case, believing that the problem with paint stock-outs is the result of poor inventory management, the owner asks the researcher to detail warehousing and shipping processes. Had it stopped there this would be a descriptive study; but if problems in the processes can be linked with sales losses due to an inability to make timely deliveries to retail or wholesale customers, then an explanatory study will emerge. The researcher tests this hypothesis by modelling the last year of business using the relationship between processes and results.

## *Predictive*

If we can provide a plausible explanation for an event after it has occurred, it is desirable for us to be able to predict when and in what situations such an event might reoccur. A **predictive study**, the fourth type, is rooted as much in theory as in explanation.

National governments in Europe are always interested in economic predictions for the coming year, as a country's economic situation largely determines the tax revenues it will receive, as well as likely government expenditure (e.g. on unemployment benefits). Economic research institutes, such as the CPB in the Netherlands, the DIW or IFO in Germany, and the

## Conflicting conclusions

On 21 May 2001, a century-long industrial relationship was severed when Bridgestone/Firestone, Inc. announced that it would stop selling tyres to Ford. Firestone CEO John Lampe said that any relationship needed to be built on 'trust and mutual respect', and that Ford's anticipated replacement of 13 million tyres – without just cause from Firestone's point of view – showed an obvious lack of trust.

These two automobile industry giants, although party to the same crash data, came to very different conclusions. Firestone claimed its tyres failed at a higher than normal rate only when installed on Ford Explorers. Ford claimed that crashes involving Explorers were far more likely with Firestone tyres. Firestone's Lampe stated, 'Our analysis suggests that there is a significant safety concern with a substantial segment of Ford Explorers.' He added that Ford 'steadfastly refused to acknowledge those concerns'.

Were the National Highway Traffic Safety Administration (NHTSA) data incorrect? Did the companies examine significantly different insurance data? Were the conflicting conclusions incorrect? The answer to each of these questions is no.

Business research is conducted to enable decision-makers to make better decisions. Both companies needed to make decisions that would protect their brand equity and offer a buffer against wrongful death and injury lawsuits. Many believe that Firestone is fighting for its very survival; Ford's situation is far less severe.

While, initially, GM reaffirmed its relationship with the tyre company (even naming Firestone its 2001 Supplier of the Year) and Nissan Motor expects to continue its relationship with Firestone, if they or other automotive companies choose to follow Ford's lead, Firestone could crumble under the effects of such a divorce.

## References and further reading

Bradsher, Keith, 'Firestone to stop sales to Ford', *New York Times on the Web*, 22 May 2001 (www.nytimes.com/2001/ 05/22/business/22TIRE.html).

'Bridgestone/Firestone proudly accepts sixth consecutive supplier of the year award from General Motors', Bridgestone/Firestone, Inc. press release, Nashville, TN, 30 July 2001 (http://www.firestone.com/homeimgs/H010730a.htm).

'Bridgestone/Firestone, Inc. ends Ford tire business in the Americas', Bridgestone/Firestone, Inc. press release, Nashville, TN, 21 May 2001 (http://www.mirror.bridgestonefirestone. com/homeimgs/H010521a.htm).

'Ford Motor Company to replace all 13 million Firestone Wilderness AT tires on its vehicles', Bridgestone/Firestone, Inc. press release, Nashville, TN, 22 May 2001 (http://media.ford.com/newsroom/release_firestone.cfm?article_id=8361&id=92&art_ids=0&bn=1).

'GM reaffirms commitment to Bridgestone/Firestone products', Bridgestone/Firestone, Inc. press release, Nashville, TN, 24 May 2001 (http://mirror.bridgestone-firestone.com/homeimgs/H010524a.htm).

'Statement by John Lampe, Chairman, CEO and President Bridgestone/Firestone, Inc.', Bridgestone/Firestone, Inc. press release, Nashville, TN, 22 May 2001 (http://www.mirror.bridgestonefirestone. com/homeimgs/H010521a.htm).

www.firestone.com

www.ford.com

research departments of banks, use complex theory-driven models to predict key economic figures (e.g. economic growth). The variables included in such models are – among many others – firms' current investments in equipment, consumer confidence, currency exchange rates and so on.

This type of study often calls for a high level of inference. Why, for example, would increasing consumer confidence stimulate economic growth in one year, while in other years the effect of consumer confidence is hardly detectable? The answer to such a question would be of great value in improving the models employed as well as future predictions. In business research, prediction is found in studies conducted to evaluate specific courses of action or to forecast current and future values.

Sometimes, we want to get an idea about how the future might look like but lack solid theories allowing such predictions. Other methods to predict the future include scenario models and expert surveys. In the former, the researcher works out different scenarios based on different assumptions on the course of key factors. For example, you might want to know how the market for private insurance will develop in China in the next 20 years. Your prediction will depend on your assumption of how many Chinese have sufficient income to be interested in such insurance. Expert surveys are mostly based on qualitative interviews with experts on a given issue and distilling the most likely from these expert opinions. Although these two latter models do not rely on an explicit theoretical model, the researcher and the experts questioned certainly work with implicit theories on which they base their assessment of the future.

The researcher is asked to predict for the York College president the success of the proposed retirement facility for alumni, based on the number of applications for residency the project will attract. This prediction will be based on the explanatory hypothesis that alumni frequent programmes and projects sponsored by the institution because they feel attached to their university and alumni associations bear the images of youthfulness as well as mental and physical stimulation.

Finally, once we can explain and predict a phenomenon, we would like to be able to control it. Being able to replicate a scenario and dictate a particular outcome is the objective of **control**. In the York College case, if we assume that the college goes ahead with its retirement community and enjoys the success predicted, the president will feel encouraged to build a similar facility to serve another group of alumni and duplicate that success.

Control is a logical outcome of prediction. The complexity of the phenomenon and the adequacy of the prediction theory, however, are largely responsible for deciding success in a control study. At York College, if a control study were carried out to examine the various promotional approaches used with alumni to stimulate images of youthfulness, the promotional tactics that drew the largest number of alumni applications for residency could be identified. Once known, this knowledge could be used successfully with different groups of alumni *only if* the researcher could account for and control all other variables influencing the applications.

## 1.3  Is research always problem-solving based?

In the four cases detailed above, researchers were asked to respond to particular 'problems' that managers needed to solve. **Applied research** has a practical problem-solving emphasis, although the need for problem-solving is not always generated by a negative circumstance. Whether the 'problem' is negative, like rectifying an inventory system that is resulting in lost sales (as in the ColorSplash case) or, say, an opportunity to increase stockholder wealth through acquiring another firm, problem-solving plays a very important part in business research.

The problem-solving nature of applied research means that it is conducted in order to reveal answers to specific questions related to action, performance or policy needs. In this respect, all four of the case examples above appear to qualify as applied research. Pure, or basic, research is also problem-solving based, but in a different sense. It aims to solve perplexing questions (i.e. problems) of a theoretical nature that have little direct impact on action, performance or policy decisions.

**Pure research** or **basic research** in the business arena might involve a researcher for, say, an advertising agency who is studying the results of the use of coupons versus rebates as demand stimulation tactics, but not in a specific instance or in relation to a specific client's product. In another pure research scenario, a researcher might study the influence on productivity of remuneration methods that pay according to a piece-work rather than a salary-plus-commission system. Both applied and pure research are, then, problem-solving based. Applied research is, however, directed much more to making immediate managerial decisions.

Some authorities equate research with basic or scientific investigations and would reject all four examples. History shows, however, that science typically has its roots in the pragmatic problems of real life. Interest in basic research comes much later, following the development of knowledge in a particular field. Research that is restricted to basic or pure research is too narrowly defined.

One respected author defines scientific research as a 'systematic, controlled, empirical, and critical investigation of natural phenomena guided by theory and hypotheses about the presumed relations among such phenomena'.[3] The terms 'systematic' and 'controlled' in this definition refer to the degree to which the observations are controlled and alternative explanations of the outcome are ruled out. The terms 'empirical' and 'critical' point to requirements for the researcher to test subjective beliefs against objective reality, and to leave the findings open to further scrutiny and testing. These qualities are what the author means by 'scientific'. Whether all business research needs to be this stringent or should be 'guided by theory and hypotheses about presumed relations' is, however, debatable.

The classical concept of basic research does call for a hypothesis,[4] but in applied research such a narrow definition omits at least two types of investigation that are highly valued. First, there is the exploratory study in which the investigator knows so little about the area of study that hypotheses have not yet emerged.[5] An equally important area of study is that which purists call merely descriptive. The importance of descriptive research to business should be reinforced as follows.

> There is no more devastating condemnation that the self-designated theorist makes of the researcher than to label his work purely descriptive. There is an implication that associates 'purely descriptive' research with empty-headedness; the label also implies that as a bare minimum every healthy researcher has at least one hypothesis to test, and preferably a whole model. This is nonsense.

> In every discipline, but particularly in its early stages of development, purely descriptive research is indispensable. Descriptive research is the stuff out of which the mind of man, the theorist, develops the units that compose his theories. The very essence of description is to name the properties of things: You may do more, but you cannot do less and still have description. The more adequate the description, the greater is the likelihood that the units derived from the description will be useful in subsequent theory building.[6]

The answer to the question posed at the beginning of this section, 'Is research always problem-solving based?' is yes. Whether basic or applied, simple or complex, all research should provide an answer to a question. If managers always knew what was causing problems or offering opportunities in their realm of responsibility, there would be little need for applied research, pure research or basic research; intuition would be all that was necessary to make effective decisions.

Any of the four types of study – reporting, descriptive, explanatory or predictive – can properly be called research. We also can conclude from the various examples that we have seen that research is a systematic inquiry aimed at providing information to solve managerial problems. This defines the basic requirements that any effort must meet in order to be called research.

All four cases match this definition, but they suggest different stages of scientific development. A rough measure of the development of science in any field is the degree to which explanation and prediction have replaced reporting and description as research objectives. By this standard, the development of business research is in a comparatively formative stage.

# 1.4  What makes good research?

Good research generates dependable data, which is derived through practices that are conducted professionally and that can be used and relied upon. In contrast, poor research is carelessly planned and conducted, resulting in data that we can't trust, i.e. we cannot be sure whether the results give an appropriate account of the reality and consequently we cannot base policy advice or any business decisions on these results. Good research follows the structure of the **scientific method**. Several defining characteristics of the scientific method are listed in Exhibit 1.1 and below, where the managerial dimensions of each are discussed.

The nine criteria summarized in Exhibit 1.1 together make up desirable, decision-oriented research. They are especially useful guidelines for managers who are performing research themselves. This is because they create barriers that prevent the researcher from adjusting his or her findings to meet their desired ends rather than allowing them to reflect reality.

## 1  Purpose clearly defined
The purpose of the research – the problem involved or the decision to be made – should be clearly defined and sharply delineated in a form that is as unambiguous as possible. Getting it down in writing is valuable even in instances where the decision-maker and researcher are the same person. Any statement of the decision or problem should include its scope, its limitations, and the precise meanings of all words and terms significant to the research. Failure of the researcher to do this adequately may raise legitimate doubts in the minds of research report readers as to whether the researcher has sufficient understanding of the problem to make a sound proposal for action.

| Characteristics of research | How can researcher achieve it? | Where to find out more |
|---|---|---|
| 1 Purpose clearly defined | In applied research, the researcher distinguishes between symptom of organization's problem, the manager's perception of the problem and the research problem; in pure research, it is also wise to clearly separate the research dilemma addressed and the research problem actually investigated | Chapter 2 |
| 2 Research process detailed | Researcher provides complete research proposal | Chapter 2 |
| 3 Research design thoroughly planned | Exploratory procedures are outlined with constructs defined<br>Sample unit is clearly described, along with sampling methodology<br>Data collection procedures are selected and designed | Chapters 2, 6–10 |
| 4 High ethical standards applied | Safeguards are in place to protect study participants, organizations, clients and researchers<br>Recommendations do not exceed the scope of the study<br>The study's methodology and limitations sections reflect researcher restraint and concern for accuracy | Chapter 3 |
| 5 Limitations frankly revealed | Desired procedure is compared with actual procedure in report<br>Desired sample is compared with actual sample in report<br>Impact on findings and conclusions is detailed | Chapters 6, 13 |
| 6 Adequate analysis for decision-maker's needs | Sufficiently detailed findings are tied to collection instruments | Chapters 14–18 |
| 7 Findings presented unambiguously | Findings are clearly presented in words, tables and graphs<br>Findings are logically organized to facilitate reaching a decision about the manager's problems<br>Executive summary of conclusions is outlined<br>Detailed table of contents is tied to the conclusions and findings presentation | Chapters 13–18 |
| 8 Conclusions justified | Decision-based conclusions are matched with detailed findings | Chapters 13–18 |
| 9 Researcher's experience reflected | Researcher provides experience/credentials with report | Chapter 13 |

*Exhibit 1.1* What actions guarantee good research?

## 2 Research process detailed

The research procedures used should be described in sufficient detail to permit another researcher to repeat the research (it should be replicable). Except when secrecy is imposed, research reports should reveal with candour the sources of the data and the means by which they were obtained. Omission of significant procedural details makes it difficult, or even impossible, to estimate the validity and reliability of the data, and justifiably weakens the confidence of the reader in the research itself as well as any recommendations based on the research.

## 3 Research design thoroughly planned

The procedural design of the research should be planned carefully to yield results that are as objective as possible. When sampling of a population is involved, the report should include evidence concerning the degree of representativeness of the sample. A survey of opinions or recollections ought not to be used when more reliable evidence is available from documentary sources or by direct observation. Bibliographic searches should be as thorough and complete as possible. Experiments should have satisfactory controls. Direct observations should be recorded in writing as soon as possible after the event. Efforts should be made to minimize the influence of personal bias in selecting and recording data.

## 4 High ethical standards applied

Researchers often work independently and have significant latitude in designing and executing research projects. A research design that includes safeguards against causing mental or physical harm to participants and that makes data integrity a first priority should be valued highly. Ethical issues in research reflect important moral concerns about the practice of responsible behaviour in society. Ethical research issues are discussed at length in Chapter 3.

Researchers frequently find themselves precariously balancing the rights of their subjects against the scientific dictates of their chosen method. When this occurs, they have a responsibility to guard the welfare of the participants in the studies and also the organizations to which they belong, their clients, their colleagues and themselves. Careful consideration must be given to those research situations in which there is the possibility of physical or psychological harm, exploitation, invasion of privacy and/or loss of dignity. The research requirements must be weighed against the potential for adverse effects. Typically, you will be able to redesign a study, but on occasion you will not. As a researcher, you should be prepared for this dilemma.

## 5 Limitations frankly revealed

The researcher should report, with complete frankness, any flaws in procedural design, and estimate their effect on the research findings. There are few perfect research designs. Some of the imperfections may have little effect on the validity and reliability of the data; others may invalidate them entirely. A competent researcher should be sensitive to the effects of imperfect design, and his or her experience in analysing the data should provide a basis for estimating their influence. As a decision-maker, you should question the value of a piece of research that reports no limitations.

## 6 Adequate analysis for decision-maker's needs

Analysis of the data should be extensive enough to reveal its significance, and the methods of analysis used should be appropriate. The extent to which this criterion is met is frequently a good measure of the competence of the researcher. Adequate analysis of the data is the most difficult phase of research for the novice. The validity and reliability of data should be checked carefully. The data should be classified in ways that assist the researcher in reaching pertinent conclusions and that clearly reveal the findings that have led to those conclusions. When statistical methods are used, the probability of error should be estimated and the criteria of statistical significance applied.

### 7  Findings presented unambiguously

Some evidence of the competence and integrity of the researcher may be found in the report itself. For example, language that is restrained, clear and precise, assertions that are carefully drawn and hedged with appropriate reservations, and an apparent effort to achieve maximum

## What are the consequences of faking data in research?

Is it more than an ethical dilemma if you falsify the description of your methodology or if you modify your sampling plan? These are ethical and procedural issues that researchers, even famous ones, face. In its December 2001 issue, *FastCompany* asked author, consultant and motivational speaker Tom Peters to revisit the writing of *In Search of Excellence*, the 1982 best-selling business title. In his confession #3, Peters is quoted as saying that he 'faked the data' that resulted in the eight underlying principles – principles that guided American business for much of the next decade.

Rather than evolving from a large study of businesses, where each was selected based on its performance metrics (a probability study), Peters switched the research design and he, along with partner and co-author Robert Waterman, asked McKinsey colleagues and other contacts to identify 'cool' companies (a non-probability, judgement sample). They conducted detailed personal interviews with contacts in those initial 62 companies, and then reduced the list to 43 by a post-interview review of performance metrics.

Peters, in confession #7, admits that he missed some of the emerging 'excellence' factors because they were 'too superficial to make an impact'. Some of the things his study missed were early signs of the growing influence of information technology and the importance that speed would come to have in business.

Do you think that his confession diminishes the importance of the results?

## References and further reading

'Tom Peters's true confessions', *FastCompany* 53 (December 2001), p. 78.

Byrne, John, 'The real confessions of Tom Peters', *Business Week*, 3 December 2001, p. 48.

Peters, Tom and Waterman, Robert, *Excellence: In Search of Excellence, Lessons from America's Best-Run Companies*. New York: Warner Books, 1982, pp. 13–24.

Tom Peters! (http://www.tompeters.com/toms_world/press_kit/excellence.asp).

www.fastcompany.com

www.mckinsey.com

www.tompeters.com

objectivity tend to give the decision-maker a favourable impression of the researcher. Generalizations that outrun the evidence on which they are based, exaggerations and unnecessary verbiage, however, tend to have the opposite effect. Such reports are not valuable. The presentation of data should be comprehensive, easily understood by the decision-maker, and organized so that the decision-maker can readily locate critical findings.

**8  Conclusions justified**

Conclusions should be limited to those for which the data provide an adequate basis. Novice researchers are often tempted to broaden the basis of induction by including personal experiences and their own interpretations – which are not, of course, subject to the controls under which the research data were gathered. Equally undesirable is the all-too-frequent practice of drawing conclusions from a study of a limited population and applying them universally. Some researchers may also be tempted to rely too heavily on data collected in a prior study and use it in the interpretation of a new one. This sometimes occurs among research specialists who confine their work to clients in a small industry. These actions tend to decrease the objectivity of the research and undermine readers' confidence in its findings. Good researchers always specify the conditions under which their conclusions are valid.

**9  Researcher's experience reflected**

Greater confidence in the research is warranted if the researcher is experienced, has a good reputation in the research field and is a person of integrity. Were it possible for the reader of a research report to obtain sufficient information about the researcher, this criterion would perhaps be one of the best bases for judging the degree of confidence a piece of research warrants and the value of any decision based upon it. For this reason, the research report should always contain information about the qualifications of the researcher.

## 1.5  Research philosophies

We introduced the importance of thinking about what research is in a rather pragmatic way. However, how research should be conducted is embedded in the broader philosophies of science. Research is based on reasoning (theory) and observations (data or information). How observations and reasoning are related to each other is a still ongoing and old philosophical debate on the development of knowledge. Although many researchers conduct sound research without a thought for underlying philosophical considerations, some knowledge of research philosophies is beneficial for you as a researcher as it helps to clarify the research design and facilitates the choice of an appropriate one. Furthermore, understanding the basic assumptions of research philosophies can enable researchers to reach designs beyond their past experience.[7] In the following, we provide an overview of the two most distinguished research philosophies, **positivism** and **interpretivism** (also called phenomonology). Between these two positions various other research philosophies exist, relying on some principles of positivism or interpretivism, while relaxing others and incorporating principles of the opposing philosophy. The most notable of these is **realism**, which will be discussed later.

Looking at the often fierce debates between positivists and interpretivists, one might get the impression that research is either conducted on planet 'positivarium' or on planet 'interpretivarium', and research has to be embedded in one philosophy. Using the survey methodology seems to imply a deductive approach rooted in positivism, and an ethnographic observational study using inductive reasoning seems to follow interpretivism. By and large, such classifications are reasonable, but research practice shows that researchers rarely subscribe consistently to one philosophy and, in management research in particular, a more pragmatic view prevails.

## Positivism

Positivism is a research philosophy adopted from the natural sciences. Its three basic principles are:

1  the social world exists externally and is viewed objectively
2  research is value-free
3  the researcher is independent, taking the role of an objective analyst.

Auguste Comte, an early proponent of positivism, said that 'all good intellects have repeated, since Bacon's time, that there can be no real knowledge but that which is based on observed facts'.[8] According to positivism, knowledge develops by investigating the social reality through observing objective facts. This view has important implications for the relationship between theory and observations, as well as for how research is conducted. Theory development starts with hypothesizing fundamental laws and deducing what kind of observations support or reject the theoretical predictions of the hypotheses. Consequently, the research process starts with identifying causalities forming the base of fundamental laws. Then research is conducted to test whether observations of the world indeed fit the derived fundamental laws and to assess to what extent detected causalities can be generalized (i.e. are applicable to the whole world). Positivism implies the following assumptions.

- The social world is observed by collecting objective facts.
- The social world consists of simple elements to which it can be reduced.

A scientist following this research tradition believes (assumes) that observable facts are objective, because they are external, that is we cannot influence them, and research is conducted value-free. This implies that different researchers observing a social phenomenon, such as the takeover battle between two firms, arrive at the same facts describing the social world. As a consequence, concepts need to be operationalized to allow a quantitative measurement of the facts. Further, the social world can be reduced to simple elements. Distilling its elements and reducing them to fundamental laws is the best way to investigate a phenomenon. This explains why studies following the positivism approach often single out one explanation in order to understand a phenomenon and deliberately neglect other aspects, which are often investigated in separate studies.

## Interpretivism

Unlike positivists, interpretivists hold the view that the social world cannot be understood by applying research principles adopted from the natural sciences and propose that social sciences require a different research philosophy. The basic principles of interpretivism are:

- the social world is constructed and is given meaning subjectively by people
- the researcher is part of what is observed
- research is driven by interests.

Interpretivists argue that simple fundamental laws are insufficient to understand the whole complexity of social phenomena. More important, however, they claim that an objective observation of the social world is impossible, as the social world has a meaning for human beings and is constructed by intentional behaviour and actions. Knowledge is developed and theory built through developing ideas inducted from the observed and interpreted social constructions. The researchers' emphasis on making sense of what is happening sometimes even generates surprising findings beyond the current common scientific knowledge. Interpretivists attempt to understand subjective realities and to offer interpretative explanations, which are meaningful for the participants of the research. The involvement of the researcher in the research is most apparent in action research (see Chapter 8), where the researchers engage in active collaboration with participants to address real-life problems in a specific context, and aim to offer and implement feasible solutions to the problem.

Interpretivists also reject the notion that research is value-free. As researchers offer an interpretation of how people interpret the social world, the researchers' interpretation is also socially constructed, reflecting their motives and beliefs. As Habermas stated, human interests not only channel our thinking, but also guide how we investigate the world (i.e. which questions we ask), and how we construct our knowledge (i.e. how we formulate the answers found).[9] Thus, our approach to research social phenomena also reflects the currently common construction of our knowledge about and basic beliefs to do with the world.

Interpretivism implies the following assumptions.

- The social world is observed by seeing what meanings people give to it and interpreting these meanings from their viewpoint.
- Social phenomena can only be understood by looking at the totality.

Gathering and measuring facts will not disclose the essence of a social phenomenon; rather, researchers need to explore why people have different experiences and to understand how these differences result in the different constructions and meanings people give to the social world. Interpretivists research social phenomena by making sense of how people interpret the social world. This requires the researcher to dig into the processes of subjective interpretation, acknowledging the specific motivations and interests of the participants. Compared to natural phenomena, social phenomena are characterized by a high complexity and are often unique, as they result from multiple circumstances constructed by many individuals. This means that interpretivism does not attach a great deal of importance to the generalizability of findings. The world, and especially the business world, is constantly changing and what seemed sensible three years ago may not hold at all now. Hence, in an ever changing world, generalization, even over short periods of time, becomes questionable.

## Realism

Realism is a research philosophy sharing principles of positivism and interpretivism. Like positivism, its exponents believe that social sciences can rely on the research approach dominant in the natural sciences. More specifically, it accepts the existence of a reality independent of human beliefs and behaviour. However, it also concedes that understanding people and their behaviour requires acknowledgement of the subjectivity inherent to humans. In the realists' view, there are social processes and forces beyond the control of humans, which affect our beliefs and behaviour. These processes and forces operate at the macro level. At the micro level (i.e. at the level of individual human beings), subjective individual interpretations of reality are important for a full understanding of what is happening. Still, most realists would accept that these subjective interpretations are not unique and that people share similar interpretations, partly because the external forces at the macro level influence everyone. Thus, research requires the identification of external factors describing general forces and processes influencing humans, as well as the investigation of how people interpret and give meaning to the setting they are situated in. Critical realism, a branch of realism, recognizes the existence of a gap between the researcher's concept of reality and the 'true' but unknown reality. This implies that research is not value-free, and is conducted within a broader framework based on our current knowledge and concept of reality.

## Research implications of positivism and interpretivism

The opposing stances taken by positivists and interpretivists are summarized in Exhibit 1.2. These differences in basic principles and assumptions have several implications for how researchers should conduct research. In the following, we will discuss how the two research philosophies affect research design.

Positivism starts from the idea that the world can be described by objective facts, which are then investigated. Therefore, one needs to assess whether observations are indeed objective facts. The constructs used are operationalized to ensure that two researchers observing the same phenomenon measure it in the same way. In practice, constructs are often operationalized in quantitative terms, as representing facts using numbers facilitates comparisons. The interpretivist is interested in subjective meanings and interpretations of phenomena to detect what is happening in a specific situation. As each observation is subjective he or she relies ideally on multiple sources and different methods to collect information on the phenomena. An example will serve to illustrate this.

Assume company performance is an essential aspect of the phenomena investigated. A study following the positivistic philosophy will ideally use a set of quantitative indicators reflecting performance, such as profit, sales, market share, growth or a relative measure such as return on assets. Interpretivists might even use financial key indicators from annual reports, but they would put more emphasis on subjective assessments of performance by management and employees. These subjective assessments can result in a quite different picture of the performance than financial indicators suggest and can even provide hints as to why a firm is or is not doing well.

A common study structure in the positivistic tradition is that researchers investigate a research problem by testing whether theoretically derived hypotheses hold for the situations investigated. If the objective facts support the hypothesis, the underlying fundamental laws are

| | Positivism | Interpretivism |
|---|---|---|
| **Basic principles** | | |
| View of the world | The world is external and objective | The world is socially constructed and subjective |
| Involvement of researcher | Researcher is independent | Researcher is part of what is observed and sometimes even actively collaborates |
| Researcher's influence | Research is value-free | Research is driven by human interests |
| **Assumptions** | | |
| What is observed? | Objective, often quantitative, facts | Subjective interpretations of meanings |
| How is knowledge developed? | Reducing phenomena to simple elements representing general laws | Taking a broad and total view of phenomena to detect explanations beyond the current knowledge |

*Exhibit 1.2* Positivism and interpretivism compared.

applicable and their validity is enforced. The value of the research usually increases with the generalizability of the findings, because a detected relationship, which cannot be linked to other similar circumstances, does not qualify as a fundamental law. This calls for large sample sizes to ensure that the findings based on the sample investigated represent the whole population. Interpretivistic studies follow a different structure. They offer a thick and rich description of the investigated phenomena, which is interpreted to understand what is happening. As they claim that generalization is of minor importance, as discussed above, smaller sample sizes (often just one) are sufficient.

Some people suggest that a 'perfect' research study combines positivism and interpretivism. However, there are major practical and theoretical restrictions questioning the feasibility of such a combined approach. Practical restrictions include the immense effort required to conduct a study in both traditions. For example, positivistic studies usually rely on larger samples while interpretivistic studies emphasize the thickness of the provided descriptions. Unfortunately, thickness of description and sample size have a substitutive relation, as shown in Exhibit 1.3. Good research not only exists in extreme forms, but is much more often an intelligent combination of the two. Good research operates on a line between the white and the light-blue area: moving too much into the blue area is, even if feasible, not efficient. Using a research design far away from the optimal line and in the white area is not sufficient to gain insight into what is happening. If your study is based on just a few cases and the information you collected on each case does not exceed what is usually obtained in large-scale surveys, your research has nothing of interest to offer. In the next section we discuss how you decide what position on the optimal line you wish to occupy.

A major theoretical restriction of combining different research philosophies is that the

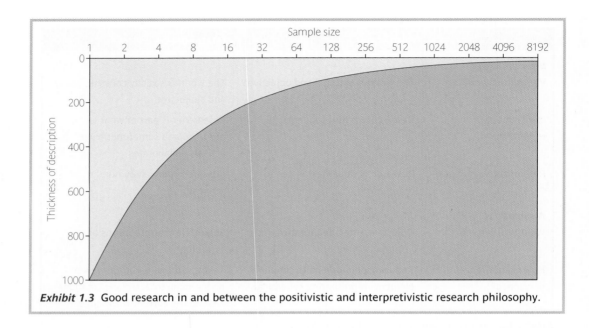

**Exhibit 1.3** Good research in and between the positivistic and interpretivistic research philosophy.

research questions asked often differ slightly between the different approaches. It is hard to design a sound interpretivistic study for a research problem framed positivistically. For example, research questions that result in testable hypotheses or that try to find out whether a single observation made holds for a broader set of situations require a positivistic approach. Finally, the different assumptions (see Exhibit 1.2) make it very difficult for researchers from different research traditions to find a common ground to start from. Interpretivists are very sceptical towards all forms of measurement and will argue that even time is not measurable, although many of us will use years to measure a person's age or hours and minutes to measure a certain activity, such as the flight time between London and Hong Kong. For positivists measuring age in years and flight times in hours and minutes is unproblematic and they might not understand what the problem is as both measurements are applied by many people across different cultures. An interpretivist would, however, argue that also time is subject to individuals' interpretations. For example, two people aged 65 years might have very different ideas about their age; one might feel young and energetic looking forward to start a lot of new initiatives as soon as she gets retired, while the other feels old and unneeded after his retirement.

## Choosing a research philosophy to be used

Characteristic of scientific research, whether it is a master's thesis, a dissertation or a large-scale government-sponsored research programme, is the inclusion of theory. The place where you introduce theory can differ. You may start with theory in order to test it or solve a theoretical contradiction, or you may close with theoretical considerations drawn from your observations. The position, or role, of theory in your research is directly linked to two different reasoning approaches: deduction and induction.

# Blue isn't blue?

At a first sight, one might think that determining which colour a car, a chair or a bottle is isn't that difficult and in many cases all of us agree that that Ferrari is red and the wooden chair is brown. However, once we have to sort empty bottles for the waste glass recycling container, we sometimes doubt whether a certain bottle is still green or already brown. Likewise, does a turquoise tone look more blue or green to you? One reason for our doubts at the waste glass container or quarrels with friends on whether turquoise is more blue or more green is that colour is a perceptual property, that is our eyes and our brain derive colours when light with different wavelengths meets our eyes and is then processed in our brain.

While dyschromatopsia (colour blindness) is caused by genetic disorders or damages to the eye and brain, how we perceive colours is also culturally determined. In Russian there is no word for blue; Russians know two words for blue, one *goluboy* describing more light-blue tones and the other *siniy* describing more dark-blue tones. This difference between Russian and English allows for an interesting experiment on whether colour is subjective. If a British person would categorize a light-blue and a dark-blue shirt under the same main colour, while a Russian might categorize it under two different main colours, this would show that colour is culturally determined and therefore also depending on subjective interpretations. An experiment set up by researchers at the MIT presented 26 Russian-speaking and 24 English-speaking participants cards, showing a blue square at the top and two blue squares at the bottom. All squares were slightly differently coloured. Then participants were asked which of the two squares at the bottom matched better with the square on the top of the card. The result was that if the two squares of the bottom belonged to the two different 'blue' categories used in Russian, the Russians were better in discriminating the colours than the British, because their language had taught them two categories of blue.

If even colour, an apparently rather objective measure, gives room for so much subjective interpretation, how about even more abstract phenomena, such as solidarity, innovation and so on.

Does it make sense to attempt to measure them despite the fact that different people have rather different understanding of them?

## References and further reading

http://www.pnas.org/cgi/reprint/104/19/7780?maxtoshow=&HITS=10&hits=10&RESULTFOR-MAT=&fulltext=color+recognition+blue&searchid=1&FIRSTINDEX=0&resourcetype=HW CIT. The website with the original article.

http://wellstyled.com/tools/colorscheme2/index-en.html – a website that allows you to see how people with different forms of dyschromatopsia will see your PowerPoint presentation.

### Deduction

**Deduction** is a form of inference that purports to be conclusive – that is, the conclusion must necessarily follow from the reasons given. These reasons are said to have led to the conclusion and therefore represent proof. This form of argument calls for a stronger link between reasons and conclusions than is found in induction. For a deduction to be correct, it must be both true and valid:

Snapshot

- premises (reasons) given for the conclusion must agree with the real world (true)
- the conclusion must necessarily follow from the premises (valid).

A deduction is valid if it is impossible for the conclusion to be false if the premises are true. Logicians have established rules by which we can judge whether a deduction is valid. Conclusions are not logically justified if one or more premise is untrue or the argument form is invalid. A conclusion may still be a true statement, but for reasons other than those given. Consider, for example, the following simple deduction.

> All regular employees can be trusted not to steal. (*Premise 1*)
> John is a regular employee. (*Premise 2*)
> John can be trusted not to steal. (*Conclusion*)

If we believe that John can be trusted, we might think that this is a sound deduction. However, this conclusion cannot be accepted as a sound deduction unless the argument form is valid and the premises are true. In this case, the form is valid and premise 2 can easily be confirmed. However, many may challenge the sweeping premise that 'All regular employees can be trusted not to steal.' While we may believe that John will not steal, such a conclusion is a sound deduction only if both premises are accepted as true. If one premise fails the acceptance test, then the conclusion is not a sound deduction. This is so even if we still have great confidence in John's honesty. Our conclusion, in this case, must be based on our confidence in John as an individual rather than on a general premise that all regular employees are honest. On reflection, it should be apparent that a conclusion that results from deduction is in a sense already 'contained in' its premises.[10]

### Induction

An inductive argument is radically different from the deductive type. It does not have the same strength of relationship between reasons and conclusions. To induce something is to draw a conclusion from one or more particular facts or pieces of evidence. The conclusion explains the facts, and the facts support the conclusion.

To illustrate this point, suppose your firm spends €1 million on a regional promotional campaign and sales do not increase. This is a fact: sales did not increase during or after the promotional campaign. Under such circumstances we might ask, 'Why didn't sales increase?'

One likely answer to this question is the conclusion that the promotional campaign was poorly executed. This conclusion is an **induction** because we know from experience that regional sales should go up during a promotional event. We also know that if the promotion is poorly executed, sales will not increase. The nature of induction, however, is that the conclusion is only a hypothesis. It is one explanation, but there are others that fit the facts just as well. For example, each of the following hypotheses might explain why sales did not increase.

- Regional retailers did not have sufficient stock to fill customer requests during the promotional period.
- A strike by the employees at the haulage firm prevented stock from arriving in time for the promotion to be effective.
- A serious hurricane caused all our retail locations in the region to be closed for 10 days during the promotion.

This example illustrates the essential nature of inductive reasoning. The inductive conclusion is an inferential jump beyond the evidence presented – that is, although one conclusion explains the fact that there was no sales increase, other conclusions can also explain this fact. It may even be the case that none of the conclusions we advanced correctly explains the failure of sales to increase.

Let's look at another example. Consider the situation of Tracy Nelson, a salesperson at the Square Box Company. Tracy has one of the poorest sales records in the company. Her unsatisfactory performance prompts us to ask the question, 'Why is she performing so poorly?' From our knowledge of Tracy's sales practices, the nature of box selling and the state of the market, we might conclude (hypothesize) that her problem is that she makes too few sales calls per day to build a good sales record. Other hypotheses might also occur to us on the basis of available evidence. These hypotheses include the following.

- Tracy's territory does not have the market potential of other territories.
- Tracy's sales-generating skills are so poorly developed that she is not able to close sales effectively.
- Tracy does not have the authority to lower prices and her territory has been subject to intense price-cutting by competing manufacturers, causing her to lose many sales to competitors.
- Some people just cannot sell boxes, and Tracy is one of those people.

Each of the above hypotheses is an induction we might base on the evidence of Tracy's poor sales record, plus some assumptions or beliefs we hold about her and about the selling of boxes. All of them have some chance of being true, but we would probably have more confidence in some than in others. All require further confirmation before they gain our confidence. Confirmation comes with more evidence. The task of research is largely to:

- determine the nature of the evidence needed to confirm or reject hypotheses, and
- design methods by which to discover and measure this other evidence.

## Combining Induction and Deduction

Induction and deduction are used in research reasoning in a sequential manner. John Dewey describes this process as the **double movement of reflective thought**.[11] Induction occurs when we observe a fact and ask, 'Why is this?' In answer to this question, we advance a tentative explanation (hypothesis). The hypothesis is plausible if it explains the event or condition (fact) that prompted the question. Deduction is the process by which we test whether the hypothesis is capable of explaining the fact.

1  You promote a product but sales don't increase. (*Fact 1*)
2  You ask the question, 'Why didn't sales increase?' (*Induction*)
3  You infer a conclusion (hypothesis) to answer the question: 'The promotion was poorly executed'. (*Hypothesis*)
4  You use this hypothesis to conclude (deduce) that the sales will not increase during a poorly executed promotion. You know from experience that ineffective promotion will not increase sales. (*Deduction 1*)

This process is illustrated in Exhibit 1.4.

This example, an exercise in circular reasoning, indicates that one must be able to deduce the initiating fact from the hypothesis advanced to explain that fact. A second critical point is also illustrated in this exhibit: to test a hypothesis, one must be able to deduce from it other facts that can then be investigated. This is what classical research is all about. We must deduce other specific facts or events from the hypothesis and then gather information to see if the deductions are true. In this example, we deduce the following.

**5** A well-executed promotion will result in increased sales. (*Deduction 2*)

**6** We run an effective promotion and sales increase. (*Fact 2*)

How would Dewey's 'double movement of reflective thought' work when applied to Tracy Nelson's problem? The process is illustrated in Exhibit 1.5. The initial observation (fact 1) leads to hypothesis 1: that Tracy is lazy. We deduce several other facts from the hypothesis. These are shown as fact 2 and fact 3. We use research to find out if fact 2 and fact 3 are true. If they are found to be true, they confirm our hypothesis. If they are not, our hypothesis is not confirmed, and we must look for another explanation.

In most research, the process is more complicated than these simple examples suggest. For instance, we often develop multiple hypotheses by which to explain the phenomenon in question. Then we design a study to test all the hypotheses at once. Not only is this more efficient, but it is also a good way to reduce the attachment (and potential bias) of the researcher to any given hypothesis.

## Reflective thought and the scientific method

Induction and deduction, observation and hypothesis testing can be combined in a systematic way to illustrate the scientific method. The ideas that follow, originally suggested by Dewey and others for problem-solving analysis, represent one approach to assessing the validity of conclusions about observable events. They are particularly appropriate for researchers whose conclusions depend on empirical data.[12] The researcher:

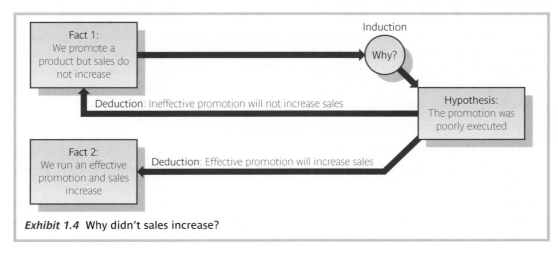

*Exhibit 1.4* Why didn't sales increase?

- encounters a curiosity, doubt, barrier, suspicion or obstacle
- struggles to state the problem – asks questions, contemplates existing knowledge, gathers facts, and moves from an emotional to an intellectual confrontation of the problem
- proposes hypotheses to explain the facts that are believed to be logically related to the problem
- deduces outcomes or consequences of the hypotheses – attempts to discover what happens if the results are (i) the opposite to those predicted or (ii) support the expectations
- formulates several rival hypotheses
- devises and conducts a crucial empirical test with various possible outcomes, each of which selectively excludes one or more hypotheses
- draws a conclusion – an inductive inference – based on acceptance or rejection of the hypotheses
- feeds information back into the original problem, modifying it according to the strength of the evidence.

Eminent scientists who claim that there is no such thing as the scientific method, or do not apply it overtly in their work, caution researchers about using template-type approaches. They are right to do so, and it should be added that the ideas presented in this book are highly inter-dependent, not sequentially fixed and may be expanded upon or eliminated according to the nature of the problem and the perspective from which it is viewed. Nevertheless, novice researchers should understand that research, when conducted scientifically, is most definitely a process.

The research process that explores the relationship between reflective thought and scientific method is described in detail in Chapter 3.

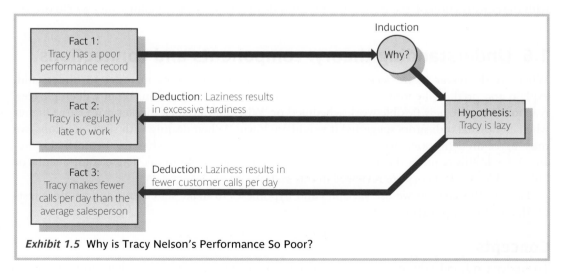

*Exhibit 1.5* Why is Tracy Nelson's Performance So Poor?

## The scientific attitude

If the tools of thinking are the 'mind' of science, then the scientific attitude is its spirit. The scientific attitude unleashes the creative drive that makes discovery possible. The stories of scientists involved in some of the most spectacular discoveries of the twentieth century – Crick, Watson, Pauling and others – are ones of imagination, intuition, curiosity, suspicion, anguish, self-doubt and the urge to know. Such predispositions are not only, however, the preserve of the natural scientist. All researchers exercise imagination in the discovery process, in capturing the most essential aspect of a problem or in selecting the technique that will reveal a phenomenon in its most natural state.

Curiosity in its many forms has long characterized persistent efforts to understand the relationship between productivity and worker satisfaction. Starting first with the Hawthorne studies, it was thought that employee satisfaction improved productivity.[13] Later research did not bear this out, and the second general conclusion was that satisfaction and productivity were not directly connected since the relationship was affected by a number of other variables. Currently, it is believed that satisfaction is sought for reasons not consistently related to work, and that productivity varies from simple to challenging tasks.

Many contextual variables are now viewed as essential to understanding the original relationship.[14] Over 30 years elapsed while this research was being sorted out. The curiosity needed to ask questions, together with the passion not to let go and an unwillingness to just accept existing answers, sustained these researchers through periods of failure and self-doubt.

Thomas Kuhn, writing in *The Structure of Scientific Revolutions*, has also addressed the question of why scientists attack their problems with such passion and devotion. Scientific inquiry, he says, attracts people for a variety of motives, 'Among them are the desire to be useful, the excitement of exploring new territory, the hope of finding order, and the drive to test established knowledge.'[15] From applied researchers addressing a manager's need to academicians fascinated with the construction of grand theories, the attitude of science is the enabling spirit of discovery.

# 1.6 Understanding theory: components and connections

When we do research, we seek to discover what we need to know in order to understand, explain and predict phenomena. We might want to answer the question 'What will employees' reaction be to the new flexible work schedule?' or 'Why did the stock market price surge higher when all normal indicators suggested it would go down?' When dealing with such questions, we must agree on definitions: which employees, what kind of reaction, what are the normal indicators? To do this requires the use of concepts, constructs and definitions. These components, or building blocks, of theory are reviewed in this section.

Later in this chapter we use variables and hypotheses to make statements and propose tests for the relationships expressed in our research questions.

## Concepts

To understand and communicate information about objects and events, there must be some common ground on which to do it. Concepts serve this purpose. A **concept** is a generally accepted collection of meanings or characteristics associated with certain events, objects, conditions, situations and behaviours. Classifying and categorizing objects or events that have common characteristics beyond any single observation create concepts. The terms 'height', 'width' and 'depth,' for example, symbolize a conception of the properties of a physical object. Similarly, the economic term 'profit' points to a property of the financial situation of an organization.

We abstract such meanings from reality and use words as labels to designate them. For example, we see a man go by and acknowledge that he is running, walking, skipping, crawling or hopping. These movements all represent concepts. We have also abstracted certain visual elements by which we identify that the moving object is an adult male, rather than an adult female or a truck or a horse. We use a host of concepts in our everyday thinking, conversing and other activities.

## Sources of Concepts

Concepts that are in frequent and general use have been developed over time through shared usage. We have acquired them through personal experience. If we lived in another society, we would hold many of the same concepts (though in a different language). Some concepts, however, are unique to a particular culture and are not readily translated into another language.

Ordinary concepts make up the bulk of communication even in research, but we will often run into difficulties when trying to deal with an uncommon concept or a newly advanced idea. One way to handle this problem is to borrow from other languages or areas (e.g. gestalt psychology) or from other fields (e.g. impressionism, say, from art). The concept of gravitation, for instance, has been borrowed from physics and used in marketing in an attempt to explain why people shop where they do. The concept of 'distance' is used in attitude measurement to describe the degree of variability between the attitudes of two or more people; the term 'threshold' is used to describe a concept in perception studies; while 'velocity' is a term borrowed by the economist from the physicist.

Borrowing is not always practical, though, so we sometimes need to adopt new meanings for words (i.e. make a word cover a different concept) or develop new labels (words) for concepts. The recent broadening of the meaning of the term 'model' is an example of the first instance; the development of concepts such as sibling and status stress are examples of the second.

When we adopt new meanings or develop new labels, we begin to develop a specialized jargon or terminology. Researchers in medicine, the physical sciences and related fields frequently use terms that are unintelligible to outsiders. Jargon no doubt contributes to the efficiency of communication among specialists, but it tends to exclude everyone else.

## The Importance of Concepts to Research

Concepts are basic to all thought and communication, yet in everyday use we pay scant attention to the problems encountered in their use. In research, special problems grow out of the need for concept precision and inventiveness. We design hypotheses using concepts. We devise measurement concepts by which to test these hypothetical statements. We gather data using these measurement concepts. We may even invent new concepts to express ideas. The success of research hinges on:

- how clearly we conceptualize, and
- how well others understand the concepts we use.

For example, when we survey people on the question of tax equity, the questions we use need to tap faithfully the attitudes of the respondents. Attitudes are abstract, yet we must attempt to measure them using carefully selected concepts.

The challenge is to develop concepts that others will clearly understand. We might, for example, ask respondents for an estimate of their family's total income. This may seem to be a simple, unambiguous concept, but we will receive varying and confusing answers unless we restrict or narrow the concept by specifying, say:

- time period (weekly, monthly or annually)
- fixed or variable income
- before or after tax
- head of family only or all family members
- salary and wages only, or also include dividends, interest and capital gains
- income in kind, such as living rent-free and employee discounts.

### *Problems in Concept Use*

The use of concepts presents difficulties that are accentuated in a research setting. First, people differ in the meanings they include under any particular label. This problem is so great in normal human communication that we often see cases where, although people use the same language, they do not understand each other. We may all agree to the meaning of concepts such as dog, table, electric light, money, employee and wife. We might encounter more difficulty, however, when we communicate concepts such as household, retail transaction, dwelling unit, regular user and debit. Still more challenging are concepts that are familiar but not well understood, such as leadership, motivation, personality, social class and fiscal policy.

Personality, for example, has been defined in the research literature in more than 400 ways.[16] Although this may seem extreme, writers are not able to express the complexity of the determinants of personality and its attributes (e.g. authoritarianism, risk-taking, locus of control, achievement orientation and dogmatism) in a fashion that leads to agreement.

The concepts described represent progressive levels of abstraction – that is, the degree to which the concept does or does not have objective referents. 'Table' is an objective concept in that we can point to a table and we can conjure up in our minds an image of a table. An abstraction like personality is much more difficult to visualize. Such abstract concepts are often called **constructs**.

## Constructs

As used in research in the social sciences, the term 'construct' refers to an image or idea specifically invented for a given research and/or theory-building purpose. We build constructs by combining the simpler concepts, especially when the idea or image we intend to convey is not directly subject to observation.

Concepts and constructs are easily confused. Here's an example to clarify the differences involved. A human resource analyst at CadSoft, an architectural software company that employs technical writers to work on its product manuals, is analysing the task attributes of a job that is in need of a redesign. She knows that the job description for a technical writer consists of three components: presentation quality, language skill and job interest. Her job analysis reveals more specific characteristics.

Exhibit 1.6 illustrates some of the concepts and constructs she is dealing with. The concepts at the right of the exhibit (format accuracy, manuscript errors and keyboarding speed) are the most concrete and easily measured. We can observe keyboarding speed, for example, and even with crude measures agree on what constitutes slow and fast 'keyboarders'. Keyboarding speed is one concept in the group that defines a construct that the human resource analyst calls 'presentation quality'. Presentation quality is in itself, though, a non-existent entity, a 'constructed type'. It is used to communicate the combination of meanings presented by the three concepts. The analyst uses it as a label for the concepts she has found empirically to be related.

Concepts in the middle of Exhibit 1.6 are vocabulary, syntax and spelling. The analyst also finds them to be related. They form a construct that she calls 'language skill'. She has chosen this term because these three concepts together define the language requirement in the job description. Language skill is placed at a higher level of abstraction in the exhibit because two of the concepts that comprise it – vocabulary and syntax – are difficult to observe and their measures more complex.

Looking at the left part of the exhibit, you will see that the analyst has not yet measured the last construct: 'job interest'. This is the least observable and most difficult to measure. It is likely to be composed of numerous concepts – many of which will be quite abstract. Researchers sometimes refer to such entities as hypothetical constructs because they can be inferred only from data; thus, they are presumed to exist but must await confirmation from further testing. If research ultimately shows the concepts and constructs in this example to be interrelated, and if the propositions that specify the connections can be supported, the researcher will have the beginnings of a **conceptual scheme**. In graphic form it would depict the relationships among the knowledge and skill requirements necessary to clarify the job redesign effort.

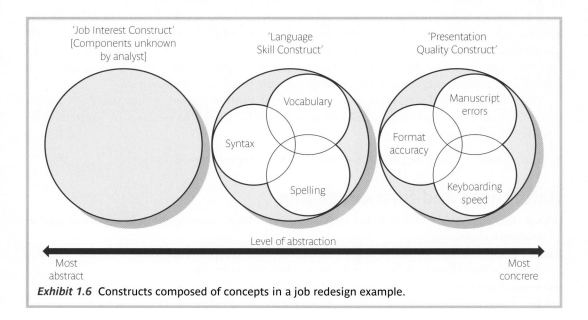

*Exhibit 1.6* Constructs composed of concepts in a job redesign example.

## Definitions

Confusion about the meaning of concepts can destroy a research study's value without the researcher or client realizing it. If words have different meanings for the different parties involved, then they will not be communicating on the same wavelength. Having a mutually acceptable set of definitions is one way to reduce this danger.

Researchers must struggle with two types of definition: dictionary definitions and operational definitions. In the more familiar dictionary definition, a concept is defined with a synonym. For example, a customer is defined as a patron; a patron, in turn, is defined as a customer or client of an establishment; a client is defined as one who employs the services of any professional and also, loosely, as patron of any shop.[17] These 'circular' definitions may be adequate for general communication but not for research. In research, we must measure concepts and constructs, and this requires more rigorous definitions.

Snapshot

## Marriott: what is concierge service?

Marriott International, Inc. is a leading hotel chain with more than 1800 properties in 53 countries and territories under various brand names (Marriott, Fairfield Inn, Residence Inn, Courtyard, TownePlace Suites, Fairfield Suites, Renaissance and ExecuStay). Due to the diversity of its operations, when managers in this company want to deliver global consistency, they turn to its sophisticated internal research division.

'We wanted to know what level of service the terms concierge, club or executive level implied. We also needed to know which term generated feelings of belonging and appreciation. We need a term that promises a level of superior service that we can deliver consistently in every property throughout the world,' says manager of marketing research Brenda Roth.

The task, then, was to find a global term for the special services floor found in Marriott and Renaissance properties. First, 'pulse groups' were conducted in the United States. Then a study was conducted that involved 40 hotel intercept interviews in Hong Kong, London and Frankfurt. Interviewers were bilingual, carrying out their interviews in the domestic language, while recording responses in English to allow for speedy data processing and analysis.

While most guests shared some common interpretations of the terms, 'one possible German connotation of concierge was as a building superintendent similar to a custodian – certainly not a desired interpretation'.

What operational definition would you develop for concierge service?

## References and further reading

'About the company', Marriott International, Inc. (http://www.marriott.com/corporateinfo/98annual/about.asp).

Brenda Roth, manager of marketing research, Marriott International, Inc., interview, January 2000, Marriott History (http://www.marriott.com/milestone.asp).

www.marriott.com

## *Operational Definitions*

An **operational definition** is one stated in terms of specific testing or measurement criteria. These terms must have empirical referents (i.e. we must be able to count, measure or in some other way gather the information via our senses). Whether the object to be defined is physical (e.g. a machine tool) or highly abstract (e.g. achievement motivation), the definition must specify characteristics and how they are to be observed. The specifications and procedures must be so clear that any competent person using them would be able to classify the objects in the same way.

For example, suppose college undergraduates are to be classified by class. No one has much trouble understanding terms such as fresher (first-year student), sophomore (second-year student), and so on; but the task may not be that simple if you must determine which students fall into which class. To do this, you need operational definitions.

Operational definitions may vary, depending on your purpose and the way you choose to measure them. Here are two different situations that require different definitions of the same concepts.

1 You conduct a survey among students and wish to classify their answers by their class status. You merely ask them to report their class status and you record it. In this case, class is divided into fresher, second-year student, junior (third-year student) or senior (fourth- or final-year student), and you accept the answer each respondent gives as correct. This is a rather casual definition process but none the less an operational definition. It is probably adequate in this case even though some of the respondents may report inaccurately.

2 You wish to make a tabulation of the class status of students for the university registrar's annual report. The measurement task here is more critical, so your operational definition needs to be more precise. You decide to define class status in terms of 'hours of credit' (i.e. the number of hours of attendance completed by the end of the spring term and recorded in each student's record in the registrar's office), as indicated below.

- Fresher: fewer than 30 hours' credit
- Second-year student: 30–59 hours' credit
- Junior: 60–89 hours' credit
- Senior: more than 90 hours' credit

The two examples given above deal with relatively concrete concepts, but operational definitions are even more critical in treating abstract ideas. Suppose you want to measure a construct called 'organizational commitment'. You may intuitively understand what this means, but it is difficult to attempt to measure it among workers. You would probably need to develop a commitment scale of your own, or you may be able to use a scale that has already been developed and validated by someone else. This scale then operationally defines the construct.

While operational definitions are needed in research, they also present some problems. One ever-present danger is thinking that a concept and its operational definition are the same thing. We forget that our definitions provide only a limited insight into what a concept or construct really is. In fact, the operational definition may be quite narrow and quite dissimilar to that someone else might use when researching the same topic. When measurements by two different definitions correlate well, this correlation supports the view that each definition measures the same concept adequately.

The problem of operational definitions is particularly difficult when dealing with constructs. Constructs have few empirical referents by which to confirm that an operational definition really measures what we hope it does. The correlation between two different definition formulations strengthens the belief that we are measuring the same thing. On the other hand, if there is little or no correlation, this may mean that we are tapping several different partial meanings of a construct. It may also mean that one or both of the operational definitions are not true labels.

Whether you use a definitional or operational definition, its purpose in research is basically the same: to provide a way of understanding and measuring concepts. You may need to provide operational definitions for only a few critical concepts, but these will almost always be the definitions used to develop the relationships found in hypotheses and theories.

## Variables

Scientists operate at both theoretical and empirical levels. At the theoretical level, there is a preoccupation with identifying constructs and their relationship to propositions and theory. At this level, constructs cannot, as we have already said, be observed. At the empirical level, where the propositions are converted to hypotheses and testing occurs, the scientist is likely to be dealing with variables. In practice, the term **variable** is used as a synonym for construct, or the property being studied. In this context, a variable is a symbol to which we assign a numeral, or value.[18]

The numerical value assigned to a variable is based on that variable's properties. For example, some variables, said to be **dichotomous variables**, have only two values, reflecting the presence or absence of a property. For example, employed/unemployed and male/female have two values, generally 0 and 1. Gender is a typical example for such a dichotomous variable. You can either be female (the value of the variable is 1) or not female, that is male (the value of the variable is 0).

Variables also take on values that represent the addition of further categories, such as the demographic variables of race or religion. All variables that produce data that fit into categories are said to be discrete, since only certain set values are possible. An automotive variable, for example, where Renault is assigned a 5 and Volkswagen a 6, provides no option for 5.5.

Income, temperature, age or a test score are examples of **continuous variables**. These variables may take on values within a given range or, in some cases, an infinite set. Your test score may range from 0 to 100, your age may be 23.5 and your present income could be €24,583.

### *Independent and Dependent Variables*

Researchers are most interested in relationships among variables. For example, does a participative leadership style (independent variable) influence job satisfaction or performance (dependent variables) or can a superior staff member's modelling of ethical behaviour influence the behaviour of her subordinates?

Exhibit 1.7 lists some terms that have become synonyms for independent variable and dependent variable. It is important to remember that there are no preordained variables waiting to be discovered 'out there' that are automatically assigned to one category or the other. As one writer notes:

| Independent variable | Dependant variable |
|---|---|
| Presumed reason | Presumed effect |
| Stimulus | Response |
| Predicted from . . . | Predicted to . . . |
| Antecedent | Consequence |
| Manipulated | Measured outcome |
| Predictor | Criterion |

*Exhibit 1.7* Defining independent and dependent variables.

> There's nothing very tricky about the notion of independence and dependence. But there is something tricky about the fact that the relationship of independence and dependence is a figment of the researcher's imagination until demonstrated convincingly. Researchers hypothesize relationships of independence and dependence: They invent them, and then they try by reality testing to see if the relationships actually work out that way.[19]

In each relationship, there is at least one **independent variable** (IV) and one **dependent variable** (DV). It is normally hypothesized that, in some way, the IV 'causes' the DV to occur. It should be noted, however, that while it is easy to establish whether an IV influences a DV, it is much harder to show that the relationship between an IV and DV is a causal relationship (see also Chapter 4). In Exhibit 1.8a, this relationship is illustrated by an arrow pointing from the independent variable to the dependent variable. For simple relationships, all other variables are considered extraneous and are ignored.

## Moderating or Interaction Variables

In actual study situations, however, such a simple one-to-one relationship needs to be conditioned or revised to take other variables into account. Often, we can use another type of explanatory variable that is of value here: the **moderating variable** (MV). A moderating or interaction variable is a second independent variable that is included because it is believed to have a significant contributory or contingent effect on the original IV–DV relationship. The arrow pointing from the moderating variable to the arrow between the IV and DV in Exhibit 1.8a exemplifies the difference between an IV directly affecting the DV and an MV affecting the relationship between an IV and the DV. For example, one might hypothesize that in an office situation:

> The introduction of a four-day working week (IV) will lead to higher productivity (DV), especially among younger workers (MV).

In this case, there is a differential pattern of relationship between the four-day week and productivity that is the result of age differences among the workers. Hence, after introducing a four-day working week the productivity gain for younger workers is higher than that for older workers. It should be noted that the effect of the moderating or interaction variable is the 'surplus' of the combined occurrence of introducing a four-day working week and being a younger worker.

To illustrate this point, assume that the productivity of younger workers is 12 percentage points higher than that for older workers, and that the productivity of workers having a four-day working week is 6 percentage points higher than those of workers having a five-day working week. If the productivity of a younger worker having a four-day working week is only 18 percentage points higher than the productivity of an older worker with a five-day working week, there is no interaction effect, because the 18 percentage points are the sum of the main effects. There would be an interaction effect if the productivity of the younger worker on a four-day week was, for example, 25 percentage points higher than the productivity of the older worker on a five-day week.

Whether a given variable is treated as an independent or moderating variable depends on the hypothesis under investigation. If you were interested in studying the impact of the length of the working week, you would make the length of week the IV. If you were focusing on the relationship between age of worker and productivity, you might use working week length as an MV.

### Extraneous Variables

An almost infinite number of **extraneous variables** (EVs) exists that might conceivably affect a given relationship. Some can be treated as IVs or MVs, but most must either be assumed or excluded from the study. Fortunately, an infinite number of variables has little or no effect on a given situation. Most can safely be ignored, as their impact occurs in such a random fashion as to have little effect. Others might influence the DV, but their effect is not at the core of the problem we investigate. Still, we want to check whether our results are influenced by them. Therefore, we include them as **control variables** (CVs) in our investigation to ensure that our results are not biased by not including them. Taking the example of the effect of the four-day working week again, one would normally think that weather conditions, the imposition of a local sales tax, the election of a new mayor, and thousands of similar events and conditions would have little effect on working week and office productivity. You should note that inclusion of control variables is especially important for research conducted in the positivistic approach, as it allows you to reduce the problem investigated and nevertheless account for additional factors. Extraneous variables can also be **confounding variables** (CFVs) to our hypothesized IV–DV relationship, similar to moderating variables. You may consider that the kind of work being done might have an effect on the impact of working week length on office productivity. This might lead you to introducing time spent in a meeting to coordinate the work as a confounding variable (CFV). In our office example, we would attempt to control for type of work by studying the effect of the four-day working week within groups attending meetings with different intensity.

 For workers less frequently asked to attend internal meetings (CFV), the introduction of a four-day working week (IV) will lead to higher productivity (DV), especially among younger workers (MV).

In Exhibit 1.8b, sunshine is shown as an extraneous variable; the broken line indicates that we included it in our research because it might influence the DV, but we consider the CV as irrelevant for the investigation of our research problem. Similarly, we included the type of work as a CFV.

### Intervening Variables

The variables mentioned with regard to causal relationships are concrete and clearly measurable – that is, they can be seen, counted or observed in some way. Sometimes, however, one may not be completely satisfied by the explanations they give. Thus, while we may recognize that a four-day working week results in higher productivity, we might think that this is not the whole story – that working week length affects some **intervening variable** (IVV) that, in turn, results in higher productivity.

An IVV is a conceptual mechanism through which the IV and MV might affect the DV. The IVV can be defined as a factor that theoretically affects the DV but cannot be observed or has not been measured; its effect must be inferred from the effects of the independent and moderator variables on the observed phenomenon.[20]

In the case of the working week hypothesis, one might view the intervening variable (IVV) to be job satisfaction, giving a hypothesis such as:

> The introduction of a four-day working week (IV) will lead to higher productivity (DV) by increasing job satisfaction (IVV).

Here we assume that a four-day working week increases job satisfaction; similarly, we can assume that attending internal meetings is an indicator negatively related to the routine character of work. Exhibit 1.8c illustrates how 'theoretical' constructs, which are not directly observed, fit into our model.

### Some Additional Examples

Let's look at some additional examples to illustrate the relationships between independent, moderating, control, extraneous and dependent variables.

The management of a bank wishes to study the effect of promotion on savings. It might advance the following hypothesis:

> A promotion campaign (IV) will increase savings activity (DV), especially when prizes are offered (MV), but chiefly among smaller savers (EV/control). The results come from enhancing the motivation to save (IVV).

Or suppose you are studying a situation that involves the causes of defective parts production. You might hypothesize as follows:

> Changing to worker self-inspection (IV) will reduce the number of defective parts (DV) when a part can be identified with its producer (MV) in electronic assembly work (EV/control), by stimulating the worker's sense of responsibility (IVV).

## 1.7 Propositions and hypotheses

We define a **proposition** as a statement about concepts that may be judged as true or false if it refers to observable phenomena. When a proposition is formulated for empirical testing, we call it a hypothesis. As a declarative statement, a **hypothesis** is of a tentative and conjectural nature.

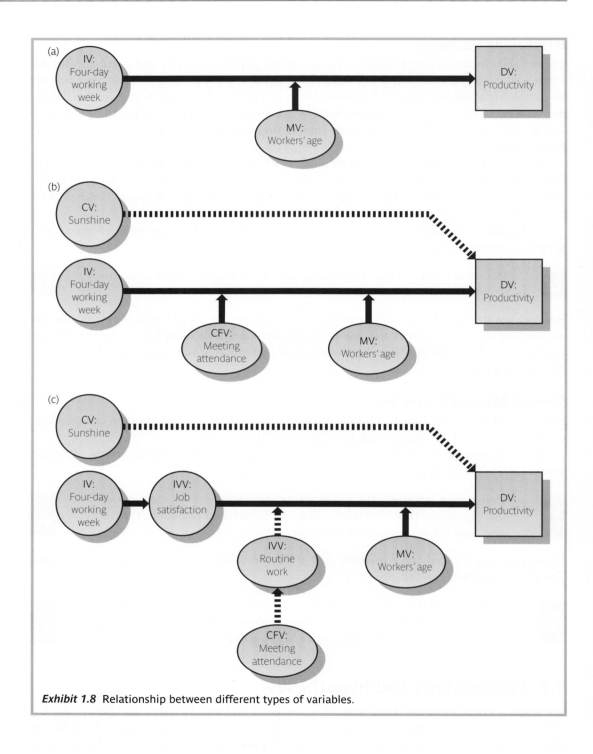

*Exhibit 1.8* Relationship between different types of variables.

Hypotheses have also been described as statements in which we assign variables to cases. A case is defined in this sense as the entity, or thing, the hypothesis talks about. The variable is the characteristic, trait or attribute that, in the hypothesis, is ascribed to the case.[21]

For example, we might form the following hypothesis:

> Executive Jones (case) has a higher than average achievement motivation (variable).

If our hypothesis were based on more than one case, it would be a generalization. For example:

> Executives in Company Z (cases) have a higher than average achievement motivation (variable).

## Descriptive hypotheses

Both of the above hypotheses are examples of **descriptive hypotheses**. These are propositions that typically state the existence, size, form or distribution of some variable. For example:

> In Denmark (case), the October seasonally adjusted unemployment rate (variable) stands at 5.8 per cent of the labour force.

> The member states of the European Union (case) are experiencing budget difficulties (variable).

> Eighty per cent of Company Z stockholders (case) favour increasing the company's cash dividend (variable).

Researchers often use a research question rather than a descriptive hypothesis. Thus, in place of the above hypotheses, we might use the following questions.

- What is the unemployment rate in Denmark?
- Are European states experiencing budget difficulties?
- Do stockholders of Company Z favour an increased cash dividend?

Either format is acceptable, but the descriptive hypothesis format has several advantages, as follows.

- It encourages researchers to crystallize their thinking about the likely relationships to be found.
- It further encourages them to think about the implications of a supported or rejected finding.
- It is useful for testing statistical significance.

## Relational hypotheses

The research question format is less frequently used with a situation calling for **relational hypotheses**. These are statements that describe a relationship between two variables with respect to a particular case. For example:

> Foreign (variable) cars are perceived by Italian consumers (case) to be of better quality (variable) than domestic cars.

In this instance, the nature of the relationship between the two variables ('country of origin' and 'perceived quality') is not specified. Is there only an implication that the variables occur in some predictable relationship, or is one variable somehow responsible for the other? The first interpretation (unspecified relationship) indicates a correlational relationship; the second (pre-dictable relationship) indicates an explanatory, or causal, relationship.

**Correlational hypotheses** state merely that the variables occur together in some specified manner without implying that one causes the other. Such weak claims are often made when we believe there are more basic causal forces that affect both variables or when we have not developed enough evidence to claim a stronger linkage. Here are three sample correlational hypotheses:

> Young machinists (under 35 years of age) are less productive than those who are 35 years of age or older.

> The height of women's hemlines varies directly with the level of the business cycle.

> People in the UK give the European Commission a less favourable rating than do people in France.

By labelling these as correlational hypotheses, we make no claim that one variable causes the other to change or take on different values. Other researchers, however, may view one or more of these hypotheses as reflecting cause-and-effect relationships.

With **explanatory (causal) hypotheses**, there is an implication that the existence of, or a change in, one variable causes or leads to a change in the other. As noted earlier, the causal vari-able is typically called the independent variable (IV) and the other the dependent variable (DV). 'Cause' means roughly to '*help* make happen'; so the IV need not be the sole reason for the existence of, or change in, the DV.

Here are three examples of explanatory hypotheses:

> An increase in family income (IV) leads to an increase in the percentage of income saved (DV).

> Exposure to the company's messages concerning industry problems (IV) leads to more favourable attitudes (DV) from production workers towards the company.

> Loyalty to a particular grocery store (IV) increases the probability of purchasing the own-label goods (DV) sponsored by that store.

In proposing or interpreting causal hypotheses, the researcher must consider the direction of influence. In many cases, this is obvious from the nature of the variables. Thus, one would assume that family income influences savings rate rather than vice versa.

Sometimes our ability to identify the direction of influence depends on the research design. In the worker attitude hypothesis, if exposure to the message clearly precedes attitude measure-ment, then the direction of exposure to attitude seems clear. If sets of information about both exposure and attitude were collected at the same time, the researcher might be justified in saying that different attitudes led to selective message perception or non-perception. Store loyalty and the purchasing of store brands, for example, appear to be interdependent. Loyalty to a store may increase the probability of buying the store's own-label goods, but satisfaction with the store's own-label goods may also lead to greater store loyalty.

## The role of the hypothesis

In research, a hypothesis serves several important functions:

- it guides the direction of the study
- it identifies those facts that are relevant and those that are not
- it suggests which form of research design is likely to be most appropriate
- it provides a framework for organizing the conclusions.

A frequent problem in research is a proliferation of interesting information. Unless the researcher curbs their urge to include additional elements, a study can be diluted by trivial concerns that do not answer the basic questions posed by the management dilemma (i.e. the focus of the research). The virtue of a hypothesis is that, if taken seriously and adhered to, it limits what will be studied.

To consider the role of the hypothesis in determining the direction of a piece of research, suppose we take this example:

> Husbands and wives agree in their perceptions of their respective roles in purchase decisions.

The hypothesis specifies who will be studied (married couples), in what context they will be studied (their consumer decision-making), and what in particular will be studied (their individual perceptions of their roles).

The nature of this hypothesis and the implications of the statement suggest that the best research design would be a communication-based study, probably a survey or interview. We have at this time no other practical means to ascertain perceptions of people except to ask about them in one way or another. In addition, we are interested only in the roles that are assumed in the purchase or consumer decision-making situation. The study should not, therefore, involve itself in seeking information about other types of role that husbands and wives might fulfil.

Reflection on this hypothesis might also reveal that husbands and wives disagree on their perceptions of their roles, but these differences may be explained in terms of additional variables, such as age, social class, background, personality differences and other factors not associated with their difference in gender.

## What makes a good hypothesis?

A good hypothesis should fulfil three conditions. It should be:

- adequate for its purpose
- testable
- better than its rivals.

For a descriptive hypothesis, adequacy for its purpose means that it clearly states the condition, size or distribution of some variable in terms of values that are meaningful to the research task. If it is an explanatory hypothesis, it must explain the facts that gave rise to the need for explanation. Using the hypothesis, plus other known and accepted generalizations, one should be able to deduce the original problem condition.

A hypothesis is testable if it meets the following conditions:

- It does not require techniques that are currently unavailable:
- It does not require an explanation that defies known physical or psychological laws.
- There are consequences or derivatives that can be deduced for testing purposes.

Generally, a hypothesis is better than its rivals if it:

- has a greater range than its rivals
- explains more facts than its rivals
- explains a greater variety of facts than its rivals
- is simple, requiring few conditions or assumptions.

## 1.8 Theory

Hypotheses play an important role in the development of **theory**. While theory development has not, historically, been an important aspect of business research, it is gradually becoming more influential.

Someone who is unfamiliar with research might use the term theory to mean the opposite of fact. In this sense, theory is viewed as being speculative. You might hear, say, that Professor X is too theoretical, that managers need to be less theoretical, or that some idea will not work because it is too theoretical. For the researcher, this gives a distorted picture of the relationship between fact and theory.

When you are too theoretical, this is likely to mean that the basis of your explanation or decision is not sufficiently attuned to specific empirical conditions. Although this may be so, it does not *prove* that theory and fact are opposites. The truth is that fact and theory are each necessary for the other to be of value. Our ability to make rational decisions, as well as to develop scientific knowledge, is measured by the degree to which we combine fact and theory.

We all operate on the basis of the theories we hold. In one sense, theories are the generalizations we make about variables and the relationships among them. We use these generalizations to make decisions and predict outcomes. For example, it is midday and you note that, outside, the natural light is dimming; dark clouds are moving rapidly in from the west, the breeze is freshening and the air temperature is getting cooler. Would your understanding of the relationship between these variables (your weather theory) lead you to predict that something decidedly wet is likely to occur at any minute?

Consider a situation where you are called upon to interview two people for possible promotion to the position of department manager. Do you have a theory about the characteristics such a person should have?

Suppose you interview Ms A and observe that she answers your questions well, openly and apparently sincerely. She also expresses thoughtful ideas about how to improve departmental functioning and is articulate in stating her views. Ms B, on the other hand, is guarded in her comments and reluctant to advance ideas for improvement. She answers questions by saying what 'Mr General Manager wants'. She is also less articulate and seems less sincere than Ms A. You would probably choose Ms A, based on the way you combine the concepts, definitions and propositions mentioned into a theory of managerial effectiveness. Your theory of managerial effectiveness, while workable, may not necessarily be a good theory because of the variables it has ignored, but it illustrates that we all use theory to guide our decisions, predictions and explanations.

A theory is a set of systematically interrelated concepts, definitions and propositions that are advanced to explain and predict phenomena (facts). In this sense, we have many theories and use them continually to explain or predict what goes on around us. To the degree that our theories are sound and fit the situation at hand, we are successful in forming explanations and predictions. Thus, while a given theory and a set of facts may not 'fit', they are not opposites. Our challenge is to build a better theory and to be more skilful in fitting together theory and fact.

The ways in which theory differs from hypothesis may also be a source of confusion. This book makes the general distinction that the difference between theory and hypothesis is one of degree of complexity and abstraction. In general, theories tend to be complex, abstract and involve multiple variables. Hypotheses, on the other hand, tend to be simple, limited-variable propositions involving concrete instances.

While researchers note a difference, at times the terms theory and hypothesis are used interchangeably. Doing this should not make much practical difference to your applied research.

## Theory and research

It is important for researchers to recognize the pervasiveness and value of theory. Theory serves us in many useful ways. It:

- narrows the range of facts we need to study
- suggests which research approaches are likely to yield the greatest meaning
- suggests a system for the researcher to impose on data in order to classify them in the most meaningful way
- summarizes what is known about an object of study, and states the uniformities that lie beyond immediate observation
- can be used to predict any further facts that may be found.

## Models

The term **model** is used in various fields of business and allied disciplines with little agreement as to its definition. This may be because of the numerous functions, structures and types of model that exist. Most definitions agree, however, that models represent phenomena through the use of analogy. A model may be defined for our purposes as the representation of a system that is constructed to study some aspect of that system or the system as a whole.

Models differ from theories in that a theory's role is explanation, whereas a model's role is representation:

> A model is not an explanation; it is only the structure and/or function of a second object or process. A model is the result of taking the structure or function of one object or process and using that as a model for the second. When the substance, either physical or conceptual, of the second object or process has been projected onto the first, a model has been constructed.[22]

Many ideas about new product adoption, for example, can be traced to rural sociology models. These describe how information and innovations spread throughout communities or cultures, starting with opinion leaders. The behaviour of a respected leader is subsequently embraced by society as a whole to express homage to that leader and retain social acceptance.

Models may be used for applied or highly theoretical purposes. Almost everyone is familiar with queuing models of service: banks, post offices, telephone voice-response units and airport security units 'feed' patrons from a single queue to multiple service points. Other models, for assembly lines, transportation and inventory, also attempt to solve immediate practical needs. A model to advance a theory of quality of working life, for example, could target employee behaviour under conditions of flexitime, permanent part-time, job-sharing and compressed working week.

Description, explication and simulation are the three major functions of modelling. Each of these functions is appropriate to applied research or theory building.

- Descriptive models: describe the behaviour of elements in a system where theory is inadequate or non-existent.
- Explicative models: extend the application of well-developed theories or improve our understanding of their key concepts.
- Simulation models: clarify the structural relationships of concepts and attempt to reveal the process relationships among them.[23]

The latter can be:

- static (i.e. represent a system at one point in time)
- dynamic (i.e. represent the evolution of a system over time).

Monte Carlo simulation models are examples of static simulations. They simulate probabilistic processes using random numbers. Redistribution of market share, brand switching and prediction of future values are just some examples of areas that can benefit from dynamic modelling.

## Research Methods in Practice 1

# Why should we cooperate?

The running case used in all chapters is the account of a government-sponsored research programme 'The management of matches' granted to Werner Raub and Jeroen Weesie (Utrecht University) in 1990. One of the authors (Blumberg) has written his Ph.D. thesis in this programme. This thesis on the management of interfirm relations in R&D is the background of the case, simply because we know more about this small part of the total programme than about the many other studies conducted within it. Still, in various chapters, we touch on some of the other studies, sometimes even rather extensively, as the thesis project did not employ all the potential research methods and methodological issues covered in the book.

In 1651, the moral philosopher Hobbes posed the simple question, why do people cooperate rather than engage in ultimate competition including the possibility of eliminating competitors by brute force, that is by killing them? You should note that publication of Hobbes' thoughts was preceded by the English Civil War (1642–1651) and that at those times legal systems did not work as they work today. Thus, you could write a contract, but a contract then differed largely from a contract today as there was no third authority that could enforce the contract; the contract was merely a written form of a promise of two parties towards each other. Still, Hobbes observed that people often cooperate with each other and he asked himself what are the reasons for that?

In 1963, the sociologist Macauley observed that many firms use contracts to structure and govern their relations with other firms, but hardly use them. Why do they use those contracts, but do not trust in their enforcement? One explanation to this particular question is that contract enforcement through the courts takes a long time and is often unpredictable, as shown in the proverb having right and getting right are two different things.

Are we nice to each other? In 2004, the European Social Survey questioned more than 40,000 people in 20 countries about their ethical attitudes and behaviour. More than 80 per cent of the respondents responded that they are ethical, that is in the last five years they had not engaged in any unethical behaviour such as keeping change money that they were not entitled to, having paid for goods or service without getting a proper invoice, made a wrong or extensive claim towards an insurance company and so on. What about the other 20 per cent, do we need to care about them?

Akerlof (1970) explained why the 'honest' dealers suffer from the phoney dealers in the used car market. For a buyer of a new car it is hard to distinguish between the honest and phoney car dealer. As a buyer you cannot detect which cars are good value for money and which are overpriced lemons. As a consequence, you are only willing to pay the price suitable for a lemon. Suppose you are an honest dealer, how can you convince sellers that the cars you sell are good ones? Would offering a warranty be a solution?

All these examples point at one very general problem affecting people for centuries, namely, why do self-interested actors cooperate with each other? Think broadly about further examples in which people and/or firms face such cooperation problems; think about situations in which it is obvious to you that people cooperate with each other and think about other situations in which it is less understandable or even puzzles you that people cooperate.

## References

Akerlof, G.A. (1970) 'The Market for "Lemons": Qualitative uncertainty and the market mechanism', *Quarterly Journal of Economics* 84, pp. 488–500.

Hobbes, T. (1651/1996) *Leviathan: World's Classics.* Oxford: Oxford University Press.

Macaulay, S. (1963) 'Non-Contractual Relations in Business', *American Sociological Review* 28, pp. 55–66.

# Summary

1 Research is any organized inquiry that is carried out in order to provide information that can be used to solve problems. Business research is a systematic inquiry that provides information to guide business decisions. This includes reporting, descriptive, explanatory and predictive studies. This book emphasizes the last three.

2 What characterizes good research? Generally, we expect good research to be purposeful, with a clearly defined focus and plausible goals, with defensible, ethical and replicable procedures, and with evidence of objectivity. The reporting of procedures – their strengths and weaknesses – should be complete and honest. Appropriate analytical techniques should be used; conclusions drawn should be limited to those clearly justified by the findings; and reports of findings and conclusions should be presented clearly and be professional in tone, language and appearance. Managers should always choose a researcher who has an established reputation for good-quality work. The research objective and its benefits should be weighed against any potentially adverse effects.

3 Research in management and business is rooted in different research philosophies. The most prominent ones are positivism and interpretivism. Positivism is the research philosophy adopted from the natural sciences. Its proponents believe that the social world exists externally and can be viewed objectively. Hence a real truth exists and it can best be understood by reducing it to the simplest possible elements. Moreover, they claim that research is value-free and that researchers should take an independent role as objective analysts. Interpretivism supposes that the social world is constructed and people give subjective meaning to it. Hence, the social world is an individual construction and, to understand it, the researcher needs to look at a total picture. Unlike positivists, interpretivists believe that research is driven by interests and that the researcher is part of what is observed.

4 The demand for information tomorrow will be much greater than it is today. Research will make a major contribution to providing this knowledge. The knowledge of research methods will be of value in many situations for managers, public policy-makers and scientific researchers. They may need to conduct research either for themselves or for others. As users and readers of research results they will need to be able to judge research quality. Finally, they may become research specialists themselves.

5 Styles of thinking are perspectives, or filters, for determining how we view and understand reality. They affect what we accept as truth and govern how rigorously we test the information we receive before endorsing it. Although the scientific method is the pre-eminent means by which we secure empirical information, it is not the only source of truth. Other styles of thinking also have an apparent, and often useful, influence on business disciplines, and give their approval to the theory-building and problem-solving approaches of those fields.

Scientific inquiry is grounded in the inference process. This process is used for the development and testing of various propositions, largely through the so-called 'double movement of reflective thinking'. Reflective thinking involves sequencing induction and deduction in order to explain inductively (by hypothesis) a puzzling condition/dilemma.

In turn, the hypothesis is used in the deduction of further facts that can be sought to confirm or deny the truth of the hypothesis.

Researchers think of 'doing science' as an orderly process that combines induction, deduction, observation and hypothesis testing into a set of reflective thinking activities. Although the scientific method consists of neither sequential nor independent stages, the problem-solving process it reveals provides insight into the way that research is conducted.

6  Scientific methods and scientific thinking are based on concepts – the symbols that we attach to bundles of meaning that we hold and share with others. We invent concepts to help us to think about and communicate abstractions. We also use higher-level concepts – constructs – for specialized scientific explanatory purposes that are not directly observable. Concepts, constructs and variables may be defined descriptively or operationally. Operational definitions, which are essential in research, must specify adequately the empirical information needed and state how it will be collected. In addition, they must have the proper scope or 'fit' for the research problem at hand.

Concepts and constructs are used at the theoretical level; variables are used at the empirical level. Variables can be allocated numerals or values for the purpose of testing and measurement. They may be classified as explanatory (independent, dependent or moderating), extraneous or intervening.

7  Propositions are of great interest in research because they may be used to assess the truth or falsity of relationships among observable phenomena. When we advance a proposition for testing, we are hypothesizing. A hypothesis describes the relationships between or among variables. A good hypothesis is one that can explain what it claims to explain, is testable, and has greater range, probability and simplicity than its rivals.

Sets of interrelated concepts, definitions and propositions that are advanced to explain and predict phenomena are called theories. Models differ from theories in that models are analogies or representations of some aspect of a system or of the system as a whole. Models are used for description, explication and simulation.

## Discussion questions

## Terms in review

1  What is research? Why should there be any question about the definition of research?

2  What is the difference between applied and basic or pure research? Use a decision about how a salesperson is to be paid, by commission or salary, and describe the question that would guide applied research versus the question that would guide pure research.

3  Distinguish among the following sets of items, and suggest the significance of each in a research context.
   a  concept and construct
   b  deduction and induction

    c  operational definition and dictionary definition
    d  concept and variable
    e  hypothesis and proposition
    f  theory and model
    g  scientific method and scientific attitude

**4** Describe the basic principles and assumptions of positivism and interpretivism.

**5** Describe the characteristics of the scientific method.

**6** Listed below are some terms commonly found in a management setting. Are they concepts or constructs? Give two different operational definitions for each.
    a  first-line supervisor
    b  employee morale
    c  assembly line
    d  overdue account
    e  line management
    f  leadership
    g  price – earnings ratio
    h  union democracy
    i  ethical standards

**7** In your company's management development programme there was a heated discussion between some people who claimed that 'Theory is impractical and thus no good' and others who claimed that 'Good theory is the most practical approach to problems.' What position would you take and why?

**8** An automobile manufacturer observes demand for its brand increasing as per capita income increases. Sales increases also follow low interest rates, which ease credit conditions. Buyer purchase behaviour is seen to be dependent on age and gender. Other factors influencing sales appear to fluctuate almost randomly (e.g. competitor advertising, competitor dealer discounts, introduction of new competitive models).
    a  If sales and per capita income are positively related, classify all variables as dependent, independent, moderating, extraneous or intervening.
    b  Comment on the utility of a model based on the hypothesis.

## Making research decisions

**9** A human resources manager needs information in order to help him decide whether to create a 'custom-built' motivation programme or purchase one offered by a human resources consulting firm. What are the dilemmas the manager faces in selecting either alternative?

**10** You are manager of the European division of a major corporation, supervising five animal feed plants scattered over four counties. Corporate headquarters asks you to conduct an investigation to determine whether any of these plants should be closed, expanded, moved or downsized. Is there a possible conflict between your roles as researcher and manager? Explain.

**11** Advise each of the following people on a specific research study that he or she might find useful. Classify each proposed study as reporting, descriptive, explanatory or predictive.
    a  When the management decision problem is known:
      i    manager of a full-service restaurant with high employee turnover

    **ii**   head of an academic department committee charged with selecting a research methods textbook.

  **b** When the management decision problem has not yet been specified:

    **i**   manager of a restaurant

    **ii**   plant manager at a shoe factory

    **iii**   director of the TV programme *Who Wants To Be A Millionaire?* in charge of sponsor recruitment

    **iv**   data analyst with ACNielsen (research specialist)

    **v**   human resources manager at a university

    **vi**   product manager for the Mercedes A Class

    **vii**   family services officer for your county

    **viii**   office manager for a paediatrician.

**12** The new president of an old, established company is facing a problem. The company is currently unprofitable and is, in the president's opinion, operating inefficiently. The company sells a wide range of equipment and supplies to the dairy industry. It manufactures some items and sells many wholesale to dairies, creameries and similar plants. Because the industry is changing in several ways, survival will become more difficult in the future. In particular, many equipment companies are bypassing wholesalers and selling direct to dairies. In addition, many independent dairies are being taken over by large food chains. How might research help the new president make the right decisions? In answering this question, consider the areas of marketing and finance as well as the company as a whole.

**13** You have received the results of a research report carried out by a consultant on behalf of your firm, a life insurance company. The study is a survey of morale in the home office and covers the opinions of about 500 secretaries and clerks, as well as about 100 executives and actuaries. You are asked to comment on its quality. What will you look for?

**14** As area sales manager for a company that manufactures and markets outboard engines, you have been assigned the responsibility of conducting a research study to estimate the sales potential of your products in the Scandinavian market. Discuss the key issues and concerns arising from the fact that you, the manager, are also the researcher.

**15** You observe the following condition: 'Our female sales representatives have lower customer defections than do our male sales representatives.'

  **a** Propose the concepts and constructs you might use to study this phenomenon.

  **b** How might any of these concepts and/or constructs be related to explanatory hypotheses?

**16** You are the office manager of a large firm. Your company prides itself on its high-quality customer service. Lately, complaints have surfaced which reveal that an increasing number of incoming calls are being misrouted or dropped. Yesterday, when passing the main reception area, you noticed the receptionist fiddling with his hearing aid. In the process, a call came in and would have gone unanswered if not for your intervention. This particular receptionist had earned an unsatisfactory review three months earlier for tardiness. Your inclination is to urge this employee – who has been with the firm for 20 years – to retire, or to fire him if retirement is rejected. However, you know the individual is well liked and seen as a fixture in the company.

  **a** Suggest several hypotheses that might account for dropped or misrouted incoming calls.

  **b** Using the 'double movement of reflective thought', show how you would test these hypotheses.

## From concept to practice

**17** Apply the principles in Exhibit 1.1 to the research scenario in question 8.

**18** Using Exhibits 1.4 and 1.5 as a guide, draw up graphs to illustrate the inductions and deductions in the following statements. (If there are gaps, supply what is needed to make them complete arguments.)

 **a** Repeated studies indicate that economic conditions vary with – and lag 6 to 12 months behind – the changes in the national money supply; therefore, we may conclude that money supply is the basic economic variable.

 **b** Research studies show that heavy smokers have a higher rate of lung cancer than do non-smokers; therefore, heavy smoking causes lung cancer.

 **c** Show me a person who goes to church regularly, and I will show you a reliable worker.

## Class discussion

**19** Suppose you are part of an international team of social experts asked to assess the organizational culture within a large life insurance company. All class members born in the months January to June should follow the positivistic research philosophy, while those class members born in the months July to December should take the interpretivism route. Discuss how the organizational culture of the company could be assessed.

**20** Business decisions are often taken under immense time pressure. Often, there is just not enough time to collect information based on good research. Discuss which criteria of good research you would compromise on if you just did enough not have enough time; or would it be better to abandon the research altogether, if it cannot be conducted well, as the obtained information is likely to be invalid and unreliable?

Online
*Learning* **Centre**

## Get started with understanding statistical techniques!

When you have read this chapter, log on to the Online Learning Centre website at ***www.mcgraw-hill.co.uk/textbooks/blumberg*** to explore chapter-by-chapter test questions, additional case studies, a glossary and more online study tools for Business Research Methods.

# Notes

[1] See, for example, Murray Levine, 'Investigative reporting as a research method: analysis of Bernstein and Woodward's *All the President's Men*', *American Psychologist* 35 (1980), pp. 626–38.

[2] See, for example, Elizabethann O'Sullivan and Gary R. Rassel, *Research Methods for Public Administrators*. New York: Longman, 1999.

[3] Fred N. Kerlinger and Howard B. Lee, *Foundations of Behavioral Research* (4th edn.). New York: HBJ College & School Division, 1999, p. 15.

[4] A hypothesis is a statement that is advanced for the purpose of testing its truth or falsity.

[5] An exploratory study describes an investigation when the final research problem has not yet been clearly fixed. Its aim is to provide the insights needed by the researcher to develop a more formal research design.

[6] Reprinted with the permission of Macmillan Publishing Co., Inc. from Robert Dubin, *Theory Building* (rev. edn., 1978). Copyright © 1969, Free Press, a division of Macmillan Co.

[7] Mark Easterby-Smith, Richard Thrope and Andy Lowe, *Management Research: An Introduction*. London: Sage, 1991, p. 20.

[8] Auguste Comte, *The Positive Philosophy of Auguste Comte*. London: Trubner & Co., 1853.

[9] Jürgen Habermas, 'Knowledge and interest', in D. Emmet and A. MacIntyre (eds.), *Sociological Theory and Philosophical Analysis*. London: Macmillan, 1970.

[10] Howard Kahane, *Logic and Philosophy* (2nd edn.). Belmont, CA: Wadsworth, 1973, p. 3.

[11] John Dewey, *How We Think*. Boston: Heath, 1910, p. 79.

[12] This section is based on Dewey, *How We Think*, and John R. Platt, 'Strong inference', *Science*, 16 October 1964, pp. 347–53.

[13] F.J. Roethlisberger and W.J. Dickson, *Management and the Worker*. Cambridge, MA: Harvard University Press, 1939.

[14] Paul R. Lawrence, 'Historical development of organizational behaviour', in Jay W. Lorsch (ed.), *Handbook of Organizational Behaviour*. Englewood Cliffs, NJ: Prentice Hall, 1987, p. 6.

[15] Thomas S. Kuhn, *The Structure of Scientific Revolutions*. Chicago: University of Chicago Press, 1970, p. 37.

[16] Kenneth R. Hoover, *The Elements of Social Scientific Thinking* (5th edn.). New York: St. Martin's Press, 1991, p. 21.

[17] *Merriam-Webster's Collegiate Dictionary* (10th edn.). Springfield, MA: Merriam-Webster, 1999, http://www.m-w.com/cgi-bin/dictionary.

[18] Fred N. Kerlinger and Howard B. Lee, *Foundations of Behavioral Research* (4th edn.). New York: HBJ College & School Division, 1999.

[19] Hoover, *Elements of Social Scientific Thinking*, p. 71.

[20] Bruce Tuckman, *Conducting Educational Research*. New York: Harcourt Brace Jovanovich, 1972, p. 45.

[21] William N. Stephens, *Hypotheses and Evidence*. New York: Thomas Y. Crowell, 1968, p. 5.

[22] Leonard C. Hawes, *Pragmatics of Analoguing: Theory and Model Construction in Communication*. Reading, MA: Addison-Wesley, 1975, p. 111.

[23] Hawes, *Pragmatics of Analoguing*, pp. 116–22.

# Recommended further reading

**Beardsley, Monroe,** *Practical Logic.* **Englewood Cliffs, NJ: Prentice Hall, 1969.** A lucid discussion of deduction and induction, as well as excellent coverage of argument analysis.

**Browne, M. Neil and Keeley, Stuart M.,** *Asking the Right Questions: A Guide to Critical Thinking* **(7th edn.). Upper Saddle River, NJ: Prentice Hall, 2003.** Addresses question-asking skills and the techniques necessary for evaluating different types of evidence.

**Bryman, Allan and Bell, Emma,** *Business Research Methods.* **Oxford: Oxford University Press, 2003.** Chapter 1 offers a fine philosophical-based introduction to research methods.

**Churchman, C.W.,** *The Design of Inquiring Systems.* **New York: Basic Books, 1971.** An essential work for understanding the connections between philosophy, science and the nature of inquiry.

**Haas, Peter J. and J. Springer, Fred,** *Applied Policy Research: Concepts and Cases.* **New York: Garland Reference Library of Social Science, No. 1051, 1998.** Chapter 2 discusses policy research strategies and contributions.

**Hoover, Kenneth R. and Donovan, Todd,** *The Elements of Social Scientific Thinking* **(6th edn.). New York: Worth Publishers, 1994.** A brief but highly readable treatise on the elements of science and scientific thinking.

**Kaplan, Abraham,** *The Conduct of Inquiry.* **San Francisco: Transaction Publications, 1998.** A good source of information on the philosophy of science and logical reasoning.

**Kerlinger, Fred N. and Lee, Howard B.,** *Foundations of Behavioral Research* **(4th edn.). New York: HBJ College & School Division, 1999.** Especially Part 1: 'Introduction to Business Research'.

**Medema, Steven G. and Samuels, Warren J. (eds.),** *Foundations of Research in Economics: How do Economists do Economics?* **Cheltenham: Edward Elgar, 1997.** This edited volume offers insights from outstanding economists on how to conduct economic research. Although it focuses on economics, the insights provided are also useful for other social sciences.

**Random, Matthew,** *The Social Scientist in American Industry.* **New Brunswick, NJ: Rutgers University Press, 1970.** A research report detailing the experiences of social scientists employed in industry. Chapter 7 presents a summary of findings.

**Remenyi, Dan** *et al.,* *Doing Research in Business and Management: An Introduction to Process and Method.* **Thousand Oaks, CA: Sage, 1998.** Chapters 1 and 2 establish the business research perspective for management students.

**Transfield, D. and Starkey, K.,** 'The nature, social organization and promotion of management research: towards policy', *British Management Journal* 9, 1998, pp. 341–53. An article emphasizing the application side of management research and the significance of cross-fertilization between science and business practice.

## Chapter 2

# The research process and proposal

## Chapter contents

## LEARNING OBJECTIVES

When you have read this chapter, you should understand:

- ☑ that research is decision- and dilemma-centred

- ☑ that the research question results from careful exploration and analysis, and sets the direction for the research project

- ☑ that planning research design demands an understanding of all stages of the research process

- ☑ the purpose of the proposal, and how it is used

- ☑ the two processes available for evaluating the quality of proposals, and when each is used.

# 2.1 The research process

The research task is usually described as a sequential process that involves several clearly defined steps. However, it does not necessarily require that each step is completed before going on to the next one: a certain amount of recycling, circumventing and skipping of steps is likely to occur. Sometimes steps are taken out of sequence, two or more may carried out at the same time, and some may be omitted altogether. Despite these real-life variations, the idea of a basic sequence is useful in developing a project and in keeping things orderly as it unfolds.

Exhibit 2.1 illustrates the sequence of the **research process**. You will be referred back to this exhibit often as we discuss each step on the subsequent pages. Our discussion of the questions that guide project planning and data-gathering is incorporated into the model (look at the elements within the down-pointing triangle in Exhibit 2.1 and compare them with what is shown in Exhibit 2.2). Exhibit 2.1 also depicts the structure of this chapter and introduces the remainder of the book.

The research process usually begins as follows. A **research dilemma** triggers the need for investigating how the dilemma can be solved (as discussed in the previous chapter). A growing number of customer complaints, poor results after an advertising campaign, increasing turnover of personnel … these are all examples of outcomes which signal that all is not well in a business. In other situations, a controversy might arise, a major commitment of resources is called for, or conditions in the environment might signal the need for a decision. Similarly, observations made in the real world may contradict common theoretical predictions. For example, how can one explain that in an industry that is characterized by a strong concentration in the number of firms, new small firms suddenly emerge and the former concentration trend is reversed.

Such events cause managers to reconsider their purpose or objectives, and researchers to question existing theories, define a problem that requires solution or develop strategies for solutions they have already identified.

For our purposes, the research question – its origin, selection, statement, exploration and refinement – is the critical activity in the research process sequence. Throughout this chapter we emphasize the problem-related steps. A well-known quote from Albert Einstein, which is no less apt today, supports this view:

> The formulation of a problem is far more often essential than its solution, which may be merely a matter of mathematical or experimental skill. To raise new questions, new possibilities, to regard old problems from a new angle requires creative imagination and marks real advance in science.[1]

Whether the researcher is involved in basic or applied research, a thorough understanding of the management question is fundamental to success in the research enterprise.

## The management research question hierarchy

A useful way to approach the research process is to state the basic dilemma that prompts the research and then try to develop other questions. This is done by, progressively, breaking down the original question into other more specific questions. Think of the outcome of this process as the **management research question hierarchy**. Exhibit 2.2 offers examples of the kinds of question

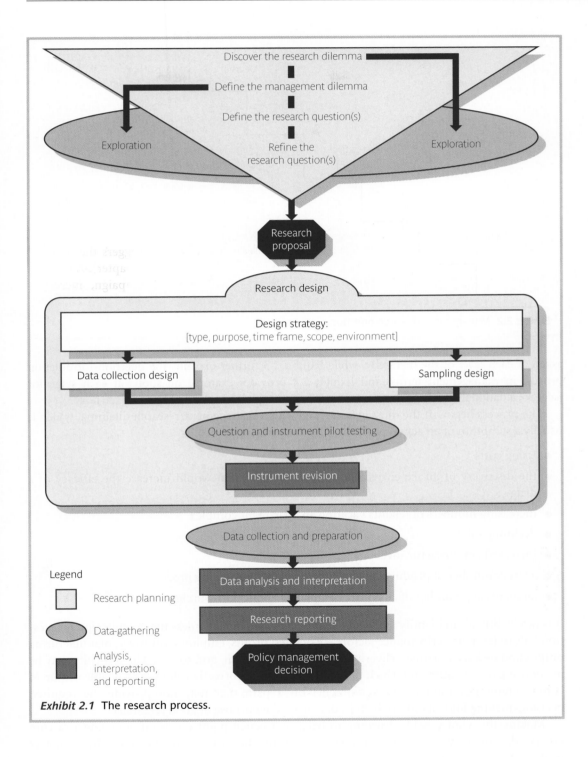

*Exhibit 2.1* The research process.

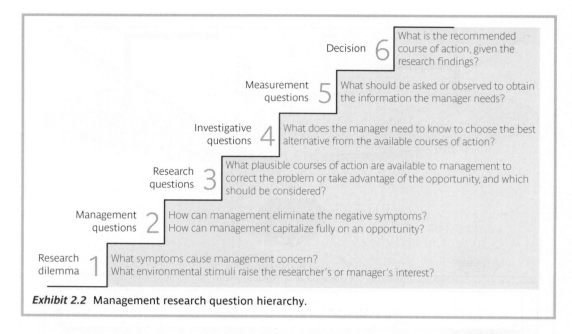

*Exhibit 2.2* Management research question hierarchy.

asked at each level of the hierarchy, while Exhibit 2.3 further explains the question-formulation process in management terms, and Exhibit 2.4 provides example questions at each stage for SalePro, a national sales organization that is facing unexplained sales variations by territory.

The process begins at the most general level with a management/research dilemma, which is usually a symptom of an actual problem. The dilemma might be:

- rising costs
- the discovery of an expensive chemical compound that would increase the efficacy of a drug
- increasing numbers of tenants vacating an apartment complex
- declining sales
- increased employee turnover
- a larger number of product defects during the manufacturing process
- an increasing number of customer complaints about post-purchase service.

It is rarely difficult to identify management/research dilemmas (unless the organization in question fails to track its performance factors – like sales, profits, employee turnover, manufacturing output and defects, on-time deliveries, customer satisfaction, and so on). The difficulty may lie in choosing one dilemma on which to focus. Choosing incorrectly will direct valuable resources (time, manpower, money and equipment) on a path that may not provide the required decision-making information (which is, of course, the purpose of good research).

Making this choice is like learning to balance a pencil point-down on your finger, a coin on its edge or a pyramid on its pinnacle. Only practice will make the researcher/manager proficient.

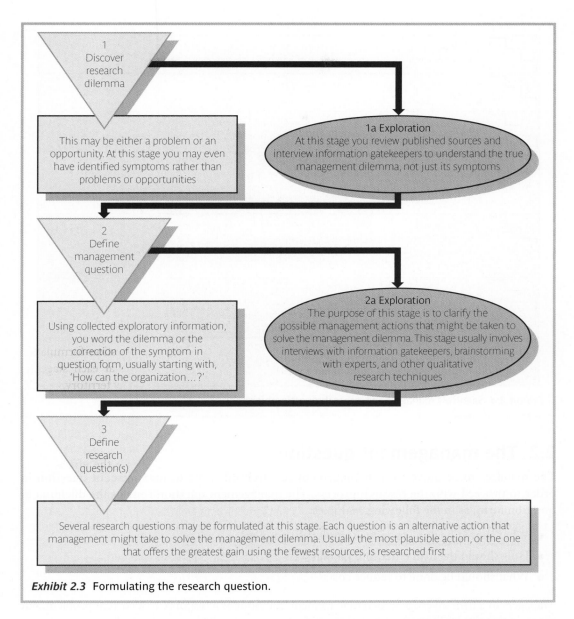

1
Discover
research
dilemma

This may be either a problem or an
opportunity. At this stage you may even
have identified symptoms rather than
problems or opportunities

1a Exploration
At this stage you review published sources and
interview information gatekeepers to understand the true
management dilemma, not just its symptoms

2
Define
management
question

Using collected exploratory information,
you word the dilemma or the
correction of the symptom in
question form, usually starting with,
'How can the organization…?'

2a Exploration
The purpose of this stage is to clarify the
possible management actions that might be taken to
solve the management dilemma. This stage usually involves
interviews with information gatekeepers, brainstorming
with experts, and other qualitative
research techniques

3
Define
research
question(s)

Several research questions may be formulated at this stage. Each question is an alternative action that
management might take to solve the management dilemma. Usually the most plausible action, or the one
that offers the greatest gain using the fewest resources, is researched first

**Exhibit 2.3** Formulating the research question.

For new managers, or established managers facing new responsibilities, developing several management research question hierarchies, each starting with a different dilemma, will assist in the choice process.

In all exhibits related to the research process model, in this and subsequent chapters, a pyramid is used to represent the management research question hierarchy and to emphasize the precarious nature of the research process's foundation decisions.

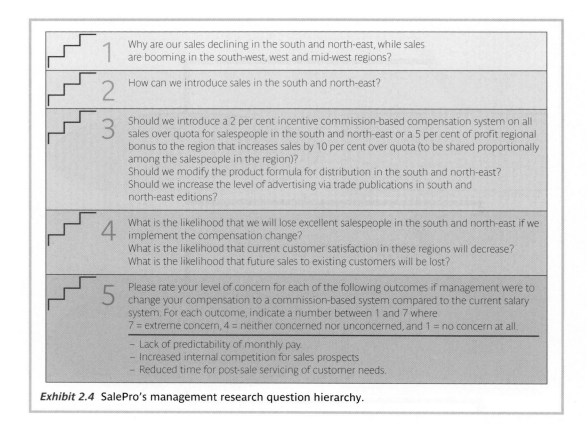

1. Why are our sales declining in the south and north-east, while sales are booming in the south-west, west and mid-west regions?

2. How can we introduce sales in the south and north-east?

3. Should we introduce a 2 per cent incentive commission-based compensation system on all sales over quota for salespeople in the south and north-east or a 5 per cent of profit regional bonus to the region that increases sales by 10 per cent over quota (to be shared proportionally among the salespeople in the region)?
Should we modify the product formula for distribution in the south and north-east?
Should we increase the level of advertising via trade publications in south and north-east editions?

4. What is the likelihood that we will lose excellent salespeople in the south and north-east if we implement the compensation change?
What is the likelihood that current customer satisfaction in these regions will decrease?
What is the likelihood that future sales to existing customers will be lost?

5. Please rate your level of concern for each of the following outcomes if management were to change your compensation to a commission-based system compared to the current salary system. For each outcome, indicate a number between 1 and 7 where 7 = extreme concern, 4 = neither concerned nor unconcerned, and 1 = no concern at all.
   - Lack of predictability of monthly pay.
   - Increased internal competition for sales prospects
   - Reduced time for post-sale servicing of customer needs.

*Exhibit 2.4* SalePro's management research question hierarchy.

## 2.2 The management question

The manager must move from **management/research dilemma** to **management question** in order to proceed with the research process. The management question restates the dilemma in question form, as in the following examples.

- What should be done to reduce employee turnover?
- How should the firm enter foreign markets?
- What should be done to reduce costs?

Managers in a firm investigate such management questions as a response to a current problem, but many management dilemmas are also researched more generally in a student's thesis or a research paper. For example, a student's thesis on human resource management, internationalization strategies or on productivity issues will address the questions stated above.

### Management question categories

Management questions are too numerous to list, but we can categorize them as follows:

- choice of purpose or objectives

- generation and evaluation of solutions
- troubleshooting or control situation.

The first type of question concerns the choice of purpose or objectives. The general question is 'What do we want to achieve?' At company level the question might be 'Should we at Metal-Works Corporation reconsider our basic corporate objectives as they concern our public image?' More narrowly, a management question on objectives might ask 'What goals should MetalWorks Corporation try to achieve in its next round of labour negotiations?' In academic research, possible objectives are attempts to explain current inconsistencies within or between theoretical considerations, testing new theoretical ideas or giving a well-reasoned, that is theoretically backed, account of an observed phenomenon.

A second category of management questions concerns the generation and evaluation of solutions. The general question is 'How can we achieve the ends we seek?' Research projects in this group usually deal with concrete problems. Projects can involve questions such as the following.

- How can we achieve our five-year goal of doubled sales and net profits?
- How can we reduce employee turnover and increase the organizational commitment of our workers?
- What should be done to reduce post-purchase service complaints?
- How can we explain new firms' successful entrance into mature and concentrated industry?
- How can we explain that the stock price of highly diversified firms is lower than the stock price of less diversified firms, even if we consider differences in returns?

A third class of management questions concerns the troubleshooting, or control, situation. The problem usually involves monitoring or diagnosing various ways in which an organization is failing to achieve its established goals. This class includes questions such as 'Why does our department incur the highest costs?' and 'How well is our programme meeting its goals?'

No matter how the management question is defined, research can take many directions. A specific question can, for example, give rise to many studies. So, concern for MetalWorks' company image might lead to:

- a survey among various groups to discover their attitude towards the company
- secondary research into what other companies are doing to enhance their images
- a study to forecast expected changes in social attitudes.

The question concerning MetalWorks' labour negotiation objectives might prompt research into recent settlements in the industry or a survey among workers to find out how well management has met its concerns about the quality of their working life. It is the joint responsibility of the researcher and the manager to choose the most productive project.

## The nature of the management question

Assume that a researcher is asked to help the new management of a bank. The president is concerned about erosion of the bank's profitability (the management dilemma) and wants to turn this situation around. BankChoice is the oldest and largest of three banks in a region with a population of about 500,000. Profits have stagnated in recent years. The president and the consultant discuss the problem facing the organization and settle on this management question: 'How can we improve our profit picture?'

This question does not specify what kind of research is to be done. It is strictly managerial in thrust. It implies that the bank's management faces the task of developing a strategy for increasing profits. The question is broad. Notice that it doesn't indicate whether management should increase profits via encouraging a larger number of deposits, by downsizing personnel, outsourcing the payroll function, or by some other means.

Further discussion between the bank president and the researcher reveals that there are really two questions to be answered. The problem of low deposit growth is linked to concerns of a competitive nature. While lowered deposits directly affect profits, another part of the profit weakness is associated with negative factors within the organization that are increasing operation costs. The experienced researcher knows that the management question as stated is too broad to guide a definitive research project. Such a broadly worded question is fine as a starting point, but BankChoice will want to refine its management question into more specific sub-questions as follows.

- How can we increase the number of deposits?
- How can we reduce costs?

This separation of the management question into two sub-questions may not have occurred had there not been a discussion between the researcher and the manager.

### Exploration

BankChoice has done no formal research in the past. It has little specific information about competitors or customers, and has not analysed its internal operations. To move forward in the management research question hierarchy and define the research question, the client needs to collect some exploratory information on:

- what factors are contributing to the bank's failure to achieve a stronger growth rate in deposits
- how well the bank is doing in terms of work climate, efficiency of operations compared to industry norms, and financial condition compared to industry norms and competitors.

To do this, a small focus-group exercise is conducted among employees, and trade association data are acquired to facilitate a comparison of financial and operating statistics from company annual reports and end-of-year division reports. From the results of these two exploratory activities, it is obvious that BankChoice's operations are not as progressive as its competitors, but that it has its costs well in line. So the revised management question becomes 'What should be done to make the bank more competitive?'

The area of **exploration** may surface within the research process in several locations (see Exhibit 2.3). An exploration typically begins with a search of published **data**. In addition, researchers often seek out people who are well informed on the topic in question, especially those who have clearly stated positions on controversial aspects of the problem.

Take the case of TechByte, a company interested in enhancing its position in a given technology that appears to have potential for future growth. This interest or need might quickly elicit a number of questions:

- How fast might this technology develop?
- What are the likely applications of this technology?
- Which companies now possess it, and which are likely to make a major effort to get it?
- How much will it take in resources?
- What are the likely payoffs?

In the above investigation of opportunities, researchers would probably start off by looking at specific books and periodicals. They would be looking only for certain aspects in this literature, such as recent developments, predictions by informed figures about the prospects of the technology, identification of those involved in the area, and accounts of successful ventures or failures by others in the field.

Having familiarized themselves with the literature, researchers might seek interviews with scientists, engineers and product developers who are well known in the field. They would pay special attention to those who represent the two extremes of opinion with regard to the prospects of the technology. If possible, they would talk with persons having information on particularly thorny problems in development and application. Although much of the information will be confidential and competitive, skilful investigation can uncover many useful indicators.

An unstructured exploration allows the researcher to develop and revise the management question and determine what is needed to secure answers to the proposed question.

## 2.3  From research to measurement question

### Research questions

Once the researcher has a clear statement of the management question, she must work with the manager to translate it into a **research question**. This step is often a rather large one, especially if you conduct research sponsored by an organization, as practioners formulate questions in terms of the problem to be solved and not in terms of the research it is necessary to conduct. Consider the research question to be a fact-oriented, information-gathering question. There are many different ways to address most management dilemmas. It is at this point in formulating research questions that the insight and expertise of the manager come into play. Only reasonable alternatives should be considered. If the researcher is not part of the manager's decision-making environment, then she may be of minimal help in this translation; the direction that the manager gives the researcher is most important. If, however, the researcher is an integral part of the decision-making environment, she may assist the manager in evaluating which courses of action should and can be researched.

Let's go back to our earlier example: MetalWorks Corporation. Currently, MetalWorks has lower productivity than comparable companies in the industry and it pays wages according to the latest contract between unions and the industry association, plus additional benefits related to tenure. A year ago MetalWorks closed an unprofitable plant in northern England. Recently, the media have published stories about disrupted relations between management and labour representatives resulting in a worrisome public image. The more specific management question reads 'What should MetalWorks Corporation achieve in the next round of labour negotiations?' In a brainstorming session MetalWorks' management hypothesized several problems that may have resulted in the lower productivity and the disturbed relations with workers. Some of these problems are not as easy to correct as others (e.g., demand for MetalWorks' products is only partly within the firm's immediate control – it is also determined by the current economic situation). If MetalWorks does not survey its employees about job satisfaction and their organizational commitment on a regular basis, an exploratory study might have to be undertaken to determine employees' major concerns.

Defining the research question incorrectly is a fundamental weakness in the research process. Time and money can be wasted studying an alternative that won't help the manager rectify the dilemma.

The researcher's task is to assist the manager in formulating a research question that fits the need to resolve the management dilemma. A research question is the hypothesis of choice that best states the objective of the research study. It is a more specific management question that must be answered. It may be just one question, or more than one. A research process that answers this more specific question will provide the manager with the information necessary to make the decision he or she is facing.

After consulting with a labour expert, MetalWorks' management identifies several credible options to be achieved in the labour negotiations:

- more flexible working hours, which will allow the company to adjust hours worked to suit current demand
- relate additional benefits for workers not to their length of tenure but to the company's profit
- establish 'round tables' of workers, management and local (labour) representatives in each plant to discuss current problems at the plant level
- start a public relations campaign to improve MetalWorks' image and secure more positive media coverage.

These choices lead to several research questions, as follows.

- What are the effects of different flexible working time systems on productivity?
- What are the effects of payment schemes for additional benefits on MetalWorks' profitability, and how should such schemes be designed?
- What are the effects of 'round tables' on MetalWorks' productivity?
- What are the effects of public relations campaigns on the perceived image of MetalWorks?

Meanwhile at BankChoice, the president has agreed that the research should be guided by the following research question: 'How does the image of BankChoice affect its number of customers and cost structure?'

## Fine-tuning the research question

The term fine-tuning might seem to be an odd usage for research, but it creates an image that most researchers come to recognize. Fine-tuning the question is precisely what a skilful practitioner must do once the initial exploration is complete. At this point, a clearer picture of the management and research questions begins to emerge. After a preliminary review of the literature, a brief exploratory study, or both, the project begins to crystallize in one of two ways:

1  it is apparent that the question has been answered and the process is finished

2  a question different from that originally addressed has become apparent.

The research question does not have to be materially different, but it will have evolved in some fashion. This is no cause for discouragement, however. The refined research question (or questions) will have better focus and will help to move the research forward with more clarity than the initial question (or questions) that were formulated.

In addition to fine-tuning the original question, other research question-related activities should be addressed in this phase in order to enhance the progress of the project. These are as follows.

1  Examine the concepts and constructs to be used in the study. Are they defined satisfactorily? Have operational definitions been employed where appropriate?

2  Review the research questions with the intent of breaking them down into specific second- and third-level questions.

3  If hypotheses are used, ensure that they meet the quality criteria mentioned in the preceding chapter.

4  Determine what evidence must be collected to answer the various questions and hypotheses.

5  Set the scope of the study by stating what is *not* part of the research question. This will establish a boundary that will help to separate contiguous problems from the primary objective.

When the characteristics or plausible causes of the problem have been defined accurately and the research question clearly stated, it is possible to develop the essential sub-questions that will guide planning of the project at this stage of the research process. However, if the research question is at all poorly defined, the researcher will need further exploration and question revision to refine the original question and generate the material necessary to construct suitable investigative questions.

## Investigative questions

Once the research question(s) has been selected, the researcher's thinking needs to move to a more specific level – that of **investigative questions** (see Exhibit 2.4). These questions reveal the specific pieces of information that the manager feels he or she needs to know in order to answer the research question.

Investigative questions are questions that the researcher must answer to arrive at a satisfactory conclusion about the research question. To formulate them, the researcher takes a general research question and breaks it into more specific questions about which to gather data. This 'fractionating' process can continue down through several levels of increasing specificity. Investigative questions should be included in the research proposal because they guide the development of the research design – they are the foundation on which the research data collection instrument is based.

The researcher working on the BankChoice project develops two major investigative questions for studying the market, with several sub-questions under each, as presented below. The questions provide insight into the lack of deposit growth.

1  What is the public's position regarding financial services and their use?
    a  What specific financial services are used?
    b  How attractive are various services?
    c  What bank-specific and environmental factors influence a person's use of a particular service?
2  What is the bank's competitive position?
    a  What are the geographic patterns of our customers and our competitors' customers?
    b  What demographic differences are revealed among our customers and those of our competitors?
    c  What words or phrases does the public (both customers and non-customers) associate with BankChoice? With BankChoice's competitors?
    d  How aware is the public of the bank's promotional efforts?
    e  What opinion does the public hold of the bank and its competitors?
    f  How does growth in services compare among competing institutions?

## Measurement questions

**Measurement questions** should be outlined by completion of the project-planning activities, but usually await pilot testing for refinement. There are two types of measurement question:

1  pre-designed or pre-tested questions
2  custom-designed questions.

Pre-designed measurement questions are those that have been formulated and tested by previous researchers, are recorded in the literature, and may be applied literally or adapted to the project at hand. Some studies lend themselves to the use of these readily available measurement devices. This provides enhanced validity and can reduce the cost of the project. More often, however, the measurement questions need to be tailored to the investigative questions. The resources required for this task will be the collective insights from all the activities in the research process completed to this point, particularly insights arising from exploration. Later, during pilot testing of the data collection instrument(s), these custom-designed questions will be refined.

Measurement questions constitute the fifth level of the hierarchy (see Exhibit 2.2). In surveys, measurement questions are the questions we actually ask the respondents. They appear on our questionnaire. In an observation study, measurement questions are the observations researchers must record about each subject studied.

BankChoice decides to conduct a survey of local residents. Its questionnaire contains many measurement questions, seeking information that will provide answers to the bank's investigative questions. A total of 200 residents complete questionnaires and the information collected is used to guide a reorientation of the bank's image.

The assumptions and facts used to structure the management research question hierarchy set the direction of the project. Using the hierarchy for guidance is a good way to think methodically about the various issues. Think of the hierarchy as six sequential levels moving from the general to the specific. While our approach suggests six discrete levels – concluding with the management decision – the hierarchy is actually more of a continuum. The investigative question stage, in particular, may involve several levels of questioning before it is possible to develop satisfactory measurement questions.

## 2.4  Research process problems

Although it is desirable for research to be thoroughly grounded in management decision priorities, studies can wander off target or be less effective than they should be. Some of the reasons for this are described below.

### The favoured technique syndrome

Some researchers are method-bound. They recast the management question so that it is amenable to their favourite methodology – a survey, for example. Others might prefer to emphasize the case study, while others still wouldn't consider either approach. Not all researchers are comfortable with experimental designs. The past reluctance of most social scientists to use experimental designs is believed to have inhibited the development of scientific research in the social science arena.

The availability of a technique is an important factor in determining how research will be done or whether a given study can be carried out. People who are knowledgeable about and skilled in some techniques but not in others are too often blinded by their special competences. Their concern for technique dominates the decisions concerning what will be studied (both investigative and measurement questions) and how (research design).

### Company database strip-mining

The existence of a pool of information, or a database, can distract a manager, seemingly reducing the need for other research. As evidence of the research-as-expense-not-investment mentality mentioned in Chapter 1, managers frequently hear this sort of thing from their superiors: 'We should use the information we already have before collecting more.' Modern management information systems are capable of providing massive volumes of data. However, this is not the same as saying modern management information systems provide substantial *knowledge*.

Each field in a database was originally created for a specific reason, a reason that may or may not be compatible with the management question facing the organization. In the Netherlands, many supermarket chains have introduced customer cards, which entitle the owner to specific special offers. Each time a customer pays at the cash register their card is scanned along with all the products purchased. The scanned information is at the root of a large database, which can be used for various market research purposes, such as customer segmentation, the identification of high-volume customers, and so on. For example, the supermarket can investigate whether specific groups of customers purchase fresh products, such as meat. However, this system does not allow one to investigate why certain customers do not purchase meat. Is a customer dissatisfied with the meat quality offered and prefers to go to a local butcher or is the customer a vegetarian?

Mining management information databases is fashionable and all types of organization increasingly value the ability to extract meaningful information from the data. While such data-mining is often the starting point in decision-based research, rarely will such activity answer all management questions related to a particular management dilemma.

## Unresearchable questions

Not all management questions are researchable, and not all research questions answerable. To be researchable, a question must be one for which observation or other data collection can provide the answer. Many questions cannot be answered on the basis of information alone.

Questions of value and policy must often be weighed in management decisions. In our MetalWorks example, management may be asking, 'Should we hold out for a liberalization of the seniority rules in our new labour negotiations?' While information can be brought to bear on this question, additional considerations such as 'fairness to the workers' or 'management's right to manage' may be important to the decision.

It may be possible for many of these questions of value to be transformed into questions of fact. With regard to 'fairness to the workers', one might first gather information from which to estimate the extent and degree to which workers will be affected by a rule change; then one could gather opinion statements from the workers about the fairness of seniority rules. Even so, substantial value elements remain. Questions left unanswered include, 'Should we argue for a policy that will adversely affect the security and well-being of older workers who are least equipped to cope with this adversity?'

Even if a question can be answered by facts alone, it might not be researchable because currently accepted and tested procedures or techniques are inadequate.

## Ill-defined management problems

Some categories of problem are so complex, value-laden and bound by constraints that they prove to be intractable to traditional forms of analysis. These questions have characteristics that are virtually the opposite of those of well-defined problems. One author describes the differences like this:

> To the extent that a problem situation evokes a high level of agreement over a specified community of problem solvers regarding the referents of the attributes in which it is given, the operations that are permitted, and the consequences of those operations, it may be termed unambiguous or well defined with respect to that community. On the other hand, to the extent that a problem evokes a highly variable set of responses concerning referents of attributes, permissible operations, and their consequences, it may be considered ill-defined or ambiguous with respect to that community.[2]

Another author points out that ill-defined research questions are least susceptible to attack from quantitative research methods because such problems have too many interrelated facets for measurement to handle with accuracy.[3] Yet another authority suggests that there are some research questions of this type for which methods do not presently exist or, if the methods were to be invented, they still might not provide the data necessary to solve them.[4] Inexperienced researchers should avoid ill-defined problems. Even seasoned researchers will want to conduct a thorough exploratory study before proceeding with the latest approaches.

## Politically motivated research

It is important to remember that a manager's motives for seeking research are not always obvious. Managers might express a genuine need for specific information on which to base a decision. This is the ideal scenario for quality research. Sometimes, however, a research study may not really be desirable but is authorized anyway, chiefly because its presence may win approval for a certain manager's pet idea. At other times, research may be authorized as a measure of 'personal protection' for a decision-maker in the event that he or she is criticized later. In these less than ideal cases, the researcher may find it more difficult to win the manager's support for an appropriate research design.

# 2.5 Designing the study

The **research design** is the blueprint for fulfilling objectives and answering questions. Selecting a design may be complicated by the availability of a large variety of methods, techniques, procedures, protocols and sampling plans. For example, you may decide on a secondary data study, case study, survey, experiment or simulation. If a survey is selected, should it be administered by mail, computer, telephone, the Internet or personal interview? Should all relevant data be collected at one time or at regular intervals? What kind of structure will the questionnaire or interview guide possess? What question wording should be employed? Should the responses be scaled or open-ended? How will reliability and validity be achieved? Will characteristics of the interviewer influence responses to the measurement questions? What kind of training should the data collectors receive? Is a sample or a census to be taken? What types of sampling should be considered?

These questions represent only a few of the decisions that have to be made when just one method is chosen. The creative researcher can, however, actually benefit from this confusing array of options. The numerous combinations spawned by the abundance of tools available may be used to construct alternative perspectives on the same problem.

By creating a design using diverse methodologies, researchers are able to achieve greater insight than if they followed the most frequent method encountered in the literature or suggested by a disciplinary bias. Although it must be conceded that students (and managers) rarely have the resources to pursue a single problem from a multi-method, multi-study strategy, the advantages of several competing designs should be considered before settling on one.

## Sampling design

Another step in planning the design is to identify the target population and select the sample if a census is not desired. The researcher must determine who and how many people to interview, what and how many events to observe, or what and how many records to inspect.

A **sample** is part of the target population, carefully selected to represent that population. When researchers undertake sampling studies, they are interested in estimating one or more population values and/or testing one or more statistical hypotheses.

If a study's objective is to examine the attitudes of British automobile assemblers about quality improvement, the population may be defined as the entire adult population of auto assemblers employed by the auto industry in the UK. Definition of the terms 'adult' and 'assembler', and the relevant job descriptions included under 'assembly' and 'auto industry', may further limit the population under investigation. The investigator may also want to restrict the research to readily identifiable companies in the market, vehicle types or assembly processes. The sampling process must then give every person within the target population a known non-zero chance of selection if probability sampling is used.

## 2.6  Resource allocation and budgets

General notions about research budgets have a tendency to single out data collection as the most costly activity. Data collection requires substantial resources but perhaps less of the budget than clients might expect. Employees must be paid, training and transport must be provided, and other expenses incurred must be paid; but this phase of the project often accounts for no more than one-third of the total research budget. The geographic scope and the number of observations required do affect the cost, but much of the cost is relatively independent of the size of the data-gathering effort. Thus, a guide might be that (i) project planning, (ii) data-gathering and (iii) analysis, interpretation and reporting each share about equally in the budget.

Without budgetary approval, many research efforts are terminated due to lack of resources. A budget may require significant development and documentation as in grant and contract research, or it may require less attention as in some in-house projects or investigations funded out of the researcher's own resources. The researcher who seeks funding must not only be able to persuasively justify the costs of the project, but also to identify the sources and methods of funding. One author identifies three types of budget in organizations where research is purchased and cost containment crucial.

- Rule-of-thumb budgeting involves taking a fixed percentage of some criterion. For example, a percentage of the prior year's sales revenues may be the basis for determining the marketing research budget for a manufacturer.

- Departmental or functional area budgeting allocates a portion of total expenditures in the unit to research activities. Government agencies, not-for-profits, and the private sector alike will frequently manage research activities out of functional budgets. Units such as human resources, marketing or engineering then have the authority to approve their own projects.

- Task budgeting selects specific research projects to support on an ad hoc basis. This type is the least proactive but does permit definitive cost–benefit analysis.[5]

## 2.7  Valuing research information

There is a great deal of interplay between budgeting and value assessment in any decision to conduct research. An appropriate research study should help managers avoid losses and increase sales or profits, otherwise research can be wasteful. The decision-maker wants a firm cost estimate for a project and an equally precise assurance that useful information will result from the study. Even if the researcher can give good cost and information estimates, the managers still must judge whether the benefits outweigh the costs. Such costs/benefit considerations are equally important in assessing the value of more academic research, as resources are limited in terms of research time and available financial means to conduct the research.

Conceptually, the value of applied research is not difficult to determine. In a business situation, the research should produce added revenues or reduce expenses in much the same way as any other investment of resources. One source suggests that the value of research information may be judged in terms of 'the difference between the result of decisions made with the information and the result that would be made without it'.[6] While such a criterion is simple to state, its actual application presents difficult measurement problems.

## Evaluation methods
### Ex post facto *evaluation*

If there is any measurement of the value of research, this is usually done as an after-the-fact (*ex-post facto*) event. Twedt reports on one such effort, an evaluation of marketing research done at a major corporation.[7] He secured 'an objective estimate of the contribution of each project to corporate profitability'. He reports that most studies were intended to help management determine which one of two (or more) alternatives was preferable. He guesses that in 60 per cent of the decision situations, the correct decision would have been made without the benefit of the research information. In the remaining 40 per cent of the cases, the research led to the correct decision. Using these data, he estimates that the return on investment in marketing research in this company was 351 per cent for the year studied. However, he acknowledges that the return-on-investment figure was inflated because only the direct research costs were included.

This effort at cost–benefit analysis is commendable even though the results come too late to guide a current research decision. However, such analysis may sharpen the manager's ability to make judgements about future research proposals. The critical problem remains, though, that of project evaluation before the study is done.

### Prior or interim evaluation

A proposal to conduct a thorough management audit of operations in a company may be a worthy one, but neither its costs nor its benefits are easily estimated in advance. Such projects are sufficiently unique that managerial experience seldom provides much aid in evaluating such a proposal. Even in these situations, however, managers can make some useful judgements. They may determine that a management audit is needed because the company is in dire straits and management does not understand the scope of its problems. The management information need may be so great as to ensure that the research is approved. In such cases, managers may decide to control the research expenditure risk by doing a study in stages. They can then review costs and benefits at the end of each stage and give or withhold further authorization.

### Option analysis

Some progress has been made in the development of methods for assessing the value of research when management has a choice between well-defined options. Managers can conduct a formal analysis with each alternative judged in terms of estimated costs and associated benefits and with managerial judgement playing a major role.

If the research design can be stated clearly, one can estimate an approximate cost. The critical task is to quantify the benefits from the research. At best, estimates of benefits are crude and largely reflect an orderly way to estimate outcomes under uncertain conditions.

## 2.8 The research proposal

Exhibit 2.1 depicts the research **proposal** as an activity that incorporates decisions made during the early project planning phases of the study, including the management research question hierarchy and exploration. The proposal thus incorporates the choices that the investigator makes in the preliminary steps, as depicted in Exhibit 2.5.

A written proposal is often required when a study is being suggested. This ensures that all the parties involved concur on the project's purpose and on the proposed methods of investigation, and each party's obligations and responsibilities are apparent. A blueprint for the construction of a house, for instance, is the proposal for conducting a research project. Proposals soliciting financial means, such as a funding request put to governmental science foundations, or tenders for commercial research, have to spell out time schedules and budgets. Depending

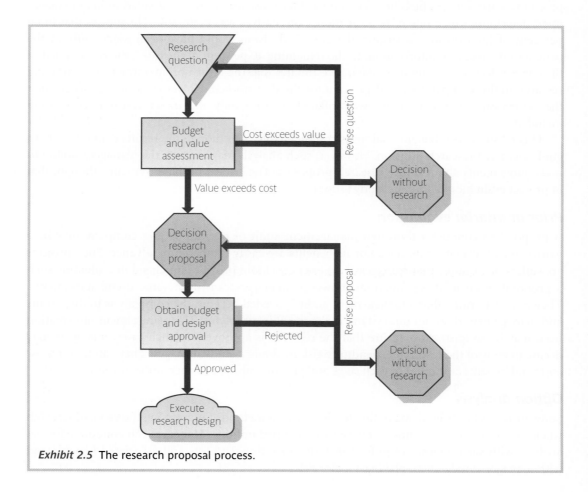

***Exhibit 2.5*** The research proposal process.

on the needs and desires of the manager, substantial background detail and elaboration of proposed techniques may be included.

The length and complexity of research proposals differ widely. Business research proposals normally range from one to ten pages. Applicants for foundation or government research grants typically file a proposal request of a few pages, often in a standardized format specified by the granting agency. A research proposal may also be oral, where all aspects of the research are discussed but not codified in writing. Proposals for student papers are sometimes presented orally to a thesis tutor, although it is also common for supervisors to ask students to prepare a written document.

## Proposal content

Every proposal, regardless of length, should include two basic sections:

1 statement of the research question
2 brief description of the research methodology.

In a brief memo-type proposal, the research question may be incorporated into a paragraph that also sets out the management dilemma, management question and categories of investigative question. The following statements present the management question facing the respective managers and indicate the nature of the research that will be undertaken.

1 BankChoice, currently the leading bank in the city, has not been growing as fast as its major competitors. Before developing a long-range plan to enhance the bank's competitive position, it is important to determine the bank's present competitive status, its advantages and opportunities, and its major deficiencies. The primary objective of this proposed research is to develop a body of benchmark information about BankChoice, its major competitors and the market for banking services.

2 ArtDeco Appliances must choose a location for a new plant to serve eastern markets. Before this location decision is made, a feasibility study should be conducted to determine, for each of five sites, the estimated:
   a costs of serving existing customers
   b building, relocation, tax and operating costs
   c availability of local labour in the six major crafts used in production
   d attractiveness of the living environment for professional and management personnel.

A second section includes a statement of what will be done: the bare bones of the research design. For BankChoice, the researcher might propose the following.

Personal interviews will be conducted with a minimum of 200 residents to determine their knowledge of, use of and attitudes toward local banks. In addition, information will be gathered about their banking and financing practices and preferences. Other information of an economic or demographic nature will also be gathered from published sources and public agencies.

Often, research proposals are much more detailed and describe specific measurement devices that will be used, time and cost budgets, sampling plans and many other details. Still, even the very brief proposals above reveal that the formulation of the research question needs to be rather specific. From the beginning of a project, it is only helpful if one has a clear understanding of what will be researched and what not.

We look at the research proposal in much greater detail below.

## 2.9  Pilot testing

The data-gathering phase of the research process typically begins with **pilot testing**. Pilot testing may be skipped if the researcher wishes to condense the project time frame. A pilot test is conducted to detect weaknesses in design and instrumentation, and to provide proxy data for selection of a probability sample. It should, therefore, draw subjects from the target population and simulate the procedures and protocols that have been designated for data collection. If the study is a survey to be executed by mail, the pilot questionnaire should be mailed. If the design calls for observation by an unobtrusive researcher, this behaviour should be practised. The size of the pilot group may range from 5 to 100 subjects, depending on the method to be tested, but the respondents do not have to be statistically selected. In very small populations or special applications, pilot testing runs the risk of exhausting the supply of respondents and sensitizing them to the purpose of the study. This risk is generally overshadowed by the improvements made to the design by a trial run.

There are a number of variations on pilot testing. Some of them are restricted, intentionally, to data-collection activities. One form, pre-testing, may rely on colleagues, respondent surrogates or actual respondents to refine a measuring instrument. This important activity has saved countless survey studies from disaster by using the suggestions of the respondents to identify and change confusing, awkward or offensive questions and techniques. One interview study was designed by a group of college professors for EducTV, an educational television consortium. In the pilot test, they discovered that the wording of nearly two-thirds of the questions was unintelligible to the target group, later found to have a median eighth-grade education. The revised instrument used the respondents' language and was successful.

Pre-testing may be repeated several times to refine questions, instruments or procedures.

## 2.10  Data collection

The gathering of data may range from a simple observation at one location to a grandiose survey of multinational corporations at sites in different parts of the world. The method selected will largely determine how the data are collected. Questionnaires, standardized tests, observational forms, laboratory notes and instrument calibration logs are among the devices used to record raw data.

But what are data? One writer defines data as the facts presented to the researcher from the study's environment. Data may be characterized further by their abstractness, verifiability, elusiveness and closeness to the phenomenon.[8] As abstractions, data are more metaphorical than real. For example, a growth in gross national product (GNP) cannot be observed directly, only the effects of it may be recorded.

Second, data are processed by our senses, which are often limited in comparison to the senses of other living organisms. When sensory experiences consistently produce the same result, our data are said to be trustworthy because they may be verified.

Third, capturing data is elusive, complicated by the speed at which events occur and the time-bound nature of observation. Opinions, preferences and attitudes vary from one milieu to another and with the passage of time. For example, attitudes about spending during the late 1980s differed dramatically one decade later within the same population, due to sustained prosperity within the final four years of the millennium.

Finally, data reflect their truthfulness by proximity (closeness) to the phenomena. Secondary data have had at least one level of interpretation inserted between the event and its recording. Primary data are sought for their proximity to the truth and control over error. These cautions remind us to exercise caution in designing data-collection procedures and generalizing from results.

Data are edited to ensure consistency across respondents and to locate omissions. In the case of survey methods, editing reduces errors in the recording, improves legibility, and clarifies unclear and inappropriate responses. Edited data are then put into a form that makes analysis possible. Because it is impractical to place raw data into a report, alphanumeric codes are used to reduce the responses to a more manageable system for storage and future processing. The codes follow various decision rules that the researcher has devised to assist with sorting, tabulating and analysing. Personal computers have made it possible to merge editing, coding and data entry into fewer steps even when the final analysis may be run on a larger system.

## 2.11  Analysis and interpretation

Readers of a study, such as managers, need information, not raw data. Researchers generate information by analysing data after its collection. **Data analysis** usually involves reducing accumulated data to a manageable amount, developing summaries, looking for patterns and applying statistical techniques. Scaled responses on questionnaires and experimental instruments often require the analyst to derive various functions, as well as to explore relationships among variables. Further, researchers must interpret these findings in light of the client's research question or determine if the results are consistent with their hypotheses and theories. Increasingly, managers are asking research specialists to make recommendations based on their interpretation of the data.

The larger the amount of data gets, the more researchers have to rely on statistical techniques to summarize them and to detect patterns. Here's an example to illustrate this point.

A telecommunications firm is interested in the question 'How well will a new mobile phone – with colour display and other features such as Internet access and e-mail – be received by (potential) customers?' The management board of the firm appoints a project team of three people to investigate this question. The project team could, for example, invite a couple of customers to a focus group meeting to reflect on the new phone. The team could also ask a market research company to interview 500 people by phone. The focus group discussion will provide mainly qualitative data, and the analysis and interpretation is likely to be a qualitative account based on the project team's observations in the focus group discussion. Even if just 10 questions are asked in the telephone survey, this would result in a data matrix with 5000 data points. Such an amount of data points exceeds human cognitive capabilities. It is just impossible to look through the phone interviews or at the data matrix and get a general idea of what the 500 respondents think about the new mobile phone. Standard statistical techniques allow the researcher to summarize the data (e.g. by calculating means for each question) and to detect patterns (e.g. by calculating the correlation between a respondent's age and the importance of a colour display in the buying decision).

## 2.12 Reporting the results

Finally, it is necessary to prepare a report and transmit the findings and recommendations to the manager for the intended purpose of decision-making. The researcher adjusts the style and organization of the report according to the target audience, the occasion and the purpose of the research. The results of applied research may be communicated via conference call, letter, written report, oral presentation, or some combination of any or all of these methods.

Reports should be developed from the manager's or information user's perspective. The sophistication of the design and sampling plan, or the software used to analyse the data may help to establish the researcher's credibility, but in the end the manager's foremost concern is solving the management dilemma. Thus, the researcher must assess the manager's needs accurately throughout the research process and incorporate this understanding into the final product: the research report.

The management decision-maker occasionally shelves a research report without taking action. Inferior communication of results is one reason for this outcome. With this possibility in mind, a research specialist should strive for:

- insightful adaptation of the information to the client's needs
- careful choice of words in crafting interpretations, conclusions and recommendations.

Sometimes, organizational and environmental forces beyond the researcher's control argue against the implementation of results.

At a minimum, a research report should contain the following:

- an executive summary consisting of a synopsis of the problem, findings and recommendations
- an overview of the research – the problem's background, literature summary, methods and procedures, and conclusions
- a section on implementation strategies for the recommendations
- a technical appendix with all the materials necessary to replicate the project.

## 2.13 The research proposal in detail
### The purpose of the research proposal

As noted earlier in this chapter, the research proposal is an individual's or company's offer to produce a product or render a service to a potential buyer or sponsor. To reiterate, the purpose of the research proposal is to:

1  present the management or research question to be researched and relate its importance
2  discuss the research efforts of others who have worked on related management questions
3  suggest the data necessary for solving the question and how the data will be gathered, treated and interpreted.

In addition, a research proposal must present the researcher's plan, services and credentials in the best possible way to encourage the proposal's selection over competitors. In contract research, the survival of companies depends on their ability to develop winning proposals.[9] A proposal is also known as a work plan, prospectus, outline, statement of intent or draft plan.[10] The proposal tells us what, why, how and where the research will be done, and whom it will approach. It must also show the benefit of doing the research.[11]

Many students and inexperienced researchers view the proposal as unnecessary work. The research proposal is essentially a road map, showing clearly the location from which a journey begins, the destination to be reached, and the method of getting there. Well-prepared proposals include potential problems that may be encountered along the way, and methods for avoiding or working around them, much as a road map indicates alternate routes for a detour. Thus, the proposal is an essential planning tool for researchers themselves. Once you know what question you exactly want to research, it is much easier to decide which books and articles should be included in a literature review and which books and articles are beyond the scope of your research. Having thought about what and how you would like to collect the data enables you to plan the data-collection process. It clarifies, for example, whether you already need to obtain a larger sample that you will approach with a questionnaire or whether you need to make appointments with key informants on a specific issue or event.

## Sponsor uses

All research has a sponsor in one form or another. The student researcher, for example, is responsible to their class instructor. In a corporate setting, whether the research is being done in-house by a research department or under contract to an external research firm, management sponsors the research. University-, government- or corporate-sponsored (grant) research uses grant committees to evaluate the work.

A research proposal allows the sponsor to assess the sincerity of the researcher's purpose, the clarity of his or her design, the extent of his or her relevant background material, and his or her suitability for undertaking the project. Depending on the type of research and the sponsor, various aspects of a standard proposal design are emphasized. The proposal displays the researcher's discipline, organization and logic. It thus allows the research sponsor to assess both the researcher and the proposed design, to compare them against competing proposals on current organizational, scholastic or scientific needs, and to make the best selection for the project.

A poorly planned, poorly written or poorly organized proposal damages the researcher's reputation more than the decision not to submit a proposal.

Comparison of the research project results with the proposal is also the first step in the process of evaluating the overall research. By comparing the final product with the stated objectives, it is easy for the sponsor to decide if the research goal – a better decision on the management question – has been achieved.

Another benefit of the proposal is the discipline it brings to the sponsor. Many managers, requesting research from an in-house, departmental research project, do not adequately define the problem they are addressing. The research proposal acts as a catalyst for discussion between the person conducting the research and the manager. The researcher translates the management question, as described by the manager, into the research question and outlines the objectives of the study.

On review, the sponsor may discover that the interpretation of the problem does not encompass all the original symptoms. The proposal, then, serves as the basis for additional discussion between the sponsor and the researcher until all aspects of the management question are understood. Parts of the management question may not be researchable, or at least not subject to empirical study. An alternate design, such as a qualitative or policy analysis study, may need to be proposed.

On completion of the discussions, the sponsor and researcher should agree on a carefully worded research question. As Exhibit 2.6 reveals, proposal development can work in an iterative fashion until the sponsor authorizes the research to proceed.

For an outside research contract, the process is different. Proposals are usually submitted in response to a request for bid, or **request for proposal (RFP)**. The researchers may wish to convince the sponsor that his or her approach to the research question differs from that indicated by the management question specified in the initial RFP. In this way, the researcher can show superior understanding of the management dilemma compared to researchers submitting competing proposals.

## Researcher benefits

A proposal is as beneficial for the researcher as for the sponsor. The process of writing a proposal encourages the researcher to plan and review the project's logical steps. Related management and research literature should be examined in developing the proposal. This review prompts the researcher to assess previous approaches to similar management questions and

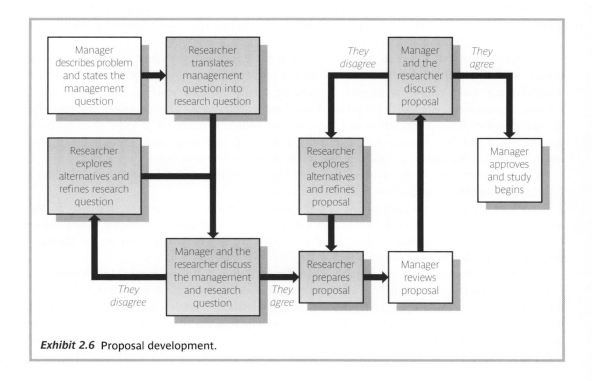

*Exhibit 2.6* Proposal development.

revise the research plan accordingly. Additionally, developing the proposal offers the opportunity to spot flaws in the logic, errors in assumptions, or even management questions that are not addressed adequately by the objectives and design.

The in-house or contract researcher uses the approved research proposal as a guide throughout the investigation. Progress can be monitored and milestones noted. On completion, the proposal provides an outline for the final research report.[12]

As in any other business, a contract researcher makes his or her profit from estimating costs correctly and pricing the research project appropriately. A thorough proposal process is likely to reveal all possible cost-related activities, thus making cost estimation more accurate. As many of these cost-associated activities are related to time, a proposal benefits a researcher by forcing a time estimate for the project. These time and cost estimates encourage researchers to plan the project so that work progresses steadily towards the deadline. Since many people are inclined to procrastinate, having a schedule helps them work methodically towards the completion of the project.

## 2.14  Types of research proposal

In general, research proposals can be divided into those generated for internal and external audiences. An internal proposal is produced by staff specialists or by the research department within the firm. External proposals sponsored by university grant committees, government agencies, government contractors, not-for-profit organizations or corporations can be classified further as either **solicited** or **unsolicited**. With few exceptions, the larger the project, the more complex the proposal. In public-sector work, the complexity is generally greater than in a comparable private-sector proposal.

There are three general levels of complexity: exploratory studies, small-scale studies and large-scale studies (these levels are illustrated in Exhibit 2.7). The exploratory study generates the most simple research proposal. More complex and common in business is the small-scale study – either an internal study or an external contract research project. The large-scale professional study is the most complex proposal we deal with here (and can be worth millions of pounds). Government agency large-scale project RFPs usually generate proposals that run to several hundred pages and use the modules that we discuss next. However, each agency has unique requirements, making generalized coverage beyond the scope of this text.

Exhibit 2.8 displays a set of modules for building a proposal. Their order can represent an outline for a proposal. Based on the type of proposal you are writing you may choose the appropriate modules for inclusion. This is a general guide, but deviations are often appropriate if they serve a specific purpose. For example, most small-scale studies do not require a glossary of terms. Terms are defined within the body of the proposal. However, if the proposal deals with a subject that is not familiar to management, it is appropriate to add a glossary. For a solicited study, the RFP will indicate both the content headings and their order.

Take some time to review Exhibit 2.8. Compare the proposal modules suggested for each type of study. This will increase your understanding of proposals.

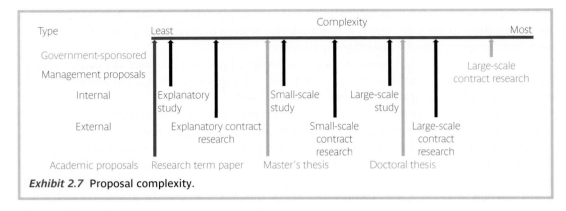

**Exhibit 2.7** Proposal complexity.

## Internal proposals

Internal proposals are more succinct than external ones. At the least complex end of the continuum shown in Exhibit 2.7, a one- to three-page memo from the researcher to management outlining the problem statement, study objectives, research design and schedule is enough to start an exploratory study. Privately and publicly held businesses are concerned with how to solve a particular problem, make a decision or improve an aspect of their business. Seldom do businesses start research studies for other reasons.

Regardless of the intended audience, in the small-scale proposal, the literature review and bibliography are consequently not emphasized and can often be stated briefly in the research design. Since management insists on brevity, an executive summary is mandatory for all but the most simple of proposals (projects that can be proposed in a two-page memo do not need an executive summary). Schedules and budgets are necessary for funds to be committed. For the smaller-scale projects, descriptions are not required for facilities and special resources, nor is there a need for a glossary. Since managers familiar with the problem sponsor small projects, the associated jargon, requirement, and definitions should be included directly in the text. The measuring instrument and project management modules are not required; managers will typically leave this detail for researchers.

## External proposals

An external proposal is either solicited or unsolicited. A solicited proposal is often in response to an RFP. The proposal is likely to be competing against several others for a contract or grant. An unsolicited proposal represents a suggestion by a contract researcher for research that might be done. An example of such a proposal might be a consulting firm proposing a research project to a client that has retained the consultancy for other purposes. Another example of an unsolicited proposal might be a research firm that proposes an omnibus study to a trade association to address problems arising from a change in the cultural or political–legal environments. The unsolicited proposal has the advantage of not competing against others but the disadvantage of having to speculate on the ramifications of a management dilemma facing the firm's management. In addition to being an outsider assessing an internal problem, the writer of an unsolicited proposal must decide to whom the document should be sent. Such proposals are often time-sensitive, so the window of opportunity might close before a redirected proposal finds its appropriate recipient.

| Proposal modules \ Proposal types | Management Internal — Exploratory study | Small-scale study | Large-scale study | Management External — Exploratory contract | Small-scale contract | Large-scale contract | Government — Large-scale contract | Student — Term paper | Master's Thesis | Doctor's thesis |
|---|---|---|---|---|---|---|---|---|---|---|
| Executive summary | | ✓ | ✓ | ✓ | ✓ | ✓ | ✓ | | (✓) | (✓) |
| Problem statement | ✓ | ✓ | ✓ | ✓ | ✓ | ✓ | ✓ | ✓ | ✓ | ✓ |
| Research objectives | ✓ | ✓ | ✓ | ✓ | ✓ | ✓ | ✓ | ✓ | ✓ | ✓ |
| Literature review | | | ✓ | | | ✓ | ✓ | | ✓ | ✓ |
| Importance/benefits of study | | | ✓ | ✓ | ✓ | ✓ | ✓ | | | ✓ |
| Research design | ✓ | ✓ | ✓ | ✓ | ✓ | ✓ | ✓ | | ✓ | ✓ |
| Data analysis | | | | | ✓ | ✓ | | | | ✓ |
| Nature and form of results | | ✓ | ✓ | | ✓ | ✓ | ✓ | | ✓ | ✓ |
| Qualification of researchers | | | | ✓ | ✓ | ✓ | ✓ | | | |
| Budget | | ✓ | ✓ | ✓ | ✓ | ✓ | ✓ | | | |
| Schedule | ✓ | ✓ | ✓ | ✓ | ✓ | ✓ | ✓ | | (✓) | ✓ |
| Facilities and special resources | | | ✓ | ✓ | ✓ | ✓ | ✓ | | ✓ | ✓ |
| Project management | | | ✓ | | | ✓ | ✓ | | | |
| Bibliography | | | ✓ | | | ✓ | ✓ | ✓ | ✓ | ✓ |
| Appendices/glossary of terms | | | ✓ | | | ✓ | ✓ | | ✓ | ✓ |
| Measurement instrument | | | ✓ | | | ✓ | ✓ | | | ✓ |

*Exhibit 2.8* Modules to include in proposals: a comparison of management-oriented proposals and student proposals.

The most important sections of the external proposal deal with the objectives, design, qualifications, schedule and budget. In contract research, the results and objectives sections are the standards against which the completed project is measured. The executive summary of an external proposal may be included within the letter of transmittal. As the complexity of the project increases, more information is required about project management and the facilities and special resources. As we move towards government-sponsored research, particular attention must be paid to each specification in the RFP. To ignore or not meet any specification is to automatically disqualify your proposal as 'non-responsive.'[13]

## 2.15  Structuring the research proposal

Look again at Exhibit 2.8. Using it for reference, you can put together a set of modules that tailors your proposal to the intended audience. Each of the following modules is flexible, so its content and length may be adapted to specific needs.

### Executive summary

You might find it valuable to revisit the management research question hierarchy and the research process model (see above) prior to reading this section.

The **executive summary** allows a busy manager or sponsor to understand quickly the thrust of a proposal. It is essentially an informative abstract, giving executives the chance to grasp the essentials of the proposal without having to read the details.[14] The goal of the summary is to secure a positive evaluation by the executive who will pass the proposal on to the staff for a full evaluation. As such, the executive summary should include brief statements of the management dilemma and management question, the research objectives/research question(s), and the benefits of your approach. If the proposal is unsolicited, a brief description of your qualifications is also appropriate.

### Problem statement

This section needs to convince the sponsor to continue reading the proposal. You should capture the reader's attention by stating the management dilemma, its background, its consequences and the resulting management question. The importance of answering the management question should be emphasized here if a separate module on the importance/benefits of study is not included later in the proposal. In addition, this section should include any restrictions or areas of the management question that will not be addressed.

Problem statements that are too broadly defined cannot be addressed adequately in one study. It is important for the management question to clearly distinguish the primary problem from related problems. Be sure your problem statement is clear, and does not use idiom or clichés. After reading this section, the potential sponsor should know the management dilemma and the question, its significance, and why something should be done to change the status quo.[15]

### Research objectives

This module addresses the purpose of the investigation. It is here that you lay out exactly what is being planned by the proposed research. In a descriptive study, the objectives can be stated as the research question. Recall that the research question can be broken down further into investigative questions. If the proposal is for a causal study, then the objectives can be restated as a hypothesis.

The objectives module flows naturally from the problem statement, giving the sponsor specific, concrete and achievable goals. It is best to list the objectives either in order of importance or in general terms first, moving to specific terms (i.e. research question followed by underlying investigative questions). The research question(s) (or hypotheses, if appropriate) should be separated from the flow of the text for quick identification.

The research objectives section is the basis for judging the remainder of the proposal and, ultimately, the final report. Verify the consistency of the proposal by checking to see that each objective is discussed in the research design, data analysis and results sections.

## Literature review

The **literature review** section examines recent (or historically significant) research studies, company data or industry reports that act as a basis for the proposed study. Begin your discussion of the related literature and relevant secondary data from a comprehensive perspective, moving to more specific studies that are associated with your problem. If the problem has a historical background, begin with the earliest references.

Avoid the extraneous details of the literature; do a brief review of the information, not a comprehensive report. Always refer to the original source. If you find something of interest in a quotation, find the original publication and ensure you understand it. In this way, you will avoid any errors of interpretation or transcription. Emphasize the important results and conclusions of other studies, the relevant data and trends from previous research, and particular methods or designs that could be duplicated or should be avoided. Discuss how the literature applies to the study you are proposing; show the weaknesses or faults in the design, discussing how you would avoid similar problems. If your proposal deals solely with secondary data, discuss the relevance of the data and the bias or lack of bias inherent in it.

A literature review might reveal that the sponsor can answer the management question with a secondary data search rather than the collection of primary data. We discuss this more fully in Chapter 10.

The literature review may also explain the need for the proposed work to appraise the shortcomings and/or informational gaps in secondary data sources. This analysis may go beyond scrutinizing the availability or conclusions of past studies and their data, to examining the accuracy of secondary sources, the credibility of these sources, and the appropriateness of earlier studies.

Close the literature review section by summarizing the important aspects of the literature and interpreting them in terms of your problem. Refine the problem as necessary in light of your findings.

## Importance/benefits of the study

In this section you describe explicit benefits that will accrue from your study. The importance of 'doing the study now' should be emphasized. Usually, this section runs to no more than a few paragraphs. If you find it difficult to write, then you have probably not clarified the research dilemma adequately. Return to the analysis of the problem and ensure – through additional discussions with your sponsor or your research team, or by a re-examination of the literature – that you have captured the essence of the problem.

## Example of a 'good' thesis proposal

*Below is an example of a good thesis proposal that a student prepared for the first meeting with a thesis supervisor. It is a good proposal, but not a perfect one and, of course, the final thesis looked different from what was originally proposed, but still investigated the problem proposed.*

### Thesis proposal
### Social Capital and Entrepreneurship

### I Introduction and problem statement

In recent years, the role of social capital and networking is no longer limited to sociology (Granovetter, 1985) as resource for social action (Baker, 1990; Burt, 1992; Coleman, 1988, 1990), but has gradually emerged as medium for understanding entrepreneurial behaviour (Liao and Welsch, 2003). Empirical research found that social capital is positively related to firm performance (Baker, 1990), product innovation and value creation (Tsai and Ghoshal, 1998), and industry-wide network formation (Walker *et al.*, 1997). According to Westlund and Bolton (2003), social capital is even as important to enterprises as financial, real and human capital. Therefore, it appears as if entrepreneurs would be well advised to develop and promote networks of all sorts (Davidsson and Honig, 2003).

> Gives a general overview of the problem and begins to name some important references, which allow the reader to immediately place the study.

However, most studies investigating the relation between social capital and entrepreneurship have focused on social capital as an individual resource and neglect another prominent perspective on social capital, namely, a resource that is nested within communities (Putnam, 2000). Henceforth, the research problem will be referred to as *social capital differences in the Netherlands*. Examining the nature of social capital across different regions in the Netherlands may help to clarify how to promote regional dynamism resulting from venture creation and entrepreneurship, which is a key concept for understanding future socio-economic changes (Yamada, 2002).

> Gives a clear motivation of the problem statement in terms of a theoretical gap.

### What is the influence of regional differences in social capital on entrepreneurship?

Furthermore, the general research question has been divided into two sub-questions with the aim of developing a comprehensive idea about social capital dynamics and regional economic development:

> Provides sub-questions to the research problem that facilitate the readers' understanding about what the proposal really is.

1 What are the necessary conditions that facilitate the creation of social capital networks and subsequently enhance entrepreneurial activity?

2 How do social capital networks interact with different business sectors?

### II Research objectives – contributions of the study

In sum, the contributions of this paper are: (1) to add an analysis of the effects of social capital at the community level on entrepreneurship, (2) to investigate the social capital at the community level, (3) to examine the interplay of regional differences in social capital networks and entrepreneurship at the same time in the analysis, (4) to identify the underlying processes that determine the contributions of entrepreneurial gestation activities, (5) to provide an integrative framework of entrepreneurship activities based on social capital, and (6) to test it empirically by means of a country-wide secondary data sets. Hence, this paper will explore social capital within the context of Dutch entrepreneurship and it will be centered on the two research questions mentioned above:

> This part briefly summarizes the motives for the study, so the reader is informed of the questions that will be addressed.

## III  Literature review

As Granovetter (1985) points out, economic action is not at all independent of the social relationships surrounding an economic actor. Strategically engaging in social activities and wisely managing social relations save significant transaction costs in the search for critical information and provide unique economic opportunities (Chung *et al.*, 2000). Abbel *et al.* (2001) also confirm that social networks provide information and contacts on how to raise capital or whom to sell goods and services to. Informal social relations and tacit social arrangements are hence a critical aspect for businesses (Spence *et al.*, 2003).

Social capital is formally defined as *'the sum of actual and potential resources embedded within, available through, and derived from the network of relationships possessed by individual or social units'* (Nahapiet and Ghoshal, 1998, p. 243), that is simply speaking, a set of social resources rooted in relationships (Burt, 1992; Loury, 1977).

Granovetter (2000) highlights the importance of informal relationships, trust and solidarity for [...] business development. In view of the fact that the accumulation of knowledge, information, and other resources through social ties open new *'productive opportunities'* (Penrose, 1959) that constitute a driving force in the growth of new ventures (Penrose, 1959), social ties raise the attention of both academics and practitioners.

Another key feature of social capital emerging from the literature is that it is crucial for effective collective action. Pinglé (2001) even goes as far as maintaining that *'at the very least, its presence appears to enable collective action needed for economic development, it is held to strengthen democracy, and promote good governance.'* However, mutual networks of trust that characterize a community might also inhibit entrepreneurship rather than facilitate it. For example, tight bonds between individuals may strangle the temptation to *'march to a different pipe'* or *'colouring outside the lines'* rather than encourage entrepreneurship (Westlund and Bolton, 2003). Heavily saturated social capital networks may result in closed recruitment opportunities or even unfair pricing agreements, representing the dark side of social capital (Putnam, 2000, pp. 350–63). By creating relationships with customers and suppliers, a firm may exploit its established network to shut out potentially more productive capital from the market.

> Previous paragraphs also highlight important references related to the topic. Here, the student clearly shows that he has a good command of the literature in this field.

Despite the recognition of social capital networks' significance on entrepreneurship, other scholars have addressed the effects of social capital on firm dissolution (Pennings *et al.*, 1998), knowledge and competence development (Zahra *et al.*, 1999), alliance formation (Chung *et al.*, 2000), or even its impact on political alliance patterns and national policy outcomes (Broadbent 2000). Although there has been much theorizing about social capital, only scant systematic attention has been paid to the development of a dynamic rather than a static concept of social capital. Among the exceptions to this are Cooke and Wills (1999), and Lyons (2002), who both examined how businesses respond to attempts by policy-makers to *create*

Granovetter, M., 'The economic sociology of firms and entrepreneurs', in Swedberg, R. (ed.) *Entrepreneurship: The Social Science View.* Oxford: Oxford University Press, 2005, pp. 244–75.

Liao, J. and Welsch, H., 'Social capital and entrepreneurial growth aspiration: a comparison of technology – and non-technology-based nascent entrepreneurs', *Journal of High Technology Management Research* 14, 2003, 149–70.

Loury, G.C., 'A dynamic theory of racial income differences', in Wallace, P.A. and Lamond, A. (eds.). *Women, Minorities and Employment Discrimination.* Lexington, MA: Lexington Books, 1977.

Lyons, T.S., 'Building social capital for rural enterprise development: three case studies', *Journal of Developmental Entrepreneurship* 7, 2002, 193–216.

Nahapiet, J., and Ghoshal, S., 'Social capital, intellectual capital, and the organizational advantage', *Academy of Management Review* 23, 1998, 242–66.

Onyx, J. and Bullen, P., 'Measuring social capital in five communities', *Journal of Applied Behavioural Science* 36, 2000, 23–42.

Pennings, L., Lee, K. and van Witteloostuijn, A., 'Human capital, social capital, and firm dissolution', *Academy of Management Journal*, 1998, 425–40.

Penrose, E.T., *The theory of the growth of the firm.* Oxford: Oxford University Press, 1959.

Pingle, V., *Identity Landscapes, Social Capital and Entrepreneurship: Small Business in South Africa.* Doornfontein: Centre for Policy Studies, 2001.

Putnam, R.D., *Making Democracy Work: Civic Traditions in Modern Italy.* Princeton, NJ: Princeton University Press, 1993.

Putnam, R.D., *Bowling Alone.* New York: Simon & Schuster, 2000.

Spence L.J., Schmidpeter, R. and Habisch, A., 'Assessing social capital: small and medium sized enterprises in the UK and Germany', *Journal of Business Ethics* 47, 2003, 17–29.

Tsai, W. and Ghoshal, S., 'Social capital and value creation: the role of intra-firm networks', *Academy of Management Journal* 41, 1998, 464–76.

Walker, G., Kogut, B. and Shan, W., 'Social capital, structural holes and the formation of an industry network', *Organization Science* 8, 1997, 109–25.

Westlund, H. and Bolton, R., 'Local social capital and entrepreneurship', *Small Business Economics* 21, 2003, 77–113.

Yamada, J., *Entrepreneurship as Knowledge and Social Capital Creation: Theoretical Analysis of the Startup Stage of Firms.* Kagawa University: The Institute of Economic Research. Working Paper Series, No. 50, 2002.

Zahra, S.A., Nielsen, A.P. and Bogner, W.C., 'Corporate entrepreneurship, knowledge, and competence development', *Entrepreneurship Theory & Practice* 23, 1999, 169–90.

## *Measurement Instrument*

For large projects, it is appropriate to include samples of the measurement instruments if they are available when you assemble the proposal. This allows the sponsor to discuss particular changes in one or more of the instruments. If the proposal includes the development of a custom-designed measurement instrument, omit this appendix section.

## Other

Any detail that reinforces the body of the proposal can be included in an appendix. This includes researcher CV, profiles of firms or individuals to which work will be subcontracted, budget details, and lengthy descriptions of special facilities or resources.

# 2.18  Evaluating the research proposal

Proposals are subject to either formal or informal reviews. Formal reviews are carried out regularly for solicited proposals. The formal review process varies, but typically includes:

- development of review criteria, using RFP guidelines
- assignment of points to each criterion, using a universal scale
- assignment of a weight for each criterion, based on importance of each criterion
- generation of a score for each proposal, representing the sum of all weighted criterion scores.

The sponsor should assign the criteria, the weights and the scale to be used for scoring each criterion before the proposals are received. The proposal should then be evaluated with this checklist of criteria to hand. Points are recorded for each criterion, reflecting the sponsor's assessment of how well the proposal meets the company's needs relative to that criterion (e.g. on a scale of 1 to 10, where 10 is the largest number of points assigned to the best proposal for a particular criterion). After the review, the weighted criterion scores are added to provide a cumulative total. The proposal with the highest number of points wins the contract.

Several people, each of whom may be assigned to a particular section, typically review long and complex proposals. The formal method is most likely to be used for competitive government, university or public-sector grants, and also for large-scale contracts.

Small-scale contracts and student proposals are more likely to be submitted to informal evaluation.

In an informal review, the project needs, and thus the criteria, are well understood but are not usually well documented. In contrast to the formal method, a system of points is not used and the criteria are not ranked.

In practice, many factors contribute to a proposal's acceptance and funding. Primarily, the content discussed above must be included to the level of detail required by the sponsor's RFP.

Beyond the required modules, other factors can quickly eliminate a proposal from consideration or improve the sponsor's reception of the proposal, among them:

- neatness
- organization, in terms of being both logical and easily understood
- completeness in fulfilling the RFP's specifications, including budget and schedule
- appropriateness of writing style
- submission within the RFP's timeline.

Although a proposal produced on a word-processor and bound with an expensive cover will not overcome design or analysis deficiencies, a poorly presented, unclear or disorganized proposal will not receive serious attention from the reviewing sponsor. Given that multiple reviewers may be evaluating only a given section, the reviewer should easily be able to skim through the proposal to any section of interest.

In terms of the technical writing style of the proposal, the sponsor must be able to understand the problem statement, the research design and the methodology. The sponsor should clearly understand why the proposed research should be funded, and the exact goals and concrete results that will come from the study.

Finally, a late proposal will not be reviewed. While current project disqualification due to lateness may appear to be the worse result here, there is a possible longer-term effect of this. Lateness communicates a level of disrespect for the sponsor – that the researcher's schedule is more important than the sponsor's. A late proposal also communicates a weakness in project management, which raises an issue of professional competence. This concern about competence may continue to plague the researcher during future project proposal reviews.

## Research Methods in Practice 2

## Boiling the problem down?

Going back to the Ph.D. thesis on the management of R&D cooperations: What are the advantages to engage in interfirm cooperations?

1  Cooperation allows realizing economies of scale by accumulating the resources of firms. Think of Nedcar, a joint venture between Volvo and Mitsubishi, operating an automotive manufacturing plant in the south Netherlands. By using the same plant for two types of car, the two mother companies of the joint venture are allowed to produce their vehicles in a plant that meets the minimum efficient plant size in the industry. If the two companies had each built a plant on their own, each plant would have been too small to produce efficiently or too large to meet the demand in the European market.

2  Cooperation allows for a smart combination of resources and capabilities two firms hold. Especially in R&D, innovations often require expertise on different domains that are not available within one firm. For example, Philips cooperated with Dupont to develop an optical disc. Philips had a long-lasting experience in the electronics around discs and Dupont contributed its knowledge in chemical research especially on polymers.

3  Given that companies are risk averse, cooperations allow for the spreading of risks. Oil companies, such as Shell or British Petroleum, often cooperate in the exploitation of a new oilfield. Even as oil companies belong to the largest corporations in the world with immense financial resources, they prefer to share the risks with other competitors when it comes to explorations of new oilfields. To explore a new field the companies need to conduct many trial drills. Each drill requires an immense investment, but it is highly uncertain how much oil they will get out of a particular hole. Rather than gambling, companies prefer to cooperate with each other and pool the drills they conduct in a given oilfield.

4  Access to new markets can be an important motive to form a cooperation. A local partner is often much better informed about the foreign market and has access to already existing distribution networks. In some developing countries, such as India and China, it is often even required to join up with a local partner in exchange for the right to access the market.

5  Standardization is another motive to form cooperations. Consumer electronics are a well-known example in which firms develop new applications but use different technologies in the beginning. Back in the 1970s it was the battle between different VCR systems: VHS, Betamax and Video2000. In the early years of DVDs not every DVD player could read all formats and the differences between TV technologies PAL in most European countries and NTSC in the USA still show that different standard coexists. Agreeing on one standard is often profitable as many buyers are reluctant to buy as long as it remains unclear what will be the dominant technology in the future. They do not like to take the risk of buying a new product that will be useless in just a few years, because a different technology dominates the market.

Given all these advantages, why is cooperation so problematic and why do so many alliances between firms fail? In general, one can identify three problems associated with cooperations.

1  Coordination problems emerge as cooperation partners need to synchronize their different activities. Communication problems are a well-known sub-category of such coordination problems.

2  Allocation problems. Cooperation problems need to agree on how they allocate the efforts and costs as well as the profits and benefits. Note that it is often hard to determine costs and profit in advance, as they are uncertain. In addition, it often depends on the structure of the cooperation which partner obtains higher profits. Take the example of the cooperation between Philips and the SaraLee division of Douwe Egberts, which developed jointly the Senseo coffee-setting machines. Both firms faced saturated markets in Europe. Almost every household already had a coffee-setting machine and would buy a new one only if the old one was broken. Similarly, almost all households could afford to buy as much coffee, once a luxury good, as they want to consume. To boost up the markets an innovation was needed. The Senseo coffee machine was such an innovation. This new type of coffee machine presses hot water through the coffee, just like the expensive Italian espresso machines, but is still much less expensive. Senseo coffee machines sell for about €100, while classical espresso machines start at €500. However, to use the machine you need to buy coffee that is pre-packed in pads. Currently, the retail price for coffee in pads is about €18 per kilo, while ordinary coffee sells for about €7 per kilo. Thus, Philips profits from the cooperation by putting a new type of coffee machine on the market and SaraLee profits by selling not more coffee but the same amount at a higher price. An important issue here is, however, how to get the innovation into the market and a lot depends on the price for the coffee machine. The usual pricing strategy in consumer electronics is a skimming strategy, that is you start with a high price of the new appliance that only a few people are willing to pay and reduce the price in subsequent years to attract more buyers. However, if Philips had chosen such a strategy, SaraLee would have suffered, as it is highly unlikely that supermarkets would include the new coffee pads on their shelves if just a small minority of consumers would buy them. Thus, for SaraLee it was essential that the market was penetrated quickly with a low price for the coffee machine. The lower the price for the coffee machine, the more coffee pads it would sell. How would you solve this problem?

3  Opportunism problems are often obstacles to cooperation. The problem emerges when a cooperation continues to lose full control and this can be exploited by the partner. Three examples illustrate typical opportunism problems.

a  Private use of information: especially in R&D, cooperation often requires that the partner disclose knowledge and know-how to each other. A well-known example is the US manufacturer of bicycles, Schwinn, once a leading manufacturer. To reduce costs Schwinn outsourced the production of frames to Giant manufacturing, a then rather unknown Taiwanese company. Through the cooperation with Schwinn, Giant not only learned how to make frames but also learned how the bicycle market worked and used this know-how to build up a bicycle manufacturing business. Currently, Giant bicycles are sold worldwide, while Schwinn is still only known in the USA. The fear of a knowledge drain and piracy of many European companies if they invest in China is another example of this problem.

b Reduced contributions to joint efforts: another form of opportunistic conduct is shrinking on your own efforts in the cooperation. Shrinking occurs if joint projects with another firm gets a lower priority than other internal projects. Staffing a joint venture with less able employees, reluctance to invest in the joint venture or the non-disclosure of knowledge are classical examples of such behaviour.

c Opportunistic exit: not so unlike marriage, interfirm cooperation does not last forever. However, how is a cooperation terminated? Sometimes it is in the interest of both parties to end the cooperation. But often one partner would like to continue, while the other wants to quit. For example, a joint venture between Liz Claiborne and Avon failed after Avon acquired Perfumes Stern, another producer of luxury fragrances. After this acquisition Liz Claiborne perceived Avon as a competitor and left the alliance against Avon's will.

This extensive list of advantages and obstacles of interfirm cooperations raises the questions of how firms should manage their cooperations to reap the benefits and reduce the costs. Thus, although the research programme started with a research dilemma (see Running Case Study in Chapter 1, p. 47), the particular Ph.D. project formulated a specific management problem.

Moving down in the management research question hierarchy from the management question to research questions involves identifying which choices are available in order to solve the problem. Economic theory and transaction costs economies in particular point at contracts as a solution to cooperation problems. Firms negotiate contracts determining the rights and duties each partner has. However, a well-known problem of contracts is that they are incomplete, that is they do not cover every possible situation that might occur in the course of the cooperation. Moreover, the enforcement of a contract in case of non-compliance is also problematic, because it takes time for legal authorities to enforce a contract. This brings us back to Hobbes, who raised the question, why do people cooperate with each other and build up a society, a process that cannot be enforced? Next to contracts, there should be other mechanisms that ensure cooperation between firms. In his seminal article, Mark Granovetter pointed out that all economic actions are embedded in the fabric of social relations. Thus, the embeddedness in social relations could be a substitute for contracting. Transaction cost economies and considerations regarding the social embeddedness of economic actions suggest a couple of factors affecting the governance of interfirm cooperations. To understand what explains the differences in the management of interfirm cooperations, we need information about the following issues. In other words, the theories that have been employed in this study inform us which investigative questions one has to ask. To answer the problem statement of the Ph.D. thesis we need to get informed about:

- How do firms manage their R&D relations?
  How do contracts used to manage R&D relations look like?
  How do firms negotiate contracts?

- What is social embeddedness of a R&D relation?
  How well is the relation embedded within other relations between the partners?
  How well is the relation embedded within a larger network of relations the partners maintain?

● What are important characteristics of the R&D relation?
   How large was the relation?
   Did it involve relation-specific investments?
   How large was the uncertainty?

The list above is just a short version of the possible investigative questions one needs to ask. Feel free to think about other investigative questions. Later on we will see how these investigative questions formed the basis for the measurement questions, that is the questions that were actually used to collect the information needed.

# Reference

Granovetter, Mark S. (1985), 'Economic action and social structure: the problem of embeddedness'. *American Journal of Sociology* 91, pp. 481–510.

4 You have been approached by the editor of *Gentlemen's Magazine* to carry out a rèsearch study. The magazine has been unsuccessful in attracting shoe manufacturers as advertisers. When members of the sales force tried to secure advertising from shoe manufacturers, they were told men's clothing stores are a small and dying segment of their business. Since *Gentlemen's Magazine* goes chiefly to men's clothing stores, the manufacturers reasoned that it was, therefore, not a good vehicle for their advertising. The editor believes that a survey (via mail questionnaire) of men's clothing stores in the UK will probably show that these stores are important outlets for men's shoes and are not declining in importance as shoe outlets. He asks you to develop a proposal for the study and submit it to him. Develop the management research question hierarchy that will help you to develop a specific proposal.

5 Based on an analysis of the last six months' sales, your boss notices that sales of beef products are declining in your chain's restaurants. As beef entrée sales decline, so do profits. Fearing beef sales have declined due to several newspaper stories reporting *E. coli* contamination discovered at area grocery stores, he suggests a survey of area restaurants to see if the situation is pervasive.

   a   What do you think of this research suggestion?

   b   How, if at all, could you improve on your boss's formulation of the research question?

6 You are the new manager of market intelligence in a rapidly expanding software firm. Many product managers and corporate officers have requested market surveys from you on various products. Design a form for a research proposal that can be completed easily by your research staff and the sponsoring manager. Discuss how your form improves communication of the research objectives between the manager and the researcher.

7 Consider the new trends in desktop publishing, multimedia computer authoring and display capabilities, and inexpensive videotaping and playback possibilities. How might these be used to enhance research proposals? Give several examples of appropriate use.

8 You are manager of research in a large department store chain. Develop a list of criteria for evaluating the types of research activities listed below. Include a point scale and weighting algorithm.

   a   Market research

   b   Advertising effectiveness

   c   Employee opinion surveys

   d   Credit card operations

   e   Computer service effectiveness at individual store level

## From concept to practice

9 Develop the management research question hierarchy (see Exhibits 2.2, 2.3 and 2.4), citing management dilemma, management question and research question(s) for each of the following:

   a   the production manager of a shoe factory

   b   the president of a home healthcare services firm

   c   the vice-president of labour relations for an auto manufacturer

   d   the retail advertising manager of a major metropolitan newspaper

   e   the chief of police in a major city.

10 Develop the management research question hierarchy for a management dilemma you face at work or with an organization for which you volunteer.

11 Develop a memo proposal for a research study in which 300 interviews are conducted to address the management question you defined in question 9.

12 Select an article from a scientific management journal. Outline a proposal for the research as if it

had not yet been performed. Make estimates of time and costs. Generate a CPM schedule for the project following the format in Exhibit 2.10.

13  Compare the example of a good proposal with a bad proposal, which is available at the online resource centre.

14  Using Exhibit 2.3 as your guide, what modules would you suggest be included in a proposal for each of the following cases?

   a  A bank interested in evaluating the effectiveness of its community contributions in dollars and loaned executive time.

   b  A manufacturer of leather custom-designed teacher development portfolios evaluating the market potential among teachers, who are now legally required to execute a professional development plan every three years.

   c  A university studying the possible calendar change from three 11-week quarters to two 16-week semesters.

   d  A dotcom that monitors clicks on banner ads interested in developing a different pricing structure for its service.

## Class discussion

15  Discuss the problems of trading off exploration and pilot testing under tight budgetary constraints. What are the immediate and long-term effects?

16  The educational board of your faculty is considering changing the rules for writing a thesis. One suggestion is that students have to write a research proposal (about five pages), which is formally assessed before a thesis supervisor is assigned. Discuss the pros and cons of writing a full proposal for a thesis and the formal assessment of it.

## Online
## *Learning* Centre

## Get started with understanding statistical techniques!

When you have read this chapter, log on to the Online Learning Centre website at ***www.mcgraw-hill.co.uk/textbooks/blumberg*** to explore chapter-by-chapter test questions, additional case studies, a glossary and more online study tools for Business Research Methods.

# Notes

[1] Albert Einstein and L. Infeld, *The Evolution of Physics.* New York: Simon & Schuster, 1938, p. 95.

[2] Walter B. Reitman, 'Heuristic decision procedures, open constraints, and the structure of ill-defined problems', in *Human Judgments and Optimality*, eds Maynard W. Shelly II and Glenn L. Bryan (New York: Wiley, 1964), p. 285.

[3] Carl M. Moore, *Group Techniques for Idea Building* (2nd edn.). Thousand Oaks, CA: Sage, 1994.

[4] Fred N. Kerlinger, *Foundations of Behavioral Research* (3rd edn.). New York: Holt, Rinehart & Winston, 1986, pp. 436–7.

[5] Walter B. Wentz, *Marketing Research: Management, Method, and Cases.* New York: Harper & Row, 1979, p. 35.

[6] Robert D. Buzzell, Donald F. Cox and Rex V. Brown, *Marketing Research and Information Systems.* New York: McGraw-Hill, 1969, p. 595.

[7] Dik Warren Twedt, 'What is the "return on investment" in marketing research?', *Journal of Marketing* 30 (January 1966), pp. 62–3.

[8] Paul D. Leedy, *How to Read Research and Understand It.* New York: Macmillan, 1981, pp. 67–70.

[9] Charles T. Brusaw, Gerald J. Alred and Walter E. Oliu, *Handbook of Technical Writing* (4th edn). New York: St. Martin's Press, 1992, p. 375.

[10] Paul D. Leedy, *Practical Research: Planning and Design* (2nd edn.). New York: Macmillan, 1980, p. 9.

[11] R. Lesikar and John Pettit, *Report Writing for Business* (9th edn.). Burr Ridge, IL: Irwin, 1995.

[12] Ibid., p. 51.

[13] William J. Roetzheim, *Proposal Writing for the Data Processing Consultant.* Englewood Cliffs, NJ: Prentice Hall, 1986, p. 106.

[14] Brusaw, Alred and Oliu, *Handbook*, p. 11.

[15] Philip V. Lewis and William H. Baker, *Business Report Writing.* Columbus, OH: Grid, 1978, p. 58.

[16] Robert G. Murdick and Donald R. Cooper, *Business Research: Concepts and Guides.* Columbus, OH: Grid, 1982, p. 112.

[17] Many texts cover project management and include details of scheduling and charting techniques such as CPM charts, which are beyond the scope of this text. See, for example, Chapter 3, 'Network analysis', in Don T. Philips, A. Ravindran and James J. Solberg, *Operations Research: Principles and Practice.* New York: Wiley, 1976; or Chapter 6, 'Network models', in K. Roscoe Davis and Patrick G. McKeon, *Quantitative Models for Management.* Boston: Kent, 1981.

[18] See, for example, Kate L. Turabian, *A Manual for Writers of Term Papers, Theses, and Dissertations.* Chicago: University of Chicago Press, 1996; Joseph Gibaldi and Walter S. Achtert, *MLA Handbook for Writers of Research Papers.* New York: Modern Language Association of America, 1999; and the *Publication Manual of the American Psychological Association.* Washington, DC: APA, 1994.

# Recommended further reading

Baker, Michael J., 'Writing up and getting published', *Marketing Review* 1(4), 2001, pp. 441–72. The last part of a series by Michael Baker on how to plan and conduct research, appearing in the first volume of *Marketing Review*.

Fox, David J., *The Research Process in Education.* New York: Holt, Rinehart & Winston, 1969. Chapter 2 includes a research process model to compare with the one in this chapter.

Krathwohl, David R., *How to Prepare a Research Proposal* (3rd edn.). Syracuse, NY: Syracuse University Press, 1988. A practical guide and framework for student projects.

Leedy, Paul D., *Practical Research: Planning and Design* (6th edn.). Englewood Cliffs, NJ: Prentice Hall, 1996. Practical and readable sections guide students through the research process.

Locke, Lawrence F., Spiduso, Waneen Wyrick and Silverman, Steven J., *Proposals That Work: A Guide to Planning Dissertations and Grant Proposals* (4th edn.). Thousand Oaks, CA: Sage, 2000. An excellent guide for students and faculty advisers covering all aspects of the proposal process.

May, Tim, *Social Research* (3rd edn.). Buckingham: Open University Press, 2001. A good overview of research processes in the social sciences.

Molfese, Victoria, Karp, Karen S. and Siegel, Linda S., 'Recommendations for writing a successful proposal from the reviewer's perspective', *Journal of Research Administration* 33(3), 2002, pp. 21–5. A case study reflecting the experience of three individuals in obtaining research funding in Canada.

Punch, Keith F., *Developing Effective Research Proposals.* Thousand Oaks, CA: Sage, 2000. A guide to how to prepare a well-constructed research proposal.

Raimond, P., *Management Projects.* London: Chapman & Hall, 1993. Chapter 4 offers a good overview of creative techniques that can be used to identify research ideas.

# Literature review

## Chapter contents

## LEARNING OBJECTIVES

When you have read this chapter, you should understand:

- ☑ what a scientific literature review is and the purposes it serves

- ☑ how to select sources and search them for information

- ☑ the structure of a good review.

## 3.1 Aims and objectives of a review

This chapter addresses an essential part of every research project: the review of the current literature. Scientific reviews of literature are rather different from the review of, say, a writer's novel, which you might find in national newspaper such as *Frankfurter Allgemeine*, *Le Monde* or *The Times*. Such reviews serve mainly to draw the attention of a potential audience to a new book and to contribute to contemporary literary debate. A scientific literature review, however, serves other purposes, namely to:

- establish the context of the problem or topic by reference to previous work
- understand the structure of the problem
- relate theories and ideas to the problem

- identify the relevant variables and relations
- show the reader what has been done previously
- show which theories have been applied to the problems
- show which research designs and methods have been chosen
- rationalize the significance of the problem and the study presented
- synthesize and gain a new perspective on the problem
- show what needs to be done in light of the existing knowledge.

## Establishing the context of the problem by reference to previous work

Progress in science is made by the continuous accumulation of knowledge. Hence, you need to embed in your study the context of the problem, by reference to previous work of others. We will use the metaphor of knowledge as a cathedral to illustrate the process. Each study and article is just another brick added to the construction of the cathedral of knowledge. Some studies just reconfirm previous knowledge, often in slightly different settings. For example, the first empirical tests of transaction cost economics were carried out in the automotive industry.[1] Later on, other scholars applied transaction cost arguments to other industries – for example, relations in the utility sector and in the rail freight sector.[2] These studies in other industries added a new brick to the chapel of transaction cost economics and demonstrated the broader applicability of the theory. Sometimes new studies lay the foundations for a new chapel and if these prove to be solid enough to build a chapel on then the contributions involved are likely to attract the highest academic merit, perhaps in the form of a Nobel Prize. Ronald Coase's article on the boundaries of a firm is one of the foundations of transaction cost economics and appeared in 1937 in *Economica*. It earned Coase the Nobel Prize in 1990, because it inspired many other scholars, who contributed to the building of the chapel of transaction cost economics.[3] For example, Williamson provided essential bricks for the further development of the theory,[4] and studies by Monteverde and Teece, Palay and Joskow (cited in notes 1 and 2 above) provided bricks of empirical testing.

So, using the metaphor of knowledge as a cathedral, the first function of a literature review is to embed the current study (the new brick) in the existing structure of knowledge (the cathedral). It allows the reader to understand much better which particular issue (chapel of the cathedral) the study addresses, where it contributes to the knowledge (foundations, walls or roof) and how it relates to the other bricks. In a complex world, isolated knowledge has no value; the value of your contribution increases if you relate it to the existing knowledge. The single brick is of limited beauty, but being part of the cathedral it contributes significantly to its overall beauty.

## Understanding the structure of the problem

Although management science is a discipline or field of its own, it is clearly embedded in the broader area of the social sciences, which includes many other disciplines, such as communication and media studies, community studies, cultural studies, economics, gender studies, economic geography, economic and social history, political studies, psychology, religious studies, social and political theory, social anthropology and sociology. This list is by no means exhaustive and could be extended by the addition of many other research fields (e.g. environmental studies). This embeddedness of management science and business studies within other disciplines creates interdependencies between these fields, which means that, to research a problem in management, it is often necessary to acquaint oneself with existing knowledge in related disciplines. In addition, seeking to familiarize oneself with these different knowledge areas offers a fruitful approach to finding new (and often better) answers to current problems.

The literature review allows you to show the reader your understanding of the problem and its structure. Taking once again the metaphor of the cathedral, you can show the reader in which chapels you are going to work and which specific aspects you will investigate. Assume that you wish to investigate the question 'Why do people become self-employed?' Plausible factors to explain the choice of self-employment include: general economic conditions, higher income than in paid labour, social background or personality traits. Each of these factors relates to a different chapel, that is theory or perspective. The first refers to macroeconomics, the second to microeconomic consideration of utility maximizing, the third to sociology and the fourth to psychology. Clearly, a single study cannot cover every perspective in the same depth and a researcher needs to choose between the possible perspectives. In a study, the literature review is a good place to argue why you selected a specific perspective, and what relationships and aspects you want to investigate within the chosen perspective.

## Showing the reader what has been done previously

The two previous objectives of a literature review positioned your study in the cathedral of science. However, the literature review is also an instrument with which you can describe the chapel to which your study (brick) contributes. It offers a brief summary of the previous work that is clearly related to the problem of your study. This is an important function of the review, because you cannot assume that every reader is as knowledgeable about the field as you are. In such a summary and discussion of the previous literature, you show which theoretical concepts others have applied to the problems, what research designs and methods they have chosen to investigate the problem, and the results that others have found. Hence, you use the literature review to present the reader with a rich description of the current state of the chapel, by pointing out the beautiful parts, but also addressing its current shortcomings.

Even for a well-informed reader (one who has read and knows most of the literature you discuss), your review is an important piece of information. The literature review allows the well-informed reader, an expert in the field, to assess at a glance how knowledgeable the writer is. For example, if a friend of yours purported to be an expert in the history of world soccer, but didn't once refer to the Brazilian team, you would have good reason to question his expertise. Similarly, a research paper that aims to investigate the 'make or buy' decisions of firms but does not mention transaction cost economics is less than convincing.

## Rationalizing the significance of the problem and the study presented

A literature review is, however, more than a summary of previous work. The summary of the status quo merely lays the foundations for a discussion of what needs to be done in the light of existing knowledge. Taking the metaphor of the cathedral once again, you use the picture of the current chapel (summary of the previous literature) to convince others that your idea for the next brick would make a valuable contribution to improving the chapel. Such improvements are usually refinements or reinforcements of current perspectives, where you fill an existing gap by adding a new brick or replacing an old brick. In the same way as a fifteenth-century master builder was likely to change the appearance of a cathedral from Roman to Gothic, by replacing Roman (round) arches with Gothic (pointed) ones, synthesizing current perspectives in a summary of the literature often gives rise to convincing ideas that will help readers gain a new perspective.

## General problems of literature review

Pulling together all the ideas that stem from different disciplines is often difficult, as authors can be rooted in certain styles of thinking and writing that are specific to certain disciplines. For example: psychological studies often place a strong emphasis on measurement issues, and are rather rigid when it comes to discussions of validity and reliability; economists are less concerned with measurement issues, but rigid in terms of model building and the usage of statistical methods; management scholars place a strong emphasis on the applicability of theories to real-world management problems, but are less bothered about theory development and rigorous methodology. There is no perfect review. Each is written from a particular perspective, often rooted in a certain discipline or school of thought. Reviews are usually written with a particular reader in mind and, consequently, the literature review of an economic study on entrepreneurs will differ a great deal from that of a sociological study on the same topic.

## 3.2  Assessment of a 'good' literature review

There is no single best structure for a review. Sometimes the literature is reviewed throughout a whole book or article; other studies review the relevant literature in a specific chapter or section. Exhibit 3.1 provides a list of the ingredients a good literature review should contain. This list falls into two parts. Adding the first three ingredients to your review ensures that it will give a decent account of the literature and inform the reader about what has been done so far in the field. The last three ingredients serve as 'seasoning'. Without this seasoning your literature review is only a description of the field, a summary of previous studies. Through the addition of seasoning it becomes your own work as it reflects your thoughts and assessment of the current literature. Further, the last three ingredients are a necessity if you plan to use the literature review to point out why your current study makes an important contribution to the field.

Exhibit 3.2 shows a short literature review, which is part of an empirical study to investigate the influence of personal networks (social capital) in the choice of whether to become self-employed. Certainly, this review is by no means complete, as the authors even acknowledge in a footnote; also, it is written from a sociological and economic perspective, hence neglecting studies that address the choice of self-employment in management science and psychology.

1 Literature mentioned and discussed relates to the problem statement of the study

**Basic ingredients**
2 Mentions (different) theoretical ideas contributing to the further exploration or explanation of the study's problem statement
3 Summarizes previous studies addressing and investigating the current study's problem statement

**'Seasoning'**
4 Discusses the theoretical ideas mentioned against the background of the results of previous studies
5 Analyses and compares previous studies in the light of their research design and methodology
6 Demonstrates how the current study fits in with previous studies, and shows its specific new contribution(s)

**Exhibit 3.1** The ingredients of a good literature review.

Looking at Exhibit 3.2 you will see that, first, the literature mentioned refers to the problem statement. The objective of the study is to advance the explanation of the choice of self-employment by investigating the role of personal networks in this decision process. As new research often bridges fields that are as yet unconnected, or extends the applicability of a theory to a new field, it is not surprising that reviews often discuss literature that does not completely tie in with the objective of the current study. Were you to read the literature cited, you would soon see that most of the studies mentioned do not cover *both* the choice of self-employment and personal networks, but all studies cited do address at least one part of the problem statement.

LITERATURE REVIEW: SOCIAL BACKGROUND AND SELF-EMPLOYMENT
The standard neo-classical economic explanation for individual self-employment is based on the rationale of utility maximization. People become self-employed if their expected utility gained from self-employment is higher than the expected utility of paid labour. At first sight this claim is supported for the Netherlands. The mean annual income of the self-employed is, at €23,400 noticeably higher than the mean annual income for paid labour, which is €17,600 (Statistics Netherlands, 1993). However, these figures are biased. First, they do not account for the fact that most self-employed people work longer than the typical eight-hour day. Hamilton (2000) shows, for example, that the hourly wages of self-employed people who have been in business for 10 years are 33 per cent lower than the hourly wages of a wage earner with comparable characteristics. Second, a few very successful entrepreneurial superstars, earning extraordinary high incomes, cause an upward bias in the mean income of business owners (Rosen, 1981). Third, market forces drive out unproductive self-employed people much quicker than firms lay off unproductive employees. This selection of successful self-employed people produces an additional upward bias. Empirical studies support the view that the expected income differences do not play a crucial role in the decision to enter self-employment, even when potential self-

selection is considered (see, e.g., Dolton and Makepeace, 1990; Rees and Shah, 1986; de Wit and van Winden 1989).

Other studies employ human capital theory (Becker, 1993 [1964]) to explain self-employment. Human capital theory is based on the idea that individuals invest in their education and working career, like a financial investor in stocks and bonds, to obtain returns later on. Applied to self-employment, it is argued that people equipped with a higher 'stock' of human capital are more productive. Self-employed people with a higher productivity can either offer better products or services, or the same products and services at a lower price. In both cases they obtain a competitive advantage above starters with lower productivity, earn above-average profits and survive. Typical indicators of one's stock of human capital are educational level, work experience or commercial training. However, empirical studies show mixed results with respect to this approach. General education has hardly any effect on the decision to enter self-employment (Carroll and Mosakowski, 1987; Dolton and Makepeace, 1990; Evans and Jovanovic, 1989; and Taylor, 1996, report no significant effect, and only Rees and Shah, 1986, report a significant positive effect). More specific forms of human capital, such as work experience, do not have a clear relationship with self-employment either. Evans and Leighton (1989) and de Wit and van Winden (1989) report significant negative effects, while Dolton and Makepeace (1990), and Evans and Jovanovic (1989) report significant positive effects. Assessing the ambiguous effects of human capital one should be aware that the self-employed comprise a very heterogeneous group. Self-employed people can be found in a wide range of occupations, from the poorly educated immigrant gardener to highly educated professionals such as lawyers or doctors. Therefore, it seems reasonable to conclude that it is not general human capital that determines self-employment but more specific entrepreneurial skills (e.g. some cooks start their own restaurants, while others prefer to be employed as chefs de cuisine in the restaurants of luxury hotels).

Within economics there exists a large body of literature that emphasizes the importance of financial capital in starting a business (see, e.g., Evans and Jovanovic, 1989; Gill, 1988; Holtz-Eakin, Joulfaian and Rosen, 1994a, 1994b). Under the conditions of a perfect market, financial capital should be freely available to entrepreneurs with promising ideas (Schumpeter, 1934). However, the risk aversion of investors, information asymmetries and moral hazards cause imperfections in financial markets, especially with respect to loans for small businesses (Evans and Jovanovic, 1989; Knight, 1921). Consequently, people with their own financial resources can more easily realize a promising business idea by becoming self-employed.

In all the studies mentioned above, it was found that parental self-employment consistently has a significant positive influence on entry into self-employment (see, e.g., Blanchflower and Oswald, 1990; Carroll and Mosakowski, 1987; Lindh and Ohlsson, 1996; Taylor, 1996). This holds even if one considers only pioneers founding an entirely new business – that is if one excludes entry into self-employment by taking over an existing family business. This suggests that self-employed parents not only bequeath the financial means, in most cases the family business, but also transfer norms, values, skills and networking resources that are beneficial to those entering self-employment. Scholars in social stratification have long acknowledged the importance of parental resources in educational and occupational success (Blau and Duncan, 1967). Recent studies on the development of self-employment in advanced economies reveal that the self-employed are also affected by the typical patterns of social mobility (Müller and Arum, 2004). Lin's (1990, 1999) 'strength of position' hypothesis links the resources of parents to social capital theory. According to Lin, the availability of networking resources is partly determined by an individual's initial network position. Several empirical studies provide additional evidence on the positive relationship between parental status and social capital (Boxman *et al.*, 1991; Lai *et al.*, 1998; Völker, 1993). Finally, next to human and financial capital, business founders can succeed only if they are able to obtain the support of third parties, such as investors and customers (Aldrich and Zimmer, 1986; Penrose, 1993 [1939]).

## References for Exhibit 3.2

Aldrich, Howard E. and Catherine Zimmer, 'Entrepreneurship through social networks', in Donald L. Sexton and Raymond W. Smilor (eds.), *The Art and Science of Entrepreneurship.* Cambridge, MA: Ballinger, 1986, pp. 3–23.

Becker, Gray S., *Human Capital: A Theoretical and Empirical Analysis with Special Reference to Education* (3rd edn.). Chicago: University of Chicago Press, 1993 [1964].

Blanchflower, David G. and Andrew J. Oswald, 'What makes an entrepreneur?' *Journal of Labor Economics* 16 (1990), pp. 26–60.

Blau, Peter M. and Otis Dudley Duncan, *The American Occupational Structure.* New York: Wiley, 1967.

Boxman, Eddy, Paul M. de Graaf and Henk Flap, 'The impact of social norms and human capital on the income attainment of Dutch managers', *Social Networks* 13 (1991), pp. 31–73.

Carroll, Glenn R. and Elaine Mosakowski, 'The career dynamics of self-employed', *Administrative Science Quarterly* 32 (1987), pp. 370–89.

Dolton, P.J. and G.H. Makepeace, 'Self-employment among graduates', *Bulletin of Economic Research* 42 (1990), pp. 33–5.

Evans, David S. and Boyan Jovanovic, 'An estimated model of entrepreneurial choice under liquidity constraints', *Journal of Political Economy* 97 (1989), pp. 808–27.

Evans, David S. and Linda S. Leighton, 'Some empirical aspects of entrepreneurship'. *American Economic Review* 79 (1989), pp. 319–33.

Gill, Andrew M., 'Choice of employment status and the wages of employees and the self-employed: some further evidence', *Journal of Applied Econometrics* 3 (1988), pp. 229–34.

Hamilton, Barton H., 'Does entrepreneurship pay? An empirical analysis of the returns to self-employment', *Journal of Political Economy* 108 (2000), pp. 604–31.

Holtz-Eakin, Douglas, David Joulfaian and Harvey S. Rosen, 'Entrepreneurial decisions and liquidity constraints', *RAND Journal of Economics* 23 (1994a), pp. 334–47.

Holtz-Eakin, Douglas, David Joulfaian and Harvey S. Rosen, 'Sticking it out: entrepreneurial survival and liquidity constraints', *Journal of Political Economy* 102 (1994b), pp. 33–73.

Knight, Frank H., *Risk, Uncertainty and Profit.* New York: Houghton Mifflin, 1921.

Lai, Gina W., Nan Lin and Shu-Yin Leung, 'Network resources, contact resources and status attainment', *Social Networks* 20 (1998), pp. 139–78.

Lin, Nan, 'Social mobility and social structure: a structural theory of status attainment', in R. Breiger (ed.), *Social Mobility and Social Structure*. Cambridge: Cambridge University Press, 1990, pp. 247–71.

Lin, Nan, 'Social networks and status attainment', *Annual Review of Sociology* 23 (1999), pp. 467–87.

Lindh, Thomas and Henry Ohlsson, 'Self-employment and windfall gains: evidence from the Swedish Lottery', *The Economic Journal* 106 (1996), pp. 1313–26.

Müller, Walter and Richard Arum (eds.) (2004), *The Re-emergence of Self-employment in Advanced Economies*. Princeton University Press.

Penrose, Edith, *The Theory of the Growth of the Firm* (3rd edn.). Oxford: Oxford University Press, 1993 [1939].

Rees, Hedley and Anup Shah, 'An empirical analysis of self-employment in the UK', *Journal of Applied Economics* 1 (1986), pp. 93–108.

Rosen, Sherwin, 'The economics of superstars', *American Economic Review* 71, pp. 845–58.

Schumpeter, Joseph, *The Theory of Economic Development*. Cambridge: Harvard University Press, 1934.

Statistics Netherlands, *Jaarboek inkomen en consumptie 1993* [*Yearbook of income and consumption 1993*] Den Haag: SDU, 1993.

Taylor, Mark P., 'Earnings, independence or unemployment: why become self-employed', *Oxford Bulletin of Economics and Statistics* 38 (1996), pp. 233–66.

Völker, Beate, *Should Acquaintances be Forgotten*. Ph.D. thesis, Utrecht University, 1993.

Wit, Gerrit de and Frans A. van Winden, 'An empirical analysis of self-employment in the Netherlands', *Small Business Economics* 1 (1989), pp. 263–72.

*Exhibit 3.2* Example of a literature review from a study on the importance of social background in the choice of self-employment.

Second, the review in Exhibit 3.2 mentions different theories that have been applied to explain self-employment. On the one hand, it mentions the more economic approach, which suggests that an individual becomes an entrepreneur if the expected utility of self-employment is higher than the expected utility of paid labour. On the other hand, it opposes this economic approach with sociological considerations, which argue that the choice of self-employment is likely to be influenced by the social background and relationships of an individual.

Third, it summarizes the literature by providing very brief accounts of the previous studies. In this particular review, the author runs through a series of factors that might explain the choice of self-employment, and briefly reports the results of previous studies concerning these factors. For example, he states that across a number of empirical studies the factor 'parental self-employment' increases the chance of an individual becoming self-employed, while the results of various studies regarding the effect of human capital (i.e. education) on the self-employment decision are much less clear, as some studies find positive effects and others negative ones. Although a literature review cannot encompass all previous literature, the selection of literature to be cited should never be based on the correspondence of previous studies' results with one's own expectations or even one's own results. Neglecting counter-evidence in other studies, of which the informed reader is often aware, leads to the conclusion that the author is not very knowledgeable about the field, and can often raise the suspicion that the paper as a whole is as incomplete and poorly put together as the literature review.

Fourth, in a literature review it is important to discuss new theories alongside the results of previous studies. This means that you use the summary of previous studies to assess the usefulness of the theories under discussion. The literature review example in Exhibit 3.2, for example, concludes that, with respect to the influence of human capital, the results of previous studies form a structure that is more like an unsorted pile of bricks than a neat, clean wall. Further, it emphasizes that the more sociological factor, 'parental self-employment', produces very consistent results, while the economic rationale of income differences has not been empirically supported. Hence, it might be more useful to investigate sociological factors than economic considerations.

Fifth, in management, economic and social science, different studies produce conflicting evidence, that is a specific hypothesis is supported by some studies and rejected by others. The reasons for such contradictions are numerous and include differences in the research design, the sample used, the measurement applied, the variables included and not included, and so on. Conflicting results can often be ascribed to such differences between previous studies. Hence, a good literature review should also analyse and compare previous studies in the light of the research design and methodology used. In the example in Exhibit 3.2, the author suggests, for example, that choosing general education as an indicator of human capital may give rise to contradictory results regarding the relationship between human capital and self-employment. Given that the group of self-employed is very heterogeneous (i.e. consists of people performing very different jobs) general education does not necessarily reflect an individual's capabilities.

Sixth, and finally, the literature review should be used to demonstrate how well the current study fits in with previous studies and to highlight the new contributions it makes.

## 3.3  Process and organization

Writing a literature review is an iterative process of three tasks:

1  searching information (literature)
2  assessing the information obtained
3  synthesizing the assessment of information.

### Literature search and sources
#### *Literature search*

It is likely that the preparation of a literature review will start with a **literature search**. A literature search calls for the use of a library's online catalogue, and one or more **bibliographic databases** or **indexes**. For some topics, it may be useful to consult a handbook or specialist encyclopaedia first to establish a list of key terms, people or events that have influenced the topic under investigation, and also to determine the major publications and the foremost authors in the field. Other reference materials will be incorporated into the search strategy as needed. In general, this literature search has five steps.

1 Define your management dilemma or management question.

2 Consult encyclopaedias, dictionaries, handbooks and textbooks to identify key terms, people or events relevant to your management dilemma or management question.

3 Apply these key terms, people or events in searching indexes, bibliographies and the web to identify specific secondary sources.

4 Locate and review specific secondary sources for relevance.

5 Evaluate the value of each source and its content.

In economic and business studies, the main problem is not finding literature that is related to a certain topic, but filtering the really relevant and good literature, and distinguishing it from irrelevant literature and dubious sources. The Internet has without doubt facilitated access to a wide range of different information, and students are now less dependent on the quality and thematic focus of their local university libraries. Using academic databases, such as ECONLIT or EBSCO, it has become much easier to find a wide range of literature related to a certain topic. Furthermore, many libraries now subscribe to services that permit electronic access to the full text of many academic journals. The amount of information available has, however, become so vast that it is impossible to read all the information to assess its quality and relevance to one's own research. Hence, researchers need some guidelines to help them decide on the relevance of available information resources. The application of such guidelines and 'filters' has the drawback that some relevant information might not be discovered and may slip through the net. That is why an iterative search-refining process is useful in ensuring search efficiency, and helps to minimize the chances of relevant information being missed. The steps to be followed are listed in Exhibit 3.3.

Before one can start the research process, one needs at least an idea of the problem involved or, better, a problem statement to give the search some direction. In this phase the search process has a broad orientation and one tries to find out what others have written on this and related topics. The primary aim is to build up a pool of potential information. One can usually distinguish two departure points for creating such a pool and you should use both. The first is your pre-knowledge. Such pre-knowledge can be based on earlier similar research you have done or simply on a course with a related topic that you have followed. You can add the literature you used in previous related research or during a related course to your pool of potential information.

Another important point of departure is the aforementioned databases of academic books and articles, such as EBSCO. You should start your search by generating a list of search terms. Words that appear in the working title of your study, and the names of the theoretical concepts you propose to use form important search terms that should be on your list. One common problem with databases is that they are often designed with a particular discipline in mind. For example, EBSCO covers mainly economic- and business-related sources, PSYCHLIT covers psychological sources and SOCIOFILE covers sociological sources. If your problem, or the perspective you want to take on the problem, bridges several disciplines you will also need to carry out the search in each of these databases or use a mega search engine that allows you to select various databases, which will be searched simultaneously. To fully utilize the potential of a database you have to learn how to use it. By using it you will learn automatically which search

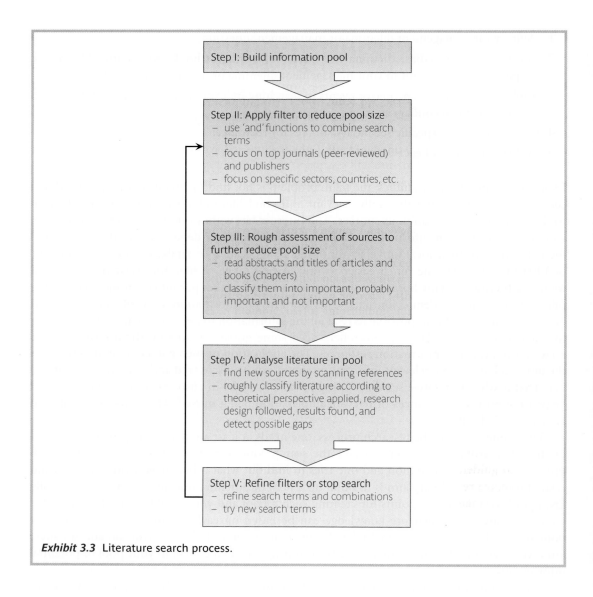

*Exhibit 3.3*  Literature search process.

strategies and terms achieve the best results, as well as the limitations of a database in terms of coverage.

Depending on the search terms used, a search can retrieve thousands of hits. Such a high number of sources can by no means be examined thoroughly. Therefore, you need to apply filters to reduce the pool size (i.e. the number of hits). Particularly for academic studies, it is often useful to restrict your search to academic peer-reviewed publications. **Peer-reviewed** publications only publish articles

For a more in-depth insight into this topic please see the Spotlight on Research section at the end of this chapter.

after other scholars – peers – have evaluated and approved the scientific quality of the work. Hence, peer review is a kind of quality mark, which ensures that the work published in such journals fulfils the quality standards of sound scientific research (see Chapter 2 to recap on these standards). More detailed information on the scientific quality of the work can be obtained from various rankings, which are often based on the Social Science Citation Index. This counts how often articles from a specific journal have been cited in other articles. Another effective method for reducing the number of hits is to combine your search terms with the logical operator 'and', and then the search system will retrieve only those sources that contain both search terms. This method is especially useful in combining search terms that are rather generic, such as utility, management, innovation, leadership, and the like. Finally, it is often also wise to limit the search to a specific application field, such as, say, an industrial sector or country. You should continue using a filter to refine this until the number of hits has reached a manageable number.

In the third stage of the process you take a first look at the sources. The main objective of this stage is to make a rough assessment of all the sources in terms of their usefulness for your study. If the number of sources is still rather high, you might just scan the titles to decide whether the book or article could be relevant for your own study. If the number of information sources is moderate, or once you have scanned the titles, you can use the abstracts (short summaries of the articles cited) of the articles and books to assess whether they are related to your study. At the end of this stage, you will have compiled a list of articles and books that are clearly related to some aspect of your own research; then you must obtain the full text of these sources.

In stage four, you read and begin to analyse your sources. To start with, it is often sufficient to skim through the text. The aim of this is to decide whether the source makes an important contribution in terms of theoretical background, research design and methods used, and qualitative or quantitative findings. Placing each article in one or more of these categories also allows you to check which part of your study still might lack literature. Although there is no golden rule as to how many articles you need overall and in each category for a comprehensive review, such a structured overview can reveal substantial imbalances in your literature coverage.

You should also check the reference section of each source to see whether it contains titles that sound promising but are not yet on your list. Such a process tends to lead to a snowball effect: references in one source point you to a new source, and that source's references in turn point you to another source, and so on. This is a very useful way to discover the (theoretical) origins of a field and to broaden your literature search across more disciplines. The main disadvantage of this system is that it is past-oriented – that is, each source will only point you to articles and books that have been published before the source itself was published. Hence, it is useful to start such a 'snowball search' with very recent articles or books. Another way to make sure your search is up to date is to identify through the snowball system prominent authors and journals. You can then search for articles that these authors have published recently and also check the latest volumes of the journals that frequently publish articles in the field in which you are interested.

Some journals, such as the *Journal of Economic Literature* or *Academy of Management Review*, publish review articles, which usually offer a good overview of the current state of affairs in a particular field. Other journals sometimes publish 'special issues' devoted to one specific theme. Guest editors, who summarize the articles and place them in the field's current scientific discussion, often introduce such special issues. Thus, review articles and special issues of journals are an extremely useful information source for determining the relevant literature for your study and literature review.

The fifth stage involves either the decision to refine your search arguments with the information obtained during stage four, or the decision to stop the search. A useful hint on

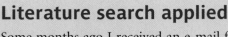

# Literature search applied

Some months ago I received an e-mail from a researcher at Erasmus University in Rotterdam. She wrote that she had read articles written by a colleague and by me, and wondered whether we would be interested in collaborating with her in a study addressing the issue of contracting between business firms. A few weeks later, we met in Eindhoven (between Rotterdam and Maastricht) to discuss our ideas on the topic.

We soon came to the conclusion that it might be worth while to investigate what different purposes business contracts serve. The economic literature assumes that firms sign contracts as safeguards against potential opportunism by the other party. However, other studies suggest that contracts may also serve other purposes than opportunism mitigation, namely coordination and signalling. Having access to a data set that assesses the contracts of exchange transactions between business firms quite extensively, we attempted to investigate the topic of 'contractual functions' more deeply, and started our collaboration. Exhibit 3.4 shows how we used the EBSCO database to get a comprehensive overview of the literature; this also formed the basis of our literature review.

| Search entries used | Result |
|---|---|
| Contract* *and* opportunism | 63 articles in peer-reviewed sources |
| Contract* *and* mitigation | 32 articles in peer-reviewed sources |
| Contract* *and* signal* | 182 articles in peer-reviewed sources |

*Note*: an asterisk (*) at the end of the search term indicates that the search engine should look not only at the specific term (e.g. contract), but also other words starting with the letters '*contract*', such as *contracts*, *contracting*, and so on.

**Exhibit 3.4**  Hits for a keyword search in EBSCO.

We quickly screened the abstracts of all these articles online to determine the relevance of each of the references for our study. We ended up with a list of about 33 articles, some of which we already knew from previous research. The articles we did not yet know were printed out and the whole text was scanned through. In this way we were able to compile a list of about 13 core articles. Then we looked at the reference lists of these core articles to see whether we had missed any important articles that were cited frequently. While checking the reference lists of the core articles we looked in particular for articles that had been published in legal journals, as our research topic deals with the interface of legal and business studies, and the database we consulted did not list legal journals. We identified another five articles that had been published in legal journals.

whether to call a halt to your search is to take a close look at the reference sections of the core articles of your literature review. When your list of literature resembles the references of the core articles and also contains some additional, more recent, articles, you know that your coverage of the relevant literature in the field is good.

## Literature sources

Literature can be found in both primary and secondary sources. **Primary sources** are full-text publications of theoretical and empirical studies, and represent the original work. **Secondary sources** are compilations of information, either in printed or digital form.

## Secondary sources

There are several bibliographic databases available to business researchers. Some of the more popular and comprehensive business bibliographic databases are listed in Exhibit 3.4 (see also Appendix A and the accompanying CD).

Most of the databases listed in Exhibit 3.5 offer numerous purchase options, both in terms of the amount and type of coverage. Some include abstracts. Nearly all the databases include the contents of around two-thirds of the indexed journals in full-text form, although the amount and the specific titles may vary widely from database to database. Full-text options vary from an exact image of the page to ASCII-text-only or text-plus-graphics. Search options also vary considerably from database to database. It is for these reasons that most libraries that support business programmes offer more than one business periodical database.

---

**ABI/INFORM Database**: a database covering more than 1000 leading business and management publications from 1971 on; from 1987 it provides full text

**EBSCO**: a database covering nearly 3800 leading business and management journals; it provides abstracts of the articles and even full text of some articles from more than 1100 peer-reviewed journals

**ECONLIT**: a database covering more than 1000 leading economic publications; it contains more than 610,000 records from 1969 to the present

**SOCIOFILE**: a database covering about 2000 leading sociological journals; it provides abstracts of the articles, and full text for some articles dating back to 1974

**psycArticles**: a database covering respected sources from 1987 to the present, including 33,000 full-text articles from publications of the American Psychological Association

*Exhibit 3.5* List of important databases.

---

The process of searching bibliographic databases and retrieving results applies to all databases.

1  Select a database appropriate to your topic.
2  Construct a **search query** (also called a **search statement**).
   a  Review and evaluate search results.
   b  Modify the search query, if necessary.
3  Save the valuable results of your search.

**4** Retrieve articles not available in the database.

**5** Supplement your results with information from web sources.

## Select a database

Most of us select the most convenient database with little regard for its scope, but considering the database contents and its limitations and criteria for inclusion at the beginning of your search will probably save you time in the long run. Remember that a library's online catalogue is a bibliographic database that will help identify books and perhaps other media on a topic. While journal or periodical titles are listed in a library's online catalogue, periodical or journal articles are rarely included. Use books for older, more comprehensive information. Use periodical articles for more current information or for information on very specific topics. A librarian can suggest one or more appropriate databases for the topic you are researching.

## The close-up

This provides direction for advanced database searches, including how initial searches are modified to obtain more relevant results.

## Save the results of the search

While the temptation to print may be overwhelming, remember that if you download your results, you can cut and paste quotations, tables and other information into your proposal without any need for rekeying. In either case, make sure you keep a note of the bibliographic information for your footnotes and bibliography. Most databases offer the choice of marking the records and printing or downloading them all at once or printing them one by one.

## Retrieve articles

For articles not available in full-text form online, retrieval will normally require the additional step of searching the library's online catalogue (unless there is a link from the database to the catalogue) to determine whether the desired issue is available and where it is located. Many libraries offer a document-delivery service for any articles that aren't available online. Some current articles may be available on the web or via a fee-based service.

There are dozens of types of information sources, each with a special function. In this section we describe five of the information types used most by business researchers. Later in this chapter we provide a more in-depth examination of three information types: bibliographic databases, government information and the World Wide Web.

## Indexes and bibliographies

Indexes and bibliographies are the mainstay of any library because they help the researcher to identify and locate a single book or journal article from among the millions published. The single most important **bibliography** in any library is its online catalogue. As with all other information types, there are many specialized indexes and bibliographies unique to business topics. These can be very useful in a literature search to find authors and titles of prior works on the topic of interest. (A list of key business resources is provided in Appendix A and on the accompanying CD.)

## Dictionaries

Dictionaries are so ubiquitous that they probably need no explanation. We all use them to verify spelling or grammar usage, or to define terms. In business, as in every field, there are many specialized dictionaries that define words, terms or jargon unique to a discipline. Most of these specialized dictionaries include in their word lists information on people, events or organizations that shape the discipline. They are also an excellent place to find acronyms. A growing number of dictionaries and glossaries (terms in a specialized field, area or topic, plus their definitions) are now available on the web. One of these is the Federal Reserve Bank of Chicago's Glossaries of Financial Terms (at www.chicagofed.org/publications/glossary/index.cfm). An example of a printed business dictionary is the *Dictionary of Business and Management*. Information from dictionaries and glossaries may be used to identify key terms for a search of an online or printed database.

## Encyclopaedias

An **encyclopaedia** can be used to find background or historical information on a topic, or to find names or terms that can enhance your search results in other sources. For example, you might use an encyclopaedia to find out when Microsoft introduced Windows, then use that date to draw more information from an index to the time period. Encyclopaedias are also helpful in identifying the experts in a field and the key writings on any topic. The *Encyclopaedia of Company Histories* and the *New Palgrave Dictionary of Economics and the Law* are two examples of specialized multivolume encyclopaedias.

## Handbooks

A **handbook** is a collection of facts unique to a topic. Handbooks often include statistics, directory information, a glossary of terms, and other data such as laws and regulations essential to a field. The best handbooks include source references for the facts they present. The *Statistical Abstract of the United States* is probably the most valuable and frequently used handbook available. It contains an extensive variety of facts, an excellent and detailed index, and a gateway to even more in-depth data for every table included.

## Directories

**Directories** are used for finding names and addresses, as well as other data. While many are available and useful in printed format, directories in digitized format, which can be searched by certain characteristics or sorted and then downloaded, are far more useful. Many are available free via the web, but the most comprehensive directories are proprietary (that is, they must be purchased). An especially useful directory available in most libraries, either in print or electronic format, is the *Encyclopedia of Associations* (called 'Associations Unlimited' on the web), which provides a list of public and professional organizations along with their locations and contact numbers.

## *Primary sources*

In science, a specific study is often pre-published in the form of a thesis, report, unpublished manuscript or conference proceeding, before it is published as an article in a scientific journal or as a chapter in a book. Such pre-publications serve two functions. First, authors circulate an unpublished manuscript among colleagues or present it at a conference to receive comments, which helps them to improve the study. Second, as the date of the pre-publication appears, the author can claim that he or she had a particular theoretical thought or empirical finding at this specific time and not later on.

Just a brief glance at the reference list of any academic article reveals that by far the greatest number of references stem from academic books or journals. Hence, these two forms of publication are the most important and relevant sources for any academic research. However, other publications, such as professional and trade journals, newspapers, and working papers or conference proceedings, often also form a rich source of information. Exhibit 3.6 offers an overview of the different literature sources and characterizes their usefulness for scientific work, their coverage in databases and their availability.

### The Internet as literature source

The World Wide Web is such a vast information, business and entertainment resource that it would be difficult, if not foolish, to overlook. Millions of pages of data are publicly available, and the size of the web doubles every few months.[5] But searching and retrieving reliable information on the web is a great deal more problematic than searching a bibliographic database. There are no standard database fields, no carefully defined subject hierarchies (known as controlled vocabulary), no cross-references, no synonyms, no selection criteria and, in general, no rules. There are dozens of search engines and they all work differently, but how they work is not always easy to determine. Nonetheless, the convenience of the web and the extraordinary amount of information to be found on it are compelling reasons for using it as an information source.

As you can see in Exhibit 3.7, the basic steps to searching the web are similar to those outlined for searching a bibliographic database. As you approach the web, you start at the same point: focusing on your management question. Are you looking for a known item (e.g. the personal website of a famous scholar)? Are you looking for information on a specific topic?

If you are looking for a specific topic, what are its parameters? For example, if your topic is managed healthcare, are you hoping to find general statistics, public policy issues, accounting standards or evidence of its impact on small businesses?

There are perfectly legitimate reasons to browse for information, and with its hypertext linking system, the web is the ultimate resource for browsing. The trick is to browse but to stay focused on the topic at hand. In the browse mode you do not have any particular target. You follow hypertext links from site to site for the sheer joy of discovery. This is somewhat analogous to window shopping at the mall or browsing the bookshelves in a library. It may or may not be fruitful. Neither is browsing likely to be efficient: researchers often work to tight deadlines, as managers often cannot delay critical decisions; therefore, researchers rarely have the luxury of undirected browsing.

Below are detailed those steps in the web search process that call for altered behaviour to that used in bibliographic searches.

### Select a search engine or directory

A search for specific information or for a specific site that will help you solve your management question requires a great deal more skill and knowledge than browsing. Start by selecting one or more Internet search engines. Web search engines vary considerably in the following ways:

- the types of Internet sources they cover (http, telnet, Usenet, ftp, etc.)
- the way they search web pages (every word? titles or headers only?)

| Source | Usefulness for scientific work | Coverage in databases, abstracts and indexes | Likely availability |
|---|---|---|---|
| (Refereed) academic journals | Form the basis of any scientific work as they contain articles reflecting the current scientific discussion, show recent theoretical developments, and provide empirical assessments of problems and theoretical ideas. Peer-reviewed academic journals in particular are a very useful source as their articles meet the high-quality standards of science | Usually very well covered. However, investigations of problems that cross different scientific disciplines call for the scanning of various databases, as most databases specialize in a particular discipline (e.g. EBSCO in management studies ECONLIT in economics, SOCFILE in sociology and PSYLIT in psychology); these comprehensive databases are available on CD-ROM for journal abstracts | University libraries usually have the most important journals in stock. Further, access to electronic databases containing the full text of journals has become more and more common recently |
| Professional and trade journals | Professional and trade journals are a useful source of information concerning the practical relevance of a problem. In addition, they often publish studies or provide data that can be useful in illustrating the background of the research or even the arguments made | Such journals are not as well covered in academic databases, although EBSCO contains a large number of these journals | Some of these journals may be included in the collections of university libraries. Furthermore, public libraries often hold some of these journals |
| Books | Books are as important as academic journal articles as sources of recent discussions, | Usually well covered in electronic databases, and in abstract and index sources. In addition, recent | University libraries have a large stock collection of academic books. If one is not available in |

| Source | Usefulness for scientific work | Coverage in databases, abstracts and indexes | Likely availability |
|---|---|---|---|
| Books (continued) | developments, theories and empirical investigations concerning a certain research topic. It often depends on the specific research field whether the relevant authors publish more in books or in journals. Edited volumes (i.e. books containing contributions from several authors) often provide a comprehensive overview of the topic. In particular a book's Introduction can often offer an assessment of the different contributions and how they fit into the bigger picture of the topic. Books written by one author are often a reflection of their own work in the last decade or so and can offer a richer and deeper description of the theoretical ideas and the empirical investigations. For example, books describing an empirical study often contain the complete questionnaire used and detailed information on the sample | books are often reviewed and discussed in academic journals, such as the *Journal of Economic Literature*, *Administrative Science Quarterly* or *Organization Studies*. These reviews usually offer a comprehensive summary of the book, and a critical assessment of the strengths and weaknesses of the book. They are very helpful when deciding whether it is worth reading the whole book. | the local university library, a copy can be sourced through inter-university lending. A common problem is that recently published books will be popular with other users and it may take some time before one can recall or reserve them. Hence, it is useful to identify as soon as possible books that are relevant to your research to ensure that you can stick to the time project |

| Source | Usefulness for scientific work | Coverage in databases, abstracts and indexes | Likely availability |
|---|---|---|---|
| Newspapers and public opinion journals | Newspapers and public opinion journals are useful sources of real-world examples (stylized facts), which will make your work much more lively. This holds especially for well-known newspapers and journals, such as the *Financial Times, Business Week, The Economist*, and so on | These days, the larger national and international newspapers in particular offer databases that will allow you to search their back issues and download specific articles at reasonable cost. However, these databases are newspaper-specific and will often require you to take out a subscription to the newspaper | National and some international newspapers are usually available in university and public libraries. In addition, some newspapers offer articles from their back issues via the Internet. However, the costs of such services can be considerable, as you may need to take out a subscription for a longer period |
| Conference proceedings/ unpublished manuscripts | Similar to refereed journals, as most articles published in academic journals have been presented before at conferences or circulated as manuscripts in the scientific community. However, not every manuscript or conference contribution will finally be published in an academic journal. Hence, the quality does not always meet the high academic standards for good research and you will have to check for yourself whether these standards really are met. The big advantage of conference proceedings and unpublished | Usually, electronic databases, abstracts and index sources do not cover this source. Information on conference contributions is, however, often available on the websites of the conferences themselves. Unpublished manuscripts are often available at the websites of university research institutes, university departments or the homepage of the researcher | University libraries will often possess printed conference proceedings from major conferences, and the unpublished manuscripts of faculty staff. Further, some well-established working paper series, such as *NBER* and *CPER*, are available via the Internet. Another alternative to sourcing unpublished manuscripts is to e-mail the author(s) directly and ask for an electronic copy of the paper or to check if they are available on the personal homepage(s) of the author(s) |

| Source | Usefulness for scientific work | Coverage in databases, abstracts and indexes | Likely availability |
|---|---|---|---|
| Conference proceedings/ unpublished manuscripts (continued) | manuscripts is that the information is much more recent as the time lag between writing down the ideas and results, and publishing is much shorter. Hence, this source becomes much more important if you are working on a problem that is rather new (e.g. research about the Internet) or fast-developing (e.g. research on AIDS) | | |
| Reports | Reports are a useful source of specific information, which you might want to use during your own research. Further, they often offer descriptive data, which are useful in illustrating the importance or relevance of a statement or argument you have made | The number of reports is indefinite, but unfortunately there is no one database that holds information on all existing reports. In academic reference databases the coverage of reports is usually quite poor. Often, you can find information on the reports themselves by looking at the websites of the institutions that published them (e.g. government agencies, industrial and professional associations, and also companies) | Many reports have been written to find answers to the very specific real-world problems of a company or state institution. Reports often contain interesting but also proprietary information and, as a consequence, are not in the public domain |
| Theses | Ph.D. theses share a number of characteristics with other | Usually very bad. There are some specialized theses databases; | The physical circulation of Ph.D. theses is very limited and often |

| Source | Usefulness for scientific work | Coverage in databases, abstracts and indexes | Likely availability |
| --- | --- | --- | --- |
| | unpublished manuscripts, and parts of some of the better ones are likely to be published in scientific journals at some point. What distinguishes Ph.D. theses from other unpublished working papers is that they are much more exhaustive and usually contain a very comprehensive literature review as well as an extensive description of the theories and methodologies used. Master's theses, except for the very good ones, often do not meet the high standards of sound academic work. However, like reports, they often offer interesting background information and descriptive data. Further, their literature review section and reference list can be used as a departure point for your own literature search | however, these are usually restricted to Ph.D. theses, and to a specific country or even university | only the Ph.D.-granting university holds a copy of the thesis in its library. The availability of Master's theses depends very much on the policy of the university involved, and many universities are rather restrictive with respect to public access to theses |

*Exhibit 3.6* Overview of primary literature.

| Bibliographic search process | Web search process |
|---|---|
| 1. Select a database appropriate to your topic | 1. Select a search engine or directory |
|  | 2. Determine your search options |
| 2. Construct a search query | 3. Construct a search query |
| • review and evaluate search results | • review and evaluate search results |
| • modify the search query | • modify the search query |
| 3. Save valuable results of your search | 4. Determine your search options |
| 4. Retrieve articles not available in the bibliographic database | 5. Supplement your results with information from non-web sources |
| 5. Supplement your results with information from web sources |  |

**Exhibit 3.7** The web search process compared to the bibliographic search process.

- the number of pages they include in their indexes
- the search and presentation options they offer
- the frequency with which they are updated.

Furthermore, some publicly indexable pages via the web are not retrievable at all using current web search engines. Among the material open to the public, but not indexed by search engines, is the following:[6]

- pages that are proprietary (that is, fee-based) and/or password-protected, including the contents of bibliographic and other databases
- pages accessible only through a search form (databases), including such highly popular web resources as library catalogues, e-commerce catalogues (such as Amazon.com and similar offerings), and the Security and Exchange Commission's EDGAR catalogue of SEC filings
- poorly designed framed pages
- some non-HTML or non-plain-text pages, especially PDF graphics files, for which no text alternative is offered. These pages cannot be retrieved using any current search engine.

The search engine, portal or directory you select may well be determined by how comprehensive you want your results to be.[7] If you want to use some major sites only, then start with a directory such as Yahoo! or Google. At least within the publicly indexable pages, one approach emphasizes selectivity, and the other comprehensiveness. If you are interested in comprehensiveness, use more than one search engine.

What is the difference between a search engine, a portal and a directory? Directories rely on human intervention to select, index and categorize web content. Subject directories build an index based on web pages or websites, but not on words within a page. Presenting a series of subject categories that are then further subdivided, Yahoo! (http://www.yahoo.com/) was the first web subject directory and is still one of the most popular choices for finding information on the web. This is because most users are satisfied with a few good sites rather than a long list of possibilities.

A search engine's different software components allow it to search and retrieve web pages. These include:

- software that automatically sends robots, sometimes called spiders, out to comb the web going from server to server to build an index of the words, pages and files that are publicly indexable
- algorithms that determine how those pages will be selected and prioritized for display
- user interface software that determines the search options available to the user.

A **portal** is, as the name suggests, a gateway to the web. A portal often includes a directory, a search engine, and other user features such as news and weather. Most Internet service providers (ISPs) are portals to the web. The AOL homepage is an example. This portal uses information based on past user search behaviour to determine what to offer on the opening screen. Therefore, some valuable search engines, indexes, directories and more may be relegated to an 'other search aids' category. Specialized portals are increasingly popular. An industry portal, one type of specialized portal, lists many different resources about a specific industry. Competia Express, the competitive intelligence site (http://www.competia.com/express/index.html), offers industry portals for many different industries.

## Determine your search options

Nearly all search services have a 'Help' button that will lead you to information about the search protocols and options of that particular search engine. How does the search engine work? Can you combine terms using Boolean operators (AND, OR, NOT) or other connectors? How do you enter phrases? Truncate terms? Determine output display? Limit by date or other characteristic? Some search engines provide a basic and an advanced search option. How do they differ?

## Construct a search query and enter your search term(s)

The web is not a database, nor does it have a controlled vocabulary. Therefore, you must be as specific as possible, using the keywords in your management question and any variations you can think of. It is up to you to determine synonyms, variant spellings, and broader or narrower terms that will help you retrieve the information you need. This may involve some trial and error. For instance, a general term (such as 'business') would be useless in a search engine that purports to index every word in every document.

## Save the results of your search

If you have found good information, you will want to keep it for future reference so that you can cite it in your proposal or refer to it later in the development of your investigative questions. If you do not keep documents, you may have to reconstruct your search. At a future time, given that some portion of the web is revised and updated daily, those same documents may no longer be available.

## Supplement your results with information from non-web sources

There is still a great deal of information in books, journals and other print sources that is not available on the web. While many novice researchers start and end here, the more sophisticated researcher knows that a web search is just one of many important options.

## Reading and evaluating research

Reading for review differs from reading for pleasure, as it requires the reader to distil the relevant information and to unravel the reasoning. Furthermore, as the number of potentially interesting books and articles is uncountable, one needs to read efficiently. Start by reading the title and then try to get an idea of the general structure of the text. In the case of a book you will study the table of contents and in the case of an article you will read the abstract. Try to identify what is the main point the book or article wants to make.

The whole reading process is guided by two questions. First, is the reading relevant for my study, that is does the article at least touch on the issues and question I wish to address? Second, if it is relevant does it add to the arguments or information I offer? (The latter question also includes information and articles opposing your own thinking.) If you are convinced that either of these two questions will be answered with a 'no' you can skip the article.

For example, if you intend to investigate the internationalization strategies of Dutch family firms, not all articles dealing either with internationalization strategies OR family businesses will be relevant for your study. However, an AND criterion could be too strict, as a study investigating growth strategies in family firms might offer useful insights. The second selection question refers to the fact that, often, the information presented in one literature source is hardly different from the information presented in another. For example, there are certainly hundreds of studies addressing the difficulties of medium-sized or family firms in following an internationalization strategy. Even a comprehensive literature review does not need to deal with all such studies. If a certain theoretical argument or empirical finding is documented in many studies, it is usually sufficient to refer to just a few of them. But, to which should you refer? There are no strict guidelines as to which studies should be taken into account and which not. However, the following are some useful criteria.

- Time of publication. One mentions the study that was published first to give credit to the author(s) who made a certain argument or presented a specific finding first. This rule explains that some classical works, written more than 100 years ago, are still often mentioned. Sometimes, it is also advisable to mention quite recent studies, especially with respect to empirical results, as effects may change over time. For example, a study from the 1930s investigating who took over a family business is likely to find that the eldest son has a higher chance of becoming the successor. With the start of the new millennium, the effects of children's gender and birth rank are likely to be much smaller.

- Most scholars will usually include articles from (top) sources in their own academic field. Thus, a sociologist is more likely to include articles published in the *American Journal of Sociology*, an economist articles published in the *Journal of Political Economy* and a business scientist articles published in the *Academy of Management Journal* or the *Strategic Management Journal*.

- The scope of the study. Particularly in the case of empirical studies, studies with a broader scope (i.e. a higher external validity) are more likely to be included in a review than studies with a rather narrow scope.

Exhibit 3.8 provides a list of criteria to help assess the relevance and value of an article, chapter or book to be included in a literature review. With the steadily increasing number of books, journals and articles available, hardly anyone can claim to write a complete literature review. It is inevitable that some literature will have to be omitted, and, often, the choice of which literature should be omitted informs us of the perspective the author has on the field. However, a good literature review needs to include references to the classical and most prominent studies. For this reason articles or (book) chapters that are frequently cited by other scholars working in the field need to be mentioned. For example, if you write a literature review on studies related to transaction cost theory, you need to include references to Coase (1937) and Williamson (1973, 1983).[8]

Another indicator of the prominence of an article or book is the relative importance of the journal or publisher. Articles that appear in one of the top management journals or in books issued by a well-known publisher usually have a greater impact (i.e. are more prominent) than articles from 'smaller' journals or publishers. In general, the more recent literature is more important, as it is built on a larger knowledge base. When writing a review of the literature, you must bear in mind that older or even outdated articles might state thoughts or ideas that were

| Criteria | Relevance or value increasing |
| --- | --- |
| Prominence of article or (book) chapter documented by citations or the source | The more an article or (book) chapter has been cited, the more it has been appreciated by other scholars |
| Recency of the article or (book) chapter | The world is changing, and so is our view of it and knowledge of it. Hence more recent articles usually offer a better idea than older ones of the current state of knowledge |
| Methodological quality of the article or (book) chapter | Any article or (book) chapter referred to should meet the criteria of good research (see Chapter 1) |
| Comparability of your arguments with the arguments put forward in the article or (book) chapter | The criterion refers to whether or not the article or (book) chapter relates to the arguments you make, either by supporting them or by contradicting them |
| Uniqueness of the articles or (book) chapter | How original (unique) is the contribution of the article? Is it a repetition of a previous study in a slightly different context or is it a fundamentally new study? |

Exhibit 3.8 Criteria for the relevance and value of articles and (book) chapters.

considered reasonable at the time the article was published, but are not acceptable today, as later evidence has clarified matters. This is not, however, the case for classical studies or books that form the foundations of the knowledge base and still hold true. The reputation of the publisher, journal and the authors is an indication of the scientific quality of a piece of work, but it is only an indicator and in the end you have to use your own judgement; many well-known authors have published less convincing pieces and many really important articles have been published by people who were little known at the time their work was published. Hence, whether you want to include a study in your review of the literature depends on your quality of judgement along the lines of the criteria for good research presented in Chapter 1.

Without a doubt, many interesting and excellent studies have been published, but that does not mean you have to include them all in your literature review. Any other study is relevant for your study if it relates clearly to the arguments you make, either by supporting them or by contradicting them. Any articles or (book) chapters that do not relate to your study sufficiently distract the reader of your study from the points you want to make and may even disappoint the reader (as every reference to a specific piece of work creates expectations, which you will be unable to fulfil if your study does not address the problem and arguments of the study referred to). Similarly, many studies in the literature largely address the same research problem. For example, there are hundreds of studies investigating why people choose to become self-employed. To decide which of these studies you want to include into your literature review, you have to assess what is the unique contribution of a study to this field of research. Who put forward a new argument, who looked at the issue from a (slightly) different angle, and so on?

## *How to read*

Once you have chosen to read an article or book for review, never start by attempting to read every sentence, but try to get the gist of the research. The following steps offer a useful strategy for quickly grasping the main issues in a piece of literature.

1 Skim through the book to discover its structure, topic, style, general reasoning, data and references.

   a Read the title.

   b Read the chapter titles or section headings.

   c Check whether empirical evidence is presented and, if so, what kind of evidence (purely theoretical work or qualitative research or quantitative research).

   d Check the references to see whether you already know some of the literature or authors cited. (Checking references becomes more important the more literature you have seen on an issue. If you are not a complete novice to an issue and read through the references of an article or book without recognizing one of the cited articles or at least authors, this should arouse your suspicions. In such a case it is likely that the article does not really address what you are interested in.)

2 Survey each chapter of the book/each section of the article.

   a Read the sub-headings and try to determine the main structure of the book/article.

   b Take a closer look at the figures and tables provided, as they often summarize (parts of) the text.

**3** Skim over and read the Preface and Introduction to identify the main ideas.

**4** Read the parts and chapters that are important to your own area of interest.

Once you have embarked upon a more thorough reading of a book or article, it is important to distil the essentials of the text. Exhibit 3.9 lists the important elements of many texts.

| Introduction, problem statement | Theoretical sections/chapters | Sections/chapters covering methodology, analysis and conclusions |
| --- | --- | --- |
| Definitions | Arguments | Techniques |
| Events | Concepts | Design |
| Evidence | Hypotheses | Results |
| Motives | Interpretations | Conclusions |
| Perspective | Justification | Summary |
| Problem | Theory | Recommendations |
| Questions | Styles of thinking | |
| Standpoints | | |

*Exhibit 3.9* The important elements of a text.

The questions you should be able to answer after reading a book or article are as follows.

**1** What is the problem addressed?

**2** What are the proposed theories or ideas?

**3** How has it been investigated?/What methods were used?

**4** What are the results in terms of the problem stated?

Writing down the answers to these questions will often take you some way towards compiling your own review.

## Synthesizing the literature

A literature review is a piece of academic writing and it must be logically structured and clear. This chapter has already talked about the aims and objectives of a review and the purposes it should serve. First, any review of the literature requires you to deliver an appropriate summary of prior work. In the sections above, we have indicated how you can scan the enormous amount of literature available efficiently, and how to select the pieces of literature most relevant to your review. A review, however, is more than a well-structured summary of the literature; a good review also contains considerable insight from the writer, as it is not only a précis, but a well-reasoned piece of criticism too.

### Criticism

Whenever you write an academic literature review or participate in a scientific discussion, it is worth considering the main points of effective criticism.

- You should base your criticism on an assessment of weaknesses and strengths.
- You should criticize theories, arguments, ideas and the methodology, but not the authors or their motives.
- You should reflect on your own critique, providing reasons for the choices you have made, and recognizing and pointing out any weaknesses in your criticism.
- You should treat the work of others with due respect, that is give a fair account of the views and arguments of others when summarizing.

Further, you must always provide reasons for your disagreement with a certain view or argument; just stating that you disagree is wrong and insufficient. Finally, you should focus on the major parts of an argument. If you base your criticism on minor details or construct hypothetical examples to show that under very specific circumstances the argument might not hold, your criticism is not usually a strong one.

## The writing process

This section cannot provide a detailed account of how to write a review, article or book. There are many books on general writing techniques that might be worth a look at (see the list of references at the end of the book). However, we will still give you a broad outline of the writing process and how you can improve your writing. As with most other tasks, doing something well requires you to make a plan, and it's a good idea to write down such a plan. Your plan should contain at least the following elements:

1  the aims and objectives of the review
2  the audience for the review
3  a brief summary of your main points
4  a draft outline
5  a list of the main material you have selected (in the case of a review, note down the main pieces of literature you will discuss in your review).

Right from the start it should be clear to you why you are writing the review. Do you just want to give a summary of the existing literature on a specific topic? Do you want to critically assess the current literature on a topic and use the conclusions of your review as a point of departure for motivating your own research?

It is clear that a review for a scientific journal, which aims to illustrate the current state of the art with regard to a specific topic, differs from a review that is part of an article investigating a particular question, and where the review is used to place the research conducted into a specific context.

The audience for your review is a crucial consideration when deciding on many aspects during the review process. The more knowledgeable your audience, the less time you need to spend planning the review. If you are writing an article for a scientific journal, where you can expect that most of the readers will know the literature as well as you do, you do not need to give a short summary of each piece of literature you include. If you are reviewing the literature for a scientific audience that does not know the specific literature involved, then you should give your readers more information on the content of the literature under review. Finally, if you are writing a review for an educational audience, which is not (yet) acquainted at all with the field, you need to provide much more information on each piece of literature included. To sum up, the better informed your audience, the more your review can be your own reasoned interpretation of the current state of affairs in the field and the less need there is to present an overview of existing studies.

Reviewing the literature usually means more than providing a brief summary of it. Every literature review should also try to make a point with regard to what the author thinks about the field. Some possible themes for points to make are as follows.

- What are the remaining unsolved puzzles in the field?
- On which aspects do most authors agree, and on which aspects do you find much disagreement?
- Given the current state of affairs, what are promising and fruitful future research directions?
- What are the current lacunae in the field?

Before you come to write down your review, you need to clarify which points you want to make, how you will use the review to support your points, and how you can structure the review to make your points.

Structuring an argument is part of drafting the outline. You should be aware that a review can be structured in many ways. It is very common to use a chronological structure, starting with the earliest studies and ending with the most recent. Such a structure works well if you want to show historical developments in a field. Sometimes a field is subdivided into different 'schools of thought'; in such a case it is often sensible to structure the review along the lines of these. In other cases, the main theoretical idea has been applied in many different fields (e.g. the idea of social capital has been used to explain differences in regional economic success, promotions in a firm, success of entrepreneurs, the forming of buyer–supplier relations, and so on). Here, the field of application can be a useful guide to the structure. Finally, you will need to select your material (i.e. decide which studies will be included in your review).

## 3.4 Meta analysis[9]

Recently, **meta analysis** has become increasingly popular to review and summarize studies addressing the same topic. It dates back to the work of Glass and Smith on psychotherapy in the 1970s.[10] Science is a cumulative activity and one research problem is explored and investigated by a large number of studies. For example, studies on who is likely to become self-employed, firms' choices of internationalization strategies, and so on, are countless. Meta analysis allows you to investigate quantitatively which outcomes are supported by most studies and which outcomes are more ambiguous. Further, you can identify whether differences in the research set-up, such as differences in sample size, different types of population, and so on, explain differences in the outcome. To some extent, a meta analysis is a very quantitative approach to a literature review.

## Advantages and disadvantages of meta analysis

Meta analysis is a particularly powerful tool for reviewing an already well-investigated research field (i.e. a field in which quantitative empirical studies have been published). It offers a very structured approach to summarize the cumulated knowledge of all the studies included and is often able to detect relationships that narrative summaries of a research field have been unable to uncover. The structured approach of meta analysis (i.e. the tracking and recording of many characteristics of the studies, such as sample size, included variables, sample population, correlations between included variables, etc.) provides a way of organizing and handling such a large amount of information, which is usually less efficient and comprehensive if you use only notes and index cards to summarize the literature. This structured approach, however, is also a disadvantage of meta analysis, as it can only take account of the quantifiable characteristics of a study. It misses other important evaluation criteria, such as the methodological quality of a study or its social context, which can be accounted for in a narrative summary.

A major criticism of meta analysis is that it compares apples and oranges, and misses. For example, a meta analysis of studies on internationalization strategies can include studies that follow distinct theoretical ideas and therefore use different sets of independent variables. This problem, however, is only substantial if you attempt to average all studies to obtain an overall mean effect size. It is less of a problem if your main objective is to compare different (groups of) studies. A final disadvantage of meta analysis is the tremendous effort involved in conducting such an analysis.

## Conducting a meta analysis

Meta analysis starts, like any research project, with the formulation of a problem statement. What is the research objective or, in other words, along what lines (criteria) do you want to compare or summarize the selected studies? A quantitative comparison and summary of studies requires that we obtain quantitative information for each study. In meta analysis this information is called the **effect size statistic**. Exhibit 3.10 provides an overview of common effect size statistics, but as a researcher you are free to develop other meaningful statistics that might serve the purpose of your meta analysis better than the common ones. Depending on the information available for each study, you can of course investigate multiple effect size statistics.

Once you have formulated your research problem and decided which effect size statistics are relevant to answering it, you need to develop a coding scheme to record the relevant information from the studies included in your meta analysis. Exhibit 3.11 provides you with an overview of possible information that could usefully be coded for each study. This and other information is then coded in a spreadsheet or data file (like Microsoft Excel) and statistical application software, with the studies in the rows and the different information items in the columns. Once you have organized all the information in one data file you can use statistical software to perform standard and sophisticated statistical analyses.

| Effect size statistic | Objective and example of an application |
|---|---|
| Central tendency description | Compares descriptive statistics of variables, such as mean, mode or proportion, describing a central tendency across various samples<br>*Suppose you analyse various studies investigating the proportion of women reaching top management positions. This statistic provides you with the distribution of the proportions in the various studies and could be analysed by relating it to other characteristics of the study and sample* |
| Pre-post contrast | Compares a central tendency at two points of time to examine changes and requires that all studies included provide information for both points of time<br>*Related to the example above, the proportion of women in top management positions in the 1990s and in the 2000s is compared and is used to examine changes* |
| Group contrast | Comparison is not between two points of time but between two groups, which can be distinguished<br>*Related to the example above, the proportion of women in top management positions in business firms and in public institutions, such as hospitals, ministries, and so on* |
| Association between variables | Comparing of the covariation between two variables, for example the correlation coefficient<br>*Related to the example above, the correlation between having a working mother and achieving a top management position* |

*Exhibit 3.10*  Common effect size statistics in meta analysis.

- Variables and their definition
- Sample size
- Time and place of data-collection (study)
- Descriptive statistics of each variable (mean, mode, standard deviation, variances)
- Reliability scores for measurements
- Correlation coefficients between two variables
- Regression coefficients and their confidence intervals
- Statistical methodology used

*Exhibit 3.11*  Useful information to collect and code for each study.

## Research Methods in Practice 3

# How do you write a literature review about a topic that has hardly been researched?

The study on the management of R&D cooperations does not only look at contracts as instruments to govern interfirm relations, but also on another ex-ante management instrument, namely search. As soon as one concedes that economic action is embedded in a social structure, one also acknowledges that there are differences between economic actors, for example more and less trustworthy partners. However, while contracts had been already studied extensively, the literature on searching is rather scarce.

A good start for any literature review is to develop a framework in which you place all the different studies you have read. A table that summarizes all studies investigating differences in organizational forms from a transaction cost perspective is shown below in Exhibit 3.12. The columns represent two categories of the dependent variable, namely studies explaining vertical integration and studies focusing on hybrid organizational forms. The rows represent different sets of independent variable. The studies in the first row focus purely on factors suggested by transaction cost economies; the studies in the second row extend their view by also looking at how the market or external environment might affect the choice to integrate or to choose for a specific hybrid form. The studies in the last row focus again on characteristics of the transaction but also take considerations regarding the social embeddedness into account. Thus, the study on the management of R&D cooperations discussed in this case would fall into the lower right cell.

The literature reviews presented here differ considerably from the literature review presented in Exhibit 3.2. While the literature review in Exhibit 3.2. gives a brief synthesis of the many studies and their results on the decision to become self-employed, the literature review below is developed from a theoretical perspective. Here, the author wants to show why it is sensitive to view searching a partner as an important form of ex-ante cooperation management and develops arguments by looking at the literature in transaction cost theory and in search theory.

## 1  Introduction

> *One should hardly have to tell academicians that information is a valuable resource: knowledge is power. And yet it occupies a slum dwelling in the town of economics. Mostly it is ignored; the best technology is assumed to be known ... There are a great many problems in economics for which this neglect or ignorance is no doubt permissible or even desirable. But there are some for which this is not true, and I hope to show that some important aspects of economic organization take a new meaning when the are considered from the viewpoint of search for information.*
>
> (Stigler 1961: 213)

This citation of Stigler certainly applies to the economic organization of interfirm cooperations, like for example co-makership, cross-licensing or joint R&D projects. Most studies addressing the problem of economic organization and market exchange use transaction cost-based arguments to explain differences in interfirm contracting (for an overview of such studies see, e.g., Blumberg, 1998; Klein and Shelanski, 1995). More recently several scholars recognized that firms are not anonymous isolated actors and extended the analysis of contractual arrangements with considerations concerning the social embeddedness of cooperations. The social embeddedness of a cooperation describes the position of the cooperating firms in a social structure formed by other firms, which are partners, customers, suppliers or

| Main Independent variables | Dependent variable | |
|---|---|---|
| | vertical integration (market versus hierarchy) | hybrid forms (contract duration, occurrence of specific clauses) |
| Characteristics of the cooperation | Anderson, 1988<br>Gatignon and Anderson, 1988<br>Globerman and Schwindt, 1986<br>Hennart, 1988<br>John and Weitz, 1988<br>Klein *et al.* 1990<br>Levy, 1985<br>Masten *et al.* 1989<br>Monteverde and Teece, 1982<br>Stuckey, 1983 | Joskow, 1985, 1987, 1990<br>Leffler and Rucker, 1991<br>Palay, 1984, 1985<br>Pittman, 1991 |
| Characteristics of the cooperation and the market | Caves and Bradburd, 1988<br>Harrigan, 1986<br>Lieberman, 1991<br>MacDonald, 1985<br>*Muris et al. 1992*<br>Pisano, 1990<br>Walker and Weber, 1984, 1987 | Crocker and Lyon, 1994<br>Davidson and McFetridge, 1984<br>Mulherin, 1986 |
| Characteristics of the cooperation and social embeddedness | *Eccles, 1981* | *Acheson, 1985*<br>Allen and Lueck, 1992<br>Gulati, 1995<br>Heide and Miner, 1992<br>*Lorenz, 1988*<br>Lyon, 1994<br>Parkhe, 1993<br>*Wilson, 1980* |

Note: Studies printed in italics are qualitative.

*Exhibit 3.12* An overview of studies on variations in organizational forms from a transaction cost perspective.

competitors. Intensive and multiple contacts between these firms indicate a strong embeddedness (Granovetter, 1985). Heide and Miner (1992) reflect on the importance of expectations with respect to future business between the partners and find that the possibility to retaliate in future relationships reduces contracting. Gulati (1995) and Lyon (1994) show that earlier relationships between the two partners also reduce contracting. Finally, Lorenz (1988), Batenburg *et al.* (2003), Buskens (1999) and Rooks *et al.*

(2000) investigated the role of social networks for the organization of buyer–supplier relations. Except for Batenburg *et al.* these studies support the notion that a strong embeddedness in social networks reduce the necessity of extended contracting, because social networks provide other mechanisms, such as implicit voice and exit threats, to govern the relation.

Transaction cost-based studies always address as a dependent variable the choice of an organizational form or contracting. Searching as a management instrument to reduce problems that arise from coordination and cooperation problems have been widely neglected. Most empirical studies implicitly assume that the best partner is already known and that this information is available at no costs. However, theoretical elaborations explicitly addressed search costs as an essential part of transaction costs and thereby recognize the importance of searching (see, e.g., Kenney and Klein, 1983; Milgrom and Roberts, 1992: 29; Furubotn and Richter, 1991: 51–2). The consideration of the social embeddedness in recent studies provides an additional argument to address search management. One consequence of social embeddedness is that firms differ in their informational basis and abilities to gather additional information (Braun, 1993: 4–5). Hence, transaction cost economics as well as considerations with regard to the social embeddedness of firms indicate that a more thorough investigation of search management within interfirm cooperations could be fruitful.

## 2  Transaction costs and search theory

Search management consists mainly of gathering information about potential partners for the intended joint project. Firms are interested in two types of information: (1) information about the technological competences of the partner and (2) information about the partner's trustworthiness and reliability. Collecting such information before entering an interfirm cooperation diminishes potential coordination and cooperation problems.

## Transaction cost economics

Before presenting a formal search model and hypotheses derived from it, I briefly reflect on the basics of transaction cost economics with regard to the organization of interfirm cooperations. Given bounded rationality and actors that (sometimes) behave opportunistically, firms entering a cooperation face the problem that the partner has incentives and opportunities to take an unilateral advantage of their cooperative attitude. These incentives and opportunities form the problem potential that has to be mitigated to achieve the benefits of a successful collaboration between the partners. According to Williamson (1985: 52–61) the problem potential is determined by three dimensions: (1) The volume of a cooperation indicates how large the gains of opportunism are as well as how large the damage of the betrayed partner can be. (2) Dependency and relation specific investments, that is investments that are not (or just partly) redeployable outside the cooperation, create a hold-up problem and enable the non-investing partner to claim the so-called quasi-rent. The quasi-rent is the part of the cooperation's earnings in excess of the amount necessary to prevent a partner from leaving the cooperation. As soon as a partner has made relation-specific investments and incurred sunk costs, the non-investing partner can appropriate the quasi-rents from this investment by threatening to terminate the relationship, because for the investing partner costs of losing the quasi-rent are smaller than the costs associated with a terminated relationship (see Richter and Furubotn, 1996: 93; Klein *et al.*, 1978: 298). (3) Uncertainty is the third dimension of the problem potential. Next to the external uncertainty, which refers to unpredictable changes in market conditions and technologies, I consider also the internal uncertainty, which refers to a firm's abilities to assess the trustworthiness and competence of a potential partner. The former type of uncertainty offers each partner margins for opportunistic behaviour, because intentional opportunism becomes difficult to distinguish from force majeure at higher levels of uncertainty. The latter type refers to monitor problems, which create opportunities for opportunism (Durkheim, 1893; Milgrom and Roberts, 1992). Given the volume of a cooperation, the necessary relation-specific investments and the uncertainty level, partners can mitigate the problem potential by choosing an adequate organizational form and agreeing on appropriate contracts. Several empirical studies support transaction cost theory-based hypotheses on the relationship between the dimensions of the problem potential and the extent of vertical integration (see, e.g., Walker and Weber, 1984; Pisano, 1990), respectively, by the use of contractual agreements (see, e.g., Joskow, 1985; Lyon, 1994). Next to problem potential issues, various more recent studies addressed the social embeddedness of cooperations, that is earlier and future relationships between the partners as well as ties towards the other partners of the partner, as an additional factor to explain the (contractual) organization of interfirm cooperations (see, e.g., Gulati, 1995).

## Search theory applied

Within economics, labour markets and brand choices of consumers have been the major applications of search models (see, e.g., Stigler, 1961 and Nelson, 1970 for consumer search behaviour and Devine and Kiefer, 1991 for an overview of labour market search). These models are based on the following idea. Given a distribution of prices (or wages) and given the search costs for evaluating each brand (or job) offer, one can determine a reservation price (or wage) and thereby optimize the number of evaluated offers. If the price (wage) of an offer is lower (higher) than the reservation price (wage) the offer is accepted and searching stops (Diamond, 1987; McCall, 1970; Stigler, 1961). These models base the choice on a single selection criterion, the price. Selecting a partner certainly involves more than one criterion, such as technological competence, trustworthiness and reliability. Thus, a slightly different search model should not optimize the number of evaluated offers but the amount of gathered information. The amount of gathered information is optimized under the assumptions that the total search costs as well as the total search benefits increase in the amount of information.

If you take Exhibit 3.1. which mentions the main ingredients for a good literature review, are the literature reviews presented in this book in the main good and what are their weaknesses?

## References

Acheson, James M. 'The Maine lobster market: between market and hierarchy'. *Journal of Law, Economics, and Organization* 1, 1985, 385–96.

Allen, Douglas W. and Lueck, Dean 'The "back forty" on a handshake: specific assets, reputation, and the structure of farmland contracts'. *Journal of Law, Economics, and Organization* 8, 1992, 366–76.

Anderson, Erin 'Transaction costs as determinants of opportunism in integrated and independent sales forces'. *Journal of Economic Behavior and Organization* 9, 1988, 247–64.

Batenburg, Ronald, Raub, Werner and Snijders, Chris. 'Contacts and Contracts: dyadic embeddedness and the contractual behaviour of firms.' *Research in the Sociology of Organizations, 20*, 2003, 135–88.

Blumberg, Boris *Das Management von Technologiekooperationen.* Wiesbaden: Gabler, 1998.

Braun, Norman *Socially Embedded Exchange.* Frankfurt am Main: Peter Lang, 1993.

Buskens, V. *Social Networks and Trust.* Utrecht: ICS dissertation, 1999.

Caves, Richard E. and Bradburd, Ralph M. 'The empirical determinants of vertical integration'. *Journal of Economic Behavior and Organization* 9, 1988, 26–79.

Crocker, Keith J. and Lyon, Thomas P. 'What do "facilitating practices" facilitate? An empirical investigation of most-favored-nation clauses in natural gas contracts'. *Journal of Law and Economics* 37, 1994, 297–322.

Davidson, W.H. and McFetridge, Donald G. 'International technology transactions and the theory of the firm'. *The Journal of Industrial Economics* 32, 1984, 253–64.

Devine, T.J. and Kiefer, N.M. 1991 *Empirical Labor Economics: The Search Approach.* New York: Oxford University Press, 1991.

Diamond, Peter A. 'Search theory', in Eatwell, John, Milgate, Murray and Newman, Peter (eds.) *The New Palgrave. Allocation, Information, and Markets.* New York: Norton, 1987, 271–86.

Durkheim, Emile *De la Division du Travail Social.* 9. Auflage. Paris: PUF 1973, 1893.

Eccles, Robert 'The quasiform in the construction industry'. *Journal of Economic Behavior and Organization* 2, 1981, 335–58.

Furubotn, Eirik and Richter, Rudolf. The new institutional economics: a collection of articles from the *Journal of Institutional and Theoretical Economics,* Texas A&M University Press.

Gatignon, Hubert and Anderson, Erin 'The multinational corporation's degree of control over foreign subsidiaries: an empirical test of a transaction cost explanation'. *Journal of Law, Economics, and Organization* 4, 1988, 305–36.

Globerman, Steven and Schwindt, Richard 'The organization of vertically related transactions in the Canadian forest products industries'. *Journal of Economic Behavior and Organization* 7, 1986, 199–212.

Granovetter, Mark S. 'Economic action and social structure: the problem of embeddedness'. *American Journal of Sociology* 91, 1985, 481–510.

Gulati, Ranjay 'Does familiarity breed trust? The implications of repeated ties for contractual choices in alliances'. *Academy of Management Journal* 38, 1995, 85–112.

Harrigan, Kathryn R. 'Matching vertical integration strategies to competitive conditions'. *Strategic Management Journal* 7, 1986, 535–55.

Heide, Jan B. and Miner, Anne S. 'The shadow of the future: effects of anticipated interaction and frequency of contact on buyer–seller cooperation'. *Academy of Management Journal* 35, 1992, 265–91.

Hennart, Jean-François 'Upstream vertical integration in the aluminium and tin industries: a comparative study of the choice between market and intrafirm coordination'. *Journal of Economic Behavior and Organization* 9, 1988, 281–99.

John, George and Weitz, Barton A. 'Forward integration into distribution: an empirical test of transaction cost analysis'. *Journal of Law, Economics, and Organization* 4, 1988, 337–55.

Joskow, Paul L. 'Vertical integration and long-term contracts: the case of coal-burning electric generating plants'. *Journal of Law, Economics, and Organization* 1, 1985, 33–80.

Joskow, Paul L. 'Contract duration and relationship-specific investments: empirical evidence from coal markets'. *American Economic Review* 77, 1987, 168–85.

Joskow, Paul L. 'The performance of long-term contracts: further evidence from coal markets'. *RAND Journal of Economics* 21, 1990, 251–74.

Kenney, R.W. and Klein, Benjamin 'The economics of block booking'. *Journal of Law and Economics* 26, 1983, 497–540.

Klein, Benjamin, Crawford, R.A. and Alchian, Armen A. 'Vertical Integration, Appropriate Rents, and the Competitive Contracting Process'. *Journal of Law and Economics* 21, 1978, 297–326.

Klein, Peter G. and Shelanski, Howard A. 'Empirical Work in Transaction Cost Economics'. *Journal of Law, Economics, and Organization* 11, 1995.

Klein, Saul, Frazier, Gary L. and Roth, Victor J. 'A transaction cost analysis model of channel integration in international markets'. *Journal of Marketing Research* 27, 1990, 196–208.

Leffler, Keith B. and Rucker, Randal R. 'Transaction Costs and the Efficient Organization of Production: A Study of Timber-Harvesting Contracts'. *Journal of Political Economy* 99, 1991, 1060–87.

Levy, David T. 'The transactions cost approach to vertical integration: an empirical explanation'. *Review of Economics and Statistics* 67, 1985, 438–45.

Lieberman, Marvin B. (1991) 'Determinants of vertical integration: an empirical test'. *The Journal of Industrial Economics* 39, 1991, 451–66.

Lorenz, Edward H. 'Neither friends nor strangers: informal networks of subcontracting in French industry', in Gambetta, Diego (ed.) *Trust: Making and Breaking Cooperative Relations.* Oxford: Basil Blackwell, 1988, 194–210.

Lyon, Bruce R. 'Contracts and specific investment: an empirical test of transaction cost theory'. *Journal of Economics and Management Strategy* 3, 1994, 257–78.

MacDonald, James M. 'Market exchange or vertical integration: an empirical analysis'. *Review of Economics and Statistics* 67, 1985, 327–31.

Masten, Scott E., Meehan, Jr. James and Snyder, Edward 'Vertical integration in the U.S. auto industry: a note on the influence of transaction specific assets'. *Journal of Economic Behavior and Organization* 12, 1989, 265–73.

McCall, J. 'Economics of information and job search'. *Quarterly Journal of Economics* 84, 1990, 113–26.

Milgrom, Paul and Roberts, John *Economics, Organization and Management.* Englewood Cliffs NJ: Prentice-Hall, 1992.

Monteverde, Kirk and Teece, David J. 'Supplier switching costs and vertical integration in the automobile industry'. *Bell Journal of Economics* 13, 1982, 206–13.

Mulherin, J. Harold 'Complexity in long-term contracts: an analysis of natural gas contractual provisions'. *Journal of Law, Economics, and Organization* 2, 1986, 105–17.

Muris, Timothy J., Scheffman, David T. and Spiller, Pablo T. 'Strategy and transaction costs: the organization of distribution in the carbonated soft drink industry'. *Journal of Economics and Management Strategy* 1, 1992, 83–128.

Nelson, Phillip 'Information and consumer behavior'. *Journal of Political Economy* 78, 1970, 311–29.

Palay, Thomas M. 'Comparative institutional economics: the governance of rail freight contracting'. *Journal of Legal Studies* 13, 1984, 265–87.

Palay, Thomas M. 'Avoiding Regulatory Constraints: Contracting Safeguards and the Role of Informal Agreements'. *Journal of Law, Economics, and Organization* 1, 1985, 155–75.

Parkhe, Arvind 'Strategic alliance structuring: a game theoretic and transaction cost examination of interfirm cooperation'. *Academy of Management Journal* 36, 1993, 794–829.

Pisano, Gary P. 'The R&D Boundaries of the Firm: An Empirical Analysis'. *Administrative Science Quarterly* 35, 1990, 153–76.

Pittman, Russell 'Specific investments, contracts, and opportunism: the evolution of railroad sidetrack agreements'. *Journal of Law and Economics* 34, 1991. 565–89.

Rooks, Gerrit, Raub, Werner, Tazelaar, Frits and Selton, Robert 'How inter-firm co-operation depends on social embeddedness'. *Acta Sociologica: Scandinavian Review of Sociology* 43, 2000, 123–38.

Stigler, George J. 'The economics of information'. *Journal of Political Economy* 69, 1961, 213–25.

Stuckey, John A. *Vertical Integration and Joint Ventures in the Aluminium Industry.* Cambridge MA: Harvard University Press, 1983.

Walker, Gordon and Weber, David 'A transaction cost approach to make-or-buy decisions'. *Administrative Science Quarterly* 29, 1984, 373–91.

Walker, Gordon and Weber, David 'Supplier Competition, Uncertainty and Make-or-Buy Decisions', *Academy of Management Journal* 30, 1987, 589–96.

Williamson, Oliver E. *The Economic Institutions of Capitalism.* New York: Free Press, 1985.

Wilson, James A. 'Adaption of uncertainty and small numbers exchange: the New England fresh fish market'. *Bell Journal of Economics* 4, 1980, 491–504.

# Summary

1 With respect to literature sources, one can distinguish primary and secondary literature. Primary literature includes all kinds of articles, books and reports in their original form. Secondary literature is a compilation of primary literature. Examples of secondary literature include indexes and bibliographies, dictionaries, encyclopaedias, handbooks and directories.

2 The process for searching bibliographic databases applies to both print and online sources.
   a Select a database appropriate to your topic.
   b Construct a search query (or search statement).
     - Review and evaluate search results.
     - Modify the search query, if necessary.
   c Save the valuable results of your search.
   d Retrieve articles not available in the database.
   e Supplement your results with information from web sources.

   Many online and web-based sources use Boolean logic to construct search queries, but protocols do differ. One reason to review the results of your original search is to modify it with newly discovered information. The researcher should check the bibliographies of cited works, check the subject headings assigned to the extracted articles, and search for works by referenced authors.

3 The basic steps for searching web-based sources include a critical last step that novice researchers often skip.
   a Select a search engine or directory.
   b Determine your search options.
   c Construct a search query and enter your search term(s).
     - Review and evaluate the search results.
     - Modify your search query, if necessary.
   d Save the valuable results of your search.
   e Supplement your results with information from non-web sources.

   When doing a web-based search, several options are available: known-item searches, 'who' searches, 'where' searches and 'what' searches. Due to the special characteristics of each type of search, each starts with a different search strategy. Several special sites have evolved to offer the researcher assistance for each type of search. These can be found in Appendix A.

4 Meta analysis allows the summarization of various empirical studies that investigate the same research problem. It is a very structured approach, which summarizes, compares and analyses the differences between studies along many characteristics of the studies including employing statistical methodology. On the one hand, the rigorous structure and quantification approach often results in the detection of patterns and relations that are unnoticed by more narrative summaries of a research field. On the other hand, the rigorous approach can often not account for important issues, such as differences in the methodological soundness of the studies included.

## Discussion questions

### Terms in review

1 Define the distinctions between primary and secondary literature.
2 Describe, briefly, the different steps in the literature review process.
3 Describe the objective, advantages and disadvantages of meta analysis.

### Making research decisions

4 What are promising search strategies?
5 How do you decide which literature should be included in a review?
6 If you have written your own literature review for a research problem in which you have an interest, do you think conducting a meta analysis on the literature covered in your narrative review would be useful? If not, why not? If so, what would you like to investigate by applying meta analysis?

### From concept to practice

7 Using Exhibits 3.6, 3.8 and 3.9, state a research question and then plan a bibliographic and web search.
8 Choose a field that you would like to review and
   a draft the outline of the review
   b select the literature that, according to you, must be included.

### Classroom discussion

9 Brainstorm within your class or sub-groups about useful search terms that could be employed to start a literature search for the following problem statements.
   a Who becomes an entrepreneur and what does it take to be a successful one?
   b What explains the differences in internationalization strategies chosen by financial institutions in Europe?
   c How effective is impression management in the consultancy industry?
10 A common problem for students starting off on a Master's thesis is that they cannot track down the relevant literature. Given the thousands of studies published every year in the field of management science, it is highly unlikely that there are no, or very few, related studies. Discuss in the class why many students, despite the vast amount of studies published, still have serious problems finding relevant literature, and what can be done to solve this problem.

## Online *Learning* Centre

### Get started with understanding statistical techniques!

When you have read this chapter, log on to the Online Learning Centre website at
***www.mcgraw-hill.co.uk/textbooks/blumberg*** to explore chapter-by-chapter test questions, additional
case studies, a glossary and more online study tools for business research methods.

## Notes

[1] Kirk Monteverde and David J. Teece, 'Supplier switching costs and vertical integration in the automotive industry', *Bell Journal of Economics* 13 (1982), pp. 206–313.

[2] Thomas M. Palay, 'Comparative institutional economics. The governance of rail freight contracting', *Journal of Legal Studies* 13 (1984), pp. 263–87; and Paul J. Joskow, 'Contract duration and relation-specific investments: empirical evidence from coal markets', *American Economic Review* 77 (1987), pp. 168–83.

[3] Ronald Coase, 'The nature of the firm', *Economica* 4 (1937), pp. 386–403.

[4] Oliver E. Williamson, *Markets and Hierarchies: Analysis and Antitrust Implications*. New York: Free Press, 1973; and Oliver E. Williamson, *The Economic Institutions of Capitalism*. New York: Free Press, 1983.

[5] Good sources for web size estimates are the studies by Steve R. Lawrence and C. Lee Giles, 'Searching the World Wide Web', *Science* 280 (April 1998), pp. 98–100, and 'Accessibility of information on the web', *Nature* 400 (8 July 1999), pp. 107–9, with updated summary data at http://www.www-metrics.com.

[6] Michael Dahm, 'Counting angels on a pinhead: critically interpreting web size estimates', *Online* 24 (January/February 2000), pp. 33–44. This article further interprets the pioneering research by authors Steve R. Lawrence and C. Lee Giles (op. cit.).

[7] The May/June 1999 issue of *Online* focuses on search engine technology. See, for example, Danny Sullivan, 'Crawling under the hood: an update on search engine technology', *Online* 23 (May/June 1999), pp. 30–8. See also Danny Sullivan's 'Search engine watch' (http://searchenginewatch.com/) and Greg Notess's 'Search engine showdown' (http://www.notess.com/search/) for current information about search engines and their features.

[8] Ronald Coase, 'The nature of the firm', *Economica* 4 (1937), pp. 386–403; Oliver E. Williamson, *Markets and Hierarchies: Analysis and Antitrust Implications*. New York: Free Press, 1973; and Oliver E. Williamson, *The Economic Institutions of Capitalism*. New York: Free Press, 1983.

[9] This section on meta analysis builds on Mark W. Lipsey and David B. Wilson, *Practical Meta Analysis*. Thousand Oaks, CA: Sage, 2000.

[10] G.V. Glass, 'Primary, secondary and meta-analysis of research', *Educational Researcher* 3 (3–8) (1976); M.L. Smith and G.V. Glass, 'Meta analysis of psychotherapy outcome studies', *American Psychologist* 32 (1977), pp. 732–60.

# Recommended further reading

Bedeian, Arthur C., 'The manuscript review process: the proper roles of authors, reviewers and editors', *Journal of Management Inquiry* 12(4), 2003, pp. 331–8. A paper investigating the experiences of authors that have published in the *Academy of Management Journal,* one of the leading journals in management science.

Bell, Judith, *Doing your Research Project* (3rd edn.). Buckingham: Open University Press, 1999. Chapter 6 offers an excellent guide on how to organize a literature review.

Hard, Chris, *Doing a Literature Review.* Thousand Oaks, CA: Sage, 1998. This book addresses issues such as searching for existing knowledge, analysing arguments and ideas, and writing a literature review.

Katz, William A., *Introduction to Reference Work, Volume I and Volume II.* New York: McGraw-Hill, 2001. An excellent text on how to work with references.

Saunders, Mark *et al., Research Methods for Business Students* (4th edn.). Harlow: Pearson Education, 2006. Chapter 3 is an excellent guide for students and lecturers alike on literature review.

Woy, James (ed.), *Encyclopedia of Business Information Sources* (14th edn.). Gale Group, 2000. An excellent database on sources containing useful information for business and management research.

# Spotlight on research 1

## Advanced searching

In advanced searches, you use your knowledge of the database to make the search more productive.

### *Construct the search query*

Use the keywords from your management question to prepare a query for the database. Bibliographic databases, including libraries' online catalogues, all have similar search options, such as a basic keyword search, an advanced search and a way to choose a subject from a browse list. Like all databases, bibliographic databases consist of several standard fields.

In most bibliographic databases, all searches are keyword searches, but it is possible to search for a specific author, title or series (a known-item search) by limiting your results to a specific field of the bibliographic record. For a list of typical research fields, see Exhibit S1.1. This is especially important if you are researching a prolific author such as Peter Drucker, who may have many works both by and about him. If you do not limit or narrow your search to a specific field, then you will conduct a general keyword search of all the records in the database. Because of the size of most databases, single-word searches generally yield results that are not very useful unless the single word is very unique. Instead, examine your management question

| Standard search fields for monographs | |
|---|---|
| Author | Publisher |
| Title | Series |
| Subject | |

| Limiters in book catalogues | |
|---|---|
| Language | Type of publication |
| Date of publication | Format (book, video, CD-ROM, etc.) |

| Standard search fields for periodical databases | |
|---|---|
| Author | Abstract |
| Title of article | Company name |
| Subject headings | ISSN code |
| Periodical title | |

| Limiters in periodical databases | |
|---|---|
| Date | Periodical title |
| Full text | Peer review |

*Exhibit S1.1* Search fields in databases.

for all relevant keywords and variations, and establish a more precise search query using the connectors described below.

The most important thing to remember about search engines for the web or for databases is that they do not all work in the same way. In fact, they have widely varying search protocols. What you do not know can act against you. So, if finding good information is important to you, take a couple of minutes to determine what special features and search options are used. For instance, if you enter a multiword term, what happens? Does the database search your term as a

| Expanding Your Search | Narrowing Your Search | |
| --- | --- | --- |
| [OR]<br>Use OR to search for plurals, synonyms, or spelling variations. Either or both terms will be present in results.<br>● woman OR women<br>● business OR corporation<br>● international OR foreign | [AND]<br>Use AND to require that all terms you specify be present in the results.<br>● child AND advertising | [Phrases]<br>Use a term consisting of two or more words. Some phrases require double quotes to enclose the phrase, while others do not.<br>● human resource management<br>● "human resource management" |
| Truncation<br>Symbols (?, *, !) that replace one or more characters or letters in a word or at the end of a word<br><br>● electr*<br>(retrieves electricity, electric, electrical)<br>● child?<br>(retrieves children, childish, child's | [NOT]<br><br>Use NOT to eliminate terms from your search. But use NOT with care. It is easy to eliminate the good with the unwanted.<br>● medicine NOT nursing<br>● Caribbean NOT Cuba | [ADJ]<br><br>ADJ requires the first term specified to immediately precede the last term specified.<br>● six ADJ sigma |
| | [Limiters]<br>Conditions (date, publication, type, language) for limiting your search. Most databases also offer *field limiting*, limiting the occurrences of your search to a specific database field, such as the author field, title, and so on. Some bibliographic databases offer the convenience of limiting the search results to peer-reviewed articles or to articles only available in full text. Use the latter with care as some significant articles may be overlooked even though they are in the library. | |

*Exhibit S1.2* Review of advanced search options.

phrase? Or does it insert a connector such as 'and' or 'or' between each word? How does it handle stopwords ('the', 'in' and other similar small words)? The results will vary considerably in these three scenarios (see Exhibits S1.2 and S1.3).

## *Search strategy options*
### Basic searching

If you have a unique term, try a basic search using that term. Most bibliographic databases will present the results list in reverse date order – that is, those items published most recently will appear first. Review the list of items your search has retrieved. Are there too many? Not enough? Are they very relevant or not very relevant? If they meet the 'Goldilocks test' of 'just right', then you can move on to the next step (saving results).

### Advanced searching

If you have retrieved too few or no relevant items, or if you have retrieved hundreds of items, you should consider modifying your search query. Start with the most relevant items in the results list. Then do one of the following:

- search for the cited works (the bibliography) of the full-text articles
- search for other works by the author or authors of the relevant citations
- check the subject headings assigned to the articles (Are there any more precise terms or synonyms that would improve your search results? More importantly, are there pairs of terms that appear in all of the most relevant items? Is there a thesaurus with the database that defines or expands the terminology used in the subject headings?).

As a result of your examination of the relevant citations and any background preparation you have done in other sources such as encyclopaedias, you should now have one or more keywords and synonyms for each concept. You can now use Boolean operators or connectors (see Exhibit S1.2) to combine terms or sets of terms to expand or narrow your search. There are four basic Boolean operators or connectors: OR, AND, NOT and ADJ.

Think of your management question as a series of keywords. For example, your management question might be 'How can I design an appropriate training or awareness programme to prevent sexual harassment lawsuits in my company?' In this example, concept A would be training, concept B would be harassment, and concept C would be lawsuits. In the most basic of keyword searches, you could use a keyword search with the operator AND to combine them:

training AND harassment AND lawsuits

If your search results are inadequate, you might need to expand your search statement with synonyms connected with the operator OR. For our sample management question, your search would look like Exhibit S.1.3. If your search results are too numerous, you will need to limit your search.

| Step 1: Build a list of synonyms for each concept in the management question | | | | |
|---|---|---|---|---|
| Concept A | Operator | Concept B | Operator | Concept C |
| training | AND | sex* harassment | AND | lawsuit* |
| awareness | | wom*n | | law |
| behaviour | | female | | courts |
| professional | | gender | | legal |
| development | | men | | |

Step 2: Create and search with a concept group by combining each term in a column with OR. Put each concept group in parentheses. Then combine each concept group with AND

(training OR awareness OR behaviour OR professional development) AND (sex* harassment OR wom*n OR men OR female OR gender) AND (lawsuit OR legal OR law OR courts)

*Exhibit S1.3*  Advanced searching process.

# Ethics in business research

## LEARNING OBJECTIVES

When you have read this chapter, you should understand:

- ☑ what issues are covered in research ethics

- ☑ the goal of 'no harm' for all research activities and what constitutes 'no harm'

- ☑ the differing ethical dilemmas and responsibilities of researchers and sponsors

- ☑ the role of ethical codes of conduct in professional associations.

# 4.1  What are research ethics?

As in other aspects of business, all parties in research should exhibit ethical behaviour. **Ethics** is the study of the 'right behaviour' and addresses the question of how to conduct research in a moral and responsible way. Thus, ethics not only address the question of how to use methodology in a proper way to conduct sound research, but also address the question of how the available methodology may be used in the 'right' way. Conducting empirical research, either quantitative or qualitative, often requires that you as a researcher have to compromise between what methodological theory recommends and what is feasible from a practical viewpoint. Likewise, you have to resolve whether the way you conduct your research is morally defensible towards all parties involved in the research.

Ethics, then, are moral principles, norms or standards of behaviour that guide moral choices about our behaviour and our relationships with others. In business research, ethical issues come to the fore whenever a conflict arises between the desire to conduct research that meets the highest quality standards or the requests of the sponsor on the one hand, and societal values – like, say, privacy, freedom and honesty – on the other.

There is no single approach to ethics. There are two dominant philosophical standpoints on research ethics: deontology and teleology. In the deontological view, the ends never justify the use of the means that are questionable on ethical grounds. For example, even if fully informing a respondent about the purpose and procedures of a study is likely to affect the (response) behaviour of this respondent in such a way that the obtained information is barely usable to answer the research question, any deception of the respondent would be unethical. German legislation forbidding certain types of medical experiment is based partly on such a deontological view, as a response to immoral, evil research conducted during the Nazi regime.

Business researchers often ascribe to the teleological principle, which posits that the morality of the means has to be judged by the ends served. Hence, the benefits of a study are weighed against the costs of harming the people involved. There are two major problems with this position. First, the benefits of a study, that is the ends served, may be morally questionable. Second, a simple comparison of the total costs and benefits cannot, however, offer a straightforward answer to an ethical dilemma, if the costs are borne by some parties, while others reap the benefits. Thus, any deviation from ethical standards, such as deceiving respondents, must be based on thorough reasoning.

As a researcher, you have the responsibility to find the middle ground between being completely code-governed and ethical relativism. The foundation for that middle ground is an emerging consensus on ethical standards for researchers. Codes and regulations guide researchers and sponsors. Review boards and peer groups help researchers examine their research proposals for ethical dilemmas. Many design-based ethical problems can be eliminated by careful planning and constant vigilance. In the end, responsible research anticipates ethical dilemmas and attempts to adjust research design, procedures and protocols during the planning process rather than treating them as an afterthought. Ethical research requires personal integrity from the researcher, the project manager and the research sponsor.

Because integrity in research is vital, we are discussing its components early in this book. This chapter is organized around the theme of ethical treatment of respondents, fellow researchers, and clients or research sponsors. Also highlighted are appropriate laws and codes, resources for ethical awareness and cases for application. Exhibit 4.1 relates each ethical issue under discussion to the research process introduced in Chapter 2.

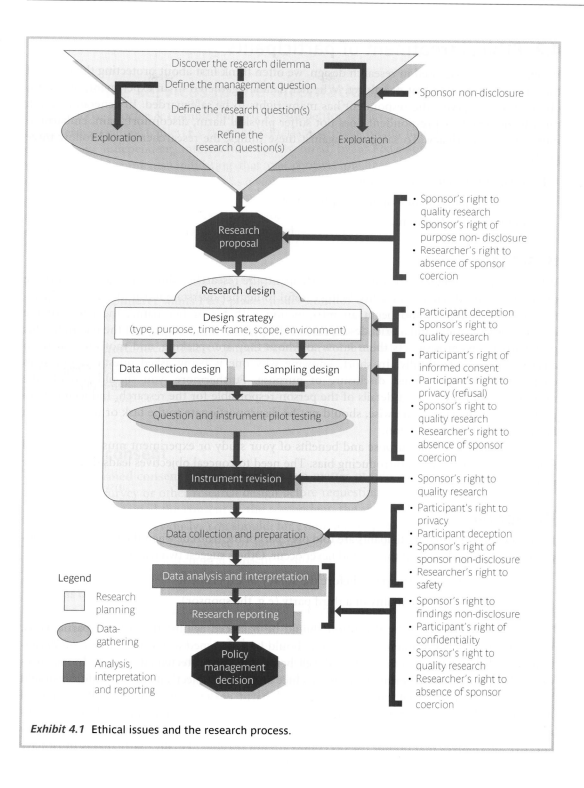

*Exhibit 4.1*  Ethical issues and the research process.

**Content**

Surveys conducted by the Lakeside University Centre for Survey Research contain the following informed consent components in their introductions.

1   Introduce ourselves – interviewer's name and Lakeside University Centre for Survey Research
2   Briefly describe the survey topic (e.g. barriers to health insurance)
3   Describe the geographic area we are interviewing (e.g. people in Wales) or target sample (e.g. mothers in a management position)
4   Tell who the sponsor is (e.g. Ministry of Welfare)
5   Describe the purpose(s) of the research (e.g. satisfaction with services received/provided by a local agency)
6   Give a 'good-faith' estimate of the time required to complete the interview
7   Promise anonymity and confidentiality (when appropriate)
8   Tell the respondent the participation is voluntary
9   Tell the respondent that item non-response is acceptable
10  Ask permission to begin

**Sample introduction**

Hello, I'm [fill in NAME] from the Centre for Survey Research at Lakeside University. We're surveying residents in Wales to ask their opinions about some health issues. This study is sponsored by the National Institute of Health and its results will be used to research the effect of community ties on attitudes towards medical practice. The survey takes about 40 minutes. Your participation is anonymous and voluntary, and all your answers will be kept completely confidential. If there is any question that you don't feel you can answer, please let me know and we'll move to the next one. So, if I have your permission, I'll continue.

**Sample conclusion**

The respondent is given information on how to contact the principal investigator. For example: John Kennedy is the principal investigator for this study. Would you like Dr Kennedy's address or telephone number in case you want to contact him about the study at any time?

*Exhibit 4.2* Informed consent procedures for surveys.

## Debriefing participants

**Debriefing** involves several activities that follow the collection of data:

- explanation of any deception
- description of the hypothesis, goal or purpose of the study
- post-study sharing of results
- post-study follow-up medical or psychological attention.

First, the researcher shares the truth of any deception with the participants, as well as the reasons for using deception in the context of the study's goals. In cases where severe reactions occur, follow-up medical or psychological attention should be provided to continue to ensure that participants remain unharmed by the research.

Even when research does not deceive participants, it is a good practice to offer them follow-up information as a matter of course. This retains the goodwill of the participant, providing an incentive to participate in future research projects. For surveys and interviews, participants can be offered a brief report on the findings. They will not usually request additional information; occasionally, though, the research will be of particular interest to a participant. A simple set of descriptive charts or data tables can be generated for such an individual.

For experiments, all participants should be debriefed in order to put the experiment into context. Debriefing usually includes a description of the hypothesis being tested and the purpose of the study. Participants who were not deceived will still benefit from a debriefing session; they will be able to understand why the experiment was created. The researchers will also gain important insight into what the participants thought about during and after the experiment. This may lead to modifications in future research designs. Like survey and interview respondents, participants taking part in experiments and observational studies should be offered a report of the findings.

### To what extent do debriefing and informed consent reduce the effects of deception?

Research suggests that the majority of participants do not resent temporary deception and may have more positive feelings about the value of the research after debriefing than those who didn't participate in the study. Nevertheless, deception is an ethically thorny issue and should be addressed with sensitivity and concern for research participants.

## Rights to privacy

Privacy laws in Europe, as well as in the United States and other countries, are taken seriously. In 2002, at its summit in Nice, the member states of the European Union (EU) signed a charter of fundamental rights. Article 8, on the protection of personal data, reads:

> 1. Everyone has the right to the protection of personal data concerning him or her.
>
> 2. Such data must be processed fairly and on the basis of consent of the person concerned or some other legitimate basis laid down by the law. Everyone has the right of access to data which have been collected concerning him or her and the right to have it rectified.

By 1995, the EU had already passed a directive and required member states to incorporate it into national laws by 1998; however, it allowed each member state to extend the directive and alter its detailed meanings.

The importance of the **right to privacy** may be illustrated with an example.

An employee of MonsterVideo, a large video company, is also a student at the local university. For a research project, this student and his team members decide to compare the video-viewing habits of a sample of customers. Using telephone interviews, the students begin their research. After enquiring about people's viewing habits and the frequency of rentals versus purchases, the students move on to the types of film people watch. They find that most respondents answer questions about their preferences for children's shows, classics, best-sellers, mysteries and science fiction. However, cooperation ceases when the students question the viewing frequency of pornographic movies. Without the guarantee of privacy, most people will not answer this kind of question truthfully, if at all. The study then loses key data.

The privacy guarantee is important not only in retaining the validity of research but also in protecting respondents. In the example above, imagine the harm that could be caused by releasing information on the viewing habits of particular citizens. Clearly, the confidentiality of survey answers is an important aspect of respondents' right to privacy.

Once the guarantee of confidentiality has been given, it is essential to protect that confidentiality. The researcher protects respondent confidentiality in several ways:

- obtaining signed non-disclosure documents
- restricting access to participant identification
- revealing participant information only with written consent
- restricting access to data instruments where the participant is identified
- non-disclosure of data sub-sets.

Researchers should restrict access to information that reveals names, telephone numbers, addresses or other identifying features. Only researchers who have signed **non-disclosure** confidentiality forms should be allowed access to the data. Links between the data or database and the identifying information file should be weakened. Individual interview response sheets should be inaccessible to everyone except the editors and data-entry personnel. Occasionally, data-collection instruments should be destroyed once the data are in a data file. Data files that make it easy to reconstruct the profiles or identification of individual participants should be carefully controlled. For very small groups, data should not be made available because it is often easy to pinpoint a person within the group. Employee satisfaction survey feedback in small units can easily be used to identify an individual through descriptive statistics alone. These last two protections are particularly important in human resources research.[5]

Privacy is more than confidentiality, however. A right to privacy means that one has the right to refuse to be interviewed or to refuse to answer any question in an interview. Potential participants have a right to privacy in their own homes, including not admitting researchers and not answering telephones. Samples of household surveys are often taken from telephone directories, which are sold by telecommunications providers. These lists of phone numbers are often incomplete, because people can request that their number is not listed. As more and more people are choosing to go ex-directory, direct marketing and research agencies are now employing random dialling – where a computer generates at random a phone number to be dialled – to approach respondents for phone interviews. Random dialling is, however, forbidden in certain countries (such as the Netherlands). People also have the right to engage in private behaviour in private places without fear of observation. In some countries, even in public places, people have to be informed that the area is under surveillance (e.g. by erecting signs which state that a property is monitored by video cameras).

The right to privacy is also an important issue regarding the linking of databases. Privacy laws restrict to what extent different databases can be combined to get a more complete picture of a respondent. In the MonsterVideo example, above, it would be undesirable if it was possible to link the information obtained through the phone interviews with the record of video rentals and purchases of a specific customer.

To address these rights to privacy, ethical researchers:

- inform participants of their right to refuse to answer any questions or participate in the study
- obtain permission to interview participants
- schedule field and phone interviews.

## Staples: held together with ethics?

Staples launched the office supplies superstore industry with the opening of its first store in Brighton (Boston), Massachusetts, in May 1986. Its goal: to provide small-business owners with the same low prices on office supplies previously enjoyed only by large corporations. Today, the company has more than 46,000 employees serving customers through more than 1000 office superstores, including branches in the UK, Germany, the Netherlands and Portugal.

In his 1996 book, *Staples for Success*, CEO Thomas Stemberg's philosophical titbits (such as 'Always think three steps ahead' and 'How you recover is more important than the mistakes you make') are sprinkled throughout. In one particular anecdote, Stemberg, who wanted to know how the company's rival managed its delivery system prior to instituting a delivery plan of its own, had his wife Dola apply for a job at the Office Depot order delivery centre. While he stopped the process before she took the job, he didn't stop before he had the desired information. So is it truly a case of 'anything goes' when it comes to collecting information about a competitor?

## References and further reading

www.staples.com

Stemberg, Thomas (1996) *Staples for Success*. Santa Monica, CA: Knowledge Exchange.

## 4.3  Data-collection in cyberspace

Some ethicists argue that the very conduct that results in resistance from participants – interference, invasiveness in their lives, denial of privacy rights – has encouraged researchers to investigate topics online that have long been the principal commodity of offline investigation. The novelty and convenience of communicating by computer has led researchers into cyberspace in search of abundant sources of data.

In a special ethics issue of *Information Society*, scholars involved in cyberspace research concluded:

> " All participants agree that research in cyberspace provides no special dispensation to ignore ethical precepts. Researchers are obligated to protect human subjects and 'do right' in electronic venues as in more conventional ones. Second, each participant recognizes that cyberspace poses complex ethical issues that may lack exact analogs in other types of inquiry. The ease of covert observation, the occasional blurry distinction between public and private venues, and the difficulty of obtaining the informed consent of subjects make cyber-research particularly vulnerable to ethical breaches by even the most scrupulous scholars. Third, all recognize that because research procedures or activities may be permissible or not precluded by law or policy, it does not follow that they are necessarily ethical or allowable. Fourth, all agree that the individual researcher has the ultimate responsibility for assuring that inquiry is not only done honestly, but done with ethical integrity.[6] "

Issues relating to cyberspace in research also relate to data-mining. The information-collection devices available today were once the tools of the spy, the science-fiction protagonist or the superhero. Smart cards, biometrics (finger printing, retinal scans, facial recognition), electronic monitoring (closed-circuit television, digital camera monitoring), global surveillance and genetic identification (DNA) are just some of the technological tools being used by today's organizations to track and understand employees, customers and suppliers. Every time you surf on the web, the hosts of the websites you visit, intentionally or even unintentionally, can make contact with your computer and monitor your activity by storing small programs, such as cookies, on it. Technically, it is possible for them to obtain a great deal of information about you in this way, such as the location of your computer, the websites you have visited in the past and even the information stored on your computer. However, despite the fact that you may have visited a certain website deliberately, this does not imply that you are willing to give personal information to the host of that website. The data-mining of all this information, collected from advanced and not necessarily obvious sources, offers infinite possibilities for research abuse.

The primary ethical data-mining issues are privacy and consent. Smart cards – those ubiquitous credit-card-sized devices that imbed personal information on a computer chip, which is then matched to purchase, employment or other behaviour data – offer the researcher implied consent to participant surveillance. The surface benefits of card use, however, may be enough to obscure from an unsuspecting user the data-mining purpose of the card (see Snapshot).

Retailers, wholesalers, medical and legal service providers, schools, government agencies and resorts, to name but a few, use smart cards or their equivalent. In most instances, participants provide, sometimes grudgingly, the personal information requested by enrolment procedures. In others – for instance, when smart technology is used to monitor those convicted of crimes and sentenced to municipal or state correction facilities, or those attending specific schools – enrolment is mandatory. In some instances, mandatory sharing of information is initially for personal welfare and safety: when, say, you admit yourself for a medical procedure and provide detailed information about medication or prior surgery. In others, enrolment is for less critical, but potentially attractive, monetary benefits – for example, free car-care services when a smart card is included with the keys to a new vehicle. The bottom line is that, whatever perceived benefit is gained by the cardholder, the organization collecting the information gains a major benefit: the potential for better understanding and competitive advantage.

## Customer privacy

Supermarkets have increasingly introduced loyalty cards to bind customers by offering price reductions or added-value rewards. However, a recent survey by IGD, a research firm specializing in the food and grocery industry, reveals that 38 per cent of British shoppers do not have any loyalty card and 40 per cent of cardholders get fed up with these cards (partly because they have serious privacy concerns). In the USA an increasing awareness of customer associations concerning loyalty cards and the associated privacy protection can be observed.

In 1998, Albert Heijn, the Dutch branch of the multinational Ahold (a retail company operating in more than 20 countries and serving 30 million customers) introduced its 'bonuscard', entitling holders to special discounts on certain products, which changed weekly. Households could obtain this card by filling in an application form, which included a short questionnaire. Then, every time the cardholder shops at Albert Heijn the card is scanned with the purchases made. Through scanning the bonuscard, information about purchasing habits can be linked to the individual profile of the customer acquired through the application form questionnaire, as well as to other information sources. For example, the company can link address information to an existing database on neighbourhood demographics.

Civil rights organizations have been harsh critics of the bonuscard and have warned that, one day, Albert Heijn and other firms might know more about their customers than even their best friends do. They even suggested strategies that would undermine the value of the information collected, such as swapping bonuscards with friends. As a consequence of this public turmoil, Albert Heijn eventually agreed to issue an anonymous bonuscard.

What are the ethical limits of combining and exploring databases?

## References and further reading

Albert Heijn bonuscard (www.ah.nl/klantenservice/bonuskaart/article.jsp?id=1282)
loyalty cards (www.igd.com/cir/ciritem_fs.asp?Menuid=33&cirid=841)
www.ah.nl
www.igd.com
www.nocards.org

General privacy laws may not be sufficient to protect the unsuspecting in the cyberspace realm of data-collection. The 15 EU countries started the new millennium by passing the European Commission's Data Protection Directive. Under this directive, commissioners can prosecute companies and block websites that fail to live up to its strict privacy standards. Specifically, the directive prohibits the transmission of names, addresses, ethnicity and other personal information to any country that fails to provide adequate data protection. This includes direct mail lists, hotel and travel reservations, medical and work records and orders for products, among a host of other examples. US industry and government agencies have resisted regulation of data flow, but the EU insists that it is the right of every citizen to find out what information about them is in a database and to correct any mistakes. Few US companies would willingly offer such access due to the high costs incurred; a perfect example of this reluctance is the diffi-culty individuals experience in correcting erroneous credit reports, even when such information is based on transactions using stolen personal identity or credit cards.

Yet questions remain regarding the definition of specific ethical behaviours for cyber research, the sufficiency of existing professional guidelines and the issue of ultimate respons-ibility for respondents. If researchers are responsible for the ethical conduct of their research, are they then solely responsible for the burden of protecting participants from every conceiv-able harm?

## 4.4 Ethics and the sponsor

There are also ethical considerations to bear in mind when dealing with the research client or sponsor. Whether undertaking product, market, personnel, financial or other research, a sponsor has the right to receive research that has been conducted ethically.

## Confidentiality

Some sponsors wish to undertake research without revealing their identity. They have a right to several types of confidentiality, including sponsor non-disclosure, purpose non-disclosure and findings non-disclosure.

Companies have a right to dissociate themselves from the sponsorship of a research project. This type of confidentiality is called **sponsor non-disclosure**. Due to the sensitive nature of the management dilemma or the research question, sponsors may hire an outside consulting or research firm to complete research projects. This is often done when a company is testing a new product idea, to avoid potential consumers being influenced by the company's current image or industry standing. Alternatively, if a company is contemplating entering a new market, it may not wish to reveal its plans to competitors. In such cases, it is the responsibility of the researcher to respect this desire and devise a plan that safeguards the identity of the research sponsor and the rights of the respondent. The sponsor's right to conceal his identity can come into conflict with the respondent's right to be fully informed about the objectives of the study. Sometimes, respondents even ask for whom the study is being conducted. The ethically correct way to deal with such a situation requires the respondent to be told that you cannot reveal the name of the sponsor, thus risking that the respondent may refuse to answer.

**Purpose non-disclosure** involves protecting the purpose of the study or its details. A research sponsor may be testing a new idea that is not yet patented and may not want the competition to know of its plans. It may be investigating employee complaints and may not want to spark union activity. Perhaps the sponsor might be contemplating a new public stock offering, where advance disclosure would spark the interest of the authorities or cost the firm thousands or even millions of euros. Finally, even if a sponsor feels no need to conceal its iden-tity or the study's purpose, most sponsors want the research data and findings to remain confi-dential, at least until the management decision has been made. Thus, sponsors usually demand and receive **findings non-disclosure** between themselves or their researchers and any interested but unapproved parties.

## Right to quality research

An important ethical consideration for the researcher and the sponsor is the sponsor's **right to quality** research. This right entails:

- providing a research design appropriate for the research question
- maximizing the sponsor's value for the resources expended
- providing data-handling and reporting techniques appropriate for the data collected.

From the proposal through the design to data analysis and final reporting, the researcher guides the sponsor on the proper techniques and interpretations. Often sponsors will have heard about a sophisticated data-handling technique and will want it used even when it is inappropriate for the problem in hand. The researcher should guide the sponsor so that this does not occur. The researcher should propose the design most suitable for the problem, and should not propose activities designed to maximize researcher revenue or minimize researcher effort at the sponsor's expense.

Finally, we have all heard the saying that there are 'lies – damn lies – and statistics'; it is the researcher's responsibility to make sure that any statistics produced are truthful. The ethical researcher always follows the analytical rules and conditions for results to be valid, and reports findings in a way that minimizes the drawing of false conclusions. The ethical researcher also uses charts, graphs and tables to show the data objectively, whatever the sponsor's preferred outcome.

## Sponsor's ethics

Occasionally, research specialists may be asked by sponsors to participate in unethical behaviour. Compliance by the researcher would be a breach of ethical standards. Some examples to be avoided are:

- violating participant confidentiality
- changing data or creating false data to meet a desired objective
- changing data presentations or interpretations
- interpreting data from a biased perspective
- omitting sections of data analysis and conclusions
- making recommendations beyond the scope of the data collected.

We now examine the effects of complying with these types of coercion. A sponsor may offer a promotion, future contracts or a larger payment for the existing research contract; or the sponsor may threaten to fire the researcher or tarnish the researcher's reputation. For some researchers, the request may seem trivial and the reward high – but of what value are distorted results?

Suppose you investigate what employees of a medium-sized service company think about the plan for a large restructuring of the company. Your research reveals that most employees understand that a major restructuring of the firm is necessary, but they have doubts that the suggested new structure will result in the predicted productivity gains, as it requires much more coordination across the different locations of the firm. Imagine now that the firm's management has asked you to focus in your research report on the first result, namely that the majority of employees understand the need for restructuring, and neglect the doubts of the employees. Maybe the management will be pleased with your report and you will be more likely to be asked to conduct future research. But how will such behaviour affect your reputation as a researcher? What will happen if others get to know that your report contains only half the truth? Finally, is it wise to confirm management's view that the employees support their restructuring plans, although you know that many employees do not agree with the management? What is the value to management of such distorted information?

### What is the ethical course?

Often, this calls for a confrontation of the sponsor's demands and for the researcher to take the following action:

- educate the sponsor in the purpose of research
- explain the researcher's role in fact-finding versus the sponsor's role in decision-making
- explain how distorting the truth or breaking faith with participants leads to future problems
- failing moral persuasion, terminate the relationship with the sponsor.

## 4.5 Researchers and team members

Another ethical responsibility of researchers is their team's safety, as well as their own. In addition, responsibility for ethical behaviour rests with the researcher who, along with his or her assistants, is charged with protecting the anonymity of both the sponsor and the participant.

## Safety

It is the researcher's responsibility to design a project so that the safety of all interviewers, surveyors, experimenters or observers is protected. It may be important to consider several factors in ensuring a researcher's **right to safety**. Some urban areas and undeveloped rural areas may be unsafe for research assistants. If, for example, the researcher must personally interview people in a high-crime district, it is reasonable to provide a second team member to protect the researcher. Alternatively, if an assistant feels unsafe after visiting a neighbourhood by car, a different researcher should be assigned to the destination.[7] It is unethical to require staff members to enter an environment where they feel threatened. Researchers who are insensitive to these concerns face both research and legal risks – the least of which involves having interviewers falsify instruments.

## Ethical behaviour of assistants

Researchers should require ethical compliance from team members just as sponsors expect ethical behaviour from the researcher. Assistants are expected to carry out the sampling plan, to interview or observe respondents without bias, and to record all necessary data accurately. Unethical behaviour, such as filling in an interview sheet without having asked the participant the questions, cannot be tolerated. The behaviour of the assistants is under the direct control of the responsible researcher or field supervisor. If an assistant behaves improperly in an interview or shares a participant's interview sheet with an unauthorized person, it is the researcher's responsibility. Consequently, all assistants should be well trained and supervised.

## Protection of anonymity

As discussed previously, researchers and assistants protect the confidentiality of the sponsor's information and the anonymity of the respondents. Each researcher handling data should be required to sign a confidentiality and non-disclosure statement.

## 4.6  Ethical obligations to the research community

As a researcher you not only have an ethical obligation towards your research fellows, who cooperate with you in specific projects, but also to the (research) community as a whole. Every piece of research is a serious attempt to shed some light on what is true. In Chapter 2, we discussed which requirements good research has to fulfil in order to claim that the research's findings are a truthful reflection of reality. While less than two centuries ago the truthfulness of an argument was proved by referring to God, these days references to scientific studies are used to prove a claim. In public debates the introductory phrase 'God said …' has been replaced by phrases such as 'Research by the University of Hull reveals that …', 'An article just published in the European Economic review shows that …' or 'Various independent scientific studies give clear evidence that …'. This increasing reference to the findings of scientific research in order to demonstrate the truth of an argument shows that the general public place great confidence in the accuracy of research.

The research community has earned this confidence in the accuracy of its findings by repeatedly showing that the public can trust the results of sound research. Despite this, however, the accuracy of research findings is often questioned. This scepticism towards the findings of research studies is fuelled by improperly conducted research.

Exhibit 4.3 gives examples of what kind of behaviour leads to poor research. Producing poor research also has an ethical element. Whenever researchers – intentionally or merely because they can't do any better – conduct a research study without complying to the standards of good research, they find themselves on ethically questionable grounds. If research is irrelevant and inconsequential, then no one will base their decisions upon it; at the very least, poor research damages the trust people have in the reliability of research in general.

As a researcher, you need to be aware that others will use the results you produce to make decisions or to convince others in a debate. Therefore, you have to ensure that people are not misled by your results and conclusions. This also requires you to be open and honest about the limitations of your research. Everybody who has ever conducted empirical research knows that it is impossible to do research that is 100 per cent perfect. Time and budget constraints, respondent's capacities and motivations, information researchers cannot access, and so on, often limit research. Ethical standards do not require the researcher to refrain from any research that cannot be conducted perfectly, but they do require the researcher to be honest and open about methodological limitations, as the revealing of limitations allows others to assess the quality and reliability of the results more efficiently.

**Speculative interpretation of the results**
- Expand the answers provided beyond the original research question

**Neglecting the limitations of the research**
- Measurement problems
- Sample biases (e.g. experiments with student participants are generalized to the whole population)
- Design deficiencies (e.g. missing control groups in experiments)

**Capitalizing on chance (reporting the best)**
- Not analysing or reporting insignificant effects
- Selecting the 'best' model out of the thousands estimated

**Fabrication of data**
- Deleting observations (to alter results)
- Modifying the answers of respondents
- Faking the results of analyses

*Exhibit 4.3* **Examples of unethical behaviour on a sliding scale.**

With modern computer techniques it has become very quick and easy to estimate thousands of models. Despite the many benefits of this, the ease with which one can analyse data also has a pitfall. As it is so easy to analyse data, the researcher might be tempted to estimate many slightly different models, change the scaling of a variable which is close to significance, use only the significant effects, and so on. Repeated analyses of data is fine as long as you use this to assess the robustness of your results (i.e. to check whether you obtain the same results if you estimate the model slightly differently). However, as soon as you re-estimate your model to search for a better one you begin to capitalize on chance. The thinking behind the problem of chance capitalization is that, in quantitative analyses, we use the 5 per cent (or sometimes even 10 per cent) significance level to establish whether or not a variable makes a difference (i.e. whether the effect of an independent on the dependent variable or the difference in the means of two variables really differs from zero). If we find that the means of two variables are different at the 5 per cent level, in 5 per cent of the cases there is no real difference in the mean. In other words, 1 in 20 mean comparisons report a difference although there is no difference. Thus, we check whether the means of two variables are different and we compare the two means 20 times, and every time they are a little bit different, it is likely that we will get one comparison suggesting a significant difference at the 5 per cent level, because once in 20 cases the laws of probability misled us.

To put it simply: you will always find a significant result if you search long enough for it. If you search long enough you will certainly, for instance, find a Portuguese person who speaks Finnish fluently. However, having found a fluent Finnish-speaking Portuguese person would not allow you to conclude that Portuguese people speak Finnish.

Sometimes, researchers restrict their analyses to the significant results, especially when their sample size is small. You should note, however, that there is a difference between excluding something from the analysis and not reporting that you excluded something for certain reasons. Often researchers have an inclination to value significant results more than non-significant ones. However, insignificant results are also very important and can be fruitful. For example, many studies including gender as an influencing factor indeed find significant differences between women and men. Suppose you investigate the motivation of employees in a firm and the results of your study show that there are no differences between men and women. Such an outcome contradicts the results of previous studies and is exciting, especially if you are able to explain why in your study you do not find differences between women and men.

Insignificant results are an important part of our knowledge; it is not only useful to know what are influencing factors, but also what factors are not influencing, although one might think they have an impact. You need to be very careful if you suppress insignificant results. All types of behaviour described so far can be justified if you assess the consequences thoroughly. It starts to become unethical as soon as you perform such activities to arrive at the results you would like to have or to suppress results that do not fit with your own perspective on the issue. Methodology and statistics are powerful tools for getting to grips with what is going on; however, they can also be misused to conceal the truth.

In recent years, major newspapers have frequently published stories on researchers who have falsified research results or indulged in **plagiarism**. Such stories mostly refer to researchers in the so-called 'hard sciences', such as physics and medicine. However, a group of US researchers argues that falsifying results might be even more common in economics and other social sciences, as the cost of falsifying results might be lower. **Falsification** of results in drug research could harm patients and even result in deaths; populations may be harmed by falsified or exaggerated reports on poverty in British cities.

A group of US researchers carried out a survey among the participants of the American Economic Association's annual meeting in Chicago in 1998. Their survey revealed that about 4 per cent of the participating economists confessed to having falsified research data.[8] Falsification or fabrication of data is unethical whatever the means. Although 4 per cent is not that great a figure, and might include research that has never been published, it is still much too high. Research falsification is a serious threat to the reputation and integrity of the research community as a whole.

In the third issue of the 1999 volume the editors of *Kyklos*, a European economic journal, informed their readers that one reader had told them that an article published by Hans W. Gottinger in *Kyklos* 1996 was identical to an article published by G.J. Watts in *Economics of Innovations and New Technology* in 1992. As Gottinger was unable to give a convincing explanation for the similarity of his work to the previously published work, the editor viewed it as a clear case of plagiarism. Plagiarism is a serious offence and is a form of unethical behaviour, because it involves stealing the intellectual property of someone else. Even if you copy just a single paragraph from the work of someone else without mentioning your source, you have crossed the line of plagiarism.

As explained in Chapter 2, new research usually builds on previous research and, consequently, you will be required to mention the ideas and results of others in your own reporting. You must identify any parts of your own work that are based on, or mention ideas, arguments or results from the work of others, and acknowledge their previous work using a system of references. This makes it quite obvious to readers which parts of the study originate from you and which parts do not.

Plagiarism is a hot issue in university communities; students may copy each other's assignments if they know different lecturers will grade them. Copying from other sources (plagiarism) has existed for a long time, but with the birth of the Internet, it has become far easier. From your own desk at home you can easily access thousands of sources, and search engines can assist you in finding appropriate sites where you will be able to locate suitable texts or even whole papers. In addition, as this information is provided digitally, you do not even have to retype the text – just using a basic copy-and-paste function will allow you to insert text from other sources into your own work in the blink of an eye.

Currently, however, the advantages offered by information technology are turning against the plagiarist. Software such as that to be found at turnitin.com or plagiarism.com,[9] allows tutors to check very easily whether text submitted by a student contains elements from uncredited sources or is very similar to something submitted by another student. Many universities are becoming better equipped to detect plagiarism and, once it has been uncovered, the consequences for plagiarists can be severe.

The most important argument against plagiarism at college and university is that students who merely copy the work of others do not learn anything, despite the fact that they go to school to advance their knowledge and to learn skills. Thus, those people who use plagiarism as an easy way of getting marks fail to achieve what they set out to do.

For a more in-depth insight into this topic please see the Spotlight on Research section at the end of this chapter.

## 4.7 Professional standards

As is the case with many other professions (accountants, estate agents and the like) the various bodies to which professional researchers belong have developed their own standards.

Many professional associations' codes have detailed research sections; one such code is the code of ethical conduct of the Academy of Management (see Exhibit 4.4); other examples are the European Federation of Psychologist Associations and the International Sociologist Association (ISA). Such bodies update their codes frequently.

Exhibit 4.4 shows sections of the code of ethical conduct of the Academy of Management, a professional organization serving scholars and practitioners in management (a full version of the code is available online at www.aomonline.org/aom.asp?ID=68&page_ID=54). The professional associations of other social science disciplines use similar codes; for example, that of the European Federation of Psychologist Associations can be viewed at www.efpa.be, and that of ISA at http://www.ucm.es/info/isa/servers.htm.

While this book commends professional societies and business organizations for developing standards, without enforcement these will be ineffectual. Effective codes:

- are regulative
- protect the public interest and the interests of the profession served by the code
- are behaviour-specific
- are enforceable.

A study that assessed the effects of personal and professional values on ethical consulting behaviour concluded:

> The findings of this study cast some doubt on the effectiveness of professional **codes of ethics** and corporate policies that attempt to deal with ethical dilemmas faced by business consultants. A mere codification of ethical values of the profession or organization may not counteract ethical ambivalence created and maintained through reward systems. The results suggest that unless ethical codes and policies are consistently reinforced with a significant reward and punishment structure and truly integrated into the business culture, these mechanisms would be of limited value in actually regulating unethical conduct.[10]

## ACADEMY OF MANAGEMENT CODE OF ETHICAL CONDUCT CREDO
We believe in discovering, sharing and applying managerial knowledge.

### PREAMBLE
Our professional goals are to enhance the learning of students, colleagues and others to improve the effectiveness of organization through our teaching, research, and practice of management. We have five major responsibilities:

1  To our students – relationships with students require respect, fairness and caring, along with recognition of our commitment to the subject matter and to teaching excellence.
2  To managerial knowledge – prudence in research design, human subject use, confidentiality, result reporting, and proper attribution of work is a necessity.
3  To the Academy of Management and the larger professional environment – support of the academy's mission and objectives, service to the Academy and our institutions, and the recognition of the dignity and personal worth of colleagues is required.
4  To both managers and the practice of management – exchange of ideas and information between the academic and organizational communities is essential.
5  To all people with whom we live and work in the world community – sensitivity to other people, to diverse cultures, to the needs of the poor and disadvantaged, to ethical issues, and to newly emerging ethical dilemmas is required.

### ADVANCEMENT OF MANAGERIAL KNOWLEDGE
Research of Academy members should be done honestly, have a clear purpose, show respect for the rights of all individuals and organizations, efficiently use resources, and advance knowledge in the field.

**Conducting and Reporting:** It is the duty of Academy members conducting research to design, implement, analyze, report, and present their findings rigorously. Research rigor includes careful design, execution, analysis, interpretation of results, and retention of data. Presentation of research should include a treatment of the data that is honest and that reveals both strengths and weaknesses of findings. When important alternate hypotheses or explanations exist, they should be noted and data that disconfirm hypotheses should be acknowledged. Authorship and credit should be shared in correct proportion to the various parties' contributions. Whether published or not, ideas or concepts derived from others should be acknowledged, as should advice and assistance received. Many management-related journals have policies prohibiting or restricting potential articles from being reviewed concurrently in other outlets. These policies should be closely observed or there should be explicit discussion with the relevant journal editors concerning the intended multiple submissions. More than one report of essentially the same data and results should not be published unless the reports are explicitly directed to different audiences through different types of outlets. When several separate but related reports result from a single study the existence of the different reports should be made known to the relevant journal editors and the reports should reference each other. Reviewer comments should be considered thoughtfully before a manuscript is submitted to a different journal.

Participants: It is the duty of Academy members to preserve and protect the privacy, dignity, well-being, and freedom of research participants. This duty requires both careful research design and informed consent from all participants. Risks and the possibility of harm to research participants must be carefully considered, and, to the extent possible, these must be minimized. When there is a degree of risk or potential harm inherent in the research, potential participants – organizations as well as individuals – must be informed. Informed consent means explaining to potential participants the purposes and nature of the research so they can freely choose whether or not to become involved. Such explanations include warning of possible harm and providing explicit opportunities to refuse to participate and to terminate participation at any time. Because students and employees are particularly subject to possible coercion, even when unintended, special care must be taken in obtaining their informed consent. Third party review is one of protecting the interests of research participants. Research plans involving human participants should be reviewed by an appropriate third party such as a university human subjects committee or a focus group of potential participants. Questions regarding Confidentiality or anonymity must be resolved between researcher and potential research participants, both individuals and organizations; if confidentiality or anonymity is requested, this must be honored. Deception should be minimized and, when necessary, the degree and effects must be mitigated as much as possible. Researchers should carefully weigh the gains achieved against the cost in human dignity. To the extent that concealment or deceptions necessary, the researcher must provide a full and accurate explanation to participants at the conclusion of the study, including counseling, if appropriate.

Dissemination: It is the duty of journal editors and reviewers to exercise their position of privilege in confidential, unbiased, prompt, constructive, and sensitive manner. They have a duty to judge manuscripts only on their scholarly merits. Conflicts of interest may arise when a reviewer is in basic disagreement with the research approach or the line of research represented by a manuscript. In such cases, a reviewer should consult with the journal editor to decide whether to accept or decline to review the manuscript. Protecting intellectual property is a responsibility of the reviewer and the editor. The content of a manuscript is the property of its author(s). It is therefore inappropriate to use ideas or show another person a manuscript one has been asked to review, without the explicit permission of its authors. Advice regarding specific, limited aspects of the manuscript may be sought from qualified colleagues so long as the author's intellectual property remains secure. Sharing of reviewing responsibilities is inappropriate. The review is the sole responsibility of the person to whom it was assigned by the journal editor. In particular, students and colleagues should not be asked to prepare reviews unless the journal's editor has given explicit approval. Anyone contributing to a review should receive formal recognition. Constructive review means providing critiques and comments in a spirit of collegiality with thoroughness, timeliness, compassion, and respect, and in ways intended to improve the quality of the manuscript.

**Grants and Contracts:** It is the duty of Academy members to accurately represent themselves and their proposed projects and to manage those projects as promised. Representation means accurate disclosure of one's level of expertise and expected actual involvement, the outcomes that can be reasonably expected, the realistic funding level needed, and any potential conflicts of interest. Grant and contract management requires independence and objectivity such that one does not compromise one's responsibilities or create conflicts of interest. One must also manage time and budget responsibly and use the funds as promised unless permission is explicitly granted to do otherwise.

## THE ACADEMY OF MANAGEMENT AND THE LARGE PROFESSIONAL ENVIRONMENT

The Mission Statement of the Academy describes member benefits and professional opportunities of members, which impose corresponding duties and service responsibilities.

**Sharing and Dissemination of Information:** To encourage meaningful exchange, Academy members should foster a climate of free interchange and constructive criticism within the Academy and should be willing to share research findings and insights fully with other members.

**Academy Participation:** The Academy is a voluntary association whose existence and operations are dependent on cooperation, involvement, and leadership from its members. Members should abide by the Constitution, Bylaws, policies, and codes of the Academy. Members should consider offering their time and talent to carry out activities necessary to maintain the Academy and its functions. Officers and members should fulfill their Academy obligations and responsibilities in a timely, diligent, and sensitive manner, without regard to friendships or personal gain. Members should honor all professional commitments, including presentation of accepted papers and participation in scheduled roles as chair, discussant, or panel member. If absence from a scheduled meeting is unavoidable, members must contact appropriate individuals and pursue suitable alternative arrangements. One should consider the impact one's projects or activities may have on the integrity or reputation of the Academy, and one should not engage in such projects or activities that may have possible negative implications. Members should not imply that their work is sanctioned by the Academy unless an appropriate Academy body has specifically done so.

**Commitment to Professional Standards of Conduct:** By this Code, the Academy provides ongoing ethical guidance for its members. Members should work to raise the consciousness of other members concerning ethical responsibilities, and they should encourage acceptance of these responsibilities. Members should notify appropriate

▶

Academy officers or committees regarding the practices or actions of members they believe may violate Academy regulations or general standards of ethical conduct. In this manner, the aspirational and educational goals of this Code are served through discussion of the ethical dilemmas and values of our profession.

**Strengthening and Renewal of the Academy:** The Academy of Management must have continuous infusions of members and new points of view to remain viable and relevant as a professional association. Members may contribute by encouraging all eligible individuals to participate in the Academy and by assisting new and prospective members in developing their skills, knowledge, and understanding of their professional obligations.

The professional environment for many Academy members includes the university community: The central values that underlie appropriate university participation are understanding, involvement, respect, fairness, and the pursuit of knowledge.

**Participation in University Leadership:** Professors should take an active interest in university governance. Professors should be aware of university policies that affect the dissemination of policies. Professors should endeavor to positively influence policies relating to the quality of education and service to students. Active organizational involvement requires exercise of personal voting rights and respect for such rights of others, without regard to rank or tenure. Professors should evaluate colleagues for purposes of promotion or tenure on the basis of appropriate academic criteria, which is fairly weighted in accordance with standards understood by the faculty and Academy members to treat their colleagues with respect and fairness. Members should safeguard confidential personnel matters and avoid disclosing opinions expressed, attribution of statements, and voting behavior outcomes. Members should address misunderstandings and conflicts with those directly involved and avoid speculative criticism that might damage the reputations of individuals or groups. When speaking or acting outside their university roles, professors should avoid creating the impression that they are speaking or acting for the university or its administration. Professors should dispose of complimentary books requested from publishers by a manner other than sale.

All Academy members, whether affiliated with a university, a business, a governmental, a service, or consulting organization have an obligation to interact with others in a professional manner.

**Membership in the Professional Community:** It is the duty of Academy members to interact with others in our community in a manner that recognizes individual dignity and merit. The responsible professional promotes and protects the rights of individuals without regard to race, color, religion, national origin, handicap, sex, sexual orientation, age, political beliefs, or academic ideology, and refrains from sexual harassment. In the spirit of intellectual inquiry, the professional should welcome suggestions and complaints openly without reprisal. Members should ensure that outside activities do not significantly diminish their availability and energy to meet their institutional obligations.

## MANAGER AND THE PRACTICE OF MANAGEMENT

Consulting with client organizations ('clients') has the potential for enriching the teaching and practice of management, for translating theory into practice, and for furthering research and community service. To maximize such potential benefits, it is essential that members who consult be guided by the ideals of competence, integrity, and objectivity.

**Credentials and capabilities:** It is the duty of consultants to represent their credentials and capabilities in an accurate and objective manner. Consultants shall accept only those assignments for which they have appropriate expertise. Consultants shall refrain from exaggerating their professional qualifications to secure prospective assignments. Consultants shall examine any factors (e.g., prior experience, capabilities, other commitments) that might limit their judgement or objectivity in carrying out an assignment. University endorsement of the consulting activities of Academy members should not be represented or implied to potential clients unless the assignment is formally under university sponsorship or is so approved.

**Obligations to Clients:** Consultants have a duty to fulfill their obligations to their present and prospective clients in a professionally responsible and timely manner. Consultants shall place the highest possible priority on their clients' interests. Consultants shall avoid or withdraw from situations in which their clients' interests come into serious conflict with their own. Consultants shall not serve two or more competing clients without the consent of all parties. Consultants shall fully inform their clients. This means presenting results and/or advice in an unbiased manner and discussing fully with the client the values, risks, and limitations of the recommendations.

**Client Relations:** Consultants must fulfill duties of confidentiality and efficiency as part of the relationship with their clients. Consultants shall maintain confidentiality with respect to their clients' identities and the assignments undertaken, unless granted permission by the client. Consultants should exercise concern for the protection of clients, employees and other stakeholders by maintaining, in particular, appropriate confidentiality. Consultants shall not take personal or financial advantage of confidential information acquired as a result of their professional relationships, nor shall they provide the basis upon which others may take such advantage. Consultants should meet their time commitments, and they should conserve the resources that are utilized.

**Remuneration:** It is the duty of consultants to negotiate clear and mutually accepted remuneration agreements for their services. Consultants shall provide a realistic estimate of the fees to be charged in advance of assignments. Fees charged shall be commensurate with the services performed.

**Societal Responsibilities:** Consultants have a duty to uphold the legal and moral obligations of the society in which they function. Consultants should report to the appropriate authorities any unlawful activities that may have been uncovered during the course of their consulting engagements (except where one's functional professional code directs otherwise.)

**Students and Employees:** It is the duty of the consultant to safeguard the rights of students and employees when they are involved in consulting assignments. Consultants may involve students in work generated by consulting engagements, especially if such work possesses learning potential, but students must not be coerced into participation. When they are so involved, students, as well as employees, should be fairly compensated, and they should be made aware of the nature of the work they are doing.

### THE WORLD COMMUNITY

As citizens of the world community, Academy members may have much to contribute in shaping global consciousness through their teaching, research, and service.

**World View:** Academy members have a duty to consider their responsibilities to the world community. In their role as educators, members of the Academy can play a vital role in encouraging a broader horizon for decision making by viewing issues from a multiplicity of perspectives, including the perspectives of those who are the least advantaged. As researchers, members of the Academy should consider, where appropriate, increasing their exposure to other cultures via travel, study, and research. Where appropriate, the research might highlight the responsible stewardship of the earth's resources. In addition, members should take as a challenge the ongoing task of identifying evolving ethical issues by listening to those whose welfare is affected and by exploring the interaction of people and technology. In fulfilling their service responsibilities members of the Academy should consider how they might lend their time and talent to enhance the world community through involvement in uncompensated public service.

*Exhibit 4.4* Example of a professional standard.

## Research Methods in Practice 4

# What to reveal?

In the research project on R&D cooperations, we examined 94 cooperations nested within a specific business unit of five Dutch multinational companies from various sectors. None of the five companies was a direct competitor to another. The typical schedule of the research looked as follows.

1  We arranged a first meeting with the general manager of the business unit and presented two research projects, namely the project on R&D cooperations and another project on buyer–supplier relations. The goal of this meeting was to ensure that the business unit was willing to participate in the research. We mentioned that the research was supported by NEVI, the Dutch Association for Purchasing Management, and that we have also approached other companies to participate in the study. We never did, however, reveal which companies did also participate in the study.

2  In a second later meeting with the general manager, we asked him to identify R&D cooperations within the business unit (see the case in Chapter 6 on sampling for more detailed information on this process). Once we had identified R&D cooperations that satisfied our criteria, we asked for the names of the employees who had full insight into this specific R&D cooperation; usually this was the project leader. These persons were our main respondents. Where possible, we tried to meet the person briefly to introduce ourselves and the project and to make an appointment for an interview. In addition, we left a written questionnaire for each cooperation for the respondent to fill in before the interview, which we would pick up at the interview and we would ask the respondent to have the contract signed with the cooperation partner during the interview.

3  On the agreed date, we visited the respondent again, picked up the written questionnaire and interviewed the person.

4  After we have compiled the data, we would return to the company and present the results of our analysis.

Exhibit 4.5 below shows a chart which we typically used in our presentations. It shows how much contracting effort the company invested (y-axis) against the problem potential, a combined measure of the different characteristics of the cooperation, such as size, dependency on the partner and uncertainty. According to our theory, we would expect that with an increasing problem potential, that is a higher chance that opportunism occurs, contracting effort goes up. The straight line is the regression line if we regress problem potential on contracting and as we expected it has a positive slope. As you can see from the figure, we observe cooperations in which under-contracting occurred and others in which over-contracting occurred.

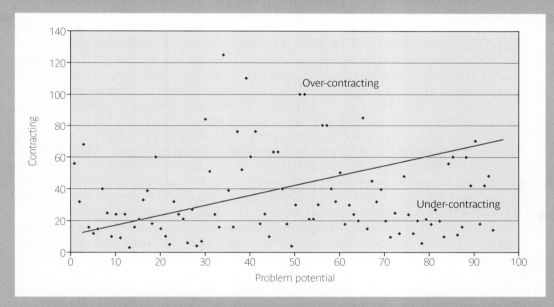

**Exhibit 4.5** Contracting efforts against the problem potential of a cooperation for 94 R&D cooperations.

*Note*: The solid straight line shows the regression line.

This question might surprise you: Is showing such a figure ethically problematic? What are the ethical considerations a researcher should make when making such a figure. The ethical problem at hand is the problem of which information to disclose. If we look at research reports, we usually only see averaged information, such as a mean or a coefficient in a regression analysis. The straight line is such an averaged information, but the dots reveal more – they show actual cases. The way we present the figure here does not reveal a lot; you know that a dot stands for a specific cooperation, but you do not know the name of the company nor the name of the cooperation partner.

In the presentations towards the companies, we revealed more.

1 We coloured the dots representing the company we presented for differently, thus the managers knew which dots represented them and which dots represented the four other companies. Thus, the management could see whether they would be more or less likely to under-contract compared to the four other companies. It should be mentioned that when we presented the project, we did not discuss the issue that the research would enable us to compare the companies involved, that is that

we would be able to conduct a benchmark study, as this was not the intention of the research project. Still, we presented company-specific results, as these were much more informative for the management than our general conclusions. Did we reveal to much? We thought not as from the information given a company only learned about itself, not about the other four companies.

2  In a further step we also attached the names of the cooperation partners to the dots of the company that we presented. Thus, the management could see which of their cooperations suffered from under-contracting and which suffered from over-contracting. In the interviews we also asked how well the cooperation was going and not surprisingly, we could show that cooperations that were not going well were mostly in the area of under-contracting.

Our research problem focused on the issue of how to mitigate (opportunism) problems through the ex-ante management of cooperations. In the discussions with the management of the firms we also talked about the over-contracting cases. These cases are less interesting for our research problem as the partners mitigated the potential problems more than sufficiently, but they are problematic from an efficiency consideration. Seeing in which cooperations a company invested more contracting effort than needed raised the question of whether a company allocates its resources, that is mainly the time people invest in a cooperation efficiently.

Naming the cooperation partners becomes problematic, because with the name of the cooperation partner it is also obvious which person is responsible for the alliance. Thus, a figure like the one presented plus the names of the cooperation partners can allow management to identify which project leaders under- or over-manage their cooperations. When we started the project we never thought about this issue, but when we prepared these figures it became clear to us that our data also contain information on the management capabilities of project leaders, the respondents.

In business research, we often investigate companies or cooperations, as in the case here. But we obtain the information from individuals, which serve as respondents. Researchers need to realize that the information they get from individuals is not only about the company or cooperation that is at the core of their investigation, but it also reveals a lot about the responding individual. In our case the respondents thought that had they reported about a cooperation and did not realize that they had also reported on how they managed the cooperation.

In our case, the management of all five companies took the results to think about how they could improve their cooperation management. Each dot in Exhibit 4.5 represents a cooperation and the straight line shows the positions that well-managed cooperations should take depending on their problem potential. Cooperations that are close to the line are well managed, cooperations that are above the line are 'over-managed' while cooperations below the line are 'under-managed'. Thus, dots that are way off the line are inefficiently managed cooperations. Importantly for us, the management did not use the result to identify which project leaders managed their cooperations inefficiently; instead, they used the results to see how they could improve their cooperation management in general.

As researchers, we produce knowledge and knowledge can be used for good and bad ends. Is a researcher responsible for how the knowledge produced is used?

## Summary

1  Ethics are norms or standards of behaviour that guide moral choices about our behaviour and our relationships with others. Ethics differ from legal constraints, in which generally accepted standards have defined penalties that are universally enforced. The goal of ethics in research is to ensure that no one is harmed or suffers adverse consequences from research activities.

   As research is designed, several ethical considerations must be balanced:
   - protect the rights of the participant or subject
   - ensure the sponsor receives ethically conducted and reported research
   - follow ethical standards when designing research
   - protect the safety of the researcher and team
   - ensure the research team follows the design.

2  In general, research must be designed so that a participant does not suffer physical harm, discomfort, pain, embarrassment or loss of privacy. Begin data-collection by explaining to respondents the benefits expected from the research. Explain that their rights and well-being will be adequately protected and say how this will be done. Be sure that interviewers obtain the informed consent of the respondent. The use of deception is questionable; when it is used, debrief any participant who has been deceived.

3  Many sponsors wish to undertake research without revealing themselves. Sponsors have the right to demand and receive confidentiality between themselves and the researchers. Ethical researchers provide sponsors with the research design needed to solve the managerial question. The ethical researcher shows the data objectively, regardless of the sponsor's preferred outcome(s).

   The research team's safety is the responsibility of the researcher. Researchers should require ethical compliance from team members in following the research design, just as sponsors expect ethical behaviour from the researcher.

4  Many corporations and research firms have adopted a code of ethics. Several professional associations have detailed research provisions. Of particular interest are those of the professional associations in the field you are working in. Federal, state and local governments have laws, policies and procedures in place to regulate research on human beings.

## Discussion questions

## Terms in review

1   Name the basic ethical considerations when conducting research and whom (you as researcher, research community, research sponsors or research participants) they affect.

## Making research decisions

2   When the manager for market intelligence of AutoCorp, a major automotive manufacturer, boarded a plane in Stuttgart, her mind was on shrinking market share and late product announcements. As she settled back to enjoy what was left of a hectic day, she reached for the in-flight magazine, which was jammed into the seat pocket in front of her.

    Crammed into this already tiny space was a report with a competitor's logo, marked 'Confidential – Restricted Circulation'. It contained a description of new product announcements for the next two years. Not only was it intended for a small circle of senior executives, it also answered the questions she had recently proposed to an external research firm.

    The proposal for the solicited research could be cancelled. Her research budget, already savaged, could be saved and it could boost her career.

    She foresaw only one problem. In the last few months, AutoCorp's newly hired ethicist had revised the firm's Business Conduct Guidelines. They now required company employees in possession of a competitor's report to return it or face dismissal. But it was still a draft and not formally approved. She had the rest of the flight to decide whether to return the document to the airline or slip it into her briefcase.

    a   What are the most prudent decisions that she can make about her responsibilities to herself and others?

    b   What are the implications of those decisions even if there is no violation of law or regulation?

3   The city commissioners of Miro Beach proposed limits on boaters who anchor offshore in waterfront areas of the St. Lucinda River adjoining the city. Residents had complained of pollution from live-aboard boaters. This 'car park' for boats created an unsightly view.

    The city based its proposed ordinance on research done by staff. The staff did not hold graduate degrees in either public or business administration, and it was not known if staff members were competent to conduct research. The staff requested a proposal from a team of local university professors who had conducted similar work in the past. The research cost was $10,000. After receiving the proposal, the staff chose to do the work themselves and not expend resources on the project. Through an unidentified source, the professors later learned that their proposal had contained enough information to guide the city's staff and suggested data-collection areas that might provide information that could justify the boaters' claims.

    Based on the staff's one-time survey of waterfront litter, 'pump-out' samples and a weekly frequency count of boats, an ordinance was drafted and a public workshop held. Shortly afterwards, a group of concerned boat owners formed Boaters Inc., an association to promote boating, raise funds and lobby the commission. The group's claims were that the boaters (i) spent thousands of dollars on community goods and services, (ii) did not create the litter, and (iii) were being unjustly penalized because the commission's fact-finding was flawed.

    With the last claim in mind, the boaters flooded the city with public record requests. The clerks reported that in some weeks the requests were one per day. Under continued pressure, the city attorney hired a private investigator (PI) to infiltrate Boaters Inc. to collect information. He rationalized this on the grounds that the boaters had challenged the city's grant applications in order to 'blackmail the city into dropping plans to regulate the boaters'.

The PI posed as a college student and worked for a time in the home of the boater organization's sponsor while helping with mailings. Despite the PI's inability to corroborate the city attorney's theory, he recommended conducting a background investigation on the organization's principal, an employee of a tabloid newspaper. The PI was not a boating enthusiast and soon aroused suspicion. Simultaneously, the organization turned up the heat on the city by requesting what amounted to 5000 pages of information: 'studies and all related documents containing the word "boat".' Failing to get a response from Miro Beach, the boaters filed a suit under the Florida Public Records Act. By this time, the city had spent $20,000.

The case stalled, went to appeal, and was settled in favour of the boaters. A year later, the organization's principal filed an invasion of privacy and slander suit against the city attorney, the PI and the PI's firm. After six months, the suit was amended to include the city itself and sought $1 million in punitive damages.

a   What are the most prudent decisions the city can make about its responsibilities to itself and others?

b   What are the implications of these decisions even if there is no violation of law or regulation?

4  It was John's first year of college teaching, and there were no summer teaching assignments available to new employees. However, the university was kind enough to steer him towards an aviation firm, Avionics, which needed help creating an organizational assessment survey. The assignment was to last five weeks, but it paid about the same as teaching all summer. The work was just about as perfect as it gets for an organizational behaviour specialist. Avionics' vice-president, who John met on his first day, was cordial and smooth. John would report to a senior manager who was coordinating the project with the human resources and legal departments.

It was soon apparent that in the 25-year history of Avionics, there had never been an employee survey. This was understandable given management's lack of concern for employee complaints. Working conditions had deteriorated without management intervention, and government inspectors counted the number of heads down at desks as an index of performance. A serious organizing effort was planned before the VP could approve the survey.

Headquarters dispatched nervous staffers to monitor the situation and generally involve themselves with every aspect of the questionnaire. Shadowed, the young researcher began to feel apprehension turn to paranoia. He consoled himself, however, with the goodwill of 500 enthusiastic, cooperative employees, who had pinned their hopes of a better working environment on the results of this project.

John's data-collection was textbook perfect. No one had asked to preview his findings or indeed shown any particular interest. In the fifth week, he travelled with the VP and senior manager to make a presentation at headquarters. Respondents at the headquarters location were invited to attend. Management was intent on showing its confidence in the isolated nature of 'a few engineers' complaints'. They had also promised to engage the participants in action planning over the next few days.

An hour into the journey, the Avionics VP turned from his reading to the young researcher and said, 'We have seen your results, you know. And we would like you to change two key findings. They are not all that critical to this round of fixing the "bone orchard", and you'll have another crack at it as a real consultant in the autumn.'

'But that would mean breaking faith with your employees,' replied John, 'people who trusted me to present the results objectively. It's what I thought you wanted.'

'Yes, well, look at it this way,' responded the VP. 'All of your findings we can live with except these two. They're an embarrassment to senior management. Let me put it plainly. We have government contracts into the foreseeable future. You could retire early with consulting income from this place. Someone will meet us with new slides just before the meeting.' How do you respond to this message from the VP?

a What are the most prudent decisions Avionics can make about its responsibilities to itself and others?

b What are the implications of those decisions even if there is no violation of law or regulation?

5 SupplyCo is a supplier to a number of firms in an industry. This industry has a structure that includes suppliers, manufacturers, distributors and consumers. Several companies are involved in the manufacturing process – from processed parts to the creation of the final product – with each firm adding some value to the product.

By carefully mining its customer data warehouse, SupplyCo reveals a plausible new model for manufacturing and distributing industry products that would increase the overall efficiency of the industry system, reduce the costs of production (leading to greater industry profits and more sales for SupplyCo), and result in greater sales and profits for some of the industry's manufacturers (SupplyCo's customers).

On the other hand, implementing the model would damage the sales and profits of other firms that are also SupplyCo's customers but that are not in a position (due to manpower, plant or equipment limitations) to benefit from the new manufacturing/distribution model. These firms would lose sales, profits and market share, and potentially go out of business.

Does SupplyCo have an obligation to protect the interests of all its customers and to take no action that would harm any of them, since it had the data within its warehouse only because of its relationship with its customers? (It would betray some of its customers if it were to use the data in a manner that would cause these customers harm.) Or does it have a more powerful obligation to its stockholders and employees to aggressively pursue the new model that research reveals would substantially increase its sales, profits and market share against competitors?

a What are the most prudent decisions SupplyCo can make about its responsibilities to itself and others?

b What are the implications of those decisions even if there is no violation of law or regulation?

## Class discussion

Split the class into two groups, for example according to the half of the year in which they have their birthday. One group has a more lenient opinion regarding ethics while the other advocates that behaviour needs to follow strict ethical rules. Discuss the following issues, or one of three questions in the section on 'Making research decisions', above.

6 Several websites on the Internet provide broad catalogues of master's theses at reasonable prices and others even offer master's theses on demand. Is there something wrong with seeking such assistance when you have to write your own thesis? In the end, your career goal is to become a manager, and you will then seek such services from professionals. Moreover, what you need to know about research you have already learned in this course.

7 'With statistics you can prove everything' and 'I only trust statistics that I faked myself' are well-

known sayings. The rules of good research are often bent to produce evidence in support of a point one wants to make, or to serve one's own purpose. What is the value of applying such research rules strictly if others apply them more leniently?

## Online *Learning* Centre

### Get started with understanding statistical techniques!

When you have read this chapter, log on to the Online Learning Centre website at ***www.mcgraw-hill.co.uk/textbooks/blumberg*** to explore chapter-by-chapter test questions, additional case studies, a glossary and more online study tools for Business Research Methods.

## Notes

[1] Elizabethann O'Sullivan and Gary R. Rassel, *Research Methods for Public Administrators*. New York: Longman, 1999.

[2] American Psychological Association, *Ethical Principles of Psychologists and Code of Conduct*. Washington, DC: APA, 1997.

[3] According to the EU Directive on Data Protection 1994, agreeing to participate in an interview is an adequate consent. However, collecting sensitive data on, say, medical records, criminal records, ethnicity, religion, trade union membership, sexual orientation, and so on, requires an 'explicit' consent. The Directive does not offer a definition of 'explicit' consent.

[4] Exhibit 4.2 shows the standard procedures used for informed consent in surveys conducted by the Indiana University Center for Survey Research. Wording and protocol by CSR IU.

[5] Robert A. Baron and Donn Byrne, *Social Psychology: Understanding Human Interaction*. Boston: Allyn & Bacon, 1991, p. 36.

[6] Floyd J. Fowler, Jr., *Survey Research Methods* (rev. edn.). Beverly Hills, CA: Sage, 1988, p. 138.

[7] Robert O'Harrow, 'Privacy rules send US firms scrambling', *Washington Post*, 20 October 1998.

[8] List, John A., Charles D. Bailey, Patricia J. Euzent and Thomas L. Martin, 'Academic economists behaving badly? A survey on three areas of ethical behavior', *Economic Inquiry* Vol. 39, January 2001, pp. 162–70.

[9] An overview of the features of plagiarism-detection software and links to the suppliers of such software is available at www.fdewb.unimaas.nl/eleum/plagiarism/plagiarism.html.

[10] Jeff Allen and Duane Davis, 'Assessing some determinant effects of ethical consulting behavior: the case of personal and professional values', *Journal of Business Ethics* (1993), p. 449.

# Recommended further reading

Carrigan, Marylyn and Kirkup, Malcolm, 'The ethical responsibilities of marketers in retail observational research: protecting stakeholders through the ethical "research covenant" ', *International Review of Retail, Distribution and Consumer Research* 11(4), 2001, pp. 415–36. This article discusses how new technologies can raise ethical issues in consumer research.

Huws, U., Dench, S. and Iphofen, R., *An EU Code of Ethics for Socio-Economic Research.* **Brighton: Institute of Employment Studies, 2004.** A report on the development of ethical guidelines for socio-economic research.

Mauthner, Melanie, Birch, Maxine, Jessop, Julie and Miller, Tina (eds.), *Ethics in Qualitative Research.* **Thousand Oaks: Sage, 2002.** Examines the practical and theoretical aspects of ethical dilemmas in qualitative research, addressing also the issue of the implications if private information becomes public.

Miles, Mathew B. and Huberman, A. Michael, *Qualitative Data Analysis.* **Thousand Oaks, CA: Sage, 1994.** Chapter 11 discusses several ethical issues from the perspective of the consequences for data analysis.

National Academy of Sciences, *On Being a Scientist: Responsible Conduct in Research* (2nd edn.). **Washington, DC: National Academy Press, 1995.** Written for beginning researchers, this source describes the ethical foundations of scientific practices, personal and professional issues, and research applications for industrial, governmental and academic settings.

Oliver, Paul, *The Student's Guide to Research Ethics.* **Buckingham: Open University Press, 2003.** A comprehensive book examining ethical issues in academic and professional research.

Rosnow, Ralph L. and Rosenthal, Robert, *People Studying People: Artifacts and Ethics in Behavioral Research.* **New York: Freeman, 1997.** A potent source of analysis and advice; particularly appropriate for Chapters 8 and 9 on observation and experimentation.

## Spotlight on research 2

## Do data warehouses challenge fair play?

By H. Jefferson Smith

One of the most popular concepts in information technology these days is data warehousing, which stores a company's data in a central repository. The information in the database is updated frequently and is made available for planning, marketing, and decision-making.

Data warehouses are designed to support online analytical processing and data-mining. These technologies have been described as akin to turning 100 statisticians loose on your data at the same time.

Many kinds of business questions can be answered through these technologies. You can find and track customers, analyse their behaviour, segment a customer base, customize products, model past attrition behaviour (thus reducing past customer defections), and refine a business strategy by massaging the warehouse data.

For example, one consumer credit company has a data warehouse that contains almost 1000 attributes per customer. The database is so large that updates take more than 48 hours and rely on 50 different feeder files. But the payback is also large: analysts are generating more than 200 queries per day, and in-depth reports on spending patterns and demographics are available to the company's marketers. The analysts and marketers have also used the warehouse to generate targeted mailings to customers.

Nevertheless, along with the potential benefits of data warehousing come some serious considerations about fair play in the use of customer data. The various issues that arise depend on whether an organization's customers are other businesses or individual consumers.

### It's just business

Almost every company has relationships with other firms. Some are suppliers that provide the company with products or services, while others distribute or purchase its products and services. In addition, a company has relationships with individual consumers who buy its products – either directly or through a distributor or retailer. Thus, when an enterprise warehouses data about its customers in business-to-business transactions, a corporation should think about what constitutes fair play from the perspective of several different players: the company that is its direct customer, the firms supplying that customer, and the firms or individual consumers buying that customer's products.

In general, the company with the data warehouse should follow a two-edged principle. It is fair to use the customer data to deduce ways in which the relationship with this business customer (or other potential customers of this type) could be strengthened.

It would be fair, for example, to create statistical profiles of current customers based on the warehouse data and to use those profiles to deduce which market segments might be most appropriate for future targeting. It would also be acceptable to conclude which additional products or services would be most appropriate for current customers and to focus special attention on creating and marketing those products or services to those customers.

On the other hand, it is unfair to use the customer data in any of the following three ways. First, it is unfair to do anything that might harm the customer's relationships with any of its suppliers or customers. Suppose, for example, that company B, after careful scrutiny of its warehoused data, realized that most of the purchases customer C made were being resold to one of C's clients, D. Obviously, both B and D could benefit if D bought its products directly from B and bypassed C. B could charge D a price that was higher than what it charged C but lower than what D paid C.

Though this scenario appears economically efficient, B's contacting D to suggest such a deal would constitute gross unfairness to C. B would be using data about its relationship with C to undercut C's position with D.

Second, it is unfair to use customer data in any way that intrudes on the customer's proprietary know-how. Suppose that its data warehouse gave company E knowledge about the specific methods and techniques that one of its customers, F, was using to design and produce its products. It would be unfair for E to reveal this information to others or to use this knowledge to take advantage of F in future negotiations.

Third, it is unfair to use customer data to change an industry structure if that change is detrimental to any of the firm's customers. Suppose, for example, that company G was a supplier to a number of firms in an industry. This industry has a value system of suppliers, manufacturers, distributors, and consumers. Several companies are involved in the manufacturing process – from raw materials to the final product – with each firm adding some value to the product.

By carefully massaging its data warehouse, G might discover a new scheme for manufacturing and distributing products that would increase the overall efficiency of the system, reduce the cost of production (leading to greater industry profits and more sales for G), and lead to greater sales and profits for some of the manufacturers (G's customers).

On the other hand, the scheme would hurt the sales and profits of other firms that are also G's customers. Although some people might disagree, I would argue that G had an obligation to protect the interests of all its customers and to take no action that would harm any of them. Since G had the data in its warehouse only because of its relationship with its customers, it would be a betrayal to use that data in a manner that would harm any of them.

## Making it personal

When a company's customers are individual consumers instead of other businesses, different rules of fairness apply because concepts of fair information use at this level are often viewed as a human rights issue. Therefore, issues related to consumer privacy – a concept quite distinct from that of corporations' right to proprietary trade knowledge – quickly come into play.

The general rules of fairness in warehousing consumer data should be the same as those that are becoming generally accepted for other applications that involve personal data.

- Consumers should be fully informed of the intended uses of data before the data are collected.
- Consumers should be allowed to opt out of any uses they find offensive.
- Data collected from consumers for one purpose should not be used for another purpose without the consumer's permission.

The rules suggest that it will be difficult to begin warehousing consumer data unless some up-front work is done to ensure that consumers are fully informed of the intended uses ahead of time and are given an opportunity to opt out.

For example, unless consumers are told in advance that transaction data will be used to assess their spending patterns and create psychographic profiles of their activities, such analysis should not be done. Fortunately, the consumer credit company discussed earlier has engaged in just such a notification programme.

Assuming that the analysts have access to a set of 'clean' consumer data (data gathered under the policies outlined above), they can proceed to mine the data, classifying consumers as appropriate, targeting specific customers for certain offers, and developing plans for soliciting new customers.

However, a word of warning is in order, based on experiences in the database marketing industry. The results of the mining activities should be carefully evaluated to ensure that they produce no socially negative outcomes or, at least, that the outcomes are grounded in business decisions rather than in unintended discrimination. For example, the targeting of specific residents in one urban area for special purchase offers has been called discriminatory because the offers were sent disproportionally to one racial group and excluded members of other groups.

It seems obvious that the use of data warehousing introduces new ethical challenges into both business-to-business and business-to-consumer relationships. However, the lines are not drawn clearly in all areas, and there is still room for judgement calls on many issues. Therefore, in the interest of fair play, corporate and IT executives who want to take advantage of this technology should pay serious attention to all the issues involved.

# PART 2

# Research approaches

## Part contents

# Chapter 5

# Quantitative and qualitative research

## Chapter contents

## LEARNING OBJECTIVES

When you have read this chapter, you should understand:

- ☑ the basic stages of research design

- ☑ the major descriptors of research design

- ☑ the major types of research design

- ☑ the relationships that exist between variables in research design and the steps for evaluating those relationships.

## 5.1 Qualitative and quantitative studies

Before we look deeper into different aspects of the research design we will discuss a widely used distinction for research study, namely the one between qualitative studies and quantitative studies. This distinction is based mainly on the kind of information used to study a phenomenon. As their names suggest quantitative studies rely on quantitative information (i.e. numbers and figures), while qualitative studies base their accounts on qualitative information (i.e. words, sentences and narratives). One textbook creates a verbal picture to help differentiate between the two:

> Quality is the essential character or nature of something; quantity is the amount. Quality is the what; quantity the how much. Qualitative refers to the meaning, the definition or analogy or model or metaphor characterizing something, while quantitative assumes the meaning and refers to a measure of it ... The difference lies in Steinbeck's [1941] description of the Mexican Sierra, a fish from the Sea of Cortez. One can count the spines on the dorsal fin of a pickled Sierra, 17 plus 15 plus 9. 'But,' says Steinbeck, 'if the Sierra strikes hard on the line so that our hands are burned, if the fish sounds and nearly escapes and finally comes in over the rail, his colors pulsing and his tail beating the air, a whole new relational externality has come into being.' Qualitative research would define the being of fishing, the ambience of a city, the mood of a citizen, or the unifying tradition of a group.[1]

Many scholars show a strong preference for either type of study. However, these preferences more likely reflect their own capabilities and experiences than a general idea about which type of research is more useful. It must be emphasized that one cannot decide whether qualitative or quantitative studies are better or more useful. It is important to note that there are no predeterminates for the appropriateness of either a qualitative or a quantitative study. Although quantitative studies seem to be more common in economics and qualitative studies in anthropology, there are plenty of examples of very insightful qualitative studies in economics and good quantitative studies in anthropology. Further, in many social sciences, such as management studies, sociology, psychology, and so on, there is no such clear predominance of qualitative or quantitative studies. Similarly, a new investigation often starts with qualitative studies exploring new phenomena and, later on, quantitative studies follow to test the validity of propositions formulated in previous qualitative studies. Although this approach is often observed in chronologically ordered studies on one phenomenon, this should not give the idea that quantitative studies are never explorative, or that it is ridiculous to combine qualitative study and tests of propositions or validity assessments.

From the above, it is obvious that many research problems can be investigated qualitatively as well as quantitatively. Chapter 2 gives the example of the project team of a telecommunications provider, which is tasked with investigating the likely market acceptance of a newly designed mobile phone with many new features. In this example the project team could either form consumer focus groups and discuss within these groups how well the new mobile phone is likely to be received, or it could phone-interview about 500 consumers about which features of a mobile phone they would appreciate. The focus-group approach is a typical example of a qualitative study, while the phone-interview approach would qualify as a quantitative study. Which study is more appropriate depends very much on what the project team seeks, as the focus-group study will provide different answers to the telephone survey.

Let's take another example. Assume that you want to investigate how the rich and the poor live in your country. A typical quantitative version of such a study would start with a numeric definition of who is considered rich and who is considered poor – for example, the rich are those people who earn at least three times the mean income and the poor are those who can spend half or less of the mean income. Your description of the rich and the poor would depend on information included in a general survey. For example, the questions in such a survey could address: demographic information on the respondent and his or her household (age, married or unmarried, number of children, etc.), the respondent's educational background and occupation, their ownership of durable consumer goods (fridge, piano, car), the respondent's norms and values, the respondent's scores on personality traits, and so on. The list of possible questions you could ask is endless and your selection among all the possible questions will be driven by the specificities of your research problem. Are you interested in how the rich and poor generate income and how they spend it, or are you more interested in their lifestyles?

A more qualitative account of such an investigation could also emphasize the generation of income and its spending, or respondents' lifestyles. However, such a qualitative investigation would not use a large-scale survey to learn something about the life of rich and poor people; rather, it would be based on observations or deeper and less structured interviews. Within an observational study, researchers could, for example, follow an average week in the life of some wealthy and some poor people. They could accompany the respondents to their workplace or to any social welfare institutions, participate in how they spend their evenings and the weekend, go shopping with them, and so on. Likewise, they could talk with a number of poor and a number of rich people, holding intensive interviews to cover the life story of each of them. In such a qualitative research setting the researchers would still, to a large extent, control the kind of information gathered. They would do this in two ways. First, they would exercise control by selecting the (leading) questions asked, or by deciding how and when the observation will be conducted. Second, qualitative research is usually much less rigorously structured than quantitative research and, consequently, the researcher is more likely to miss some information. Even by taking the utmost care, researchers will not be able to note down all the information available; rather, they will choose – subconsciously and deliberately – some of the information provided and neglect other parts of it. However, compared to a quantitative study, a qualitative study is more likely to obtain unexpected information, as the more structured approach of quantitative study directs the researcher more, leaving less leeway to explore other avenues. That is why explorative studies often have a more qualitative character, although quantitative research, for example data-mining (see Chapter 8), is also used for explorations.

You should be aware that there are no general guidelines as to when a qualitative or quantitative research approach is more appropriate. When making the choice as to whether to conduct a qualitative or quantitative study you need to consider the following questions.

● What is your research problem?
● Are you attempting to conduct an explorative, descriptive, causal or predictive study?
● What is the objective (i.e. what kind of outcomes are you looking for)?
● What kind of information do you want to obtain and what do you already have access to?

Nevertheless, two researchers with similar, or even the same, answers to these questions may still come to different conclusions regarding the choice between qualitative and quantitative study. It is often impossible to determine whether a qualitative or quantitative study would be best able to answer a research problem, as a cost–benefit calculation of the trade-off between the two options does not always provide an unambiguous answer. The quality of any research study does not so much depend on whether it is qualitative or quantitative, but rather it depends on the quality of its design and how well it is conducted. In scientific and business research, there are plenty of examples of excellent qualitative and quantitative studies; unfortunately, however, there are also many examples of poorly conducted studies.

## We do not need market research and consumer surveys

Aldi is one of the largest discount retail chains in Europe and also has operations in the USA. Every day millions of consumers visit one of their over 7500 shops worldwide to buy groceries, but increasingly also non-food articles such as textiles, stationery, toys, and so on. Regularly, the organization opens new shops, adds new products to its regular or incidental portfolio of products sold. In 2005, the word 'Aldisierung' [Aldization] was announced as word of the year in Switzerland. The word describes a recent trend that more and more people, including those with rather high income, have become very price sensitive for almost all consumer goods and they buy frozen pizza, coffee beans, DVD players and suncream where they can pay the lowest price and ALDI is often their final choice.

Surprisingly, ALDI has never spent a cent on external market research. They also do not track what individual customers buy through registering their purchases and combine it with information stored on a customer card. They can't because they do not have customer cards. But what do they do? The ALDI management decides on common sense. Even top-level executives visit stores and talk to store managers and employees on a weekly basis. According to Dieter Brandes, a former ALDI manager, the best market research is to shop in your own stores and keep your eyes open. Then you will understand immediately why some articles sell well and others do not and you will learn much more than any figures that market research can tell you.

How does the management decide whether a new product should be added, which is a very strategic decision, as a typical ALDI holds just about 1000 products compared to 20,000 in their competitors' stores. The management board of ALDI, consisting of the general managers of their regional subsidiaries each overseeing about 70 stores, will decide by discussing the proposal and trying the product, but no extensive market research is involved.

## References and further reading

Brandes, D. (2004) *Bare essentials: The ALDI Way of Retailing.* London: Cyan/Campus.
*Business Week, 26 April 2004,* 'The next Wal-Mart?'

## 5.2 What is research design?

There are many definitions of research design, but no one definition imparts the full range of important aspects. Several examples from leading authors can be cited:

> The research design constitutes the blueprint for the collection, measurement, and analysis of data. It aids the scientist in the allocation of his limited resources by posing crucial choices: Is the blueprint to include experiments, interviews, observation, the analysis of records, simulation, or some combination of these? Are the methods of data collection and the research situation to be highly structured? Is an intensive study of a small sample more effective than a less intensive study of a large sample? Should the analysis be primarily quantitative or qualitative?[2]

And:

> Research design is the plan and structure of investigation so conceived as to obtain answers to research questions. The plan is the overall scheme or program of the research. It includes an outline of what the investigator will do from writing hypotheses and their operational implications to the final analysis of data. A structure is the framework, organization, or configuration of … the relations among variables of a study. A research design expresses both the structure of the research problem and the plan of investigation used to obtain empirical evidence on relations of the problem.[3]

These definitions differ in detail, but together they give the essentials of research design:

- the design is an activity- and time-based plan
- the design is always based on the research question
- the design guides the selection of sources and types of information
- the design is a framework for specifying the relationships among the study's variables
- the design outlines procedures for every research activity.

Thus, the design provides answers for questions such as these:

- What kind of answers is the study looking for and which methods will be applied to find them?
- What techniques will be used to gather data?
- What kind of sampling will be used?
- How will time and cost constraints be dealt with?

## Classification of designs

Early in any research study, one faces the task of selecting the specific design to use. A number of different design approaches exist but, unfortunately, no simple classification system defines all the variations that must be considered. Exhibit 5.1 classifies research design using eight different descriptors.[4] Following on from this, a brief discussion of these descriptors serves to illustrate their nature and contribution to research.

| Category | Options |
|---|---|
| The degree to which the research question has been crystallized | Exploratory study |
| | Formal study |
| The method of data-collection | Monitoring |
| | Interrogation/communication |
| | Archival sources |
| The power of the researcher to influence the variables under study | Experimental |
| | *Ex-post facto* |
| The purpose of the study | Descriptive |
| | Causal |
| | Predictive |
| The time dimension | Cross-sectional |
| | Longitudinal |
| The topical scope – breadth and depth – of the study | Case |
| | Statistical study (sample or census) |
| The research environment | Field setting |
| | Laboratory research |
| | Simulation |
| The participants' perceptions of research activity | Actual routine |
| | Modified routine |

**Exhibit 5.1** Descriptors of research designs.

## Degree of research question crystallization

A study may be viewed as exploratory or formal. The essential distinctions between these two options are the degree of structure and the immediate objective of the study. **Exploratory studies** tend towards loose structures with the objective of discovering future research tasks. The immediate purpose of exploration is usually to develop hypotheses or questions for further research. The **formal study** begins where the exploration leaves off – it begins with a descriptive account of the current situation followed by the hypothesis or research question, and involves precise procedures and data source specifications. The goal of a formal research design is to provide a valid representation of the current state and to test the hypotheses or answer the research questions posed.

The exploratory–formal study dichotomy is less precise than some other classifications. All studies have elements of exploration in them, and few are completely uncharted. The results of quantitative studies often raise new research questions and contain therefore an explorative element. Likewise, qualitative studies very often provide convincing evidence for theoretical explanations. The sequence discussed in Chapter 2 (see Exhibit 2.1) suggests that more formalized studies contain at least an element of exploration before the final choice of design. More detailed consideration of exploratory research is found later in this chapter.

## Method of data-collection

This classification distinguishes between the monitoring and interrogation/communication processes. **Monitoring** includes studies in which the researcher inspects the activities of a subject or the nature of some material without attempting to elicit responses from anyone. Traffic counts at an intersection, licence plates recorded in a restaurant car park, a search of the library collection, an observation of the actions of a group of decision-makers – all are examples of monitoring. In each case the researcher notes and records the information available from observations.

In the **interrogation/communication study**, the researcher questions the subjects and collects their responses by personal or impersonal means. The collected data may result from (i) interview or telephone conversations, (ii) self-administered or self-reported instruments sent through the mail, left in convenient locations, or transmitted electronically or by other means, or (iii) instruments presented before and/or after a treatment or stimulus condition in an experiment. As discussed in Chapter 10, the researcher is not always required to collect data. Often, the information required to answer a research problem is already available and the researcher can rely on these secondary data.

Qualitative and quantitative studies can rely on both methods of data-collection. A quantitative study does not need to rely on communication, observational studies (see Chapter 8) can for example be also qualitative. Likewise, good qualitative study should be based on monitoring and communication (see Chapter 9).

## Researcher control of variables

In terms of the researcher's ability to manipulate variables, we must differentiate between experimental and *ex-post facto* designs. In an **experiment**, the researcher attempts to **control** and/or manipulate the variables in the study. It is enough that we can cause variables to be changed or held constant in keeping with our research objectives. Experimental design is appropriate when one wishes to discover whether certain variables produce effects in other variables. Experimentation provides the most powerful support possible for a hypothesis of causation.

With an *ex-post facto* **design**, investigators have no control over the variables in the sense of being able to manipulate them. They can only report what has happened or what is happening. It is important that the researchers using this design do not influence the variables, as to do so introduces bias. The researcher is limited to holding factors constant by judicious selection of subjects according to strict sampling procedures and by the statistical manipulation of findings.

## The purpose of the study

The essential difference between a **descriptive study** and a **causal study** lies in their objectives. If the research is concerned with finding out who, what, where, when or how much, then the study is descriptive. If it is concerned with learning why – that is, how one variable produces changes in another – it is causal. Research on crime is descriptive when it measures the types of crime committed, how often, when, where and by whom. A causal study tries to explain relationships among variables – for instance, why the crime rate is higher in Paris than in Oslo. Descriptive and causal studies can be both quantitative and qualitative. For example, the reports published by governments' statistical agencies are often quantitative descriptive studies, as they

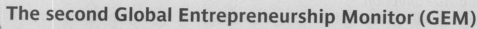

## The second Global Entrepreneurship Monitor (GEM)

Researchers at the Kauffman Center for Entrepreneurial Leadership (Babson College) and the London Business School joined forces in 1997 to try to prove or disprove a conceptual model of cultural, economic, physical and political factors to predict economic growth. The research design compensated for lack of control by using 'a variety of nations with diversity in frame-work conditions, entrepreneurial sectors, business dynamics and economic growth'. The 1999 longitudinal study conducted in eight countries included various data-collection methods:

- standardized national primary data collected by each national research team
- two rounds of adult phone surveys of at least 1000 adults per country (face to face in Japan) to measure entrepreneurial activity and attitude, completed and coordinated by an international market survey firm
- hour-long interviews with 4–39 experts (key informants) for each country
- a detailed 12-page questionnaire completed by each key informant.

Market Facts (Arlington Heights, IL) did the first round of data-collection in June 1998 (Canada, Finland, Germany, the UK and the USA). Audience Selection Ltd (London) con-ducted the second round in March 1999 in all 10 countries. The 2000 study employed research teams from more than 21 countries, including 10 countries from the 1999 study.

For the purposes of the study, entrepreneurship was defined as 'any attempt to create a new business enterprise or to expand an existing business'. Employing regression analysis, a weight was assigned to each factor of influence. The researchers discovered in the 1999 study that per-ception of opportunity (.79) and two measures of entrepreneurial potential – capacity (0.64) and motivation (0.93) – positively correlate with business start-up rates. The 2000 study created a Total Entrepreneurial Activity Index, combining the nascent start-up rate (percentage of adults engaged in activities related to starting a business) and the new firm rate (percentage of adults reporting managing an owned business without payroll to additional employees).

This study is ongoing, but researchers thus far conclude that 'support for the conceptual model is encouraging, although clearly not conclusive'.

## References and further reading

*GEM: 1999 UK Executive Report*, London Business School, ©1999.

'New study on entrepreneurship reveals US is awash in capital for new business start-ups: report indicates that start-up activity is more prevalent than previously believed' (at http://www.businesswire.com/cgi-bin/fheadline.cgi?day0/192090158&ticker=).

Reynolds, P., Hay, M. and Camp, S. *GEM: 1999 Executive Report*, Babson College and London School of Business, ©1999.

Reynolds, Paul, Levie, J. and Autio, E. 'Data collection – analysis strategies operations manual', *Babson College–London Business School Global Entrepreneurship Monitor: 1999*, ©1999.

Reynolds, Paul, Levie, J., Autio, E., Hay, M. and Bygrave, W. '1999 research report: entrepreneur-ship and national economic well-being', ©1999 (at www.babson.edu/entrep/index.html).

www.london.edu

www2.babson.edu/babson/babsoneshipp.nsf/Public/HomePage

Zacharakis, A., Reynolds, P. and Bygrave, W. *GEM: National Entrepreneurship Assessment – United States of America – 1999 Executive Report*, Babson College, ©1999.

Zacharakis, A., Bygrave, W. and Shepard, D. *National Entrepreneurship Assessment – United States of America: 2000 Executive Report*, Babson College, ©2000.

only provide a sketch of the current situation. Qualitative case studies can be descriptive if the emphasis is on reporting what has been observed, like in many anthropological studies, or causal if the case study explores a case to present new theoretical explanations.

## The time dimension

**Cross-sectional studies** are carried out once and represent a snapshot of one point in time. **Longitudinal studies** are repeated over an extended period. The advantage of a longitudinal study is that it can track changes over time. Further, longitudinal studies are also more powerful regarding tests of causality, as a causal relationship between A and B requires that A happened before B. Having measurements of A at time $t = 0$ and B at time $t = 1$ ensures that A indeed happened before B. The distinction between cross-sectional and longitudinal studies is again not related to the distinction between qualitative and quantitative studies. Both time dimensions are possible for both studies. However, good case studies, as an example for a qualitative study, are usually longitudinal, that is the investigated phenomena is observed over a certain time span.

In longitudinal studies of the panel variety, the researcher may study the same people over time. In marketing, panels are set up to report consumption data on a variety of products. These data, collected from national samples, provide a major databank on relative market share, consumer response to new products, and new promotional methods. Other longitudinal studies, such as cohort groups, use different subjects for each sequenced measurement. The service industry might have looked at the needs of ageing baby boomers by sampling 40–45 year olds in 1990 and 50–55 year olds in 2000. Although each sample would be different, the population of 1945–1950 cohort survivors would remain the same.

Some types of information, once collected, cannot be collected a second time from the same person without the risk of bias. The study of public awareness of an advertising campaign over a six-month period, for example, would require different samples for each measurement.

While longitudinal research is important, the constraints of budget and time impose the need for cross-sectional analysis. Some benefits of a longitudinal study can be revealed in a cross-sectional study by adroit questioning about past attitudes, history and future expectations. Responses to these kinds of question should be interpreted with care, however.

## The topical scope

The statistical study differs from the case study in several ways. **Statistical studies** are designed for breadth rather than depth. They attempt to capture a population's characteristics by making inferences from a sample's characteristics. Hypotheses are tested quantitatively. Generalizations about findings are presented based on the representativeness of the sample and the validity of the design. A special case of statistical studies are census studies, which are based on the whole population.

**Case studies** place more emphasis on a full contextual analysis of fewer events or conditions and their interrelations. Although hypotheses are often used, the reliance on qualitative data makes support or rejection more difficult. An emphasis on detail provides valuable insight for problem-solving, evaluation and strategy. This detail is secured from multiple sources of information. It allows evidence to be verified and avoids the problem of data being missed.

Although case studies have been maligned as 'scientifically worthless' because they do not meet minimal design requirements for comparison,[5] they have a significant scientific role. It is known that 'important scientific propositions have the form of universals, and a universal can be falsified by a single counterinstance'.[6] Thus, a single well-designed case study can provide a major challenge to a theory and provide, simultaneously, a source of new hypotheses and constructs.

### The research environment

Designs also differ as to whether they occur under actual environmental conditions (**field conditions**) or under staged or manipulated conditions (**laboratory conditions**) or even artificially (**simulations**).

In the field condition, we observe or interrogate people in the usual environment, such as their homes, their workplaces or the shops they visit. In the laboratory condition, we are able to manipulate the environment although the laboratory might be designed as the usual environment, for example the laboratory might look like a shopping aisle in a supermarket. To simulate is to replicate the essence of a system or process. **Simulations** are used increasingly in research, especially in operations research. The major characteristics of various conditions and relationships in actual situations are often represented in mathematical models. Role-playing and other behavioural activities may also be viewed as simulations.

### Participants' perceptions

The usefulness of a design may be reduced when people in a disguised study perceive that research is being conducted. **Participants' perceptions** influence the outcomes of the research in subtle ways, or even more dramatically, as demonstrated by the pivotal Hawthorne studies of the late 1920s. Although there is no widespread evidence of attempts by participants or respondents to please researchers through successful hypothesis-guessing or evidence of the prevalence of sabotage, when participants believe that something out of the ordinary is happening, they may behave less naturally. There are three levels of perception.

1  Participants perceive no deviations from everyday routines.

2  Participants perceive deviations, but as unrelated to the research.

3  Participants perceive deviations as researcher-induced.[7]

The 'mystery shopper' scenario is the perfect example of the final level of perception noted in the above list. If a retail sales associate knows that she is being observed and evaluated – with consequences in terms of future remuneration, scheduling or work assignment – she is likely to change her performance. In all research environments and control situations, researchers need to be vigilant with regard to effects that may alter their conclusions. Participants' perceptions serve as a reminder to classify one's study by type, to examine validation strengths and weaknesses, and to be prepared to qualify results accordingly.

## Exploratory studies

The **exploratory study** (**exploration**) is particularly useful when researchers lack a clear idea of the problems they will meet during the study. Through exploration, researchers develop concepts more clearly, establish priorities, develop operational definitions and improve the final research design. Exploration may also save time and money: if the problem is found not to be as important as it was first thought, subsequent more formal studies can be cancelled.

Exploration serves other purposes as well. The area of investigation may be so new or so vague that a researcher needs to do an exploration just to learn something about the research or management dilemma. Important variables may not be known or may not be defined thoroughly. Hypotheses for the research may be needed. Also, the researcher may explore to be sure that it is practical to do a formal study in the area. A federal government agency, the Office of Industry Analysis, proposed that research be done on how executives in a given industry made decisions about raw material purchases. Questions were planned asking how (and at what price spreads) one raw material was substituted for another in certain manufactured products. An exploration to discover if industry executives would divulge adequate information about their decision-making on this topic was essential for the study's success.

Despite its obvious value, researchers and managers alike pay exploration less attention than it deserves. There are strong pressures for quick answers. Moreover, exploration is sometimes linked to old biases about qualitative research: accusations of subjectiveness, non-representativeness and non-systematic design. More realistically, exploration saves time and money, and should not be slighted.

### *Qualitative techniques*

The objectives of exploration may be accomplished with different techniques. Both qualitative and quantitative techniques are applicable, although exploration relies more heavily on **qualitative techniques**.

When we consider the scope of qualitative research, several approaches are adaptable for exploratory investigations of management questions:

- in-depth interviewing (usually conversational rather than structured)
- participant observation (to perceive at first hand what participants in the setting experience)
- films, photographs and videotape (to capture the life of the group under study)
- projective techniques and psychological testing (such as a thematic apperception test, projective measures, games or role-playing)

- case studies (for an in-depth contextual analysis of a few events or conditions)
- street ethnography (to discover how a cultural sub-group describes and structures its world at street level)
- elite or expert interviewing (for information from influential or well-informed people in an organization or community)
- document analysis (to evaluate historical or contemporary confidential or public records, reports, government documents and opinions)
- proxemics and kinesics (to study the use of space and body-motion communication respectively).[8]

When these approaches are combined, four exploratory techniques emerge with wide applicability for the management researcher:

1. secondary data analysis
2. experience surveys
3. focus groups
4. two-stage designs.

### Secondary data analysis

The first step in an exploratory study is a search of the secondary literature. Studies made by others for their own purposes represent **secondary data**. It is inefficient to discover anew through the collection of **primary data** or original research what has already been done and reported at a level sufficient to solve the research question.

Within secondary data exploration, a researcher should start with an organization's own data archives. Reports of prior research studies often reveal an extensive amount of historical data or decision-making patterns. By reviewing prior studies, you can identify methodologies that proved successful and unsuccessful.

Another source of secondary data is published documents prepared by authors outside the sponsor organization. There are tens of thousands of periodicals and hundreds of thousands of books on all aspects of business. Data from secondary sources help us decide what needs to be done and can be a rich source of hypotheses.

If one is creative, a search of secondary sources will supply excellent background information as well as many good leads. Yet if we confine the investigation to obvious subjects in bibliographic sources we will often miss much of the best information. Suppose the Copper Industry Association is interested in estimating the outlook for the copper industry over the next 10 years. We could search through the literature under the headings 'copper production' and 'copper consumption'. However, a search restricted to these two topics would miss more than it finds. When a creative search of the copper industry is undertaken, useful information turns up under the following reference headings: mines and minerals; non-ferrous metals; forecasting; planning; econometrics; consuming industries such as automotive and communications; countries where copper is produced, such as Chile; and companies prominent in the industry, such as Anaconda and Kennecott.

## *Experience survey*

While published data are a valuable resource, it is seldom the case that more than a fraction of the existing knowledge in a field is put into writing. A significant portion of what is known on a topic, while in writing, may be proprietary to a given organization and thus unavailable to an outside searcher. Also, internal data archives are rarely well organized, making secondary sources, even when known, difficult to locate. Thus, we will profit by seeking information from persons experienced in the area of study, tapping into their collective memories and experiences.

When we interview persons in an **experience survey**, we should seek their ideas about important issues or aspects of the subject, and discover what is important across the subject's range of knowledge. The investigative format we use should be flexible enough to allow us to explore various avenues that emerge during the interview.

- What is being done?
- What has been tried in the past without success? With success?
- How have things changed?
- What are the change-producing elements of the situation?
- Who is involved in decisions and what role does each person play?
- What problem areas and barriers can be seen?
- What are the costs of the processes under study?
- Whom can we count on to assist and/or participate in the research?
- What are the priority areas?

The product of such questioning may be a new hypothesis, the discarding of an old one, or information about the practicality of doing the study. Probing may show whether certain facilities are available, what factors need to be controlled and how, and who will cooperate in the study.

Discovery is more easily carried out if the researcher can analyse cases that provide special insight. Typical of exploration, we are less interested in getting a representative cross-section than in getting information from sources that might be insightful. Assume we study Star-Auto's automobile assembly plant. It has a history of declining productivity, increasing costs and a growing number of quality defects. People who might provide insightful information include:

- newcomers to the scene – employees or personnel who may recently have been transferred to this plant from similar plants
- marginal or peripheral individuals – persons whose jobs place them on the margin between contending groups (first-line supervisors and lead workers are often neither management nor worker but something in between)
- individuals in transition – recently promoted employees who have been transferred to new departments
- deviants and isolates – those in a given group who hold a different position from the

majority, as well as workers who are happy with the present situation, highly productive departments and workers, and loners of one sort or another

- 'pure' cases or cases that show extreme examples of the conditions under study – the most unproductive departments, the most antagonistic workers, and so forth

- those who fit well and those who do not – the workers who are well established in their organizations versus those who are not, those executives who fully reflect management views and those who do not

- those who represent different positions in the system – unskilled workers, assemblers, superintendents, and so forth.[9]

## Focus groups

Originating in sociology, **focus groups** became widely used in marketing research during the 1980s and are used for increasingly diverse research applications today.[10] The most common application of focus-group research continues to be in the consumer arena. However, many corporations are using focus-group results for diverse exploratory applications.

The topical objective of a focus group is often a new product or product concept. The output of the session is a list of ideas and behavioural observations, with recommendations by the moderator. These are often used for later quantitative testing. As a group interview tool, focus groups have applied-research potential for other functional areas of business, particularly where the generation and evaluation of ideas or the assessment of needs is indispensable. In exploratory research, the qualitative data that focus groups produce may be used for enriching all levels of research questions and hypotheses, and for comparing the effectiveness of design options.

Focus groups are also a useful approach in the research process regarding pre-testing questionnaires, experiments, and so on. A prior focus-group discussion of the research design and the instruments used in the research can improve the research considerably, as sources of error and misunderstanding are handled before the study is conducted. Using a focus group to assess the research design and instruments before they are put into a pilot test is advantageous because pilot groups usually only contain people who could be respondents. For example, one of the authors of this book conducted a survey among business starters. Before the questionnaire was tested in pilot interviews with entrepreneurs, it was also discussed in focus groups. These focus groups included entrepreneurs (the potential respondents), but also people close to business starters, such as bankers, accountants and people from the Chamber of Commerce.

A focus group is a panel of people, led by a trained moderator, who meet for 90 minutes to two hours. The facilitator or moderator uses group dynamics principles to focus or guide the group in an exchange of ideas, feelings and experiences on a specific topic. Typically the focus group panel is made up of six to ten respondents. Too small or too large a group results in less effective participation. The facilitator introduces the topic and encourages the group members to discuss it among themselves.

Following a topical guide, the moderator will steer the discussion to ensure that all the relevant information desired by the client is considered by the group. The facilitator also keeps gregarious individuals from dominating the conversation, ensuring that each person enters the discussion. In ideal situations, the group's discussion will proceed uninterrupted; however, if the discussion begins to lag, the facilitator moves it along by introducing another facet of the topic that the group has not yet considered. In some groups a questionnaire is administered to the participants before the group work begins, to gather additional data. Typically, one or more representatives of the client will sit behind a one-way mirror in the focus group room to observe the verbal and non-verbal interactions and responses of participants.

## Homogeneity within the focus group

It is often preferable, depending on the topic, to run separate focus groups for different sub-sets of the population. For example, a study on nutritional advice may begin with separate consumer and physician focus groups to determine the best ways to provide the advice. This type of homogeneous grouping tends to promote more intense discussion and freer interaction.[11] For consumer groups, consideration should also be given to such factors as gender, ethnicity, employment status and education. In a recent US exploratory study of discount shoppers, the attitudes about the economy and personal finances expressed by east coast respondents and west coast respondents were widely divergent. The client sponsor was able to use this information to build a marketing strategy tailored to each geographic area.[12]

Since most focus groups are homogeneous, the sourcing of respondents for focus groups is usually done through informal networks of colleagues, community agencies and the target group. Sometimes researchers advertise to attract a wider range of opinions.[13]

## Telephone focus groups

Traditional focus-group participants meet face to face, usually in specialized facilities that enable respondents to interact in a comfortable setting while being observed by a sponsoring client. However, there is often a need to reach people that traditional focus groups cannot attract. With modern telephone conferencing facilities, telephone focus groups can be particularly effective when:

- it is difficult to recruit desired participants – members of elite groups and hard-to-find respondents such as experts, professionals, physician specialists, high-level executives and store owners
- target group members are rare, 'low incidence' or widely dispersed geographically – directors of a medical clinic, celebrities, early adopters and rural practitioners
- issues are so sensitive that anonymity is needed but respondents must be from a wide geographical area – people suffering from a contagious disease, people using non-mainstream products, high-income individuals, competitors
- you want to conduct only a couple of focus groups but want nationwide representation.

Telephone focus groups are usually less expensive than face-to-face focus groups by up to 40 per cent. In contrast to face-to-face groups, heterogeneous telephone groups can be productive. People in traditional superior–subordinate roles can be mixed as long as they are not from the same city. A telephone focus group is less likely to be effective when:

- participants need to handle a product
- an object of discussion cannot be sent through the mail in advance

- the sessions run are likely to be long
- the participants are groups of young children.

## Online focus groups

An emerging technique for exploratory research is to approximate group dynamics using e-mail, websites, Usenet newsgroups or an Internet chat room. Emerging technology also makes it possible to do 'live' voice chats online, reducing or eliminating the cost associated with telephone focus groups. Posting questions to a newsgroup with an interest in the research problem can generate considerable discussion. However, online discussions are not confidential unless they take place on an intranet. Although online forum discussions are unlikely to reflect the average participants, they can be a good way of getting in touch with populations that have special interests (e.g. BMW Club members or 'power computer users').

## Videoconferencing focus groups

The third type of non-face-to-face focus group is conducted via videoconferencing. Many anticipate growth for this medium. Like telephone focus groups, videoconferencing offers significant savings. By reducing the travel time for the facilitator and the client, it means more focus groups can be accomplished in a shorter time. However, videoconferencing retains the barrier between the moderator and participants, although less so than telephone focus groups. Since large corporations and universities often have their own internal videoconferencing facilities, most videoconferencing focus groups will tend to occur within such settings.

## Recording, analysis and reporting

In face-to-face settings, some moderators use large sheets of paper to record trends on the wall of the focus group room; others use a personal notepad. Producing both video- and audiotapes enables a full analysis of the interview. The recorded conversations and moderator notes are summarized across several focus-group sessions using content analysis. This analysis provides the research sponsor with a qualitative picture of the respondents' concerns, ideas, attitudes and feelings.

## Advantages and disadvantages

The primary advantage of the focus group as an exploratory research tool is its ability to quickly and inexpensively grasp the core issues of a topic. Focus groups are brief, relatively inexpensive and extremely flexible. They provide the researcher or client with a chance to observe reactions to their research questions in an open-ended group setting. Participants respond in their own words, rather than being forced to fit into a formalized method. Because they can react freely to each other's responses, the unexpected often occurs.

Focus groups best enable the exploration of surprise information and new ideas. Agendas can be modified as the research team moves on to the next focus group. Even within an existing focus group, an adept facilitator can build on the ideas and insights of previous groups, getting to a greater depth of understanding. However, because they are qualitative devices, with limited sampling accuracy, results from focus groups should not be considered a replacement for quantitative analyses.

## Two-stage design

A useful way to design a research study is as a two-stage design. With this approach, exploration becomes a separate first stage with limited objectives: (i) clearly defining the research question and (ii) developing the research design.

In arguing for a two-stage approach, we recognize that much about the problem is not known but should be known before effort and resources are committed. In these circumstances, one is operating in unknown areas, where it is difficult to predict the problems and costs of the study. Proposals that acknowledge the practicality of this approach are particularly useful when the research budget is inflexible. A limited exploration for a specific modest cost carries little risk for both sponsor and researcher, and often uncovers information that reduces the total research cost.

An exploratory study is finished when the researchers have achieved the following:

- established the major dimensions of the research task
- defined a set of subsidiary investigative questions that can be used as guides to a detailed research design
- developed several hypotheses about possible causes of a management dilemma
- learned that certain other hypotheses are such remote possibilities that they can be safely ignored in any subsequent study
- concluded that additional research is not needed or is not feasible.

## Descriptive studies

In contrast to exploratory studies more formalized studies are typically structured with clearly stated hypotheses or investigative questions. Formal studies serve a variety of research objectives:

- descriptions of phenomena or characteristics associated with a subject population (the who, what, when, where and how of a topic)
- estimates of the proportions of a population that have these characteristics
- discovery of associations among different variables.

The third study objective is sometimes labelled a correlational study, a sub-set of descriptive studies. A descriptive study may be simple or complex; it may be done in many settings. Whatever the form, a descriptive study can be just as demanding of research skills as the causal study, and we should insist on the same high standards for design and execution.

The simplest descriptive study concerns a univariate question or hypothesis in which we ask about, or state something about, the size, form, distribution or existence of a variable. For example, in an account analysis at BankChoice, we might be interested in developing a profile of savers. We may first want to locate them in relation to the main office. The question might be 'What percentage of the savers live within a two-mile radius of the office?' Using the hypothesis format, we might predict that '60 per cent or more of the savers live within a two-mile radius of the office'.

We may also be interested in securing information about other variables, such as the relative size of accounts, the number of accounts for minors, the number of accounts opened within the last six months, and the amount of activity (number of deposits and withdrawals per year) in accounts. Data on each of these variables, by themselves, may have value for management decisions. Bivariate relationships between these or other variables may be of even greater interest. Cross-tabulations between the distance from the account owner's residence or employment to the branch and account activity may suggest that differential rates of activity are related to account owner location. A cross-tabulation of account size and gender of account owner may also show interrelation. Such findings do not imply a causal relationship. In fact, our task is to determine if the variables are independent (or unrelated) and if they are not, then to determine the strength or magnitude of the relationship. Neither procedure tells us which variable is the cause. For example, we might be able to conclude that gender and account size are related but not that gender is a causal factor in account size.

Descriptive studies are often, however, much more complex than this example suggests. One study of savers began as described and then went into much greater depth. Part of the study included an observation of account records that revealed a concentration of nearby savers. Their accounts were typically larger and more active than those whose owners lived at a distance. A sample survey of savers provided information on stages in the family life cycle, attitudes towards savings, family income levels and other matters. Correlation of this information with known savings data showed that women owned larger accounts. Further investigation suggested that women with larger accounts were often widowed or working single women who were older than the average account holder. Information about their attitudes and savings practices led to new business strategies at the bank.

Some evidence collected led to causal questions. The correlation between proximity to the office and the probability of having an account at the office suggested the question 'Why would people who live far from the office have an account there?' In this type of question a hypothesis makes its greatest contribution by pointing out directions that the research might follow. It might be hypothesized that:

1 distant savers (operationally defined as those with addresses more than two miles from the office) have accounts at the office because they once lived near the office; they were 'near' when the account decision was made

2 distant savers actually live near the office, but the address on the account is outside the two-mile radius; they are 'near', but the records do not show this

3 distant savers work near the office; they are 'near' by virtue of their work location

4 distant savers are not normally near the office but responded to a promotion that encouraged savers to bank via computer; this is another form of 'nearness' in which this concept is transformed into one of 'convenience'.

When these hypotheses were tested, it was learned that a substantial portion of the distant savers could be accounted for by hypotheses 1 and 3. The conclusion: location was closely related to saving at a given association. The determination of cause is not so simple, however, and these findings still fall within the definition of a descriptive study.

# Causal studies

The correlation between location and probability of account holding at BankChoice looks like strong evidence to many, but the researcher with scientific training will argue that correlation is not causation. Who is right? The essence of the disagreement seems to lie in the concept of cause.

## *The concept of cause*

One writer asserts that:

> There appears to be an inherent gap between the language of theory and research which can never be bridged in a completely satisfactory way. One thinks in terms of theoretical language that contains notions such as causes, forces, systems, and properties. But one's tests are made in terms of covariations, operations, and pointer readings.[14]

The essential element of causation is that A 'produces' B or A 'forces' B to occur. But that is an artefact of language, not what happens. Empirically, we can never demonstrate an A–B causality with certainty. This is because we do not 'demonstrate' such causal linkages deductively or use the form or validation of premises that deduction requires for conclusiveness. Unlike deductive syllogisms, empirical conclusions are inferences – inductive conclusions. As such, they are probabilistic statements based on what we observe and measure. But we cannot observe and measure all the processes that may account for the A–B relationship.

In Chapter 1 we discussed the example of sales failing to increase following a promotion. Having ruled out other causes for the flat sales, we were left with one inference that was probably, but not definitely, the cause: a poorly executed promotion.

Meeting the ideal standard of causation requires that one variable always causes another and no other variable has the same causal effect. The method of agreement, proposed by John Stuart Mill in the nineteenth century, states, 'When two or more cases of a given phenomenon have one and only one condition in common, then that condition may be regarded as the cause (or effect) of the phenomenon.'[15] Thus, if we can find Z and only Z in every case where we find C, and no others (A, B, D or E) are found with Z, then we can conclude that C and Z are causally related. Exhibit 5.2 illustrates this method.

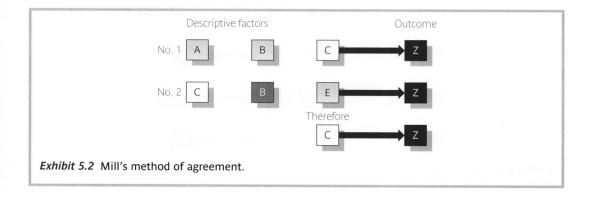

*Exhibit 5.2* Mill's method of agreement.

An example of the method of agreement might be the problem of occasional high absenteeism on Mondays in a factory. A study of two groups with high absenteeism (1 and 2 in Exhibit 5.2) shows no common job, department, demographic or personal characteristics (A, B, D and E). However, membership in a camping club (C) is common across both groups. The conclusion is that club membership is associated with high absenteeism (Z). (We return to this example in the following section.)

The method of agreement helps rule out some variables as irrelevant. In Exhibit 5.2, A, B, D and E are unlikely to be causes of Z. However, there is an implicit assumption that there are no variables to consider other than A, B, C, D and E. One can never accept this supposition with certainty because the number of potential variables is infinite. In addition, while C may be the cause, it may instead function only in the presence of some other variable not included.

The negative canon of agreement states that where the absence of C is associated with the absence of Z, there is evidence of a causal relationship between C and Z. Together with the method of agreement, this forms the basis for the method of difference:

> If there are two or more cases, and in one of them observation Z can be made, while in the other it cannot; and if variable C occurs when observation Z is made, and does not occur when observation Z is not made; then it can be asserted that there is a causal relationship between C and Z.[16]

The method of difference is illustrated in Exhibit 5.3. Although these methods neither ensure discovery of all relevant variables nor provide certain proof of causation, they help advance our understanding of causality by eliminating inadequate causal arguments.[17]

A more refined cause-and-effect model proposes that individual variables are not the cause of specific effects but that processes are the cause of processes.[18] Evidence for this position is illustrated in Exhibit 5.4. Here various cause-and-effect relationships between sales performance and feedback clarify the differences between simple and more complex notions of causality.[19]

In model A, we contend that feedback causes an increase in sales performance. An equally plausible explanation is shown in model B: improvement in sales performance causes the salesperson to behave in a proactive way, seeking more feedback to apply to the next experience.

Model C suggests the reinforcement history of the salesperson is the cause of both initiation

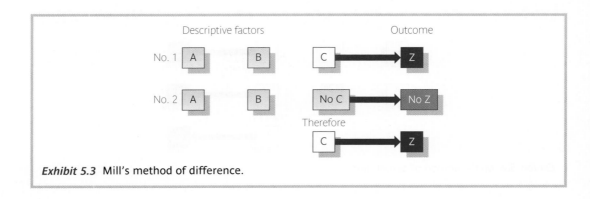

**Exhibit 5.3** Mill's method of difference.

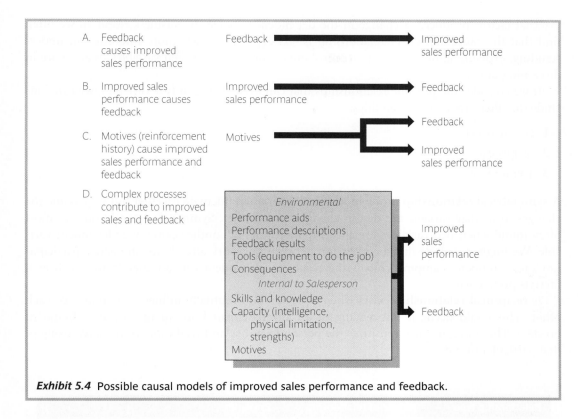

A. Feedback causes improved sales performance

B. Improved sales performance causes feedback

C. Motives (reinforcement history) cause improved sales performance and feedback

D. Complex processes contribute to improved sales and feedback

Feedback ➡ Improved sales performance

Improved sales performance ➡ Feedback

Motives ➡ Feedback / Improved sales performance

Environmental
Performance aids
Performance descriptions
Feedback results
Tools (equipment to do the job)
Consequences
Internal to Salesperson
Skills and knowledge
Capacity (intelligence, physical limitation, strengths)
Motives

➡ Improved sales performance

➡ Feedback

**Exhibit 5.4** Possible causal models of improved sales performance and feedback.

of self-administered feedback and working harder to improve performance. In model D, we suggest that complex processes contribute to changes in feedback and performance. They are in the salesperson's environment and are unique to the person. Other examples could show how positive versus negative reinforcement could create upward or downward sequences that would affect both feedback and performance. Yet all of them make predictions about presumed causal relationships among the variables.

Contemporary authors describe the way researchers substitute 'prediction' for '**causation**'. When scientists speak of causation, they are often referring to a kind of prediction. Predictions can be considered to reflect cause only when all the relevant information is considered. Of course, we can never know all the relevant information, so our predictions are, consequently, presumptive. Hence, the disillusionment in science with the concept of cause. Scientists do use the word 'cause' from time to time, but do not be misled into thinking that they mean cause in the absolute sense.[20]

Causal inferences are going to be made. Although they are neither permanent nor universal, they allow us to build knowledge of presumed causes over time. Such empirical conclusions provide us with successive approximations to the truth. Recognizing this caveat, let's look further at the types of causal relationship of interest to business researchers.

## Causal relationships

Our concern in causal analysis is with how one variable affects, or is 'responsible for', changes in another. The stricter interpretation of causation, found in experimentation, is that some external factor 'produces' a change in the dependent variable. In business research, we often find that the cause-and-effect relationship is less explicit. We are more interested in understanding, explaining, predicting and controlling relationships between variables than we are in discerning causes.

If we consider the possible relationships that can occur between two variables, we can conclude that there are three possibilities:

1  symmetrical
2  reciprocal
3  asymmetrical.[21]

A **symmetrical relationship** is one in which two variables fluctuate together but we assume the changes in neither variable are due to changes in the other. Symmetrical conditions are most often found when two variables are alternate indicators of another cause or independent variable. We might conclude that a correlation between low work attendance and active participation in a company camping club is the result of (dependent on) another factor, such as a lifestyle preference.

A **reciprocal relationship** exists when two variables mutually influence or reinforce each other. This could occur if the reading of an advertisement leads to the use of a brand of product. The usage, in turn, sensitizes the person to notice and read more of the advertising of that particular brand.

| Relationship type | Nature of relationship | Examples |
|---|---|---|
| Stimulus – response | An event or change results in a response from some object | • A change in work rules leads to a higher level of worker output<br>• A change in government economic policy restricts corporate financial decisions<br>• A price increase results in fewer unit sales |
| Property – disposition | An existing property causes a disposition | • Age and attitudes about saving<br>• Gender and attitudes towards social issues<br>• Social class and opinions about taxation |
| Disposition – behaviour | A disposition causes a specific behaviour | • Opinions about a brand and its purchase<br>• Job satisfaction and work output<br>• Moral values and tax cheating |
| Property – behaviour | An existing property causes a specific behaviour | • Stage of the family life cycle and purchases of furniture<br>• Social class and family savings patterns<br>• Age and sports participation |

*Exhibit 5.5* Four types of asymmetrical causal relationship.

Most research analysts look for **asymmetrical relationships**. With these we postulate that changes in one variable (the independent variable, or IV) are responsible for changes in another variable (the dependent variable, or DV). The identification of the IV and DV is often obvious, but sometimes the choice is not clear. In these latter cases we evaluate independence and dependence on the basis of:

1 the degree to which each variable may be altered – the relatively unalterable variable is the independent variable (IV) (e.g. age, social status, present manufacturing technology)

2 the time order between the variables – the independent variable (IV) precedes the dependent variable (DV).

Exhibit 5.5 describes the four types of asymmetrical relationship: stimulus–response, property–disposition, disposition–behaviour and property–behaviour. Experiments usually involve stimulus–response relationships. Property–disposition relationships are often studied in business and social science research. Much of *ex-post facto* research involves relationships between properties, dispositions and behaviours.

## Testing causal hypotheses

While no one can ever be certain that variable A causes variable B to occur, one can gather some evidence that increases the belief that A leads to B. In testing causal hypotheses, we seek three types of evidence.

1 Covariation between A and B.
- Do we find that A and B occur together in the way hypothesized?
- When A does not occur, is there also an absence of B?
- When there is more or less of A, does one also find more or less of B?

2 Time order of events moving in the hypothesized direction.
- Does A occur before B?

3 No other possible causes of B.
- Can one determine that C, D and E do not covary with B in a way that suggests possible causal connections?

### Causation and experimental design

In addition to these three conditions, successful inference-making from experimental designs must meet two other requirements. The first is referred to as control. All factors, with the exception of the independent variable, must be held constant and not confounded with another variable that is not part of the study. Second, each person in the study must have an equal chance of exposure to each level of the independent variable. This is **random assignment** of subjects to groups.

Here is a demonstration of how these factors are used to detect causation. Assume you wish to conduct a survey of Utrecht College's alumni to enlist their support for a new programme. There are two different appeals, one largely emotional and the other much more logical in its approach. Before mailing out appeal letters to 50,000 alumni, you decide to conduct an experiment to see whether the emotional or the rational appeal will draw the greater response. You choose a sample of 300 names from the alumni list and divide them into three groups of 100 each. Two of these groups are designated as experimental groups. One gets the emotional appeal and the other gets the logical appeal. The third group is the **control group** and receives no appeal.

Covariation in this case is expressed by the percentage of alumni who respond in relation to the appeal used. Suppose 50 per cent of those who receive the emotional appeal respond, while only 35 per cent of those receiving the logical appeal respond. Control group members, unaware of the experiment, respond at a 5 per cent rate. We would conclude that using the emotional appeal enhances response probability.

The time sequence of events does not pose a problem to the causality between sending the letter, which was done first, and receiving alumni support, which followed the letter. There is no chance that the alumni support prompted the sending of letters requesting that support. However, have other variables confounded the results? Could some factor other than the appeal have produced the same results? One can anticipate that certain factors are particularly likely to confound the results. One can control some of these to ensure that they do not have this confounding effect. If the question studied is of concern only to alumni who attended the university as undergraduates, those who only attended graduate school are not involved. Thus, you would want to be sure the answers from the latter group did not distort the results. Control would be achieved by excluding graduate students.

**Randomization** is the basic method by which equivalence between experimental and control groups is determined. Experimental and control groups must be established so that they are equal. Matching and controlling are useful, but they do not account for all unknowns. It is best to assign subjects to either experimental or control groups at random (this is not to say haphazardly – randomness must be secured in a carefully controlled fashion according to strict rules of assignment). If the assignments are made randomly, each group should receive its fair share of different factors. The only deviation from this fair share would be that which results from random variation (the 'luck of the draw'). The possible impact of these unknown extraneous variables on the dependent variables should also vary at random. The researcher, using tests of statistical significance, can estimate the probable effect of these chance variations on the DV and can then compare this estimated effect of extraneous variation to the actual differences found in the DV in the experimental and control groups.

A second approach to control uses **matching**. There might be a reason to believe that different ratios of alumni support will come from various age groups. To control by matching, we need to be sure that the age distribution of alumni is the same in all groups. In a similar way, control could be achieved by matching alumni from engineering, liberal arts, business and other schools. Even after using such controls, however, one cannot match or exclude other possible confounding variables. These are dealt with through random assignment.

We emphasize that random assignment of subjects to experimental and control groups is the basic technique by which the two groups can be made equivalent. Matching and other control forms are supplemental ways of improving the quality of measurement. In a sense, matching and controls reduce the extraneous 'noise' in the measurement system and in this way improve the sensitivity of measurement of the hypothesized relationship.

## Causation and *ex-post facto* design

Most research studies cannot be carried out experimentally by manipulating variables. Yet we still are interested in the question of causation. Instead of manipulating and/or controlling exposure to an experimental variable, we study subjects who have been exposed to the independent factor and those who have not.

Consider the following question: Are innovative firms more profitable? A lot of anecdotic evidence suggests that innovation stimulates profits, such as Apple's recent success story of the iPod® introduction. But the question is whether the statement that innovation drives profits holds in general. Obviously, it is not practical to set up an experiment in which we would randomly determine which firms are innovative and which not.

The better approach would be to get a list of firms and measure their innovativeness and profitability. The results might look something like those found in Exhibit 5.6. The data suggest that a firm's innovativeness could be a cause for higher profitability. The covariation evidence is consistent with this conclusion. But what other evidence will give us an even greater confidence in our conclusion?

We would like some evidence of the time order of events. It is logical to expect that if innovation causes profitability, there will be a temporal relationship. If we could establish that profitable firms had been innovative before profits rose, it would be good evidence in support of our hypothesis. Also, if high profitability occurs before a company has been innovative, the time order does not support our hypothesis any more and would suggest that profitability may cause innovation; perhaps because more profitable firms have more resources to invest in innovation.

Of course, many other factors could be causing the high profitability of innovative firms. Here again, the use of control techniques will improve our ability to draw firm conclusions. First, in drawing a sample of innovative as well as non-innovative firms, we can build a random sample. In this way, we can be more confident of a fair representation of average firms' profitability.

We cannot use assignment of subjects in *ex-post facto* research as we did in experimentation. However, we can gather information about potentially confounding factors and use these data to make cross-classification comparisons; in this way we can determine whether there is a relationship between innovation, profitability and other factors. Assume we also gather data on firm size and introduce it as a cross-classification variable; the results might look like those in Exhibit 5.7. These data suggest firms size is also a factor. Larger firms are more likely to be profitable. Part of the high profitability among more innovative firms seems to be associated with

| | Innovativeness | |
|---|---|---|
| Profitability | Yes | No |
| High | 20 | 35 |
| Low | 10 | 140 |

*Exhibit 5.6* Data on employee absenteeism.

| | Less innovative | | More innovative | |
|---|---|---|---|---|
| Profitability | Low | High | Low | High |
| Small firm | 85 | 10 | 6 | 3 |
| Medium-sized firm | 45 | 10 | 3 | 5 |
| Large firm | 10 | 15 | 1 | 12 |

Exhibit 5.7  Cross-tabulated data on employee absenteeism.

the fact that most innovative firms are larger. Within size groups, it is also apparent that innovative firms have a higher incidence of higher profits than less innovative firms of the same size.

### The post hoc fallacy

While researchers must necessarily use *ex-post facto* research designs to address causal questions, a word of warning is in order. High innovation rates among firms with high profitability is weak evidence for claiming a causal relationship. Similarly, the covariation found between variables must be interpreted carefully when the relationship is based on *ex-post facto* analysis. The term **post hoc fallacy** has been used to describe these frequently unwarranted conclusions.

The *ex-post facto* design is widely used in business research and is often the only approach feasible. In particular, one seeks causal explanations between variables that are impossible to manipulate. Not only can the variables not be manipulated, but the subjects usually cannot be assigned to treatment and control groups in advance. We often find that there are multiple causes rather than one. Be careful using the *ex-post facto* design with causal reasoning. Thorough testing, validating of multiple hypotheses and controlling for confounding variables are essential.

## Research Methods in Practice 5

## Social embeddedness a new concept

The project on R&D cooperations, which we mentioned in the first four chapters had a clear quantitative focus. One important reason for setting up a quantitative study has been that a main objective of the project was to test simultaneously hypotheses derived from transaction cost economics and hypotheses based on considerations regarding the social embeddedness. The idea was to show that there is something beyond contracts as classical institutional economics suggests. At the time of the study, the knowledge as well as the number of empirical studies on transaction cost economics and hybrid forms of governance, such as contracts, joint ventures, and so on, was already rather large. The central idea of transaction cost economies, namely that frequency, relation specific investments and uncertainty drive the choice a governance structure along the continuum markets to hierarchies, was widely acknowledged. There is an overwhelming number of studies supporting the main issues of transaction cost economies, while studies presenting results that would contradict transaction cost theory were hardly existing. If scholars criticized the theory, they mainly argued that restricting the governance of interfirm relations to contractual governance was too narrow.

While transaction cost economies is an already well-established theory, the arguments of social embeddedness were well received at that time but not established. Not surprising that the initial article of transaction cost theory (Ronald Coase: 'The nature of the firm') was published in 1937, while the idea of social embeddedness is much younger; one important article was published in 1985 by Mark Granovetter.

One consequence of the relative newness of the concept of social embeddedness is certainly that there is some general common understanding of what is meant by social embeddedness, but as soon as one becomes more specific, many unanswered questions arise. For example, does social embeddedness only refer to current relations or does it also refer to previous and future relations? What is socially embedded? Is the firm socially embedded or the cooperation between two firms? What are the effects of social embeddedness on profit, efficiency, productivity, sales, and so on? Is the performance effect of social embeddedness positive or inverted u-shaped? All these questions show that the concept of social embeddedness is still in a rather early development stage, which offers ample opportunities for qualitative explorative studies.

At the same time, Richard Blundel (2002) has investigated the reproduction on knowledge in English artisanal farmhouse cheesemaking between 1850 and 2000. More specifically, he explores the growth trajectories of two cheesemakers and their embeddedness in business networks, that is their relations to other firms and institutions. Thus, while in the study on R&D cooperations social embeddedness was seen as a rather static concept, Blundel looked at the dynamics of networks to understand how artisanal cheesemakers reproduce their knowledge and withhold the economic pressure of cheesemakers employing modern technologies to produce mass-market cheese at low prices.

## References

Coase, Ronald (1937) 'The nature of the firm', *Economica* 4, pp. 386–405.

Blundel, Richard K. (2002) 'Network evolution and the growth of artisanal firms: a tale of two regional cheesemakers', *Entrepreneurship and Regional Development* 14, 1: pp. 1–30.

Granovetter, Mark S. (1985) 'Economic action and social structure: the problem of embeddedness', *American Journal of Sociology* 91, pp. 481–510.

# Summary

1 A frequently used and important distinction of research studies is quantitative versus qualitative. Which approach you choose will have consequences for your research in terms of the research problems you can investigate and the kind of answers you expect. However, in business research, quantitative as well as qualitative research approaches are appropriate for investigating business research problems. What matters is not the choice between quantitative and qualitative, but the quality of the research design and how well the study is conducted.

2 If the direction of a research project is not clear, it is often wise to follow a two-step research procedure. The first stage is exploratory, aimed at formulating hypotheses and developing the specific research design. The general research process contains three major stages: (i) exploration of the situation, (ii) collection of data, and (iii) analysis and interpretation of results.

3 A research design is the strategy for a study and the plan by which the strategy is to be carried out. It specifies the methods and procedures for the collection, measurement and analysis of data. Unfortunately, there is no simple classification of research designs that covers the variations found in practice. Some major descriptors of designs are:
   ● exploratory versus formalized
   ● observational versus interrogation–communication
   ● experimental versus *ex-post facto*
   ● descriptive versus causal
   ● cross-sectional versus longitudinal
   ● case versus statistical
   ● field versus laboratory versus simulation
   ● subjects perceive no deviations, some deviations or researcher-induced deviations.

4 Exploratory research is appropriate for the total study in topic areas where the developed data are limited. In most other studies, exploration is the first stage of a project, and is used to orient the researcher and the study. The objective of exploration is the development of hypotheses, not testing.

   Formalized studies, including descriptive and causal, are those with substantial structure, specific hypotheses to be tested or research questions to be answered. Descriptive studies are those used to describe phenomena associated with a subject population or to estimate proportions of the population that have certain characteristics.

   Causal studies seek to discover the effect that a variable(s) has on another (or others) or why certain outcomes are obtained. The concept of causality is grounded in the logic of hypothesis testing, which, in turn, produces inductive conclusions. Such conclusions are probabilistic and thus can never be demonstrated with certainty. Current ideas about causality as complex processes improve our understanding of Mill's canons, though we can never know all the relevant information necessary to prove causal linkages beyond doubt.

5 The relationships that occur between two variables may be symmetrical, reciprocal or asymmetrical. Of greatest interest to the research analyst are asymmetrical relationships, which may be classified as any of the following types:

- stimulus–response
- property–disposition
- disposition–behaviour
- property–behaviour.

We test causal hypotheses by seeking to do three things: (i) measure the covariation among variables, (ii) determine the time-order relationships among variables, and (iii) ensure that other factors do not confound the explanatory relationships.

The problems of achieving these aims differ somewhat in experimental and *ex-post facto* studies. Where possible, we try to achieve the ideal of the experimental design with random assignment of subjects, matching of subject characteristics, and manipulation and control of variables. Using these methods and techniques, we measure relationships as accurately and objectively as possible.

## Discussion questions

## Terms in review

1 Distinguish between the following:
   a exploratory and formal studies
   b experimental and *ex-post facto* research designs
   c descriptive and causal studies.
2 Establishing causality is difficult, whether conclusions have been derived inductively or deductively.
   a Explain and elaborate on the implications of this statement.
   b Why is ascribing causality more difficult when conclusions have been reached through induction?
   c Correlation does not imply causation. Illustrate this point with examples from business.
3 Using yourself as the subject, give an example of each of the following asymmetrical relationships:
   a stimulus – response
   b property – disposition
   c disposition – behaviour
   d property – behaviour.
4 Why not use more control variables rather than depend on randomization as the means of controlling extraneous variables?
5 Researchers seek causal relationships by either experimental or *ex-post facto* research designs.
   a In what ways are these two approaches similar?
   b In what ways are they different?

## Making research decisions

6 You have been asked to determine how hospitals prepare and train volunteers. Since you know relatively little about this subject, how will you find out? Be as specific as possible.

7 You are the administrative assistant for a division chief in a large holding company that owns several hotels and theme parks. You and the division chief have just come from the CEO's office, where you were informed that guest complaints related to housekeeping and employee attitude are increasing. Your on-site managers have mentioned some tension among the workers but have not considered it unusual. The CEO and your division chief instruct you to investigate. Suggest at least three different types of research that might be appropriate in this situation.

8 Propose one or more hypotheses for each of the following variable pairs, specifying which is the IV and which is the DV. Then develop the basic hypothesis to include at least one moderating variable or intervening variable.

 a The Index of Consumer Confidence and the business cycle.

 b Level of worker output and closeness of worker supervision.

 c Student GPA and level of effort in a class required by student's major.

## From concept to practice

9 Use the eight design descriptors in Exhibit 5.1 to profile the research described in the Snapshots in this chapter.

## Class discussion

10 Discuss the following provocative statements.

 a Qualitative research is very much like telling stories in the local pub.

 b Quantitative research is a sub-branch of higher mathematics, nice for some whizz-kids, but irrelevant in practice.

 c Explorative research explores phenomena about which we already know a lot.

 d The predictive power of causal studies in the management sciences is so low that their value is close to zero.

# Online *Learning* Centre

## Get started with understanding statistical techniques!

When you have read this chapter, log on to the Online Learning Centre website at ***www.mcgraw-hill.co.uk/textbooks/blumberg*** to explore chapter-by-chapter test questions, additional case studies, a glossary and more online study tools for Business Research Methods.

# Notes

[1] John Van Maanen, James M. Dabbs Jr. and Robert R. Faulkner, *Varieties of Qualitative Research*. Beverly Hills, CA: Sage, 1982, p. 32.

[2] Reprinted with permission of Macmillan Publishing from *Social Research Strategy and Tactics* (2nd edn.), by Bernard S. Phillips, p. 93. Copyright ©1971 by Bernard S. Phillips.

[3] Fred N. Kerlinger, *Foundations of Behavioral Research* (3rd edn.). New York: Holt, Rinehart & Winston, 1986, p. 279.

[4] The complexity of research design tends to confuse students as well as writers. The latter respond by forcing order on the vast array of design types through the use of classification schemes or taxonomies. Generally, this is helpful, but because the world defies neat categorization, this scheme, like others, may either include or exclude too much.

[5] Kerlinger, *Foundations of Behavioral Research*, p. 295.

[6] Abraham Kaplan, *Conduct of Inquiry*, San Francisco: Chandler, 1964, p. 37.

[7] W. Charles Redding, 'Research setting: field studies', in *Methods of Research in Communication*, eds. Philip Emmert and William D. Brooks, Boston: Houghton Mifflin, 1970, pp. 140–2.

[8] Catherine Marshall and Gretchen B. Rossman, *Designing Qualitative Research*. Newbury Park, CA: Sage, 1989, pp. 78–108.

[9] This classification is suggested in Claire Selltiz, Lawrence S. Wrightsman and Stuart W. Cook.

[10] Rick H. Hoyle, *Research Methods in Social Relations* (3rd edn.). New York: Holt, Rinehart & Winston, 1976, pp. 99–101.

[11] A comprehensive and detailed presentation may be found in Richard A. Krueger, *Focus Groups: A Practical Guide for Applied Research* (2nd edn.). Thousand Oaks, CA: Sage, 1994; and David L. Morgan, *Successful Focus Groups: Advancing the State of the Art*. Thousand Oaks, CA: Sage, 1993. See also Thomas L. Greenbaum, 'Focus group spurt predicted for the '90s', *Marketing News* 24(1) (8 January 1990), pp. 21–2.

[12] P. Hawe, D. Degeling and J. Hall, *Evaluating Health Promotion: A Health Worker's Guide*. Artarmon, NSW: MacLennan & Petty, 1990. 'Shoppers speak out in focus groups', *Discount Store News* 36(5) (3 March 1997), pp. 23–6.

[13] Hawe, Degeling and Hall, *Evaluating Health Promotion*, p. 176.

[14] Hubert M. Blalock Jr., *Causal Inferences in Nonexperimental Research*. Chapel Hill: University of North Carolina Press, 1964, p. 5.

[15] As quoted in William J. Goode and Paul K. Hatt, *Methods in Social Research*. New York: McGraw-Hill, 1952, p. 75.

[16] From *Methods in Social Research* by William J. Goode and Paul K. Hatt. Copyright ©1952, McGraw-Hill Book Company. Used with the permission of McGraw-Hill Book Company.

[17] Morris R. Cohen and Ernest Nagel, *An Introduction to Logic and Scientific Method*. New York: Harcourt Brace, 1934, Chapter 13; and Blalock, *Causal Inferences*, p. 14.

[18] R. Carnap, *An Introduction to the Philosophy of Science*. New York: Basic Books, 1966.

[19] Content adapted from Thomas F. Gilbert, *Human Competence*. New York: McGraw-Hill, 1978.

Tabular concept based on Emanuel J. Mason and William J. Bramble, *Understanding and Conducting Research* (2nd edn.). New York: McGraw-Hill, 1989, p. 13.

[20] Mason and Bramble, *Understanding and Conducting Research*, p. 14.

[21] Morris Rosenberg, *The Logic of Survey Analysis*. New York: Basic Books, 1968, p. 3.

# Recommended further reading

**Babbie, Earl R., *The Practice of Social Research* (9th edn.). Belmont, CA: Wadsworth, 2000.** Contains a clear and thorough synopsis of design.

**Bartunek, Jean M. and Myeong-Gu, Seo, 'Qualitative research can add new meaning to quantitative research', *Journal of Organizational Behaviour* 23(2), 2002, pp. 237–42.** The authors explore how a study might have differed if a quantitative instead of a qualitative approach had been used.

**Bryman, Alan and Bell, Emma, *Business Research Methods*. Oxford: Oxford University Press, 2003.** A good textbook on research methods, with a clear emphasis on qualitative methods.

**Creswell, John W., *Qualitative Inquiry and Research Design* (5th edn.). Thousand Oaks, CA: Sage Publishing, 1997.** A creative and comprehensive work on qualitative research methods.

**Gill, J. and P. Johnson, *Research Methods for Managers* (3rd edn.). Thousand Oaks, CA: Sage, 2002.** Chapters 3, 9 and 10 discuss different research approaches by assessing the philosophical and theoretical assumptions of each approach.

**Krathwohl, David R., *Social and Behavioral Science Research: A New Framework for Conceptualizing, Implementing, and Evaluating Research Studies*. San Francisco: Jossey-Bass, 1985.** Chapter 9, on causality, is insightful, well reasoned and highly recommended.

**Mason, Emanuel J. and Bramble, William J., *Understanding and Conducting Research* (2nd edn.). New York: McGraw-Hill, 1989.** Chapter 1 has an excellent section on causation; Chapter 2 provides an alternative classification of the types of research.

**Morgan, David L. and Kruger Richard A. (eds.), *The Focus Group Kit*. Thousand Oaks, CA: Sage, 1997.** A six-volume set including an overview guidebook, planning, developing questions, moderating, involving community members, and analysing results.

**Oakshott, Lee, *Essential Quantitative Methods for Business, Management and Finance*. London: Palgrave Macmillan, 2001.** One of the best-selling books on quantitative methods in the UK.

**Silverman, David, *Doing Qualitative Research*, Thousand Oaks, CA: Sage, 1999.** Another of the best-selling books on qualitative research in the UK.

**Strauss, Anselm and Corbin, Juliet, *Basics of Qualitative Research* (2nd edn.). Thousand Oaks, CA: Sage, 1998.** A step-by-step guide with particularly useful sections on coding procedures.

# Chapter 6

# Sampling strategies

*From one case to the whole population*

## Chapter contents

## LEARNING OBJECTIVES

When you have read this chapter, you should understand:

- ☑ the importance of the unit of analysis
- ☑ why case studies are a very useful research approach and how they are conducted
- ☑ the two premises on which sampling theory is based
- ☑ the characteristics of accuracy and precision for measuring sample validity
- ☑ the two main categories of sampling techniques and their varieties
- ☑ the six questions that must be answered to develop a sampling plan
- ☑ the critical issues and formulas that determine the appropriate sample size.

# 6.1 Unit of analysis

An important step in designing research is the decision on the **unit of analysis**. The unit of analysis describes the level at which the research is performed and which objects are researched. People or individuals are a common unit of analysis. However, in business research we often apply other units of analysis than people, individuals or employees. Frequently occurring examples of other units of analysis at a 'higher' level than people are organizations, divisions, departments or more general groups. At a 'lower' level, we can think of management decisions, transactions or contracts as units of analysis.

It is important to note, however, that the unit of analysis and the kind of respondent the researcher questions to obtain information are not the same thing. For example, in a study of the internationalization strategies of medium-sized companies we might interview the general managers of such companies, but the unit of analysis is the company and not the general manager. Similarly, we might question heads of purchasing departments about a firm's contracts with its suppliers. Although we question heads of purchasing departments, the unit of analysis is the contract governing the relationship between the firms and the supplier.

Thinking carefully about a study's unit of analysis is an important way of avoiding the difficulties and errors that may occur later in problem definition and research design; this is because the unit of analysis is closely linked to all parts of the research process. When researchers define the research problem, they already need to be thinking about the unit of analysis. Is it the entire organization, or specific departments, work groups, employees or decisions? The unit of analysis is derived from the research question. However, one research question often allows for more than one unit of analysis, so the researcher has to choose.

Read through the two examples of research questions provided below.

**1. Why do the self-employment rates differ so much in the countries of the EU?**
At first sight the appropriate unit of analysis for this research question seems obvious. It should be countries, as we want to compare the self-employment rate of different countries. Choosing countries is not a bad idea, but whether it is really a good choice depends largely on which possible reasons we would like to investigate as explanations for the differing self-employment rates. Are the explanations we advance also at the unit level of countries? If we want to investigate whether differences in the legal system, the national culture or the industry structure of the economy do affect the self-employment rate, countries is a good choice as unit of analysis. If our explanation of the differing rates in self-employment is more rooted in individuals (e.g. differences in risk attitude or how entrepreneurs cope with difficulties in the start-up phase), it is better to use individuals or the firms they have started as the unit of analysis.

**2. What are the effects of pay systems on an employee's job satisfaction?**
One can derive two units of analysis from this question. First, the pay system, which might apply to the whole company or to certain work groups within the company, although it's unlikely that the company has a different pay system for every employee. Second, the question mentions the job satisfaction of the employee, which is at the level of the employee. Which unit of analysis would you choose? The entire organization, work groups or employees? There is no straightforward answer to this question – the choice of unit of analysis depends very much on the research objectives and has serious implications for further elements of the research design.

Choosing the entire organization would require that the data are collected in many organizations. Furthermore, we would need to ensure that all other variables (e.g. job satisfaction) are also measured at the organizational level, that is we would need a kind of mean job satisfaction for every organization. To obtain such a mean job satisfaction we would either have to measure the job satisfaction of a representative group of employees in each organization ourselves or we would need to have secondary information, say from previous surveys on job satisfaction among employees in the selected organizations. Further, we would have to ensure that employees within one organization are paid according to the same pay systems. Thus, the choice of entire organizations as unit of analysis entails a more complex and more costly research design. However, entire organizations as unit of analysis would also allow us to expand our research problem. For example, we could investigate whether other organizational characteristics, such as, say, centralization of decision-making have a more significant effect on job satisfaction than pay systems. We could also research whether differences in pay systems and resulting differences in job satisfaction also lead to differences in organizational performance.

Alternatively, we could use work groups as unit of analysis. Again we would have to ensure that just one pay system applies to a work group. We would also need information on the job satisfaction of each work group. Choosing work groups as unit of analysis is likely to have the following implications for the research design.

- Depending on the number of work groups and applied pay systems in a firm, we may still need to investigate more than one organization to achieve a sufficient number of work groups (sample size).
- To obtain a sound measurement of job satisfaction it may be necessary to question individual employees in each work group selected.

Finally, we could also use employee as unit of analysis. For example, we could survey people who are currently employed in paid labour and ask them about their job satisfaction and which system their employer uses to determine their pay. In such a design, people employed at very different organizations will be interviewed. In this design we need to ensure that differences in job satisfaction are indeed caused by differences in the payment system and not by other differences between these organizations, in areas such as labour conditions, type of company, level of payments, and so on. Furthermore, as we only ask the employees and not the firms, our assessment of the payment systems is purely based on the respondent's answers to our questions about the system. However, what happens if respondents do not know the ins and outs of the payment system used in their company?

The examples above demonstrate that the choice of unit of analysis is strongly related to the following three questions.

## 1. What Is our research problem and what do we really want to answer?
Taking the second example, on the relationship between payment systems and job satisfaction, we need to decide whether we are more interested in job satisfaction and how a firm can improve the satisfaction of its employees, or whether we are more interested in finding out about the effects of different payment systems and which factors a firm needs to take into account when designing an optimal payment system.

**2. What do we need to measure to answer our research problem?**

Answering this question also allows us to define the unit of analysis. First, we identify the information needed to answer the research problem, that is what variables do we need? Then, we have to determine which objects (decisions, individuals, organizations, etc.) are described by the variables we want to measure.

**3. What do we want to do with the results of the study/whom do we address in our conclusions?**

In the first example, it makes a difference whether our study is part of policy advice for a government or whether its results should help entrepreneurs. In the former case, the unit of analysis is countries and in the latter entrepreneurs.

## 6.2 The nature of sampling

Before we discuss the different **sampling** issues in detail, please read through the experience of Erik van de Duivel, who works for the Belgian Tourist Authority, which is presented in the accompanying Snapshot. Suppose that, in this case, the unit of analysis is individuals, although you could argue that decisions on holidays are made at the household level and not at the individual level.

## Erik van de Duivel and international holidaymakers

The Belgian Tourist Authority wants to promote the Belgian coast as a vacation destination for short breaks and longer holidays to people from its neighbouring countries – France, Germany, the Netherlands and the UK. An important part of this promotional campaign is a survey among (potential) visitors from these four countries. The survey's aims include an assessment of the general image of the Belgian coast as a vacation destination as well as the respondents' specific opinion on the price and quality of the accommodation on offer, restaurants, shopping and sport facilities.

Erik van de Duivel is in charge of this survey and asks himself how he should approach visitors from these countries. He thinks about distributing Dutch, English, French and German versions of the questionnaires, along with a nice pencil, among the many people spending the day on the terraces of restaurants and cafés along the beach. Everybody who fills in a questionnaire and returns it to him or one of his assistants can keep the nice pencil, which is in the colours of the Belgian flag. To prepare the survey he has made several appointments with people working in the tourism industry on the Belgian coast.

In the morning, Erik meets Justine de Clerck, who works at the Tourist Information Office in Knokke, a major resort on the Belgian coast. He tells her that he would like to start the data-collection at the end of April/beginning of May, and that this should take about two weeks. Justine tells him that his idea sounds great and that never before has someone tried to find out what the visitors think, and in such a systematic way. However, she expresses the hope that the sun will shine during his collection days, as if it does not many visitors will plan day trips to nearby towns of Antwerp, Brugge and Gent instead. She also tells him that she expects that, at the end of April/beginning of May, there will be many British and Dutch tourists, but relatively few Germans and French. These two countries have a public holiday during this period: the Dutch celebrate their Queen's birthday on 30 April and Deliberation Day on 5 May; the British have a bank holiday on 3 May. The German and French people, on the other hand, cannot use a public holiday to have a long weekend, because Labour Day on 1 May and the French celebration on 8 May fall on Saturdays. Finally, she adds that at this time of year most visitors only visit for a short break (i.e. fewer than five days), while in the summer months (July and August) many people, especially families, spend two or three weeks of their main vacation here.

Justine's information is valuable to Erik, but what should he do? Should he collect information one week in May and one week in July, even though this would delay the completion of his research for two months? If he only collects data in May, how can he ensure that his sample contains sufficient German and French respondents? Before he can think more deeply about this question, he has an appointment with Theo Verbeeck, the owner of a well-known seafood restaurant at the beach. Theo says that most restaurant owners would not object to Erik conducting the survey among guests on their premises, but that he must inform the restaurant owners and managers beforehand. Further, he mentions that the Belgian coast plays host to many holidaymakers who rarely spend money in the restaurants and pubs there. In particular, families with children rent holiday homes, prepare most of their own food and rarely visit restaurants, although they are more likely to frequent the local snack bars offering world-famous Belgian fries.

The next day, Erik van de Duivel returned to his office in Brussels, and thought again about the goals of the image campaign for the Belgian coast. The campaign's main goal is to achieve an increase in the number of nights visitors spend at the coast. Erik remembers a slide presentation given by Tom Dellaert, a professor of marketing in the hospitality industry. One slide mentioned three approaches to increasing the number of 'visitor nights':

1  convince current visitors to stay longer
2  convince current visitors to return more often
3  convince new visitors to give the Belgian coast a try.

Interviewing visitors on the restaurant terraces along the beach would tell him how much current visitors like the Belgian coast and what they would like to see change, but how can he get information on new visitors, who have never visited the Belgian coast before? How can he approach them? When he talks about this issue with his colleague, Miranda Appels, she tells him that she recently visited the website of the dairy company Countrylove, to check out some of the lovely recipes posted there. When she clicked on to the recipe section a window popped up inviting her to participate in a consumer survey that promised the chance to win some great prizes, ranging from picnic baskets to holidays in France. Miranda suggests that it might be worth conducting an Internet survey like this on their own website to draw in those people who have never visited the Belgian coast, but do have an interest in Belgium. Why else would they surf the website of the Belgian Tourist Authority?

Most people intuitively understand the idea of sampling. One taste of a drink tells us whether it is sweet or sour. If we select a few employment records out of a complete set, we usually assume our selection reflects the characteristics of the full set. If some of our staff members favour a flexible work schedule, we infer that others will too. These examples vary in their representativeness, but each is a sample.

The basic idea of sampling is that by selecting some of the elements in a population, we may draw conclusions about the entire population. A **population element** is the subject on which the measurement is being taken. It is the unit of study, as explained above. A **population** is the total collection of elements about which we wish to make some inferences. All office workers in the firm compose a 'population of interest'; all 4000 files define a population of interest. A **census** is a count of all the elements in a population. If 4000 files define the population, a census would obtain information from every one of them.

## Why sample?

There are several compelling reasons for sampling, including:

- lower cost
- greater accuracy of results
- greater speed of data-collection
- availability of population elements.

We now look at each of these in turn.

### Lower cost

The economic advantages of taking a sample rather than conducting a census are massive. Consider the cost of conducting a census. For example, the cost of the British census in 2001 was about £255 million (€387 million).[1] Is it any wonder that researchers in all types of organization ask, 'Why should we spend thousands of euros interviewing all 4000 employees in our company if we can find out what we need to know by asking only a few hundred?'

### Greater accuracy of results

Deming argues that the quality of a study is often better with sampling than with a census. He suggests that 'Sampling possesses the possibility of better interviewing [testing], more thorough investigation of missing, wrong or suspicious information, better supervision, and better processing than is possible with complete coverage.'[2] Research findings substantiate this opinion. More than 90 per cent of the total survey error in one study was from non-sampling sources and only 10 per cent or less was from random sampling error.[3] The US Bureau of the Census shows its confidence in sampling by taking sample surveys to check the accuracy of its census. However, while it is politically correct to take a census of the population, we know that segments of the population are seriously under-counted.

### Greater speed of data-collection

Sampling's speed of execution reduces the time between the recognition of a need for information and the availability of that information. If it takes a clothing company until autumn to receive the

# How complete is a census?

In the UK, the first official census was held on 10 March 1801, and revealed that its population was then nine million. This was a much more precise estimate than previous ones, which had ranged between eight and eleven million. But, how sure can the census takers be that they have really counted every inhabitant once? Hence, are census data really the perfect reflection of the population? For example, overall form-returning rates for England and Wales in the 2001 (1991) census were 94 per cent (96 per cent), and the figure was even worse in inner London with a response rate of 78 per cent in 2001 and 88 per cent in 1991.

This non-response is a serious threat to the representativity of the census, which is of utmost importance as census data are used in many areas of public policy: for example, they are used to determine the funding local authorities are entitled to receive from government. As the census takers expected an increase in non-responses in 2001, they developed a new strategy known as 'One Number Census' (ONC) to obtain a representation of the whole population. The central idea of this strategy is to complement the census with a follow-up survey, the 'Census Coverage Survey' (CCS), which consisted of a sample of 320,000 households who were questioned in face-to-face interviews. The Census Coverage Survey was conducted independently of the census, that is the CCS interviewers had no access to census data, in 16,000 postcode areas, achieving an overall response rate of 91 per cent.

Combining the results of the census and the CCS results in a very high precision ±0.2 per cent (i.e. the error margin for the whole population is 104,000 people). For local authority areas, this error margin varies from 6.1 per cent in Luton to 0.6 per cent in Dudley, East Dorset, Redcar and Cleveland. More importantly, the idea of checking the census data with large-scale survey data allowed an estimate of the census's precision to be made for the first time.

The issues of non-response and coverage are still at the heart of census researchers' concerns, and in 2011, when the next census is taken, a completely new methodology for collecting data will be applied. Instead of using a large field force to deliver and collect forms, the forms will be posted after several measures have been taken to obtain a complete database of current addresses.

## References and further reading

Office for National Statistics, *The 2011 Census: A Proposed Design for England and Wales.* Discussion paper, 2003.

Office for National Statistics (http://www.statistics.gov.uk/census2001).

Teague, Andy 'New methodologies for the 2001 Census in England and Wales', *International Journal of Social Research Methodology* 3, 2000, pp. 245–55.

first results of a survey among retailers about how they perceived the company's latest spring collection, it will be too late for any adjustments and the information from the survey will be useless. Furthermore, the larger the sample size, the longer the data-collection itself will take. Long collection periods can cause biases as, within the period, events might occur that influence respondents' answer behaviour (see Chapters 7 and 12). Political opinion polls are a good example of the latter problem. In particular, in the last few months before an election voters are very sensitive.

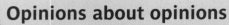

# Opinions about opinions

On 26 June 2006, the Dutch government, under Prime Minister Balkenende, known as 'cabinet Balkenende III' fell but remained in charge of the government as a new general election was already planned for 26 November 2006. Election races are good times for opinion polls and surveys to set questions on which party or person you are going to vote for belong to the most well-known public surveys. Before the 2006 general election in the Netherlands, three different research agencies polled the voting behaviour of the Dutch population every week and the outcomes of their polls were headline news for three months. Moreover, journalists frequently asked politicians to comment on the results. Thus, the polls became part of the political discussion.

In election polls particularly, history has shown famous examples of successes and failures to predict the outcome of elections. One of the most famous is the 1948 US presidential race between Harry S. Truman (Democrat) and Thomas E. Dewey (Republican). Almost all opinion polls predicted that Dewey would win the election. The confidence in Dewey's victory was so strong that the *Chicago Tribune* even printed 'Dewey defeats Truman' as a headline before the official result was known. Truman became the 33rd president of the USA when he gained more than two million votes than Dewey. Later it turned out that many opinion polls were based on telephone surveys and in 1948 Republican voters were much more likely to own a telephone.

From 1948 in the USA to 2006 in the Netherlands – again an election year and three agencies polled the opinions of the Dutch voting population, namely Interview-NSS, Maurice de Hond (peil.nl) and TNS-NIPO. What is interesting to observe is that each agency has a different approach. TNS-NIPO polls every day of the week and calculates a weekly average, while Interview-NSS and Maurice de Hond poll on a specific day in the week. The biggest difference is, however, that Interview-NSS and TNS-NIPO telephone a new set of random landline telephone numbers every week, while Maurice de Hond uses an Internet panel that everybody can subscribe to if they want. Thus, the sample of de Hond is not random and certainly biased. Is the availability of a computer in 2006 similar to the availability of a telephone in 1948?

You should not be so naïve as to believe that the percentage of votes for each party reported by polling organizations is based on the frequency of the answers to the question 'Which party would you vote for if we had a general election now?' Thus, if opinion polls report that the Liberal party will get 22 per cent of the vote, that does not mean that 22 per cent of the respondents answered 'Liberal party' to the above question. The process from the raw data to the actual reported figure is much more complex. Mori, a British polling organization, is well known for their strategy to consider only those respondents who answer that they are likely going to vote. Other polling organizations use complex weighting schemes to correct for difference in actual voting among different parties, because Conservative voters are more likely to actually vote than Labour voters. In Germany, for example, it is said that sunshine on election day is good for the Social Democrats because fewer of their voters stay home if the sun shines, while Conservative voters walk to the voting booth regardless of the weather. Another important factor is that voters who intend to vote for an extreme party on the left or right are less likely to disclose their choice to interviewers, creating a systematic underestimation of more extreme parties.

Still what you see in Exhibit 6.1 is surprising, as the objective of all polling organizations is to give a correct prediction of how many seats a party would gain during the elections. The

Dutch parliament has 150 seats. The two largest parties were the CDA (Conservative) Prime Minister Jan-Peter Balkenende as candidate for the prime minister and the PvdA (Labour) with Wouter Bos as candidate for the prime minister. The solid lines represent the weekly predictions of Interview-NSS, the dashed lines the predictions of Maurice de Hond and the dotted lines the predictions of TNS-NIPO. How do you explain why the polling organizations differ so much in their weekly predictions?

The final outcome of the elections was that the CDA won 41 seats and the PvdA 33 seats. A remarkable outcome as neither of the two parties was able to build a majority with smaller parties nor did the two largest parties together reach the 76 seats. On 22 February 2007 a new cabinet under Prime Minister Balkenende was officially instated with ministers from the CDA, PvdA and the CU (a small party that bases its political beliefs on Christian values).

A few days after the election, Interview-NSS published a press release stating that 'they were delighted about the congratulations of Maurice de Hond and TNS-NIPO, but that they also had a kind of Balkenende feeling – although you lose you are still the biggest'. This is remarkable considering the election outcome. The Interview-NSS polls assigned 14 seats (out of 150) incorrectly, that is an error of 10 per cent. The Maurice de Hond polls assigned 16 seats incorrectly and the TNS-NIPO polls even as many as 20 seats. Have you thought about why Maurice de Hond with the self-selected Internet panel did not score worse? If even the opinion polls based on a rather large sample differ so much with respect to the answer to an easily understandable question, how much can we trust the results of polls on more complex questions?

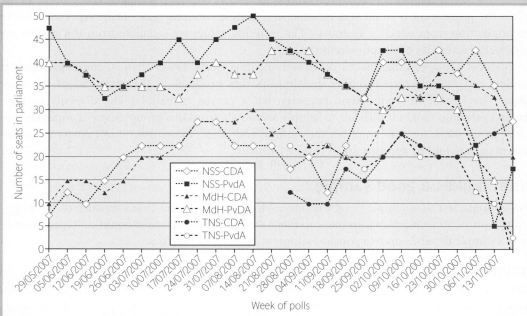

**Exhibit 6.1** Number of seats obtained by CDA (Conservative) and PVdA (Labour) according to the polls of Interview-NSS (NSS) and Maurice de Hond (MdH) and TNS-NIPO (INS) between 29 May 2007 and 13 November 2007.

# References and further reading

www.mori.com
www.peil.nl (website Maurice de Hond)
www.politiekbarometer.nl (website Interview-NSS)
www.tns-nipo.com

### Availability of population elements

Some situations require sampling. When we test the breaking strength of materials, we must destroy them; a census of this type would, therefore, mean complete destruction of all materials. Sampling is also the only process possible if a population is infinite.

## 6.3  Sample versus census

The advantages of sampling over census studies are less compelling when the population is small and the variability within the population high. Two conditions are appropriate for a census study:

1  feasible when the population is small

2  necessary when the elements are quite different from each other.[4]

When the population is small and variable, any sample we draw may not be representative of the population from which it is drawn. The resulting values we calculate from the sample are incorrect as estimates of the population values.

Consider European manufacturers of stereo components. Fewer than 50 companies design, develop and manufacture amplifier and loudspeaker products at the high end of the price range. The size of this population suggests that a census is feasible. The diversity of their product offerings makes it difficult to sample accurately from this group. Some companies specialize in speakers, some in amplifier technology, and others in compact disc transports. In this case, then, it would be appropriate to choose a census.

### What makes a good sample?

The ultimate test of a sample design is how well it represents the characteristics of the population it purports to represent. In measurement terms, the sample must be valid. Representativity of a sample depends on two considerations: accuracy and precision.

### Accuracy

Accuracy is the degree to which bias is absent from the sample. When the sample is drawn properly, some sample elements underestimate the population values being studied and others overestimate them. Variations in these values offset each other; this counteraction results in a sample value that is generally close to the population value. For these offsetting effects to occur, however, there must be sufficient elements in the sample, and they must be drawn in a way that favours neither overestimation nor underestimation.

An accurate (unbiased) sample is one in which the underestimators and the overestimators are balanced among the members of the sample. There is no **systematic variance** with an accurate sample. Systematic variance has been defined as 'the variation in measures due to some known or unknown influences that 'cause' the scores to lean in one direction more than another'.[5] Homes on the corner of a block, for example, are often larger and more valuable than those within a block. Thus, a sample that selects corner homes only will cause us to overestimate house values in an area. Erik van Duivel (see the Snapshot on p. 226) learned that the season of the year in which a survey is conducted dramatically could reduce the accuracy and representativity of a sample among foreign holidaymakers.

Even the large size of some samples cannot counteract systematic bias. The classic example of a sample with systematic variance was the *Literary Digest* presidential election poll in 1936, in which more than 2 million people participated. The poll predicted that Alfred Landon would defeat Franklin Roosevelt for the presidency of the USA. Yes, your memory is correct: there has never been a US president named Alfred Landon. It was discovered later that the poll had drawn its sample from telephone owners who were in the middle and upper classes – at the time, bastions of the Republican Party – while Roosevelt appealed to the much larger working class, who didn't own telephones and typically voted for the Democratic Party candidate.

### Precision

A second criterion of a good sample design is precision of estimate. No sample will fully represent its population in all respects. The numerical descriptors that describe samples may be expected to differ from those that describe populations because of random fluctuations inherent in the sampling process. This is called sampling error and reflects the influence of chance in drawing sample members. Sampling error is what is left after all known sources of systematic variance have been accounted for. In theory, sampling error consists of random fluctuations only, although some unknown systematic variance may be included when too many or too few sample elements possess a particular characteristic.

Precision is measured by the standard error of estimate, a type of standard deviation measurement; the smaller the standard error of estimate, the greater the precision of the sample. The ideal sample design produces a small standard error of estimate. However, not all types of sample design provide estimates of precision, and samples of the same size can produce different amounts of error variance.

## 6.4 Types of sample design

The researcher makes several decisions when designing a sample. These are represented in Exhibit 6.2. The sampling decisions flow from two decisions made in the formation of the management research question hierarchy: the nature of the management question and the specific investigative questions that evolve from the research question.

A variety of sampling techniques is available. The one the researcher should select depends on the requirements of the project, its objectives and the funds available. In the discussion that follows, we will use two examples:

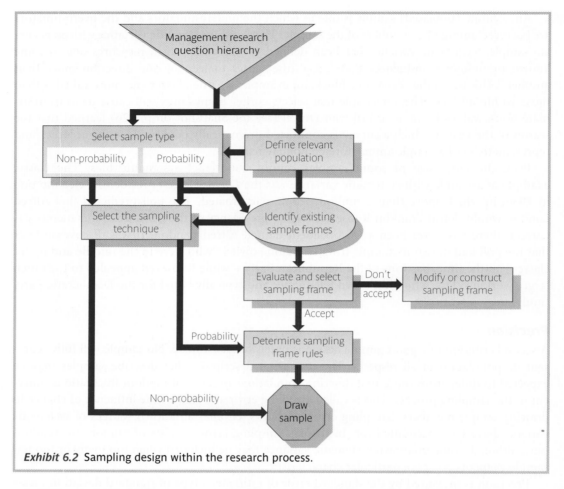

*Exhibit 6.2* Sampling design within the research process.

1 Erik van de Duivel's survey among international holidaymakers at the Belgian coast (see Snapshot on p. 226)

2 a study of the feasibility of starting a dining club near the campus of Lake University.

The researchers at Lake University are exploring the feasibility of creating a dining club, whose facilities would be available on a membership basis. To launch this venture, they will need to make a substantial investment. Research will allow them to reduce many risks. Thus, the research question is 'Would a membership dining club be a viable enterprise?' Some investigative questions that flow from the research question include the following.

1 Who would patronize the club and on what basis?

2 How many would join the club under various membership and fee arrangements?

3 How much would the average member spend per month?

4 What days would be most popular?

5 What menu and service formats would be most desirable?

| Element selection | Representation basis | |
|---|---|---|
| | **Probability** | **Non-probability** |
| Unrestricted<br>Restricted | Simple random<br>Complex random<br>Systematic<br>Cluster<br>Stratified<br>Double | Convenience<br>Purposive<br>Judgement<br>Quota<br>Snowball |

*Exhibit 6.3* Types of sampling designs.

**6** What lunch times would be most popular?

**7** Given the proposed price levels, how often per month would each member have lunch or dinner?

**8** What percentage of the people in the population say that they would join the club, based on the projected rates and services?

We will use the last three investigative questions as examples, and focus specifically on questions 7 and 8 in assessing the project's risks. First, we will digress a little to look at other information and examples of sample design, coming back to Lake University in the next section.

In decisions to do with sample design, the representation basis and the element-selection techniques, as shown in Exhibit 6.3, classify the different approaches.

## Representation

The members of a sample are selected on a probability basis or by another means. **Probability sampling** is based on the concept of random selection – a controlled procedure which ensures that each population element is given a known non-zero chance of selection.

In contrast, **non-probability sampling** is arbitrary (non-random) and subjective. Each member does not have a known non-zero chance of being included. Allowing interviewers to choose sample elements 'at random' (meaning 'as they wish' or 'wherever they find them') is not random sampling. Only probability samples provide estimates of precision. While we are not told how Erik van de Duivel will select respondents from the people having a drink on a terrace along the beach, it is clear that he has not used probability sampling techniques.

## Element selection

Whether the elements are selected individually and directly from the population – viewed as a single pool – or when additional controls are imposed, element selection may also classify samples. If each sample element is drawn individually from the population at large, it is an unrestricted sample. Restricted sampling covers all other forms of sampling.

Selecting a random sample is accomplished with the aid of computer software, a table of random numbers or a calculator with a random number generator. Drawing slips out of a hat or ping-pong balls from a drum serves as an alternative if every element in the **sampling frame** has an equal chance of selection. Mixing the slips (or balls) and returning them between every selection ensures that every element is just as likely to be selected as any other.

A table of random numbers (such as Appendix E, Exhibit E.10) is a practical solution when no software program is available. Random number tables contain digits that have no systematic organization. Whether you look at rows, columns or diagonals, you will find neither sequence nor order. Exhibit E.10 in Appendix E is arranged into 10 columns of five-digit strings, but this is solely for readability.

Assume the researchers want a special sample from a population of 95 elements. How will the researcher begin?

1  Assign each element within the sampling frame a unique number from 01 to 95.

2  Identify a random start from the random number table (drop a pencil point first on to the table with closed eyes. Let's say the pencil dot lands on the eighth column from the left and 10 numbers down from the top of Exhibit E.10, marking the five digits 05067).

3  Determine how the digits in the random number table will be assigned to the sampling frame to choose the specified sample size (researchers agree to read the first two digits in this column downwards until 10 are selected).

4  Select the sample elements from the sampling frame (05, 27, 69, 94, 18, 61, 36, 85, 71 and 83) using the above process. The digit 94 appeared twice and the second instance was omitted; 00 was omitted because the sampling frame started with 01.

Other approaches to selecting digits are endless: horizontally right to left, bottom to top, diagonally across columns, and so on. Computer selection of a simple random sample will be more efficient for larger projects.

*Exhibit 6.4* How to choose a random sample.

## Probability sampling

The unrestricted, **simple random sample** is the simplest form of probability sampling. Since all probability samples must provide a known non-zero chance of selection for each population element, the simple random sample is considered a special case in which each population element has a known and equal chance of selection. In this section, we use the simple random sample to build a foundation for understanding sampling procedures and choosing probability samples. Exhibit 6.4 provides an overview of the steps involved in choosing a random sample.

## 6.5  Steps in sampling design

There are several decisions to be made in securing a sample. Each requires unique information. While the questions presented here are sequential, an answer to one question often forces a revision to an earlier one. In this section we consider the following questions.

1  What is the relevant population?

2  What are the parameters of interest?

3  What is the sampling frame?

4  What is the type of sample?

5  What size sample is needed?

6  How much will it cost?

## What is the relevant population?

The definition of the population may be apparent from the management problem or the research question(s), but often it is not. Is the population for the dining club study at Lake University defined as 'full-time day students on the main campus of Lake University'? Or should the population include 'all persons employed at Lake University'? Or should townspeople who live in the neighbourhood be included? Without knowing the target market chosen for the new venture, it is not obvious which of these is the appropriate sampling population.

There may also be confusion about whether the population consists of individuals, households or families, or a combination of these. If a communication study needs to measure income, then the definition of the population element as individual or household can make quite a difference. In an observation study, a sample population might be non-personal: displays within a store or any ATM a bank owns or all single-family residential properties in a community. Good operational definitions are crucial in choosing the relevant population.

Assume the Lake University dining club is to be solely for the students and employees on the main campus. The researchers might define the population as 'all currently enrolled students and employees on the main campus of Lake University'. However, this does not include family members. They may want to revise the definition to make it 'current students and employees of Lake University, main campus, and their families'.

In the non-probability sample, Erik van de Duivel seems to have defined his relevant population as Dutch, British, French and German visitors. He presumes that he has an equal need to investigate the needs of holidaymakers who regularly spend their holidays at the Belgian coast and those who come infrequently or even those who have never visited the Belgian coast before. The regular visitors he can reach easily by distributing questionnaires in the restaurants and cafes along the beach; he is certain to miss those people who have not yet visited the Belgian coast, but who might still be an important target group for future promotion campaigns.

## What are the parameters of interest?

**Population parameters** are summary descriptors (e.g. incidence proportion, mean, variance) of variables of interest in the population. **Sample statistics** are descriptors of the relevant variables computed from sample data. Sample statistics are used as estimators of population parameters. The sample statistics are the basis of our inferences about the population. Depending on how measurement questions are phrased, each may collect a different type of data (see Exhibit 6.5). Each different type of data also generates different sample statistics. Data types are discussed in greater detail in Chapter 5.

| Parameter of interest | Type of data | Example scale |
|---|---|---|
| Attendance at a special event | Nominal | Participation in a promotion (yes, no) |
| Percentage of patrons who order their steak cooked rare | Ordinal | How meat is cooked (well done, medium, rare) |
| Mean temperature of ideal vacation destination | Interval | Temperature in degrees |
| Average number of store visits per month | Ratio | Actual number of store visits |

*Exhibit 6.5* Parameter of interest and type of data.

When the variables of interest in the study are measured on interval or ratio scales, we use the sample mean to estimate the population mean and the sample standard deviation to estimate the population standard deviation. Asking Lake University affiliates to reveal their frequency of eating on or near campus (less than five times per week, greater than five but less than ten times per week or greater than ten times per week) would provide an interval data estimator.

When the variables of interest are measured on nominal or ordinal scales, we use the sample proportion of incidence to estimate the population proportion and the $pq$ to estimate the population variance ($pq$ is the product term of the population proportion $p$ and $q$, which equals $1 - p$; if the population proportion $p$ is 0.5, $q$ is also $0.5 = 1 - 0.5$ and $pq$ equals $0.25 = 0.5 \times 0.5$; if $p$ is below or above 0.5, $pq$ is smaller than 0.25; see also the Snapshot on research 3 for further explanation). The **population proportion of incidence** 'is equal to the number of elements in the population belonging to the category of interest, divided by the total number of elements in the population'.[6]

Proportion measures are necessary for nominal data and are widely used for other measures too. The most frequent proportion measure is the percentage. In the Lake University study, examples of nominal data are the proportion of a population that expresses interest in joining the club (e.g. 30 per cent; therefore p is equal to .3 and $q$, those not interested, equals .7) or the proportion of married students who report that they now eat in restaurants at least five times a month. The Belgian Tourist Authority tries to examine which proportion of holidaymakers has visited the Belgian coast already in the two previous years and which proportion plans to return in the next year. These measures would result in nominal data. Exhibit 6.6 indicates population parameters of interest for our two example studies. We discuss proportion estimators in more detail later in this chapter.

There may also be important sub-groups in the population about whom we would like to make estimates. For example, we might want to draw conclusions about the extent of dining club use that could be expected from married students versus single students, residential students versus commuter students, and so on. Such questions have a strong impact on the nature of the sampling frame we accept, the design of the sample, and its size. Erik van de Duivel should be more interested in reaching infrequent rather than regular international visitors.

| Example | Population parameter of interest (type data) | Scale |
|---|---|---|
| Belgian coast | Frequency of previous holidays at the Belgian coast (interval) | More than 5 times, 3 to 5 times, once or twice, none |
| | Proportion of French, German and British tourists (nominal) | Actual percentage |
| Lake University | Frequency of eating on or near the campus within seven days (ratio data) | Actual eating experience |
| | Proportion of students/employees expressing interest (nominal data) | Actual percentage interest |

Exhibit 6.6 Sample population parameters.

# What is the sampling frame?

The sampling frame is closely related to the population. It is the list of elements from which the sample is actually drawn. Ideally, it is a complete and correct list of population members only. As a practical matter, however, the sampling frame often differs from the theoretical population.

For the dining club study, the Lake University directory would be the logical first choice as a sampling frame. Directories are usually accurate when published in the autumn, but suppose the study is being done in the spring. The directory will contain errors and omissions because some people will have withdrawn or left since the directory was published, while others will have enrolled or been hired. Usually university directories don't mention the families of students or employees.

Just how much inaccuracy one can tolerate in choosing a sampling frame is a matter of judgement. You might use the directory anyway, ignoring the fact that it is not a fully accurate list. However, if the directory is a year old, the amount of error might be unacceptable. One way to make the sampling frame for the Lake University study more representative of the population would be to secure a supplemental list of the new students and employees, as well as a list of the withdrawals and terminations from Lake University's registrar and human resources databases. You could then add and delete information from the original directory. Or, if privacy policies permit, you might just request a current listing from each of these offices and use these lists as your sampling frame.

A greater distortion would be introduced if a branch campus population were included in the Lake University directory. This would be an example of a too inclusive frame – that is, a frame that includes many elements other than the ones in which we are interested. A university directory that includes faculty and staff retirees is another example of a too inclusive sampling frame.

Often you have to accept a sampling frame that includes people or cases beyond those in whom you are interested. You may have to use a telephone directory to draw a sample of

## How much will it cost?

Cost considerations influence decisions about the size and type of sample, and also the data-collection methods. Almost all studies have some budgetary constraints, and this may encourage a researcher to use a non-probability sample. Probability sample surveys incur list costs for sample frames, call-back costs, and a variety of other costs that are not necessary when more haphazard or arbitrary methods are used. But when the data-collection method is changed, the amount and type of data that can be obtained also change. Note the effect of a €2000 budget on sampling considerations.

- Simple random sampling: €25 per interview; 80 completed interviews.
- Geographic cluster sampling: €20 per interview; 100 completed interviews.
- Self-administered questionnaire: €12 per respondent; 167 completed instruments.
- Telephone interviews: €10 per respondent; 200 completed interviews.[8]

Opening a dining club at Lake University is a major investment and hence a more careful but also more costly sampling design is justified. The research by the Belgian Tourist Authority to improve its promotional campaign will hopefully be beneficial to all tourism-related businesses at the Belgian coast. However, the Tourist Authority itself only benefits indirectly from an increase in visitors. In this case any spend on the research is not available later for the promotional campaign.

# 6.6 Complex probability sampling

Simple random sampling is often impractical. Reasons for this include the following.

- It requires a population list (sampling frame) that is often not available.
- It fails to use all the information about a population, thus resulting in a design that may be wasteful.
- It may be expensive to implement in terms of both time and money.

These problems have led to the development of alternative designs that are superior to the simple random design in their statistical and/or economic efficiency.

A more efficient sample in a statistical sense is one that provides a given precision (**standard error of the mean** or proportion) with a smaller sample size. A sample that is economically more efficient is one that provides a desired precision at a lower monetary cost. We achieve this with designs that enable us to lower the costs of data-collection, usually through reduced travel expenses and interviewer time.

In the discussion that follows, four alternative probability sampling approaches are considered:

1 systematic sampling
2 stratified sampling
3 cluster sampling
4 double sampling.

# Systematic sampling

A versatile form of probability sampling is **systematic sampling.** In this approach, every $k^{th}$ element in the population is sampled, beginning with a random start of an element in the range of 1 to $k$. The $k^{th}$ element is determined by dividing the sample size into the population size to obtain the skip pattern applied to the sampling frame. The major advantage of systematic sampling is its simplicity and flexibility. It is easier to instruct fieldworkers to choose the dwelling unit listed on every $k^{th}$ line of a listing sheet than it is to use a random number table. With systematic sampling, there is no need to number the entries in a large personnel file before drawing a sample.

To draw a systematic sample you merely need to follow the steps listed below.

- Identify the total number of elements in the population.
- Identify the sampling ratio ($k$ = total population size divided by size of the desired sample).
- Identify the random start.
- Draw a sample by choosing every $k^{th}$ entry.

Invoices or customer accounts can be sampled by using the last digit or a combination of digits of an invoice or customer account number. Time sampling is also easily accomplished.

While systematic sampling has some theoretical problems, from a practical point of view it is usually treated as a simple random sample. When similar population elements are grouped within the sampling frame, systematic sampling is statistically more efficient than a simple random sample. This might occur if the listed elements are ordered chronologically, by size, by class, and so on. Under these conditions, the sample approaches a proportional stratified sample. The effect of this ordering is more pronounced on the results of cluster samples than for element samples and may call for a proportional stratified sampling formula.[9]

One concern with systematic sampling is the possible periodicity in the population that parallels the sampling ratio. In sampling days of the week, a 1-in-7 sampling ratio would give biased results. A less obvious case might involve a survey in an area of apartment-type houses where the typical pattern is eight apartments per building. Many systematic sampling fractions, such as 1 in 8, could easily over-sample some types of apartment and under-sample others. The only protection against this is constant vigilance on the part of the researcher.

Another difficulty may arise when there is a monotonic trend in the population elements. That is, the population list varies from the smallest to the largest element, or vice versa. Even a chronological list may have this effect if a measure has trended in one direction over time. Whether a systematic sample drawn under these conditions provides a biased estimate of the population mean or proportion depends on the initial random draw. Assume that a list of 2000 commercial banks is created, arrayed from the largest to the smallest, from which a sample of 50 must be drawn for analysis. A sampling ratio of 1 to 40 (begun with a random start at 16) drawing every 40th bank would exclude the 15 largest banks and give a small-size bias to the findings. Ways to deal with this concern include:

- randomize the population before sampling
- change the random start several times in the sampling process
- replicate a selection of different samples.

## Stratified sampling

Most populations can be segregated into several mutually exclusive sub-populations or strata. The process by which the sample is constrained to include elements from each of the segments is called **stratified random sampling**. University students, for example, can be divided by class level, school or specialism, gender, and so on. Once a population has been divided into the appropriate strata, a simple random sample can be taken within each stratum. The sampling results can then be weighted and combined into appropriate population estimates.

There are three reasons why a researcher chooses a stratified random sample:

1  to increase a sample's statistical efficiency
2  to provide adequate data for analysing the various sub-populations
3  to enable different research methods and procedures to be used in different strata.[10]

Stratification is usually more efficient statistically than simple random sampling and, at worst, equal to it. With the ideal stratification, each stratum is homogeneous internally and heterogeneous with other strata. This might occur in a sample that includes members of several distinct ethnic groups. In this instance, stratification makes for a pronounced improvement in statistical efficiency.

It is also useful when the researcher wants to study the characteristics of certain population sub-groups. Thus, if one wishes to draw some conclusions about activities in the different classes of a student body, stratified sampling would be used. Stratification is also called for when different methods of data-collection are applied in different parts of the population. This might occur when we survey company employees at the home office with one method but must use a different approach with employees scattered over the country.

If data are available on which to base a stratification decision, how should we go about it?[11] The ideal stratification would be based on the primary variable under investigation. If the major concern is to learn how often per month patrons would use the dining club in our example, then one would like to stratify on this expected number of use occasions. The only difficulty with this idea is that if we knew this information, we would not need to conduct the study. We must, therefore, pick a variable for stratifying that we believe will correlate with the frequency of club use per month, something like work or class schedule as an indication of when a sample element might be near campus at lunch-times.

Researchers often have several important variables about which they want to draw conclusions. A reasonable approach is to seek some basis for stratification that correlates well with the major variables. It might be a single variable (class level) or it might be a compound variable (class by gender). In any event, we will have done a good stratifying job if the stratification base maximizes the difference among strata means and minimizes the within-stratum variances for the variables of major concern.

The more strata used, the closer you come to maximizing interstrata differences (differences between strata) and minimizing intrastratum variances (differences within a given stratum). You must base the decision partially on the number of sub-population groups about which you wish to draw separate conclusions. Costs of stratification also enter the decision. There is little to be gained in estimating population values when the number of strata exceeds six.[12]

The size of the strata samples is calculated with two pieces of information:

1  how large the total sample should be

2  how the total sample should be allocated among strata.

In deciding how to allocate a total sample among various strata, there are proportionate and disproportionate options.

## *Proportionate versus disproportionate sampling*

In **proportionate stratified sampling**, each stratum is properly represented so that the sample drawn from it is proportionate to the stratum's share of the total population. This approach is more popular than any of the other stratified sampling procedures. Some reasons for this include:

- it has higher statistical efficiency than a simple random sample

- it is much easier to carry out than other stratifying methods

- it provides a self-weighting sample; the population mean or proportion can be estimated simply by calculating the mean or proportion of all sample cases, eliminating the weighting of responses.

On the other hand, proportionate stratified samples often gain little in statistical efficiency if the strata measures and their variances are similar for the major variables under study.

Any stratification that departs from the proportionate relationship is disproportionate. There are several disproportionate allocation schemes. One type is a judgmentally determined disproportion based on the idea that each stratum is large enough to secure adequate confidence levels and interval range estimates for individual strata.

A researcher makes decisions regarding **disproportionate stratified sampling**, however, by considering how a sample will be allocated among strata. One author states that, 'In a given stratum, take a larger sample if the stratum is larger than other strata; the stratum is more variable internally; and sampling is cheaper in the stratum.'[13]

If one uses these suggestions as a guide, it is possible to develop an optimal stratification scheme. When there is no difference in intrastratum variances and when the costs of sampling among strata are equal, the optimal design is a proportionate sample.

While disproportionate sampling is theoretically superior, there is some question as to whether it has wide applicability in a practical sense. If the differences in sampling costs or variances among strata are large, then disproportionate sampling is desirable. It has been suggested that 'differences of several-fold are required to make disproportionate sampling worthwhile'.[14]

The process for drawing a stratified sample is as follows.

- Determine the variables to use for stratification.

- Determine the proportions of the stratification variables in the population.

- Select proportionate or disproportionate stratification based on project information needs and risks.

- Divide the sampling frame into separate frames for each stratum.

- Randomize the elements within each stratum's sampling frame.

- Follow random or systematic procedures to draw the sample.

| Stratified sampling | Cluster sampling |
|---|---|
| 1  We divide the population into a few sub-groups, each with many elements in it. The sub-groups are selected according to some criterion that is related to the variables under study | 1  We divide the population into many sub-groups, each with a few elements in it. The sub-groups are selected according to some criterion of ease or availability in data-collection |
| 2  We try to secure homogeneity within sub-groups, heterogeneity between sub-groups | 2  We try to secure heterogeneity within sub-groups and homogeneity between sub-groups |
| 3  We randomly choose elements from within each sub-group | 3  We randomly choose a number of the sub-groups, which we then typically study in depth |

*Exhibit 6.7* Stratified sampling versus cluster sampling.

## Cluster sampling

In a simple random sample, each population element is selected individually. The population can also be divided into groups of elements with some groups randomly selected for study. This is known as **cluster sampling**. Cluster sampling differs from stratified sampling in several ways (for a comparison of these, see Exhibit 6.7).

When done properly, cluster sampling also provides an unbiased estimate of population parameters. Two conditions foster the use of cluster sampling:

1  the need for more economic efficiency than can be provided by simple random sampling, and

2  the frequent unavailability of a practical sampling frame for individual elements.

Statistical efficiency for cluster samples is usually lower than for simple random samples chiefly because clusters are usually homogeneous. Families in the same block (a typical cluster) are often similar in social class, income level, ethnic origin, and so on.

While statistical efficiency in most cluster sampling may be low, economic efficiency is often great enough to overcome this weakness. The criterion, then, is the net relative efficiency resulting from the trade-off between economic and statistical factors. It may take 690 interviews with a cluster design to give the same precision as 424 simple random interviews, but if it costs only €5 per interview in the cluster situation and €10 in the simple random case, the cluster sample is more attractive (€3450 versus €4240).

## Area sampling

Much research involves populations that can be identified with some geographic area. When this occurs, it is possible to use **area sampling**, the most important form of cluster sampling. This method overcomes both the problems of high sampling cost and the unavailability of a practical sampling frame for individual elements. Area sampling methods have been applied to national populations, county populations, and even smaller areas where there are well-defined political or natural boundaries.

Suppose you want to survey the adult residents of a city. You would seldom be able to secure a listing of such individuals. It would be simple, however, to get a detailed city map that shows the blocks of the city. If you take a sample of these blocks, you are also taking a sample of the adult residents of the city.

## Design

In designing cluster samples, including area samples, we must answer several questions.

1  How homogeneous are the clusters?

2  Shall we seek equal or unequal clusters?

3  How large a cluster shall we take?

4  Shall we use a single or multi-stage cluster?

5  How large a sample is needed?

We now look briefly at the answers to each of these questions.

### 1. How homogeneous are the clusters?

Clusters are homogeneous. This contributes to low statistical efficiency. Sometimes one can improve this efficiency by constructing clusters to increase intracluster variance. In our dining club study, the students might have constructed clusters that included members from all classes. In area sampling, they could combine adjoining blocks that contain different income groups or social classes. Area cluster sections do not have to be contiguous, but the cost saving is lost if they are not near each other.

### 2. Shall we seek equal or unequal clusters?

A cluster sample may be composed of clusters of equal or unequal size. The theory of clustering is that the means of sample clusters are unbiased estimates of the population mean. This is more likely to be true when clusters are equal. It is often possible to construct artificial clusters that are approximately equal, but natural clusters, such as households in city blocks, often vary substantially. While one can deal with clusters of unequal size, it may be desirable to reduce or counteract the effects of unequal size. There are several approaches to this, as outlined below.

- Combine small clusters and split large clusters until each approximates an average size.
- Stratify clusters by size and choose clusters from each stratum.
- Stratify clusters by size and then sub-sample using varying sampling fractions to secure an overall sampling ratio.

In the latter case, we may seek an overall sampling fraction of 1/60 and desire that sub-samples contain five elements each. One group of clusters might average about 10 elements per cluster. In the '10 elements per cluster' stratum, we might choose 1 in 30 of the clusters and then sub-sample each chosen cluster at a 1/2 rate to secure the overall 1/60 sampling fraction. Among clusters of 120 elements, we might select clusters at a 1/3 rate and then sub-sample at a 1/20 rate to secure the 1/60 sampling fraction.[15]

### 3. How large a cluster shall we take?

There is no a priori answer to this question. Even with single-stage clusters, say of 5, 20 or 50, it is not clear which size is superior. Some have found that in studies using single-stage clusters, the optimal cluster size is no larger than the typical city block.[16] Comparing the efficiency of the above three cluster sizes requires that we discover the different costs for each size and estimate the different variances of the cluster means.

### 4. Shall we use a single-stage or multistage cluster?

For most area sampling, especially large-scale studies, the tendency is to use multi-stage methods.

There are four reasons that justify sub-sampling in preference to the direct creation of smaller clusters and their selection in one-stage cluster sampling.

1  Natural clusters may exist as convenient sampling units, yet may be larger than the desired economic size.

2  We can avoid the cost of creating smaller clusters in the entire population and confine it to the selected sampling units.

3  The effect of clustering is often less in larger clusters. For example, a compact cluster of four dwellings from a city block may bring into the sample similar dwellings, perhaps from one building; but four dwellings selected separately can be spread around the dissimilar sides of the block.

4  The sampling of compact clusters may present practical difficulties. For example, independent interviewing of all members of a household may seem impractical.[17]

### 5. How large a sample is needed?

Answering this question involves deciding how many subjects must be interviewed or observed, and depends heavily on the specific cluster design. These details can be complicated. Unequal clusters and multi-stage samples are the chief complications, and their statistical treatment is beyond the scope of this book.[18] Here we will treat only single-stage samples with equal-size clusters (known as **simple cluster sampling**). This is analogous to simple random sampling. The simple random sample is really a special case of simple cluster sampling. We can think of a population as consisting of 20,000 clusters of one student each or 2000 clusters of 10 students each, and so on. The only difference between a simple random sample and a simple cluster sample is the size of cluster. Since this is so, we should expect that the calculation of a probability sample size would be the same for both types.

## Double sampling

It may be more convenient or economical to collect some information by sample and then use this information as the basis for selecting a sub-sample for further study. This procedure is called **double sampling, sequential sampling** or **multi-phase sampling**. It is usually found with stratified and/or cluster designs. The calculation procedures are described in more advanced texts.

Double sampling can be illustrated by our dining club example. You might use a telephone survey or another inexpensive survey method to discover who would be interested in joining

| Type | Description | Advantages | Disadvantages |
|---|---|---|---|
| Simple random | Each population element has an equal chance of being selected into the sample. Sample drawn using random number table/generator | Easy to implement with automatic dialling (random digit dialling) and with computerized voice response systems | Requires a listing of population elements. Takes more time to implement. Uses larger sample sizes. Produces larger errors. Expensive |
| Systematic | Selects an element of the population at a beginning with a random start and following the sampling fraction selects every $k^{th}$ element | Simple to design. Easier to use than the simple random. Easy to determine sampling distribution of mean or proportion. Less expensive than simple random | Periodicity within the population may skew the sample and results. If the population list has a monotonic trend, a biased estimate will result based on the start point |
| Stratified | Divides population into sub-populations or strata and uses simple random on each strata. Results may be weighted and combined | Researcher controls sample size in strata. Increased statistical efficiency. Provides data to represent and analyse sub-groups. Enables use of different methods in strata | Increased error will result if sub-groups are selected at different rates. Expensive. Especially expensive if strata on the population have to be created |
| Cluster | Population is divided into internally heterogeneous sub-groups. Some are randomly selected for further study | Provides an unbiased estimate of population parameters if properly done. Economically more efficient than simple random. Lowest cost per sample, especially with geographic clusters. Easy to do without a population list | Often lower statistical efficiency (more error) due to sub-groups being homogeneous rather than heterogeneous |
| Double (sequential or multiphase) | Process includes collecting data from a sample using a previously defined technique. Based on the information found, a sub-sample is selected for further study | May reduce costs if first stage results in enough data to stratify or cluster the population | Increased costs if used indiscriminately |

*Exhibit 6.8* Comparison of probability sampling designs.

such a club and the degree of their interest. You might then stratify the interested respondents by degree of interest and sub-sample among them for intensive interviewing on expected consumption patterns, reactions to various services, and so on. Whether it is more desirable to gather such information by one or two-stage sampling depends largely on the relative costs of the two methods.

Because of the wide range of sampling designs available, it is often difficult to select an approach that meets the needs of the research question and helps to contain the costs of the project. To help with these choices, Exhibit 6.8 may be used to compare the various advantages and disadvantages of probability sampling.

Non-probability sampling techniques are covered in the next section. They are used frequently and offer the researcher the benefit of low cost. However, they are not based on a theoretical framework and do not operate from statistical theory; consequently, they produce selection bias and non-representative samples. Despite these weaknesses, their widespread use demands their mention here.

# 6.7 Non-probability sampling

Any discussion of the relative merits of probability versus non-probability sampling clearly shows the technical superiority of the former. In probability sampling, researchers use a random selection of elements to reduce or eliminate sampling bias. Under such conditions, we can have substantial confidence that the sample is representative of the population from which it is drawn. In addition, with probability sample designs, we can estimate an interval range within which the population parameter is expected to fall. Thus, we can not only reduce the chance of sampling error but also estimate the range of probable sampling error present.

With a subjective approach like non-probability sampling, the probability of selecting population elements is unknown. There are several ways that can be used to choose persons or cases to include in the sample. Often we allow the choice of subjects to be made by fieldworkers on the scene. When this occurs, there is greater opportunity for bias to enter the sample selection procedure and to distort the findings of the study. Also, we cannot estimate any range within which to expect the population parameter. Given the technical advantages of probability sampling over non-probability sampling, why would anyone choose the latter?

Some researchers suggest that the bias of non-probability samples can be reduced by post-stratification and propensity scoring. The first method, post-stratification, requires that we have some information (usually personal (age, gender) or firm (size, industry)) demographics that are available for the whole population. If the distribution on these demographic characteristics differs between the sample and the population you can calculate weights correcting for the over- or under-representation of these characteristics. There are some practical reasons for using these less precise methods. Propensity scoring, the second method, does not require information on the whole population but a second sample from a previous research is believed to be more representative for the population than the sample you use. Comparing your sample with the second sample allows calculating propensity scores reflecting the chance that a subject of the second, more representative sample, would also be included in your sample. It should, however, be noted that both methods rely on the heavy assumption that the weights or propensity scores are really related to the variables of interest in your research. Even if you are able to apply one of these two measures you will never eliminate the bias of the non-probability sample.

## Usefulness of non-probability samples

Do you really need a probability sample? The answer to this question depends crucially on the objective of your research and more specifically on the kind of conclusion you want to draw. If you want to generalize, that is you attempt to find out what percentage of students think about starting an own company or if you are interested in the accurate size of an effect, for example how much less cigarettes would be sold if tobacco taxes were to be increased by €1, you need to draw a probability sample.

Often, however, you are not so much interested in the accurate size of an effect, but rather in whether there is a positive or negative effect. This holds especially for research that employs concepts (variables) that do not know a common scale. Demand in cigarettes and price can be measured in commonly accepted numbers (packages sold and price in euros), but many concepts in business research do not have a common scale, such as motivation, competitiveness, and so on. What you want to know is for example whether more motivated employees or more competitive firms really perform better. To investigate such a hypothesis, we do not need probability samples. All we need is a sample that contains well- and less-motivated employees (competitive firms). Thus, we just need a sample whose subjects vary sufficiently on the variables under investigation.

Let's take on the example on tobacco usage and cigarettes prices. With a non-probability sample among smoking students you could investigate which factors (e.g. friends, information on the long-term effects of smoking, price) would encourage smoking students to stop. A possible result of such a study could be that the price effect is relatively small compared to the effects of friends and information. With a probability sample you could show how many students quit smoking if taxes are increased. The non-probability study would be useful for organizations attempting to find out how they could convince students to stop smoking. The probability study would help the minister of finance to calculate the effects of a tobacco tax increase. Next to this considerations regarding the objective of the study, non-probability sample also offer practical advantages.

## Practical considerations for non-probability samples

We may use non-probability sampling procedures because they meet the sampling objectives satisfactorily. While a random sample will give us a true cross-section of the population, this may not be the objective of the research. If there is no desire or need to generalize to a population parameter, then there is much less concern about whether the sample fully reflects the population. Often researchers have more limited objectives. They may be looking only for the range of conditions or for examples of dramatic variations. This is especially true in exploratory research where one may wish to contact only certain persons or cases that are clearly atypical. Erik van de Duivel, in our Belgian coast example, would probably have wanted a probability sample if the decision resting on the data was a full restructuring of the Belgian Tourist Authority to better serve international visitors. However, the decision as to which features of the Belgian coast one should emphasize in a promotional campaign has relatively less impact and involves less in the way of costs.

Additional reasons for choosing non-probability over probability sampling are cost and time. Probability sampling clearly calls for more planning and repeated call-backs to ensure that each selected sample member is contacted. These activities are expensive. Carefully controlled non-probability sampling often seems to give acceptable results, so the investigator may not even consider probability sampling. Erik's results from his fieldwork in the restaurants would generate questionable data, but he seemed to realize the fallacy of many of his assumptions once he had spoken with a couple of local experts in the tourism industry.

While, in theory, probability sampling may be superior, there can be breakdowns in its application. Even carefully stated random sampling procedures may be subject to careless application by the people involved. Thus, the ideal probability sampling may be only partially achieved because of the human element.

It is also possible that non-probability sampling may be the only feasible alternative. In particular, if the relevant population remains vague and difficult to define, it may be unfeasible even to attempt to construct a probability sample. Erik wants to approach potential holiday-makers by inviting visitors to his website to fill in an online questionnaire. Obviously, this method will miss all those potential visitors who have not used the Internet to obtain information on the Belgian coast. As participants of online surveys are often offered a small reward or the chance to win a larger reward, these surveys may attract respondents who are not remotely interested in the Belgian coast, but only in the chance of winning a prize. In addition, the total population may not be available for study in certain cases. At the scene of a major event, it may be impractical to even attempt to construct a probability sample. A study of past correspondence between two companies, for instance, must use an arbitrary sample because the full correspondence is not usually available.

In another sense, those who are included in a sample may select themselves. In mail surveys, those who respond may not represent a true cross-section of those who receive the questionnaire. The receivers of the questionnaire decide for themselves whether they will participate. There is some element of self-selection in almost all surveys because every respondent chooses whether or not to be interviewed.

## Convenience sampling

Non-probability samples that are unrestricted are called **convenience samples**. They are the least reliable design but normally the cheapest and easiest to conduct. Researchers or fieldworkers have the freedom to choose whoever they can find, hence the word 'convenience'. Examples include informal pools of friends and neighbours, people responding to a newspaper's invitation for readers to state their positions on some public issue, a TV reporter's 'man-in-the-street' intercept interviews, and using employees to evaluate the taste of a new snack food.

While a convenience sample has no controls to ensure precision, it may still be a useful procedure. Often you will take such a sample to test ideas or even to gain ideas about a subject of interest. In the early stages of exploratory research, when you are seeking guidance, you might use this approach. The results may present evidence that is so overwhelming that a more sophisticated sampling procedure is unnecessary. In an interview with students concerning some issue of campus concern, you might talk to 25 students selected sequentially. You might discover that the responses are so overwhelmingly one-sided that there is no incentive to interview further.

# Purposive sampling

A non-probability sample that conforms to certain criteria is called purposive sampling. There are two major types – judgement sampling and quota sampling.

**Judgement sampling** occurs when a researcher selects sample members to conform to some criterion. In a study of labour problems, for example, you may want to talk only with those who have experienced on-the-job discrimination. Another example of judgement sampling occurs when election results are predicted from only a few selected precincts that have been chosen because of their predictive record in past elections. Erik van de Duivel, in our Belgian coast example, thinks about collecting data in May and July, because he believes he will reach short-break visitors mainly in May, and people spending two or more weeks in July.

When used in the early stages of an exploratory study, a judgement sample is appropriate. When one wishes to select a biased group for screening purposes, this sampling method is also a good choice. Companies often try out new product ideas on their employees. The rationale is that one would expect the firm's employees to be more favourably disposed towards a new product idea than the public. If the product does not pass this group, it does not have any prospect of success in the general market.

**Quota sampling** is the second type of purposive sampling. We use it to improve representativeness. The logic behind quota sampling is that certain relevant characteristics describe the dimensions of the population. If a sample has the same distribution on these characteristics, then it is likely to be representative of the population regarding other variables over which we have no control. Suppose the student body of Lake University is 55 per cent female and 45 per cent male. The sampling quota would call for sampling students at a ratio of 55 to 45 per cent. This would eliminate distortions due to a non-representative gender ratio. Erik van de Duivel could use quota sampling to ensure that the distribution over different nationality of his sample reflects the current nationality distribution of visitors. For example, he might know from previous studies or tourist registration data that 35 per cent of the visitors are Dutch, 30 per cent are German, 20 per cent are British and 15 per cent are French.

In most quota samples, researchers specify more than one control dimension. Each should meet two tests. It should:

1 have a distribution in the population that we can estimate
2 be pertinent to the topic studied.

We may believe that responses to a question should vary, depending on the gender of the respondent. If so, we should seek proportional responses from both men and women. We may also feel that undergraduates differ from graduate students, so this would be a dimension. Other dimensions – such as a student's academic discipline, ethnic group, religious affiliation and social group affiliation – may also be chosen. Only a few of these controls can be used. To illustrate, suppose we consider the following example.

Gender: two categories – male, female

Class level: two categories – graduate, undergraduate

College: six categories – arts and science, agriculture, architecture, business, engineering, other

Religion: four categories – Protestant, Catholic, Jewish, other

Fraternal affiliation: two categories – member, non-member

Family socio-economic class: three categories – upper, middle, lower

In an extreme case, we might ask an interviewer to find a male undergraduate business student who is Catholic, a fraternity member and from an upper-class home. All combinations of these six factors would call for 576 ($2 \times 2 \times 6 \times 4 \times 2 \times 3 = 576$) such cells to consider. This type of control is known as precision control. It gives greater assurance that a sample will be representative of the population. However, it is costly and too difficult to carry out with more than three variables.

When we wish to use more than three control dimensions, we should depend on frequency control. With this form of control, the overall percentage of those with each characteristic in the sample should match the percentage holding the same characteristic in the population. No attempt is made to find a combination of specific characteristics in a single person. In frequency control, we would probably find that the accompanying sample array (see Exhibit 6.9) is an adequate reflection of the population, although the population may contain a considerable yet small number of married female students who are campus residents, while in our sample not a single person meets these combined characteristics.

Quota sampling has several weaknesses. First, the idea that quotas on some variables assume a representativeness on others is argument by analogy. It gives no assurance that the sample is representative of the variables being studied. Often, the data used to provide controls may also be outdated or inaccurate. There is also a practical limit on the number of simultaneous controls that can be applied to ensure precision. Finally, the choice of subjects is left to fieldworkers to make on a judgemental basis. They may choose only friendly-looking people, people who are convenient to them, and the like.

Despite the problems with quota sampling, it is widely used by opinion pollsters, and marketing and other researchers. Probability sampling is usually much more costly and time-consuming. Advocates of quota sampling argue that while there is some danger of systematic bias, the risks are usually not that great. Where predictive validity has been checked (e.g. in election polls), quota sampling has generally been satisfactory.

|  | Population | Sample |
|---|---|---|
| Male | 65% | 67% |
| Married | 15 | 14 |
| Undergraduate | 70 | 72 |
| Campus resident | 30 | 28 |
| Independent | 75 | 73 |
| Protestant | 39 | 42 |

*Exhibit 6.9* Distributions of characteristics in the sample and the population.

## Snowball sampling

This design has found a niche in recent years in applications where respondents are difficult to identify and are best located through referral networks. In the initial stage of **snowball sampling**, individuals are discovered, and may or may not be selected through probability methods. This group is then used to locate others who possess similar characteristics and who, in turn, identify others. Similar to a reverse search for bibliographic sources, the 'snowball' gathers subjects as it rolls along. Various techniques are available for selecting a non-probability snowball with provisions for error identification and statistical testing.

Snowball sampling is especially useful if you want to sample subjects that are difficult to identify, because they are nowhere registered as a population. Two examples of master theses illustrate the power of this sampling strategy. (1) A student wanted to investigate how informal investors select the companies they invest in. Through personal relations with a few start-up companies, he was able to obtain the contact information of six informal investors, but six informal investors are certainly too few for an appropriate sample. However, in the first interviews he conducted it appeared that those six informal investors know many other informal investors. He asked his initial contacts whether they would be willing to provide the contact information of the investors they know and finally succeeded in interviewing 59 informal investors. (2) A student was interested in how people who recently joined a company build up their network within the company. He started by contacting graduates that he already knew and asked them whether they would forward his questionnaire to colleagues who also joined the company recently. Using snowball sampling, he was able to build a sample that was not restricted to graduates from his own university and also included non-graduates, who moved from another company to the current company. Both examples point at another advantage of snowball sampling, namely the referral effect. The chance that a targeted person would be willing to cooperate with you as a respondent would be, of course, much higher if there was some kind of (in)direct relation. In the study of informal investors, the initial contacts often did not only provide the contact information but also phoned and informed them about the research or agreed to be named when the researcher contacted them.

## 6.8 Sampling on the Internet

The popularity of the Internet has increased significantly in the past decade and almost every firm and more and more households have direct access to it. As a result, researchers have also explored the possibility of using the Internet for research. To assess the advantages and disadvantages of using the Internet for sampling issues, it is useful to distinguish between building up a population list and sampling (selecting) respondents through the Internet.

## Internet populations

Definitions of the Internet population are still unclear. A wide definition includes all individuals and organizations who have access to it, while narrower definitions restrict the population to those that maintain a website, are member of a mailing list, and so on. Regardless of which definition a researcher chooses, one needs to be aware that the Internet population differs considerably from the general population, just like a city's telephone directory does not fully reflect the general population of that city. Although the access to and usage of the Internet has increased enormously in recent years, the general opinion is that Internet users are still compared to the general population younger, better educated and wealthier.

As discussed earlier, researchers often have a population in mind, but it is difficult to obtain a complete list of all members of the population that can be used to draw a sample. The Internet can be a source of such lists, as many websites offer listings and directories, sometimes even with contact information. Furthermore, the Internet plays host to many databases that offer such information, sometimes free of charge and often at a reasonable cost.

Suppose you want to survey business-consulting companies on their codes of ethics and how they have implemented these codes in their daily work. How could you use the Internet to build up a list of consulting firms to draw a sample?

First, the Internet can direct you to the professional associations of consulting firms, which can then be asked for their membership directories if these are not available online. Furthermore, it can be used to identify those firms that are not members of any association, by searching for the websites of consulting firms.

In terms of building up a population list the Internet is a very useful tool. It can be used as a departure point, but it can also be used to supplement a list you already have. The main advantage of the Internet is that it provides information independent of your location. Suppose you study at Leeds University and you want to conduct the survey mentioned above among consulting firms in the UK. In this case you are very likely to find information and directories for this population in your local university library. However, how could you easily obtain information on consulting firms in the Czech Republic if you are located in Leeds? The Internet is one solution to this problem.

Whether using the Internet to build up a population list is a good idea depends crucially on how well the intended population is represented on the Internet. As mentioned above, the Internet does not offer a good representation of the general population of a country or a city. But it is often useful for more specific populations, such as the population of consulting firms as in the example above or the student population of your faculty based on the faculty's email list.

## Internet sampling

With respect to the issue of sampling or selecting respondents by using the Internet, one has to distinguish probabilistic and non-probabilistic samples. Regarding probabilistic samples, it is of utmost importance to ensure that the Internet population reflects the targeted population. If the target population has members who are not part of the Internet population, those members have a zero chance of being included, which violates the basic principles of probability samples.

Second, you can use the Internet for drawing a non-probability sample. Take the example of dairy company, Countrylove, which invited Miranda Appels to participate in an online survey. The specific problem with this sampling approach is that you do not have any control over which people participate in the survey. Such non-probability samples may contain respondents who do not belong to your population. Countrylove assumes that mainly buyers of its products visit its website, but it does not know for sure. Visitors to its website could also be people who are interested in finding a job at Countrylove or students writing a term paper on the dairy industry. Filter questions such as 'Why did you come to our website?' are a possible measure that will help to identify types of respondent in your sample. Another problem is that it is difficult to ascertain whether a group of people voluntarily responding to online questionnaires is representative of the population as a whole, or even the population of Internet users. For example, elderly people are, in general, under-represented in Internet samples, while younger males are over-represented (see also the section on non-response error in Chapter 7, p. 289).

Conducting data-collection through the Internet has a considerable cost advantage as the sending and returning of questionnaires is virtually without cost. One problem that needs to be considered, however, is whether the response rates are comparable to the expected response to mail or phone survey, which we discuss in Chapter 7.

For a more in-depth insight into this topic please see the Spotlight on Research section at the end of this chapter.

## Research Methods in Practice 6

# Purposive sampling

In business research, we often apply convenience or purposive samples, for two main reasons: (1) A simple letter or telephone call with the remark that a firm has just been chosen to participate in an interesting research is rarely successful and will not give access to the information the researcher seeks. Thus, many researchers use their own personal network to contact firms. (2) Even if we take a less personal approach to contact firms, the population size is often not very large. The Netherlands has a population of 16.2 million people living in 7 million households, but the number of firms that maintain a whole portfolio of R&D cooperations is much smaller. The exact figure is unknown, but will be not larger than 1000. Even if one takes a less personal approach to contact firms, business researchers often contact the whole population, that is they make a census of that well-defined population.

In the project on R&D cooperations, we had to select firms and cooperations. To select firms, we used purposive judgement sampling and defined the following criteria that a firm needed to fulfil:

1  The firm has to be Dutch. We had two reasons for this criteria. First, extending the research to other countries would raise the question whether differences in the legal institutions would start to play a larger role, although we know that the majority of the cooperations we investigated were with non-Dutch partners. Second, it was obvious that we had to visit each company several times and that visits to companies far away would have been rather costly. From the base of the research centre in Utrecht we could reach all destinations in the Netherlands within a one-day trip.

2  The firm needs to have a substantial portfolio of R&D cooperations. Thus, we were only interested in firms that have their own R&D department.

3  We also focused on manufacturing firms, as we believed that the R&D process in a typical service firm, such as an insurance company, would look completely different from the R&D process of a manufacturing company producing machinery. Thus, we wanted to preclude that possible differences in the cooperation management would mainly be explained by a firm's sector and that the sector would overshadow all other results.

With these criteria in mind, we started to think about firms that we could easily contact. First, we looked at whether members of the research team had a good link to such a firm through his or her personal network. We used these personal contacts as a direct route to access the company. We also thought about whether we could link this specific project on R&D cooperations to a project on purchasing management that was sponsored by the NEVI Dutch Associations for Purchasing Management. This project had a similar design as it was also set up as a multi-firm study and in each firm different relations to suppliers would be examined. From the set of firms that participated in the NEVI research we identified four firms that also had their own substantial R&D cooperations.

In each firm, we had to identify the R&D cooperations. Although we approached rather large firms, the number of R&D cooperations they maintained was not hundreds but rather dozens. Thus, we employed again purposive sampling but with a quota system. We employed this quota system to ensure that we got sufficient variance on the independent variables. To obtain a list of potential R&D cooperations we asked the general manager the following questions:

1  Please name the three largest R&D cooperations you maintained in the last three years in terms of the yearly budget. Then name three mid-sized cooperations and three smaller cooperations. This selection ensures that we had at least some variance on the problem potential of the cooperation and forced the manager also to name some smaller cooperations that are otherwise easily overseen.

2  For each cooperation we asked whether the firm had known the partner before, for example through a previous cooperation to ensure variance in the social embeddedness. Depending on whether the existing sample of nine cooperations was imbalanced towards cooperations with new or old partners, we asked for additional cooperations to balance the sample.

3  In a third step we asked whether the manager could name some cooperations in which at least some problems whether solved or not had occurred after the formation. We asked that question to ensure that our sample would not suffer from an unintended bias towards successful cooperations.

4  In the last step we tried to identify a person within the firm that could answer our questions regarding the cooperation and that had been heavily involved in the cooperation in the phases of searching for a partner, negotiations and contracting, and the operation of the cooperation. For some cooperations we could not find such a person, as some people who played a central role in the early phases had changed jobs in the meantime.

From the sampling procedures we employed, it is obvious that we do not have a random sample that is representative for R&D cooperations in Dutch manufacturing firms. But is it really necessary to have such a representative random sample to investigate the research problem appropriate?

# Summary

1 The unit of analysis is a key concept in research and its choice determines what kind of problems and questions the research can answer and how the results of the research can be applied. Sound research requires that either the unit of analysis is kept the same or that differences in the unit of analysis are controlled.

2 Case study research is an important, and in business science also widely used, research approach. Unlike survey research it does not follow the sampling logic but the replication logic, and case study results are therefore not generalizable to a population but to a theoretical proposition. The main advantages of the case study approach compared to other approaches is that it relies on multiple sources of evidence, such as interviews, observations and documents.

3 Sampling is based on two premises. One is that there is enough similarity among the elements in a population that a few of these elements will adequately represent the characteristics of the total population. The second premise is that while some elements in a sample underestimate a population value, others overestimate this value. The result of these tendencies is that a sample statistic such as the arithmetic mean is generally a good estimate of a population mean.

4 A good sample has both accuracy and precision. An accurate sample is one in which there is little or no bias or systematic variance. A sample with adequate precision is one that has a sampling error that is within acceptable limits for the study's purpose.

5 A variety of sampling techniques is available. They may be classified by their representation basis and element selection techniques, as shown in the table.

   Probability sampling is based on random selection – a controlled procedure that ensures that each population element is given a known non-zero chance of selection. In contrast, non-probability selection is 'not random'. When each sample element is drawn individually from the population at large, it is unrestricted sampling. Restricted sampling covers those forms of sampling in which the selection process follows more complex rules.

| Element selection | Representation basis | |
| --- | --- | --- |
| | Probability | Non-probability |
| Unrestricted | Simple random | Convenience |
| Restricted | Complex random | Purposive |
| | Systematic | Judgement |
| | Cluster | Quota |
| | Stratified | Snowball |
| | Double | |

   **c** Using the finite population adjustment factor?

   **d** A disproportionate stratified probability sample?

**7** You plan to conduct a survey using unrestricted sampling. What subjective decisions must you make?

**8** You draw a random sample of 300 employee records from the personnel file and find that the average length of service per employee is 6.3, with a standard deviation of 3.0 years.

   **a** What percentage of the workers would you expect to have more than 9.3 years of service?

   **b** What percentage would you expect to have more than 5.0 years of service?

# Making research decisions

**9** You are working for Kiddybooks, a small publisher of children books. Although Kiddybooks children's books have won many awards, the exposure of your books in book shops is shoddy. Book shops claim that despite the awards you have won parents are not demanding your books. Apparently the relationship between awards for good books and sales of good books does not work in your case.

   How could you investigate why the relationship between awards and book sales does not work for Kiddybooks? Formulate different research questions and identify the unit of analysis.

**10** Your task is to interview a representative sample of attendees for the large concert venue where you work. The new-season schedule includes 200 live concerts featuring all types of musicians and musical groups. Since neither the number of attendees nor their descriptive characteristics are known in advance, you decide on non-probability sampling. Based on past seating configurations, you can calculate the number of tickets that will be available for each of the 200 concerts. Thus, collectively, you will know the number of possible attendees for each type of music. From attendance research conducted at concerts held during the previous two years, you can obtain gender data on attendees by type of music.

   How would you conduct a reasonably reliable non-probability sample?

**11** A Vietnamese sports shoemaker produces shoes in two grades for the European and Russian markets. European retailers require the size labelling to be precise, while for the Russian market it does not matter. Up to now the firm has mainly produced shoes for the Russian market, but it has the chance to contract with a large shoe discounter in Europe if it is able to comply with the specified quality requirement (i.e. the labelled shoe size is the actual shoe size).

   Explain how these facts affect decisions regarding quality control in sample design, confidence intervals and sample size.

**12** You wish to take an unrestricted random sample of undergraduate students at Lake University to ascertain their levels of spending per month on food purchased off-campus and eaten on the premises where purchased. You ask a test sample of nine students about their food expenditure and find that on average they report spending €20, with two-thirds of them reporting spending from €10 to €30.

   What size sample do you think you should take? (Assume your universe is infinite.)

**13** You wish to adjust your sample calculations to reflect the fact that there are only 2500 students in your population. How does this additional information affect your estimated sample size in question 12?

**14** Your large firm is facing its first union negotiation. Your superior wants an accurate evaluation of the morale of its large number of computer technicians. What size sample would you draw if it was to be an unrestricted sample?

## From concept to practice

15 Design an alternative non-probability sample that will be more representative of people who have not yet visited the Belgian coast.

16 How would you draw a cluster sample for the Belgian Tourist Authority project?

17 Using Exhibit 6.7 as your guide, for each sampling technique describe the sampling frame for a study of employers' skill requirements of new employees using the industry in which you are currently working or wish to work.

### Classroom discussion

18 Discuss how the problem of non-response can affect the results of analyses based on randomly selected samples, and how these problems can eventually be eased.

Online
*Learning* Centre

## Get started with understanding statistical techniques!

When you have read this chapter, log on to the Online Learning Centre website at ***www.mcgraw-hill.co.uk/textbooks/blumberg*** to explore chapter-by-chapter test questions, additional case studies, a glossary and more online study tools for Business Research Methods.

## Notes

[1] Office for National Statistics, 3 August 2004 (at http://www.statistics.gov.uk/census2001/cb_2.asp).

[2] W.E. Deming, *Sample Design in Business Research*. New York: Wiley, 1960, p. 26.

[3] Henry Assael and John Keon, 'Nonsampling versus sampling errors in survey research', *Journal of Marketing Research*, Spring 1982, pp. 114–23.

[4] A. Parasuraman, *Marketing Research* (2nd edn.). Reading, MA: Addison-Wesley, 1991, p. 477.

[5] Fred N. Kerlinger, *Foundations of Behavioral Research* (3rd edn.). New York: Holt, Rinehart & Winston, 1986, p. 72.

[6] Amir D. Aczel, *Complete Business Statistics*. Burr Ridge, IL: Irwin, 1996, p. 180.

[7] The correction for a finite population is shown in the example below.

If a finite population of 20,000 is considered, the sample size is 256 for an interval of ±.5 meals and 95 per cent confidence.

$$\sigma_{\bar{X}} = \frac{s}{\sqrt{n-1}} = \sqrt{\frac{N-n}{N-1}} = 0.255 = \frac{4.1}{\sqrt{n-1}} \times \sqrt{\frac{20,000-n}{20,000-1}} \ or$$

$$n = \frac{s^2 N + \sigma_{\bar{X}}^2 (N-1)}{s^2 N + \sigma_{\bar{X}}^2 (N-1)}$$

where
$N$ = size of the population
$n$ = size of the sample

[8] All estimates of costs are hypothetical.

[9] Leslie Kish, *Survey Sampling*. New York: Wiley, 1965, p. 188.

[10] Ibid., pp. 76–7.

[11] Typically, stratification is carried out before the actual sampling, but when this is not possible, it is still possible to stratify after the fact. Ibid., p. 90.

[12] W.G. Cochran, *Sampling Techniques* (2nd edn.). New York: Wiley, 1963, p. 134.

[13] Ibid., p. 96.

[14] Kish, *Survey Sampling*, p. 94.

[15] For detailed treatment of these and other cluster sampling methods and problems, see Kish, *Survey Sampling*, pp. 148–247.

[16] J.H. Lorie and H.V. Roberts, *Basic Methods of Marketing Research*. New York: McGraw-Hill, 1951, p. 120.

[17] Kish, *Survey Sampling*, p. 156.

[18] For specifics on these problems and how to solve them, the reader is referred to the many good sampling texts available. Two that have been mentioned already are Kish, *Survey Sampling*, Chapters 5, 6 and 7; and Cochran, *Sampling Techniques*, Chapters 9, 10 and 11.

[19] A proportion is the mean of a dichotomous variable when members of a class receive the value of 1 and non-members receive a value of 0.

# Recommended further reading

**Barnett, Vic, *Sample Survey* (3rd edn.). London: Hodder & Stoughton, 2002.** A text offering a good overview of classic sampling techniques as well as recent developments, such as sampling on the Internet.

**Best, Samuel J. and Krueger, Brian S. *Internet Data Collection*, Thousand Oaks: Sage, 2004.** Chapter 3 offers a concise overview on Internet sampling.

**Diamantopolous, Adamantios and Schlegelmilch, Bodo B., *Taking the Fear out of Data Analysis*. Thomson Learning, 1998.** Chapter 2 discusses sampling issues in an entertaining manner.

**Deming, W. Edwards, *Sample Design in Business Research*. New York: Wiley, 1990.** A classic by the late author, an authority on sampling.

**Kish, Leslie, *Survey Sampling*. New York: Wiley, 1995.** A widely read reference on survey sampling, recently updated.

**Simsek, Zeki and Veiga, John F., 'A primer on internet organizational surveys', *Organizational Research Methods* 4(3), 2001, pp. 218–35.** This paper presents and discusses strategies for using Internet samples.

**Yates, Frank, *Sampling Methods for Censuses and Surveys* (4th edn.). New York: Oxford University Press, 1987.** A readable text with an emphasis on sampling practices.

# Spotlight on Research 3

## Applying concepts

In the Lake University dining club study, we explore probability sampling and the various concepts used to design the sampling process.

Exhibit S3.1 shows the Lake University dining club study population ($n = 20,000$) consisting of five sub-groups based on their preferred lunch times. The values 1 to 5 represent the preferred lunch times of 11.00 a.m., 11.30 a.m., 12.00 noon, 12.30 p.m. and 1.00 p.m. The frequency of response ($f$) in the population distribution, shown beside the population sub-group, is what would be found if a census of the elements was taken. Normally, population data are unavailable or are too costly to obtain. We are faking omniscience for the sake of the example.

Now assume that we sample 10 elements from this population without knowledge of the population's characteristics. We use a sampling procedure from a statistical software program, a random number generator or a table of random numbers. Our first sample ($n_1 = 10$) provides us with the frequencies shown below sample $n_1$ in Exhibit S3.1. We also calculate a mean score, $\overline{X}_n = 3.0$, for this sample. This mean would place the average preferred lunch time at 12.00 noon. The mean is a point estimate and our best predictor of the unknown population mean, $\mu$ (the arithmetic average of the population). Assume further that we return the first sample to the population and draw a second, third and fourth sample by the same procedure. The frequencies, means and standard deviations are as shown in the exhibit. As the data suggest, each

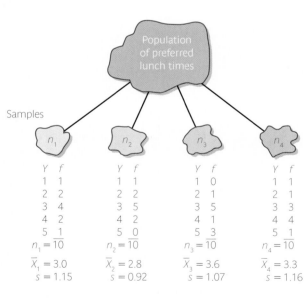

*Exhibit S3.1* Random samples of preferred lunch times.

sample shares some similarities with the population, but none is a perfect duplication because no sample perfectly replicates its population.

We cannot judge which estimate is the true mean (accurately reflects the population mean). However, we can estimate the interval in which the true $\mu$ will fall by using any of the samples. This is accomplished by using a formula that computes the standard error of the mean.

$$\sigma_{\bar{X}} = \frac{\sigma}{\sqrt{n}}$$

where

$\sigma_{\bar{X}}$ = standard error of the mean or the standard deviation of all possible $\bar{X}$ s
$\sigma$ = population standard deviation
$v$ = sample size

The standard error of the mean measures the standard deviation of the distribution of sample means. It varies directly with the standard deviation of the population from which it is drawn. If the standard deviation is reduced by 50 per cent, the standard error will also be reduced by 50 per cent. It also varies inversely with the square root of the sample size. If the square root of the sample size is doubled, the standard error is cut by one-half, provided the standard deviation remains constant.

Let's now examine what happens when we apply sample data ($n'$) from Exhibit S3.1 to the formula. The sample standard deviation will be used as an unbiased estimator of the population standard deviation.

$$\sigma_X = \frac{s}{\sqrt{n}}$$

where

$s$ = standard deviation of the sample $n_1$
$s_1 = 1.15$
$\bar{X}_1 = 3.0$
$v_1 = 10$
substituting into the equation
$$\sigma_X = \frac{s}{\sqrt{n}} = \frac{1.15}{\sqrt{10}} = .36$$

How does this improve our prediction of $\mu$ from $\bar{X}$? The standard error creates the interval

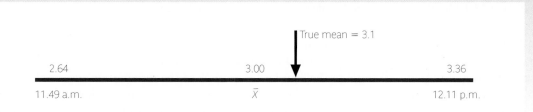

range that brackets the point estimate. In this example, $\mu$ is predicted to be 3.0 or 12.00 noon (the mean of $n_1$) ±.36. This range may be visualized on a continuum:

We would expect to find the true $\mu$ between 2.64 and 3.36 – between 11.49 a.m. and 12.11 p.m. (If 2 = 11.30 a.m. and .64 (of 30 minutes) = 19.2 minutes, then 2.64 = 11.30 a.m. + 19.2 minutes or 11.49 a.m.) Since we assume omniscience for this illustration, we know the population average value is 3.1. Further, because standard errors have characteristics like other standard scores, we have 68 per cent confidence in this estimate – that is, one standard error encompasses ±1 $Z$ or 68 per cent of the area under the normal curve (see Exhibit 6.11). Recall that the area under the curve also represents the confidence estimates that we make about our results. The combination of the interval range and the degree of confidence creates the **confidence interval**. To improve confidence to 95 per cent, multiply the standard error of .36 by ±1.96 ($Z$), since 1.96 Z covers 95 per cent of the area under the curve (see Exhibit

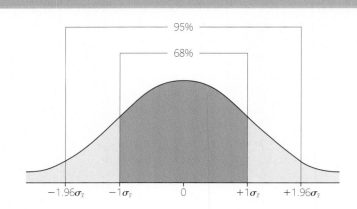

**Exhibit S3.2** Confidence levels and the normal curve.

|  | Reducing the standard deviation | Doubling the square root of the sample size |
|---|---|---|
|  | $\sigma_x = \dfrac{.74}{\sqrt{10}} = .234$ | $\sigma_x = \dfrac{.8}{\sqrt{25}} = .16$ |
| $\sigma_x = \dfrac{s}{\sqrt{n}}$ | $\sigma_x = \dfrac{.37}{\sqrt{10}} = .117$ | $\sigma_x = \dfrac{.8}{\sqrt{100}} = .08$ |

**Exhibit S3.3** Effects of changes in the standard deviation or sample size.

S3.4). Now, with 95 per cent confidence, the interval in which we would find the true mean increases to ±.70 (from 2.3 to 3.7 or from 11.39 a.m. to 12.21 a.m.).

Parenthetically, if we compute the standard deviation of the distribution of sample means (3.0, 2.8, 3.6, 3.3), we will discover it to be .35 (see Exhibit S3.4). Compare this to the standard error from the original calculation (.36). The result is consistent with the second definition of the standard error: the standard deviation of the distribution of sample means ($n_1$, $n_2$, $n_3$, and

| Standard error ($Z$) | Percent of area* | Approximate degree of confidence |
|---|---|---|
| 1.00 | 68.27 | 68 % |
| 1.65 | 90.10 | 90 |
| 1.96 | 95.00 | 95 |
| 3.00 | 99.73 | 99 |
| Note: *includes both tails in a normal distribution. | | |

*Exhibit S3.4* Standard errors associated with areas under the normal curve.

$n_4$). Now let's return to the dining club example and apply some of these concepts to the researchers' problem.

If the researchers were to interview all the students and employees in the defined population, asking them, 'How many times per month would you eat at the club?' they would get a distribution of something like that shown in Part A of Exhibit S3.5. The responses would range from 0 to as many as 30 lunches per month with $\mu$ and $\sigma$.

However, they cannot take a census, so $\mu$ and s remain unknown. By sampling, the researchers find the mean to be 10.0 and the standard deviation to be 4.1 eating experiences (how often they would eat at the club per month). Turning to Part C of Exhibit S3.5, three observations about this sample distribution are consistent with our earlier illustration. First, it is shown as a histogram; it represents a frequency distribution of empirical data, while the smooth curve of Part A is a theoretical distribution. Second, the sample distribution (Part C) is similar in appearance but is not a perfect duplication of the population distribution (Part A). Third, the mean of the sample differs from the mean of the population.

If the researchers could draw repeated samples as we did earlier, they could plot the mean of each sample to secure the solid line distribution found in Part B. According to the **central limit theorem**, for sufficiently large samples ($n = 30$), the sample mean will be distributed around the population mean approximately in a normal distribution. Even if the population is not normally distributed, the distribution of sample means will be normal if there is a large enough set of samples.

### Estimating the interval for the Lake University dining club sample

Any sample mean will fall within the range of the distribution extremes shown in Part B of Exhibit S3.4. We also know that about 68 per cent of the sample means in this distribution will fall between $x_3$ and $x_4$ and 95 per cent will fall between $x_1$ and $x_2$.

If we project points $x_1$ and $x_2$ up to the population distribution (Part A of Exhibit S3.4) at points $x'_1$ and $x'_2$, we see the interval where any given mean of a random sample of 64 is likely to fall 95 per cent of the time. Since we will not know the population mean from which to measure the standard error, we infer that there is also a 95 per cent chance that the population mean is within two standard errors of the sample mean (10.0). This inference enables us to find the sample mean, mark off an interval around it, and state a confidence likelihood that the population mean is within this bracket.

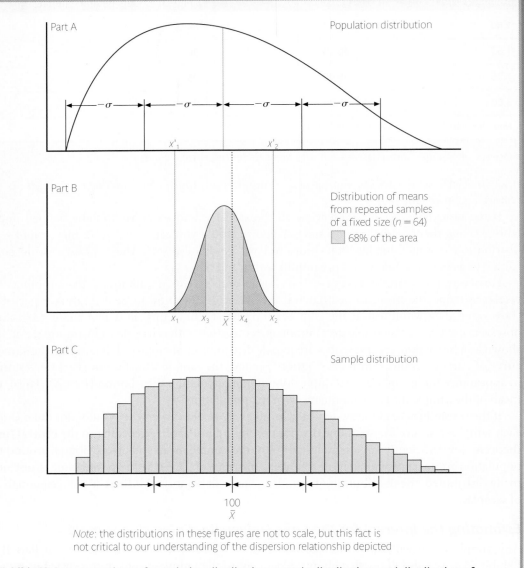

**Exhibit S3.5** A comparison of population distribution, sample distribution, and distribution of sample means of the lake university dining club study.

Because the researchers are considering an investment in this project, they would want some assurance that the population mean is close to the figure reported in any sample they take. To find out how close the population mean is to the sample mean, they must calculate the standard error of the mean and estimate an interval range within which the population mean is likely to be.

Given a sample size of 64, they still need a value for the standard error. Rarely will one have the value for the standard deviation of the population ($\sigma$), so we must use a proxy figure. The best proxy for s is the standard deviation of the sample (s). Here the standard deviation ($s = 4.1$) was obtained from a pilot sample, as outlined overleaf.

$$\sigma_X = \frac{s}{\sqrt{n}} = \frac{4.1}{\sqrt{64}} = 5.1$$

If one standard error of the mean is equal to 0.51 visits, then 1.96 standard errors (95 per cent) are equal to 1.0 visit. The students can estimate with 95 per cent confidence that the population mean of expected visits is within $10.0 \pm 1.0$ visit or from 9.0 to 11.0 meal visits per month.

## Changing confidence intervals

The above estimate may not be satisfactory in two ways. First, it may not represent the degree of confidence the researchers want in the interval estimate, considering their financial risk. They might want a higher degree of confidence than the 95 per cent level used here. By referring to a table of areas under the normal curve, they can find various other combinations of probability. Exhibit S3.6 summarizes some of those more commonly used. Thus, if the students want a greater confidence in the probability of including the population mean in the interval range, they can move to a higher standard error, say, $\overline{X} \pm 3s_X$. Now the population mean lies somewhere between $10.0 \pm 3 (0.51)$ or from 8.47 to 11.53. With 99.73 per cent confidence, we can say this interval will include the population mean.

We might wish to have an estimate that will hold for a much smaller range – for example, $10.0 \pm 0.2$. To secure this smaller interval range, we must either:

1  accept a lower level of confidence in the results, or

2  take a sample large enough to provide this smaller interval with the higher desired confidence level.

If one standard error is equal to 0.51 visits, then 0.2 visits would be equal to 0.39 standard errors ($0.2/0.51 = .39$). Referring to a table of areas under the normal curve (Appendix E, Exhibit E.1), we find that there is a 30.3 per cent chance that the true population mean lies within $\pm 0.39$ standard errors of 10.0. With a sample of 64, the sample mean would be subject to so much error variance that only 30 per cent of the time could the researchers expect to find the population mean between 9.8 and 10.2. This is such a low level of confidence that the

| Approximate degree of confidence | Interval range of dining visits per month |
| --- | --- |
| 68% | $\mu$ is between 9.48 and 10.52 visits |
| 90 | $\mu$ is between 9.14 and 10.86 visits |
| 95 | $\mu$ is between 8.98 and 11.02 visits |
| 99 | $\mu$ is between 8.47 and 11.53 visits |

*Exhibit S3.6* Estimates associated with various confidence levels in the Lake University dining club study.

| Decision issues | Lake University Decisions | |
|---|---|---|
| | **'Meal Frequency' (interval, ratio data)** | **'Joining' (nominal, ordinal data)** |
| 1. The precision desired and how to quantify it | | |
| ● The confidence researcher wants in the estimate (selected based on risk) | 95% confidency ($Z$ = 1.96) | 95% confidency ($Z$ = 1.96) |
| ● The size of the interval estimate the researcher will accept (selected based on risk) | ±.5 meals per month per person | ±.10 (10%) |
| 2. The expected dispersion in the population for the question used to measure precision | 0 to 30 meals | 0 to 100% |
| ● Sample mean | 4.1 meals | |
| ● Standard deviation | | |
| ● Sample proportion of population with the given attribute being measured | | 30% |
| ● Measure of the sample dispersion | | $pq$ = .30(1 − .30) = 0.21 |
| 3. Whether a finite population adjustment should be used | No | No |
| 4. Estimate of standard deviation of population | | |
| ● Standard error of mean | .5/1.96 = 2.55 | |
| ● Standard error of the proportion | | .10/1.96 = 0.051 |
| 5. Sample size formula | Formula from pages 273/274 | Formula from page 275 |
| 6. Sample size | $n$ = 259* | $n$ = 96 |

Note: *because both investigative questions were of interest, the researcher would use the larger of the two sample sizes calculated, $n$ = 259, for the study.

*Exhibit S3.7* Lake University sampling design decisions on 'meal frequency' and 'joining' constructs.

researchers would normally move to the second alternative; they would increase the sample size until they could secure the desired interval estimate and degree of confidence.

## Calculating the sample based on critical investigative questions

The researchers have selected two investigative question constructs as critical – 'frequency of patronage' and 'interest in joining' – because they believe both to be crucial IN making the correct decision on the Lake University dining club opportunity. The first requires a point estimate, the second a proportion. By way of review, decisions needed and decisions made by Lake University researchers are summarized in Exhibit S3.7.

With regard to precision, the 95 per cent confidence level is often used, but more or less confidence may be needed in light of the risks of any given project. Similarly, the size of the interval estimate for predicting the population parameter from the sample data should be decided. When a smaller interval is selected, the researcher is saying that precision is vital, largely because inherent risks are high. For example, on a five-point measurement scale, one-tenth of a point is a very high degree of precision in comparison to a one-point interval. Given that a patron could eat up to 30 meals per month at the dining club (30 days times one meal per day), anything less than one meal per day would be asking for a high degree of precision in the Lake University study. The high risk of the Lake University study warrants the 0.5 meal precision selected.

The next factor that affects the size of the sample for a given level of precision is the population dispersion. The smaller the possible dispersion, the smaller will be the sample needed to give a representative picture of population members. If the population's number of meals ranges from 18 to 25, a smaller sample will give us an accurate estimate of the population's average meal consumption. However, with a population dispersion ranging from 0 to 30 meals consumed, a larger sample is needed for the same degree of confidence in the estimates. Since the true population dispersion of estimated meals per month eaten at Lake University dining club is unknowable, the standard deviation of the sample is used as a proxy figure. Typically, this figure is based on any of the following:

- previous research on the topic
- a pilot test or pre-test of the data instrument among a sample drawn from the population
- a rule of thumb (one-sixth of the range based on six standard deviations within 99.73 per cent confidence).

If the range is from 0 to 30 meals, the rule-of-thumb method produces a standard deviation of five meals. The researchers want more precision than the rule-of-thumb method provides, so they take a pilot sample of 25 and find the standard deviation to be 4.1 meals.

A final factor affecting the size of a random sample is the size of the population. When the size of the sample exceeds 5 per cent of the population, the finite limits of the population constrain the sample size needed. A correction factor is available in that event.

The sample size is computed for the first construct, meal frequency, as follows.

$$\sigma_{\bar{x}} = \frac{s}{\sqrt{n}}$$

$$\sqrt{n} = \frac{s}{\sigma_{\bar{X}}}$$

$$n = \frac{s^2}{\sigma_{\bar{X}}^2}$$

$$n = \frac{(4.1)^2}{(.255)^2}$$

$$n = 258.5 \text{ or } 258$$

where

$$\sigma_{\bar{X}} = 0.255 \left( \frac{0.5}{1.96} \right)$$

If the researchers are willing to accept a larger interval range (±1 meal), and thus a larger amount of risk, then they can reduce the sample size to $n = 65$.

## Calculating the sample size for the proportions' question

The second key question concerning the dining club study was 'What percentage of the population says it would join the dining club, based on the projected rates and services?' In business, we often deal with proportion data. An example is a Gallup poll that projects the percentage of people who expect to vote for or against a proposition or a candidate. This is usually reported with a margin of error of ±5 per cent.

In the Lake University study, a pre-test answers this question using the same general procedure as before. But instead of the arithmetic mean, with proportions, it is p (the proportion of the population that has a given attribute)[20] – in this case, interest in joining the dining club. And instead of the standard deviation, dispersion is measured in terms of $p \times q$ (in which $q$ is the proportion of the population not having the attribute, and $q = (1 - p)$). The measure of dispersion of the sample statistic also changes from the standard error of the mean to the standard error of the proportion $s_p$.

We calculate a sample size based on this data by making the same two subjective decisions – deciding on an acceptable interval estimate and the degree of confidence. Assume that from a pilot test, 30 per cent of the students and employees say they will join the dining club. We decide to estimate the true proportion in the population within 10 percentage points of this figure ($p = 0.30 \pm 0.10$). Assume further that we want to be 95 per cent confident that the population parameter is within ±0.10 of the sample proportion. The calculation of the sample size proceeds as before.

±0.10 = desired interval range within which the population proportion is expected (subjective decision)

1.96 $\sigma_{\pi}$ = 95 per cent confidence level for estimating the interval within which to expect the population proportion (subjective decision)

$s_p = -0.051$ = standard error of the proportion (0.10/1.96)

$pq$ = measure of sample dispersion (used here as an estimate of the population dispersion).

$$\sigma_p = \sqrt{\frac{pq}{n}}$$

$$n = \frac{pq}{\sigma_p^2}$$

$$n = \frac{.3 \times .7}{(.051)^2} = 81$$

The sample size of 81 persons is based on an infinite population assumption. If the sample size is less than 5 per cent of the population, there is little to be gained by using a finite population adjustment. The students interpreted the data found with a sample of 81 chosen randomly from the population as 'We can be 95 per cent confident that 30 per cent of the respondents would say that they would join the dining club with a margin of error of ±10 per cent'.

Previously, the researchers used pilot testing to generate the variance estimate for the calculation. Suppose this is not an option. Proportions data have a feature concerning the variance that is not found with interval or ratio data. The $pq$ ratio can never exceed 0.25. For example, if $p = 0.5$, then $q = 0.5$, and their product is 0.25. If either $p$ or $q$ is greater than 0.5, then their product is smaller than 0.25 ($0.4 \times 0.6 = 0.24$, and so on). When we have no information regarding the probable $p$ value, we can assume that $p = 0.5$ and solve for the sample size.

$$n = \frac{pq}{\sigma_p^2}$$

$$n = \frac{0.25}{(0.51)^2} = 96$$

If we use this maximum variance estimate in the dining club example, we find the sample size needs to be 96 persons.

# Survey research

## Chapter contents

## LEARNING OBJECTIVES

When you have read this chapter, you should understand:

☑ the process for selecting the appropriate and optimal communication approach

☑ what factors affect participation in survey studies

☑ the major sources of error in survey studies, and how to minimize them

☑ the major advantages and disadvantages of the three communication approaches.

## 7.1 Characteristics of the communication approach

The researcher determines the data-collection approach largely by identifying the types of information needed – investigative questions the researcher must answer – and the desired data type (nominal, ordinal, interval or ratio) for each of these questions. The characteristics of the sample unit – specifically, whether a participant can articulate his or her ideas, thoughts and experiences – also play a role in the decision. Part A of Exhibit 7.1 shows the relationship of these decisions to the research process detailed in Chapter 2 (p. 56). Part B of Exhibit 7.1 indicates how the researcher's choice of a communication (versus an observation) approach affects the following:

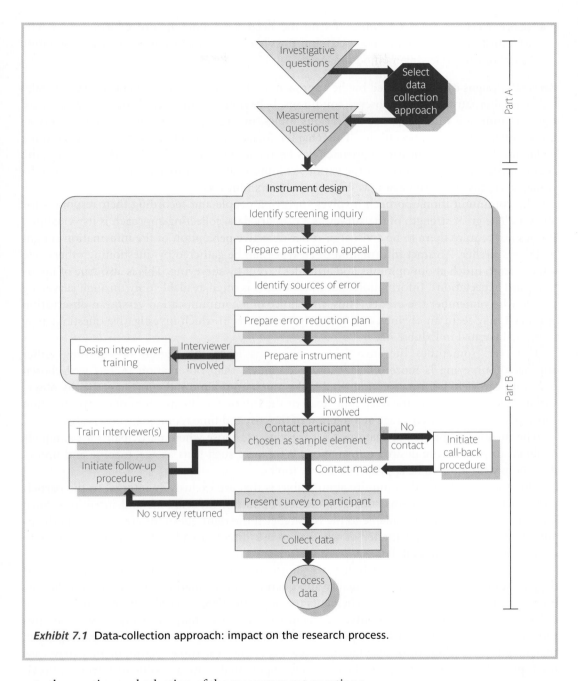

*Exhibit 7.1* Data-collection approach: impact on the research process.

- the creation and selection of the measurement questions
- sampling issues (explored in Chapter 6), which drive contact and call-back procedures
- instrument design (discussed in Chapter 13), which incorporates attempts to reduce error and create participant-screening procedures

- data-collection processes, which create the need for follow-up procedures (when self-administered instruments are used) and possible interviewer training (when personal or telephone interviewing methods are used).

Research designs can be classified by the approach used to gather primary data. There are really only two alternatives: we can observe conditions, behaviour, events, people or processes; or we can communicate with people about various topics, including participants' attitudes, motivations, intentions and expectations. This chapter focuses on the choices the researcher must make once the **communication approach** has been chosen (see Exhibit 7.2), by discussing the characteristics and applications of the various communication approaches as well as their individual strengths and weaknesses (as summarized in Exhibit 7.4).

The communication approach involves surveying people and recording their responses for analysis. The great strength of the **survey** as a primary data-collecting approach is its versatility. It does not require there to be a visual or other objective perception of the information sought by the researcher. Abstract information of all types can be gathered by questioning others. We seldom learn much about opinions and attitudes except by surveying. This is also true of intentions and expectations. Information about past events is often available only through surveying people who remember the events. Thus, the choice of a communication versus an observation approach may seem an obvious one, given the directions in which investigative questions may lead, as illustrated in Exhibit 7.2.

However, sometimes the investigative questions leave the option of choosing either approach. Surveying is more efficient and economical than observation. A few well-chosen questions can yield information that would take much more time and effort to gather by observation. A survey that uses the telephone, mail or the Internet as the medium of communication can expand geographic coverage at a fraction of the cost and time required by observation.

The most appropriate applications for surveying are those where participants are uniquely qualified to provide the desired information. We expect such facts as age, income and immediate family situation to be appropriate survey topics.

Questions can be used to inquire about subjects that are exclusively internal to the participant. Included here are items such as attitudes, opinions, expectations and intentions. Such information can be made available to the researcher if the right questions are asked of participants. It becomes, finally, a matter of whether to ask direct or indirect questions in order to collect the most meaningful data.

The communication approach has its shortcomings, however. Its major weakness, as depicted in Exhibit 7.3, is that the quality and quantity of information secured depends heavily on the ability and willingness of participants to cooperate. Often, people refuse an interview or fail to reply to a mail- or computer-delivered survey. There may be many reasons for this unwillingness to cooperate. Certain people at certain times fail to see any value in participation; they may be suspicious of or fear the interview experience for some reason; or they may view the topic as too sensitive and thus the interview as potentially embarrassing or intrusive. Previous encounters with marketers who have attempted to disguise their sales pitch as a research survey can also erode participants' willingness to cooperate.

Even if individuals agree to participate, they may not possess the knowledge that is being sought. If we ask participants to report on events that they have not experienced personally, we

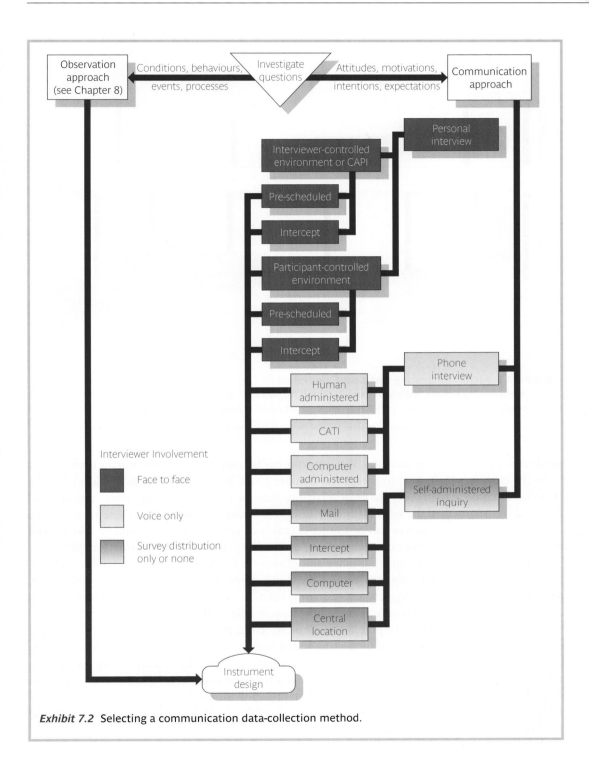

*Exhibit 7.2* Selecting a communication data-collection method.

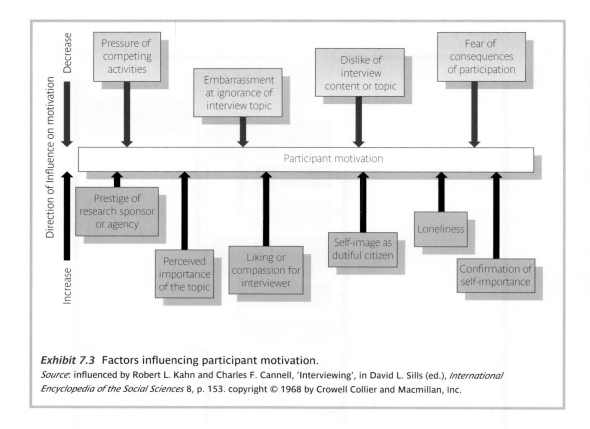

***Exhibit 7.3*** Factors influencing participant motivation.

*Source*: influenced by Robert L. Kahn and Charles F. Cannell, 'Interviewing', in David L. Sills (ed.), *International Encyclopedia of the Social Sciences* 8, p. 153. copyright © 1968 by Crowell Collier and Macmillan, Inc.

need to assess their replies carefully. If our purpose is to learn what the participant understands to be the case, it is legitimate to accept the answers given, but if our intent is to learn what the event or situation actually was, we must recognize that the participant is reporting second-hand data and the accuracy of the information declines. We should not depend on these second-hand sources if a more direct source can be found. A family or group member should be asked about another member's experience only when there is no other way to get the information directly.

Sometimes a participant may not have an opinion on the topic of concern. Under such circumstances, their proper response should be 'don't know' or 'have no opinion'. Too often, though, participants feel obliged to express some opinion even if they do not have one. In such cases, it is difficult for researchers to know how true or reliable the answers are.

Participants may also interpret a question or concept in a way that differs from the researcher's intention. This occurs when the individual answers a question that differs from the one being asked. Also, a participant may intentionally mislead the researcher by giving false information. It is difficult for a researcher to identify these occasions. Thus, survey responses should be accepted for what they are: statements by individuals that reflect varying degrees of truth. Despite these weaknesses, communicating with research participants is a principal method of management research.

## 7.2  Choosing a communication method

Once the researcher has determined that surveying is the appropriate data-collection approach, various means may be used to secure information from individuals. A researcher can conduct a survey by personal interview, telephone, mail, computer or a combination of these. As noted in Exhibit 7.4, while there are commonalities among these approaches, several considerations are unique to each.

## 7.3  Personal interviewing

A **personal interview** (i.e. face-to-face communication) is a two-way conversation initiated by an interviewer to obtain information from a participant. The differences in the roles of interviewer and participant are pronounced. They are typically strangers, and the interviewer generally controls the topics and patterns of discussion. The consequences of the event are usually insignificant for the participant, who is asked to provide information but has little hope of receiving any immediate or direct benefit from this cooperation.

### Evaluation of the personal interview

There are real advantages as well as clear limitations to personal interviewing. The greatest value lies in the depth of information and detail that can be secured. It far exceeds the information secured from telephone and self-administered studies via intercepts (e.g. shoppers in malls or visitors to a trade fair at the exit gate of the fair), **mail surveys** or computer (both intranet and Internet). The interviewer can also do more things to improve the quality of the information received than with another method.

The absence of assistance in interpreting questions is a clear weakness that can be improved by the presence of an interviewer. Interviewers can note conditions of the interview, probe with additional questions and gather supplemental information through observation.

Interviewers also have more control than is the case when using other kinds of interrogation. They can pre-screen to ensure the correct participant is replying, and they can set up and control interviewing conditions. They can use special scoring devices and visual materials, as is done with **computer-assisted personal interviewing (CAPI)**. Interviewers can also adjust the language of the interview as they observe any problems and the effects the interview is having on the participant.

With such advantages, why would anyone want to use any other survey method? Probably the greatest reason is that personal interviewing is costly, in terms of both money and time. A personal interview may cost anything from a few euros to several hundred for an interview with a hard-to-reach person. Costs are particularly high if the study covers a wide geographic area or has stringent sampling requirements.

An exception to this is the **intercept interview** that targets participants in centralized locations, such as shoppers in retail malls. Intercept interviews reduce the costs associated with travel. Product and service demonstrations can also be coordinated, further reducing costs. Their cost-effectiveness, however, is offset when representative sampling is crucial to the study's outcome. Exhibit 7.5 offers some helpful tips when intercept interviews are an appropriate research design.

| | Personal Interviews | Telephone Interviews | Self-administered Surveys |
|---|---|---|---|
| Description | People selected to be part of the sample are interviewed in person by a trained interviewer | People selected to be part of the sample are interviewed on the telephone by a trained interviewer | Questionnaires are:<br>**a** mailed, faxed or couriered to be self-administered – with return mechanism generally included<br>**b** computer-delivered via intranet, Internet and online services – computer stores/forwards completed instruments automatically<br>**c** people intercepted/studied via paper or computerized instrument in central location – without interviewer assistance |
| Advantages | • Good cooperation from respondents<br>• Interviewer can answer questions about survey, probe for answers, use follow-up questions, and gather information by observation<br>• Special visual aids and scoring devices can be used<br>• Illiterate and functionally illiterate respondents can be reached<br>• Interviewer can pre-screen respondent to ensure he or she fits the population profile<br>• CAPI – computer-assisted personal interviewing: responses can be entered into a portable microcomputer to reduce error and cost | • Lower costs than personal interview<br>• Expanded geographic coverage without dramatic increase in costs<br>• Uses fewer, more highly skilled interviewers<br>• Reduced interviewer bias<br>• Fastest completion time<br>• Better access to hard-to-reach respondents through repeated call-backs<br>• Can use computerized random-digit dialling<br>• CATI – computer-assisted telephone interviewing: responses can be entered directly into a computer file to reduce error and cost | • Allows contact with otherwise inaccessible respondents (e.g. CEOs)<br>• Incentives may be used to increase response rate<br>• Often lowest-cost option<br>• Expanded geographic coverage without increase in costs (a)<br>• Requires minimal staff (a)<br>• Perceived as more anonymous (a)<br>• Allows respondents time to think about questions (a)<br>• More complex instruments can be used (b)<br>• Fast access to the computer-literate (b)<br>• Rapid data-collection (b, c)<br>• Respondent who cannot be reached by phone (voice) may be accessible (b, c) |

| | | | |
|---|---|---|---|
| Disadvantages | • High costs<br>• Need for highly trained interviewers<br>• Longer period needed in the field collecting data<br>• May be wide geographic dispersion<br>• Follow-up is labour intensive<br>• Not all respondents are available or accessible<br>• Some respondents are unwilling to talk to strangers in their homes<br>• Some neighbourhoods are difficult to visit<br>• Questions may be altered or respondent coached by interviewers | • Response rate is lower than for personal interview<br>• Higher costs if interviewing geographically dispersed sample<br>• Interview length must be limited<br>• Many phone numbers are unlisted or not working, making directory listings unreliable<br>• Some target groups are not available by telephone<br>• Responses may be less complete<br>• Illustrations cannot be used | • Sample frame lists viable locations rather than prospective respondents (b, c)<br>• Visuals may be used (b, c)<br>• Low response rate in some modes<br>• No interviewer intervention available for probing or explanation (a)<br>• Cannot be long or complex (a)<br>• Accurate mailing lists needed (a)<br>• Often respondents returning survey represent extremes of the population – skewed responses (a)<br>• Anxiety among some respondents (b)<br>• Directions/software instruction needed for progression through the instrument (b)<br>• Computer security (b)<br>• Need for low-distraction environment for survey completion (c) |

*Exhibit 7.4* Comparison of communication approaches.

1   When screening for multiple studies at the same time, make your questionnaire distinctive:

   a  use coloured paper

   b  use paper with a distinctive colour or patterned edge

2   Make surveys clipboard-friendly:

   a  never print questions on both sides of the paper

   b  keep font style and point size legible in inconsistent and dim light

   c  confine your questionnaire to four pages or fewer

3   Write the 'respondent approach' section to include answers to the following often-asked questions.

   a  What's the study about?

   b  What's in it for me if I participate?

   c  How long will it take?

4   Limit the number of screening questions (also known as 'screeners') to avoid participant termination:

   a  keep screening question(s) to the point – ask only for critical data

   b  build screening questions on facts, not assumptions or generalities

   c  if you need to speak with the primary purchaser, don't specify gender, family status or age in the screeners

5   Keep screening question(s) safe from respondents' eyes:

   a  choose normal, not bold, type style

   b  put these in parentheses or use another separation device

6   Don't overuse skip patterns: the more cumbersome the patterns, the more likely they won't be followed consistently or effectively.

7   Don't force the interviewer to remember responses to questions on previous pages in order to ask questions on the current page.

8   Tally where respondents terminate the screening process or survey:

   a  include a horizontal string of question numbers at the bottom of each page so that the interviewer can circle the number of the next question after termination.

*Exhibit 7.5* Tips on intercept survey design.

*Source*: www.quirks.com/CGI-BIN/SM40i.exe?docid=3000:58911&%70assArticleId=52; E.B. Feltser, 'Pain-free mall intercepts', *Quirk's Marketing Research Review*, November 1996

Costs have risen rapidly in recent years for most communication methods because changes in the social climate have made personal interviewing more difficult. Many people today are reluctant to talk with strangers or to permit visits to their homes. Interviewers are reluctant to visit unfamiliar neighbourhoods alone, especially for evening interviewing. Finally, results of personal interviews can be affected adversely by interviewers who alter the questions asked or in other ways bias the results. (Interviewer bias is discussed in more depth later in this chapter.) If we are to overcome these deficiencies, we must appreciate the conditions necessary for interview success.

## Requirements for success

Three broad conditions must be met in order to have a successful personal interview.

1 The participant must possess the information being targeted by the investigative questions.
2 The participant must understand his or her role in the interview as the provider of accurate information.
3 The participant must perceive adequate motivation to cooperate.

The interviewer can do little about the participant's information level. Screening questions can qualify participants when there is doubt about their ability to answer. This is the study designer's responsibility. Furthermore, the researcher can ask prospective respondents, in a letter announcing the study and confirming the interview date, to have certain information to hand. In a study on the contracting behaviour of business firms in alliances, for example, one of the authors asked the respondents to have the contract at hand during the interview.

## Increasing participation[1]

Interviewers can influence participants in many ways. An interviewer can explain what kind of answer is sought, how complete it should be, and in what terms it should be expressed. Interviewers can even do some coaching in the interview, although this can be a biasing factor.

Participant motivation is a responsibility of the interviewer. Studies of reactions to many surveys show that participants can be motivated to participate in personal interviews and, in fact, can even enjoy the experience. In one study, more than 90 per cent of participants said the interview experience was interesting, and three-quarters reported that they were willing to be interviewed again.[2] In intercept/self-administered studies, the interviewer's primary role is to encourage participation as the participant completes the survey on his or her own.

## Increasing participants' receptiveness

As depicted in Exhibit 7.4, a variety of forces can affect participant motivation in an interview. Many of these involve the interviewer. At first, it may seem easy to question another person about various topics, but research interviewing is not so simple. What we do or say as interviewers can make or break a study. Participants often react more to their feelings about the interviewer than to the content of the questions. It is also important for the interviewer to ask the questions properly, record the responses accurately, and probe meaningfully. To achieve these aims, he or she must be trained to carry out those procedures that foster a good interviewing relationship.

The first goal in an interview is to establish a friendly relationship with the participant. Three factors will help with participant receptiveness.

1 The participant must believe that the experience will be pleasant and satisfying.
2 The participant must believe that answering the survey is an important and worthwhile use of his or her time.
3 The participant must dismiss any mental reservations that he or she might have about participation.

Whether the experience will be pleasant and satisfying depends heavily on the interviewer. Typically, participants will cooperate with an interviewer whose behaviour reveals confidence and who engages people on a personal level. Effective interviewers are differentiated not by demographic characteristics but by these interpersonal skills. By confidence, we mean that most participants are immediately convinced that they will want to participate in the study and cooperate fully with the interviewer. An engaging personal style is one where the interviewer instantly establishes credibility by adapting to the individual needs of the participant.

For the participant to think that answering the survey is important and worth while, some explanation of the study's purpose is necessary, although the extent of this will vary. It is the interviewer's responsibility to discover what explanation is needed and to supply it. Usually, the interviewer should state the purpose of the study, say how the information will be used and suggest what is expected of the participant. Participants should feel that their cooperation would be meaningful to themselves and to the survey results. When this is achieved, more participants will express their views willingly.

Participants often have reservations about being interviewed that must be overcome. They may suspect that the interviewer is a salesperson in disguise or has an illegitimate purpose. In addition, they may also feel inadequate or fear the questioning will embarrass them. Techniques for the successful interviewing of participants in environments they control – particularly their homes – follow.

### The introduction

The participant's first reaction to the request for an interview is at best a guarded one. Interviewer appearance and action are critical in forming a good first impression. Interviewers should immediately identify themselves by name and organization, and provide any special identification necessary (introductory letters or other information to confirm the study's legitimacy). In this brief but critical period, the interviewer must display friendly intentions and stimulate the participant's interest.

The interviewer's introductory explanations should be no more detailed than necessary. Too much information can introduce a bias. However, some participants will demand more detail. For them, the interviewer might explain the objective of the study, its background, how the participant was selected, the confidential nature of the interview (if it is confidential), and the benefits of the research findings. Typical questions that might be asked when they are invited to participate in a research are: 'How did you happen to pick me?' 'Who gave you my name?' 'Why don't you go next door?' 'Why are you doing this study?' or a comment such as 'I don't know enough about this'.[3]

### If the participant is busy or away

If it is obvious that the participant is busy, it may be a good idea to give a general introduction and try to stimulate enough interest to arrange an interview at another time. If the designated participant is not at home, the interviewer should briefly explain the proposed visit to the person who is contacted. It is desirable to establish good relations with intermediaries since their attitudes can help in contacting the desired participant. Interviewers contacting participants door to door often leave calling or business cards, which have details of their affiliation and a number where they can be reached to reschedule the interview.

## Establishing a good relationship

The successful interview is based on rapport – meaning a relationship of confidence and understanding between interviewer and participant. Interview situations are often new to participants, and they need help in defining their roles. The interviewer can help by conveying that the interview is confidential (if it is) and important, and that the participant can discuss the topics with freedom from censure, coercion or pressure. Under these conditions, the participant can obtain much satisfaction from 'opening up' without pressure being exerted.

## Gathering the data

Up to this point, the communication aspects of the interviewing process have been stressed. Having completed the introduction and established an initial rapport, the interviewer can turn to the technical task of gathering information. The interview centres on a pre-arranged question sequence. The technical task is well defined in studies with a structured survey procedure (in contrast to an exploratory interview situation). The interviewer should follow the exact wording of the questions, ask them in the order presented and ask every question that is specified. If any questions are misunderstood or misinterpreted, they should be repeated.

A difficult task in interviewing is to make certain the answers satisfy the question's objectives adequately. To do this, the interviewer must learn the objectives of each question from a study of the survey instructions or by asking the research project director. It is important to bear this information in mind because many first responses are inadequate even in the best-planned studies.

The technique of stimulating participants to answer more fully and relevantly is termed **probing**. Since it presents a great potential for bias, a probe should be neutral and appear as a natural part of the conversation. Appropriate probes (those that, when used, will elicit the desired information while injecting a limited amount of bias) should be specified by the designer of the data-collection instrument. There are several different probing styles, as outlined below.

- A brief assertion of understanding and interest: with comments such as 'I see', 'yes' or 'uh' or 'aha', the interviewer can let the participant know that she or he is listening and is interested in hearing more.

- An expectant pause: the simplest way to encourage the participant to say more is to pause, along with an expectant look or a nod of the head. This approach must be used with caution.

- Some participants have nothing more to say, and frequent pausing could create some embarrassing silences and make them feel uncomfortable, reducing their willingness to participate further.

- Repeating the question: this is particularly useful when the participant appears not to understand the question or has strayed from the subject.

- Repeating the participant's reply: the interviewer can do this while writing it down. Such repetition often serves as a good probe. Hearing thoughts restated often promotes revision or further comment.

- A neutral question or comment: such comments make a direct bid for more information.

- Examples are 'How do you mean?' 'Can you tell me more about your thinking on that?' 'Why do you think that is so?' and 'Anything else?'[4]

- Question clarification: when the answer is unclear or is inconsistent with something already said, the interviewer may suggest that the participant failed to understand fully. Typical of such probes is 'I'm not quite sure I know what you mean by that – could you tell me a little more?' or 'I'm sorry, but I'm not sure I understand. Did you say previously that …?' It is important that the interviewer take the blame for this failure to understand so as not to appear to be cross-examining the participant.

A specific type of response that requires persistent probing is the 'I don't know' answer. This is a satisfactory response if the participant really does not know. Too often, however, 'I don't know' means the participant does not understand, wants time to think or is trying to evade the question. The interviewer can best probe this type of reply by using the expectant pause or by making a reassuring remark such as 'We are interested in your ideas about this.'[5]

### Recording the interview

While the methods used in recording will vary, the interviewer usually writes down the participant's answers. The following guidelines show how to make this task more efficient. First, record responses as they occur. If the interviewer waits until later, they will lose much of what is said. If there is a time constraint, the interviewer should use some sort of shorthand system that will preserve the essence of the participant's replies without converting them into the interviewer's paraphrases. Abbreviating words, leaving out articles and prepositions, and using only keywords are good ways to do this.

Another technique is for the interviewer to repeat the response while writing it down. This helps to hold the participant's interest during the writing and checks the interviewer's understanding of what the participant said. Normally the interviewer should start the writing when the participant begins to reply. The interviewer should also record all probes and other comments on the questionnaire in parentheses to separate them from the responses.

Study designers sometimes create a special interview instrument for recording participant answers. This may be integrated with the interview questions or may be a separate document. In such instances the likely answers are anticipated, allowing the interviewer to check participant answers or to record ranks or ratings. However, all interview instruments must permit the entry of unexpected responses.

## Selection and training

The job requirements for interviewers include at least intermediate education, good communication skills, flexible schedules, willingness to tolerate intermittent work hours and mobility. These requirements result in an interviewer profile that is largely composed of white females who have few childcare responsibilities.[6] Little research evidence suggests that other profiles would increase performance or reduce error, except in studies where the question directly involves ethnicity or religion, or where volunteer interviewers are used. The former would imply that matching for race or religion should be considered, and the latter cautions against the use of volunteers because of attrition, recording error and training-related problems.

Field interviewers receive varying degrees of training, ranging from brief written instructions to extensive sessions. Commercial research firms often provide lower levels of training, while governmental, educational and similar research organizations provide more extensive training. Evidence supports the value of training. In one widely cited study, intensive training produced significant improvements in interviewer performance. The training effect was so great that the performance of individual interviewers before training was a poor predictor of post-training performance.[7]

Written instructions should be provided in all studies. Instructions should cover at least the general objectives of the study and mention something about the problems encountered in tests of the interview procedure and how they were solved. In addition, most questions should be discussed separately, giving the interviewer some insight into the purpose of the question, examples of adequate and inadequate responses, and other suggestions such as how to probe for more information. Definitions of concepts or constructs should be included so interviewers can explain and interpret in a standardized manner.

An interview training programme should accomplish the following:

- provide new interviewers with the principles of measurement; give them an intellectual grasp of the data-collection function and a basis for evaluating interviewing behaviour
- provide practice in introductions and introductory materials
- teach the techniques of interviewing
- teach wording and 'skip' instructions to help with a smooth and consistent flow of questions
- teach how to probe
- provide experience in recording answers of different types and on different scales
- provide the opportunity for practice and evaluation by conducting interviews under controlled conditions
- offer careful evaluation of interviews, especially at the beginning of actual data-collection; such evaluation should include a review of interview protocols.[8]

## Interview problems

In personal interviewing, the researcher must deal with bias and cost. While each is discussed separately, they are interrelated. Biased results grow out of three types of error: sampling error, non-response error and response error. We have dealt with the first of these in Chapter 6 but will discuss the other two below.

### Non-response error

In communication studies, **non-response error** occurs when the responses of participants differ in some systematic way from the responses of non-participants. This occurs when the researcher (i) cannot locate the person (the predesignated sample element) to be studied or (ii) is unsuccessful in encouraging that person to participate. This is an especially difficult problem when you are using a probability sample of subjects. If the researcher must interview predesignated persons, the task is to find them. Failure to locate a predesignated participant can be due to inaccessibility. In central cities, getting access to the participant can be a problem, as apartment security and locations that produce safety problems for night-time follow-up may complicate household access.[9] One study of non-response found that only 31 per cent of all first calls (and 20 per cent of all first calls in major metropolitan areas) were completed.

Solutions to reduce errors of non-response include:

- establishing and implementing call-back procedures
- creating a non-response sample and weighting results from this sample
- substituting another individual for the missing participant.

### Call-backs

The most reliable solution to non-response problems is to make call-backs. If enough attempts are made, it is usually possible to contact most target participants, although unlimited call-backs are expensive.[10] An original contact plus three call-backs should usually secure about 85 per cent of the target participants. Yet in one study, 36 per cent of central city residents had still not been contacted after three call-backs.[11] One way to improve the productivity of call-backs is to vary them by time of day and day of week. Sometimes neighbours can suggest the best time to call.

### Weighting

Another approach that has been used successfully is to treat all remaining non-participants as a new sub-population after a few call-backs. A random sample is then drawn from this group, and every effort is made to complete this sample with a 100 per cent response rate. Findings from this non-participant sample can then be weighted into the total population estimate.[12] In a survey in which central city residents are under-represented, we can weight the results of interviews that are completed with such residents to give them full representation in the results. The weakness of this approach is that weighted returns often differ from those that would be secured if successful call-backs were made. Thus, an unknown – but possibly substantial – bias is introduced. Weighting for non-response after only one contact attempt will probably not overcome non-response bias, but participant characteristics converge on their population values after two to three call-backs.[13]

### Substitution

A third way to deal with the non-response problem is to substitute someone else for the missing participant. This is, however, dangerous. 'At home' participants are likely to differ from 'not at home' persons in systematic ways. One study suggested that 'not at home' persons are younger, better educated, more urban and have a higher income than the average.[14]

If it is absolutely necessary to substitute, it is better for the interviewer to ask others in the household about the designated participant. This approach has worked well 'when questions are objective, when informants have a high degree of observability with respect to participants, when the population is homogeneous, and when the setting of the interview provides no clear-cut motivation to distort responses in one direction or another'.[15]

## Response error

When the data reported differ from the actual data, **response error** occurs. Response error can occur during the interview (created by either the interviewer or participant) or during the preparation of data for analysis.

**Participant-initiated error** occurs when the participant fails to answer fully and accurately – either by choice, or because of inaccurate or incomplete knowledge. One study found that participants typically underestimated cash and other liquid assets by as much as 25–50 per cent. Other data, such as income and purchases of consumer durables, are more accurately reported. Participants also have difficulty in reporting fully and accurately on topics that are sensitive or involve ego matters. Consistent control or elimination of this bias is a problem that has yet to be solved. The best advice is to use trained interviewers who are knowledgeable about such problems.

**Interviewer error** is also a major source of response bias. From the introduction to the conclusion of the interview, there are many points where the interviewer's control of the process can affect the quality of the data. Study designers should strive to eliminate several different kinds of error, as outlined below, evolving from the interview techniques discussed above.

- Failure to secure full participant cooperation: the sample loses credibility and is likely to be biased if interviewers do not do a good job of enlisting participant cooperation.

- Failure to consistently execute interview procedures: the precision of survey estimates will be reduced and there will be more error around estimates to the extent that interviewers are inconsistent in ways that influence the data. Interview procedures are especially important if the interviews are conducted by different interviewers, as is common in larger surveys.

- Failure to establish appropriate interview environment: answers may be systematically inaccurate or biased when interviewers fail to 'train' and motivate participants appropriately or fail to establish a suitable interpersonal setting.[16]

- Falsification of individual answers or whole interviews: perhaps the most insidious form of interviewer error is cheating. Surveying is difficult work, often done by part-time employees, usually with only limited training and under little direct supervision. At times, falsification of an answer to an overlooked question is perceived as an easy solution to counterbalance the incomplete data. This easy, seemingly harmless first step can be followed by more pervasive forgery. It is not known how much of this occurs, but it should be of constant concern to research directors as they develop their data-collection design, and to those organizations that outsource survey projects. Falsifications of the interview also include the skipping of questions, either because they are difficult to ask or because they take a lot of time. One of the authors of this book recalls being interviewed for a market research survey on travel. One of the questions asked him to list all the foreign countries he had visited in the past two years. When he had named five countries, the interviewer stopped him saying that for each named country he now wished to ask a couple of additional questions.

- Inappropriate influencing behaviour: it is obvious that an interviewer can distort the results of any survey by inappropriate suggestions, word emphasis, tone of voice, body language and question rephrasing. These activities, whether premeditated or merely due to carelessness, are widespread. This problem was investigated using a simple structured questionnaire and 'planted' participants, who then reported on the interviewers. The conclusion was that 'the high frequency of deviations from instructed behavior is alarming'.[17]

In the travel survey mentioned above, the interviewer also suggested that the author answer a question on the total costs of a trip to a specific country with the option 'don't know', as – according to him – nobody knows exactly the total costs of such a trip. He was right: most people will have difficulty in recollecting the exact cost of a trip. However, a good interviewer will never suggest the 'don't know' option, but will instead ask for a reasonable estimate if the respondent does not know the exact answer.

- Failure to record answers accurately and completely: error may result from an interview recording procedure that forces the interviewer to summarize or interpret participant answers, or that provides insufficient space to record answers as provided by the participant.

- Physical presence bias: interviewers can influence participants in unperceived ways. Older interviewers are often seen as authority figures by young participants, who modify their responses accordingly. Some research indicates that perceived social distance between interviewer and participant has a distorting effect, although the studies do not fully agree on just what this relationship is.[18]

In light of the numerous studies on the various aspects of interview bias, the safest course for researchers is to recognize that there is constant potential for response error.

## Costs

While professional interviewers' wage scales are typically not high, interviewing is costly, and these costs continue to rise. Much of the cost results from the substantial interviewer time taken up with administrative and travel tasks. Participants are often geographically scattered, and this adds to the cost. Repeated contacts (recommended at six to nine per household) are expensive. In recent years, some professional research organizations have attempted to gain control of these spiralling costs. Interviewers have typically been paid an hourly rate, but this method rewards inefficient interviewers and often results in field costs exceeding budgets.[19] The US Bureau of the Census and the National Opinion Research Center have experimented with production standards and a formula pay system that provide an incentive for efficient interviewers. This approach has cut field costs by about 10 per cent and has improved the accuracy of the forecasts of fieldwork costs.

A second approach for reducing field costs has been to pre-schedule personal interviews. Telephone calls to set up appointments for interviews are reported to reduce personal calls by 25 per cent without reducing cooperation rates.[20] Telephone screening is also valuable when a study is concerned with a rare population. In one such case, where blind persons were sought, it was found that telephone screening of households was one-third of the cost of screening on a face-to-face basis.[21]

A third means of reducing high field costs is to use self-administered questionnaires. In one study, a personal interview was conducted in the household with a self-administered questionnaire left for one or more other members of the household to complete. In this study, the cost per completed case was reduced by half when compared to conducting individual personal interviews. A comparison between a personal interview and a self-administered questionnaire seeking the same data showed that there was generally sufficient similarity of answers to enable them to be combined.[22]

Snapshot

# Counting eggs

The living conditions that egg-laying hens are forced to endure are cruel. Most hens are held in cages that offer less space per hen than the size of a page of this book. Photos showing how hens produce our breakfast eggs have appeared in the media and animal activists have used them to draw consumers' attention to this issue. Although poultry associations argue that the current usage of cages for hens does not violate animal rights, the European Commission has decided that, from 2006, egg producers must provide more space for their hens. The EU directive distinguishes three egg production conditions offering increasing levels of space for hens – (1) cage, (2) barn and (3) free-range – and egg producers have to mark each egg according to the production conditions. In this way, consumers can have a say in the hens' living conditions by revealing their preference at the supermarket checkout.

Exhibit 7.6 shows which eggs German consumers say they prefer (inner circle) and which eggs they actually buy (outer circle). The difference between the two circles (derived from different data sources, namely a consumer survey and secondary statistics) is astonishing. Only 1 out of 20 consumers concedes preferring cage eggs, yet 12 out of 20 eggs sold come from caged hens. How can these differences be explained? Is social desirability of answering behaviour the only explanation? What do you think about the explanation that the 5 per cent of consumers confessing that they buy eggs from caged hens are heavy egg consumers, while those that buy free-range eggs consume fewer eggs? What do you think about the comment that the population between the two statistics differs – the one on buying preferences consists only of households, while the purchase statistic also includes small businesses, such as restaurants, who buy their eggs from retailers?

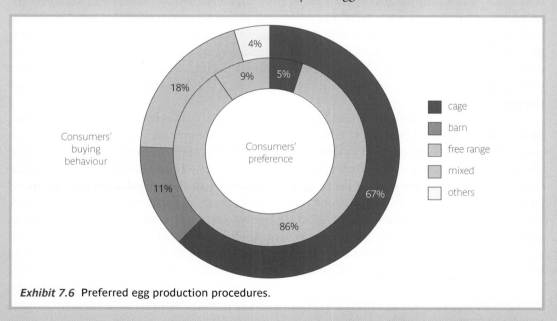

**Exhibit 7.6**  Preferred egg production procedures.

# References and further reading

*Der Spiegel.*

# 7.4  Telephone interviewing

The telephone can be helpful in arranging personal interviews and screening large populations for unusual types of participants. Studies have also shown that making prior notification calls can improve the response rates of mail surveys. However, the telephone interview makes its greatest contribution in survey work as a unique mode of communication to collect information from participants.

## Evaluation of the telephone interview

Of the advantages that telephone interviewing offers, probably none ranks higher than its moderate cost. One study reports that sampling and data-collection costs for telephone surveys can run from 45 to 64 per cent lower than comparable personal interviews.[23] Much of this saving comes from cuts in travel costs and administrative savings from training and supervision. When calls are made from a single location, the researcher may use fewer yet more skilled interviewers. Telephones are especially economical when call-backs to maintain probability sampling are involved and participants are widely scattered. Long-distance service options make it possible to interview nationally at a reasonable cost.

With the widespread use of computers, telephone interviewing can be combined with immediate entry of responses into a data file by means of terminals, personal computers or voice data entry. This brings added savings in time and money. **Computer-assisted telephone interviewing (CATI)** is used in research organizations throughout the world. A CATI facility consists of acoustically isolated interviewing carrels organized around supervisory stations. The telephone interviewer in each carrel has a personal computer or terminal that is networked to the telephone system and to the central data-processing unit. A software program that prompts the interviewers with introductory statements, qualifying questions and pre-coded questionnaire items drives surveying. These materials appear on the interviewers' monitors. CATI works with a telephone number management system to select numbers, dial the sample and enter responses.

Another means of securing immediate response data is the **computer-administered telephone survey**. Unlike CATI, there is no interviewer. A computer calls the telephone number, conducts the interview, places data into a file for later tabulation and terminates the contact. The questions are voice-synthesized, and the participant's answer and computer timing trigger continuation or disconnect. This mode is often compared to the self-administered questionnaire (discussed later in this chapter) and offers the advantage of participant privacy. One study showed that the **non-contact rate** for the electronic survey mode is similar to other telephone interviews when a random telephone list is used. It also found that rejection of this mode of data-collection affects the **refusal rate** (and thus non-response bias) because people will hang up more readily on a computer than on a human.[24] The non-contact rate is a ratio of potential but unreached contacts (no answer, busy, answering machine, and disconnects but not refusals) to all potential contacts. The refusal rate refers to the ratio of participants who decline the interview to all potential contacts.

When compared to either personal interviews or mail surveys, the use of telephones brings a faster completion of a study, sometimes taking only a day or so for the fieldwork. When compared to personal interviewing, it is also likely that interviewer bias – especially bias caused by the physical appearance, body language and actions of the interviewer – is reduced by using the telephone.

Almost 91 per cent of British households have a fixed telephone service, while in eastern European countries, such as Romania, only 20 per cent of households have access to a fixed line.[25] Access to participants through low-cost, efficient means has made telephone interviewing a very attractive alternative for marketing, public opinion and academic researchers. Finally, behavioural norms work to the advantage of telephone interviewing. If someone is present, a ringing phone is usually answered, and it is the caller who decides the purpose, length and termination of the call.[26] New technology, notably caller identification systems where the receiver can decide whether a call is answered based on caller identity, is expected to increase the non-contact rate associated with telephone surveys.

There are also disadvantages to using the telephone for research. A skilled researcher will evaluate the use of a telephone survey to minimize the effect of the following disadvantages:

- inaccessible households (no telephone service)
- inaccurate or non-functioning numbers
- limitation on interview length (fewer measurement questions)
- limitations on use of visual or complex questions
- ease of interview termination
- less participant involvement
- distracting physical environment.

We will now look at each of these in turn.

## Inaccessible households

Many households move each year, generating many obsolete numbers and new households for which numbers have not yet been published. Also, individuals increasingly opt to have unlisted numbers. Another recent problem encountered in telephone surveys is the increasing number of people who only have a mobile telephone, but no fixed line subscription. In some European countries (e.g. in the UK, Belgium and Portugal) the number of main fixed telephone lines is actually declining, while subscriptions to mobile telephone services are rising every year. In 2000, subscription to mobile telephones (235 million) exceeded the number of main telephone lines (204 million) for the first time in the EU member states.[27] In Finland – a front-runner in mobile telephone penetration, 29 per cent of households already only have a mobile telephone connection (i.e. no fixed telephone connection). Respective figures for France are 16 per cent, the UK 6 per cent, and 4 per cent in Germany and Sweden.[28] Although people carry their mobile telephones with them most of the time and are therefore easily contactable, most research agencies have been reluctant to contact people on their mobile telephones, as it is impossible to know what they are doing and where they are when called. Such variations in participant availability by telephone can be a source of bias.

## Inaccurate or non-functioning numbers

Several methods have been developed to overcome the deficiencies of directories; among them are techniques for choosing telephone numbers by using random-digit dialling or combinations of directories and random-digit dialling.[29] **Random dialling** procedures normally require choosing telephone exchanges or exchange blocks and then generating random numbers within these blocks for calling.[30] However, increasing demand for multiple telephone lines by both households and individuals has generated new telephone area codes and local exchanges. This too increases the inaccuracy rate. It should also be noted that using random dialling procedures is forbidden by law in some countries, such as the Netherlands.

### Limitation on interview length

A limit on interview length is another disadvantage of the telephone, but the degree of this limitation depends on the participant's interest in the topic. Ten minutes has generally been thought of as ideal, but interviews of 20 minutes or more are not uncommon. Interviews ran for one and a half hours in one long-distance survey.[31]

### Limitations on use of visual or complex questions

In telephone interviewing, it is difficult to use maps, illustrations, visual aids, complex scales or measurement techniques (however, in some instances, these might be supplied via fax or e-mail prior to the pre-scheduled interview). The medium also limits the complexity of the survey and the use of visualization techniques possible with personal interviewing. For example, in personal interviews, participants are sometimes asked to sort or rank an array of cards containing different responses to a question. For participants who cannot visualize a scale or other measurement device that the interview is attempting to describe, one solution has been to employ a nine-point scaling approach and to ask the participant to visualize it by using the telephone dial or keypad.[32]

### Ease of interview termination

Some studies suggest that the response rate in telephone studies is lower than for comparable face-to-face interviews. One reason is that participants find it easier to terminate a telephone interview. Telemarketing practices may also contribute. Public reaction to investigative reports of wrongdoing and unethical behaviour within telemarketing activities places an added burden on the researcher, who must try to convince a participant that the telephone interview is not a pretext for soliciting contributions or selling products.

### Less participant involvement

Telephone surveys can result in less thorough responses, and those interviewed by telephone find the experience to be less rewarding than a personal interview. Participants report less rapport with telephone interviewers than with personal interviewers. Given the growing costs and difficulties of personal interviews, it is likely that an even higher share of surveys will be by telephone in the future. Thus, it is the responsibility of management researchers using telephone surveys to attempt to improve the enjoyment of the interview. One authority suggests that:

> We need to experiment with techniques to improve the enjoyment of the interview by the participant, maximize the overall completion rate, and minimize response error on specific measures. This work might fruitfully begin with efforts at translating into verbal messages the visual cues that fill the interaction in a face-to-face

interview: the smiles, frowns, raising of eyebrows, eye contact, etc. All of these cues have informational content and are important parts of the personal interview setting. We can perhaps purposefully choose those cues that are most important to data quality and participant trust and discard the many that are extraneous to the survey interaction.[33]

### Distracting physical environment

Speculation has also surfaced with regard to the increasing practice of substituting one's home or office phone with cellular and wireless phones. In terms of telephone surveys, this raises concerns about the changing environment in which such surveys might be conducted, the resulting quality of data collected under possibly distracting circumstances, and the possible increase in refusal rates.

## Telephone interview trends

Future trends in telephone interviewing bear watching. Answering machines and multi-line households will affect sampling, as will variations among telephone companies' services and the degree of cooperation that will be extended to researchers. There is also concern about the ways in which random-digit dialling can be made to deal with non-functioning and ineligible numbers.[34]

Answering machines could pose potentially complex response-rate problems since they are estimated to have substantial penetration in residential households. Previous research discovered that most answering-machine households are accessible; the subsequent contact rate was greater in answering-machine households than in no-machine households and about equal with busy-signal households. Other findings suggested that:

- individuals with answering machines were more likely to participate
- machine use was more prevalent on weekends than on weekday evenings
- machines were more commonplace in urban than in rural areas.

Voicemail options offered by local telephone service providers have less market penetration but are gaining increasing acceptance. Questions about the socio-demographics of users and non-users and the relationship of answering-machine/voicemail technology to the rapid changes in the wireless market remain to be answered.[35] Caller identification technology, the assignment of facsimile machines or computer modems to dedicated telephone lines, and technology that identifies computer-automated diallers and sends a disconnect signal in response are all expected to have an impact on the non-contact rate of telephone interviews.

## 7.5 Self-administered surveys

The **self-administered questionnaire** has become ubiquitous in modern living. Service evaluations of hotels, restaurants, car dealerships and transportation providers furnish ready examples. Often, a short questionnaire is left to be completed by the participant in a convenient location or is packaged with a product. Self-administered mail surveys are delivered not only by national mail firms, such as Royal Mail and Deutsche Post, but also via fax and courier service. Other methods of distribution include computer-delivered and intercept studies.

Intercept studies may use a traditional paper questionnaire or a computer-delivered survey. The participant participates without interviewer assistance, usually in a predetermined environment such as a shopping mall. All modes have special problems and unique advantages (see Exhibit 7.4).

## Evaluation of self-administered surveys

Much of what researchers know about self-administered surveys has been learned from experiments conducted with mail surveys and personal experience. So as we explore the strengths and weaknesses of the various self-administered methods, we will start with this body of knowledge.

### Costs

Self-administered surveys of all types typically cost less than personal interviews. This is true of mail surveys, as well as computer-delivered and intercept studies. Telephone and mail costs are in the same general range, although in specific cases either may be lower. It should be noted, however, that the time involved in collecting the information is much greater for telephone surveys, which increases the costs substantially if the interviewers have to be paid. The more geographically dispersed the sample, the more likely it is that self-administered surveys via computer or mail will be the low-cost method. A mail or computer-delivered study can cost less because it is often a one-person job. In addition, computer-delivered studies (including CAPI and CATI studies) eliminate the cost of printing surveys, a significant element of both mail studies and personal interviewing.

### Sample accessibility

Another advantage of using mail is that researchers can contact participants who might otherwise be inaccessible. Some people – such as major corporate executives or doctors – are difficult to reach in person or by telephone, as gatekeepers (secretaries, office managers and assistants) limit access. Researchers can, however, often access these special participants by mail or computer. When the researcher has no specific person to contact – say, in a study of corporations – the mail or computer-delivered survey may be routed to the appropriate participant. Questionnaires sent to a corporation without a personal name will often not be returned as the general mail office of the corporation might not know to whom the questionnaire should be forwarded. Furthermore, the researcher cannot control whether the appropriate person answered the questionnaire. If you do not have personal names, the second best solution is to address the questionnaire to a certain job function, such as 'head of the sales department'. This is more effective if the corporation is not too large, because large corporations may have hundreds of heads of sales department. In general it is advisable to put considerable effort into finding out the personal names of the people you want to contact.

### Careful consideration

While intercept studies still pressure participants for a relatively quick turnaround, in a mail survey the participant can take more time to collect facts, talk with others or consider replies at length than is possible in a telephone or personal interview. Computer-delivered studies, especially those accessed via e-mail links to the Internet, usually have time limitations on both access and completion once started. And once started, computer-delivered studies cannot easily be interrupted by the participant to seek information not immediately known.

## Anonymity

Mail surveys are typically perceived as more impersonal, providing greater anonymity than the other communication modes, including other methods for distributing self-administered questionnaires. For example, in the Dutch Family Survey, researchers interviewed the head of the household and his or her spouse with a combination of personal interview and self-administered questionnaire. The self-administered questionnaire included questions on satisfaction with their relationship and their partner, which respondents might understandably have been reluctant to answer honestly if the partner were present!

## Topic coverage

A major limitation of self-administered surveys concerns the type and amount of information that can be secured. Researchers normally do not expect to obtain large amounts of information and cannot probe too deeply into topics. Participants will generally refuse to cooperate with a long and/or complex mail, computer-delivered or intercept questionnaire unless they perceive a personal benefit. Returned mail questionnaires with many questions left unanswered testify to this problem, but there are also many exceptions. One general rule of thumb is that the participant should be able to answer the questionnaire in no more than 10 minutes (similar to the guidelines proposed for telephone studies). On the other hand, one study of the general population found more than a 70 per cent response to a questionnaire calling for 158 answers.[36]

## Non-response error

Another major weakness of the self-administered study is non-response error. Many studies have shown that better-educated participants and those more interested in the topic answer mail surveys. A high percentage of those who reply to a given survey have usually replied to others, while a large share of those who do not respond are habitual non-participants.[37] Response rates of business firms also differ considerably between countries: in general they are higher in Japan than in Europe, and higher in Europe than in the US.[38] In either case, there are many non-respondents, and we usually know nothing about how those who answer differ from those who do not.

## Reducing non-response error

The research literature is filled with ways to improve mail survey returns, and much of this knowledge may be applied to other modes of delivering self-administered surveys. Seemingly every possible variable has been studied. Over 200 methodological articles have been published on efforts to improve mail response rates. Three review articles concluded that few variables consistently showed positive response rates.[39] Several practical suggestions emerge from the conclusions.[40]

### Follow-ups

Follow-ups, or reminders, are very successful in increasing response rates. Since each successive follow-up produces more returns, the very persistent (and well-financed) researcher can potentially achieve an extremely high total response rate. However, the value of additional information thus obtained must be weighed against the costs required for successive contacts.

## Preliminary notification

There is evidence that advance notification, particularly by telephone, is effective in increasing response rates; it also serves to accelerate the rate of return. However, follow-ups are a better investment than preliminary notification.

## Concurrent techniques

1 Questionnaire length: although common sense suggests that short questionnaires should obtain higher response rates than longer questionnaires, research evidence does not support this view.

2 Survey sponsorship: there is little experimental evidence concerning the influence of survey sponsorship on response rates; however, the sparse evidence that does exist suggests that official or 'respected' sponsorship increases response rates.

3 Return envelopes: the inclusion of a stamped addressed envelope encourages response because it simplifies questionnaire return.

4 Postage: many tests regarding postage are reported in the literature, but few studies have tested the same variables. The existing evidence shows that expedited delivery is very effective in increasing response rates. Findings do not show a significant advantage for first class over third class, for commemorative stamps over ordinary postage, for stamped mail over metered mail or for multiple small denomination stamps over single larger denomination stamps.

5 Personalization: personalization of the mailing has no clear-cut advantage in terms of improved response rates. Neither personal inside addresses nor individually signed cover letters significantly increased response rates; personally typed cover letters proved to be somewhat effective in most but not all cases cited. The one study that tested the use of a titled signature versus one without a title did show a significant advantage in favour of the title.

6 Cover letters: the influence of the cover letter on response rates has received almost no experimental attention, although the cover letter is considered an integral part of the mail survey package. It is the most logical vehicle for persuading individuals to respond, yet the few studies that are reported offer no insights as to its formulation.

7 Anonymity: experimental evidence shows that the promise of anonymity to participants, either explicit or implied, has no significant effect on response rates.

8 Size, reproduction and colour: the few studies that examined the effects of questionnaire size, method of reproduction and colour found no significant difference in response rates.

9 Money incentives: a monetary incentive sent with the questionnaire is very effective in increasing response rates. Larger sums bring in added response, but at a cost that may exceed the value of the added information. In studies among organizations in particular, an interesting incentive is to promise the respondent a report highlighting the findings of the research. You might even choose to offer a customized report, which compares the respondent's answers with the average of the sample or a specified sub-sample.

10 Deadline dates: the few studies that tested the impact of deadline dates found that they did not increase the response rate; however, they did serve to accelerate the rate of questionnaire return.

Researchers are equivocal about the above suggestions and conclusions because 'the manipulation of one or two techniques independently of all others may do little to stimulate response'.[41] Efforts should be directed towards the more important question of maximizing the overall probability of response. The Total Design Method (TDM), consisting of two parts, is proposed to meet this need.[42] First, the researcher must identify the aspects of the survey process that affect the response rate, either qualitatively or quantitatively. Each aspect must be shaped to obtain the best response. Second, the researcher must organize the survey effort so the design intentions are carried out in detail. The results achieved in 48 surveys using TDM showed response rates of 50–94 per cent, with a median response rate of 74 per cent.[43] TDM procedures suggest minimizing the burden on participants by designing surveys that:

- are easy to read
- offer clear response directions
- include personalized communication
- provide information about the survey in a cover letter (or via advance notification)
- are followed by researcher contacts to encourage response.[44]

## Maximizing the mail survey

To maximize the overall probability of response, attention must be given to each point of the survey process where the response may break down.[45] For example:

- the wrong address and wrong postage can result in non-delivery or non-return
- the envelope or fax cover sheet may look like junk mail and be discarded without being opened
- lack of proper instructions for completion may lead to non-response
- the wrong person may open the envelope or receive the fax and fail to call it to the attention of the right person
- a participant may find no convincing explanation for completing the survey and thus discard it
- a participant may temporarily set the questionnaire aside and fail to complete it
- the return address may be lost so the questionnaire cannot be returned.

Efforts to overcome these problems will vary according to the circumstances, but some general suggestions can be made for mail surveys and, by extension, for self-administered questionnaires using different delivery modes. With a questionnaire, a cover letter and return mechanism should be sent. Incentives, such as euro notes, gift coupons or prepaid phone cards, are often attached to the letter in commercial studies. Follow-ups are usually needed to get the maximum response. Opinions differ about the number and timing of follow-ups – in general, the timing of follow-ups should be adapted for different delivery modes. TDM uses the follow-ups described below.

1  One week later: a pre-printed postcard is sent to all recipients thanking them for returns and reminding others to complete and mail the questionnaire.

**2** Three weeks after the original mailing: a new questionnaire is sent, along with a letter telling non-participants that the questionnaire has not been received and repeating the basic appeal of the original letter.

**3** Seven weeks after the original mailing: a third cover letter and questionnaire are sent by certified mail to the remaining non-participants.

An appeal for cooperation is essential and may be altruistic or more expedient. The former is often found when the questionnaire is short, easy to complete and does not require much effort from a participant. Anonymity may or may not be mentioned. A brief letter emphasizes the 'Would you do me a favour?' approach. Often a token is sent to symbolize the researcher's appreciation. Sometimes this is not powerful enough. Then an appeal must stress how important the problem is to a group with which the participant identifies.

The cover letter should also convey that the participant's help is needed to solve a problem. Researchers are portrayed as reasonable people making a reasonable appeal for help. They are intermediaries between the person asked for help and an important issue. The total effect must be personalized to convey to participants that they are important to the study. The standard is to make the appeal comparable in appearance and content to what one would expect in a business or professional letter.

Finally, a mixed model can be used to improve response. One study compared the use of 'drop-off' delivery of a self-administered questionnaire to a mail survey.[46] Under the drop-off system, a lightly trained survey-taker personally delivered the questionnaires to target households and returned in a couple of days for the completed instrument. Response rates for the drop-off system were typically above 70 per cent – much higher than for comparable mail surveys. In addition, the cost per completed questionnaire was from 18 to 40 per cent lower than for mail surveys.

Beyond a higher response rate and lower cost per response, the drop-off delivery gives greater control over sample design, permits thorough identification of the participants' geographic location and allows the researcher to eliminate those who fall outside a predefined sample frame (persons of the wrong age, income or other characteristics). Additional information can be gathered by observation on the visits. However, the cost advantage is probably restricted to studies where participants can be reached with little travel.

Drop-off delivery has much in common with intercept studies that employ self-administered completion of a questionnaire. The researcher can encourage the selected participant to complete the questionnaire, stressing the importance of his or her participation and the ease of completion, and then indicate the procedure for returning it. These activities are likely to increase response rates and reduce non-response error.

In business research, the respondents are often organizations – for example individuals representing a company – and not private persons. As the respondents are representatives of an organization their willingness to respond does not only depend on their motivation, but also on their capacity and authority to respond (in large organizations in particular, the required knowledge is often spread over different persons and departments). Authority to respond is another problem when approaching organizations (e.g. subsidiaries are less likely to respond). Surveying organizations require that specificities of organizational research are considered in the survey design. In particular, researchers should take into account the following points.[47]

- Is asking for financial information really necessary for the purpose of the study? Asking for such information can trigger non-response.

- If you approach a subsidiary, you need to clarify that you are interested in the specific subsidiary and not the company as a whole. Otherwise such organizations might not respond as they feel that they are not authorized to respond or think that they do not have the information.

- As with all other surveys, people might be reluctant to answer as filling in the survey takes time. A very useful strategy in this context is to ask the top management for cooperation in the study. They can help to identify respondents in the organization but, more importantly, if they support a survey in their organization people feel obliged to answer.

# 7.6 Web-based surveys

Computer-delivered self-administered questionnaires use organizational intranets, the Internet or online services to reach their participants. Participants may be targeted (as when BizRate, an online e-business rating service, sends an e-mail to a registered e-purchaser to participate in a survey) or self-selecting (as when a computer screen pop-up window offers a survey to an individual who clicks on a particular website or when a potential participant responds to a postcard inquiry looking for participants). In 2002, 135 million people used the Internet (i.e. 36 per cent of the population) in the 15 EU member states. However, the percentage of Internet use differs considerably between countries: while in Scandinavian countries more than 50 per cent of the population uses the Internet, in Greece and Spain less than 20 per cent of the population use the web.[48] Is it any wonder that computer-delivered self-administered surveys have caught the imagination of business (see Exhibit 7.7)?

The computer-delivered survey, however, has made the collective execution of many of these suggestions more attractive. Once the computer-delivered survey is crafted, the cost of re-delivery via computer – thereby decreasing non-response error – is very low. Preliminary notification via e-mail is also accomplished in a more timely and less costly way than by phone or mail. The return mechanism for the computer-delivered study is usually the click of a mouse or a single keystroke. Personalization of the survey cover letter – the e-mail that links the participant to the survey – is easily accomplished. The computer also makes the use of colour within a survey, even colour photographs, a viable option – one not often considered with paper surveys due to cost. In addition, video clips – never an option with a mail survey – are possible with a computer-delivered survey. Even the delivery of monetary and other incentives has been simplified with the use of e-currencies. However, employing all the stimulants for participation that have been researched cannot overcome a participant's inability to complete an Internet survey due to technological problems. Such glitches are likely to continue to plague participation as long as researchers and participants use different computer platforms, operating systems and software.

Computer surveying is surfacing at trade shows, where participants complete surveys while making a visit to a company's stand. Continuous tabulation of results provides a stimulus for attendees to visit a particular exhibit as well as giving the exhibitor detailed information for evaluating the productivity of the show. This same technology transfers easily to other situations where large groups of people congregate.

| Web Attractions | Example |
|---|---|
| Short turnaround of results; results are tallied as respondents complete surveys | A soft-drink manufacturer got results from a web survey in just five days |
| Ability to use visual stimuli | Florida's tourism office used eye-movement tracking to enhance its website and improve its billboard and print ads |
| Ability to do numerous surveys over time | A printer manufacturer did seven surveys in six months during the development of one of its latest products |
| Ability to attract participants who wouldn't participate in another research project, including international respondents | An agricultural equipment manufacturer did a study using two-way pagers provided free to farmers to query users about its equipment – respondents usually unavailable by telephone or PC |
| Respondents feel anonymous | Anonymity was the necessary ingredient for a study on impotence conducted by a drug manufacturer |
| Shortened turnaround from survey draft to execution of survey | A Hewlett-Packard survey using Greenfield Online's *QuickTake* took two weeks to write, launch, and field – not the standard three months using non-web venues |
| Experiences unavailable by other means | One major advertising agency is conducting Web research using virtual supermarket aisles that respondents wander through, reacting to client products and promotions LiveWorld has developed a packaging study showing more than 75 images of labels and bottle designs |
| **Web Drawbacks** | |
| Recruiting the right sample is costly and time-consuming; unlike telephone and mail sample frames, no lists exist | TalkCity, working for Whitton Associates and Fusion5, set up a panel of 3700 teens for a survey to test new packaging for a soft drink using telephone calls, referrals, e-mail lists, banner ads and website visits. It drew a sample of 600 for the research. It cost more than $50,000 to set up the list |
| Converting surveys to the web can be expensive | LiveWorld's teen study cost $50,000–$100,000 to set up, with additional fees with each focus group or survey. The total price tag was several hundred thousand dollars |
| It takes technical as well as research skill to field a web survey | A 10–15 minute survey can take up to five days of technical expertise to field and test |
| While research is more compatible with numerous browsers, the technology isn't perfect | A well-known business magazine did a study among a recruited sample only to have the survey abort on question 20 of a larger study |

**Exhibit 7.7** The web as a research venue.[49]

*Note*: if you understand HTML standards and web-survey programming, you will find a very useful web-survey tutorial at http://www.researchinfo.com.

Companies are now using intranet capabilities to evaluate employee policies and behaviour. Ease of access to electronic mail systems makes it possible for both large and small organizations to use computer questioning with both internal and external participant groups. Many techniques of traditional mail surveys can easily be adapted to computer-delivered questionnaires (e.g. follow-ups to non-participants are more easily executed and are less expensive).

It is not unusual to find registration procedures and full-scale surveying being done on World Wide Websites. University sites are asking prospective students about their interests, and university departments are evaluating current students' use of online materials. A short surf on the Internet reveals organizations using their sites to evaluate customer service processes, build sales-lead lists, evaluate planned promotions and product changes, determine supplier and customer needs, discover interest in job openings, evaluate employee attitudes, and more. Advanced and easier-to-use software for designing web surveys can also be found.

The **web-based questionnaire** has the power of CATI systems, but without the expense of network administrators, specialized software or additional hardware. As a solution for Internet or intranet websites, you need only a personal computer and web access. Most products are browser-driven with design features that allow custom survey creation and modification.

Two primary options are proprietary solutions offered through research firms and off-the-shelf software designed for researchers who possess the knowledge and skills described here and in Chapter 12. With fee-based services, you are guided (often online) through problem formulation, questionnaire design, question content, response strategy, and wording and sequence of questions. Staff then generate the questionnaire HTML code, host the survey at their server, and provide data consolidation and reports. Off-the-shelf software is a strong alternative. *PC Magazine* has reviewed six packages containing well-designed user interfaces and advanced data preparation features.[50] The advantages of these software programs are:

- questionnaire design in a word-processing environment
- ability to import questionnaire forms from text files
- a coaching device to guide you through question and response formatting
- question and scale libraries
- automated publishing to a web server
- real-time viewing of incoming data
- ability to edit data in a spreadsheet-type environment
- rapid transmission of results
- flexible analysis and reporting mechanisms.

Ease of use is not the only influence pushing the popularity of web-based instruments – cost is a major factor and web-based research is much less expensive than conventional survey research. Although fees are based on the number of completions, a sample of 100 might cost one-sixth of a conventional telephone interview. Bulk mailing and e-mail data-collection have also become more cost-effective because any instrument may be configured as an e-mail questionnaire.

## 7.7 Selecting an optimal method

The choice of a communication method is not as complicated as it might first appear. By comparing your research objectives with the strengths and weaknesses of each method, you will be able to choose one that is suited to your needs. The summary of advantages and disadvantages of personal interviews, telephone interviews and self-administered questionnaires presented in Exhibit 7.4 should be useful in making such a comparison.

When your investigative questions call for information from hard-to-reach or inaccessible participants, the telephone interview, mail- or computer-delivered survey should be considered. However, if data must be collected very quickly, the mail survey is likely to be ruled out because of lack of control over the returns. Alternatively, you may decide that your objective requires extensive questioning and probing – then the personal interview should be considered.

If none of the choices turns out to be a particularly good fit, it is possible to combine the best characteristics of two or more alternatives into a mixed mode. Although this decision will incur the costs of the combined modes, the flexibility of tailoring a method to your unique needs is often an acceptable trade-off.

Ultimately, all researchers are confronted by the practical realities of cost and deadlines. As Exhibit 7.4 suggests, on average, personal interviews are the most expensive communication method and take the most field time unless a large field team is used. Telephone interviews are moderate in cost and offer the quickest option, especially when CATI is used. Questionnaires administered by mail are the least expensive, although these traditionally require a longer data-collection period. When your desired sample is available via the Internet, emerging Internet surveying may prove to be the least expensive communication method with the most rapid (simultaneous) data availability. The use of the computer to select participants, and reduce coding and processing time will continue to improve the cost-to-performance profiles of these methods in the future.

Most of the time an optimal method will be apparent. However, managers' needs for information often exceed their internal resources. Factors such as specialized expertise, a large field team, unique facilities or a rapid turnaround prompt organizations to seek assistance from research vendors of survey-related services.

## 7.8 Outsourcing survey services

Commercial suppliers of research services vary from full-service operations to speciality consultants. When confidentiality is likely to affect competitive advantage, the manager or staff will sometimes prefer to bid only a phase of the project. Alternatively, the organization's staff members may possess such unique knowledge of a product or service that they must fulfil a part of the study themselves. Regardless of this, the exploratory work, design, sampling, data-collection or processing and analysis may be contracted separately or as a whole.

Research firms also offer special advantages that their clients do not typically maintain in-house. Centralized location interviewing, focus group facilities or computer-assisted telephone facilities may be particularly desirable for certain research needs. A professionally trained staff with considerable experience in similar management problems is another benefit. Data processing and statistical analysis capabilities are especially important for some projects. Other vendors have specially designed software for interviewing and data tabulation.[51] Panel suppliers provide another type of research service with an emphasis on longitudinal survey work.[52] By using the same participants over time, **panels** can track trends in attitudes towards issues or products, product adoption or consumption behaviour, and myriad other research interests. Suppliers of panel data can secure information from personal and telephone interviewing techniques as well as from the mail and mixed modes. Diaries are a common means of chronicling events of research interest by the panel members. These are mailed back to the research organization. Point-of-sale terminals and scanners aid electronic data-collection for panel-type participant groups. Mechanical devices placed in the homes of panel members may be used to evaluate media usage.

## Research Methods in Practice 7

## Combining written surveys and interviews

The set-up of the research required that we needed a lot of information. Our final questionnaire was 38 pages long (see Chapter 13 for more information on the questionnaire used). We did not want to compromise further on the length of the questionnaire. Our main arguments were that the theories we employ contain a number of rather complex concepts, such as relation-specific investments, uncertainty, social embeddedness, contracts, contracting effort, and so on. Sound measurement of those concepts requires that we cover each concept with more than just one or two questions, as otherwise the validity of our study would be threatened.

Although a questionnaire of 38 pages might be acceptable, you should be aware that for each cooperation one questionnaire had to be filled in. Many of our respondents were involved in more than just one cooperation and had to fill in the questionnaire more than once, also we tried to limit it to three cooperations for one respondent.

What to do? As the general management of the participating firms agreed to support the study, we were not afraid that people would refuse to answer; they could not as they were asked by management to do it. But still, if respondents are not allowed to refuse, they might become careless in answering the questions.

Given the nature of many questions, we also thought that it was not advisable to use a written questionnaire, as some questions just needed further explanations. Thus, our initial intention was to use the 38-page questionnaire in an interview session. But how long does it take to go through a 38-page questionnaire with a respondent? In a pre-test, it took much more than an hour. Thus, if a respondent informed us about three cooperations, we would need to have an interview of four hours or more, which is just too long.

To reduce the interview time to about 45 minutes, we developed the idea of splitting the questionnaire into a written part and an oral part. As described earlier, we handed the respondents a written questionnaire for each cooperation at one of our first visits to the company. We asked the respondents to answer the questions in the questionnaire with regard to the cooperation mentioned on the cover page. This written questionnaire contained mainly questions that resembled statements that the respondents had to react to on a Likert Scale. These questions are usually easy to answer. Moreover, the questions we asked in the written questionnaire were only questions on independent variables, variables that mainly refer to characteristics of the cooperation and the relation with the partner. All other questions were then asked in a latter interview that took between 30 and 60 minutes per cooperation.

▶

▶

Still, it should be mentioned that our decision to ask one respondent about more than one coopera-tion proved to be problematic. In the related research on buyer–supplier relations, some of the people from the purchasing departments had to fill in up to five questionnaires. Once, we arrived for the personal interview with such a purchasing employee and asked whether he had already filled out the five written questionnaires. His answer was 'yes of course as you have asked me to do.' He handed us one question-naire and on the cover page he had also put the names of all five suppliers and added. 'All these five rela-tions are the same, I manage every supplier the same way'. We then went through the written questionnaire supplier by supplier and somehow he suddenly realized that not all relations were the same.

# Summary

1 The communication approach involves questioning or surveying people and recording their responses for analysis. Communication is accomplished via personal interviews, telephone interviews or self-administered surveys, with each method having its specific strengths and weaknesses. The optimal communication method is the one that is instrumental in answering your research question, and dealing with the constraints imposed by time, budget and human resources. The opportunity to combine several survey methodologies makes the use of the mixed mode desirable in many projects.

2 Successful communication requires that we seek information the participant can provide, and that the participant understands his or her role and is motivated to play that role. Motivation, in particular, is a task for the interviewer. Good rapport with the participant should be established quickly, and then the technical process of collecting data should begin. The latter often calls for skilful probing to supplement the answers volunteered by the participant. Simplicity of directions and instrument appearance are additional factors to consider in encouraging response in self-administered communication studies.

3 Two factors can cause bias in interviewing. One is non-response. It is a concern with all types of survey. Some studies show that first calls often secure less than 20 per cent of the designated participants. Various methods are useful for increasing this representation, the most effective being making call-backs until an adequate number of completed interviews has been secured. The second factor is response error, which occurs when the participant fails to give a correct or complete answer. The interviewer can also contribute to response error. However, the interviewer can provide the main solution to both types of error.

4 The major advantages of personal interviewing are the ability to explore topics in great depth, achieve a high degree of interviewer control and provide maximum interviewer flexibility for meeting unique situations. However, this method is costly and time-consuming, and its flexibility can result in excessive interviewer bias.

   Telephone interviewing has become much more popular in recent years because of the diffusion of the telephone service in households and the low cost of this method compared with personal interviewing. Long-distance telephone interviewing has grown. There are also disadvantages in telephone interviewing: many telephone numbers are unlisted, and directory listings become obsolete quickly; there is also a limit on the length and depth of interviews conducted using the telephone.

   The self-administered questionnaire can be delivered by the national postal service, facsimile, a courier service, a computer or intercept. Computer-delivered self–administered questionnaires use organizational intranets, the Internet or online services to reach their participants. Participants may be targeted or self-selecting. Intercept studies may use a traditional questionnaire or a computerized instrument in environments where interviewer assistance is minimal.

5 Outsourcing survey services offers special advantages to managers. A professionally trained research staff, centralized location interviewing, focus group facilities and computer-assisted facilities are among them. Speciality firms offer software and computer-based assistance for telephone and personal interviewing as well as for mail and mixed modes. Panel suppliers produce data for longitudinal studies of all varieties.

## Discussion questions

### Terms in review

1 Distinguish among response error, interviewer error and non-response error.
2 How do environmental factors affect response rates in personal interviews? How can we overcome these environmental problems?

### Making research decisions

3 Assume you are planning to interview shoppers in a shopping centre about their views on increased food prices and what the government should do about them. In what different ways might you try to motivate shoppers to cooperate in your survey?

4 In recent years, in-home personal interviews have grown more costly and more difficult to complete. Suppose, however, you have a project in which you need to talk with people in their homes. What might you do to hold down costs and increase the response rate?

5 In the following situations, decide whether you would use a personal interview, telephone survey or self-administered questionnaire. Give your reasons.

   a A survey of the residents of a new subdivision on why they happened to select that area in which to live. (You also wish to secure some information about what they like and do not like about life in the subdivision.)

   b A poll of students at Metro University on their preferences among three candidates who are running for presidency of the Student Union.

   c A survey of 58 wholesale grocery companies in Sweden on their personnel management policies for warehouse personnel.

   d A survey of financial officers of the Fortune 500 corporations to learn their predictions for the economic outlook in their industries in the next year.

   e A study of applicant requirements, job tasks and performance expectations as part of a job analysis of student work-study jobs on a college campus of 2000 students, where 1500 are involved in the work-study programme.

6 You decide to take a telephone survey of 100 families with children in Manchester to learn how community services facilitate the combination of work and childcare. You want a good representation of all families with children in Manchester. Explain how you will carry out the sampling for such a study.

7 You plan to conduct a mail survey of the traffic managers of 1000 major manufacturing companies across the country. The study concerns their company policies regarding the payment of moving expenses for employees who are transferred. What might you do to improve the response rate of such a survey?

8 A major corporation agrees to sponsor an internal study on sexual harassment in the workplace. This is in response to concerns expressed by its female employees. How would you handle the following issues?

   a Sample selection

   b The communication approach (self-administered, telephone, personal interview and/or mixed)

   c The purpose: fact-finding, awareness, relationship building and/or change

   d Minimization of response and non-response error

## Classroom discussion

**9** Divide the class into sub-groups of up to four people. Each sub-group has the task of developing a questionnaire on the learning behaviour of students. The first group develops a mail questionnaire, the second group a phone questionnaire, the third group a questionnaire to be used in a personal interview, the fourth group a mail questionnaire, and so on. Ask each group to use their communication approach in such a way that they will obtain answers that groups using other communication approaches are less likely to obtain.

**10** Non-response can create serious biases in samples. Brainstorm the following questions in your class group.
   **a** When does non-response create larger and when smaller biases?
   **b** How can you design a study in a way that reduces non-response?
   **c** How can you assess the effects of non-response once the study has been conducted?

Online
*Learning* Centre

## Get started with understanding statistical techniques!

When you have read this chapter, log on to the Online Learning Centre website at **www.mcgraw-hill.co.uk/textbooks/blumberg** to explore chapter-by-chapter test questions, additional case studies, a glossary and more online study tools for business research methods.

# Notes

[1] One of the top research organizations in the world is the Survey Research Center of the University of Michigan. The material in this section draws heavily on the *Interviewer's Manual* (rev. edn.). Ann Arbor, Survey Research Center, University of Michigan, 1976; and Floyd J. Fowler, Jr., *Survey Research Methods*. Beverly Hills, CA: Sage, 1988, Chapter 7.

[2] Robert L. Kahn and Charles F. Cannell, *The Dynamics of Interviewing*. New York: Wiley, 1957, pp. 45–51.

[3] Survey Research Center, *Interviewer's Manual*, p. 8.

[4] Ibid., pp. 15–16.

[5] Ibid., p. 17.

[6] Fowler, *Survey Research Methods*, p. 112.

[7] S.A. Richardson, B.S. Dohrenwend and D. Klein, *Interviewing: Its Forms and Functions*. New York: Basic Books, 1965, pp. 328–58.

[8] Reproduced by special permission from Charles F. Cannell and Robert L. Kahn, 'Interviewing', in G. Lindzey and E. Aronson (eds.), *The Handbook of Social Psychology* (2nd edn.), Vol. 2. Reading, MA: Addison-Wesley, 1968. See also Fowler, *Survey Research Methods*, p. 115; P.J. Guenzel, T.R.

Berkmans and Charles F. Cannell, *General Interviewing Techniques*. Ann Arbor: Institute for Social Research, University of Michigan, 1983.

[9] In one study, 5.5 per cent of white participants and 11 per cent of non-white respondents were still not contacted after six calls. See W.C. Dunkleberg and G.S. Day, 'Nonresponse bias and callbacks in sample surveys', *Journal of Marketing Research*, May 1974, Table 3.

[10] Ibid.

[11] Fowler, *Survey Research Methods*, p. 50.

[12] C.H. Fuller, 'Weighting to adjust for survey nonresponse', *Public Opinion Quarterly*, Summer 1974, pp. 239–46.

[13] Dunkleberg and Day, 'Nonresponse bias', Table 3.

[14] Ibid., pp. 160–8.

[15] Eleanore Singer, 'Agreement between inaccessible respondents and informants', *Public Opinion Quarterly*, Winter 1972/73, pp. 603–11.

[16] Fowler, *Survey Research Methods*, p. 111.

[17] B.W. Schyberger, 'A study of interviewer behavior', *Journal of Marketing Research*, February 1967, p. 35.

[18] B.S. Dohrenwend, J.A. Williams, Jr. and C.H. Weiss, 'Interviewer biasing effects: toward a reconciliation of findings', *Public Opinion Quarterly*, Spring 1969, pp. 121–9.

[19] Seymour Sudman, *Reducing the Costs of Surveys*. Chicago: Aldine, 1967, p. 67.

[20] Ibid., p. 59.

[21] Ibid., p. 63.

[22] Ibid., p. 53.

[23] Robert M. Groves and Robert L. Kahn, *Surveys by Telephone*. New York: Academic Press, 1979, p. 223.

[24] Michael J. Havice, 'Measuring nonresponse and refusals to an electronic telephone survey', *Journalism Quarterly*, Fall 1990, pp. 521–30.

[25] www.telecommagazine.com/default.asp?journalid=28&fune=articles&page:0310i10&year =2003&month=10; www.dmeurope.com/default.asp?articleid=1464

[26] See, for example, J.H. Frey, Jr., *Survey Research by Telephone*. Beverly Hills, CA: Sage, 1983.

[27] Statistical Office of the European Communities, 'Statistics on the information society in Europe: data 1996–2002', 2003, pp. 42–4.

[28] www.commil.com/industryquotes.htm

[29] G.J. Glasser and G.D. Metzger, 'Random digit dialing as a method of telephone sampling', *Journal of Marketing Research*, February 1972, pp. 59–64; Seymour Sudman, 'The uses of telephone directories for survey sampling', *Journal of Marketing Research*, May 1973, pp. 204–7.

[30] A block is defined as an exchange group composed of the first four or more digits of a seven-digit number, such as 721–0, 721–1, and so on.

[31] Sudman, *Reducing the Costs of Surveys*, p. 65.

[32] J.J. Wheatley, 'Self-administered written questionnaires or telephone interviews', *Journal of Marketing Research*, February 1973, pp. 94–5.

[33] Groves and Kahn, *Surveys by Telephone*, p. 223.

[34] Paul J. Lavrakas, *Telephone Survey Methods: Sampling, Selection, and Supervision* (2nd edn.). Thousand Oaks, CA: Sage, 1993, p. 16.

[35] Peter S. Tuckel and Barry M. Feinberg, 'The answering machine poses many questions for telephone survey researchers', *Public Opinion Quarterly*, Summer 1991, pp. 200–17.

[36] Don A. Dillman, *Mail and Telephone Surveys.* New York: Wiley, 1978, p. 6.

[37] D. Wallace, 'A case for and against mail questionnaires', *Public Opinion Quarterly*, Spring 1954, pp. 40–52.

[38] Harzing, Anne-Will, 'Response rates in international mail surveys: results of a 22 country study', *International Business Review* 6 (1997), pp. 641–65.

[39] Leslie Kanuk and Conrad Berenson, 'Mail surveys and response rates: a literature review', *Journal of Marketing Research*, November 1975, pp. 440–53; Arnold S. Linsky, 'Stimulating responses to mailed questionnaires: a review', *Public Opinion Quarterly* 39 (1975), pp. 82–101; Julie Yu and Harris Cooper, 'A quantitative review of research design effects on response rates to questionnaires', *Journal of Marketing Research* 20 (1983), pp. 36–44.

[40] Kanuk and Berenson, 'Mail surveys', p. 450. Reprinted from the *Journal of Marketing Research*, published by the American Marketing Association.

[41] Dillman, *Mail and Telephone Surveys*, p. 8.

[42] Ibid., p. 12.

[43] Ibid., pp. 22–4.

[44] Total Design Method (http://survey.sesrc.wsu.edu/tdm.htm), 4 February 2000. Don Dillman is Professor of Sociology and Rural Sociology and Deputy Director of Research and Development of the Social and Economic Sciences Research Center at Washington State University.

[45] Dillman, *Mail and Telephone Surveys*, pp. 160–1.

[46] C.H. Lovelock, Ronald Still, David Cullwick and Ira M. Kaufman, 'An evaluation of the effectiveness of drop-off questionnaire delivery', *Journal of Marketing Research*, November 1976, pp. 358–64.

[47] Donald Tomaskovic-Devey, Jeffrey Leiter and Shealy Thompson, 'Organizational survey nonresponse', *Administrative Science Quarterly*, 1994, pp. 439–57.

[48] Statistical Office of the European Communities, 'Statistics on the information society in Europe: data 1996–2002', 2003, p. 50.

[49] These examples are drawn from the personal experience of the authors, as well as from Noah Shachtman, 'Why the web works as a market research tool', *AdAge.com*, Summer 2001 (http://adage.com/tools2001).

[50] Nelson King, '[Web-based surveys] how they work', *PC Magazine*, 18 January 2000 (http://www.pcmag.com).

[51] There are a number of sources for research services, some of which are annotated. For current listings, consult the latest edition of the *Marketing Services Guide; The American Marketing Association Membership Directory*. Chicago: American Marketing Association; *Consultants and Consulting Organizations Directory*. Detroit: Gale Research Corporation; or the research section of *Marketing News*.

[52] A list of panel vendors is provided in Duane Davis, *Business Research for Decision Making* (4th edn.). Belmont, CA: Wadsworth, 1996, p. 283.

# Recommended further reading

**Arksey, Hilary and Knight, Peter T.,** *Interviewing for Social Scientists: An Introductory Resource with Examples.* **Thousand Oaks, CA: Sage, 1999.** Covers design, improvization, success rates, specialized contexts and transforming findings into results.

**Dillman, Don A.,** *Mail and Internet Surveys: The Tailored Design Method.* **New York: Wiley, 1999.** The Tailored Design Method, which expands on the Total Design Concept of Dillman's classic work, takes advantage of computers, electronic mail and the Internet to better our understanding of survey requirements.

**Fowler, Floyd J., Jr.,** *Survey Research Methods* **(2nd edn.). Thousand Oaks, CA: Sage, 1993.** An excellent overview of all aspects of the survey process.

**Groves, Robert M.** *et al., Telephone Survey Methodology.* **New York: Wiley, 2001.** Distinguished survey experts present the latest developments in phone surveys from different national contexts.

**Harzing, Anne-Will,** 'Response rates in international mail surveys: results of a 22 country study', *International Business Review* **6(6), 1997, pp. 641–62.** An investigation into response effects in different countries, including the USA and the UK.

**Jobber, David, Saunders, John and Mitchell, Vince-Wayne,** 'Prepaid monetary incentive effects on mail survey response', *Journal of Business Research* **57(4), 2004, pp. 347–50.** A study investigating the trade-off between increased costs for offering incentives and the marginal benefits of a higher response rate.

**Lavrakas, Paul J.,** *Telephone Survey Methods: Sampling, Selection, and Supervision* **(2nd edn.). Thousand Oaks, CA: Sage, 1993.** This specialized work takes an applied perspective of interest to students and managers. Chapters 3, 5 and 6 on supervision are particularly useful.

**Nesbary, Dale, K.,** *Survey Research and the World Wide Web.* **Needham Heights, MA: Allyn & Bacon, 1999.** Screen shots from Windows and FrontPage, e-mail survey construction and Internet orientation for survey research.

**Welch, Catherine, Marschan-Piekkari, Rebecca, Penttine, Heli and Tahvanainen, Marja,** 'Corporate elites as informants in qualitative international business research', *International Business Review* **11(5), 2002, pp. 661–78.** An article discussing methodologies on how interviews with elite informants during the fieldwork can be incorporated into the research.

# Secondary data and archival sources

## LEARNING OBJECTIVES

When you have read this chapter, you should understand:

- ☑ the difference between primary and secondary data

- ☑ the typical sources of secondary data, and how to select them

- ☑ how secondary data can be used

- ☑ what data-mining is and how it works

- ☑ what meta analysis is.

## 8.1 Secondary data

In Chapters 5, 6, 7, 9, 10 and 11, the different aspects and issues involved in conducting research by collecting primary information or data are discussed (i.e. how you, the researcher, can gather the information necessary to answer your research problem). An alternative to gathering information oneself is to use secondary data. Secondary data is information or data that has already been collected and recorded by someone else, usually for other purposes. A lot of information gathered by the government, for instance, is publicly available and accessible either at no or low cost.[1] Information pertaining to financial markets, such as stock prices and trading volumes, is widely available in financial newspapers or online at various financial portals. The annual reports of public companies are another source that is often used for secondary data.

Sometimes, the information you seek is not all available from one source but can be compiled from several sources, as the following example illustrates. Tobias Ricke works in the marketing department of a large publishing company. He would like to know whether the sales volumes of political books are related to the political orientation and participation of customers. Of course, Tobias could hold a survey among potential customers, but it would take time to set up such a survey and Tobias is not sure whether his boss would be willing to give him the budget required. So, he thinks about which of the data that are already available he could use to investigate his question. He can obtain the weekly sales data for each title and each bookstore from internal sources. Further, he knows that the results of the last national and regional elections for every constituency are available from government sources. Thus, by combining these two data sources he can build up a data file that contains, per constituency, the number of books sold and the party preferences and participation of the population in the last regional and national elections. Instead of using the election results from the government source, he might also choose to buy existing data on voting intentions from commercial research agencies that conduct opinion polls.

This strategy of supplementing existing data from internal sources, as in the example above, or obtained through primary data-collection with secondary data can produce interesting data sets. For example, many primary surveys among business firms record the sector the firm belongs to. Secondary data containing information on different sectors can then be used to enrich the information regarding the external environment in which a firm operates.

## The advantages of secondary data

The main advantages of using secondary data are that this approach saves time and money. As secondary data are usually already available, the researcher can immediately start to analyse the data and try to find an answer to his or her research problem. The often time-consuming activities of setting up the research, approaching the respondents, collecting information from respondents and recording any information obtained in a way suitable for analysis is not necessary. As a researcher, you will need, however, to identify potential sources of secondary data. You need to know whether the information you require to answer your research problem is available, where you can find it, and whether and how you can access it.

Identifying sources of secondary data can become time-consuming, especially if obtaining the desired data calls for the consultation of multiple sources, the data need to be reorganized to be suitable for analysis and if the data are not available in electronic form. Often, you might find secondary data that contain only partly the information you need to answer your research problem, because either information (variables) are missing or the information is only available in aggregated form (e.g. the firm rather than the employee is the observation unit). If the deficiencies are not too large you might choose to reformulate your research problem by focusing on aspects that can be investigated with the available data or by addressing the problem with a different unit of analysis. A common problem in the usage of multiple sources is merging the different sources involved into one data file.

The accessibility of secondary data is often problematic too, as access to the data may be restricted. Business firms, like commercial research agencies, are unlikely to share data they have generated, because this information is a valuable asset that creates a competitive advantage. Even researchers at universities are reluctant to grant access to 'their' data, as they have invested time and effort in their collection, and want to milk them for their own studies and publications. However, if you have a good idea how existing data can be used to investigate a specific research problem, suggesting collaboration, such as writing a joint paper or setting up a project that also benefits the data owner can open doors.

Governments and other international institutions (see Exhibit 10.3 for a list of such information sources) often offer access to data free of charge, especially if the collection of the data has been financed with public funds. Other information sources are accessible at a fee that is substantially lower than the costs that would be involved if you were to collect the data for yourself. Sometimes a reduced fee will be charged if the data are to be used for academic purposes, such as a Master's or Ph.D. thesis. Whenever you need to pay for access to secondary data, you need to calculate – provided that you have the funds to pay for the access – whether the benefits of the data are worth the investment.

Another advantage of secondary data is that, depending on the source of the data, such data are often of fairly high quality. This holds in particular for data offered by well-respected institutions such as local, national and international governmental institutions, or well-known research agencies. This high-quality data stems from the facts that (i) such institutions often have better access to information providers, and (ii) many experts were involved in the research and data-collection process.

## The disadvantages of secondary data

The main problem with using secondary data is that they were not collected with your specific research problem in mind. Thus, they might not fit perfectly with the requirements of your research problem. In assessing the usefulness of secondary data you need to address the following questions.

1 Is the information provided in the secondary data sufficient to answer your research problem?
   a Do the secondary data cover all the information you need?
   b Is the information available detailed enough?
   c Do the data follow the definitions you apply in your research problem?
   d Are the data accurate enough?
2 Do the secondary data address the same population you want to investigate?
   a Do the secondary data refer to the unit of analysis you want to investigate?
   b Is the sample on which the secondary data are based a good representation of the population you wish to address?
3 Were the secondary data collected in the relevant time period?

### Information quality

If you cannot answer yes to all of the questions above, the usefulness of the secondary data is questionable. Question 1 and its sub-questions refer to the most common problem with secondary data. As secondary data have usually been collected for another purpose, they often do not cover all the information you need. For example, secondary data sources on the financial information of public companies often contain only the information published in annual reports. But if you are interested in how the strategic choices of firms affect their financial performance, these secondary data are insufficient, as the source contains detailed information on the latter but no information on strategic choices.

Similarly, information in secondary data is often not detailed enough. For example, population statistics may sometimes contain information on how many non-nationals live in a certain region, but do not distinguish between the different nationalities involved. Hence, if you want to investigate the economic position of Turkish immigrants in Germany, secondary data are useless, as you can only identify non-nationals but not non-nationals who are Turkish citizens. A related problem is that the definitions used in the secondary data do not match with the definitions you wish to apply. Suppose, again, you want to investigate the economic position of Turkish immigrants in Germany and the available data *are* detailed enough and contain information on respondents' nationality. This would mean that all immigrants from Turkey who have acquired German nationality are not counted as Turkish in the secondary data. As your study objective is the economic position of Turkish immigrants, your definition of 'Turkish' is broader than the definition applied in the secondary data and consequently the data do not fit.

Accuracy can be a serious problem when using secondary data if the source of the data is unknown. Earlier, we noted that secondary data can often be of a high quality if they come from official sources or well-known research agencies. Secondary data might also come from other sources, however, so before using the data you need to evaluate their source.

## Sample quality

Another common problem with secondary data sources is that they often provide information on an aggregate level. For example, there are many **secondary sources** that provide a wide range of information on the level of the industrial sector, but fewer secondary sources that have the same information at company or even establishment level. The quality of the sample is another problem associated with secondary data. In particular, if the intention of your research is to predict or to generalize to a larger population, the data need to be representative. Finally, the timeliness of the data is important, as secondary data are often out of date.

Librarians evaluate and select information sources based on five factors that can be applied to any type of source, whether printed or electronic. These are:

1 purpose
2 scope
3 authority
4 audience
5 format.

Exhibit 8.1 summarizes the critical questions a researcher asks when applying these factors during information **source evaluation**.

| Evaluation factor | Questions to answer |
|---|---|
| Purpose | • Why does the information exist?<br>• How evident is the purpose it is trying to convey?<br>• Does it achieve its purpose?<br>• How does its purpose affect the type and bias of information presented? |
| Scope | • How old is the information?<br>• How often is it updated?<br>• How much information is available?<br>• Is it selective or comprehensive?<br>• What are the criteria for inclusion?<br>• If applicable, what geographic area, time period or language does it cover?<br>• How does the information presented compare with similar information sources?<br>• What information did you expect to find that was missing?<br>• Is there additional documentation on the data, such as detailed descriptions of the variables, information on the data-collection process (e.g. sampling), information on the definitions applied, and so on? |
| Authority | • What are the credentials of the author, institution or organization sponsoring the information?<br>• Does the information source give you a means of contacting anyone for further information?<br>• If facts are supplied, where do they come from? |
| Audience | • To whom does the information source cater?<br>• What level of knowledge or experience is assumed?<br>• How does this intended audience affect the type and bias of the information? |
| Format | • How quickly can you find the required information?<br>• How easy to use is the information source?<br>• Is there an index?<br>• Is the information downloadable into a spreadsheet or word-processing program if desired? |

*Exhibit 8.1* Evaluating information sources.

## Purpose

The **purpose** of the source is what the author or institution is trying to accomplish. In general, the purpose may be to enlighten or to entertain. Among purposes in the enlighten subset, authors may be attempting to establish credibility, broaden knowledge within a field or discipline, or establish a company image. Once you have determined the purpose of the source, you will also want to determine whether or how it provides a bias to the information presented. Bias is the absence of a balanced presentation of information. Most researchers expect company websites to be biased in favour of the company; however, we expect sources offered by independent organizations to be more balanced, presenting both positive and negative information about relevant organizations without favouring one or the other.

## Scope

Tied closely to the purpose of the source is its **scope**. What is the date of publication? What time period does this source cover? How much of the topic is covered and in what depth? Is the material covered local, regional, national or international? If the source is bibliographic, how comprehensive is it? If it is a biographical source, a directory or bibliography, what are the criteria for inclusion? If you do not know the scope of your information sources, you may miss essential information by relying on an incomplete source.

## Authority

Of major concern to any information user is the **authority** of the source. We have already noted that **primary sources** are the most authoritative. In any source, both the author and the publisher are indicators of the authority. Authority also applies to web resources where anyone can post anything. In this environment it is always important to check the credentials of the site. For instance, data and statements about economic indicators on Thailand are much more likely to be authoritative if they come from a Thai government source or an international institution, such as the World Bank, than from a personal page with no information about the author or producer.

## Audience

**Audience** is also an important factor in evaluating an information source and it too is tied to the purpose of the source. The audience for this textbook is college students – more specifically, college students who are studying or majoring in business or public administration, some of whom are practising managers. While others – for example, educators – may benefit from the information, the authors have taken great care to select appropriate examples and to write in terms that management students will easily relate to. Brokerage firm Charles Schwab has no confusion in terms of purpose or audience. In a recent ad, Charles Schwab is quoted as follows: 'I see the Internet as the single most empowering force for the individual investor'.[2] The Schwab.com website is designed to empower every single Charles Schwab customer, with rapid market summary updates, and research on companies and funds. The numerous awards Schwab has won for its website indicate that it is doing well in achieving its aims. It also uses an intranet to provide key information to its employees.[3]

## Format

**Format** factors may vary from source to source but, in general, relate to how the information is presented and how easy it is to find a specific piece of information. In a printed source, the arrangement of the information – alphabetical? hierarchical? chronological? – nearly always has an impact on the retrieval of information. Indexes are usually essential. Do cross-references link one term to related terms? How are acronyms handled? Is the reference to an item? Table number? Page? How do type fonts or colour help you find information? Furthermore, it is often important whether and how the information can be downloaded. In particular, if you are looking for quantitative information, whether the information is available in an electronic format and can be stored in a data matrix (preferably in the format readable by the software you use for analysis) is important, because otherwise you will have to record the information manually, which can be very time-consuming and boring.

## 8.2  Sources of secondary data

Exhibit 8.2 provides an overview of the different types of source of secondary data. One important distinction is whether each is an internal or external source. The data format, written or electronic, is another useful distinction criteria. These two dimensions create a 2 × 2 matrix. The two cells covering external sources can be subdivided further by the nature of the data publisher.

The distinction between written and electronic data sources has become more vague with the increasing use of information technology, as information that had formerly been stored on paper is increasingly stored electronically. E-mails and written documents that have been scanned and stored in an electronic file are examples of this sort of development. How information is stored electronically, however, still makes a difference to the researcher. Therefore, deciding on which data sources to use on the basis of how easily the stored information can be processed further might be a better idea.

Secondary information that is organized in a database or stored in a data-matrix format can be processed much more easily than a collection of tables containing the same information but only available as PDF files. Similarly, it makes a difference if financial information on the 50 EUROSTOXX companies is stored in one data file, such as a MicrosoftExcel spreadsheet or SPSS data file, or in 50 different files (one for each company). In the latter case you would need to check whether the organization of all the files is identical, that is do they use the same labels for different items in the financial statements and do they all report in the same currency? Only after such a check and a probable reorganization of the files can you merge them.

Secondary data sources can either be internal or external. Internal sources are built up and maintained by the organization or institution for which the researcher is working. They are available only to members of this organization. All the information stored in management information systems, such as personnel records or accounting records, are clearly internal secondary data. They are mostly recorded for other purposes than research, but often provide sufficient information to investigate certain research problems. For example, the information stored in a customer relationship management (CRM) system is stored, among other reasons, to control the sales force and to register customer orders. Such a CRM database, however, is also likely to contain information that will be useful in investigating research questions, such as 'How do the efforts of the sales force relate to the volume of orders customers place?' or 'What characterizes our high-volume customers?' In larger organizations in particular, a vast amount of information is stored for different purposes and researchers often fail to spot the potential value of such sources to their research. What complicates the usage of such data sources is that information is often stored in separate places, and the different departments of a company are often unaware of what information is available in other departments.

The term 'external secondary data source' refers to all data sources outside an organization

| | Internal | External |
|---|---|---|
| Written | • Memos<br>• Contracts<br>• Invoices | Publishers of books and periodicals:<br>• indexes<br>• yearbooks<br><br>Government and supranational institutions:<br>• white books<br>• reports<br><br>Professional and trade associations:<br>• (annual) reports<br><br>Media sources:<br>• newspapers and magazines<br>• special reports (supplements)<br><br>Commercial sources:<br>• (annual) reports |
| Electronic | • Management information systems<br>• Accounting records | Publishers of books and periodicals:<br>• bibliographic databases<br><br>Government and supranational institutions:<br>• websites (of statistical offices)<br>• CD-ROMs<br><br>Professional and trade associations:<br>• websites<br><br>Media sources:<br>• websites<br>• CD-ROMs of complete volumes<br><br>Commercial sources:<br>• websites<br>• datasets of previous studies |

*Exhibit 8.2* Sources of secondary data.

or institution. As Exhibit 8.2 shows, external sources can be further distinguished by who provides the data. Publishers of books and journals are an important source of secondary data. The idea that books and journals mostly contain merely the analysis and interpretation of existing data is a misconception. For those studies that seek to investigate a longer time period, these are a vital source of information. Suppose you are interested in finding out how top managers and boards have changed in the last century. For such a study it would be a good idea to dig out information from books on the history of certain companies, or the biographies of (former) top managers. Periodicals and **indexes** such as yearbooks are an even more commonly used source of secondary data. Suppose you want to investigate what determines the level of transfer payments for European football players. Football yearbooks provide plenty of information on who sold and bought what player in the last season, and on characteristics of the players (such as age, position, number of internationals played and goals scored). Increasingly, such information is also available in electronic form, which often helps to ease the process of working with and processing the information.

Making up one of the most important sources of secondary data are governments and supranational institutions, such as the European Union (EU), Organization for Economic Co-operation and Development (OECD), International Monetary Fund (IMF), World Bank and the United Nations (UN). As mentioned earlier, the main advantage of such sources is that they provide data that is of a distinct high quality and accuracy. This information is available in the form of books and reports, but increasingly online and often at no cost. As well as national government and supranational institutions, regional governmental institutions also provide secondary information. For example, the US Federal Reserve Bank is subdivided into 12 districts (Atlanta, Boston, Cleveland, Chicago, Dallas, Kansas City, Minneapolis, New York, Philadelphia, Richmond, San Francisco and St. Louis) and each maintains a research department to prepare reports. In Europe, many sub-national governmental bodies (e.g. the provinces in the Netherlands or the *Länder* in Germany) as well as cities collect regional information.

Trade and professional associations can also be a valuable source of secondary data if you are interested in specific industries or professions. Compared to secondary data from government sources, information obtained through trade and professional associations should be assessed carefully, however. Many trade and professional associations serve a lobbying function and hence may only publish favourable and biased information. This problem also applies to political interest groups and parties. Suppose you want to investigate whether and how oil companies, such as British Petroleum, Statoil or Shell, consider environmental issues in their strategy. Certainly, the information you might obtain from these oil companies would differ considerably from information obtained from environmental groups such as Greenpeace.

Every day, print media, radio and TV stations publish a vast amount of information. The *Financial Times* and *Business Week* are two examples of a daily and a weekly print source of information on a wide array of business and economic issues. This information is based partly on press announcements from firms, governments, and so on, but also on the publications' own analyses via their journalists. In addition, many media commission research studies to commercial research agencies to learn about various aspects of a country's economic, political and social life. 'Top 100' lists are usually the outcome of such media studies commissioned to commercial research agencies (see the following Snapshot for an example). As almost all media have a website, a great deal of information is available online. Some media even maintain online archives with supplementary data and back issues, which can be very useful for research purposes, although to access them you sometimes need to subscribe to the service and pay a fee. Furthermore, most media have useful information on their readers, listeners or viewers, as this is essential for attracting advertisers. Although the information contained in such media kits may be less complete than one might wish, it can still be useful for research purposes, and is mostly available free of charge.

Snapshot

## How to buy the Pope's car

For centuries auctions have been a well-known institution to match a seller and a buyer. However, the types of product that were auctioned rather than exchanged through the usual retail channels were mostly limited to expensive and rare goods, such as antiques. The main disadvantage of auctions was that the seller and the interested buyer had to meet each other at a specified time. Thus, sellers would only auction their goods if they could be certain that sufficient potential buyers would be willing to attend the auction at the specified time.

The Internet has changed the market for auctions as it has enabled access to virtual auctions. Now sellers and buyers are virtually matched. Internet auctions typically end a specified time, but buyers do not need to be present at the specified time and can place their initial bids beforehand and even increase their bids as long as the auction has not finished. Probably the most well-known online auction platform is eBay. On eBay nearly everything is auctioned, even products that you cannot obtain in a shop. For example:

- A second-hand Volkswagen Golf, a popular car that is often auctioned on eBay but is also available at second-hand car dealers. But one Golf auction was particularly special as this Golf was formerly owned by Pope Benedict XVI. It was sold for €189,000 to the Golden Palace Casino in Austin, Texas.

- On 25 October 2007, the inaugural flight of the Airbus A380 left Singapore and arrived in Sydney. Singapore Airlines auctioned all tickets for this flight and the return leg on eBay. Everyone could have been part of this historical event in aviation history, at least if they had been willing to spend €402 for an economy seat or €72,172 for a first-class suite. In total, the auction of the flight tickets raised close to €1,000,000, which was donated to charity.

What makes online auctions appealing for researchers is that they can follow thousands of real bidding processes. Everybody with an eBay account can see the following information during and at the end of the auction: number of buyers who inspected the product, number of bids, time and height of each bid and the final price. Moreover, it is revealed how experienced the sellers and bidders are (indicated by the number of auctions completed successfully) and the reputation of sellers and bidders (indicated by the percentage of previous well-proceeded auctions).

Therefore, it is not surprising that recently many scientific articles investigating auction theory used eBay as a source for secondary data. For example, one study discussed how the reputation of a seller affects the final price achieved at an auction. Daniel Houser and John Wooders followed different offers of an identical product, a Pentium III 500 processor, to see whether sellers with a higher reputation achieved a higher price. As this and other studies show, ebay is a fruitful source for secondary data.

But what are the limits of these secondary data? What cannot be investigated?

## References and further reading

Houser, Daniel and Wooders John (2006) 'Reputation in auctions: theory, and evidence from ebay'. *Journal of Economics and Management Strategy* 15(2), pp. 353–68.
www.ebay.de
http://news.bbc.co.uk/2/hi/europe/4518939.stm
http://www.singaporeair.com/saa/en_UK/content/company_info/press_release/NE_3507.jsp

The final category of external sources of secondary data is the commercial source. Although every commercial firm is a potential source of secondary data – at least of data about the firm itself – we usually refer to companies that sell and publish information for a fee as commercial sources. With respect to business research in particular, the number of firms providing such services is huge and the differences between them also vast. Many companies in this field are mainly vendors of addresses and contact information that other companies need for direct marketing. For research purposes, such information is only useful for sampling purposes, especially if the address database covers (almost) the full population. Other commercial sources provide much more information than just addresses. Research firms such as Gallup and Infratest specialize in public opinion polls and surveys on consumer attitudes. Media often use these professional research services and publish the results (e.g. people's answers to that evergreen question 'Which party would you vote for if there was a general election today?').

Financial data and stock market information make up another area that is well covered by commercial sources. Standard & Poor and Moody are well-known research firms that provide all kinds of financial data and studies. Both firms have a reputation for the high-quality financial assessment of firms, as reflected in the breadth of acknowledgement of their credit rating for government and company bonds. Other research firms, such as GfK and ACNielsen, specialize in marketing research, collecting information on consumer attitudes and behaviour, market shares, and so on. From a researcher's perspective the main problem with commercial sources is that accessing them is either not possible or often very costly. Commercial research companies earn their money by providing and collecting information. Many business firms commission studies to them as they have a wealth of expertise in the area of conducting research; however, these firms will usually insist on exclusive rights to any information collected.

## 8.3  How to use secondary data efficiently

We have looked at the advantages and disadvantages, as well as sources of secondary data, and illustrated numerous problems using them. Those occasions when you can identify and ensure full access to secondary data that enable you to answer your initial research problem fully are quite rare. However, if budget constraints do not allow you to collect primary information, you will have to rely on secondary data and put up with the imperfections. The following three considerations can ease the burden of living with these imperfections:

| **Publishers of books and periodicals (see also Exhibit 3.4)** | | |
|---|---|---|
| McGraw-Hill | Publisher of scientific books and academic textbooks, and *Business Week* | http://www.mcgraw-hill.com |
| Prentice Hall | Publisher of scientific books and academic textbooks, and the *Financial Times* | http://www.prenhall.com |
| Oxford University Press | Publisher of scientific books and academic textbooks | http://www.oup.co.uk |
| **Government and supranational institutions** | | |
| Statbase | UK national statistics | http://www.statistics.gov.uk/statbase/mainmenu.asp |
| Statline | Dutch national statistics | http://www.cbs.nl/statline |
| OECD Statistics | Economic statistics at an international level | http://www.oecd.org |
| **Government and supranational institutions** | | |
| European Social Survey | Information on the values and social background of people in more than 20 European countries | http://www.europeansocialsurvey.org |
| Eurostat | Statistical agency of the European Union | http://www.eurostat.eu |
| Federal Reserve Bank | Economic data on federal reserve system and government time series | http://www.stls.frb.org |
| National Trade Data Bank of the US Department of Commerce | Offers access to various databases covering topics such as price indices, export opportunities per industry, country and product, political and socio-economic conditions, and so on | Available on CD-ROM |
| **Professional and trade associations** | | |
| British Furniture Manufacturers | Membership directories, industry information | www.bfm.org.uk |
| CBI (Confederation of British Industry) | Business surveys (not free), studies on British industry | www.cbi.org.uk |
| European Express Service Providers | Industry information, studies on the sector | www.euroexpress.org |
| **Media sources** | | |
| *FT Info* | Company information | http://www.info.ft.com/companies |
| *Business Week* | Company information, special reports on selected issues, news | http://www.businessweek.com |
| **Commercial sources** | | |
| TNS-NIPO | Market and opinion research, offers some of the results of its studies free of charge | http://tns-nipo.com |

*Exhibit 8.3* Secondary data sources (selected examples).

- merging of multiple secondary data sources
- adjusting your research problem to the available data
- investigating which research problems can be investigated with the available data.

A common problem when using secondary data sources is that they do not contain the information required. In some cases, the information required *is* available but not stored in one source. As we have already seen, this is when the merging of different sources is a solution. For example, a firm's internal sources might provide sufficient information on how the firm's operations perform in different countries, but contain no information concerning the external environment. Combining the internal data with external data on economic, social and political country factors will create a much richer data set, which will permit the investigation of how different external conditions affect the firm's performance or internal procedures. It should be noted that using information from external sources is also a good strategy for enriching any primary data collected. You are often likely to record nominal information, such as country or industrial sector, in a primary survey. Such information becomes much more meaningful if you combine it with externally available information on countries or sectors.

Merging information from different sources into one database requires you to have some information that is available in all sources. If such 'matching' information is missing, you cannot merge the information, but you can still use different sources of secondary data to investigate your research problem. In Chapter 10, we discuss case studies and mention the method of triangulation (i.e. looking for evidence not just in one source but in multiple sources). Finding supporting evidence in multiple sources increases the validity of your results as, for example, it becomes less likely that the outcome is the result of a method or sample bias.

Adjusting your research problem to the available data is a very delicate strategy, as it carries the risk that the data and not the management problem drive your research. When cutting the research problem down to 'fit' the data, the most important question is always 'Does it still make sense to embark on a research venture with such a "cleaned-up" research problem?' Generally speaking, the larger the deficiencies of the secondary data with regard to the original research problem, the less helpful it will be to adjust the research problem. Secondary data deficiencies can exist in terms of what information is available and how detailed that information is. An initial research question may refer to subjects in the secondary data. If the sampled subjects in the secondary data do not correspond with the population you are interested in, you need to ask yourself whether you can still learn something if you investigate the sub-optimal non-corresponding sample. For example, if you want to investigate the economic position of immigrants in your country, but the secondary data only contain information on immigrants from Mediterranean countries such as Italy, Turkey, Egypt and Morocco, it might be reasonable to use this data only if immigrants from Mediterranean countries form a large proportion of the immigrants in your country. Thus, secondary data on Mediterranean immigrants are reasonably useful in studying the economic position of immigrants in a western European country, but much less useful for a study in the USA.

If secondary data miss information or are less detailed, you again need to assess how severe the data problem is. For example, in an explanatory or predictive study it is very serious if you miss information on the dependent variable, but less serious if information on an independent or control variable is unavailable. Sometimes, it is even possible to use other available information as a proxy or indicator for missing information. For example, in a study investigating why people choose to become self-employed, the authors wanted to know whether their respondents came from wealthy families or not. Unfortunately, the secondary data did not contain information on the wealth of their families, but it did offer information on the educational level of respondents' fathers. As educational level is highly correlated with income, the authors decided to use 'father's educational level' as a proxy for the wealth of the family.[4]

The third consideration suggests data availability as the point of departure for any research venture. Rather than starting from a specific management dilemma, which is then reformulated to a researchable question, you start by looking at the available data and thinking about what interesting question it could be used to answer. Such a strategy does not aim to provide answers and solutions to a specific management problem, rather it intends to use existing information more efficiently. With the spread of information and communication technology, the amount of information collected and recorded has become infinite. However, this information is still underutilized. Data-mining, which will be discussed in the following sections, improves the utilization of existing information bases by applying advanced techniques.

## 8.4 Secondary data in qualitative research

Secondary data have a prominent role in qualitative research: for example, case studies usually rely on multiple data sources, such as personal interviews with key people in an organization and also internal documents or, say, newspaper clippings connected with the organization being investigated in the case. Moreover, official statistics provide useful information for determining general context, such as general or sector-specific economic conditions, and so on. Qualitative researchers often make use of secondary data, which were originally produced without any intention of analysing them. Secondary data from official statistics, but also from internal databases, are usually collected in order to conduct only a descriptive analysis of a current situation. Many other secondary data, such as letters, memos, autobiographies, newspapers and journals, are produced with a completely different intention. However, researchers can still use the information contained in these sources in their qualitative analysis. Information from such sources becomes extremely valuable if the problem statement addresses developments that may have started off or occurred a long time ago. The growing field of business history is a typical example of research relying heavily on such secondary data sources.

In business research, organizational documents are another important source of secondary data. Many organizational documents are freely accessible, such as annual reports, information supplied to shareholders, press releases, public relations material and advertisements, either in printed or electronic form. Other documents, such as newsletters, memos, internal and external letters, manuals, company procedures and the like are not public and the researcher needs to ask permission from the organization to access them (e.g. through company archives).

As with any secondary data the researcher needs to assess the quality of the data, and their relevance and usefulness for the research problem addressed. An obvious problem with organizational documents is that they are mostly written for a specific purpose and may present information strategically. This is obviously the case with advertisements and public relations material, which is produced to present a company and its products or activities in the most favourable light. However, even accounts of internal communication (e.g. e-mails exchanged within a department) are often written with a hidden agenda in mind, of which you as a researcher may be unaware.

## 8.5  Data-mining

Every day, organizations at all levels collect a tremendous amount of information and record it in databases. Such information is not gathered to investigate specific research problems; rather, it is part of an advanced control and monitoring process. Although the objective of collecting and recording the information is not related to business research, such information can be very useful in investigating research problems.

The term **data-mining** describes the process of uncovering knowledge from databases stored in data warehouses. The purpose of data-mining is to identify valid, novel, useful and ultimately understandable patterns in data.[5] Similar to traditional mining, where miners search beneath the surface for valuable ore, data-mining searches large databases for information that is indispensable to managing an organization. Both types of mining call for a large amount of material to be sifted before a profitable vein is discovered. Data-mining is a useful tool; it is an approach that combines exploration and discovery with confirmatory analysis. An organization's own internal historical data is often an underutilized source of information in the exploratory phase. While digging through data archives can be as simplistic as sorting through a file containing past shipping manifests or rereading company reports that have grown dusty with age, we will concentrate the remainder of our discussion on more sophisticated structures and techniques.

A **data warehouse** is an electronic repository for databases that organizes large volumes of data into categories to facilitate retrieval, interpretation and sorting by end-users. The data warehouse provides an accessible archive to support dynamic organizational intelligence applications. The key phrase here is 'dynamically accessible'. Data warehouses that offer archaic methods of data retrieval are seldom used. Data in a data warehouse must be updated continuously to ensure that managers have access to data appropriate for real-time decisions. In a data warehouse, the contents of departmental computers are duplicated in a central repository where standard architecture and consistent data definitions are applied. These data are available to departments or cross-functional teams for direct analysis, or through intermediate storage facilities or **data marts** that compile locally required information. The entire system must be constructed for integration and compatibility among the different data marts.

The more accessible the databases that comprise the data warehouse, the more likely it is that a researcher will use such databases to reveal patterns. Thus, researchers are more likely to mine electronic databases than paper ones. It is useful to remember that data in a data warehouse were once primary data, collected for a specific purpose. When researchers data-mine a company's data warehouse, all the data contained within that database become secondary data. The patterns revealed will be used for purposes other than those originally intended. For example, in an archive of sales invoices, we have a wealth of data about what was sold, how much of each item or service, at what price level, to whom, and where, when and how the products were shipped. Initially, the company generated the sales invoice to facilitate the process of getting paid for the items shipped. When a researcher mines that sales invoice archive, the search is for patterns of sales, by product, category, region of the country or world, price level, shipping method, and so on.

Traditional database queries are unidimensional and historical – for example, 'How many chocolate bars were sold during December 2003 in the Netherlands?' In contrast, data-mining attempts to discover patterns and trends in the data, and to infer rules from these patterns. For example, an analysis of retail sales by the Dutch supermarket chain Edah identified products that are often purchased together – like candy bars and soft drinks – although they may appear to be unrelated. With the rules discovered from the data-mining, a manager is able to support, review and/or examine alternative courses of action for solving a management dilemma, alternatives that may later be studied further in the collection of new primary data.

## The evolution of data-mining

The complex algorithms used in data-mining have existed for more than two decades. Customized data-mining software using neural networks, fuzzy logic and pattern recognition has been employed to spot tax fraud, eavesdrop on foreign communications and process satellite imagery.[6] Until recently, these tools have been available only to very large corporations or agencies due to their high costs. However, this is changing rapidly. In the evolution from business data to information, each new step has built on previous ones. For example, large database storage is crucial to the success of data-mining. The four stages listed in Exhibit 8.4 were revolutionary because each allowed new management questions to be answered accurately and quickly.[7]

| Evolutionary step | Investigative question | Enabling technology | Characteristics |
|---|---|---|---|
| Data-collection (1960s) | What was my average total revenue over the last five years? | Computer, tapes, disks | Retrospective static data delivery |
| Data access (1980s) | What were the unit sales in Sweden last December? | Relational databases, structured query language | Retrospective, dynamic data delivery at record level |
| Data navigation (1990s) | What were the unit sales in Sweden last December? Drill down to Uppsala. | Online analytical processing, multidimensional databases, data warehouses | Retrospective, dynamic data delivery at multiple levels |
| Data-mining (2000s) | What is likely to happen with Uppsala sales next month? Why? | Advanced algorithms, multiprocessor computers, massive databases | Prospective, proactive information delivery |

*Exhibit 8.4* The evolution of data-mining.

The process of extracting information from data has been present in some industries for years. Insurance companies often compete by finding small market segments where the premiums paid greatly outweigh the risks. They then issue specially priced policies to a particular segment with profitable results. However, two problems have limited the effectiveness of this process: getting the data has been both difficult and expensive; and processing it into information has taken time – making it historical rather than predictive. Now, instead of incurring high data-collection costs in order to resolve management questions, secondary data are available to assist the manager's decision-making.

### Pattern recognition

Data-mining tools can be programmed to sweep regularly through databases and identify previously hidden patterns. An example of **pattern recognition** is the detection of stolen credit cards based on the analysis of credit card transaction records. MasterCard processes 12 million transactions daily and uses data-mining to detect fraud.[8] Other uses include finding retail purchase patterns (used for inventory management), identifying call centre volume fluctuations (used for staffing), and locating anomalous data that could represent data-entry errors (used to evaluate the need for training, employee evaluation or security).

## Google it

What do you do if you want to know the gross national product (GNP) per head of Brazil, the profits between 1980 and 2006 of Vodafone or the number of students enrolled in your university. The simple answer is: 'google it'. The answer to these and many other (descriptive) questions is just a few mouse clicks away. Every time you enter a search query into Google or any other search engine, the query is registered and newspapers often report on the most frequent questions.

Newspapers often report which questions are most often entered into Google in a given month. In 2006 Google even opened a subsite called 'Google trends' where you can follow which search queries have gained in popularity, that is the ranking does not list generic search terms that have been used frequently for a long time, such as sex, football, and so on. Currently (September 2007), the site only refers to the trends in the USA, but that can change. In the trends lab you can see how the popularity of a term has changed over time. For example, you can see that Tony Blair was much more often googled the days when he announced his resignation and the day he actually stepped down.

Would it be possible to use the google trend to predict the outcome of an election? Could you use that information to assess how the image of a company changed after it had become involved in a corporate scandal?

## Reference
google.com/trends

### Predicting trends and behaviours

A typical example of a predictive problem is targeted marketing. Using data from past promotional mailings to identify the targets most likely to maximize return on investment, future mailings can be made more effective. The Bank of America uses data-mining software to pinpoint marketing programmes that attract high-margin, low-risk customers.[9] Other predictive problems include forecasting bankruptcy and loan default, and finding population segments with similar responses to a given stimulus. Data-mining tools can also be used to build risk models for a specific market, such as discovering the top 10 most significant buying trends each week.

## Data-mining

An understanding of statistics is essential to the data-mining process. Data-mining tools perform exploratory and confirmatory statistical analysis to discover and validate relationships. Data-mining tools even extend confirmatory statistical approaches by allowing the automated examination of large numbers of hypotheses. Suppose that there are 12 variables in a survey and we have a process, the outcome of which can be predicted when three variables are in a particular range. However, we are unfamiliar with the process and don't know which variables are relevant. With this small problem there are $12 \times 11 \times 10 = 1320$ combinations. If you spent a minute examining a plot of each pair of variables, you could easily spend 22 hours on the problem.

Numerous techniques are used in data-mining; often they are used together. The type of data available and the nature of information sought determine the technique used. Here we explore the first five techniques listed below and mention several others (to be covered in later chapters):

- data visualization
- clustering
- neural networks
- tree models
- classification
- estimation
- association
- market-basket analysis
- sequence-based analysis
- fuzzy logic
- genetic algorithms
- fractal-based transformation.

### Data visualization

By viewing aggregated data on multiple dimensions (e.g. product, brand, date of sale and region), both the analyst and the end-user gain a deeper, more intuitive understanding of the data in picture form. This is known as **data visualization**. A multidimensional database typically contains three axes: (i) dimensions, like the fields in a table; (ii) measurements, aggregate computations to be viewed; and (iii) hierarchies, which impose structure on the dimensions. For example, a set consisting of months, quarters, years is a time-based hierarchy.[10] Using this approach, the researcher views the data at various levels ('drill down/drill up'). Starting with a total of sales of breakfast cereal by region, say, the researcher observes that one region is more profitable than others. Next, she drills down to sales by store and discovers that one store is out-performing all others. Looking deeper yet reveals that this store spends the most on training warehousing personnel.

## Clustering

**Clustering** enables the researcher to segment a population. This approach assigns each data record to a group or segment. The assignment process is performed automatically by clustering algorithms that identify the similar characteristics in the data set and then partition them into groups often referred to as the 'nearest neighbours'. Clustering is often used as the first step in data-mining. For example, it may be used to segment a customer database for further analysis of customers' buying habits to decide which segments to target for a new sales campaign.

## Neural networks

**Neural networks**, or artificial neural networks (ANN), are collections of simple processing nodes that are connected. Each node operates only on its local data and on the inputs it receives via the connections. The result is a non-linear predictive model that resembles biological neural networks and learns through training. The neural model has to train its network on a training data set. One drawback is that no explanation of the results is available. Neural networks are best used where a predictive model is more useful than an explanatory model. For database marketing, a neural network can be constructed that predicts whether a specific person is likely to purchase a particular product. This enables the marketing organization to be very specific in its target marketing, reducing costs and dramatically improving sales 'hits'.

## Decision tree models

This technique segregates data by using a hierarchy of if-then statements based on the values of the variables, and creates a tree-shaped structure that represents the segregation decisions. **Decision tree models** are faster and easier to understand than neural networks, but the data must be interval or categorical. Specific decision tree methods include classification and regression trees (CART) and chi-square automatic interaction detection (CHAID), a type of Automatic Interaction Detection model.

## Classification

**Classification** uses a set of preclassified examples to develop a model that can classify the population of records at large. Fraud detection and risk assessments of credit applications are particularly well suited to this type of analysis. Classification frequently employs decision trees or neural network-based classification algorithms (see the descriptions below). Classification begins with training the software with a set of preclassified sample transactions. For a fraud-detection application, this would include complete records of both fraudulent and valid activities. The algorithm uses these cases as criteria to set the parameters for proper discrimination. Once developed, the model can correctly classify new records into the same predefined classes. For example, a model capable of classifying loan applicants may generate a rule stating, 'If applicant earns €45,000, is between 35 and 45 years old, and lives in a specific area, then the applicant is a good credit risk.' Estimation is a variation of classification. Instead of using a binary classifier (e.g. a loan applicant is a good risk or a bad risk), estimation generates a score (e.g. of credit-worthiness) based on a prescored training set.

## Other mining techniques

Association is the process used to recognize and understand patterns in the data. The goal is to find, across large numbers of small transactions, trends that can be used to understand and exploit natural buying patterns. The most common form of association is **market-basket analysis**. A classic example of market-basket analysis was the discovery that beer and nappies are often purchased during the evening in the same transaction. Presumably this is not because babies like beer before bed, but because the baby's father buys the nappies and chooses to purchase beer at the same time. Information from market-basket analysis can lead stores to change their layout, adjust their inventories or introduce a targeted promotional campaign. In the financial sector, association can be used to analyse customers' accounts. The patterns identified may be used to create a 'bundle' of service offerings.

A variant of traditional market-basket analysis, **sequence-based analysis** ties together a series of activities or purchases (e.g. using an account number, a credit card or a frequent-flyer number). The association algorithm takes into account not only the combination of items but also the order of the items. Rules derived from these relationships can be used to predict a specific purchase based on previous purchases. In healthcare, such methods can be used to predict the course of a disease and to order preventative care.

Fuzzy logic, genetic algorithms and fractal transforms are used in more complex mining operations. **Fuzzy logic**, an extension of conventional (Boolean) logic, handles the concept of partial truth – truth values between 'completely true' and 'completely false'. **Genetic algorithms** are optimization techniques that use processes analogous to mutation, natural selection and genetics for search and identification of meaningful relationships. Fractal geometry was originally applied to the compression of topographic images. It is a mathematical means of compressing data with no data. Models using **fractal-based transformation** can work on many gigabytes of data, offering the possibility of identifying tiny sub-sets of data that have common characteristics. For example, fractal-based transformations would enable a researcher to discover the five customers out of five million who responded to a Neckermann catalogue offering.

## The data-mining process

Data-mining, as illustrated in Exhibit 8.5, involves a five-step process.[11]

1 Sample: decide between census and sample data.
2 Explore: identify relationships within the data.
3 Modify: modify or transform data.
4 Model: develop a model that explains the data relationships.
5 Assess: test the model's accuracy.

To better visualize the connections between the techniques just described and the process steps listed in this section, you may want to download a demonstration version of data-mining software from the Internet, such as the SAS Enterprise Miner (http://www.sas.com/service/consult/usconsult/miningcompaq.html), Compaq Advanced Data Mining Center (http://www.compaq.com, keyword search: data mining) or the SPSS demo (http://www.spss.com/lementine/newshow/sld003.htm).

## Sample

Exhibit 8.5 suggests that the researcher must decide whether to use the entire data set or a sample of the data.[12] If the data set in question is not large, if the processing power is high or if it is important to understand patterns for every record in the database, sampling should not be done. However, if the data warehouse is very large (terabytes of data), the processing power is limited or speed is more important than complete analysis, it is wise to draw a sample (see Chapter 6 on sampling). In some instances, researchers may use a data mart for their sample – with local data that are appropriate for their geography. Alternatively, the researcher may select

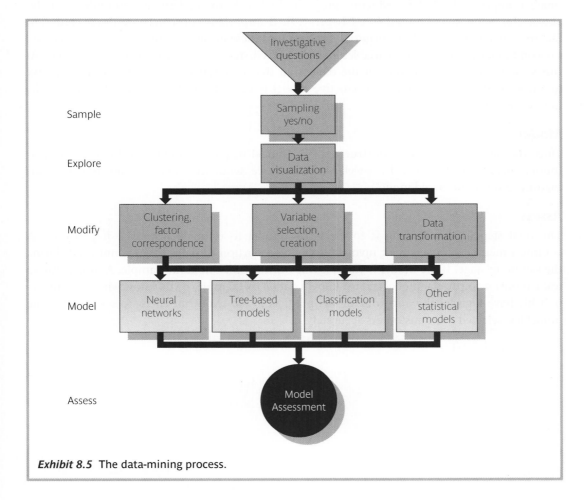

*Exhibit 8.5* The data-mining process.

an appropriate sampling technique. Since fast turnaround for decisions is often more important than absolute accuracy, sampling is appropriate. If general patterns exist in the data as a whole, these patterns will be found in the sample. If a niche is so tiny that it is not represented in a sample yet is so important that it influences the big picture, it will be found using exploratory data analysis (EDA).

### Explore

After the data are sampled, the next step is to explore them visually or numerically for trends or groups. Both visual and statistical exploration (data visualization) can be used to identify trends. The researcher also looks for outliers to see if the data need to be cleaned, cases need to be dropped or a larger sample needs to be drawn.

### Modify

Based on the discoveries in the exploration phase, the data may require modification. Clustering, fractal-based transformation and the application of fuzzy logic are completed during this phase as appropriate. A data-reduction program, such as factor analysis, correspondence analysis, or clustering, may be used (see Chapter 19). If important constructs are discovered, new factors may be introduced to categorize the data into these groups. In addition, variables based on combinations of existing variables may be added, recoded, transformed or dropped. At times, descriptive segmentation of the data is all that is required to answer the investigative question. However, if a complex predictive model is needed, the researcher will move to the next stage of the process.

### Model

Once the data are prepared, construction of a model begins. Modelling techniques in data-mining include neural networks as well as decision tree, sequence-based, classification and estimation, and genetic-based models.

### Assess

The final step in data-mining is to assess the model to estimate how well it performs. A common method of assessment involves applying a portion of data that was not used during the sampling stage. If the model is valid, it will work for this 'holdout' sample. Another way to test a model is to run the model against known data. For example, if you know which customers in a file have high loyalty and your model predicts loyalty, you can check to see whether the model has selected these customers accurately.

## Research Methods in Practice 8

# Digging contract and other archives

In the case description of the previous chapters, we have already mentioned that we were very interested in the contracts the cooperating firms had signed. Asking and answering questions about contracts is not an easy task for the interviewer as well as for the respondent. Thus, before we started to develop questions directed at the contract we needed to know how we could assess the content of contracts with an extensive set of questions. To obtain a better understanding of interfirm contracts, we needed to examine some of the contracts and we also needed to understand the structure of these contracts.

Thus, we tried to obtain access to archives that would hold contracts or model contracts. We thought about checking the following sources:

1 Check with the law faculty whether they have an archive of interfirm contracts.
2 Check with the EU how they design the contracts of the thousands of research and development (R&D) cooperations they sponsor.
3 Check with the firms we had already contacted whether they have model contracts and whether we could see a couple of actual contracts.

It should be noted that we did not want to have an informative talk with someone knowledgeable, but we wanted actual written documents that we could look at to learn how cooperations look like, how they differ, and so on.

Regarding all three sources mentioned above, we were successful but each source provided us with something different.

Law faculty
Initially, we thought that the law faculty should have something like an archive of contracts, but at least the one we contacted did not have any archive of contracts between firms. However, what they had were booklets of model contracts. These booklets show what are typical standard clauses in a private contract in general and standard clauses for particular issues. Moreover, these booklets informed us of the subtle differences in juridical wording. One example of such subtlety is the difference between the Dutch terms 'in overleg' and 'na overleg'. These terms are for example used in clauses about whether one of the partners may engage with another partner in a similar project. 'In overleg' means actually that a firm has only to inform the other party if it wants to form a similar cooperation, while 'na overleg' means that the firm needs to have the consent of the partner for forming a similar relation.

Model contracts of the EU
The EU provided us with a lot of very detailed model contracts especially fine-tuned for the governance of joint R&D projects. Combined with the model contract we found at the faculty of law, we could build from both sources something like a general framework on which aspects might be covered in a contract for an R&D cooperation.

Model contracts of firms
Through our first contacts with companies, we were also able to obtain some real contracts just before we started our investigations. These real contracts helped us tremendously in checking whether the model contracts suggested by law experts or provided by the European Commission did somehow match with reality. Our comparison showed that our model contracts had much more clauses than the real contracts, which was good news. Now, we could be pretty sure that our questions developed from the model

contracts would cover even more than the actual contract and that we did not leave out important contractual aspects.

Another lesson we draw from the use of archives to retrieve information is that you need people who know the archives. We did not find the model contracts by ourselves; rather experts in the fields pointed us in the direction of these sources. Moreover, these experts were also very helpful in helping us to understand what was in the archives. Thus, after we had studied the archive material, we would again contact legal experts and discuss with them how we read the information obtained and whether that was a sensible reading.

Later on, I dug again into secondary data sources to find real-life examples that would spice up the introduction chapter of the study. Academic writing is sometimes rather prosaic, real-life examples light it up and often help to illustrate a problem. Moreover, such examples show that the problem investigated has relevance beyond the academic community. Where did I search for examples? First, some examples were mentioned in the academic literature I looked at. Second, I looked through more practice-oriented academic journals, such as *Harvard Business Review* or *McKinsey Quarterly* and finally I scanned management magazines, such as *Businessweek*. The examples mentioned in the Running Case Study in Chapter 2 are a result of this search.

# Summary

1 Secondary data are an important information source in all research phases. In the exploratory phase of the research process, secondary data allow you to expand your understanding of the research dilemma. Secondary data can also be used to test theories or arguments. Moreover, secondary data often deliver fruitful information on the context of the study.

2 The main advantages of using secondary data rest in time and money savings as well as the high quality of secondary data if they originate from reputable sources, such as government statistics. The use of secondary data is problematic if the information therein does not fit the research problem well.

3 One of the harder tasks associated with using secondary sources is evaluating the quality of the information. Five factors to consider when evaluating the quality of the source are purpose, scope, authority, audience and format.

4 Secondary data play an important role in qualitative research, as they are frequently based on multiple sources. Moreover, secondary data can provide useful information on the context of the phenomena investigated and therefore add more to the total perspective.

5 Managers faced with current decisions requiring immediate attention often overlook internal data in a company's data warehouse. Data-mining refers to the process of discovering knowledge from databases. Data-mining technology provides two unique capabilities to the researcher or manager: pattern discovery, and the prediction of trends and behaviours. Data-mining tools perform exploratory and confirmatory statistical analyses to discover and validate relationships. These tools even extend confirmatory statistical approaches by allowing the automated examination of large numbers of hypotheses. The type of data available and the nature of information sought determine which of the numerous data-mining techniques to select. Data-mining involves a five-step process: sample, explore, modify, model and assess.

## Discussion questions

### Terms in review

1 Explain how each of the five evaluation factors for a secondary source influences its management decision-making value:
   a purpose
   b scope
   c authority
   d audience
   e format.

# Recommended further reading

Atkinson, Anthony B. and Brandolini, Andrea, 'Promises and pitfalls in the use of "secondary" data-sets: income inequality in OECD countries as a case study', *Journal of Economic Literature* 39(3), 2001, pp. 771–99. This article highlights the problems and opportunities of using secondary data, particularly for cross-country studies.

Berry, Michael J.A. and Linoff, Gordon, *Mastering Data-mining: The Art and Science of Customer Relationship Management.* New York: John Wiley & Sons, 2000.

Cowton, Christopher J., 'The use of secondary data in business ethics research', *Journal of Business Ethics* 17(4), 1998, pp. 423–34. This article demonstrates the many forms of secondary data that can be used in research.

Fayyad, U.M. and Piatesky-Shapiro, G., *Advances in Knowledge Discovery and Data-mining.* Cambridge, MA: AAAI Press–MIT Press, 1996. An excellent text that provides an overview of knowledge discovery and data-mining using statistical methods.

Katz, William A. (ed.), *Introduction to Reference Work Volume I and II* (8th edn.). New York: McGraw-Hill, 2001. The two volumes explain the basis of the reference process and all kinds of information sources.

Levitas, Ruth and Guy, Will (eds.), *Interpreting Official Statistics.* London: Routledge, 1996. This book provides information about official statistics in the UK since 1979, and many methodological issues associated with statistics, such as the Labour Force Survey.

Woy, James (ed.), *Encyclopedia of Business Information Sources* (14th edn.). Farmington Hills: Gale Group, 2000. A bibliographic guide to more than 20,000 citations covering more than 1000 interest areas in business.

# Chapter 9

# Observations, content analysis, action and ethnographic research

## LEARNING OBJECTIVES

When you have read this chapter, you should
understand:

☑ when observation studies are most useful

☑ the distinctions between monitoring non-behavioural and behavioural activities

☑ the strengths and weaknesses of the observation approach in research design

☑ the various designs of observation studies

☑ the basics of action research

☑ the basics of ethnographic research.

## 9.1 The uses of observation

Much of what we know comes from observation. We notice co-workers' reactions to political intrigue, the sounds of the assembly area, the smell of perfume, the taste of office coffee, the smoothness of the vice-president's marble desk, and a host of other stimuli. While such observation may be a basis for knowledge, the collection processes are often haphazard.

Observation qualifies as scientific inquiry when it is conducted specifically to answer a research question, is systematically planned and executed, uses proper controls, and provides a reliable and valid account of what happened. The versatility of observation makes it an indis-

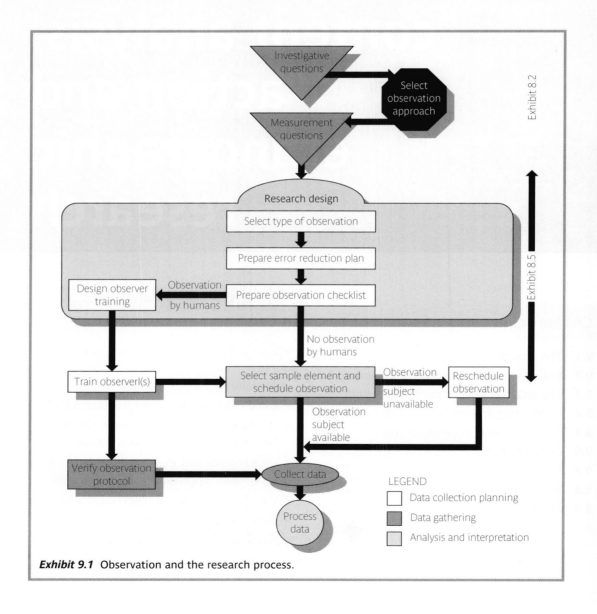

***Exhibit 9.1*** Observation and the research process.

pensable primary source method and a supplement for other methods. Many academics have a limited view of observation, relegating it to a minor technique of field data-collection. This ignores its potential for forging business decisions and denies its historic stature as a creative means of obtaining primary data. Exhibit 9.1 illustrates the use of observation in the research process.

In Chapter 7, we said that research designs are classified by the approach used to gather primary data: we can observe or we can communicate. Exhibit 9.2 describes the conditions under which observation is an appropriate method for data-collection. It also contrasts those conditions with ones we are familiar with from the communication modes discussed in Chapter 7: personal interview, telephone interview and self-administered survey (see Exhibit 7.2).

Besides collecting data visually, observation involves listening, reading, smelling and touching. Behavioural scientists define observation in terms of animal or human behaviour, but this too is limiting. As used in this text, observation includes the full range of monitoring

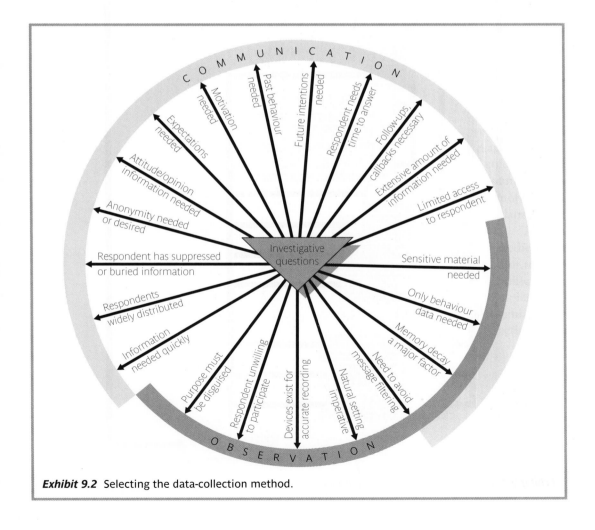

*Exhibit 9.2* Selecting the data-collection method.

behavioural and non-behavioural activities and conditions, which, as shown in Exhibit 9.3, can be classified roughly as follows.

Behavioural observation:

- non-verbal analysis
- linguistic analysis
- extra-linguistic analysis
- spatial analysis.

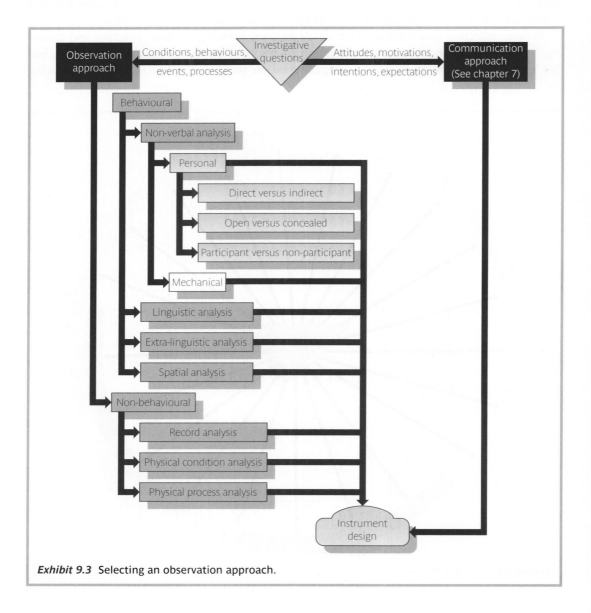

***Exhibit 9.3*** Selecting an observation approach.

Non-behavioural observation:

- record analysis
- physical condition analysis
- physical process analysis.

## Non-behavioural observation

A prevalent form of observation research is **record analysis**. This may involve historical or current records, and public or private records. They may be written, printed, sound-recorded, photographed, videotaped or any records generated by information and communication technology devices. Historical statistical data are often the only sources used for a study. Other examples of this type of observation are the content analysis (described in this chapter) of competitive advertising and the analysis of personnel records.

Physical condition analysis is typified by store audits of merchandise availability, studies of plant safety compliance, analysis of inventory conditions and analysis of financial statements. **Process (activity) analysis** includes time/motion studies of manufacturing processes and analysis of traffic flows in a distribution system, paperwork flows in an office and financial flows in the banking system. It should be noted that non-behavioural observations sometimes allow inferences on behaviour. For example, the 'cookies' stored temporarily on a personal computer reflect the web-surfing behaviour of the user. Similarly, counting the oil spots on the ground in a public car park tells us something about which car parks are used most often.

## Behavioural observation

The observational study of persons can be classified into four major categories.[1] **Non-verbal behaviour** is the most prevalent of these and includes body movement, motor expressions and even exchanged glances. At the level of gross body movement, one might study how a salesperson travels a territory. At a fine level, one can study the body movements of a worker assembling a product, or time-sample the activity of a department's work force to discover the share of time each worker spends in various ways. More abstractly, one can study body movement as an indicator of interest or boredom, anger or pleasure in a certain environment. Motor expressions such as facial movements can be observed as a sign of emotional states. Eye-blink rates are studied as indicators of interest in advertising messages. Exchanged glances are of interest in studies of interpersonal behaviour.

**Linguistic behaviour** is a second frequently used form of behaviour observation. One simple type familiar to most students is the tally of 'ahs' or other annoying sounds or words a professor makes or uses during a class. More serious applications are the study of a sales presentation's content or the study of what, how and how much information is conveyed in a training situation. A third form of linguistic behaviour involves interaction processes that occur between two people or in small groups. Bales has proposed one widely used system for classifying such linguistic interactions.[2]

Behaviour may also be analysed on an extra-linguistic level. Sometimes **extra-linguistic**

## Snapshot

### Shopping together ends in quarrels

Tim Denison conducted an extensive observational study on the shopping behaviour of women and men, looking at about 2000 people who shopped alone or in company with someone else. Overall, he observed that men stop their shopping after 72 minutes, while women still have the energy or pleasure to continue for another half an hour. Denison also observed other gender differences. Men are hunters, who know what they want, target their object, buy it and leave. Women are collectors, they look around, inspect this product and that product, and compare them. They take their time. This difference in observable behaviour is also supported by the physical state of the shoppers. The blood pressure of men rises at the start of the shopping process, reaches rather high levels, but drops considerably as soon as the product is bought. Women's blood pressure rises less quickly, does not reach as high a level as that of men, but continues to be high even 15 minutes after the purchase. These different patterns in shopping behaviour explain the friction that emerges if men and women shop together. On average, it is less than half an hour before they begin to argue.

The description of behavioural differences provided above supports common wisdom (and experience) on shopping.

But is this study any more than a rich description? What can we infer from the observed differences in physical condition (blood pressure) between women and men?

### References and further reading

Intermediair. 'Samen winkelen: niet te lang [Shopping together: not for too long]', Intermediair (2 October 2003), p. 11.

is being assessed. Even when sample sizes are small, observation records can be disproportionately large and difficult to analyse.

Fifth, observation is limited as a way to learn about the past. It is similarly limited as a method by which to learn what is going on in the present at some distant place. It is also difficult to gather information on such topics as intentions, attitudes, opinions or preferences. Nevertheless, any consideration of the merits of observation confirms its value when used with care and understanding.

## 9.3  The observer – participant relationship

Interrogation presents a clear opportunity for interviewer bias. The problem is less pronounced with observation but is still real. The relationship between observer and participant may be viewed from three perspectives:

1  whether the observation is direct or indirect
2  whether the observer's presence is known or unknown to the participant
3  what role the observer plays.

## Directness of observation

**Direct observation** occurs when the observer is physically present and personally monitors what takes place. This approach is very flexible because it allows the observer to react to and report subtle aspects of events and behaviours as they occur. He or she is also free to shift places, change the focus of the observation, or concentrate on unexpected events if they occur. A weakness of this approach is that observers' 'perception circuits' may become overloaded as events move quickly, and observers must later try to reconstruct what they were not able to record. Also, observer fatigue, boredom and distracting events can reduce the accuracy and completeness of observation.

**Indirect observation** occurs when the recording is done by mechanical, photographic or electronic means. For example, a special camera that takes one frame every second may be mounted in a department of a large store to study customer and employee movement. Indirect observation is less flexible than direct observation but is also much less biasing and may be less erratic in terms of accuracy. Another advantage of indirect observation is that the permanent record can be re-analysed to include many different aspects of an event. Electronic recording devices, which have improved in quality and declined in cost, are being used more frequently in observation research.

## Concealment

A second factor affecting the observer–participant relationship concerns whether the participant should know of the observer's presence. When the observer is known, there is a risk of atypical activity by the participant. The initial entry of an observer into a situation often upsets the activity patterns of the participants, but this influence usually dissipates quickly, especially when participants are engaged in some absorbing activity or the presence of observers offers no potential threat to the participants' self-interest. The potential bias from participant awareness of observers is always a matter of concern, however.

Observers use **concealment** to shield themselves from the object of their observation. Often technical means such as one-way mirrors, hidden cameras or microphones are used. These methods reduce the risk of observer bias but bring up the question of ethics. Hidden observation is a form of spying, and the propriety of this action must be reviewed carefully.

A modified approach involves partial concealment. The presence of the observer is not concealed, but the objectives and participant of interest are. A study of selling methods may be conducted by sending an observer with a salesperson who is making calls on customers. However, the observer's real purpose may be hidden from both the salesperson and the customer (e.g. he or she may pretend that he or she is analysing the display and layout characteristics of the stores they are visiting).

## Participation

The third observer–participant issue is whether the observer should participate in the situation while observing. A more involved arrangement, **participant observation**, exists when the observer enters the social setting and acts as both an observer and a participant. Sometimes, he or she is known as an observer to some or all of the participants; at other times the true role is concealed. While reducing the potential for bias, this again raises an ethical issue. Often participants will not have given their consent and will not have knowledge of or access to the findings. After being deceived and having their privacy invaded, what further damage could come to the participants if the results became public? This issue needs to be addressed when concealment and covert participation are used.

Participant observation makes a dual demand on the observer. Recording can interfere with participation, and participation can interfere with observation. The observer's role may influence the way others act. Because of these problems, participant observation is used less in business research than, say, in anthropology or sociology. It is typically restricted to cases where non-participant observation is not practical – for example, a study of the functioning of a travelling auditing team.

## 9.4  Conducting an observational study
### The type of study

Observation is found in almost all research studies, at least at the exploratory stage. Such data-collection is known as **simple observation**. Its practice is not standardized, as one would expect, because of the discovery nature of exploratory research. The decision to use observation as the major data-collection method may be made as early as the moment the researcher moves from research questions to investigative questions. The latter specify the outcomes of the study – the specific questions the researcher must answer with collected data. If the study is to be something other than exploratory, **systematic observation** employs standardized procedures, trained observers, schedules for recording and other devices for the observer that mirror the scientific procedures of other primary data methods. Systematic studies vary in the emphasis placed on recording and encoding observational information:

> At one end of the continuum are methods that are unstructured and open-ended. The observer tries to provide as complete and nonselective a description as possible. On the other end of the continuum are more structured and predefined methods that itemize, count, and categorize behavior. Here the investigator decides beforehand which behavior will be recorded and how frequently observations will be made. The investigator using structured observation is much more discriminating in choosing which behavior will be recorded and precisely how [it is] to be coded.[4]

One author classifies observational studies by the degree of structure in the environmental setting and the amount of structure imposed on the environment by the researcher,[5] as reflected in Exhibit 9.4. The researcher conducting a class 1, completely unstructured, study would be in a natural or field setting endeavouring to adapt to the culture. A typical example would be an ethnographic study in which the researcher, as a participant-observer, becomes a part of the culture and describes in great detail everything surrounding the event or activity of interest. Donald Roy, in the widely used case on organizational behaviour, 'Banana Time', took a punch-press job in a factory to describe the rituals that a small work group relied on to make their highly repetitive, monotonous work bearable.[6] With other purposes in mind, business researchers may use this type of study for hypothesis generation.

| Research class | Environment | Purpose | Research tool |
|---|---|---|---|
| 1 Completely unstructured | Natural setting | Generate hypotheses | |
| 2 Unstructured | Laboratory | | |
| 3 Structured | Natural setting | | Observation checklist |
| 4 Completely structured | Laboratory | Test hypotheses | Observation checklist |

*Exhibit 9.4* Classification of observation studies.

Class 4 studies – completely structured research – are at the opposite end of the continuum from completely unstructured field investigations. The research purpose of class 4 studies is to test hypotheses; therefore, a definitive plan for observing specific, operationalized behaviour is known in advance. This requires a measuring instrument, called an **observational checklist**, which is analogous to a questionnaire. Exhibit 9.5 shows the parallels between survey design and checklist development. Checklists should possess a high degree of precision in defining relevant behaviour or acts, and should have mutually exclusive and exhaustive categories. The coding is frequently closed, thereby simplifying data analysis. The participant groups being observed must be comparable and the laboratory conditions identical. The classic example of a class 4 study was Bales' investigation into group interaction.[7] Many team-building, decision-making and assessment centre studies follow this structural pattern.

The two middle classes (2 and 3) of observation studies emphasize the best characteristics of either researcher-imposed controls or the natural setting. In class 2, the researcher uses the facilities of a laboratory – videotape recording, two-way mirrors, props and stage sets – to introduce more control into the environment while simultaneously reducing the time needed for observation. In contrast, a class 3 study takes advantage of a structured observational instrument in a natural setting.

## Content specification

Specific conditions, events or activities that we want to observe determine the observational reporting system (and correspond to measurement questions). To specify the observation content, we should include both the major variables of interest and any other variables that may affect them. From this cataloguing, we then select those items we plan to observe. For each variable chosen, we must provide an operational definition if there is any question of concept ambiguity or special meanings. Even if the concept is a common one, we must make certain that all observers agree on the measurement terms by which to record results. For example, we may agree that variable X will be reported by count, while variable Y will be counted and the effectiveness of its use judged qualitatively.

Observation may be at either a factual or an inferential level. Exhibit 9.6 shows how we could separate the factual and inferential components of a salesperson's presentation. This table is suggestive only. It does not include many other variables that might be of interest, including data on customer purchase history; company, industry and general economic conditions; the

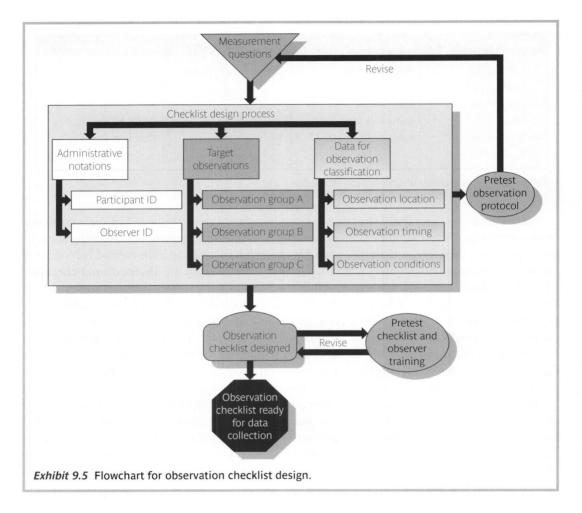

***Exhibit 9.5*** Flowchart for observation checklist design.

order in which sales arguments are presented; and specific words used to describe certain product characteristics. The particular content of observation will also be affected by the nature of the observation setting.

## Observer training

There are a few general guidelines for the qualification and selection of observers.

- Concentration: ability to function in a setting full of distractions.
- Detail-oriented: ability to remember details of an experience.
- Unobtrusive: ability to blend with the setting and not be distinctive.
- Experience level: ability to extract the most from an observation study.

An obviously attractive observer may be a distraction in some settings but ideal in others. The same can be said for the characteristics of age or ethnic background.

| Factual | Inferential |
|---|---|
| Introduction/identification of salesperson and customer | Credibility of salesperson/qualified status of customer |
| Time and day of the week | Convenience for the customer; welcoming attitude of the customer |
| Product presented | Customer interest in product |
| Selling point presented per product | Customer acceptance of selling points per product |
| Number of customer objections raised per product | Customer concerns about features and benefits |
| Salesperson's rebuttal of objection | Effectiveness of salesperson's rebuttal attempts |
| Salesperson's attempts to restore control | Effectiveness of salesperson's control attempt; consequences for customers who prefer interactions |
| Length of interview | Customer's/salesperson's degree of enthusiasm for the interview |
| Environmental factors interfering with the interview | Level of distraction for customer |
| Customer purchase decision | General evaluation of sales presentation skill |

*Exhibit 9.6* Content of observation: factual versus inferential.

If observation is at the surface level and involves a simple checklist or coding system, then experience is less important. Inexperience may even be an advantage if there is a risk that experienced observers may have pre-set convictions about the topic. Regardless, most observers are subject to fatigue, halo effects and observer drift, which refers to a decay in reliability or validity over time that affects the coding of categories.[8] Only intensive videotaped training relieves these problems.

The observers should be thoroughly versed in the requirements of the specific study. Each observer should be informed of the outcomes sought and the precise content elements to be studied. Observer trials with the instrument and sample videotapes should be used until a high degree of reliability is apparent in their observations. When there are interpretative differences between observers, they should be reconciled.

## Data-collection

The data-collection plan specifies the details of the task. In essence, it answers the questions: who, what, when, how and where.

## *Who?*

What qualifies a participant to be observed? Must each participant meet a given criterion – those who initiate a specific action? Who are the contacts to gain entry (in an ethnographic study), the intermediary to help with introductions or the contacts to reach if conditions change or trouble develops? Who has responsibility for the various aspects of the study? Who fulfils the ethical responsibilities to the participants?

Snapshot

## Envirosell: studies reveal left-hand retail

World retailers collect and subscribe to numerous data sources, but they need knowledge from that data to craft their merchandising, staffing and promotion strategies, as well as their store designs. Retail giants (such as GAP, Limited, Starbucks, Radio Shack and McDonald's) turn to consultant Paco Underhill when they want to know how consumers buy what they do and what barriers prevent or discourage buying. Underhill describes himself as a 'commercial researcher, which means I am part scientist, part artist, and part entrepreneur'. His company, Envirosell, has offices in the USA, Milan, Sidney and São Paulo. Envirosell concentrates on the third segment of retail information, drawn from observation (segment 1 is register data and segment 2 is communication studies). In a recent ABC News live e-chat, Underhill said, 'the principal differences in first-world shopping patterns are governed more by education and income than by ethnicity … but the Brits and Aussies [do] tend to walk as they drive [i.e. in the same way]. This sets up some very peculiar retail [shopping] patterns, because their walking patterns set up a left-hand dominance, whereas in the US and much of the rest of the world, our walking patterns set up a right-hand dominance.'

## References and further reading

Live e-chat with Paco Underhill, 8 July 1999 (http://www.abcnews.go.com/sections/politics/DailyNews/chat_990511underhill.html).
McGraw-Hill video library.
www.envirosell.com

## *What?*

The characteristics of the observation must be set as sampling elements and units of analysis. This is achieved when event–time dimension and 'act' terms are defined. In **event sampling**, the researcher records selected behaviour that answers the investigative questions. In **time sampling**, the researcher must choose among a time-point sample, continuous real-time measurement or a time-interval sample. For a time-point sample, recording occurs at fixed points for a specified length. With continuous measurement, behaviour or the elapsed time of the behaviour is recorded. Like continuous measurement, time-interval sampling records every behaviour in real time but counts the behaviour only once during the interval.[9]

Assume the observer is instructed to observe a quality-control inspection for 10 minutes out of each hour (a duration of two minutes each, five times). Over a prolonged period, if the samples are drawn randomly, time sampling can give a good estimate of the pattern of activities. In a time-interval sampling of workers in a department, the outcome may be a judgement of how well the department is being supervised. In a study of sales presentations using continuous real-time sampling, the research outcome may be an assessment of a given salesperson's effectiveness or the effectiveness of different types of persuasive message.

Other important dimensions are defined by acts. What constitutes an act is established by the needs of the study. It is the basic unit of observation. Any of the following could be defined as an act for an observation study:

- a single expressed thought
- a physical movement
- a facial expression
- a motor skill.

Although acts may be well defined, they often present difficulties for the observer. A single statement from a sales presentation may include several thoughts about product advantages, a rebuttal to an objection about a feature or some remark about a competitor. The observer is hard pressed to sort out each thought, decide whether it represents a separate unit of observation and then record it quickly enough to follow continued statements.

## When?

Is the time of the study important, or can any time be used? In a study of out-of-stock conditions in a supermarket, the exact times of observation may be important. Inventory is shipped to the store on certain days only, and buying peaks occur on other days. The likelihood of a given product being out of stock is a function of both time-related activities.

## How?

Will the data be directly observed? If there are two or more observers, how will they divide the task? How will the results be recorded for later analysis? How will the observers deal with various situations that may occur – when expected actions do not take place, say, or when someone challenges the observer in the setting?

## Where?

Within a spatial confine, where does the act take place? In a retail traffic pattern study, the proximity of a customer's pause space to a display or directional sign might be recorded. Must the observation take place in a particular location within a larger venue? The location of the observation, such as a sales approach observation within a chain of retail stores, can significantly influence the acts recorded.

Observers face unlimited variations in conditions. Fortunately, most problems do not occur simultaneously. When the plans are thorough and the observers well trained, observational research is quite successful.

Up to this point, our discussion has focused on direct observation as a traditional approach to data-collection. Like surveys and experiments, some observational studies – particularly participant observation – require the observer to be physically present in the research situation.

This contributes to a **reactivity response**, a phenomenon where participants alter their behaviour in response to the researcher. (You are familiar with the historic research at Western Electric and the so-called Hawthorne effect – introduced in Chapter 6 – and the reactions interviewers produce in participants that bias the findings of a study.)

## 9.5  Designing an observational study

The design of an observational study follows the same pattern as other research. Once the researcher has specified the investigative questions, it is often apparent that the best way to conduct the study is through observation. Guidance for conducting an observation and translating the investigative question(s) into an observational checklist is the subject of this section. We first review the procedural steps and then explain how to create a checklist.

Most studies that use the observational method follow a general sequence of steps that parallel the research process. Here we adapt these steps to the terminology of the observational method.

- Define the content of the study.
- Develop a data-collection plan that identifies the observational targets, sampling strategy and acts (operationalized as a checklist or coding scheme).
- Secure and train observers.
- Collect the data.
- Analyse the data.

Suppose you are working for ProSec Electronics and its management is concerned about a deterioration in the quality in its assembled product – security cameras – towards the end of each day. The management question is, 'Why are products failing quality assurance in the afternoon?' The following research question might be stated, 'What factors affect the quality of assembled cameras?' Although we presume that management is correct about the time, we will allow the data to confirm this. The investigative questions could then include: 'What is the variability due to changes in parts vendors?' 'Inventory?' 'Does the manufacturing procedure change during the day?' 'Is it shift-dependent?' 'To what extent is the failure rate contingent on time of day?' 'What is the role of workplace conditions?' 'Is it linked to assembler performance?'

Further assume that, through interviewing, we isolate the content of the study to assembler behaviour in the natural environment. The major variables of interest will be operationalized from the assembler's job description and the environmental conditions of the assembly area.

The observational targets will be the assemblers and their acts (physical behaviour consistent with the job description). We have chosen to sample during the late afternoon, initially, and we will use time sampling on a continuous basis. This allows us to record all relevant behaviour and complete an environmental checklist. The observation will be direct, and we will operate from concealment using the one-way mirror on the door to the assembly area.

A tour of the assembly area reveals a rectangular room with east- and west-facing windows. The workstations run the length of the rectangle, splitting the room in half and facing north. Comfortable chairs are present, and parts bins are to the right of each workstation, requiring the assembler to turn westwards to select parts. The windows have shades, and there is both general and task lighting.

The variables to be measured (measurement questions) were derived from the investigative questions on workplace conditions and assembler performance. Notes taken on the tour improved our understanding of contextual variables. By examining the workplace first, we can assess and begin to rule out environmental variables (lighting, temperature, noise and other variables controlled by the production facility) before moving on to behavioural characteristics. Both checklists will be revised after pre-testing. The observational checklist for the assembly environment features a range of measures from graphic rating scales to category scales. It is shown in Exhibit 9.7.

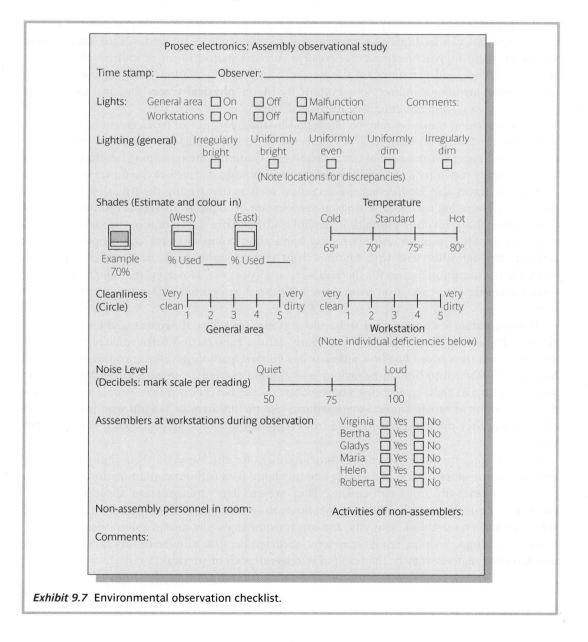

*Exhibit 9.7* Environmental observation checklist.

The assemblers are subject to periodic and unscheduled supervisory visits, and normal workplace rules for a drug-free environment. Nevertheless, the foremost ethical concern is restricting the observations to assembly activities. Using the company's cameras, we will run one on wide angle for context and the other zoomed in to capture individual assembler behaviour on a time-interval sampling. The observation will be videotaped so a consistent stimulus may be used to train observers, pre-test and refine the checklists, and obtain a benchmark for later comparison. The behavioural checklist will be devised after studying the job descriptions and viewing the preliminary videotape.

Webb and his colleagues have given us an insight into some very innovative observational procedures that can be both non-reactive and inconspicuously applied. Called **unobtrusive measures**, these approaches encourage creative and imaginative forms of indirect observation, archival searches, and variations on simple and contrived observation.[10] Of particular interest are measures involving indirect observation based on **physical traces** that include erosion (measures of wear) and accretion (measures of deposit).

Natural erosion measures may be illustrated by the frequency of replacement of vinyl floor tiles in front of museum exhibits as an indicator of exhibit popularity. The study of wear and tear on book pages is a measure of library book use. Counting the remaining brochures in a car dealer's display rack after a favourable magazine review suggests levels of consumer interest.

Physical traces also include natural accretion such as discovering the listenership of radio stations by observing car radio settings as vehicles are brought in for service. Another type of unobtrusive study involves estimating alcohol and magazine consumption by collecting and analysing domestic rubbish. An interesting application compared beer consumption reports acquired through interviews with findings from sampled rubbish. If the interview data were valid, the consumption figures for the area were at 15 per cent. However, the validity was questioned when the beer can count from domestic rubbish supported a 77 per cent consumption rate.[11]

William Rathje is a professor of archaeology at the University of Arizona, and founder of the Garbage Project in Tucson. His study of trash, refuse, rubbish and litter resulted in the sub-discipline that the *Oxford English Dictionary* has dubbed 'garbology'. By excavating landfills, he has gained insight into human behaviour and cultural patterns – sometimes sorting the contents of up to 150 coded categories. His previous studies have shown that 'people will describe their behaviour to satisfy cultural expectations, like the mothers in Tucson who unanimously claimed that they made their baby food from scratch, but whose garbage told a very different tale'.[12]

Physical trace methods present a strong argument for use based on their ability to provide low-cost access to frequency, attendance and incidence data without contamination from other methods or reactivity from participants. They are excellent 'triangulation' devices for cross-validation. Thus, they work well as supplements to other methods. Designing an unobtrusive study can test a researcher's creativity, and one must be especially careful about inferences made from the findings. Erosion results may have occurred because of wear factors not considered, and accretion material may be the result of selective deposit or survival.

# 9.6  Content analysis

Content analysis is a technique based on the manual or automated coding of transcripts, documents, (newspaper) articles or even audio and video material. The basic assumption of content analysis is that words or phrases that occur more frequently reflect a text's concern. The core idea of the method is to count specific words and phrases or to investigate which other words occur close to specific words, for example which words occur together within one sentence.

In applied business research, content analysis is often used to measure the success of public relations efforts. For example, on 29 June 2007, Apple Inc. started selling the iPhone® through its stores in the USA. But long before the first iPhone® was sold it had received tremendous media coverage. Content analysis is a method that allows you to systematically investigate the media coverage. In a first step you might simply count how often the word 'iPhone' occurs in articles of major national newspapers and magazines. A simple content analysis would count the word iPhone by analysing how often the product name is mentioned in different media. Advanced forms of content analysis also investigate in which context the word 'iPhone' appears. The information could be used to answer the following types of question:

1 What are the antecedents of media coverage? For example, why does the media coverage vary over time? Is there a relation with press announcements by Apple?

2 What are the characteristics of the media coverage? For example, why do some newspapers report positively about the iPhone and others negatively? Is there a relation with the political orientation of the newspaper?

3 What are the effects of the media coverage? For example, why do some newspapers report about the iPhone later than others? How can we explain the diffusion of certain information through the media?

The general forms of the three questions above describe the basic categories of content analysis, namely the analysis of antecedents, the analysis of characteristics and the analysis of effects. You should note that content analysis is more than a tool for descriptive analysis; it also enables us to investigate explorative and explanative questions.

## The process of content analysis

The process of content analyses is similar to the process of any research.

### Define the population of sources and design sampling procedure

What are the sources used for the content analysis? If we are interested in media coverage, we would have to define the set of media of interest, for example all newspapers or only weekly women's magazines, and so on. In other studies our population could be press releases of a company. Depending on the size of the population, we might either use all sources, for example all press releases in 2007 of Barclays Bank, or sample sources out of the population, for example a random sample of women's magazines published in Sweden.

### Define the coding procedure

Do we pursue a prescriptive analysis or an open analysis. In a prescriptive analysis, we need to define words and phrases that we search for in the text. In an open analysis, we attempt to distil the general message of the text. You should note that this step is of utmost importance for the validity of your study, because through coding text elements are categorized to allow for making inferences. Valid inferences require that the classification procedure is reliable in the sense of consistency. Thus, different people should code a text in the same way.

### *Usage of predefined dictionaries*

In prescriptive analyses we either create a dictionary of key words or we might even use standard dictionaries, that is we count, for example, the frequency of words listed in any common dictionary. Open analysis usually do not rely on dictionaries, but apply qualitative analysis with the focus on finding out what are the intentions and implications of the text.

### Type of text analysis

Different types of text analysis can be classified along the following dimensions:

1 Language use

   a linguistic

   b data banks with word lists or key word in context approaches

2 Content of analysis

   a qualitative: looking for regularities and differences in the text by exploring the whole text

   b event data: analysis of events and their sequences in textual data

   c quantitative content analysis generates data matrices appropriate to test hypotheses

   d category systems: analyses with directories to search for specific words or patterns

   e no category systems are based on the co-occurrences of words or phrases

3 What is the target of the inferences?

Content analysis is one of the methodological tools that can be used in qualitative and quantitative studies as well. In the former case content analysis mainly attempts to distil the overall meaning, the intentions of a text. In the latter case, content analysis is a tool to transform textual information into numerical data that can be used in further statistical analyses.

### *Software packages for content analysis*

Currently, many software packages are available to automate the coding. Exhibit 9.8 provides examples of common software packages and their main properties. The main features distinguishing the packages are whether they can handle only text as input or also other formats, such as multimedia sources. All packages count words and phrases, but some packages are also able to detect more complex patterns or investigate the context key words are occurring in. A last important difference between the packages is whether they have a built-in dictionary or whether the researcher has to create one. Clearly, a built-in dictionary saves time in creating your own, but limits the researcher to the analysis of words contained in the dictionary. For example, in 2007 the Dutch bank ABN Amro is the target of a takeover battle between Barclays Bank, on the one hand and a consortium lead by Royal Bank of Scotland, on the other hand. You could analyse the public statement made by ABN Amro CEO, Rijkman Groenink, and

| Package | Input data | Counting, pattern recognition | Others | More information available at |
|---|---|---|---|---|
| ATLAS.ti | Text, audio and video | Counts words and phrases, connects segments, semantic editor | | http://www.atlasti.com/index.html |
| General Inquirer | Text | Word counts | Combined with a dictionary | http://www.wjh.harvard.edu/~inquirer/ |
| Intext | Text | Word counts | Public domain software | http://www.intext.de/eindex.html |
| Qualrus | Text and multimedia | Word counts and language scripting | Provides support for coding | http://www.ideaworks.com/qualrus/index.html |
| SPSS text analysis for surveys | Text | Word counts | SPSS module | http://www.spss.com/textanalysis_surveys/ |
| Textpack | Text | Word counts and key words in contexts | | http://www.gesis.org/en/software/textpack/index.htm |

*Exhibit 9.8* An (incomplete) overview of software packages for content analysis.

check how often and in what context he mentions Barclays and the Royal Bank of Scotland. For such an analysis you would need a package that allows you to create your own dictionary which you could fill with the names of the involved firms, and also names of key players associated with the two British banks.

## 9.7 Narrative analysis

Narrative analysis is a qualitative research method allowing for in-depth investigations. Labov defined narratives as one method of recapitulating past experience by matching verbal sequences of clauses to the sequences of events which actually occurred.[13] Thus, narrative analysis examines stories focusing on how its elements are sequenced and how they are evaluated. It is important that the respondents are part of the stories they tell and that they are more than a mere observer of events.

Of course, narrative accounts are subjective, but they tap rich anecdotal information that allow the researcher to get an insight into the perspective of the respondents. Narrative analysis is usually based on in-depth interviews, but one can also base it on secondary data, such as biographies. As narrative analysis misses elements such as representative sampling, operationalization of variables, and so on, it is unsuitable for explanatory research, but a very powerful approach for explorative research.

## Procedures in narrative analysis

While content analysis often emphasizes smaller elements of a text or story, narrative analysis has a strong emphasis on understanding the narrative as a whole. In the following we describe different procedures providing a researcher with a better insight into the narrative.

### Key segments of a narrative

The following key segments of any narrative build the structural categories.

1 Abstract statement
2 Orientation segments informs us about when (time) and where (place) the story took place, which situation is described and who is involved (participants)
3 Complicating action builds up the sequence of events as actions have events as antecedents and cause new events.
4 Evaluation describes how the respondent assesses the actions and informs the researcher about the respondent's attitude. The evaluation segment provides the researcher with the meaning of the actions from the respondent's perspective.
5 Resolution describes what finally happened or what the conclusion of the story is.
6 Coda segments offer insights into the importance of the story, thus they indicate which current phenomena or actions relate to the story told.

Although other categories for structuring a narrative are possible the one above is a widely used one in narrative analysis.

## Temporal organization

Another technique of narrative analysis is to examine the temporal organization of the story. Thus, the researcher cuts the story into smaller pieces (events) and orders these pieces sequentially, deciding which events occurred simultaneously and which sequentially.

## Contextual analysis

Given that narrative analysis is a qualitative method, it should incorporate the specific context in its analysis. Narratives vary within contexts, how a respondent tells others about an accident will differ depending on whether the story is told at work, at home or to team mates at a sporting club. Likewise, how a story is told might differ across different times. How do you tell a story about a conflict with a high school teacher that will change over time. When you tell the story as a pupil, directly after the conflict, it will differ from how you tell it as a student and from how you will tell the story to your grandchildren. The differences in the stories told in different contexts particularly yield insights into the evaluation segments, and by considering the context we are better able to understand the process as a whole.

# 9.8 Action research

**Action research** has its origins in the social sciences, and Kurt Lewin introduced the term in 1943 when US authorities commissioned a study on the use of tripe as part of the regular diet of American families.[14] The objective of the research was to find out how housewives could be encouraged to include tripe rather than beef, which was scarce during wartime, in their cooking. Lewin's set-up for the study was to start by training a number of housewives in how to use tripe in their cooking and, later, look at how this training affected their cooking behaviour. While the main objectives of the research methods discussed so far emphasize the acquisition of knowledge, that is you as a researcher mainly explain want to explain, action research focuses on another objective, namely social change or the production of socially desirable outcomes. In the case of Lewin's study, the main objective was to change the diet of Americans by substituting beef with tripe.

After the Second World War, action research also became prominent in management science, especially in Europe. The Tavistock Institute in the UK and the Norwegian Industrial Democracy Project employed this methodology to encourage social change on the shop floor. Researchers from the Tavistock Institute wanted to find out why the introduction of new technologies in British coalmines did not result in the expected productivity gains. Based on action research they came up with the finding that the work organization, which still followed the Tayloristic idea of dividing labour into small sub-activities, was no longer suited to new technologies, which required greater coordination and communication between work groups.[15]

Exhibit 9.9 summarizes the core characteristics of action research and mirrors them against the more traditional research methods discussed in previous chapters. One main difference between action research and other more traditional research approaches is that the latter attempt to identify general principles, which are useful in explaining phenomena in different contexts. Action research cares less about general principles, although those can be the outcome of a project, as in the case of the coalmining study mentioned above, but places a strong emphasis on the interplay between action and research to achieve desired changes.

| Action research | Other research methods |
|---|---|
| Addresses real-life problems and is bounded by the context | Address real-life as well as scientific problems, and attempt to identify general principles and their contingencies |
| Collaborative venture of researchers, participants and practitioners | Clear division of roles between researchers, participants and practitioners |
| Continuous reflecting process of research and Action | Usually clear division between the research process and implementation processes |
| Credibility – the validity of action research is measured on whether the actions solve the problems and realize the desired change | Credibility – the validity of research is established by statistical core figures and successful replications |

**Exhibit 9.9** Characteristics of action research compared with those of other research methods.

The main criticism of action research is that the findings produced are just anecdotal evidence, and transferring the knowledge acquired in one research project to another context is difficult and sometimes even impossible.[16] As action research is often very context dependent, the research approach becomes problematic if, say, one wishes to investigate problems within a larger context, such as rising unemployment rates in the European Union (EU). Another substantial criticism concerns the problems associated with the direct participation of the researcher and attempts to integrate research with organizational goals, which neglects the critical distance of a researcher essential for conducting good academic research.[17] Further, although action research is designed to change the environment, the researchers rarely have full control over the environment. As one author pointed out, 'Rarely will an organization cede ultimate authority to an external researcher. This guarded commitment is reasonable since the researcher's motives are divided between research goals and organizational problem-solving goals.'[18]

# 9.9 Ethnographic studies

**Ethnographic studies** are usually associated with other social sciences, especially anthropology and sociology, and most people hearing the term ethnography think of studies on isolated tribes at the Amazon or in the African bush. But ethnography is used to study business phenomena more often than one might imagine – however, not usually by scholars in economics and business, and more often by business journalists. Books describing the history, or certain period in the history, of a company often share many characteristics with ethnographic study, especially concerning the gathering of information and presentation of the facts. What distinguishes a popular book describing the history of a corporation from an ethnographic study is that the former omits any problem statement and, consequently, the analysis and interpretation of the information gathered in the light of the problem statement.

| Element | Examples |
|---|---|
| Multiple information sources | Combine interviews with observations, informal talks and archive studies |
| Employing different perspectives | Obtain information from different types of information provider, such as management, employees, labour unions, industry experts, economic media |
| Record and present different types of information | Simple quantitative information (frequencies), qualitative verbal information (citations from interviews or documents), qualitative behavioural information (anecdotes on specific behaviours or descriptions of habits), qualitative non-behavioural information (visualizations of the company's structure or observational accounts of the architecture of the company buildings or the office furniture) |

*Exhibit 9.10* Elements of an ethnographic study.

A main characteristic of ethnographic studies is its richness in the description of the world it studies. Rather than describing, for example, a firm with a couple of key figures, such as sales, profit, growth, number of employees, sector, and so on, as you would in a survey study, an ethnographic study considers many more aspects. Exhibit 9.10 shows how an ethnographic study of an organization, such as a business firm, would achieve this richness and 'thickness' of information.

## Research Methods in Practice 9

### Observing cooperative behaviour

Let us leave the project on the management of R&D cooperations for a moment, because hardly any of the methods described in this chapter was employed in the project. Although we visited the companies on a regular basis, we did not maintain detail protocols of our visits, nor did we tape record our talks and discussions in the early phases. Probably, it would have been very fruitful if we had recorded all the talks we had. However, our focus was in setting up a quantitative research and therefore we needed a lot of information that we could easily compare across the different cooperations and firms.

Pure observational studies are rare in business research and occur much more often in biology, child psychology and anthropology, probably because in these fields it is often impossible to interview people. In business studies, however, observational studies are often combined with interviews. We give you below a couple of good examples of qualitative studies on cooperation that are partly based on interviews.

Robert Ellikson (1991), a law professor at Yale, has investigated how cattle farmers cooperate and settle conflict in Shasta County (California). Ellikson shows how rarely ranchers and farmers use the legal system to settle conflicts and rely instead on norms of common sense. For example, if the cattle of one farmer grasses on the land of another farmer, the former was expected to apologize, take measures that it would not happen again and pay for any serious damage. All well as interviews and digging through archival sources, Ellickson makes use of aerial photographs. He uses these photos, observational images, to obtain information on land use and fence building, to obtain a better understanding of the situations in which disputes have arisen.

In 2002 Stewart Clegg, Tyrone Pitsis, Thekla Rura-Polley and Marton Marosszeky published a study based on a case study about a large infrastructure construction project (a sewage system) that had to be finished before the summer Olympics in Sydney in 2000. Large construction projects are always a joint effort of different firms and institutions and many of them end in fiascos of tremendous over-budgeting or very late delivery. Despite immense time pressure and a tight budget, the project was completed successfully in time and within budget, because the firms and institutions involved created a culture putting the common interest above the individual interest. During the fieldwork the researchers observed meetings and artefacts that provided evidence on how this culture was generated.

A study of Robert Sutton and Andrew Hargadon (1996) explores the effectiveness of brainstorming in a group. Previous studies had showed that brainstorming in a group of 10 is less effective than asking 10 people to brainstorm in isolation and then take their outcomes together. They wanted to explore why group brainstorming is still popular in business practice although academic study built up evidence that group brainstorming generated fewer ideas of a lower quality. Their field study was conducted in a product design firm that used group brainstorming frequently. Sutton and Hargadon participated in several brainstorming sessions as observers and noticed the processes going on there. The goal of these observations was to find out what other effects next to the number of quality of ideas group brainstorming could have. Based on their observations, they suggest that conducting brainstorming in groups had other positive effects, such as enhancing cooperation between the employees as all developed an organizational memory.

What is common in all three examples is that the researchers present cases that went against common knowledge. In the examples of the farmers in Shasta county, one would have expected to see much more reliance on the legal system or bargaining and Ellickson explored why cattle farmers did not rely on the legal system. Clegg and his colleagues presented a cooperation that was managed very differently from other large-scale construction projects allowing them to explore new ways of management that overcome the many problems cooperations have. And finally Sutton and Hargadon showed why previous studies on the ineffectiveness of brainstorming in groups are short-sighted as they did not take into account other positive effects group brainstorming has.

What can be learned from these studies? When is using the observational method most promising?

# References

Clegg, Stewart R., Pitsis, Tyrone S., Rura-Polley, Thekla and Marosszeky, Marton (2002) 'Governmentality matters: designing an alliance culture of inter-organizational collaboration for managing projects', *Organization Studies* 23(3), pp. 317–337.

Ellickson, Robert (1991) *Order Without Law: How Neighbors Settle Disputes.* Cambridge, MA: Harvard University Press.

Sutton, Robert and Andrew Hargadon (1996) 'Brainstorming ideas in context. Effectiveness in a product design firm'. *Administrative Science Quarterly* 41, pp. 685–718.

# Summary

1 Observation is one of the few options available for studying records, mechanical processes, lower animals, small children and complex interactive processes. We can gather data as the event occurs and can come closer to capturing the whole event than with interrogation. On the other hand, we have to be present to 'capture' the event or have some recording device on the scene to do the job.

2 Observation includes a variety of monitoring situations that cover non-behavioural and behavioural activities.

3 The strengths of observation as a data-collection method include:
   - securing information about people or activities that cannot be derived from experiments or surveys
   - avoiding participant filtering and forgetting
   - securing environmental context information
   - optimizing the naturalness of the research setting
   - reducing obtrusiveness.

4 Observation may be limited by:
   - the expense of observer costs and equipment
   - the reliability of inferences from surface indicators
   - the problems of quantification and disproportionately large records
   - limitations presenting activities and inferences about cognitive processes.

5 We can classify observation in terms of the observer–participant relationship. This relationship may be viewed from three perspectives: (i) is the observation direct or indirect? (ii) is the observer's presence known or unknown? (iii) is the observer a participant or non-participant?

6 The design of an observational study follows the same general pattern as other research. Observational studies fall into four general types based on the degree of structure and the nature of the observational environment. The researcher must define the content of the study; develop a data-collection plan that identifies participants, sampling strategy and 'acts' (often operationalized as a checklist or coding scheme); secure and train observers; and launch the study.

   Unobtrusive measures offer an unusual and creative approach to reducing reactivity in observational research by indirect observation and other methods. Measures of erosion and accretion serve as ways to confirm the findings from other methods or operate as singular data sources.

7 Content analysis is a qualitative or quantitative approach to systematically analyse texts. The latter approach is based on counting the occurrence of words and phrases as well as detecting how far specific words stand apart in a text. The former approach puts more emphasis on detecting the general meaning of a text to categorize it.

8 Narrative analysis is based on stories. It is a qualitative explorative approach that allows a researcher to understand phenomena from the respondents perspective.

Action research is a research approach that, unlike more traditional research approaches, places an emphasis on the objective of inducing social change in the research process. Further, it relies heavily on continuous interaction between researchers, participants and practitioners.

## Discussion questions

### Terms in review

1 Compare the advantages and disadvantages of the survey to those of observation. Under which circumstances could you make a case for using observation?
2 What ethical risks are involved in observation? In the use of unobtrusive measures?
3 Based on your present or past work experience, suggest problems that could be resolved by using observation-based data.
4 Distinguish between the following:
   a the relative value of communication and observation
   b non-verbal, linguistic and extra-linguistic analysis
   c factual and inferential observation.
5 Distinguish between content and narrative analysis
6 Describe what action research is about.

### Making research decisions

7 The observer – participant relationship is an important consideration in the design of observational studies. What kind of relationship would you recommend in each of the following cases?
   a Observations of professional conduct in the classroom by the student author of a course-evaluation guide.
   b Observation of retail shoppers by a researcher who is interested in determining customer purchase time by type of goods purchased.
   c Observation of a focus group interview by a client.
   d Effectiveness of individual farmworker organizers in their efforts to organize employees of grape growers.
8 Assume you are a manufacturer of modular office systems and furniture, as well as office-organization elements (desktop and wall organizers, filing systems, etc.). Your company has been asked to propose an observational study to examine the use of office space by white-collar and managerial workers for a large insurance company. This study will be part of a project to improve office efficiency and paperwork flow. It is expected to involve the redesign of office space, and the purchase of new office furniture and organization elements.
   a What are the varieties of information that might be observed?
   b Select a limited number of content areas for study, and operationally define the observation acts that should be measured.

9  Develop a checklist to be used by observers in the previous study.
   a  Determine how many observers you need and assign two or three to a specific observation task.
   b  Compare the results of your group members' checklists for stability of recorded perceptions.
10 You wish to analyse the pedestrian traffic that passes a given store in a major shopping centre. You are interested in determining how many shoppers pass by this store, and you would like to classify these shoppers on various relevant dimensions. Any information you secure should be obtainable from observation alone.
   a  What other information might you find useful to observe?
   b  How would you decide what information to collect?
   c  Devise the operational definitions you would need.
   d  What would you say in your instructions to the observers you plan to use?
   e  How might you sample this shopper traffic?

## From concept to practice

11 Using Exhibit 9.3, identify the type of study described in each of the Snapshots featured in this chapter.
12 Obtain a current copy of a popular management magazine and a copy of the same management magazine 10 years ago. Use content analysis to establish which were the hot management phrases at both times.
13 Develop a sketch for an action research plan to investigate a management problem. Pay particular attention to the issue of how the desired change can be induced by the research project itself.

## Classroom discussion

14 Discuss in class how students' and teacher's behaviour would change if it were being recorded on video.
15 Discuss the difference in scientific contributions for the following pairs of observational and survey research.
   a  Observe the living patterns of long-term unemployed by spending a whole week with the person, compared to a large-scale mail survey among 1000 long-term unemployed people.
   b  Observe the surfing behaviour of Internet users through placing small tracking programs on their computers, compared to a large-scale phone survey among Internet users.
   c  Observe how a development team in a high-tech company works by meeting the team members several times, taking part in team discussions and even joining the team members for a beer after work, compared to personal interviews with 150 leaders of different development teams.

# Chapter 10

# Case studies and qualitative interviews

## Chapter contents

### LEARNING OBJECTIVES

When you have read this chapter, you should understand:

- ☑ why case studies are a very useful research approach and how they are conducted
- ☑ what distinguishes unstructured from structured interviews
- ☑ how to conduct unstructured interviews

## 10.1 Case studies

In the following sections, you will learn more about what case study research is about and how it differs from archive research, survey research and experiments. We have decided to discuss it here very extensively, as case study research is widely used and very effective in management research. Furthermore, it is a very popular approach among students preparing their final theses, as it combines business practice with science and also allows them to supplement their studies, (i.e. writing a thesis), with gaining practical experience (e.g. by following an internship).

Case study research is suitable for explanatory, descriptive and exploratory research, like the other approaches. The suggestion that case study research is especially, or even only, appropriate for exploratory research is a prejudiced view held by people who have little experience with case studies. Yin defines a case study as 'an empirical inquiry that investigates a contemporary phenomenon within its real-life context; when the boundaries between phenomenon and context are not clearly evident; and in which multiple **sources of evidence** are used'.[1] This definition shows clearly how case study research differs from other research approaches. Experiments usually deliberately divide the phenomenon from the context and often isolate the phenomenon from the natural context that is replaced by a laboratory setting, while case study research emphasizes the embeddedness of a phenomenon in its real-life context. Although survey researchers can account for the context, their ability to do so is limited as the number of variables they can investigate is limited. Historical studies also broadly acknowledge the context, but contrary to historic studies case studies focus on contemporary phenomena.

The role and function of case study research within scientific research are areas that are often disputed; the most common prejudices to be heard concerning case studies are that they do not contribute to building and testing theories, and that their results are often biased.

Case studies, however, offer a useful approach for use in theory development as they are especially appropriate for answering 'Why?' and 'How?' questions, although they are less useful in investigating 'What?' and 'How much?' questions. We can use the Snapshot on aggressive behaviour at the Nedcar manufacturing plant to illustrate this (see p. 376). Suppose you were interested in how often this aggressive conduct occurred, how many of the employees were directly and indirectly affected by it, and investigating the level of damage it has caused to the company. A survey among employees or an **analysis** of archival sources could be appropriate. For example, you could ask respondents whether they had been victims of physical violence, blackmail, and so on in the previous year, or whether they had heard about other colleagues who had been victimized. Further, you could check production log books and accounting information to count the number of sabotage incidents, how long it took until a machine was made operational again and what costs were involved in repairing it. The data collected would be helpful in answering the questions posed above. However, if you are interested in the reasons behind such a high level of aggressive behaviour, case study research would be more appropriate, provided that before beginning your study you had formulated a theoretical account of possible explanations for violent behaviour within firms.

In terms of theory, development case studies are akin to experiments. The results of both can be generalized to a theoretical disposition but not to a population. While a sample of 1000 respondents from the Swedish population allows you to make inferences on the whole Swedish population, a couple of case studies in Swedish households do not tell you how all Swedish people live, but do tell you a lot about the power of your theory. With case studies, theories are developed and tested in a sequential, step-by-step, manner. Starting with a previously developed theory the researcher compares the results of the case study with the theory, just as an experimenter designs experiments with the objective of testing one or a few specific theoretical predicted relations. Just as an experiment is not sufficient to support or reject a theory, one case study cannot test a theory – however, a series of experiments or case studies permits the assessment of a theory.

The choice of whether to use either case study research or survey research to investigate a specific problem depends very much on the personal preferences of the researchers, which are likely to be rooted in the traditions of the academic schools at which they were trained and in the approaches that they have used in previous studies. This is why similar problem statements

## Violence in companies

Nedcar, a car manufacturing company in Born (Netherlands), has quite a long history in car-making. In 1967, Dutch car manufacturer DAF relocated its factory from Eindhoven to Born, a city situated in the south of the Netherlands, at a point situated conveniently between Belgium and Germany, and at the intersection of major motorways, railways and waterways. In 1975, Swedish car company Volvo acquired DAF and, 16 years later, the factory in Born became the newly formed joint venture, Nedcar, owned in equal proportions by the Dutch state, Volvo and Mitsubishi. The Dutch state split its share equally between Volvo and Mitsubishi in 1999.

Shortly before that, stories about Nedcar had reached the public, revealing that within the company employees had been subject to the aggressive and even criminal conduct of a small group of colleagues, in the form of physical violence and blackmail. This aggressive behaviour was not only directed at fellow employees but also against Nedcar itself, and sabotage was a rather frequent occurrence. This was not the first time that the Nedcar factory had been connected with negative stories in the media. A few years prior to the incidents reported above, it had become public knowledge that family and friends of the president of Nedcar had obtained Volvo cars on very favourable terms, while at the same time people in the company's canteen were being sacked because some sausages had gone missing from storage.

How would you investigate the violence at Nedcar? What would interest you?

## References and further reading

www.nedcar.com

may be investigated using different approaches. Although many problems can be investigated using case studies or surveys, case study research is usually more appropriate if the number of variables that needs to be considered is quite large. With the survey approach, a large number of relevant variables also calls for a similarly large number of observations.

### Single versus multiple case studies

Within case study research it is possible to distinguish between single and multiple case studies (**single versus multiple** case studies). The former rely on one single case (as the name suggests), while the latter call for the investigation of several cases. Of course, investigating an issue in more than one context (i.e. case) is usually better than basing results on just one case. There are, however, occasions when a single case study is quite sufficient. If the intended case study research provides the closing critical study to a longer series of case studies, a single case is adequate. Such a critical case study requires of course, and as well as previous studies, a well-developed theory, and the case should be an acceptable real-life example of the circumstances in which the theoretical propositions need to be investigated.

Single case studies are also appropriate for investigating extreme or unique cases. Extreme cases (i.e. extreme combinations of circumstances) occur, according to the rules of probability, very rarely, hence there is often no more than one case available. An example is the tragic accident that befell the space shuttle *Challenger* in 2003, which was the first accident to have occurred in the landing phase of a space mission.

Moreover, a single case study may be justified for pragmatic reasons (which do not include the researcher's laziness!). For example, if a researcher is able to access information that is rarely accessible to researchers, a single case study is sufficient as it will offer as yet unknown insights. Suppose, for example, you had been allowed to carry the briefcase of Klaus Esser, former Chief Executive Officer (CEO) of Mannesmann, and observe all his actions while he resisted an unfriendly takeover bid from Vodafone until he finally accepted that company's offer on 4 February 2000. The opportunity to follow one of the key players in one of Europe's biggest takeover battles would be a unique case, for which pragmatic reasons advocate a single case study.

As mentioned above, multiple case studies are more appealing, though, as their results are considered more robust. Conducting multiple case studies requires considerable thought on which cases to select, however. Contrary to survey research the selection of cases – or, if you will, observational units – is not based on sampling logic but on **replication logic**. It is important to note here that the results of case studies are not generalized to populations, but to theoretical propositions. The main idea behind replication logic is that based on one's theory one expects that the same phenomenon occurs in the same circumstances or that the phenomenon differs if the circumstances change.

Suppose you shadow some information technology (IT) consultants who are implementing new CRM (customer relationship management) in several pharmaceutical firms. In a series of case studies you wish to investigate how employees in different jobs respond to the new system, why resistance occurs and how employees utilize the new system. In each of the pharmaceutical firms, the consultants use, on the whole, the same step-by-step implementation approach (i.e. each implementation case is a literal replication of the previous cases). If your study of these implementation projects reveals that the processes and outcomes are about the same in each case, the generalization of the case results to the theoretical propositions becomes more robust – that is, you are more convinced that your theoretical idea provides a helpful explanation of real-world phenomena.

A literal replication of case studies aims to select very similar case studies, and predicts that the processes and outcomes discovered in each study are also similar. Another kind of replication logic – theoretical – does not select similar cases but explicitly selects cases that differ from each other on theoretically important dimensions. Again, take the example of the implementation of CRM projects mentioned above, and suppose that you have the idea that organizational culture influences the course of the processes and the outcomes. Rather than selecting firms with a similar culture, you would select firms with different cultures.

## The richness of evidence sources

The main advantage of case studies compared to other approaches is that they permit the combination of different sources of evidence. It is possible to distinguish roughly three sources of evidence:

1 interviews
2 documents and archives
3 observation.

## Interviews

Interviews are the most widely used source for collecting information for evidence. Unlike interviews carried out with respondents to a survey, case study interviews are often unstructured, or even in the form of quite informal discussions with a key informant for the case. Informal discussions, or open-ended interviews with key informants, are a crucial part of many case studies, as the key informants provide valuable insights into the case's issues and can also point the case researcher towards other sources of evidence, such as relevant documents, archival surveys, or an existing internal survey or study.

The importance of discussions with key informants can also, however, give rise to the threat of the researcher becoming too dependent on them. Relying too much on just a few key informants can jeopardize the validity of a study if the informants present a biased picture of the case issue. For example, a case study on increased violence among employees at Nedcar (see Snapshot on p. 376), which is mainly based on accounts given by Nedcar's management or on interviews with the perpetrators, is likely to present a biased picture of the situation.

Semi-structured, or focused, interviews are another type of interview that is often used in case study research. In such cases, the researcher schedules interviews with people who possess relevant information on the case issues, and follows a particular structure (i.e. a set of open questions) in order to collect information. Semi-structured interviews have two main objectives: on the one hand, the researcher wants to know the informant's perspective on the issue but, on the other, they also want to know whether the informant can confirm insights and information the researcher already holds. This latter aspect, in particular, calls for a knowledgeable and socially competent interviewer. It is easy to ask people for their view on certain events and issues – confronting them with other views and asking them to reflect on their own view is more difficult. It requires a socially competent interviewer, who is able to dig deeper into the mind of the interviewee without starting an argument and ruining the cooperative atmosphere of the interview.

Finally, an interview within a case study can take the form of a structured interview as it is used in survey research, where the respondent is asked to respond to a fixed set of (mostly) closed questions. For the Nedcar Snapshot, a case study on the occurrence of violence within a firm could be supplemented with a survey among employees on their satisfaction with their jobs and colleagues. Sometimes case study researchers get lucky and can gain access to secondary survey data.

## Documents and archives

Documents including archival sources form a rich source of evidence, which is rarely exploited in other research approaches and plays a crucial role in case study research. Documents can take many forms, including letters, internal memos and reports, newspaper articles, agendas, and so on. Documents and interviews supplement each other. On the one hand, documents – such as reports and newspaper articles – are very useful in preparing the outline of any interview and in discovering and identifying issues relevant to the case. On the other hand, interviewees can lead the researcher to documents that will corroborate information obtained in an interview. Getting hold of documents for a case study requires a systematic search approach, and the researcher should use interviews to locate them and ask for permission to access them.

Although documents are an essential source of evidence, you should also be aware of their shortcomings. As most documents are in written form, they appear to be objective and truthful; however, most documents are written with a specific purpose in mind, and addressed to a specific audience. For example, the views expressed in an internal memo from the head of the procurement department on the performance of a specific supplier could differ markedly from an assessment of the same supplier by the production department.

Archival records, which are often available in digital form rather than in print, are another important source. Examples of archival sources are survey data (e.g. surveys on customer satisfaction), internal records (e.g. production statistics, personnel files, databases of customer complaints), charts and maps (e.g. charts relating to the organization) and personal records (e.g. diaries, notes on phone conversations). With respect to such archival records, you should also consider the purpose of their creation and explore their usefulness for your case study. However, if you can obtain access to relevant archives containing reliable information, you will have an extremely valuable source.

## *Observation*

Observation is a research approach in itself (see Chapter 9). As with information obtained from documents, information from observations augments other sources and is especially useful in providing tacit information.

Suppose you are interested in the culture of an organization. Documents and interviews give the impression of a dynamic and innovative company. Just examining the architecture and furniture of the office will tell you whether this image is reflected in the appearance of the company. You look around and observe that the last redecoration of the offices took place about 20 years ago, the office furniture reminds you of sorts of chairs and desks you would see in a 1960s movie, and when you ask an interviewee for his or her e-mail address the answer given is that it would be better to send a fax as the whole department has only one computer that is connected to the Internet. This discrepancy (or 'lack of fit') between your own observations and what you have read in documents and heard in interviews is very valuable to your analysis of the firm's culture.

Two general types of observation can be distinguished: direct observation and participant observation. The latter describes the situation in which you as a researcher are a member of the organization under investigation. Examples of participant observations are:

- a student writes a thesis on how to integrate a recently acquired company, while simultaneously holding an internship in the project team overseeing the process of integrating a German insurance company into a Dutch bank
- a student writes a thesis on student associations and is also the president of one.

The major advantage of participant observation is that it often offers access to information that is not available to other researchers. This deep involvement in the organization, however, also carries with it a risk: the researcher may lose their neutral, objective view.

For both types of observation, either a systematic or a more casual approach may be used. 'More casual' means that your collection of observational information is a by-product of being involved in the organization, or a by-product of your visits to the organization to hold interviews and sift through documents and archives. How to collect observational information systematically is explained in Chapter 9.

# How to conduct good case study research

One often hears the suspicion voiced that case studies produce biased evidence. Without doubt there are many case studies that follow highly questionable procedures in collecting information, apply dubious methods in analysing the information and finish with questionable conclusions. Unfortunately, however, this is also true of studies based on experiments, surveys or any other approach. It is not the approach that determines the quality of a study, but how the study is conducted. The quality of a case study depends very much on the skilful exploitation of its advantages and the rigorousness of its conducting.

Chapter 1 looked at the criteria for good research; Exhibit 10.1 applies these criteria to case study research. We now look at each of the points addressed in Exhibit 10.1 in more detail.

## *Purpose clearly defined*

A clear definition of purpose requires an explicit formulation of the study's objectives and the problem under investigation. Try to be as specific as possible in defining the purpose. In the case study on CRM systems mentioned above, the purpose should be more than just an attempt to investigate the implementation of a CRM system. The researcher should also define what aspects of this implementation process he or she wants to investigate. Are they interested in responses including the resistance of employees affected by the new system? Are they interested in how the employees utilize the new system? Are they interested in the interactions between the IT consultants and the firm's management in the implementation process?

It is also of utmost importance that you as a researcher clearly disclose any theoretical expectation you have, because any pre-considerations you have about the piece of research will largely determine the design of your study (i.e. to whom you will talk, which questions you will ask, which documents you will look at). It doesn't matter if the theoretical expectation you had at the start of the research does not match the study's outcome. In fact, good case studies often start with a well-reasoned theoretical proposition, which is sequentially broken down in the course of the study by presenting findings that point to other explanations.

## *Research process detailed*

A detailed description of the research process increases the accountability of the research, as readers are thus better able to assess it. As survey studies should inform the reader of the population used, the sampling method and the communication approach used with respondents, a case study researcher also has to describe in detail how he or she obtained the information presented. This means that you should provide information on your interview partners: who are they, what role they have in the issue investigated, how you approached them, how often and how long you talked with them, and so on. Similarly, you should describe in detail the documents and archives you have consulted, by showing what kind of information they contained, how you accessed them, why they were written and kept, and so on.

## *Research design thoroughly planned*

Case study research involves careful planning of its design. For example, if you visit a firm rather wet behind the ears, and don't know exactly what you want to investigate, your own opinion on the relevant issues or the kind of information that you are looking for, the chances of you obtaining valuable information for your study will be close to zero. You are the

| Criteria for good research | How may these be achieved in case studies? |
|---|---|
| Purpose clearly defined | • Be explicit in the formulation of the research objectives and research problem. In particular, formulate unambiguously the theoretical propositions you want to generalize to |
| Research process detailed | • Provide all information pertaining to the research process, including information on who you interviewed, what documents you obtained, what archives you looked through, which secondary data you used |
| Research design thoroughly planned | • Explain clearly the thinking behind your selection of the case(s)<br>• Plan carefully how you are going to obtain information from different sources of evidence. Who do you want to interview? How long will those interviews take? In what kind of documents and archives are you interested? Who can you ask for help in finding and accessing them?<br>• Design a case study information base that clearly distinguishes the information obtained from the case study report |
| High ethical standards applied | • Protect the rights of other actors involved in the study, such as sponsors and respondents or interviewees<br>• Ensure that your research fulfils the quality standards of good research by (i) giving an accurate account of the observation you have obtained, (ii) mentioning any information that does not fit with your theoretical proposition(s), and (iii) basing your conclusions and recommendations on the findings of the case study, and resisting the desire to exceed the scope of your study |
| Limitations frankly revealed | • Discuss to what extent the picture your case study reveals can be considered a complete one<br>• Mention when you deviated from the planned procedures in order to collect information |
| Adequate analysis of decision-maker's needs | • Explain, in detail, how you assessed the information obtained through observations<br>• Explain, in detail, how you combined and weighted evidence from different sources<br>• Do not get bogged down in details – keep the line of your argument(s) in mind at all times |
| Findings presented unambiguously | • Use a clear structure that allows you to include all relevant details, and that prevents the reader from getting lost<br>• Use tables and graphs to support the presentation of your findings |
| Conclusion justified | • Ensure that the conclusions you make are always supported by your findings and do not go beyond what you have researched. |

*Exhibit 10.1* Producing good-quality case study research.

researcher, and you have to find and impart the relevant information. This task cannot be done even by people within the firm. So, before you approach a firm or person for an interview, define clearly what you want to get out of the interview.

Do not forget that case studies thrive on the multiple sources of evidence used, and that you have to find out what sources exist and how you can arrange access to them. The rationale behind using multiple sources of evidence is that you develop converging lines of inquiry, and can apply a process of **triangulation** (i.e. the different sorts of evidence provide different measurements of the same phenomenon and increase the construct validity). The principle of triangulation increases the power of your evidence only if the sources are independent from each other.

The independence of two separate sources of evidence becomes doubtful if both can be traced back to the same origin. For example, if you obtain certain information about employee resistance during an interview with a member of the workers' union and this information is also supported by information found in a report, these two sources of evidence are not independent if the report was compiled by the same member of the union that you interviewed.

Sound case study research should delineate clearly a line between the information obtained and the report. In survey research the information obtained in the course of the survey is stored in data files, which do not usually form part of the study report. Likewise, as a case study researcher you should build up a database in which is stored all the information you obtained electronically, written or in any other form. Be aware that any notes you make during interviews or after visiting an organization are not part of the report, but part of your database.

### High ethical standards applied

As with any other research a researcher has to meet certain ethical standards when conducting a case study. In Chapter 4, we discussed which ethical standards a researcher needs to comply with. Briefly, these ethical standards can be summarized in terms of two main guidelines. First, the researcher needs to ensure that the rights of other people involved are not infringed by his or her action, or the research itself. Privacy issues can be critical in case study research, as case studies usually reveal a great deal of information. If you promised confidentially to the sponsor, you will need to ensure that well-informed third parties, such as competitors, cannot identify the sponsor, especially if your report is made publicly available. For the same reason, the right to confidentiality of informants can be at stake in case studies. In the Snapshot example of investigating violence on the shop floor at Nedcar, you would have to promise confidentiality to your informants (e.g. to a foreman who confesses to having blackmailed subordinates) and not provide sufficient information on them to enable people within the company to identify them.

Second, researchers need to be honest in their assessment and interpretation of the information obtained. A researcher should always raise the question of whether every other researcher would come to the same conclusions and interpretations of the information arrived at. If the answer to this question is yes, you will know that your assessment and interpretation of the information is a reasonable and justifiable account of the issue under investigation.

### Limitations frankly revealed

Any study, case study or not, should frankly reveal its limitations. This revelation refers first of all to whether procedures desired from a methodological viewpoint could really be followed during the research. Were the researchers able to fully obtain all information they required (i.e. did they have access to all written documents, could they interview all persons they were interested in)? For example, assume you study the effects of a firm's reorganization. Certainly, interviewing people who had been laid off in that reorganization would be important. However, it might be difficult to trace such people, as they may have moved to another city or may be less than willing to share their experiences and opinions with researchers. Furthermore, you should report and discuss any doubts you have concerning the reliability and quality of your information – for example, if you suspect that certain information has been strategically distorted or an important piece of information is unavailable for any reason.

Limitations also refer to the general applicability of the study. Although case studies do not attempt to give a representative picture of an issue, they still attempt to reveal certain effects or mechanisms that are likely to occur in other similar settings. For this reason a case researcher needs to make sure that findings in a case study are not based just on the idiosyncrasies of a specific case.

Please note that revealing and discussing limitations is not the same thing as undermining the results of a study; rather, it should serve to reinforce the reader's confidence in the study.

## Adequate analysis of decision-maker's needs

Survey researchers can use quantitative analysis methods – a rich, standardized and advanced toolkit – to analyse their information. Case study researchers are still bereft of such finely honed equipment; however, their toolkit is far from empty. They have tools that will enable them to analyse adequately any information obtained – via, for example, pattern matching and time-series analysis.

The general rationale behind pattern matching is to form a general picture of the case by detecting patterns in the information. There are several approaches to this. One is to split the theoretical dependent variables into different non-equivalent variables. In our example of the implementation of a CRM system mentioned above, we might expect a certain pattern between organizational structure and resistance, and could, for example, arrive at the following propositions.

1 Employees affected by the new CRM system will approach the workers union representative and rely on him to discuss the implications of the new system for the shop floor rather than discussing the new system directly with management.

2 Departments affected by the new CRM system will experience an increase in sickness leave days and resignations, and a reduced willingness to work extra hours.

3 The atmosphere in meetings becomes more controversial and formal, and informal communication becomes less open.

Each of these three propositions refers to an aspect of resistance in the company. If the information provided by the case study supports each of these propositions, the researcher can argue more convincingly that resistance in the investigated case is high.

The second approach is closely related to the theoretical replication of a case study, by looking for patterns with rival explanations. Thus, in the CRM implementation example, the researchers formulate rival explanations for the occurrence of resistance by defining for each explanation an exclusive set of independent variables. Then they check either within a single case study or across multiple case studies whether the case points to one of the rival explanations, as the case, in reality, matches with this explanation's set of independent variables.

Time-series analysis is often conducted in experiments and quasi-experiments (see also Chapter 11). Time-series analysis can be very simple – for example, following the trend of a certain variable over time. This trend is then compared to a theoretical explanation and a rival explanation, and any other trends, based on certain artefacts. More complex time-series analysis involves looking at the trend over time of multiple variables, and investigating whether changes in one variable are followed by changes in others. More complex time-series analyses are suitable bases for theoretical propositions on causes and effects between variables.

Suppose you wish to study on-the-job training in a plaster factory and, among others, you have the proposition that it takes between one and three months for on-the-job training to result in productivity gains. If you built up a time-series analysis of on-the-job training and productivity changes, the line representing the training must precede changes in the productivity line, and the lag between the two should be between one and three months. So, for example, if your interviews and documents reveal that the firm had on-the-job training programmes in place in the Wolshire plant in February 2002 and in the Moerdijk plant in September 2002, you should observe an increase in productivity in the Wolshire plant around April 2002 and in the Moerdijk plant around November 2002.

### Findings presented unambiguously

In a good case study the findings are presented unambiguously. As mentioned already in the section on ethical standards above, this includes disclosing all insights that you have arrived at, including those that contradict your proposition. Furthermore, it is important that the reader of the study can easily identify the main points you wish to make. This requires that you attempt to state your outcomes unconditionally, and if the outcome is conditional this is made explicit. In case study research in particular the researcher often presents so much information that the reader can get easily lost in it. For this reason, you need to distinguish clearly between your main findings and any additional findings and information. Graphs, tables and figures are useful devices in helping to summarize findings and facilitate a quick understanding of them. You could, for example, provide a table in which the columns represent different sources of evidence and each row a different theoretical proposition. In the cells of the table you can then indicate the information obtained through a source and whether it supports or rejects your proposition.

### Conclusion justified

You need to be careful that your conclusion is justified and does not expand the scope of your study. In particular you should not generalize the case study conclusion to much broader theoretical propositions. So, if your case study supports the proposition that less hierarchical organizations experience lower resistance during the implementation of a new CRM system, you must reveal that your study is on the relationship between organizational structure and resistance to new IT systems, but not on the relationship between organizational structure and resistance to change in general.

As mentioned above, case studies permit generalization to theoretical propositions but not to populations. Therefore, it is important that you resist the temptation to generalize results from your case study to others. For example, the public image of railway companies has suffered in many European countries, as tragic accidents have occurred, trains have kept time poorly, and so on. Suppose a researcher investigated this issue with a case study at DB, the main German rail company. In the final chapter of the study, the findings for DB are applied to NS, the main Dutch rail company, which is facing similar problems. The report suggests that NS could solve many of its current problems if it followed the suggestions made for DB. Such a final chapter would be unreasonable. Instead, the researcher should have made it clear that the study is limited to DB and that any suggestions arising from the study cannot be applied to other rail companies without a consideration of the specific situations they face.

Case study research offers a very valuable approach to investigating scientific and business problems, and the results of case studies will provide essential insights into how and why certain processes work as they do, and what is required to get things moving in the intended direction. However, case studies will only provide useful insights if they are conducted well. The poor quality of case studies is a major facet in the many prejudices surrounding this method.

Business students often prefer to take the case study approach in their own research projects (e.g. in a Master's thesis), as they believe that conducting case study research is easier than setting up an experiment or designing a survey. The opposite is in fact true. Good case studies call for immense effort. Just interviewing three or four people in a company does not make a case study. It is necessary to collect information from a range of other sources, such as documents and archives, or by observation, as noted above. Analysis of the information that has been collected is also more difficult than may be supposed. Although the outcome of a quantitative survey can be summarized and correlated fairly easily with widely available statistics software packages, such as SPSS or STATA, for case studies such standard techniques – which can summarize, categorize and present information – do not exist. Furthermore, there are no generally accepted rules that determine whether a detected pattern is really a 'deliberate' one (i.e. as opposed to merely random). Neither do case study researchers have the benefit of levels of significance. With each study they do, they have to convince others that the observations they have made do or do not fit with theoretical explanations. Case study research might appear easy to do and the soft option, but the reality is that, because its structure is so flexible and its points of reference vague, conducting a good piece of case study research is in fact the hard road to take, especially for the inexperienced researcher.

## 10.2 Qualitative interviews

In Chapter 7 we discussed the different communication approaches used in survey research. Common to all these communication approaches is that the interview, either face to face or by phone, is highly structured. All respondents are asked the same questions with exactly the same wording and often the respondent's answer possibilities are predetermined by the researcher. In qualitative research, the interview can be structured, semi-structured or unstructured. In a **structured interview**, the researcher uses a very detailed interview guide line similar to a questionnaire in quantitative studies. **Semi-structured interviews** usually start with rather specific questions but allow the interviewee to follow his or her own thoughts later on. Probing techniques are widely used to evoke additional information from the respondents. A well-known example for a semi-structured interview is the TV interview of a journalist with a political decision-maker in a newscast. **Unstructured interviews** mostly start with a respondent's narrative and may not have any specific question or topic list to be covered. In most qualitative studies, researchers hold semi-structured or unstructured interviews.

Exhibit 10.2 lists the main differences between structured and semi-structured or unstructured interviews. Structured interviews are useful if the goal of your study is to describe or explain, but they do not allow you to explore a topic, as the questions and answer possibilities for the respondents are predefined by the researcher. Exploring a topic needs at least a semi unstructured approach that gives the respondent the possibility to turn the interview in different directions and to come up with new sub-topics that the researcher often has not thought about beforehand. The differences between structured and unstructured interviews are partly connected with the aforementioned methodological polarizations concerning the underlying research philosophy (positivism versus interpretivism), the data-collection strategy (quantitative versus qualitative) and the sampling strategy (sample versus case study).[2]

Semi-structured or unstructured interviews are particularly useful if the research problem refers to a wide-ranging problem area and you as a researcher need to detect and identify the issues relevant to understanding the situation. The central idea of unstructured interviews is that you as a researcher want to gain insight into what the respondents consider relevant and how they interpret the situation. Possible explanations or causes of the situation are not predefined and hence the course of the interview itself is left open. In fully unstructured interviews, the interviewer usually has a mental list of relevant topics or themes to be addressed and this will be especially useful if the interview peters out. In semi-structured interviews, researchers use an interview guide containing a list of rather more specific questions to ensure that the interviewer covers the necessary areas and asks the questions in a similar, if not identical, way in all interviews. An interview guide is especially useful if interviews are conducted by different interviewers, the interviews are conducted in different settings (e.g. at two different companies), and the researchers already have an idea about which aspects are important to an understand-

|  | Structured | Semi-structured or Unstructured |
|---|---|---|
| Type of study | Explanatory or descriptive | Exploratory and explanatory (semi-structured) |
| Purpose | Providing valid and reliable measurements of theoretical concepts | Learning the respondent's viewpoint regarding situations relevant to the broader research problem |
| Instrument | Questionnaire (i.e. specified set of predefined questions) | Memory list Interview guide |
| Format | Fixed to the initial questionnaire | Flexible depending on the course of the conversation, follow-up and new questions raised |

*Exhibit 10.2* Structured and unstructured interviews.

ing of the situation under investigation. In both cases, the researcher is, however, free to ask additional questions and to change the order of the questions.

Suppose you want to investigate the working climate in a call centre. In a structured interview, you would, for example, ask respondents to rate their level of agreement with statements such as, 'I enjoy coming to work' on Likert scales; you would ask how many calls a respondent handles per hour, and so on. An unstructured interview would start with a question such as, 'Tell me something about your job; please describe to me what a typical day is like and whatever else is important.' Depending on the answers, you would ask follow-up questions such as, 'You just mentioned that at certain times of the day the call centre is very busy and callers have to wait for a long time and get annoyed. How do you deal with such stressful moments?'

A major criticism of structured interviews is that they stifle communication as the interviewer has little opportunity to resolve any communication problems.[3] For example, even the rather simple survey question, 'Have you worked in the last month?' can lead to responses such as 'What do you mean by work?' among participants who do not have a paid job, but might have worked as a volunteer or followed a programme to reintegrate the long-term unemployed. Unclear terms pose a more serious threat in structured interviews, as some respondents will not report that terms are unclear and as interviewers often clarify terms in a way that differs from the researcher's intention. In unstructured interviews the problem of unclear questions is alleviated because how a question is interpreted is part of the answer.

The response opportunities of unstructured interviews are often appreciated by respondents very much, because they allow them to frame a story the way they want it and they are not pressed in the corset of a structured questionnaire. Moreover, unstructured interviews are often more rewarding for the respondent than a structured interview, as it often takes elements of a discussion between the respondent and interviewer/researcher, that is the interview itself can become interesting for the respondent, because he or she learns through comments and points made by the interviewer.

## Questions in semi-structured and unstructured interviews

Writing an interview guide is an important part of semi-structured and unstructured interviewing as the intended interview moves from a fully unstructured interview to a semi-structured interview. An objective of unstructured interviews is to learn the respondents' viewpoints regarding phenomena relevant to the broader research problem. The main functions of an interview guide are that:

- it serves as a memory list to the interviewer to ensure that the same issues are addressed in every interview and not forgotten in some interviews
- it increases the comparability of multiple unstructured interviews by ensuring that the questions are asked similarly.

Designing an interview guide, however, involves a trade-off. The more specific the interview guide gets, that is the less structured the interview becomes, the less flexible the interviewer is in responding to the suggestions of the respondents. Thus, more structured guides improve the comparability of the answers, but reduce the explorative character of the interview.

A good starting point for an interview guide is to ask yourself the question, 'What do I want to know or why does the phenomenon interest me?' The basic principles of writing an interview guide are not very different from the principles of good questionnaire design (see Chapter 13) and you should ensure that:

- your guide contains questions that deal with all topics that could be important and order them so that they flow well, but be prepared to deviate from this path of questioning in the interview
- you formulate your questions in a language that is easily understood by the interviewees
- the questions you ask are not too specific and that the interviewee has ample opportunity to reflect on the issue at hand
- you reduce your influence as an interviewer as much as possible by avoiding leading or suggestive questions
- you also record some general and some specific demographics or facts about the respondent (such as age, gender, department they are working in, years with the company, etc.).

## Question types

In unstructured interviews several different question types (as outlined below) can be distinguished, each serving a different purpose, and it should be emphasized that a researcher's primary task in interviewing is *listening*.[4]

- *Introductory questions* – usually rather general questions that get the interview started, such as, 'Please, tell me something about the department you are working in.'
- *Follow-up questions* are used to ask the respondent to elaborate further on a given question or to clarify whether you have understood them correctly. Examples are: 'That is interesting. Please, could you say a little bit more on this?' Can you illustrate this with an example?' and 'What exactly do you mean by …?'
- *Probing questions* are similar to follow-up questions, but refer more specifically to a part of the answer. For example, if the respondent has just mentioned that the firm entered the Hungarian market recently: 'How was the decision to enter the Hungarian market made?' 'Why did you choose to enter the Hungarian market?'
- *Specifying questions* ask the interviewee to elaborate on the answer and to offer more information. Examples include: 'What happened after the decision was taken?' 'How did the trade unions react to this announcement?'
- *Direct questions* provide information on how interviewees assess a situation from their viewpoint and often ask them to describe an opinion or feeling. For example: 'What was your point of view regarding entering the Hungarian market?' 'Do you consider yourself an influential person in the organization?'
- *Indirect questions* are not directed at the interviewee personally, but ask for a general assessment sometimes followed up by a similar direct question. For example: 'What do people around here think about the entry into the Hungarian market?'
- *Structuring questions* are used when you have the feeling that the topic talked about has been covered sufficiently. One way of avoiding moving on too early is to ask: 'If we have not missed any important aspects of this subject, I would like to move on to [next topic].'

- *Silence* (i.e. pausing) is an important way of letting the interviewee know that you would like to hear more.

- *Interpreting questions* are asked in order to confirm that you have interpreted the information provided correctly. For example: 'Do you mean that without your efforts the decision to enter the Hungarian market would have been made much later or not at all?'

Unstructured interviews provide such an immense amount of information that it is hard to make a note of it all during the interview. This is why unstructured interviews are usually tape-recorded. The main advantages of tape-recording the interview are that as an interviewer you can focus on the course of the conversation rather than on taking notes. In addition, you (and others who did not take part in the actual interview) can listen to it again and make an accurate transcript of the interview. Moreover, direct quotes from interviewees, which often provide the 'spice' in a qualitative report, may more easily be collected. The disadvantage with tape-recording interviews is that many people feel uncomfortable when their responses are recorded and, consequently, this may influence their answering behaviour. For example, their answers might be less controversial. Technical problems with equipment and the need to change tapes after a certain time can also disturb the course of the interview. Finally, transcribing the information held on tape is very time-consuming, especially if the interviews are fairly long. The process of transcribing can, however, be shortened by only transcribing the relevant parts of interviews and leaving out answers that cannot be related to the research problem.

### Projective techniques

In qualitative studies, researchers often look for hidden or suppressed meanings that sometimes even the interviewee is not aware of. Detecting those meanings is simply possible with questions typical for survey questionnaires, but projective techniques provide a helpful tool.

## Individual and group interviews

Unstructured interviews can be held with an individual or with a group of people. The first is often referred to as an in-depth or depth interview, while the latter is also referred to as a focus group interview. Individual In-Depth Interview take the form of an unstructured one to one discussion with a well-chosen respondent, who has a deep insight in the relevant topic. In group interviews, a panel of experts is asked to discuss some open questions and topics.

Individual as well as group interviews are equally capable of exploring a new topic in order to develop new hypotheses, to clarify and operationalize a new concept or to identify important characteristics and drivers of a phenomenon. And both are not appropriate to gather information for testing hypotheses. But how do they differ? Individual depth interviews work much better if one needs to discuss sensitive issues that a respondent would be afraid of talking openly about in a group. The only exception to this rule is if you ensure that all the participants of a focus group have a similar experience background. For example, talking about sexual harassment is certainly a sensitive topic in any organizations. It is unthinkable to organize focus groups on such a topic along the lines of departments or hierarchical levels, as it becomes very likely that the victim and the perpetrator would be in the same group, but it is thinkable to talk about sexual harassment in a group that only consists of victims or perpetrators.

Another advantage of individual interviews is that the respondent is not influenced by other respondents. In focus groups people might hold back their own ideas if someone else just stated a contrary idea probably reinforced by a 'hmm, interesting' of the researcher or group moderator. Thus, focus interviews can be biased towards what the majority of the focus group thinks or feels because the members influence each other. Still, it must be noted that interactions between members are also an advantage of focus groups as each group member can build upon the contributions made by others. As in a group brainstorming session, the group members can also inspire each other and develop novel ideas through a lively discussion.

Finally, group interviews are considered more economical, as you talk within one interview to more people. However, one should be cautious about this economic benefit, because if you talked for three hours with 10 people or with just one person, this does not automatically mean that you obtained tenfold more information from the group interview, as even in a group interview only one person can talk at a time.

## Interviewer qualifications

The demands on the interviewer are much higher in an unstructured than in a structured interview. In structured interview, the interviewers' main task is to convince the respondent to participate, to read clearly the questions and answer possibilities and to keep the respondent motivated and perfectly willing to continue. Of course, it is better if the interviewer has some background knowledge on the study and the topic, but he or she does not need to be an expert. The situation in the unstructured interview is completely different. Here the interviewer should be an expert in the field and therefore unstructured interviews are mostly done by the researchers involved in the study, while structured interviews are often outsourced to research agencies.

The interviewer for an unstructured interview needs to be well informed if not an expert for the following reasons:

1 One of interviewer's tasks is to direct the interview, which is crucial if a respondent deviates from the interview's topic. Then you have to decide to let the respondent continue, because the new route chosen might bring up some interesting novel ideas or to stop the respondent and redirect the interview. You cannot make such a decision if you have no knowledge on the topic.

2 In unstructured interviews, it is often necessary to probe respondents, that is ask them to continue on a topic through asking the same or a similar question again. Thus, here you need to decide whether what you have heard so far is sufficient or whether it would be better to get more, and again you cannot make this decision without knowing the topic well.

3 In unstructured interviews, respondents often expect you to be an expert. People do not like to waste their time talking with people who do not know anything about the topic.

Additional interviewer characteristics that are beneficial in unstructured interviews are that interviewers should be good at active listening. Active listening is more than listening, because it requires making short comments and clarifying questions. Doing so signals to the respondent that you are interested in him or her and what is said. Moreover, the capability to establish trust and a good atmosphere is an important asset, because respondents will simply tell you more if they trust you.

## Research Methods in Practice 10

### Could we have done a case study?

As mentioned previously, the project's title has been 'the management of R&D alliances'. In the project, we have attempted to explain how firms search for cooperation partners, how much effort they put in the negotiation and contracting phase and what contracts they design. Thus, we have looked at the cooperation specific management (searching and contracting) of 94 cooperations that also have formed our unit of analysis. These 94 cooperations are nested in five large Dutch manufacturing companies. It is an idea to move the unit of analysis upward to the five firms and investigate the management of cooperations at the firm level and not at the cooperation level.

Of course, five firms would be too few to conduct any meaningful analysis, but five firms are an ideal setting for a multiple case study. At the time of the research, we did not explore this possibility, but we could have explored a case study research more. What would be a possible research strategy for conducting such a multiple case study? Whether you conduct a quantitative study or a case study affects many methodological aspects. I want to be clear about the fact that most times you cannot redesign a quantitative study to a case study or vice versa; often this will imply a complete different study The study on research and development (R&D) cooperations is, however, probably one of the few examples where we could do it with some additional efforts.

Suppose we explore the possibility of expanding the project on R&D cooperations to conduct a multiple case study in the five firms. Moving the research problem from the management of cooperations to the cooperation management of a firm already affects the research problem. Now we are no longer interested in how a firm can manage its cooperations, but are interested in how a firm should design its cooperation management. In the original project, we assumed that the answer to an optimal management of cooperations rests in searching for and finding a good partner and in negotiating and designing an optimal contract with the chosen partner. However, we did not explore firms' capabilities to do the searching and contracting well.

During our research, we heard several times that searching for and contracting with a particular partner was not slowed down by discussions with the prospective partner, but by internal discussions within the firm. A typical example is a R&D cooperation with a supplier. In high-tech, it is often not possible to purchase a standard component from a supplier; rather a firm looks for a supplier that can make a component according to its specifications. In such a cooperation the purchasing and the R&D department are involved and both have different objectives and cultures. The purchasing department is used to negotiate a low price, while the R&D department is interested in an innovative supplier. The same split within a firm can be observed at the buyer's side. The buyer's sales department is interested in a high profit margin and its R&D department appreciates the challenge to produce a new component that enhances the buyer's technological capabilities. Thus, managing cooperations is not so much a matter of finding equilibrium between the involved firms, but between finding it between the involved departments. In informal discussions with respondents, several R&D managers mentioned that they cooperated well with the supplier's engineers but were often called back by the purchasing department on the buyer side or sales department on the supplier side.

In the study on R&D cooperations, we did not explore these observations. We still assumed that a firm is one actor and does not consist of different actors. A crucial assumption, which is often made in business research, but which might turn out to be invalid, as within firms managers obstruct each other, departments follow different goals and business units compete with each other. How internal disarrays affect the management of cooperations would be a research problem that could have been investigated

▶

in a case study like research. One could have explored how these internal disarrays affect the specific cooperation management or whether and how it leads to some general management principles regarding cooperation.

Suppose we had set up such a case study with the five companies. What would have changed from the research design? Let us look at the following issues: sampling strategy, survey, archival sources, observations and interviews.

Sampling strategy: Although we moved our unit of analysis from the cooperation to the firm, it is still advisable to look at specific cooperations, because we know that a firm does not manage all its cooperations the same way. Thus, we are still interested in talking about specific cooperations, but we will select them differently. In the previous project we stratified the sample along the dimensions' cooperation size and previous relationship with the partner. Now we are interested in the internal communication and this suggests that we look for cooperations in which only one department has been involved and cooperations with different combinations of more than one department. Moreover, it might not be necessary to check 94 cooperations within the five firms and eight to ten cooperations in each firm would be sufficient.

Survey: We could still think about holding a small survey, but it should take much less time and we could certainly sacrifice a substantial number of questions. The consequence of sacrificing questions is that the validity of our measurements decreases, but we compensate for this decrease by using multiple sources of evidence. Thus, our information of what happened is not only based on the survey but also on archival sources and qualitative interviews. In addition, we can also ask more than just one respondent regarding a specific cooperation. For example, we could give the survey to a person from the R&D department and from the purchasing department. Another possibility that is often called for would be to send a survey to the partner.

Archival sources: If possible we would try to obtain not only access to the contracts, but also to any other documentation available, such as letters and emails exchanged between the firm and its partner or notes and memos from meetings, and so on. These documents provide a second source of evidence and we can cross-check the information provided in the survey with the documents.

Observations: As mentioned in the previous chapter, observations are hardly used as a sole source in business research, but can provide interesting additional information. In our case study, we can, for example, look for any artefacts that indicate that one department has a higher standing within the organization than the other one. Possible artefacts include location in the building, differences in office furniture, frequency of contact with general management, differences in the distribution of salary ranks, and so on.

Qualitative interviews: A central part of the case study would be to extend the number of qualitative interviews. On one hand, we would still collect specific information on a predefined set of cooperations, but we would add qualitative interviews with the topics of the general cooperation management and cooperation and competition between the departments. Next to the managers, responsible for specific cooperations, we would seek to have in-depth interviews with general management, the department heads and people from the legal department. To assess the atmosphere and culture towards external partners and other departments, we could also hold focus group discussions within the involved departments.

You should note that in the original explanatory project some of these elements have already been conducted.

## Summary

Case study research is an important, and in business science also widely used, research approach. Unlike survey research it does not follow the sampling logic but the replication logic, and case study results are therefore not generalizable to a population but to a theoretical proposition. The main advantages of the case study approach compared to other approaches is that it relies on multiple sources of evidence, such as interviews, observations and documents.

## Discussion questions

### Terms in review

1 What distinguishes the case study research approach from other research approaches?
2 Describe the sources of evidence that should be used in case study research, and how to collect and analyse the information.

### Making research decisions

3 The company relations office at your university offers an internship at IKEA. The intern will work for the project team assigned to prepare IKEA's expansion to China. You are lucky and get this job, and you are even luckier because one of your professors is willing to supervise your thesis on entry strategies for China.
  a How would you design case study research combining your internship at IKEA and your thesis on entry strategies?
  b To whom would you like to talk?
  c What documents would be valuable to you?
  d How could you ensure that you are not biased?

### Classroom discussion

4 Discuss in the classroom or in sub-groups what would be needed to write a good case study on the following topics. Discuss what information you need, which sources you could approach, and so on.
  a The emergence of standards and their consequences in the telecommunications industry.
  b The effects of developments in information and communication technologies on the music recording industry.
  c The basis of Ryanair's success as a low-cost airline.

## Online Learning Centre

### Get started with understanding statistical techniques!

When you have read this chapter, log on to the Online Learning Centre website at **www.mcgraw-hill.co.uk/textbooks/blumberg** to explore chapter-by-chapter test questions, additional case studies, a glossary and more online study tools for Business Research Methods.

## Notes

1  Robert K. Yin, *Case Study Research: Design and Methods.* Newbury Park: Sage, 1989, p. 23.

2  Ray Pawson, 'Theorizing the interview', *British Journal of Sociology* 47, 1996, pp. 295–314.

3  Paul Beatty, 'Understanding the standardized/non-standardized interviewing controversy', *Journal of Official Statistics* 11(2), 1995, pp. 147–60.

4  Steinar Kvale, *Interview: An Introduction to Qualitative Research Interviewing.* Thousand Oaks: Sage, 1996.

## Recommended further reading

**Eisenhardt, Kathleen M., 'Building theory from case study research',** *Academy of Management Review* **14(4), 1989, pp. 532–50.** This article describes the process of inducting theory, from case studies to writing conclusions, and discusses when case study is particularly useful.

**Gomm, Roger, Hammersley, Martyn and Foster, Peter (eds.),** *Case Study Method*: **Thousand Oaks, CA: Sage, 2000.** This edited volume offers a broad discussion of the case study method and its role in scientific research.

**Yin, Robert K.,** *Case Study Research. Design and Methods* **(3rd edn.). Newbury Park, CA: Sage, 2002.** An excellent guide and one of the standard references for case study research. Designing and conducting a case study along the lines suggested in this text almost guarantees a good case study.

# Chapter 11

# Experimentation

## Chapter contents

### LEARNING OBJECTIVES

When you have read this chapter, you should understand:

- ☑ the uses for experimentation

- ☑ the advantages and disadvantages of the experimental method

- ☑ the seven steps of a well-planned experiment

- ☑ internal and external validity with experimental research designs

- ☑ the three types of experimental design, and the variations of each.

## 11.1  What is experimentation?

Why do events occur under some conditions and not under others? Research methods that answer such questions are called **causal methods** (recall the discussion of causality in Chapter 4). *Ex-post facto* research designs – where a researcher interviews respondents or observes what is or what has been – also have the potential for discovering causality. The distinction between these methods and experimentation is that the researcher is required to accept the world as it is found, whereas an experiment allows the researcher to alter systematically the variables of interest and observe what changes follow.

In this chapter we define experimentation, and discuss its advantages and disadvantages. Next to the classical laboratory experiment, we also discuss field and quasi-experiments. An outline for the conduct of an experiment is presented as a vehicle to introduce important concepts. The questions of internal and external validity are also examined:

- Does the experimental treatment determine the observed difference or was some extraneous variable responsible?
- How can one generalize the results of the study across times, settings and persons?

The chapter concludes with a review of the most widely accepted designs and a 'Spotlight' example.

**Experiments** are studies involving intervention by the researcher beyond that required for measurement.[1] The usual intervention is to manipulate a variable in a setting and observe how it affects the subjects being studied (e.g. people or physical entities). The researcher manipulates the independent or explanatory variable and then observes whether the hypothesized dependent variable is affected by the intervention. (You may wish to revisit the discussion of causality in Chapter 4.)

An example of such an intervention is the study of bystanders and thieves.[2] In this experiment, students were asked to go to an office where they had an opportunity to see a fellow student steal some money from a receptionist's desk. A confederate of the experimenter, of course, did the stealing. The major **hypothesis** concerned whether people observing a theft would be more likely to report it (i) if they observed the crime alone or (ii) if they were in the company of someone else.

There is at least one **independent variable (IV)** and one **dependent variable (DV)** in a causal relationship. We hypothesize that in some way the IV 'causes' the DV to occur. The independent or explanatory variable in our example was the state of either being alone when observing the theft or being in the company of another person. The dependent variable was whether the subjects reported observing the crime. The results suggested that bystanders were more likely to report the theft if they observed it alone rather than in another person's company.

On what grounds did the researchers conclude that people who were alone were more likely to report crimes observed than people in the company of others? Three types of evidence form the basis for this conclusion. First, there must be an agreement between independent and dependent variables. The presence or absence of one is associated with the presence or absence of the other. Thus, more reports of the theft (DV) came from lone observers ($IV_1$) than from paired observers ($IV_2$).

Second, beyond the correlation of independent and dependent variables, the time order of the occurrence of the variables must be considered. The dependent variable should not precede the independent variable. They may occur almost simultaneously or the independent variable should occur before the dependent variable. This requirement is of little concern since it is unlikely that people could report a theft before observing it.

The third important support for the conclusion comes when researchers are confident that other extraneous variables did not influence the dependent variable. To ensure that these other variables are not the source of influence, researchers control their ability to confound the planned comparison. Under laboratory conditions, standardized conditions for control can be arranged. The crime observation experiment was carried out in a laboratory set up as an office. The entire event was staged without the observers' knowledge. The receptionist whose money was to be stolen was instructed to speak and act in a specific way. Only the receptionist, the observers and the 'criminal' were in the office. The same process was repeated with each trial of the experiment.

While such controls are important, further precautions are needed so that the results achieved reflect only the influence of the independent variable on the dependent variable.

## 11.2  An evaluation of experiments

### Advantages

When we elaborated on the concept of cause in Chapter 4, we said causality could not be proved with certainty but the probability of one variable being linked to another could be established convincingly. The experiment comes closer than any primary data-collection method to accomplishing this goal. The foremost advantage is the researcher's ability to manipulate the independent variable. Consequently, the probability that changes in the dependent variable are a function of that manipulation increases. Further, a **control group** serves as a comparison to assess the existence and potency of the manipulation and **pre-** and **post-test** measurements allow checking that the manipulation occurred before the outcome.

The second advantage of the experiment is that contamination from extraneous variables can be controlled more effectively than in other designs. This helps the researcher isolate experimental variables and evaluate their impact over time.

Third, the convenience and cost of experimentation are often superior to other methods. These benefits allow the experimenter opportunistic scheduling of data-collection, and the flexibility to adjust variables and conditions that evoke extremes not observed under routine circumstances. In addition, the experimenter can assemble combinations of variables for testing rather than having to search for their fortuitous appearance in the study environment.

Fourth, **replication** (repeating an experiment with different subject groups and conditions) leads to the discovery of an average effect of the independent variable across people, situations and times.

Finally, researchers can use naturally occurring events and, to some extent, **field experiments** to reduce subjects' perceptions of the researcher as a source of intervention or deviation in their everyday lives.

### Disadvantages

The artificiality of the laboratory is arguably the primary disadvantage of the experimental method. However, many subjects' perceptions of a contrived environment can be improved by investment in the facility.

Second, generalization from non-probability samples can pose problems despite **random assignment**: the extent to which a study can be generalized, say, from college students to managers or executives is open to question; and when an experiment is disguised unsuccessfully, volunteer subjects are often those with the most interest in the topic.

Third, the number of variables one can include in an experiment is much more limited than, for example, in survey research. Experiments are not appropriate to research problems that involve many influential factors.

Fourth, despite the low costs of experimentation, many applications of experimentation far outrun the budgets for other primary data-collection methods.

Fifth, experimentation is most effectively targeted at problems of the present or immediate future. Experimental studies of the past are not feasible, and studies about intentions or predictions are difficult. Furthermore, the factors included in the investigation should be easy to manipulate. This requirement is hard to meet if the factors considered are characteristics of the respondent, such as education, social competence and the like.

Finally, management research is often concerned with the study of people. There are limits to the types of manipulation and control that are ethical.

## 11.3 Conducting an experiment[3]

In a well-executed experiment, researchers must complete a series of activities to carry out their craft successfully. Although the experiment is the premier scientific methodology for establishing causation, the resourcefulness and creativeness of the researcher are needed to make the experiment live up to its potential. In this section, we discuss seven activities the researcher must accomplish in order to make the endeavour successful:

1 select relevant variables
2 specify the level(s) of the treatment
3 control the experimental environment
4 choose the experimental design
5 select and assign the subjects
6 pilot-test, revise and test
7 analyse the data.

We now look at each of these in turn.

### Selecting relevant variables

Throughout the book we have discussed the idea that a research problem can be conceptualized as a hierarchy of questions starting with a management problem. The researcher's task is to translate an amorphous problem into the question or hypothesis that best states the objectives of the research. Depending on the complexity of the problem, investigative questions and additional hypotheses can be created to address specific facets of the study or data that need to be gathered. Further, we have mentioned that a hypothesis is a relational statement because it describes a relationship between two or more variables. It must also be **operationalized**, a term we used earlier in discussing how concepts are transformed into variables to make them measurable and subject to testing.

Consider the following research question as we work through the seven points listed above:

> Do homogeneous teams, that is groups of people with the same nationality, perform better in a management game?

# Business experiments on the web?

We all know that the Internet is useful for data-collection. But what about using it to conduct experiments? Web samples are not usually representative of the populations we want to make inferences about. There are other concerns: web access, uninvited participants, multiple trials by the same individual, 'team' responses, distracting environments and the lack of a probability sample for statistical inference. All these issues currently stir debate. However, for some business studies, there are advantages to using a web experiment.

Eric DeRosia, a marketing Ph.D. student at the University of Michigan, has devised the 'e-Experiment'. According to DeRosia, 'The software's purpose is to facilitate primary research over the web in fields such as psychology and consumer behaviour.' He claims advantages and disadvantages over traditional laboratory experiments. In a pilot study of 125 marketing students who were randomly assigned to a supervised group lab and an outside lab on the web, responses to stimuli from attitude and brand honesty scales revealed strikingly similar reliability coefficients. In some ways, DeRosia notes, web experiments provide more control over stimulus timing, response code verification (out-of-range responses), and participants who peek ahead or change previous answers. By randomly assigning participants to experimental treatments and by controlling which questions are presented and their order, many objections to web experiments can be tackled. For the e-Experiment to work properly, it needs a small CGI program on a web server. Such programs pose security risks for universities and businesses, thus requiring a third-party vendor to host the research. Future programming will make this unnecessary.

In the meantime, other software is being released that continues the promise of the e-Experiment: rapid data-collection, graphical interface, open- and closed-question programming, randomization, estimation of participant loss rates, response time calculation, and authentication of participation (for rewards or incentives).

## References and further reading

DeRosia, Eric 'True experiments on the web', Working Paper 99.021, Ann Arbor, MI: University of Michigan Business School (http://www-personal.umich.edu/~ederosia/e-exp).
www-personal.umich.edu/~ederosia/e-exp/

Since a hypothesis is a tentative statement – a speculation – about the outcome of the study, it might take this form:

> Homogeneous teams, that is groups of people with the same nationality, perform better than mixed teams, groups of people with different nationalities, in a management game.

The researchers' challenges at this step are as follows.

1 Select variables that are the best operational representations of the original concepts.
2 Determine how many variables to test.
3 Select or design appropriate measures for them.

The researchers would need to select variables that best operationalize the concepts, 'homogeneous team', 'performance' and 'management game'. The product's classification and the nature of the intended audience should also be defined. In addition, the term 'better' could be operationalized statistically by means of a significance test.

The number of variables in an experiment is constrained by the project budget, the time allocated, the availability of appropriate controls and the number of subjects being tested. For statistical reasons, there must be more subjects than variables.[4]

The selection of measures for testing requires a thorough review of the available literature and instruments. In addition, measures must be adapted to the unique needs of the research situation without compromising their intended purpose or original meaning.

## Specifying the levels of treatment

The treatment levels of the independent variable are the distinctions that the researcher makes between different aspects of the treatment condition. For example, if salary is hypothesized to have an effect on employees exercising stock purchase options, it might be divided into high, middle and low ranges to represent three levels of the independent variable.

The levels assigned to an independent variable should be based on simplicity and common sense. In the management game example, the experimenter should not define homogenous teams as groups of people with the same nationality and mixed teams as a group, in which all members but one share the same nationality. Thus, in the first trial, the researcher is likely to form teams in which all people have the same nationality and teams in which each team member has a different nationality.

Under an entirely different hypothesis, several levels of the independent variable may be needed to test order-of-presentation effects. Here we use only two. Alternatively, a control group could provide a base level for comparison. The control group is composed of subjects who are not exposed to the independent variable(s), in contrast to those who receive the **experimental treatment** (manipulation of the independent variable(s)).

## Controlling the experimental environment

Chapter 1 discussed the nature of extraneous variables and the need for their control.

In our management game experiment, extraneous variables can appear as differences in age, gender, business experience, communications competence and many other characteristics of the game or the situation. These have the potential for distorting the effect of the treatment on the dependent variable and must be controlled or eliminated. However, at this stage we are principally concerned with **environmental control**, holding constant the physical environment of the experiment. All participants in the experiment would get the same written instruction and play exactly the same management game. The arrangement of the room, the time of administration, the experimenter's contact with the subjects, and so on, must all be consistent across each administration of the experiment.

Other forms of control involve subjects and experimenters. When subjects do not know if they are receiving the experimental treatment, they are said to be **blind**. When the experimenters do not know if they are giving the treatment to the experimental group or to the control group, the experiment is said to be **double blind**. Both approaches control unwanted complications such as subjects' reactions to expected conditions, or experimenter influence.

## Choosing the experimental design

Many of the experimental designs are diagrammed and described later in this chapter.

Unlike the general descriptors of research design that were discussed in Chapter 4, experimental designs are unique to the experimental method. They serve as positional and statistical plans to designate relationships between experimental treatments and the experimenter's observations or measurement points in the temporal scheme of the study. In the conduct of the experiment, the researchers apply their knowledge to select one design that is best suited to the goals of the research. Judicious selection of the design improves the probability that the observed change in the dependent variable was caused by the manipulation of the independent variable and not by another factor. It simultaneously strengthens the generalizability of results beyond the experimental setting.

## Selecting and assigning subjects

The subjects selected for the experiment should be representative of the population to which the researcher wishes to generalize the study's results. This may seem self-evident, but the authors of this book have witnessed several decades of experimentation with second-year college students which contradict that assumption. In the management game example, managers in a decision-making capacity, or at least management trainees, would provide better generalizing power than undergraduate college students.

The procedure for random sampling of experimental subjects is similar in principle to the selection of respondents for a survey. The researcher first prepares a sampling frame and then assigns the subjects for the experiment to groups using a randomization technique. Systematic sampling may be used if the sampling frame is free from any form of periodicity that parallels the sampling ratio. Since the sampling frame is often small, experimental subjects are recruited; thus, they are a self-selecting sample. However, if randomization is used, those assigned to the experimental group are likely to be similar to those assigned to the control group. Random assignment to the groups is required to make the groups as comparable as possible with respect to the dependent variable. Randomization does not guarantee that if a pre-test of the groups was conducted before the treatment condition the groups would be pronounced identical, but it is an assurance that those differences remaining are randomly distributed. In our example, we would need two randomly assigned groups. (Random sampling is discussed in Chapter 6.)

When it is not possible to randomly assign subjects to groups, **matching** may be used. Matching employs a non-probability quota sampling approach. The object of matching is to have each experimental and control subject matched on every characteristic used in the research. This becomes more cumbersome as the number of variables and groups in the study increases. Since the characteristics of concern are only those that are correlated with the treatment condition or the dependent variable, they are easier to identify, control and match.[5] In the management game experiment, if a large part of the sample was composed of female financial managers who recently completed training in strategic financial management, we would not want the characteristics of gender, function and training to be disproportionately assigned to one group.

Some authorities suggest a **quota matrix** as the most efficient means of visualizing the matching process.[6] In Exhibit 11.1, one-third of the subjects from each cell of the matrix would be assigned to each of the three groups. If matching does not alleviate the assignment problem, a combination of matching, randomization and increasing the sample size would be used.

## Pilot-testing, revising and testing

The procedures for this stage are similar to those for other forms of primary data-collection. Pilot-testing is intended to reveal errors in the design, and improper control of extraneous or

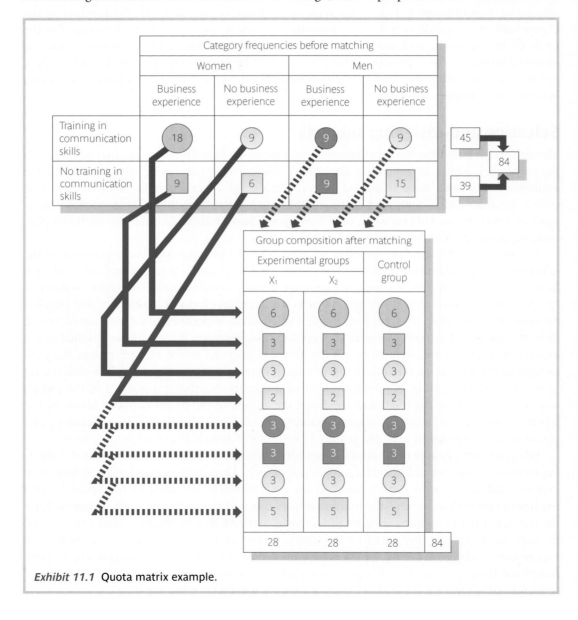

*Exhibit 11.1* Quota matrix example.

environmental conditions. Pre-testing the instruments permits refinement before the final test. This is the researcher's best opportunity to revise scripts, look for control problems with laboratory conditions and scan the environment for factors that might confound the results. In field experiments, researchers are sometimes caught off guard by events that have a dramatic effect on subjects: the test marketing of a competitor's product announced before an experiment or a reduction in force, reorganization or merger before a crucial organizational intervention. The experiment should be timed so that subjects are not sensitized to the independent variable by factors in the environment.

## Analysing the data

If adequate planning and pre-testing have occurred, the experimental data will take an order and structure uncommon to surveys and unstructured observational studies. It is not that data from experiments are easy to analyse – they are simply more conveniently arranged because of the levels of the treatment condition, pre-tests and post-tests, and the group structure. The choice of statistical techniques is commensurately simplified.

Researchers have several measurement and instrument options with experiments. Among them are:

- observational techniques and coding schemes
- paper-and-pencil tests
- self-report instruments with open-ended or closed questions
- scaling techniques (e.g. Likert scales, semantic differentials, Q-sort)
- physiological measures (e.g. galvanic skin response, EKG, voice pitch analysis, eye dilation).

# 11.4  Validity in experimentation

Even when an experiment is the ideal research design, it is not without problems. There is always a question about whether the results are true. We defined validity earlier as whether a measure accomplishes its claims. While there are several different types of validity, here only the two major varieties are considered: **internal validity** – do the conclusions we draw about a demonstrated experimental relationship truly imply cause? – and **external validity** – does an observed causal relationship generalize across people, settings and times?[7] Each type of validity has specific threats that must be guarded against.

## Internal validity

Among the many threats to internal validity, we now consider the following seven:

1  history
2  maturation
3  testing

4  instrumentation

5  selection

6  statistical regression

7  experimental mortality.

## History

During the time that an experiment is taking place, some events may occur that confuse the relationship being studied. In many experimental designs, we take a control measurement ($O_1$) of the dependent variable before introducing the manipulation ($X$). After the manipulation, we take an after-measurement ($O_2$) of the dependent variable. The difference between $O_1$ and $O_2$ is the change that the manipulation has caused.

A company's management may wish to find the best way to educate its workers about the financial condition of the company before this year's pay negotiations. To assess the value of such an effort, managers give employees a test on their knowledge of the company's finances ($O_1$). Then they present the educational campaign ($X$) to these employees, after which they again measure their knowledge level ($O_2$). This design, known as a pre-experiment because it is not a very strong design, can be diagrammed as follows:

| $O_1$ | $X$ | $O_2$ |
|---|---|---|
| Pre-test | Manipulation | Post-test |

Between $O_1$ and $O_2$, however, many events could occur to confound the effects of the education effort. A newspaper article might appear about companies with financial problems, a union meeting might be held at which this topic is discussed or another occurrence could distort the effects of the company's education test.

## Maturation

Changes also may occur within the subject that are a function of the passage of time and are not specific to any particular event. These are of special concern when the study covers a long time, but they may also be factors in tests that are as short as an hour or two. A subject can become hungry, bored or tired in a short time, and this condition can affect response results. In our management game example, teams that performed poorly in the first rounds of the game may become less enthusiastic about the game than those who perform well.

## Testing

The process of taking a test can affect the scores of a second test. The mere experience of taking the first test can have a learning effect that influences the results of the second test.

## Instrumentation

This threat to internal validity results from changes between observations in either the measuring instrument or the observer. Using different questions at each measurement is an obvious source of potential trouble, but using different observers or interviewers also threatens validity. There can even be an instrumentation problem if the same observer is used for all measurements. Observer experience, boredom, fatigue and anticipation of results can all distort the results of separate observations.

## Selection

An important threat to internal validity is the differential selection of subjects for experimental and control groups. Validity considerations require that the groups should be equivalent in every respect. If subjects are randomly assigned to experimental and control groups, this selection problem can largely be overcome. Additionally, matching the members of the groups on key factors can enhance the equivalence of the groups.

## Statistical regression

This factor operates especially when groups have been selected by their extreme scores. Suppose we measure the output of all workers in a department for a few days before an experiment and then conduct the experiment with only those workers whose productivity scores are in the top 25 per cent and bottom 25 per cent. No matter what is done between $O_1$ and $O_2$, there is a strong tendency for the average of the high scores at $O_1$ to decline at $O_2$ and for the low scores at $O_1$ to increase. This tendency results from imperfect measurement that, in effect, records some people abnormally high and abnormally low at $O_1$. In the second measurement, members of both groups score more closely to their long-run mean scores.

## Experiment mortality

This occurs when the composition of the study groups changes during the test. Attrition is especially likely in the experimental group and with each drop-out, the group changes. Because members of the control group are not affected by the testing situation, they are less likely to withdraw. In a compensation incentive study, some employees might not like the change in compensation method and may withdraw from the test group; this action could distort the comparison with the control group that has continued working under the established system, perhaps without knowing a test is under way.

## Further threats

All the threats mentioned to this point are generally, but not always, dealt with adequately in experiments by random assignment. However, five additional threats to internal validity are independent of whether or not one randomizes[8] (the first three have the effect of equalizing experimental and control groups).

1   Diffusion or imitation of treatment: if people in the experimental and control groups talk, then those in the control group may learn of the treatment, eliminating the difference between the groups.
2   Compensatory equalization: where the experimental treatment is much more desirable, there may be an administrative reluctance to deprive the control group members. Compensatory actions for the control groups may confound the experiment.
3   Compensatory rivalry: this may occur when members of the control group know they are in the control group. This may generate competitive pressures, causing the control group members to try harder.
4   Resentful demoralization of the disadvantaged: when the treatment is desirable and the experiment is obtrusive, control group members may become resentful of their deprivation and lower their cooperation and output.

5 Local history: the regular history effect already mentioned impacts both experimental and control groups alike. However, when one assigns all experimental persons to one group session and all control people to another, there is a chance for some idiosyncratic event to confound results. This problem can be handled by administering treatments to individuals or small groups that are randomly assigned to experimental or control sessions.

## External validity

Internal validity factors cause confusion about whether the experimental treatment ($X$) or extraneous factors are the source of observation differences. In contrast, external validity is concerned with the interaction of the experimental treatment with other factors and the resulting impact on the ability to generalize to (and across) times, settings or persons. Among the major threats to external validity are the following interactive possibilities.

### The reactivity of testing on X

The reactive effect refers to sensitizing subjects via a pre-test so that they respond to the experimental stimulus ($X$) in a different way. A before-measurement of a subject's knowledge about, say, the ecology programmes of a company will often sensitize the subject to various experimental communication efforts that might be made about the company. This before-measurement effect can be particularly significant in experiments where the $IV$ is a change in attitude.

### Interaction of selection and X

The process by which test subjects are selected for an experiment may be a threat to external validity. The population from which one selects subjects may not be the same as the population to which one wishes to generalize results. Suppose you use a selected group of workers in one department for a test of the piece-work incentive system. The question may remain as to whether you can extrapolate those results to all production workers. Or consider a study in which you ask a cross-section of a population to participate in an experiment, but a substantial number refuses. If you conduct the experiment only with those who agree to participate (self-selection), can the results be generalized to the total population?

### Other reactive factors

The experimental settings themselves may have a biasing effect on a subject's response to $X$. An artificial setting can obviously produce results that are not representative of larger populations. Suppose the workers who are given the incentive pay are moved to a different work area to separate them from the control group. These new conditions alone could create a strong reactive condition.

If subjects know that they are participating in an experiment, there may be a tendency to role-play in a way that distorts the effects of $X$. Another reactive effect is the possible interaction between $X$ and subject characteristics. An incentive pay proposal may be more effective with persons in one type of job, with a certain skill level or with a certain personality trait. Problems of internal validity can be solved by the careful design of experiments, but this is less true for problems of external validity. External validity is largely a matter of generalization, which, in a logical sense, is an inductive process of extrapolating beyond the data collected. In generalizing, we estimate the factors that can be ignored and that will interact with the experimental variable. Assume that the closer two events are in time, space and measurement, the more likely they are to follow the same laws. As a rule of thumb, first seek internal validity. Try to secure as much external validity as is compatible with the internal validity requirements by making experimental conditions as similar as possible to conditions under which the results will apply.

# 11.5  Experimental research designs

The many experimental designs vary widely in their power to control contamination of the relationship between independent and dependent variables. The most widely accepted designs are based on this characteristic of control:

- pre-experiments
- true experiments
- extensions of true experiments
- field and quasi-experiments
- quasi-experiments

We now look at each of these in turn.

## Pre-experimental designs

All three pre-experimental designs are weak in their scientific measurement power – that is, they fail to control adequately the various threats to internal validity. This is especially true of the one-shot case study.

### One-shot case study

This may be diagrammed as follows (see Exhibit 11.2 for a key to the symbols used in the design diagrams in this chapter):

| | | |
|---|---|---|
| *X* | *O* | (1) |
| Treatment or manipulation of independent variable | Observation or measurement of dependent variable | |

An example is an employee education campaign about a company's financial condition without a prior measurement of employee knowledge. Results would reveal only how much the employees know after the education campaign, but there is no way to judge the effectiveness of the campaign. How well do you think this design would meet the various threats to internal validity? The lack of a pre-test and control group makes this design inadequate for establishing causality.

### One-group pre-test – post-test design

This is the design used earlier in the educational example. It meets the various threats to internal validity better than the one-shot case study, but it is still a weak design. How well does it control for history? Maturation? Testing effect? The others?

$$O \; X \; O \qquad\qquad\qquad (2)$$

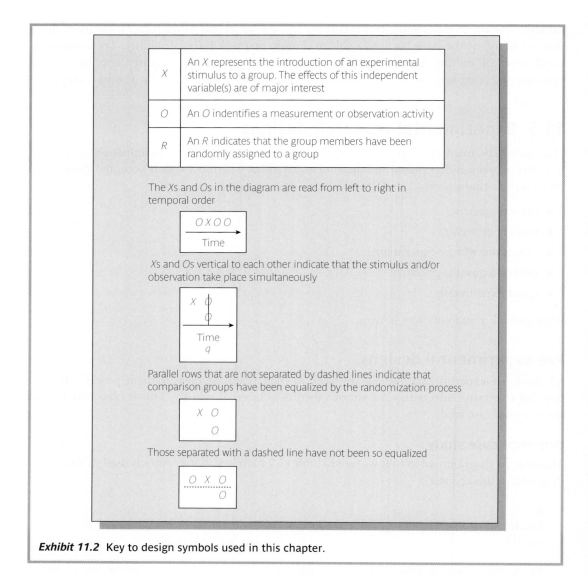

*Exhibit 11.2* Key to design symbols used in this chapter.

## *Pre-test manipulation post-test*
## Static group comparison

This design provides for two groups, one of which receives the experimental stimulus while the other serves as a control. In a field setting, imagine this scenario. A forest fire or other natural disaster is the experimental treatment, and psychological trauma (or property loss) suffered by the residents is the measured outcome. A pre-test before the forest fire would be possible, but not on a large scale (as in the recent forest fires in California). Moreover, timing of the pre-test would be problematic. The control group, receiving the post-test, would consist of residents whose property was spared.

$$\frac{X \ O_1}{O_2} \tag{3}$$

The addition of a comparison group creates a substantial improvement over the other two designs. Its chief weakness is that there is no way to be certain that the two groups are equivalent.

# True experimental designs

The major deficiency of pre-experimental designs is that they fail to provide comparison groups that are truly equivalent. The way to achieve equivalence is through matching and random assignment. With randomly assigned groups, we can employ tests of statistical significance of the observed differences.

It is common to show an $X$ for the test stimulus and a blank for the existence of a control situation. This is an oversimplification of what really occurs. More precisely, there is an $X_1$ and an $X_2$, and sometimes more. The $X_1$ identifies one specific independent variable while $X_2$ is another independent variable that has been chosen, often arbitrarily, as the control case. Different levels of the same independent variable may also be used, with one level serving as the control.

## *Pre-test – post-test control group design*

This design consists of adding a control group to the one-group pre-test–post-test design and assigning the subjects to either of the groups by a random procedure ($R$). The diagram is:

$$R \ O_1 \ X \ O_2 \tag{4}$$
$$R \ O_3 \ \ \ \ O_4$$

The effect of the experimental variable is:

$$E = (O_2 - O_1) - (O_4 - O_3)$$

In this design, the seven major internal validity problems are dealt with fairly well, although there are still some difficulties. Local history may occur in one group and not the other. Also, if communication exists between people in test and control groups, there can be rivalry and other internal validity problems.

Maturation, testing and regression are handled well because one would expect them to be felt equally in experimental and control groups. Mortality, however, can be a problem if there are different dropout rates in the study groups. Selection is adequately dealt with by random assignment.

The record of this design is not as good on external validity, however. There is a chance for a reactive effect from testing. This might be a substantial influence in attitude change studies where pre-tests introduce unusual topics and content. Nor does this design ensure against reaction between selection and the experimental variable. Even random selection may be defeated by a high decline rate by subjects. This would result in using a disproportionate share of people who are essentially volunteers and who may not be typical of the population. If this occurs, we will need to replicate the experiment several times with other groups under other conditions before we can be confident of external validity.

## Post-test-only control group design

In this design, the pre-test measurements are omitted. Pre-tests are well established in classical research design but are not really necessary when it is possible to randomize. The design is:

$$R \quad X \quad O_1 \qquad\qquad\qquad (5)$$
$$R \quad\quad\quad O_2$$

The experimental effect is measured by the difference between $O_1$ and $O_2$, $E = O_1 - O_2$. The simplicity of this design makes it more attractive than the pre-test–post-test control group design. Internal validity threats from history, maturation, selection and statistical regression are adequately controlled by random assignment. Since the subjects are measured only once, the threats of testing and instrumentation are reduced, but different mortality rates between experimental and control groups continue to be a potential problem. The design reduces the external validity problem of testing **interaction effect**, although other problems remain. Our earlier management game example comes close to this design.

# Extensions of true experimental designs

True experimental designs have been discussed in their classical forms, but researchers normally use an operational extension of the basic design. These extensions differ from the classical design forms in (i) the number of different experimental stimuli that are considered simultaneously by the experimenter, and (ii) the extent to which assignment procedures are used to increase precision.

Before we consider the types of extension, some terms that are commonly used in the literature of applied experimentation must be introduced. **Factor** is widely used to denote an independent variable. Factors are divided into **treatment levels**, which represent various subgroups. A factor may have two or more levels, such as (1) male and female, (2) large, medium and small, or (3) no training, brief training and extended training. These levels should be operationally defined.

Factors may also be classified by whether the experimenter can manipulate the levels associated with the subject. **Active factors** are those the experimenter can manipulate by causing a subject to receive one level or another. Treatment is used to denote the different levels of active factors. With the second type, the **blocking factor**, the experimenter can only identify and classify the subject on an existing level. Gender, age group, customer status and organizational rank are examples of blocking factors, because the subject comes to the experiment with a pre-existing level of each.

Up to this point, the assumption is that experimental subjects are people, but this is often not so. A better term for subject is **test unit**; this can refer equally well to an individual organization, geographic market, animal, machine type, mix of materials and innumerable other entities.

Check the following website for examples of industrial experiments: http://www.statsoft.com/textbook/stathome.html.

## Completely randomized design

The basic form of the true experiment is a completely randomized design. To illustrate its use, and that of more complex designs, consider a decision now facing the pricing manager at Top

Cannery. He would like to know what the ideal difference in price is between Top's private brand of canned vegetables and national brands such as Unox and Lacroix.

It is possible to set up an experiment on price differentials for canned tomato soup. Eighteen company stores and three price spreads (treatment levels) of 7 cents, 12 cents and 17 cents between the company brand and national brands are used for the study. Six of the stores are assigned randomly to each of the treatment groups. The price differentials are maintained for a period, and then a tally is made of the sales volumes and gross profits of the canned tomato soup for each group of stores.

This design can be diagrammed as follows:

$$R \quad O_1 \ X_1 \ O_2$$
$$R \quad O_3 \ X_3 \ O_4 \qquad\qquad\qquad (6)$$
$$R \quad O_5 \ X_5 \ O_6$$

Here, $O_1$, $O_3$ and $O_5$ represent the total gross profits for canned tomato soup in the treatment stores for the month before the test. $X_1$, $X_3$ and $X_5$ represent 7-cent, 12-cent and 17-cent treatments, while $O_2$, $O_4$ and $O_6$ are the gross profits for the month after the test started.

It is assumed that the randomization of stores to the three treatment groups was sufficient to make the three store groups equivalent. Where there is reason to believe this is not so, we must use a more complex design.

## Randomized block design

When there is a single major extraneous variable, the randomized block design is used. Random assignment is still the basic way to produce equivalence among treatment groups, but something more may be needed for two reasons. The more critical of these is that the sample being studied may be so small that it is risky to depend on random assignment alone to guarantee equivalence. Small samples, such as the 18 company stores, are typical in field experiments because of high costs or because few test units are available. Another reason for blocking is to learn whether treatments bring different results among various groups of subjects.

Consider again the canned tomato soup pricing experiment. Assume that there is reason to believe that lower-income families are more sensitive to price differentials than are higher-income families. This factor could seriously distort our results unless we stratify the stores by customer income. Therefore, each of the 18 stores is assigned to one of three income blocks and randomly assigned, within blocks, to the price difference treatments. The design is shown in Exhibit 11.3.

In this design, one can measure both **main effects** and interaction effects. The main effect is the average direct influence that a particular treatment has independent of other factors. The interaction effect is the influence of one factor on the effect of another. The main effect of each price differential is secured by calculating the impact of each of the three treatments averaged over the different blocks. Interaction effects occur if you find that different customer income levels have a pronounced influence on customer reactions to the price differentials (see Chapter 16 on hypothesis testing). Whether the randomized block design improves the precision of the experimental measurement depends on how successfully the design minimizes the variance within blocks and maximizes the variance between blocks. If the response patterns are about the same in each block, there is little value to the more complex design. Blocking may be counterproductive.

| Active factor – price difference | Blocking factor – customer income | | | |
|---|---|---|---|---|
| | | High | Medium | Low |
| 7 cents | R | $X_1$ | $X_1$ | $X_1$ |
| 12 cents | R | $X_2$ | $X_2$ | $X_2$ |
| 17 cents | R | $X_3$ | $X_3$ | $X_3$ |

*Note*: the *O*s have been omitted. The horizontal rows no longer indicate a time sequence, but various levels of blocking factor. However, before-and-after measurements are associated with each treatment.

**Exhibit 11.3** An example of randomized block design (7).

## Latin square design

The Latin square design may be used when there are two major extraneous factors. To continue with the pricing example, assume we decide to block on the size of store and on customer income. It is convenient to consider these two blocking factors as forming the rows and columns of a table. Each factor is divided into three levels to provide nine groups of stores, each representing a unique combination of the two blocking variables. Treatments are then randomly assigned to these cells so that a given treatment appears only once in each row and column. Because of this restriction, a Latin square must have the same number of rows, columns and treatments. The design looks like the example shown in Exhibit 11.4.

Treatments can be assigned by using a table of random numbers to set the order of treatment in the first row. For example, the pattern may be 3, 1, 2, as shown above. Following this, the other two cells of the first column are filled similarly, and the remaining treatments are assigned to meet the restriction that there can be no more than one treatment type in each row and column.

The experiment is carried out, sales results are gathered and the average treatment effect is calculated. From this, we can determine the main effect of the various price spreads on the sales of company and national brands. With cost information, we can discover which price differential produces the greatest margin.

A limitation of the Latin square is that we must assume that there is no interaction between treatments and blocking factors. Therefore, we cannot determine the interrelationships among

| Store size | Customer income | | |
|---|---|---|---|
| | High | Medium | Low |
| Large | $X_3$ | $X_1$ | $X_2$ |
| Medium | $X_2$ | $X_3$ | $X_1$ |
| Small | $X_1$ | $X_2$ | $X_3$ |

**Exhibit 11.4** An example of Latin square design (8).

store size, customer income and price spreads. This limitation exists because there is not an exposure of all combinations of treatments, store sizes and customer income groups. To do so would take a table of 27 cells, while this one has only 9. This can be accomplished by repeating the experiment twice to furnish the number needed to provide for every combination of store size, customer income and treatment. If one is not especially interested in interaction, the Latin square is much more economical.

## Factorial design

One commonly held misconception about experiments is that the researcher can manipulate only one variable at a time. This is not true: with factorial designs, you can deal with more than one treatment simultaneously. Consider again the pricing experiment. The managing director of the chain might also be interested in finding the effect of posting unit prices on the shelf to aid shopper decision-making. Exhibit 11.5 can be used to design an experiment that includes both the price differentials and the unit pricing.

This is known as a $2 \times 3$ factorial design in which we use two factors: one with two levels and one with three levels of intensity. The version shown here is completely randomized, with the stores being randomly assigned to one of six treatment combinations. With such a design, it is possible to estimate the main effects of each of the two independent variables and the interactions between them. The results can help to answer the following questions.

1  What are the sales effects of the different price spreads between company and national brands?

2  What are the sales effects of using unit-price marking on the shelves?

3  What are the sales-effect interrelations between price spread and the presence of unit-price information?

## Covariance analysis

We have discussed direct control of extraneous variables through blocking. It is also possible to apply some degree of indirect statistical control on one or more variables through analysis of covariance. Even with randomization, one may find that the before-measurement shows an average knowledge level difference between experimental and control groups. With covariance analysis, one can adjust statistically for this before-difference. Another application might occur if the canned tomato soup pricing experiment were carried out with a completely randomized design, only to reveal a contamination effect from differences in average customer income levels. With covariance analysis, one can still do some statistical blocking on average customer

| | Price spread | | |
|---|---|---|---|
| Unit price information | 7 cents | 12 cents | 17 cents |
| Yes | $X_1 Y_1$ | $X_1 Y_2$ | $X_1 Y_3$ |
| No | $X_2 Y_1$ | $X_2 Y_2$ | $X_2 Y_3$ |

*Exhibit 11.5*  Example of factorial design (9).

income even after the experiment has been run. (The statistical aspects of covariance analysis are discussed in Chapter 18, where an analysis of variance (ANOVA) is presented.)

The experimental approach is even used in survey research, especially to investigate methodological issues. For example, the effects of question wording or ranking can be investigated by sending different questionnaires to parts of the survey sample. Similarly, differences in response can be investigated by offering no and different incentives to respondents. Statistics Netherlands, for example, discovered by applying such a design that young males – who make up a group that has a notably low response rate – are much more likely to respond if the incentive (a prepaid phone card) is sent to them along with the request to fill in a questionnaire; this works better than promising that an incentive will be sent once the questionnaire has been returned.

Another example of implementing experimental designs into surveys is the **factorial survey**, also known as **vignette research**.[9] In factorial surveys, the researcher presents the respondent with a brief and explicit description of a situation and then asks him or her to assess the situation or to make a decision. The description of the situation contains the independent variables, while the respondent's answer is the dependent variable. In a study investigating the contracting behaviour of firms in business-to-business transactions, respondents (purchasing managers of firms) were asked to assess how much time would be needed to negotiate and draft a contract with a partner described in the vignette. Furthermore, the vignette contained information on characteristics of the transaction, such as the money involved, and so on.[10] Factorial surveys have also been used to investigate which incomes people perceive as justified for certain professions or to investigate discrimination of ethnic minorities when applying for a job.

## Field and quasi-experiments[11]

Most people imagine a scientist mixing chemical substances or a rat running through a maze when they hear about research experiments. Even when they know that humans are the test units, they still think of a laboratory. The advantages of laboratory experiments are unmistakable: the researcher's ability to fully control the research setting and to exclude any unwanted external influences. However, this control comes at the cost of an artificial setting. Even if researchers attempt to simulate reality as far as possible in the laboratory (e.g. by building a 'normal' office as in the theft/bystander example), participants are at least sensitized to the fact that they are participating in an experiment, and the behaviour that they exhibit might differ from their behaviour in the 'real' world. Field experiments are conducted in a natural setting and, often, participants do not know that their behaviour is being monitored.

A modern version of the bystander-and-thief field experiment mentioned at the beginning of this chapter involves the use of electronic article surveillance to prevent shrinkage due to shoplifting. In a proprietary study, a shopper came to the optical counter of an upmarket store and asked the salesperson if they could look at some special designer frames. The salesperson, a confederate of the experimenter, replied that she would get them from a case in the adjoining department, and disappeared. The 'thief' selected two pairs of sunglasses from an open display, deactivated the security tags at the counter, and walked out of the store; 35 per cent of the subjects (store customers) reported the theft on the return of the salesperson; 63 per cent reported

## Science-fiction shopping on the Rhine

Metro, the fifth largest retailer in the world, has cooperated with SAP, Intel and IBM, as well as other partner companies from the information technology (IT) and consumer goods industries, to develop the store of the future. The initiative is a platform for technical and process-related developments and innovations in retailing. These technologies enrich the service to consumers and improve processes in retailing. Technologies to aid the customer include a personal shopping assistant, intelligent scales, self-checkout and information terminals. Radio-frequency identifiers (RFIDs) are the basis of smarter inventory management.

These technologies have already been realized and, in April 2003, Metro opened a 'future store' in Rheinberg, Germany. This store had been a normal supermarket chain since 1977, but now is the prototype of a future store, where new technologies can be tested under real conditions. About 2500 customers visit this shopping laboratory each day.

When those customers holding a personal loyalty card enter the store, they pick up a mobile computer – the personal shopping assistant (PSA) – which can be fixed to their shopping trolley. The PSA recalls the customer's last shopping list, guides the customer through the shopping aisles if they cannot find a certain product, allows the customer to self-scan their purchases and, finally, offers customized information on its display (details of special offers, etc.). When the customer has finished shopping, she or he proceeds to the checkout, the PSA transmits details of the purchases to the cash register and the customer can then pay without having to unload their purchases onto the conveyor belt and then back into their trolley again.

In October 2003, the Boston Consulting Group surveyed the customers of this future store. Some key results of this survey were that 77 per cent of customers used at least one technology, the share of customers highly or fully satisfied with the store had risen from 34 per cent to 52 per cent since the store's 'smart' reopening, and 31 per cent of current customers are new customers.

Is the future store in Rheinberg a sophisticated laboratory experiment or a field experiment? What are the potential problems when conducting experiments in the future store?

## References and further reading

http://www.future-store.org/servlet/PB/menu/1002284_l2/index.html
http://www.future-store.org/servlet/PB/show/1002036/03–12–19_BCG-Studie3.pdf

it when the salesperson asked about the shopper. Unlike previous studies, the presence of a second customer did not reduce the willingness to report a theft.

Compare the bystander/thief experiment conducted in a laboratory that has been made to resemble an office and that conducted in a shop in an upmarket shopping centre. First, the participants in the laboratory experiment are very likely to be students or employees of the university. In the field experiment, the participants are people who usually visit shops in a shopping centre at a given day and time, which the researcher can vary. By and large, in the field experiment the participants form a much more heterogeneous group, which reflects the population better than the laboratory experiment. Second, as people in the field experiment are not aware of their participation, they are less likely to conceal or adjust their behaviour. People who know that they are participating in a laboratory experiment might, for example, observe their environment more carefully. Third, in laboratory experiments, the experimenter effect is more problematic, as experimenter and participants interact more – for example, when the experimenter introduces the procedures of the experiment.

Given these advantages of field experiments, we now turn to the disadvantages. The researcher's ability to manipulate the independent variables is the most interesting and distinguished feature of experiments. In field experiments, this advantage is partly lost, as the researcher has fewer opportunities to control the research setting. In the bystander/thief experiment conducted in the shop, the researcher has hardly any influence on who approaches the instructed salesperson in the shop and becomes a participant. Further, the number of bystanders in the shop might even vary during the experiment as people leave or enter the shop. Another problem of field experiments is that they raise ethical questions. Participants have usually not given their prior consent to participate in the research.

# Quasi-experiment

As we have discussed previously, the most important and distinguished characteristics of an experiment are (i) the researcher's ability to control the experimental setting and to manipulate the independent variables, and (ii) the random assignment of subjects (test units) to the experimental and control groups. However, there are many occasions when the researcher cannot meet these prerequisites of true experiments, as it is not feasible to assign subjects at random or to fully control the research setting. In a quasi-experiment, we often cannot know when or to whom to expose the experimental treatment. Usually, however, we can decide when and whom to measure. A **quasi-experiment** is inferior to a true experimental design, but is usually superior to pre-experimental designs if it is conducted with caution. Quasi-experimental designs are especially useful in studying the effects of well-defined events, such as the introduction of a new law, the succession of a chief executive officer (CEO), a natural disaster, and the like. The occurrence of such events is beyond the influence of the researcher and it is often unfeasible to assign subjects randomly. Two groups of quasi-experimental designs may be distinguished:

1 non-equivalent control group designs
2 time-series design.

We look at each of these now.

## *Non-equivalent control group design*

This is a strong and widely used quasi-experimental design. It differs from the pre-test–post-test control group design because the test and control groups are not randomly assigned. The design is diagrammed as follows:

$$\frac{O_1 \ X \ O_2}{O_3 \ \ O_4} \tag{10}$$

Note that the members of the two groups are not assigned randomly, but that the researcher either investigates two natural groups, for example different classes in a school or two different plants of a company or asks volunteers to apply for the experimental group experiencing a treatment and compares them with non-volunteers. For example, employees applying for a certain training programme. The more the experimental and the control group are alike the better and comparison of pre-test results ($O_1 - O_3$) is one indicator of the degree of equivalence between test and control groups. If the pre-test results are significantly different, there is a real question about the groups' comparability. On the other hand, if pre-test observations are similar between groups, there is more reason to believe that the internal validity of the experiment is good.

## Separate sample pre-test – post-test design

This design is most applicable when we cannot know when and to whom to introduce the treatment but we can decide when and whom to measure. The basic design is:

$$R \ O_1 \ (X) \hfill (11)$$
$$R \ X \ O_2$$

The bracketed treatment ($X$) is irrelevant to the purpose of the study but is shown here to suggest that the experimenter cannot control the treatment. This is not a strong design because several threats to internal validity are not handled adequately. History can confound the results but can be overcome by repeating the study at other times in other settings. In contrast, it is considered superior to true experiments in external validity. Its strength results from its being a field experiment in which the samples are usually drawn from the population to which we wish to generalize our findings. We would find this design more appropriate if the population were large, if a before-measurement were reactive or if there were no way to restrict the application of the treatment.

Assume that a company is planning an intense campaign to change its employees' attitudes towards energy conservation. It might draw two random samples of employees, one of which is interviewed about energy use attitudes before the information campaign. After the campaign the other group is interviewed.

## Time series and comparison groups

A time-series design introduces repeated observations before and after the treatment, and allows subjects to act as their own controls. The single treatment group design has before-after-measurements as the only controls. There is also a multiple design with two or more comparison groups, as well as the repeated measurements in each treatment group. The time-series format is especially useful where regularly kept records are a natural part of the environment and are unlikely to be reactive. The time-series approach is also a good way to study unplanned events in an *ex-post facto* manner. If the federal government suddenly begins price controls, for example, we could still study the effects of this action later if we had collected records regularly for the period before and after the advent of price control.

The different charts in Exhibit 11.6 show the hypothetical share price development of different firms in the oil and gas sector between April 2005 and November 2006.[12] In September 2005 UK Oil announced that Jody Jolly, 49 years old, had been appointed as the new CEO to commence in December 2005. Jody Jolly is believed to be one of, if not *the*, best managers in the world, a fact that is supported by several Manager of the Year awards from business magazines. Our research question here is whether Jody is indeed such an exceptional manager.

**Exhibit 11.6** Different hypothetical scenarios of UK Oil's share price development compared to some indices.

(c)

UK Oil — WSI

(d)

UK Oil — OSI

*Exhibit 11.6* continued

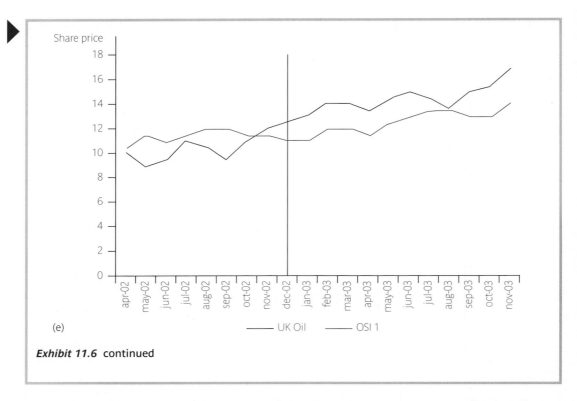

(e)

UK Oil      OSI 1

***Exhibit 11.6*** continued

Exhibit 11.6a is a chart such as you might see accompanying a portrait of Jody Jolly in a popular business magazine. It shows the share price of UK Oil, the vertical line marks the month during which Jody became the new CEO of the company. It shows that the share price of UK Oil increased from September 2002 (when Jody's appointment was announced) and has continued to rise since then. Can you deduce from this chart that Jody really made a difference? From an experimental viewpoint Exhibit 11.6a is a single interrupted time series, comparable to the pre-test–post-test design. As there is no control group with which we can compare the share price development of UK Oil, it is hard to conclude that the share price increase can be ascribed to Jody Jolly. We would have to rule out alternative explanations. But can we? A possible alternative explanation could, for example, be that the stock markets as a whole performed better in 2003. A better quasi-experimental design would include a control group, such as a stock index.

Exhibits 11.6b and 11.6c compare the development of UK Oil's share price with the World Stock Index (WSI). Suppose the WSI has moved as displayed in Exhibit 11.6b. In this case we speak of a non-effect outcome, that is the appointment of Jody had no effect, as the price of other stocks increased as well. However, how would we answer the research question if the WSI developed as shown in Exhibit 11.6c? Since the appointment of Jody Jolly, the share price of UK Oil has increased, while the performance of the WSI is roughly a horizontal line. Can we conclude from Exhibit 11.6c, then, that Jody Jolly made a difference? An alternative explanation could be that oil companies in general outperformed the WSI in 2003. The fact that the ups and downs of the share price and the index are not parallel suggests that factors other than the appointment of a new CEO affect the share price. For instance, favourable conditions in the oil business and not the appointment of Jody Jolly might be the cause of UK Oil's rising share price.

Exhibits 11.6d and 11.6e compare the share price of UK Oil with an index averaging the share price of other major oil companies. In Exhibit 11.6d the average share price of other oil companies is substantially lower than that of UK Oil, and from 2003 onwards, UK Oil's share price increases while the average share price of other oil companies does not increase as much. In the hypothetical case of Exhibit 11.6d, the conclusion that Jody made a difference is much stronger than if we base this conclusion on Exhibit 11.6c, as by choosing a more similar control group we have excluded some alternative explanations, such as industry effects. However, the initial difference in the share prices might point to the fact that UK Oil as a company has competitive advantages above other oil companies. Thus, the better stock market performance of UK Oil is caused by firm characteristics and not Jody Jolly.

Suppose Exhibit 11.6e offered a comparison between UK Oil and other oil companies. In this case, the share prices move parallel until December 2002, but after that UK Oil has performed better. Thus, from the moment Jody Jolly was appointed, UK Oil's share price took a different path from that of the other oil companies.

A quasi-experimental outcome as in Exhibit 11.6e gives strong support to the hypothesis that Jody Jolly is an exceptional manager. Any alternative explanation would have to explain why UK Oil's share price took off at the moment of Jody Jolly's appointment.

Compared to true experiments, a major deficiency of the quasi-experiment is that the test units are not assigned at random to the treatment. Often, the treatment – such as the appointment of a new CEO, as in the example above, or the introduction of a new law – is a response to developments in the past: companies appoint a new CEO because the old one performed poorly; a government tightens immigration laws as a response to an increase in the number of (economic) refugees seeking entry to a country. Interventions (treatments) as a response to previous developments – that is no random assignments – impede the interpretation of the outcomes of time series with comparison groups.

Referring again to the example of Jody Jolly, Exhibit 11.7 displays the share price development of UK Oil and Petrol US, its main competitor. The vertical line in the exhibit indicates once again the appointment of Jody Jolly. Before Jody Jolly was appointed, UK Oil's share price was much more volatile than that of Petrol US, and Jody Jolly might have been appointed as a reaction to this unstable and poor performance. Indeed, we see that after Jody Jolly's appointment UK Oil's share price rose from a three-year low and even exceeded that of Petrol US. Is Jody Jolly's appointment the explanation for the share price rise in 2003? This is hard to conclude from Exhibit 11.7, because we have to deal with 'reversion to the trend', which is similar to reversion of the mean.

Whenever a time-series reaches extreme points, it is very probable that in the following period the series moves again towards the trend, that is after reaching an extreme high (or low) the time series falls (or rises). While this regression artefact can explain the better performance of UK Oil in 2003, it cannot explain the better performance in 2004 and 2005. Hence, we can conclude that the appointment of Jody Jolly is a reasonable explanation for the better performance of UK Oil since 2003.

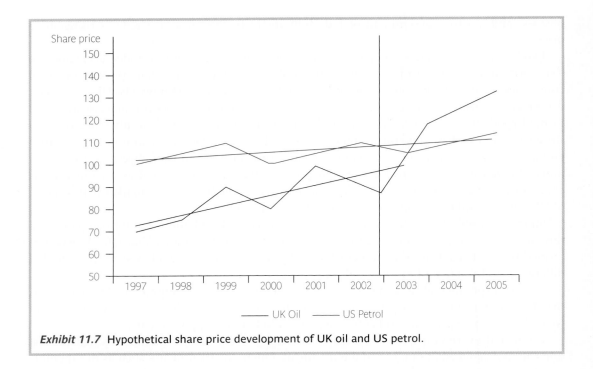

*Exhibit 11.7* Hypothetical share price development of UK oil and US petrol.

## Airports take off

Exhibit 11.8 shows annual passenger numbers for the four main German airports: Frankfurt, Munich, Düsseldorf and Hamburg. In 1992 Munich Airport moved from its old location, Riem, to a newly constructed airport at Erdinger Moos, about 30 km north-east of Munich. One of the major objectives for building a new airport at a new location was to establish Munich as the second largest airport (after Frankfurt) in Germany. Similarly, currently Berlin-Schoenefeld is being further developed to become the main international airport for Berlin, while the city airport Tegel will be closed in the near future. Could you conclude from Exhibit 11.8 that the construction of an airport at a new location is essential for further airport growth?

Our attitudes to and methods of flying have changed dramatically in the last decade. A number of European airlines, such as Ryanair, AirBerlin and easyJet, have copied the successful business concept of SouthWest Airlines in the USA. The basic idea behind these airlines is to offer low fares by following a cost leadership approach and removing costly added services. The price differences are substantial, but the classical airlines are also offering competitive prices especially if booked well in advance as Exhibit 11.10 shows.

The emergence of these so-called no-frills airlines has also affected the airports. Exhibit 11.9 shows again annual passenger numbers for a couple of German airports. Some of these airports are mainly served by no-frills and charter airlines Munster (Air Berlin), Lübeck (Ryanair), Hahn (Ryanair) and Paderborn (Air Berlin)), some are mainly served by national flag carriers

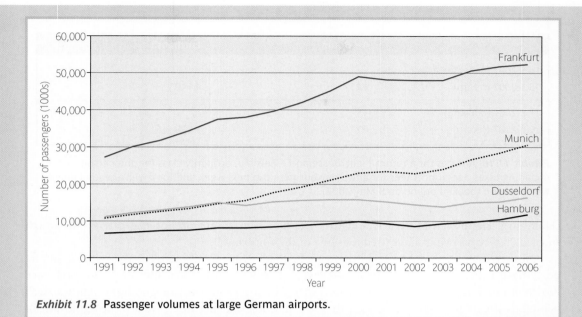

*Exhibit 11.8* Passenger volumes at large German airports.

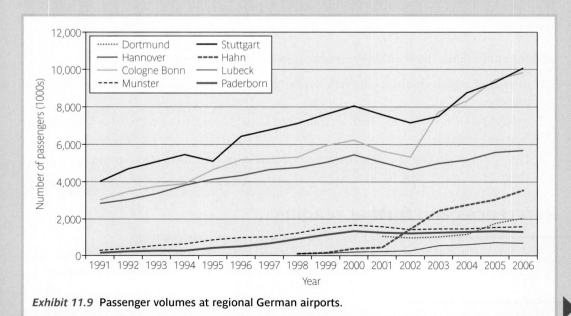

*Exhibit 11.9* Passenger volumes at regional German airports.

| | Air Berlin | Lufthansa |
|---|---|---|
| 14.5.2007 (outward)<br>15.5.2007 (return) | €257 | €1405 |
| 17.8.2007 (outward)<br>19.8.2007 (return) | €214 | €198 |

*Exhibit 11.10*  Airfares for a return flight Dusseldorf – Helsinki, economy class for one person including taxes and airport fees for a two-day business trip next week and for a well-ahead planned weekend trip (booked online on 8 May 2007).

(Hamburg, Hannover, Stuttgart) and Cologne has been an airport for flag carriers, although since 2003 Germanwings have used it as one of their hubs.

Another interesting observation that can be made from Exhibit 11.9 is that almost all airports have experienced a growth in passenger numbers since 2003, but some airports have grown at much higher rates than other airports. The top grower is Cologne Bonn that was well behind Stuttgart for years but closed that gap in 2003. Furthermore, we see the explosion of passenger numbers in Frankfurt-Hahn, the largest Ryanair base in Germany, although the airport is about 120 km or a 90-minute drive from Frankfurt and other large cities such as Cologne. Ryanair is also the main cause for the revival of Lübeck's small regional airport that has tripled its passenger volume in the last five years. However, airports can grow without being a Ryanair destination as well, as the example of Dortmund shows that it has attracted a number of no-frills and charter airlines and recently overtook the airports of Munster and Paderborn - two airports that are rather close to Dortmund.

Looking at this figure, how would you assess the following statements?

1  Attracting a no-frills airline to one's airport guarantees a substantial rise in the number of passengers.

2  Newly established airports, such as Hahn and Lübeck, draw passengers away from already existing airports.

3  The figure shows convincingly that the market airports operate in has changed from public governance to dynamic competition.

# References and further reading

For a more in-depth insight into this topic please see the Spotlight on Research section at the end of this chapter.

http://www.adv-net.org/eng/gfx/stats2000.php
www.flughafen-paderborn-lippstadt.de/pop_ups/pdf/image+ pad.
pdfwww.luebeck.org/upload/kunden/20/cmsdokus/passagiere_
flughafen_090104.pdf 12000

## Research Methods in Practice 11

# Trust games

The underlying central question of the research programme was to investigate why people or firms cooperate and how they manage to ensure cooperation despite the fact there are incentives to defect, that is to take advantage. Game theory is a powerful economic approach to model such cooperation problems. Probably, the most well-known game-theoretical cooperation model is the prisoner's dilemma (see Exhibit 11.11). If you do not know it, the situation sketched in the model is as follows: suppose you and a friend have been arrested on the charge that you have committed a crime, but the authorities do not have sufficient evidence to convict you and offer you and your friend the same deal. If you confess as a witness against your friend, he gets the maximum sentence of 15 years and you will be released after 1 year. If you both confess, they will reward your cooperation and sentence both of you to eight years and if neither of you confess they will sentence you to two years on a minor charge.

The general issue here is that the optimal outcome would be if both do not confess, but if you do not confess and the other does, you are worse off. Thus, both of you have an incentive to confess resulting in a eight-year sentence for you both. The structure of the game can be found back in real-life situations. Escape groups in cycling races such as the Tour de France face a similar situation. If they cooperate with each other well and each takes his turn in cycling at the front, the whole group has a better chance to stay ahead of the peloton with the strong sprinters who are most likely to win a stage. The incentive not to cooperate, that is not to cycle at the front, is that if the escape group stays ahead of the peloton until the finish, you will have the most energy for the sprint in the escape group. But if every cyclist spares himself, that is defects, the peloton will catch the escape group easily.

Derived from the prisoner's dilemma is another game, the trust game, in which the two players do not decide simultaneously, but sequentially. The situation is as follows and resembles partly the situation companies face when they need to decide to cooperate with a partner. Exhibit 11.12 below explains the situation. In the first stage, *Player One* can decide whether she trusts or distrusts *Player Two*. If *Player One* distrusts *Player Two*, the game stops and both gain, for example 2. If *Player One* trusts *Player Two*, they enter the second stage. Now it is upon *Player Two* whether he honours the trust of *Player One* by trusting her or whether he dishonours *Player One* by distrusting her. If *Player Two* dishonours *Player Two* he gains an opportunistic rent of 8, while *Player One* gets nothing. If *Player Two* honours the trust of *Player One*, both players get the cooperative rent, for example 5 for each. Important for the structure of

| | Your Friend | Do not confess | Confess |
|---|---|---|---|
| You | | | |
| Do not confess | | Both get two years | You get 15-year sentence Your friend gets one year sentence |
| Confess | | You get one-year sentence Your friend gets 15-year sentence | Both get eight-year sentence |

*Exhibit 11.11* Prisoner's dilemma.

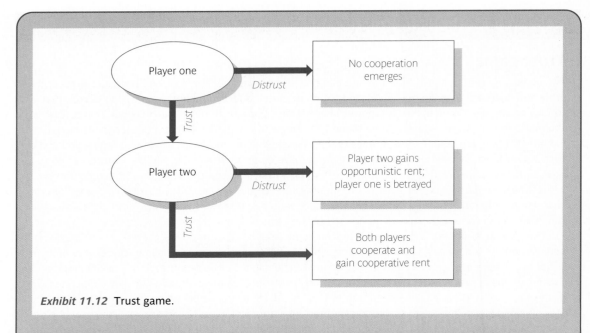

*Exhibit 11.12* Trust game.

the trust game is that the opportunistic rent is higher than the cooperative rent for *Player Two* and that *Player One* gains more for distrust than from dishonoured trust.

During the project, we were a couple of times invited to give pre-dinner talks on trust in buyer–supplier relations to purchasing managers following a training with the Dutch Association of Purchasing Management. We used these contacts with purchasing managers to collect experimental data. Before the talk, we distributed a small booklet containing 10 pages and on each page there was a figure like the one shown in Exhibit 11.12. In the straight boxes, we put outcomes; the means rewards in €. Thus, each of the 10 scenarios in the booklet had a slightly different reward structure. In most of the scenarios the opportunistic rent ranged between €20 and €50, but in one the opportunistic rent was €500. Similarly, the ratio between the cooperative and opportunistic rent varied from 0.9 to 0.4. Before we gave our talk, we asked the managers to fill in the booklet as follows:

1  Assume that you are *Player One*; circle in each scenario your choice, either 'trust' or 'distrust' as *Player One*
2  Now assume that you are *Player Two* and *Player One* trusted you; circle in each scenario your choice, either 'trust' (honour *Player One*'s trust) or 'distrust' (dishonour *Player One*'s trust).

The managers were told that we would collect the booklet and then we would randomly choose a scenario and choose a *Player One* and a *Player Two* out of their group and these two people would get the rewards according to the choice that they made.

Surprisingly, we found that most managers behaved cooperatively, although at least economic theory predicts that distrust is the most rational behaviour. What could explain the cooperative behaviour of the managers?

# Summary

1 Experiments are studies involving intervention by the researcher beyond that required for measurement. The usual intervention is to manipulate a variable (the independent variable) and observe how it affects the subjects being studied (the dependent variable).

   An evaluation of the experimental method reveals several advantages: (i) the ability to uncover causal relationships, (ii) provisions for controlling extraneous and environmental variables, (iii) the convenience and low cost of creating test situations rather than searching for their appearance in business situations, (iv) the ability to replicate findings and thus rule out idiosyncratic or isolated results, and (v) the ability to exploit naturally occurring events.

2 Some advantages of other methods that are liabilities for the experiment include: (i) the artificial setting of the laboratory, (ii) generalizability from non-probability samples, (iii) disproportionate costs in select business situations, (iv) a focus restricted to the present and immediate future, and (v) ethical issues related to the manipulation and control of human subjects.

3 Consideration of the following activities is essential for the execution of a well-planned experiment:
   a select relevant variables for testing
   b specify the levels of treatment
   c control the environmental and extraneous factors
   d choose an experimental design suited to the hypothesis
   e select and assign subjects to groups
   f pilot-test, revise and conduct the final test
   g analyse the data.

4 We judge various types of experimental research design by how well they meet the tests of internal and external validity. An experiment has high internal validity if one has confidence that the experimental treatment has been the source of change in the dependent variable. More specifically, a design's internal validity is judged by how well it meets seven threats. These are history, maturation, testing, instrumentation, selection, statistical regression and experiment mortality.

   External validity is high when the results of an experiment are judged to apply to some larger population. Such an experiment is said to have high external validity regarding that population. Three potential threats to external validity are testing reactivity, selection interaction, and other reactive factors.

5 Experimental research designs include (i) pre-experiments, (ii) true experiments and (iii) quasi-experiments. The main distinction among these types is the degree of control that the researcher can exercise over validity problems.

   Three pre-experimental designs are presented in this chapter. These designs represent the crudest form of experimentation and are undertaken only when nothing stronger is possible. Their weakness is the lack of an equivalent comparison group; as a result, they fail to meet many internal validity criteria. They are (i) the one-shot control study, (ii) the one-group pre-test–post-test design and (iii) the static group comparison.

Two forms of the true experiment were also presented. Their central characteristic is that they provide a means by which we can assure equivalence between experimental and control groups through random assignment to the groups. These designs are (i) pre-test–post-test control group and (ii) post-test-only control group.

The classical two-group experiment can be extended to multi-group designs in which different levels of the test variable are used as controls rather than the classical non-test control. In addition, the true experimental design is extended into more sophisticated forms that use blocking. Two such forms – the randomized block and the Latin square – were discussed. Finally, the factorial design was discussed in which two or more independent variables can be accommodated.

Between the extremes of pre-experiments, with little or no control, and true experiments, with random assignment, there is a grey area in which we find quasi-experiments. These are useful designs when some variables can be controlled, but equivalent experimental and control groups cannot usually be established by random assignment. There are many quasi-experimental designs, but only three are covered in this chapter: (i) non-equivalent control group design, (ii) separate sample pre-test–post-test design; and (iii) group time-series design.

## Discussion questions

## Terms in review

1  Distinguish between the following:
   a  internal validity and external validity
   b  pre-experimental design and quasi-experimental design
   c  history and maturation
   d  random sampling, randomization and matching
   e  active factors and blocking factors
   f  environmental variables and extraneous variables.
2  Compare the advantages of experiments with the advantages of survey and observational methods.
3  Why would a noted business researcher say, 'It is essential that we always keep in mind the model of the controlled experiment, even if in practice we have to deviate from an ideal model'?
4  What ethical problems do you see in conducting experiments with human subjects?
5  What essential characteristics distinguish a true experiment from other experimental research designs?

## Making research decisions

6  A lighting company seeks to study the percentage of defective glass shells being manufactured. Theoretically, the percentage of defectives is dependent on temperature, humidity and the level of artisan expertise. Complete historical data are available for the following variables on a daily basis for a year:

a temperature (high, normal, low)

b humidity (high, normal, low)

c artisan expertise level (expert, average, mediocre).

Some experts feel that defectives also depend on production supervisors. However, data on supervisors in charge are available for only 242 of the 365 days. How should this study be conducted?

7 Suppose you want to investigate whether groups are more effective in generating ideas than the same number of people working independently. Thus, is it in terms of idea generation more effective to ask six people to brainstorm for 45 minutes or to ask six people to take 45 minutes to generate ideas individually? Describe how you would operationalize variables for an experiment investigating this research question.

8 You are asked to develop an experiment for a study of the effect that compensation has on the response rates secured from personal interview subjects. This study will involve 300 people, who will be assigned to one of the following conditions: (i) no compensation, (ii) €1 compensation and (iii) €3 compensation. A number of sensitive issues will be explored concerning various social problems, and the 300 people will be drawn from the adult population. Describe how your design would be set up if it were (a) a completely randomized design, (b) a randomized block design, (c) a Latin square and (d) a factorial design (suggest another active variable to use). Which would you use? Why?

9 What type of experimental design would you recommend in each of the following cases? Suggest in some detail how you would design each study.

a A test of three methods of compensation of factory workers. The methods are hourly wage, incentive pay and weekly salary. The dependent variable is direct labour cost per unit of output.

b A study of the effects of various levels of advertising effort and price reduction on the sale of specific branded grocery products by a retail grocery chain.

c A study to determine whether it is true that the use of fast-paced music played over a store's public address system will speed up the shopping rate of customers without an adverse effect on the amount spent per customer.

d A study investigating to what extend the terrorist attacks in New York and Washington on 11 September 2001 and Madrid on 11 March 2004 have affected the stock market.

## From concept to practice

10 Using Exhibit 11.2, diagram an experiment described in one of the Snapshots featured in this chapter using research design symbols.

11 For experiments and surveys on the web, visit http://www.psych.upenn.edu/links.html#webexpts and participate in an online experiment. Prepare a short paper describing your experience and make suggestions for improving the experimental design.

## Classroom discussion

12 Discuss the practice relevance of results obtained from experimental studies. How large is the trade-off between controlled conditions and a good representation of real-life situations?

**Online**
*Learning* **Centre**

## Get started with understanding statistical techniques!

When you have read this chapter, log on to the Online Learning Centre website at
*www.mcgraw-hill.co.uk/textbooks/blumberg* to explore chapter-by-chapter test questions, additional
case studies, a glossary and more online study tools for Business Research Methods.

## Notes

[1] As we will see later, in quasi-experiments it is often not the researcher who intervenes, rather he or she frames an existing situation as an experiment and defines the occurrence of an event as intervention.

[2] Bibb Latane and J.M. Darley, *The Unresponsive Bystander: Why Doesn't He Help?* New York: Appleton-Century-Crofts, 1970, pp. 69–77. Research into the responses of bystanders who witness crimes was stimulated by an incident in New York City where Kitty Genovese was attacked and killed in the presence of 38 witnesses who refused to come to her aid or summon the authorities.

[3] This section is largely adapted from Julian L. Simon and Paul Burstein, *Basic Research Methods in Social Science* (3rd edn.). New York: Random House, 1985, pp. 128–33.

[4] For a thorough explanation of this topic, see Helena C. Kraemer and Sue Thiemann, *How Many Subjects? Statistical Power Analysis in Research.* Beverly Hills, CA: Sage, 1987.

[5] Kenneth D. Bailey, *Methods of Social Research* (2nd edn.). New York: Free Press, 1982, pp. 230–33.

[6] The concept of a quota matrix and the tabular form for Exhibit 9.1 were adapted from Earl R. Babbie, *The Practice of Social Research* (5th edn.). Belmont, CA: Wadsworth, 1989, pp. 218–19.

[7] Donald T. Campbell and Julian C. Stanley, *Experimental and Quasi-experimental Designs for Research.* Chicago: Rand McNally, 1963, p. 5.

[8] Thomas D. Cook and Donald T. Campbell, 'The design and conduct of quasi-experiments and true experiments in field settings', in Marvin D. Dunnette (ed.), *Handbook of Industrial and Organizational Psychology.* Chicago: Rand McNally, 1976, p. 223.

[9] For more information on factorial surveys see Rossi, P.H. and S.L. Nock (eds.), *Measuring Social Judgments: The Factorial Survey Approach.* Beverly Hills, CA: Sage, 1982.

[10] See Rooks, G., Raub, W., Selten, R. and Tazelaar, F., 'How inter-firm cooperation depends on social embeddedness: a vignette study', *Acta Sociologica* 43 (2000), 123–37.

[11] For an in-depth discussion of many quasi-experiment designs and their internal validity, see ibid., pp. 246–98.

[12] The hypothetical example used here is based on an idea presented in Campbell and Stanley, Chapter 7. For more detailed information, students interested in quasi-experimental designs are referred to this source and other publications by Campbell and Stanley.

[13] William J. Paul, Jr., Keith B. Robertson and Frederick Herzberg, 'Job enrichment pays off', *Harvard Business Review* (March–April 1969), pp. 61–78.

[14] Frederick J. Herzberg, 'One more time: how do you motivate employees?' *Harvard Business Review* (January–February 1968), pp. 53–62.

# Recommended further reading

Campbell, Donald T. and Russo, M. Jean, *Social Experimentation.* Thousand Oaks, CA: Sage, 1998. The evolution of the late Professor Campbell's thinking on validity control in experimental design.

Campbell, Donald T. and Stanley, Julian C., *Experimental and Quasi-experimental Designs for Research.* Chicago: Rand McNally, 1963. A universally quoted discussion of experimental designs in the social sciences.

Cook, Thomas D. and Campbell, Donald T., 'The design and conduct of quasi-experiments and true experiments in field settings', in Marvin D. Dunnette and Leaetta M. Hough (eds.), *Handbook of Industrial and Organizational Psychology* (2nd edn.). Palo Alto, CA: Consulting Psychologists Press, 1990; and *Quasi-Experimentation: Design and Analysis Issues for Field Settings.* Chicago: Rand McNally, 1979. Major authoritative works on both true and quasi-experiments and their design. Already classic references.

Green, Paul E., Tull, Donald S. and Albaum, Gerald, *Research for Marketing Decisions* (6th edn.). Englewood Cliffs, NJ: Prentice-Hall, 1991. A definitive text with sections on the application of experimentation to marketing research.

Greenberg, Jerald and Tomlinson, Edward C., 'Situated experiments in organizations: transplanting the lab to the field', *Journal of Management* 30(5), 2004, pp. 702–24. The article discusses the strengths and weaknesses of laboratory and field experiments, and explains a mixed form combining the strengths of the lab with those of the field.

Kagel, John and Roth, Alvin (eds.), *Handbook of Experimental Economics.* Princeton, NJ: Princeton University Press, 1998. A collection of essays reflecting all areas where experimental research plays a prominent role in economic research.

Kirk, Roger E., *Experimental Design: Procedures for the Behavioral Sciences* (3rd edn.). Belmont, CA: Brooks/Cole, 1994. An advanced text on the statistical aspects of experimental design.

Shadish, William R., Cook, Thomas D. and Campbell, Donald T., *Experimental and Quasi-experimental Designs for Generalised Causal Inference.* Willmington, MA: Houghton Mifflin, 2001. A completely rewritten version of the best-selling 1979 edition, with more emphasis on design issues than on data analysis and statistics.

Shaughnessy, John J., Zechmeister, Eugene B. and Zechmeister, Jeanne S., *Research Methods in Psychology* (6th edn.). New York: McGraw-Hill, 2003. Parts III and IV of the book offer a broad coverage of issues related to experimental designs, conducting experiments as well as quasi-experiments.

## Spotlight on research 4

## A job-enrichment quasi-experiment[13]

One theory of job attitudes holds that 'hygiene factors' – which include working conditions, pay, security, status, interpersonal relationships and company policy – can be a major source of dissatisfaction among workers, but have little positive motivational power. This theory says that the positive motivator factors are intrinsic to the job; they include achievement, recognition for achievement, the work itself, responsibility, and growth or advancement.[14]

A study of the value of job enrichment as a builder of job satisfaction was carried out with laboratory technicians, or 'experimental officers' (EOs), at British Chemical. The project was a multiple-group time-series quasi-experiment.

Two sections of the department acted as experimental groups and two acted as control groups. It is not clear how these groups were chosen, but there was no mention of random assignment. One of the experimental groups and one of the control groups worked closely together, while the other two groups were separated geographically and were engaged in different research. Hygiene factors were held constant during the research, and the studies were kept confidential to avoid the tendency of participants to act in artificial ways.

A before-measurement was made using a job reaction survey instrument. This indicated that the EOs typically had low morale, and many wrote of their frustrations. All EOs were asked to write monthly progress reports, and these were used to assess the quality of their work. The assessment was made against eight specifically defined criteria by a panel of three managers who were not members of the department. These assessors were never told which laboratory technicians were in the experimental group and which were in the control group.

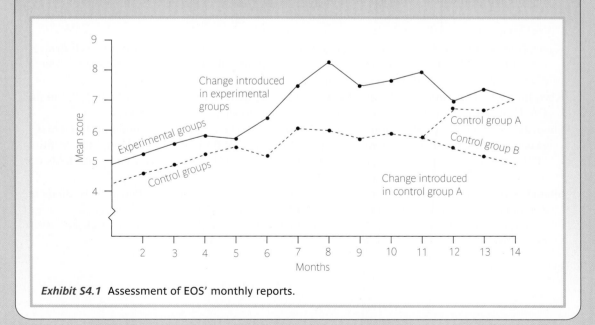

*Exhibit S4.1* Assessment of EOS' monthly reports.

The study extended over a year, with the treatments introduced in the experimental groups at the start of the 12-month study period. Changes were made to give experimental group EOs important chances for achievement; these changes also made the work more challenging. Recognition of achievement was given, authority over certain aspects was increased, new managerial responsibilities were assigned to the senior EOs, added advancements were given to others, and the opportunity for self-initiated work was provided. After about six months, these same changes were instituted with one of the control groups, while the remaining group continued for the entire period as a control. Several months of EO progress reports were available as a prior base line for evaluation. The results of this project are shown in Exhibit S4.1

# PART 3

# Research instruments

## Part contents

# 12.1 The nature of measurement

In everyday usage, **measurement** occurs when an established yardstick verifies the height, weight or another feature of a physical object. How well you like a song, a painting or the personality of a friend is also a measurement. In a dictionary-definition sense, to measure is to discover the extent, dimensions, quantity or capacity of something, especially by comparison with a standard. We measure casually in daily life, but in research the requirements for measurement are rigorous. Measurement in research consists of assigning numbers to empirical events in compliance with a set of rules. This definition implies that measurement is a three-part process:

1 selecting observable empirical events

2 developing a set of mapping rules – a scheme for assigning numbers or symbols to represent aspects of the event being measured

3 applying the mapping rule(s) to each observation of that event.[1]

Assume you are studying people who attend a car show where all of the year's new models are on display. You are interested in learning the male-to-female ratio among attendees. You observe those who enter the show area. If a person is female, you record an F; if male, an M. Any other symbols, such as 0 and 1 or # and %, may also be used if you know what group the symbol identifies. Exhibit 12.1 uses this example to illustrate the above components.

Researchers may also wish to measure, say, the desirability of the styling of the new Espace van. With this in mind, they interview a sample of visitors and assign, with a different mapping rule, their opinions to the following scale.

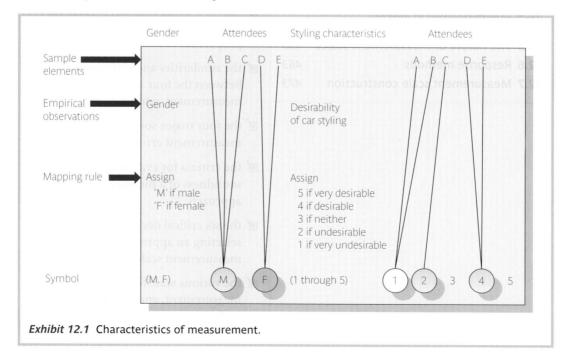

***Exhibit 12.1*** Characteristics of measurement.

What is your opinion of the styling of the Espace van?

Very desirable                    Very undesirable
5     4     3     2     1

All measurement theorists would call the above opinion rating scale a form of measurement, but some would challenge the male/female classification. Their argument is that measurement must involve quantification – that is, 'the assignment of numbers to objects to represent amounts or degrees of a property possessed by all of the objects'.[2] Our discussion endorses the more general view that numbers as symbols within a mapping rule can reflect both qualitative and quantitative concepts. The goal of measurement – indeed, the goal of 'assigning numbers to empirical events in compliance with a set of rules' – is to provide the highest-quality, lowest-error data for testing hypotheses. Researchers deduce from a hypothesis that certain conditions should exist. Then they measure these conditions in the real world. If found, the data lend support to the hypothesis; if not found, researchers conclude the hypothesis is faulty. An important question at this point is 'Just what does one measure?'

## What is measured?

Variables being studied in research may be classified as objects or as properties. **Objects** include the things of ordinary experience, such as tables, people, books and cars. Objects also include things that are not as concrete as these, such as attitudes, opinions and peer-group pressures. **Properties** are the characteristics of the objects. A person's physical properties may be stated in terms of weight, height and posture. Psychological properties include attitudes and intelligence. Social properties include class affiliation, status, number or kind of friends. These and many other properties of an individual can be measured in a research study.

In a literal sense, researchers do not measure either objects or properties. They measure indicants of the properties or indicants of the properties of objects. It is easy to observe that A is taller than B and that C participates more than D in a group process. Or suppose you are analysing members of a sales force of several hundred people to learn what personal properties contribute to sales success. The properties are age, years of experience and number of calls made per week. The indicants in these cases are so accepted that one considers the properties to be observed directly.

In contrast, it is not easy to measure properties like 'motivation to succeed', 'ability to stand stress', 'problem-solving ability' and 'persuasiveness'. Since each property cannot be measured directly, one must infer its presence or absence by observing some indicant or pointer measurement. When you begin to make these inferences, there is often disagreement about how to operationalize the indicants.

Not only is it a challenge to measure such constructs, but a study's quality depends on what measures are selected or developed, and how they fit the circumstances. The nature of measurement scales, sources of error and characteristics of sound measurement are considered next.

## 12.2  Data types

In measuring, one devises a mapping rule and then translates the observation of property indicants using this rule. For each concept or construct, several types of data are possible; the appropriate choice depends on what you assume about the mapping rules. Each data type has its own set of underlying assumptions about how the numerical symbols correspond to real-world observations.

**Mapping rules** have four characteristics as follows.

1  Classification: numbers are used to group or sort responses. No order exists.

2  Order: numbers are ordered and transitivity applies. A is greater than (>), less than (<) or equal to (=) B and if A > B > C, then A is also greater than (>) C.

3  Distance: differences between numbers are ordered. The difference between any pair of numbers is greater than, less than or equal to the difference between any other pair of numbers.

4  Origin: the number series has a unique origin indicated by the number zero.

Combinations of these characteristics of classification, order, distance and origin provide four widely used classification of measurement scales:

1  nominal

2  ordinal

3  interval

4  ratio.

The characteristics of these measurement scales are summarized in Exhibit 12.2. Deciding which data type is appropriate for your research needs should be seen as a process (see Exhibit 12.3).

| Type of data | Characteristics of data | Basic empirical operation | Example |
|---|---|---|---|
| Nominal | Classification but no order, distance or origin | Determination of equality | Gender (male, female) |
| Ordinal | Classification and order but no distance or unique origin | Determination of greater | or lesser value Doneness of meat (well, medium-well, medium-rare, rare) |
| Interval | Classification, order and distance but no unique origin | Determination of equality of intervals or differences | Temperature in degrees |
| Ratio | Classification, order, distance and unique origin | Determination of equality of ratios | Ages in years |

*Exhibit 12.2* Types of data and their measurement characteristics.

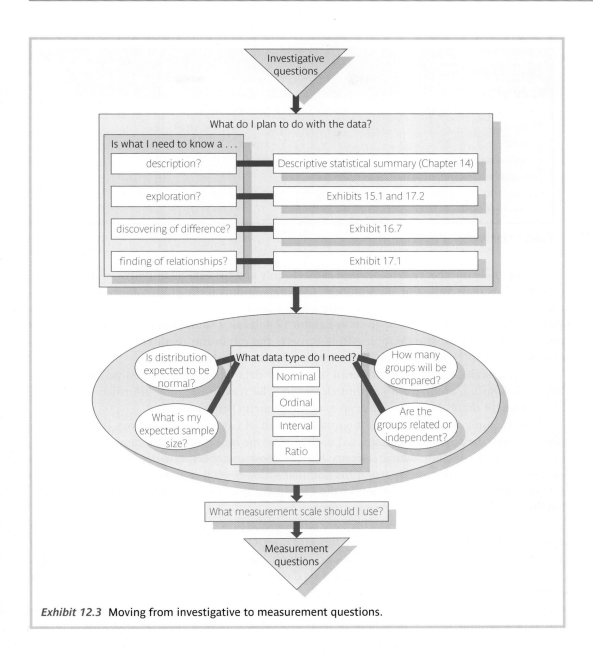

*Exhibit 12.3*  Moving from investigative to measurement questions.

## Nominal data

In business and social science research, **nominal data** are probably quite often collected. With nominal data, you are collecting information on a variable that naturally or by design can be grouped into two or more categories that are mutually exclusive and collectively exhaustive.

The counting of members in each group is the only possible arithmetic operation when a nominal scale is employed. If we use numerical symbols within our mapping rule to identify

| Religious preferences | |
| --- | --- |
| **Mapping Rule A** | **Mapping Rule B** |
| 1 = agriculture and fishing | 1 = manufacturing |
| 2 = utility | 2 = wholesale and retail |
| 3 = food | 3 = service |
| 4 = manufacturing | 4 = other |
| 5 = hotels and restaurant | |
| 6 = transport | |
| 7 = business services | |

*Exhibit 12.4* Mapping rules.

categories, these numbers are recognized as labels only and have no quantitative value. Nominal classifications may consist of any number of separate groups if the groups are mutually exclusive and collectively exhaustive. Thus, one might classify the businesses in a city according to their industry. Mapping Rule A, given in Exhibit 12.4, is not a sound nominal scale because it is not collectively exhaustive. Mapping Rule B meets the minimum requirements, although this classification may be more useful for some research purposes than others.

Nominal scales are the least powerful of the four data types. They suggest no order or distance relationship, and have no arithmetic origin. The scale wastes any information a sample element might share about varying degrees of the property being measured.

Since the only quantification is the number count of cases in each category (the frequency distribution), the researcher is restricted to the use of the mode as the measure of central tendency.[3] You can conclude which category has the most members, but that is all. There is no generally used measure of dispersion for nominal scales. Several tests for statistical significance may be utilized; the most common is the chi-square test. For measures of association, phi, lambda or other measures may be appropriate.

While nominal data are weak, they are still useful. If no other scale can be used, one can almost always classify one set of properties into a set of equivalent classes. Nominal measures are especially valuable in exploratory work where the objective is to uncover relationships rather than secure precise measurements. This data type is also widely used in survey and other *ex-post facto* research when data are classified by major sub-groups of the population. Classifications such as participants' marital status, gender, political persuasion or exposure to a certain experience abound. Cross-tabulations of these and other variables provide insight into important data patterns. Researchers often classify their objects into nominal categories and (implicitly) assume that a category reflects certain characteristics that can at least be interpreted as ordinal. An example will serve to illustrate this.

Suppose you investigate customer loyalty to a specific bank and you discover that customers living in a rural area are less likely to switch to another bank than customers living in cities. Interpretations of this result are that competition between banks in rural areas is lower and, consequently, customers have fewer banks to choose from, or that people living in rural areas have a stronger attitude to maintaining existing relationships and are more reluctant to make any changes. Both interpretations seem reasonable and additional research may indeed reveal that competition among banks is lower in rural areas and that the attitudes of rural people differ from those of city people. Strictly speaking, though, both interpretations are not backed up by data and it would be necessary to measure the competition in the specific regions, for example the number of banks operating there, or a direct measurement of the respondent's openness to change using a psychological scale. Interpreting the nominal scale 'rural and city' as an ordered scale is questionable, because not every rural area is characterized by low competition between banks and because not every rural resident has a high resistance to change.

Sometimes, however, interpreting a nominal scale as an ordinal scale can be reasonable. Suppose you divide a group of employees into those with a university degree and those without. The statement that the former group has gained a higher education is very reasonable, because the nominal categorization is basically derived from the construct 'educational level' or 'years of schooling'.

## Ordinal data

**Ordinal data** include the characteristics of the nominal scale plus an indicator of order. Ordinal data are possible if the transitivity postulate is fulfilled. This postulate states that 'if a is greater than b and b is greater than c, then a is greater than c'.[4] The use of an ordinal scale implies a statement of 'greater than' or 'less than' (an equality statement is also acceptable) without stating *how much* greater or less. While ordinal measurement speaks of 'greater than' and 'less than' measurements, other descriptors may be used – 'superior to', 'happier than', 'poorer than' or 'above'. Like a rubber yardstick, this can stretch varying amounts at different places along its length. Thus, the difference between ranks 1 and 2 on a happiness scale may be larger or smaller than the difference between ranks 2 and 3.

An ordinal concept can be generalized beyond the three cases used in the simple illustration of a > b > c. Any number of cases can be ranked.

A third extension of the ordinal concept occurs when more than one property is of interest. We may, for example, ask a taster to rank varieties of wine in terms of acid, flavour, colour and a combination of these characteristics. We can secure the combined ranking either by asking the participant to base his or her ranking on the combination of properties or by constructing a combination ranking of the individual rankings on each property. To develop this overall index, the researcher typically adds and averages ranks for each of the three properties. This procedure is technically incorrect for ordinal data and, especially for a given participant, may yield misleading results. When the number of participants is large, however, these errors average out. A more sophisticated way of combining a number of dimensions into a total index is to use a multidimensional scale (see Chapter 18).

The researcher faces another difficulty when combining the rankings of several participants. Here again, it is not uncommon to use weighted sums of rank values for a combined index. If there are many observations, this approach will probably give adequate results, though it is not theoretically correct. A better way is to convert ordinal data into **interval data**, the values of which can then be added and averaged. One well-known example is Thurstone's Law of Comparative Judgement.[5] In its simplest form, Thurstone's procedure says that the distance between scale positions of two objects, A and B, depends on the percentage of judgements in which A is preferred to B.

Examples of ordinal data include opinion and preference scales. Because the numbers of such scales have only a rank meaning, the appropriate measure of central tendency is the median. A percentile or quartile measure reveals the dispersion. Correlation is restricted to various rank-order methods. Measures of statistical significance are technically confined to that body of methods known as non-parametric methods.[6]

Researchers in the behavioural sciences differ about whether more powerful parametric significance tests are appropriate with ordinal measures. One position is that this use of parametric tests is incorrect on both theoretical and practical grounds:

> If the measurement is weaker than that of an interval scale, by using parametric methods tests the researcher would 'add information' and thereby create distortions.[7]

At the other extreme, some behavioural scientists argue that parametric tests are usually acceptable for ordinal data:

> The differences between parametric and rank-order tests were not great insofar as significance level and power were concerned.[8]

A view between these extremes recognizes that there are risks in using parametric procedures on ordinal data, but these risks are usually not great:

> The best procedure would seem to be to treat ordinal measurements as though they were interval measurements but to be constantly alert to the possibility of gross inequality of intervals.[9]

Because non-parametric tests are abundant, simple to calculate, have good power efficiencies and do not force the researcher to accept the assumptions of parametric testing, we advise their use with nominal and ordinal data. It is understandable, however, that because parametric tests (such as the t-test or analysis of variance) are so versatile, accepted and understood, they will continue to be used with ordinal data when those data approach interval data characteristics.

## Interval data

Interval data have the power of nominal and ordinal data plus one additional strength: they incorporate the concept of equality of interval (the distance between 1 and 2 equals the distance between 2 and 3). Calendar time is one such scale. For example, the elapsed time between 3 and 6 a.m. equals the time between 4 and 7 a.m. One cannot say, however, that 6 a.m. is twice as late as 3 a.m., because 'zero time' is an arbitrary origin. Centigrade and Fahrenheit temperature scales are other examples of classical interval scales. Both have an arbitrarily determined zero point. Many attitude scales are presumed to be interval. Thurstone's differential scale was an early effort to develop such a scale.[10] Users also treat intelligence scores, semantic differential scales and many other multipoint graphical scales as interval.

When a scale is interval, you use the arithmetic mean as the measure of central tendency. You can compute the average time of first arrival of trucks at a warehouse or the average attitude value on an election for union workers versus non-union workers. The standard deviation is the measure of dispersion for arrival times or worker opinions. Product moment correlation, t-tests, F-tests and other parametric tests are the statistical procedures of choice.[11]

When the distribution of scores computed from interval data lean in one direction or the other (skewed right or left), we use the median as the measure of central tendency and the interquartile range as the measure of dispersion. The reasons for this are discussed in Chapter 14.

## Ratio data

Ratio data incorporate all the powers of the previous data types plus the provision for absolute zero or origin. Ratio data represent the actual amounts of a variable. Measures of physical dimensions such as weight, height, distance and area are examples. In the behavioural sciences, few situations satisfy the requirements of the ratio scale – the area of psychophysics offering some exceptions. In business research, we find ratio scales in many areas. There are money values, population counts, distances, return rates, productivity rates and amounts of time in a time-period sense.

All statistical techniques mentioned up to this point are usable with ratio scales. Other manipulations carried out with real numbers may be done with ratio-scale values. Thus, multiplication and division can be used with this scale but not with the others mentioned. Geometric and harmonic means are measures of central tendency, and coefficients of variation may also be calculated.

Researchers often encounter the problem of evaluating variables that have been measured at different data levels. The gender of an accountant is a nominal, dichotomous variable, and salary is a ratio variable. Certain statistical techniques require the measurement levels to be the same.

Since the nominal variable does not have the characteristics of order, distance or point of origin, we cannot create them artificially after the fact. The ratio-based salary variable, on the other hand, can be reduced. Rescaling salary downwards into high-low, high-medium-low or another set of categories simplifies the comparison of nominal data. This example may be generalized to other measurement situations – that is, converting or rescaling a variable involves reducing the measure from the more powerful and robust level to a lesser one.[12] The loss of measurement power accompanying this decision is sometimes costly in that only non-parametric statistics can then be used in data analysis. Thus, the design of the measurement questions should anticipate such problems and avoid them where possible.

## 12.3  Sources of measurement differences

The ideal study should be designed and controlled for precise and unambiguous measurement of the variables. Since 100 per cent control is unattainable, error does occur. Much potential error is systematic (results from a bias) while the remainder is random (occurs erratically). One authority has pointed out several sources from which measured differences can come.[13]

Assume you are conducting an *ex-post facto* study of the residents of a major city. The study concerns the Prince Corporation, a large manufacturer with its headquarters and several major plants located in the city. The objective of the study is to discover the public's opinions about the company and the origin of any generally held adverse opinions.

# Error sources

Ideally, any variation of scores among the participants would reflect true differences in their opinions about the company. Attitudes towards the firm as an employer, as an ecologically sensitive organization or as a progressive corporate citizen would be expressed accurately. However, four major error sources may contaminate the results:

1 participant

2 situational factors

3 measurer

4 data-collection instrument.

We now look at each of these in turn.

## *Participant*

Opinion differences that affect measurement come from relatively stable characteristics of the participant. Typical of these are employee status, ethnic group membership, social class and nearness to plants. The skilled researcher will anticipate many of these dimensions, adjusting the design to eliminate, neutralize or otherwise deal with them. However, even the skilled researcher may not be as aware of less obvious dimensions. The latter variety might be a trau-matic experience a given participant had with the Prince Corporation or its personnel. Participants may be reluctant to express strong negative (or positive) feelings, or opinions that they perceive as being different from those of others, or they may have little knowledge about Prince but be reluctant to admit this ignorance. This reluctance can lead to an interview of 'guesses'.

Participants may also suffer from temporary factors like fatigue, boredom, anxiety or other distractions; these limit the ability to respond accurately and fully. Hunger, impatience or general variations in mood may also have an impact.

## *Situational factors*

These potential problem areas are legion. Any condition that places a strain on the interview or measurement session can have a serious effect on the interviewer–participant rapport. If another person is present, that person can distort responses by joining in, by distracting or merely by their very presence. If the participants believe anonymity is not guaranteed, they may be reluctant to express certain feelings. Curbside or intercept interviews are unlikely to elicit elaborate responses, while in-home interviews do so more often.

## *Measurer*

The interviewer can distort responses by rewording, paraphrasing or reordering questions. Stereotypes in appearance and action introduce bias. Inflections of voice and conscious or unconscious prompting with smiles, nods, and so on, may encourage or discourage certain replies. Careless mechanical processing – checking the wrong response or failure to record full replies – will obviously distort findings. In the data analysis stage, incorrect coding, careless tab-ulation and faulty statistical calculation may introduce further errors.

### *Data-collection instrument*

A defective instrument can cause distortion in two major ways. First, it can be too confusing and ambiguous. The use of complex words and syntax beyond participant comprehension is typical. Leading questions, ambiguous meanings, mechanical defects (inadequate space for replies, response choice omissions, poor printing, etc.), and multiple questions suggest the range of problems.

A more elusive type of instrument deficiency is poor selection from the universe of content items. Seldom does the instrument explore all the potentially important issues. The Prince Corporation study might treat company image in areas of employment and ecology but omit the company management's civic leadership, its support of local education programmes or its position on minority issues. Even if the general issues are studied, the questions may not cover enough aspects of each area of concern. While we might study the Prince Corporation's image as an employer in terms of salary and wage scales, promotion opportunities and work stability, perhaps such topics as working conditions, company management relations with organized labour, and retirement and other benefit programmes should also be included.

## 12.4  Characteristics of sound measurement

What are the characteristics of a good measurement tool? An intuitive answer to this question is that the tool should be an accurate counter or indicator of what we are interested in measuring. In addition, it should be easy and efficient to use. There are three major criteria for evaluating a measurement tool: validity, reliability and practicality.

- Validity refers to the extent to which a test measures what we actually wish to measure.
- Reliability has to do with the accuracy and precision of a measurement procedure.
- Practicality is concerned with a wide range of factors of economy, convenience and interpretability.[14]

In the following sections, we discuss the nature of these qualities and how researchers can achieve them in their measurement procedures.

## Validity

Many forms of **validity** are mentioned in the research literature, and the number grows as we expand the concern for more scientific measurement. This text features two major forms: external and internal validity.[15] The external validity of research findings refers to the data's ability to be generalized across persons, settings and times; we discussed this in reference to sampling in Chapter 6, and more will be discussed about this in Chapter 13.[16] In this chapter, we discuss only the internal validity of measurements. Hence, internal validity is further limited in this discussion to the ability of a research instrument to measure what it is purported to measure. Does the instrument really measure what its designer claims it does?

Validity in this context is the extent to which differences found with a measuring tool reflect true differences among participants being tested. We want the measurement tool to be sensitive to all the nuances of meaning in the variable and to changes in nuances of meaning over time.

# Measuring attitudes to copyright infringement

In the midst of the Napster file-swapping controversy, and in connection with an issue centring on privacy issues, the editors of *American Demographics* hired TNS Intersearch to conduct a study of adults regarding their behaviour and attitudes relating to copyright infringement. The survey instrument for the telephone study asked 1051 adult respondents several questions about activities that might or might not be considered copyright infringement. The lead question asked about specific copyright-related activities:

Do you know someone who has done or tried to do any of the following?

1  Copying software not licensed for personal use.
2  Copying a prerecorded videocassette such as a rental or purchased video.
3  Copying a prerecorded audiocassette or compact disc.
4  Downloading music free of charge from the Internet.
5  Photocopying pages from a book or magazine.

A subsequent question asked respondents, 'In the future, do you think that the amount of (ACTIVITY) will increase, decrease or stay the same?' Each respondent was also asked to select a phrase from a list of four 'that best describes how you feel about (ACTIVITY)', and to select a phrase from a list of four phrases that 'best describes what you think may happen as a result of (ACTIVITY)'. The last content question asked the degree to which respondents would feel favourably towards a company that provided 'some type of media content for free': more favourable, less favourable or 'it wouldn't impact your impression of the company'.

As you might expect, younger adults had different behaviours and attitudes compared to older adults on some indicants.

What measurement issues were involved in this study?

## References and further reading

**Data tabulation generated by TaylorNelson Sofres Intersearch.**
**John Fetto, 'Americans voice their opinions on intellectual property rights violations'**, *American Demographics*, September 2000, p. 8.
**Measurement instrument prepared by TaylorNelson Sofres Intersearch.**
**www.americandemographics.com**
**www.intersearch.tnsofres.com**

The difficulty in meeting the test of validity is that usually one does not know what the true differences are. Without direct knowledge of the dimension being studied, you must face the question, 'How can one discover validity without directly confirming knowledge?' A quick answer is to seek other relevant evidence that confirms the answers found with the measurement device, but this leads to a second question: 'What constitutes relevant evidence?' There is no short answer this time. What is relevant depends on the nature of the research problem and the researcher's judgement. One way to approach this question is to organize the answer according

| Type | What is measured | Methods |
|---|---|---|
| Content | Degree to which the content of the items adequately represents the universe of all relevant items under study | Judgemental or panel evaluation with content validity ratio |
| Criterion-related | Degree to which the predictor is adequate in capturing the relevant aspects of the criterion | Correlation |
| Concurrent | Description of the present; criterion data are available at the same time as predictor scores | |
| Predictive | Prediction of the future; criterion data are measured after the passage of time | |
| Construct | Answers the question, 'What accounts for the variance in the measure?' | Judgemental correlation of proposed test with established ones |
| | Attempts to identify the underlying construct(s) being measured and determine how well the test represents it (them) | Convergent-discriminant techniques |

Exhibit 12.5 Summary of validity estimates.

to measure-relevant types. One widely accepted classification consists of three major forms of validity (see Exhibit 12.5):

1  content validity
2  criterion-related validity
3  construct validity.[17]

We now look at each of these in turn.

## Content validity

The **content validity** of a measuring instrument (the composite of measurement scales) is the extent to which it provides adequate coverage of the investigative questions guiding the study. If the instrument contains a representative sample of the universe of subject matter of interest, then content validity is good. To evaluate the content validity of an instrument, one must first agree on what elements constitute adequate coverage. Let us use an example: suppose you are interested in the question, 'How ethical are managers?' We must decide what behaviours, attitudes and opinions are relevant to the measurement of ethics, that is which topics cover managers' ethics. One could limit the topics to issues corresponding to legal offences, such as falsifying documents or using insider information. one could also include actions that are not legal offences but considered 'wrong', such as intentionally gossiping or taking advantage of legal holes. If the data-collection instrument adequately covers the topics that have been defined as the relevant dimensions, we conclude that the instrument has good content validity.

Determination of content validity is judgemental and can be approached in several ways. First, the designer may determine it through a careful definition of the topic of concern, the items to be scaled and the scales to be used. This logical process is often intuitive and unique to each research designer.

A second way to determine content validity is to use a panel of people to judge how well the instrument meets the standards. A panel independently assesses the test items for a performance test. It judges each item to be essential, useful but not essential, or not necessary, in assessing performance of a relevant behaviour. The 'essential' responses on each item from each panel list are evaluated by a content validity ratio, and those meeting a statistical significance value are retained. In both informal judgements and in this systematic process, 'content validity is primarily concerned with inferences about test construction rather than inferences about test scores'.[18] It is important not to define content too narrowly. If you were to secure only superficial expressions of opinion in the study of managers' ethics, it would probably not have adequate content coverage.

### Criterion-related validity

**Criterion-related validity** reflects the success of measures used for prediction or estimation. You may want to predict an outcome or estimate the existence of a current behaviour or condition. These are predictive and concurrent validity, respectively. They differ only in a time perspective. An opinion questionnaire that correctly forecasts the outcome of a union election has predictive validity. An observational method that correctly categorizes families by current income class has concurrent validity. While these examples appear to have simple and unambiguous validity criteria, there are difficulties in estimating validity. Consider the problem of estimating family income. There clearly is a knowable true income for every family. However, we may find it difficult to secure this figure, because next to wage incomes the family income can also consist of income from capital or other irregular income streams, such as profits from incidental sales on eBay, for instance. Respondents are more likely to forget reporting such smaller and less frequent parts of their income. Thus, while the criterion is conceptually clear, it may be unavailable.

In other cases, there may be several criteria, none of which are completely satisfactory. Consider again the problem of judging success among the sales force at SalePro (which we looked at in Chapter 2). A researcher may want to develop a pre-employment test that will predict sales success. There may be several possible criteria, none of which individually tells the full story. Total sales per salesperson may not adequately reflect territory market potential, competitive conditions or the different profitability rates of various products. One might rely on the sales manager's overall evaluation, but how unbiased and accurate are those impressions? The researcher must ensure that the validity criterion used is itself 'valid'. One source suggests that any criterion measure must be judged in terms of four qualities:

1 relevance
2 freedom from bias
3 reliability
4 availability.[19]

A criterion is relevant if it is defined and scored in the terms we judge to be the proper measures of salesperson success. If you believe sales success is adequately measured by monetary sales volume achieved per year, then it is the relevant criterion. If you believe success should include a high level of penetration of large accounts, then sales volume alone is not fully relevant. In making this decision, you must rely on your judgement in deciding what partial criteria are appropriate indicants of salesperson success.

Freedom from bias is attained when the criterion gives each salesperson an equal opportunity to score well. The sales criterion would be biased if it did not show adjustments for differences in territory potential and competitive conditions.

A reliable criterion is stable or reproducible. An erratic criterion (using monthly sales, which are highly variable from month to month) can hardly be considered a reliable standard by which to judge performance on a sales employment test. Yet if an unreliable criterion is the only one available, it is often chosen for the study's purpose. In such a case, it is possible to use a 'correction for attenuation' formula that lets you see what the correlation between the test and the criterion would be if they were made perfectly reliable.[20]

Finally, the information specified by the criterion must be available. If it is not available, how much will it cost to access it and how difficult will it be to secure? The amount of money and effort that should be spent on development of a criterion depends on the importance of the problem for which the test is used.

Once there are test and criterion scores, they must be compared in some way. The usual approach is to correlate them. For example, you might correlate test scores of 40 new salespeople with first-year sales achievements adjusted to reflect differences in territorial selling conditions.

### Construct validity

One may also wish to measure or infer the presence of abstract characteristics for which no empirical validation seems possible. Attitude scales, and aptitude and personality tests generally concern concepts that fall into this category. Although this situation is much more difficult, some assurance is still needed that the measurement has an acceptable degree of validity.

In attempting to evaluate **construct validity**, we consider both the theory and the measuring instrument being used. If we were interested in measuring the effect of ceremony on organizational culture, the way in which 'ceremony' was operationally defined would have to correspond to an empirically grounded theory. Once assured that the construct was meaningful in a theoretical sense, we would next investigate the adequacy of the instrument. If a known measure of ceremony in organizational culture was available, we might correlate the results obtained using this measure with those derived from our new instrument. Such an approach would provide us with preliminary indications of convergent validity.

Returning to our example above, another method of validating the ceremony construct would be to separate it from other constructs in the theory or related theories. To the extent that ceremony could be separated from stories or symbols, we would have completed the first steps towards discriminant validity. Established statistical tools such as factor analysis and multitrait–multimethod analysis help determine the construct adequacy of a measuring device.[21]

In the Prince Corporation study, you may be interested in securing a judgement of 'how good a citizen' the firm is. Variations in participant ratings may be drastically affected if substantial differences exist among the participants regarding what constitutes proper corporate citizenship. One participant may believe that any company is an economic organization designed to make profits for its stockholders. She sees a relatively little role for corporations in the wide-ranging social issues of the day. At the other end of the continuum, another participant views the corporation as a leader in solving social problems, even at the expense of profits.

Both of these participants might understand Prince's role in the community but judge it quite differently in light of their differing views about what its role should be. If these different views were held, you would theorize that other information about these participants would be logically compatible with their judgements. You might expect the first participant to oppose high corporate taxes, to be critical of increased involvement of government in family affairs, and to believe that a corporation's major responsibility is to its stockholders. The second participant would be more likely to favour high corporate income taxes, to opt for more governmental involvement in daily life, and to believe that a corporation's major responsibility is a social one.

Participants may not be consistent on all questions because the measurements may be crude and the 'theory' may be deficient. When hypothesized tests do not confirm the measurement scale, you are faced with a two-sided question: 'Is your measurement instrument invalid or is your theory invalid?' These answers require more information or the exercise of judgement.

We discuss the three forms of validity separately, but they are interrelated, both theoretically and operationally. Predictive validity is important for a test designed to predict employee success. In developing such a test, you would probably first postulate the factors (constructs) that provide the basis for useful prediction. For example, you would advance a theory about the variable in employee success – an area for construct validity. Finally, in developing the specific items for inclusion in the success prediction test, you would be concerned with how well the specific items sample the full range of each construct (a matter of content validity).

In the corporate image study for the Prince Corporation, both content and construct validity considerations have been discussed, but what about criterion-related validity? The criteria are less obvious than in the employee success prediction, but judgements will be made of the quality of evidence about the company's image. The criteria used may be both subjective – 'Does the evidence agree with what we believe?' – and objective – 'Does the evidence agree with other research findings?'

Looking at Exhibit 12.6, we can approach the concepts of validity and reliability by using an archer's bow and target as an analogy. High reliability means that repeated arrows shot from the same bow would hit the target in essentially the same place – although not necessarily the intended place (first row of the graphic). If we had a bow with high validity as well, then every arrow would hit the bull's-eye (upper-left panel). If reliability is low or decreases for some reason, arrows would be more scattered (lacking similarity or closeness, like those shown in the second row).

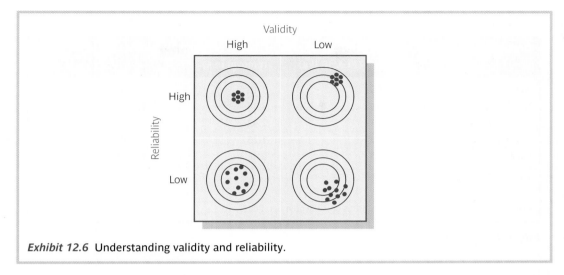

*Exhibit 12.6* Understanding validity and reliability.

High validity means that the bow would shoot true every time. It would not pull to the right or send an arrow careening into the woods. Arrows shot from a high-validity bow will be clustered around a central point (the bull's-eye), even when they are dispersed by reduced reliability (first column of the graphic). We wouldn't hit the bull's-eye we were aiming at because the low-validity bow – like the flawed data-collection instrument – would not perform as planned. When low validity is compounded by low reliability, the pattern of arrows is not only off bull's-eye but is also dispersed (lower-right panel).

# Footprint prices

That carbon dioxide is one of the main causes for global warming is now a fact rather than a suspicion. Most scientists agree that carbon dioxide is causing global warming. Carbon dioxide is always emitted if we use fossil-based fuel, such as oil and gas, to generate energy for heating, cooling or moving. Every time we use fossil-based fuel we leave a footprint, a carbon footprint, symbolizing the damage to our planet.

How can we measure the size of our footprints and the removal costs. Although air travel accounts for less than 5 per cent of the total carbon dioxide emissions, it has become a primary target for non-profit organizations to increase our awareness that consuming energy has external effects. A possible reason is certainly that kerosene, the fuel aircrafts need, is less taxed, if at all, than fuel for cars. For example, many German petrol stations inform their customers that the tax share of each litre of petrol is 86 per cent, more than for any other goods that individuals purchase. The common rationale for taxing petrol is that riding a car creates external effects (costs) that need to be covered.

Aircraft fuel has not been taxed yet and this raises the question of how to measure the external costs of air travel. Recently, a couple of organizations offered certificates for emitting carbon dioxide to individuals. Thus, everybody can voluntary buy certificates that cover the environmental costs of emitting carbon dioxide. Some airlines, for example British Airways or Air

**Snapshot**

| Organization (website) | Footprint of airtravel LHR-TXL-LHR [kg] | Costs of footprint removal in € | Costs per ton in € |
|---|---|---|---|
| www.terrapass.com | 480 | 3.19 | 6.65 |
| www.co2balance.com.uk | 540 | 7.34 | 13.61 |
| www.carbonify.com | 575 | 2.42 | 4.21 |
| www.conservationfund.org | 520 | 1.25* | 2.40 |
| www.ba.com (climatecare) | 210 | 2.46 | 11.71 |

*Note:*
* without administration costs
Calculations based on accessing the websites on 12 September, 2007.

*Exhibit 12.7* Prices of footprints.

Canada, even offer on their websites links to organizations that sell certificates covering the environmental costs of a flight booked with British Airways or Air Canada. From a methodological point of view, it would be interesting to find out how the carbon dioxide emissions of air travel are measured and furthermore how the costs associated with air travel are determined.

Suppose you live in London and plan a weekend trip to Berlin. You buy a return ticket from London Heathrow (LHR) to Berlin Tegel (TXL) and you want to pay off your carbon footprint. Exhibit 12.7 above shows you how different organizations assess the size of your footprint (in kg of emitted carbon dioxide) and the price they charge to remove that footprint.

What do we see? First, we see that the emission caused by the trip differ for each organization. While British Airways calculates 210 kg of carbon dioxide emissions, all organizations not related to an airline calculate more than double; co2 balance mentions that they have doubled the size of the footprint, because producing the fuel used also requires energy. Although this is true, you might argue that the energy to produce the aircraft fuel is already taxed, that is you have already paid for this part of your footprint.

The next step, transforming emissions to a price, even increases the differences between the certificate's prices.

Do these differences suggest that conservationfund found a more efficient way to remove the footprint? Or more to the point, which organization should you purchase a certificate from to ensure that your footprint of your trip to Berlin has really been removed?

# References and further reading

www.ba.com
www.carbonify.com
www.co2balance.com.uk
www.conservationfund.org
www.terrapass.com

# Reliability

**Reliability** means many things to many people, but in most contexts the notion of consistency emerges. A measure is reliable to the degree that it supplies consistent results. Reliability is a necessary contributor to validity but is not a sufficient condition for validity. The relationship between reliability and validity can be simply illustrated with the use of a bathroom scale. If the scale measures your weight correctly (using a concurrent criterion such as a scale known to be accurate), then it is both reliable and valid. If it consistently overweighs you by six pounds, then the scale is reliable but not valid. If the scale measures erratically from time to time, then it is not reliable and therefore cannot be valid. So if a measurement is not valid, it hardly matters if it is reliable – because it does not measure what the designer needs to measure in order to solve the research problem. In this context, reliability is not as valuable as validity, but it is much easier to assess.

Reliability is concerned with estimates of the degree to which a measurement is free of random or unstable error. Reliable instruments can be used with confidence that transient and situational factors are not interfering. Reliable instruments are robust; they work well at different times under different conditions. This distinction of time and condition is the basis for frequently used perspectives on reliability: stability, equivalence and internal consistency (see Exhibit 12.8).

# Stability

A measure is said to possess **stability** if you can secure consistent results with repeated measurements of the same person with the same instrument. An observational procedure is stable if it gives the same reading on a particular person when repeated one or more times. It is often possible to repeat observations on a subject and to compare them for consistency. When there is much time between measurements, there is a chance for situational factors to change, thereby

| Type | Coefficient | What is measured | Methods |
|------|-------------|------------------|---------|
| Test-retest | Stability | Reliability of a test or instrument inferred from examinee scores. Same test is administered twice to same subjects over an interval of less than six months | Correlation |
| Parallel forms | Equivalence | Degree to which alternative forms of the same measure produce same or similar results. Administered simultaneously or with a delay. Inter-rater estimates of the similarity of judges' observations or scores | Correlation |
| Split-half KR20 alpha | Internal consistency | Degree to which instrument items are homogeneous and reflect the same underlying construct(s) | Specialized correlational formulas |

*Exhibit 12.8* Summary of reliability estimates.

affecting the observations. The change would appear incorrectly as a drop in the reliability of the measurement process.

Stability measurement in survey situations is more difficult and less easily executed than in observational studies. While you can observe a certain action repeatedly, you usually can resurvey only once. This leads to a test-retest arrangement – with comparisons between the two tests to learn how reliable they are. Some of the difficulties that can occur in the test-retest methodology and cause a downward bias in stability include:

- time delays between measurements – leads to situational factor changes (also a problem in observation studies)
- insufficient time between measurements – permits the participant to remember previous answers and repeat them, resulting in biased reliability indicators
- participant's discernment of a disguised purpose – may introduce bias if the respondent holds opinions related to the purpose but not assessed with current measurement questions
- topic sensitivity – occurs when the participant seeks to learn more about the topic, or to form new and different opinions, before the retest
- introduction of extraneous moderating variables between measurements – may result in a change in the participant's opinions from factors unrelated to the research.

A suggested remedy is to extend the interval between test and retest (from two weeks to a month). While this may help, the researcher must be alert to the chance that an outside factor will contaminate the measurement and distort the stability score. Consequently, stability measurement through the test-retest approach has limited applications. More interest has centred on equivalence.

## Equivalence

A second perspective on reliability considers how much error may be introduced by different investigators (in observation) or different samples of items being studied (in questioning or scales). Thus, while stability is concerned with personal and situational fluctuations from one time to another, **equivalence** is concerned with variations at one point in time among observers and samples of items. A good way to test for the equivalence of measurements by different observers is to compare their scoring of the same event. An example of this is the scoring of Olympic figure skaters by a panel of judges.

In studies where a consensus among experts or observers is required, the similarity of the judges' perceptions is sometimes questioned. How does a panel of supervisors render a judgement on image improvements, a new product's packaging or future business trends? Inter-rater reliability may be used in these cases to correlate the observations or scores of the judges and render an index of how consistent their ratings are.

The major interest with equivalence is typically not how participants differ from item to item but how well a given set of items will categorize individuals. There may be many differences in response between two samples of items, but if a person is classified the same way by each test, then the tests have good equivalence. One tests for item sample equivalence by using alternative or parallel forms of the same test administered to the same persons simultaneously.

# Figure skating: a sport on thin ice

Figure skating is among the best-loved events at any Winter Olympics. The (gold) medal winners in the women's single, men's single, mixed pairs and ice dance often become the superstars of the games. In addition, an Olympic medal in figure skating really pays off. Medal winners can easily switch from amateur status to professional, presenting their skills and talents on ice at commercial ice shows, such as *Holiday on Ice*. Such professional ice show contracts pay very well.

Such a background makes figure skating an ideal setting for drama. But to complicate matters further, figure skating lacks by its very nature an objective instrument to measure the athletes' performance. Nine judges determine who wins the competition by casting scores simultaneously (from 0 to 6) on technical performance (weight: one-third) and on presentation (weight: two-thirds).

In 2002, at the Winter Olympics in Salt Lake City, USA, another drama was added to the history of figure skating. The Russian pair, Elena Berezhnaya and Anton Sikharulidze, emerged on to the ice and skated to the classical music piece 'Thais' by Jules Massenet. Although their performance contained several surprising and innovative elements, it also contained six technical errors. Next, Jamie Sale and David Pelletier came on to the ice and skated to the theme from *Love Story*, presenting a programme that was similar to those showcased in two previous international competitions. The judges from Canada, Germany, Japan and the USA usually prefer more 'traditional' presentations and marked the Canadian pair in first place. The judges from China, Poland, Russia and the Ukraine ranked the Russian pair first. The French judge, Marie-Reine La Gougne, had the decisive position and voted for Berezhnaya and Sikharulidze, who were awarded the gold medal. The spectators in the ice hall were outraged and responded to the decision of the judges with whistles and boos.

A few hours later, it was reported that La Gougne had been pressured to vote for the Russian pair by Didier Gailhaguet, president of the French Skating Federation, as part of a 'contra-deal' to secure votes for the French couple, Marina Anissina and Gwendal Peizarat, who were to appear in the ice dance competition. Although La Gougne later recast her vote, a scandal was unavoidable.

At another Winter Olympics 1998 in Nagano, Jean Senf, a Canadian judge, produced audio-taped evidence to prove that he had been approached by Yuri Balkov, a Ukrainian judge, to agree on a similar vote-swapping arrangement. The International Skating Federation took action and immediately suspended La Gougne as a judge and Gailhaguet as a member of the French Skating Federation, and decided that the Salt Lake City gold medal in pairs' figure skating would be awarded jointly to Berezhnaya/Sikharulidze and Sale/Pelletier.

The current system of assessing athletes' performances obviously does not work well at all.

How could the International Skating Federation improve the system?

# References and further reading

Figure skating: a sport on thin ice (at http://www.time.com/time/olympics2002/article0,8599, 203477-2,00).

The results of the two tests are then correlated. Under this condition, the length of the testing process is likely to affect the subjects' responses through fatigue, and the inferred reliability of the parallel form will be reduced accordingly. Some measurement theorists recommend an interval between the two tests to compensate for this problem. This approach, known as delayed equivalent forms, is a composite of test-retest and the equivalence method. As in test-retest, one would administer form X followed by form Y to half the examinees and form Y followed by form X to the other half to prevent 'order-of-presentation' effects.[22]

The researcher can include only a limited number of measurement questions in an instrument. This limitation implies that a sample of measurement questions from a content domain has been chosen and another sample producing a similar number will need to be drawn for the second instrument. It is frequently difficult to create this second set. Yet if the pool is initially large enough, the items may be randomly selected for each instrument. Even with the more sophisticated procedures used by publishers of standardized tests, it is rare to find fully equivalent and interchangeable questions.[23]

## Internal consistency

A third approach to reliability uses only one administration of an instrument or test to assess the **internal consistency** or homogeneity among the items. The split-half technique can be used when the measuring tool has many similar questions or statements to which the subject can respond. The instrument is administered and the results are separated by item into even and odd numbers, or into randomly selected halves. When the two halves are correlated, if the results of the correlation are high the instrument is said to have high reliability in an internal consistency sense. The high correlation tells us that there is similarity (or homogeneity) among the items. The potential for incorrect inferences about high internal consistency exists when the test contains many items, which inflates the correlation index.

The Spearman–Brown correction formula is used to adjust for the effect of test length and to estimate the reliability of the whole test. A problem with this approach is that the way the test is split may influence the internal consistency coefficient. To remedy this, other indexes are used to secure reliability estimates without splitting the test's items. The Kuder–Richardson Formula 20 (KR20) and Cronbach's coefficient alpha are two frequently used examples. Cronbach's alpha has the most utility for multi-item scales at the interval level of measurement. The KR20 is the method from which alpha was generalized and is used to estimate reliability for dichotomous items (see Exhibit 12.7).

## Improving reliability

The researcher can improve reliability by choosing among the following options.

- Minimize external sources of variation.
- Standardize conditions under which measurement occurs.
- Improve investigator consistency by using only well-trained, supervised and motivated persons to conduct the research.
- Broaden the sample of measurement questions used by adding similar questions to the data-collection instrument, or adding more observers or occasions to an observational study.

- Improve internal consistency of an instrument by excluding data from analysis drawn from measurement questions eliciting extreme responses. This approach requires the assumption that a high total score reflects high performance and a low total score, low performance. One selects the extreme scorers – say, the top 20 per cent and bottom 20 per cent – for individual analysis. By this process, you can distinguish those items that differentiate high and low scorers. Items that have little discriminatory power can then be dropped from the test.

## Practicality

The scientific requirements of a project call for the measurement process to be reliable and valid, while the operational requirements call for it to be practical. **Practicality** has been defined as economy, convenience and interpretability.[24] While this definition refers to the development of educational and psychological tests, it is meaningful for business measurements too.

### Economy

Some trade-off usually occurs between the ideal research project and the budget. Instrument length is one area where economic pressures dominate. More items give more reliability, but in the interests of limiting the interview or observation time (and therefore costs), we hold down the number of measurement questions. The choice of data-collection method is also often dictated by economic factors. The rising cost of personal interviewing first led to an increased use of long-distance telephone surveys and, subsequently, to the current rise in online surveys. In standardized tests, the cost of test materials alone can be such a significant expense that it encourages multiple reuse. Add to this the need for fast and economical scoring, and you can see why computer scoring and scanning are attractive.

### Convenience

A measuring device passes the convenience test if it is easy to administer. A questionnaire with a set of detailed but clear instructions, with examples, is easier to complete correctly than one that lacks these features. In a well-prepared study, it is not uncommon for the interviewer instructions to be several times longer than the interview questions. Naturally, the more complex the concepts, the greater the need for clear and complete instructions. We can also make the instrument easier to administer by paying close attention to its design and layout. Crowding of material, poor reproduction of illustrations, and the carry-over of items from one page to the next make completion of the instrument more difficult.

### Interpretability

This aspect of practicality is relevant when persons other than the test designers must interpret the results. It is usually, but not exclusively, an issue with standardized tests. In such cases, the designer of the data-collection instrument provides several key pieces of information to make interpretation possible:

- a statement of the functions the test was designed to measure and the procedures by which it was developed
- detailed instructions for administration

- scoring keys and instructions
- norms for appropriate reference groups
- evidence about reliability
- evidence regarding the inter-correlations of sub-scores
- evidence regarding the relationship of the test to other measures
- guides for test use.

For a more in-depth insight into this topic please see Spotlight on Research 5 at the end of this chapter.

## 12.5 The nature of measurement scales

When you develop measurement questions for your research study, you will often be called upon to choose between standardized scales and custom-designed ones. When what you measure is concrete (e.g. the length of an assembly line), you will usually choose a standardized measure (like measuring the assembly line with an electronic range-finder or tape-measure). When what you want to measure is a more abstract and complex construct (like customer attitudes about a product service programme), standardized measures may neither exist nor provide a close enough fit to a particular manager's scenario. In these situations, developing a customized scale to measure the construct is the only option. Otherwise, you are left to measure a construct with a tool designed for something else. This would be like measuring the length of the assembly line with your forearm instead of visible laser-beam technology.

The remainder of this chapter covers procedures that will help you to understand measurement scales, so that you can select or construct measures that are appropriate to your research. We will concentrate on the problems of measuring more complex constructs, like attitudes and opinions.

### Scaling defined

**Scaling** is a 'procedure for the assignment of numbers (or other symbols) to a property of objects in order to impart some of the characteristics of numbers to the properties in questions'.[25]

### What is scaled?

Procedurally, we assign numbers to indicants of the properties of objects. Thus one assigns a number scale to the various levels of heat and cold, and calls it a thermometer. If you want to measure the temperature of the air, you know that a property of temperature is that its variation leads to an expansion or contraction of mercury. A glass tube with mercury provides an indicant of temperature change by the rise or fall of the mercury in the tube.

In another context, you might devise a scale to measure the durability (property) of paint. You secure a machine with an attached scrub brush that applies a predetermined amount of pressure as it scrubs. You then count the number of brush strokes that it takes to wear through a 10 mm thickness of paint. The scrub count is the indicant of the paint's durability. Or you may judge a person's supervisory capacity (property) by asking a peer group to rate that person on various questions (indicants) that you create.

## Scale selection

Scaling may be reviewed in several ways, but here we cover those approaches that are of greatest value for management research.[26] Selection or construction of a measurement scale requires decisions in six key areas:

1  study objective
2  response form
3  degree of preference
4  data properties
5  number of dimensions
6  scale construction.

We now look at each of these in turn.

### Study objective

Researchers face two general study objectives:

1  to measure certain characteristics of the participants who complete the study
2  to use participants as judges of the objects or indicants presented to them.

Assume you've been contracted by the city of Munch Beach to conduct a study supposedly of voters' approval or disapproval of one or more regulatory programmes. In the first type of study, your scale would measure the voters' political orientation as conservative or liberal. You might combine each person's answers to form an indicator of that person's political orientation. The emphasis in this first study objective is on measuring attitudinal differences among people. With the second study objective, you might use the same data but in this case you are really interested in how satisfied people are with different governmental programmes. In this study objective, your real interest is in the differences in the acceptance level of one or more regulatory programmes.

### Response form

Measurement scales are of three types: rating, ranking and categorization. A rating scale is used when participants score an object or indicant without making a direct comparison to another object or attitude. For example, they may be asked to evaluate the styling of a new car on a five-point rating scale. Ranking scales constrain the study participant to make comparisons among two or more indicants or objects. Participants may be asked to choose which one of a pair of cars has the more attractive styling. They could also be asked to order the importance of comfort, ergonomics, performance and price for the target vehicle. **Categorization** asks participants to put themselves or property indicants in groups or categories. Asking car show participants to identify their gender or ethnic background, or to indicate whether a particular prototype car design would attract a youthful or mature clientele, would require a categorization response strategy.

## Degree of preference

Measurement scales may involve preference measurement or non-preference evaluation. In the former, each participant is asked to choose the object he or she favours or the solution he or she would prefer. In the latter, participants are asked to judge which object has more of some characteristic or which solution takes the most resources, without reflecting any personal preference towards objects or solutions.

## Data properties

Measurement scales may also be viewed in terms of the data properties generated by each scale. Earlier, we saw that data are classified as nominal, ordinal, interval or ratio. The assumptions underlying each data type determine how a particular measurement scale's data can be handled statistically.

## Number of dimensions

Measurement scales are either unidimensional or multidimensional. With a **unidimensional scale**, one seeks to measure only one attribute of the participant or object. One measure of employee potential is promotability. It is a single dimension. Several items may be used to measure this dimension and, by combining them into a single measure, a manager may place employees along a linear continuum of promotability. Multidimensional scaling recognizes that an object might be better described in an attribute space of $n$-dimensions rather than on a unidimensional continuum. The employee promotability variable might be better expressed by three distinct dimensions: managerial performance, technical performance and teamwork.

## Scale construction

We can classify measurement scales by the methods used to build them. Five construction approaches are used in research practice.

1 Arbitrary: a scale is custom-designed to measure a property or indicant.

2 Consensus: judges evaluate the items to be included.

3 Item analysis: measurement scales are tested with a sample of participants.

4 Cumulative: scales are chosen for their conformity to a ranking of items with ascending and descending discriminating power.

5 Factoring: scales are constructed from inter-correlations of items from other studies.[27]

Arbitrary scales may measure the concepts for which they have been designed, but the researcher has no advance evidence of a particular scale's validity and reliability. Nevertheless, researchers commonly choose this construction approach. Consensus scales are developed by a panel of judges, who evaluate the items to be included based on topical relevance and lack of ambiguity.

In item analysis, after administering the test, a total score is calculated for each scale. Individual items (a scale or part of a scale) are then analysed to determine which best discriminate between persons or objects with high total scores and low total scores.

In the cumulative approach, the endorsement of an item that represents an extreme position results in the endorsement of all items of less extreme positions.

Finally, in factoring, common factors account for the relationships. The relationships are measured statistically through factor analysis or cluster analysis.

The business researcher studies both the type of measurement scale and the scale's construction when selecting an appropriate scale. These topics form the basis for the remainder of the chapter.

# 12.6  Response methods

We said that questioning is a widely used stimulus for measuring concepts and constructs. A manager, for example, may be asked his or her views concerning an employee. The response could be 'a good machinist', 'a troublemaker', 'a union activist', 'reliable' or 'a fast worker with a poor record of attendance'. These answers, because they represent such different frames of reference for evaluating the worker, and thus lack comparability, would be of limited value to the researcher.

Two approaches improve the usefulness of such replies. First, various properties may be separated and the participant asked to judge each specific facet. Here, the researcher would substitute several distinct questions for a single one. Second, the researcher can replace the free-response reply with structuring devices. To quantify dimensions that are essentially qualitative, rating or ranking scales are used.

## Rating scales

You can use **rating scales** to judge properties of objects without reference to other similar objects. These ratings may be in such forms as 'like–dislike', 'approve–indifferent–disapprove' or other classifications using even more categories.

### Number of scale points

There is little conclusive support for choosing a three-point scale over scales with five or more points. Some researchers think that the greater the number of points on a rating scale, the greater the sensitivity of measurement and extraction of variance. The most widely used scales range from three to seven points, but it does not seem to make much difference which number is used – with two exceptions.[28] First, a larger number of scale points is needed to produce accuracy when using single-dimension versus multiple-dimension scales. Second, in cross-cultural measurement, the culture may condition participants to a standard metric. In Italy and the Netherlands school marks are given on a ten-point scale (scores of five and lower are insufficient), while Germans use a six-point scale (scores of five and higher are considered insufficient). Hence, if you used the same six-point scale for a survey conducted both in the UK and Germany, the Germans would interpret the values of the scale in a different way to the British.

### Alternative scales

Examples of rating scales are shown in Exhibit 12.9. This exhibit amplifies the overview presented in this section.[29] Later in the chapter, construction techniques for some commonly used rating scales are presented.

The **simple category scale** (also called a dichotomous scale) offers two mutually exclusive response choices. In Exhibit 12.9 they are 'yes' and 'no', but they could just as easily be 'import-

| | |
|---|---|
| **Simple category scale**<br>[dichotomous]<br>data: nominal | 'Have you ever been self employed?'<br>☐ Yes<br>☐ No |
| **Multiple choice single-response scale**<br>data: nominal | 'For which department are you working?<br>☐ Production<br>☐ Service<br>☐ Marketing and Sales<br>☐ Research and Development<br>☐ Other (Specify: _____ ) |
| **Multiple-choice multiple-response scale**<br>[checklist]<br>data: nominal | 'Check any of the sources where you collect information on potential suppliers'<br>☐ Visit to suppliers<br>☐ Visit from suppliers<br>☐ Trade fairs<br>☐ Magazines<br>☐ Informal talk with others<br>☐ Consulting service firms<br>☐ Other (Specify: _____ ) |
| **Likert scale summated rating**<br>data: interval | 'The internet is superior to traditional libraries for comprehensive searches'<br><br>STRONGLY AGREE (5)　　AGREE (4)　　NEITHER AGREE OR DISAGREE (3)　　DISAGREE (2)　　STRONGLY DISAGREE (1) |
| **Semantic differential scale**<br>data: interval | Heathrow Airport<br>FAST ____:____:____:____:____:____:____ : SLOW<br>HIGH QUALITY ____:____:____:____:____:____:____ : LOW QUALITY |
| **Numerical scale**<br>data: ordinal or* interval | EXTREMELY FAVOURABLE　　5　4　3　2　1　　EXTREMELY UNFAVOURABLE<br>Employee's cooperation in teams _____<br>Employee's knowledge of task _____<br>Employee's planning effectiveness _____ |

*Exhibit 12.9* Sample rating scales.

*Note*: *earlier in the chapter we noted that researchers differ in the ways that they treat data from certain scales. If you are unable to establish the linearity of the measured variables or you cannot be confident that you have equal intervals, it is proper to treat data from these scales as ordinal.

| Multiple rating list scale data: interval | 'Please indicate how important or unimportant each service characteristic is' |
|---|---|

'Please indicate how important or unimportant each service characteristic is'

|  | IMPORTANT |  |  |  |  |  | UNIMPORTANT |
|---|---|---|---|---|---|---|---|
| Fast reliable repair | 7 | 6 | 5 | 4 | 3 | 2 | 1 |
| Service at my location | 7 | 6 | 5 | 4 | 3 | 2 | 1 |
| Maintenance by manufacturer | 7 | 6 | 5 | 4 | 3 | 2 | 1 |
| Knowledgeable technicians | 7 | 6 | 5 | 4 | 3 | 2 | 1 |
| Notification of upgrades | 7 | 6 | 5 | 4 | 3 | 2 | 1 |
| Service contract after warranty | 7 | 6 | 5 | 4 | 3 | 2 | 1 |

**Fixed sum scale**
data: ratio

'Taking all the supplier characteristics we've just discussed and now considering *cost*, what is their relative importance to you (dividing 100 units between)?'

Being one of the lowest-cost suppliers

All other aspects of supplier performance

Sum  100

**Stapel scale**
data: ordinal or* interval

(Company name)

| +5 | +5 | +5 |
| +4 | +4 | +4 |
| +3 | +3 | +3 |
| +2 | +2 | +2 |
| +1 | +1 | +1 |
| Technology leader | Exciting products | World-class reputation |
| +1 | +1 | +1 |
| +2 | +2 | +2 |
| +3 | +3 | +3 |
| +4 | +4 | +4 |
| +5 | +5 | +5 |

**Graphic rating scale**
data: ordinal or* interval or ratio

'How likely are you to recommend British Airways to others?'
(Place an X at the position along the line that best reflects your judgement)

VERY LIKELY |————————————| VERY UNLIKELY

(Alternative with graphic)

*Exhibit 12.9* Continued.

ant' and 'unimportant', 'male and female' or another set of discrete categories had the question been different. This response strategy is particularly useful for demographic questions or where a dichotomous response is adequate.

When there are multiple options for the rater but only one answer is sought, the **multiple-choice, single-response scale** is appropriate. Our example has five options. The primary alternatives should encompass 90 per cent of the range with the 'other' category completing the participant's list. When there is no possibility for 'other', or exhaustiveness of categories is not critical, the 'other' response may be omitted. Both the multiple-choice, single-response and the simple category scale produce nominal data.

A variation, the **multiple-choice, multiple-response scale** (also called a checklist) allows the rater to select one or several alternatives. In the example of Exhibit 12.9 we are measuring seven items with one question, and it is possible that all seven sources were consulted. The cumulative feature of this scale can be beneficial when a complete picture of the participant's choices is desired. This scale generates nominal data. Answers to a multiple-response scale can be transformed in one single numeric score by assigning unique values to each answer category following the numeric series $2^n$ with $n$ representing the number of categories (i.e. 1, 2, 4, 8, 16, …) and then adding the values of all ticked answer categories.

The **Likert scale** is the most frequently used variation of the summated rating scale. Summated scales consist of statements that express either a favourable or unfavourable attitude towards the object of interest. The participant is asked to agree or disagree with each statement. Each response is given a numerical score to reflect its degree of attitudinal favourableness, and the scores may be totalled to measure the participant's attitude. In our example, the participant chooses one of five levels of agreement. The numbers indicate the value to be assigned to each possible answer with 1 the least favourable impression of Internet superiority and 5 the most favourable. These values are not normally printed on the instrument but are shown in Exhibit 12.9 to indicate the scoring system. Between 20 and 25 properly constructed questions about an attitude object would be required for a reliable Likert scale.

Likert scales help us to compare one person's score with a distribution of scores from a well-defined sample group. This measurement scale is useful for a manager when, say, an organization plans to conduct an experiment or undertake a programme of change or improvement. The researcher can measure attitudes before and after the experiment or change, or judge whether the organization's efforts have had the desired effect. This scale produces interval data.

The **semantic differential scale** measures the psychological meanings of an attitude object. Managers use this scale for brand image and other marketing studies of institutional images, political issues and personalities, and organizational studies. It is based on the proposition that an object can have several dimensions of connotative meaning. The meanings are located in multidimensional property space, called semantic space. The method consists of a set of bipolar rating scales, usually with seven points, by which one or more participants rate one or more concepts on each scale item. In the example in Exhibit 12.9, two sets of bipolar pairs are shown, one from the traditional source and one adapted to the research purpose. Based on the construction requirements discussed later, we might choose 10 scale items to score Heathrow Airport.

The semantic differential has several advantages. It produces interval data, and offers an efficient and easy way to secure attitudes from a large sample. These attitudes may be measured in both direction and intensity. The total set of responses provides a comprehensive picture of the meaning of an object and a measure of the subject doing the rating. It is a standardized technique that is easily repeated, but escapes many problems of response distortion found with more direct methods.

**Numerical scales** have equal intervals that separate their numeric scale points. The verbal anchors serve as the labels for the extreme points. Numerical scales are often five-point scales, as shown in Exhibit 12.9, but may have seven or ten points. The participant writes a number from the scale next to each item. If numerous questions about employee performance were included in the example, the scale would provide both an absolute measure of importance and a relative measure (ranking) of the various items rated. The scale's linearity, simplicity and production of ordinal or interval data make it popular with managers and researchers.

The **multiple rating list scale** is similar to the numerical scale but differs in two ways:

1  it accepts a circled response from the rater

2  the layout permits the visualization of the results.

The advantage is that a mental map of the participant's evaluations is evident to both the rater and the researcher. This scale produces interval data.

A scale that helps the researcher discover proportions is the **fixed sum scale**. In the example, two categories are presented that must sum to 100. Up to 10 categories may be used, but both participant precision and patience suffer when too many stimuli are proportioned and summed. A participant's ability to add up is also taxed in some situations; thus this is not a response strategy that can be used effectively with children or the uneducated. The advantage of the scale is its compatibility with per cent (100 per cent) and the fact that continuous data (versus discrete categories) can be compared for the alternatives. The scale is used to record attitudes, behaviour and behavioural intent. It produces interval data.

The **stapel scale** is used as an alternative to the semantic differential, especially when it is difficult to find bipolar adjectives that match the investigative question. In the example in Exhibit 12.9 there are three attributes of corporate image. The scale is composed of the word (or phrase) identifying the image dimension and a set of 10 response categories for each of the three attributes. Fewer response categories are sometimes used. Participants select a plus number for the characteristic that describes the named company. The more accurate the description, the larger is the positive number. Similarly, the less accurate the description, the larger is the negative number chosen. Ratings range from +5 to –5, very accurate to very inaccurate. Like the semantic differential, stapel scales usually produce interval data.

The **graphic rating scale** was created to enable researchers to discern fine differences. Theoretically, an infinite number of ratings is possible if the participant is sophisticated enough to differentiate and record them. The participant checks his or her response at any point along a continuum. Usually, the score is a measure of length (e.g. millimetres) from either end point. The results are usually treated as interval data. The difficulty is in coding and analysis. This response strategy requires more time than scales with predetermined categories. Other graphic rating scales use pictures, icons or other visuals to communicate with the rater, and represent a variety of data types. Graphic scales are often used with children, whose more limited vocabulary prevents the use of scales anchored with words.

## *Errors to avoid with rating scales*

The value of rating scales for measurement purposes depends on the assumption that a person can and will make good judgements. Before accepting participants' ratings, we should consider their tendencies to make errors of three types:[30]

1 leniency
2 central tendency
3 halo effect.

### Leniency

The error of **leniency** occurs when a participant is either an 'easy rater' or a 'hard rater'. The latter is an error of negative leniency. Raters are inclined to score higher people they know well and with whom they are 'ego involved'. The opposite case also applies: where acquaintances are rated lower because one is aware of the tendency towards positive leniency and attempts to counteract it. One way to deal with positive leniency is to design the rating scale to anticipate it. An example might be an asymmetrical scale that has only one unfavourable descriptive term and four favourable terms (poor – fair – good – very good – excellent). The scale designer expects that the mean ratings will be near 'good' and that there will be a symmetrical distribution about that point.

### Central tendency

Raters are reluctant to give extreme judgements, and this fact accounts for the error of **central tendency**. This is most often seen when the rater does not know the object or property being rated. To counteract this type of error try taking the following steps.

- Adjust the strength of descriptive adjectives.
- Space the intermediate descriptive phrases further apart.
- Provide smaller differences in meaning between the steps near the ends of the scale than between the steps near the centre.
- Use more points in the scale.

### Halo effect

The **halo effect** is the systematic bias that the rater introduces by carrying over a generalized impression of the subject from one rating to another. You may expect the student who does well on the first question of an examination to do well on the second, for instance. You conclude a report is good because you like its form or you believe someone is intelligent because you agree with him or her. Halo is a pervasive error. It is especially difficult to avoid when the property being studied is not clearly defined, not easily observed, not frequently discussed, involves reactions with others or is a trait of high moral importance.[31] One way to counteract the halo effect is to rate one trait at a time for all subjects or to have one trait per page.

Rating scales are widely used in management research and generally deserve their popularity. The results obtained with careful use compare favourably with other methods.

# Ranking scales

In **ranking scales**, the subject directly compares two or more objects and makes choices among them. Frequently, the participant is asked to select one as the 'best' or the 'most preferred'. When there are only two choices, this approach is satisfactory, but it often results in 'ties' when more than two choices are found. For example, assume participants are asked to select the most preferred among three or more models of a product. In response, 40 per cent choose model A, 30 per cent choose model B, and 30 per cent choose model C. Which is the preferred model? The analyst would be taking a risk to suggest that A is most preferred. Perhaps that interpretation is correct, but 60 per cent of the participants chose some model other than A. Perhaps all B and C voters would place A last, preferring either B or C to it. This ambiguity can be avoided by using some of the techniques described in this section.

Using the **paired-comparison scale**, the participant can express attitudes unambiguously by choosing between two objects. Typical of paired comparisons would be the car preference example (see Exhibit 12.11). The number of judgements required in a paired comparison is $[(n)(n-1)/2]$, where n is the number of stimuli or objects to be judged. When four cars are evaluated, the participant evaluates six paired comparisons $[(4)(3)/2 = 6]$.

# Comparing apples and oranges: the PISA report

On 4 December 2001, the Organization for Economic Co-operation and Development (OECD) published the PISA (Programme for International Student Assessment) report, describing a study comparing educational performance in 23 countries. The report is based on a standardized test assessing the reading, mathematical and scientific literacy of students in the participating countries. The sample size in each country ranged from 3372 in Iceland to 29,687 in Canada.

The results of the report attracted a great deal of attention, especially in countries whose performance was significantly below the average, such as Germany. The poor German outcomes were even covered in the international press. An article in the *Economist* on 15 December 2001 was titled 'Dummkopf!'

Germans have long been proud of their schooling – too long it seems, and an article in the *Independent* on 5 December 2001 was entitled 'Germany is out of date (and I say that with only a little Schadenfreude)'. The study's outcomes shocked the German public, and politicians of all hues called for immediate action. The suggested actions, however, differed considerably. To back their view proponents of certain actions usually referred to the educational systems of top PISA countries. For example, experts suggesting that schools should once again place more emphasis on the learning of facts referred to Korea. Others highlighting full boarding schools and a late selection of children in different school types used Finland as a model example.

Overall, it seems that most educational experts did not try to learn from the PISA report, but hand-picked the results that supported the view they held before the report was published. In many countries, the PISA report had a major impact on the political agenda. Therefore, it seems fair to ask how valid and reliable the results are.

The PISA study is a cross-country measurement of students' performance by asking students (respondents) to answer open and closed test questions. One of the important questions in any cross-country study is whether you measured the same in each country. Two measurement issues arise. First, as the tests were taken in countries with a different mother language, the original questions had to be translated. Half of the original test questions were formulated in French and half in English. To ensure the quality of the translation, the researchers used three independent translators. For example, the first translated the original English question into German, the second would get the German translation and was asked to translate it back into English without knowing anything about the original text and the third would assess the differences between the two previous translations. However, critics point to the fact that countries with French or English as mother tongue score better, on average, than countries with another mother tongue. Does this support the claim that it is purely the language of the test that influences the results?

In addition, students had to answer the questions with a time constraint: the whole test should not exceed two hours. However, German instructions are on average about one-third longer than the same instructions in English. Hence, students taking the test in German needed more time to read the questions and had as a consequence less time to think about the answers. Are differences in country scores caused by using different languages in the measurement?

Some of the test questions are open questions, and markers had to assess the quality of the answers. Of course, these people were instructed as to how to mark answers. A cross-country comparison of markings reveals that in 92 per cent of cases an international verifier agreed with the assessment of the national markers. This result implies that 8 per cent of the markings are somehow ambiguous.

How does this measurement error translate into the significant differences in the performance scores as shown in Exhibit 12.10?

In another example we might compare two bargaining proposals available to union negotiators (see Exhibit 12.12). Generally, there are more than two stimuli to judge, resulting in a potentially tedious task for participants. If 15 suggestions for bargaining proposals are available, 105 paired comparisons would be made.

Reducing the number of comparisons per participant without reducing the number of objects can lighten this burden. You can present each participant with only a sample of the stimuli. In this way, each pair of objects must be compared an equal number of times. Another procedure is to choose a few objects that are believed to cover the range of attractiveness at equal intervals. All other stimuli are then compared to these few standard objects. If 36 automobiles are to be judged, four may be selected as standards and the others divided into four groups of eight each. Within each group, the eight are compared to each other. Then the 32 are individually compared to each of the four standard automobiles. This reduces the number of comparisons from 630 to 240.

Paired comparisons run the risk that participants will tire to the point that they give ill-considered answers or refuse to continue. Opinions differ about the upper limit, but five or six stimuli are not unreasonable when the participant has other questions to answer. If the data-collection consists only of paired comparisons, as many as 10 stimuli are reasonable.

While a paired comparison provides ordinal data, there are methods for converting it to interval data. The Law of Comparative Judgement involves converting the frequencies of preferences (such as in Exhibit 12.10) into a table of proportions, which are then transformed into a Z

| | Reading literacy (country score in parentheses) | Mathematical literacy (country score in parentheses) | Scientific literacy (country score in parentheses) |
|---|---|---|---|
| Countries scoring significantly above the average score | Finland (546)<br>Canada (534)<br>New Zealand (529)<br>Australia (528)<br>Ireland (527)<br>Korea (525)<br>UK (523)<br>Japan (522)<br>Sweden (516)<br>Austria (507)<br>Belgium (507)<br>Iceland (507) | Japan (557)<br>Korea (547)<br>New Zealand (537)<br>Finland (536)<br>Australia (533)<br>Canada (533)<br>Switzerland (529)<br>UK (529)<br>Belgium (520)<br>France (517)<br>Austria (515)<br>Denmark (514)<br>Iceland (514)<br>Liechtenstein (514)<br>Sweden (510) | Korea (552)<br>Japan (550)<br>Finland (538)<br>UK (532)<br>Canada (529)<br>New Zealand (528)<br>Australia (528)<br>Austria (519)<br>Ireland (513)<br>Sweden (512)<br>Czech Republic (511) |
| Countries with a score not significantly different from the average | Norway (505)<br>France (505)<br>USA (504)<br>Denmark (497)<br>Switzerland (494) | Ireland (503)<br>Norway (499)<br>Czech Republic (498)<br>USA (493) | France (500)<br>Norway (500)<br>USA (499)<br>Hungary (496)<br>Iceland (496)<br>Belgium (496)<br>Switzerland (496) |
| Countries scoring significantly below the average score | Spain (493)<br>Czech Republic (492)<br>Italy (487)<br>Germany (484)<br>Liechtenstein (483)<br>Hungary (480)<br>Poland (497)<br>Greece (474)<br>Portugal (470)<br>Russia (462)<br>Latvia (458)<br>Luxembourg (441)<br>Mexico (422)<br>Brazil (396) | Germany (490)<br>Hungary (488)<br>Russia (478)<br>Spain (476)<br>Poland (470)<br>Latvia (463)<br>Italy (457)<br>Portugal (454)<br>Greece (447)<br>Luxembourg (446)<br>Mexico (387)<br>Brazil (334) | Spain (491)<br>Germany (487)<br>Poland (483)<br>Denmark (481)<br>Italy (478)<br>Liechtenstein (476)<br>Greece (461)<br>Russia (460)<br>Latvia (460)<br>Portugal (459)<br>Luxembourg (443)<br>Mexico (422)<br>Brazil (375) |

*Exhibit 12.10* Rating of countries in PISA study.

*Source*: Knowledge and Skills for Life. First results from the OECD Programme for International Student Assessment (PISA) 2000, available online at www.pisa.oecd.org/Docs/Download/PISA2001(English).pdf

Paired-comparison scale
data : ordinal

'For each pair of cars listed, place a tick beside the one you would most prefer if you had to choose between the two'

— VW golf                — Peugeot 307
— Opel Astra             — Opel Astra

— Peugeot 307            — Opel Astra
— VW golf                — Volvo 540

— Peugeot 307            — Volvo 540
— Volvo 540              — VW golf

Forced ranking scale
data : ordinal

'Rank the radar detection features in your order of preference. Place the number 1 next to the most preferred, 2 by the second choice, and so forth'

___ User programming
___ Cordless capability
___ Small size
___ Long-range warning
___ Minimal false alarms

Comparative scale
data : ordinal

'Compared to your previous mutual fund's performance, the new one is'

| SUPERIOR | | ABOUT THE SAME | | INFERIOR |
|---|---|---|---|---|
| — | — | — | — | — |
| 1 | 2 | 3 | 4 | 5 |

**Exhibit 12.11**  Examples of ranking scales.

matrix by referring to the table of areas under the normal curve.[32] Guilford's composite-standard method is another alternative.[33]

The **forced ranking scale** shown in Exhibit 12.11 lists attributes that are ranked relative to each other. This method is faster than paired comparisons and is usually easier and more motivating to the participant. With five items, it takes 10 paired comparisons to complete the task, and the simple forced ranking of five is easier. Also, ranking has no transitivity problem where A is preferred to B, and B to C, but C is preferred to A.

A drawback to forced ranking is the number of stimuli that can be handled by this method. Five objects can be ranked easily, but participants may grow careless in ranking 10 or more items. In addition, rank ordering produces ordinal data since the distance between preferences is unknown.

Often the manager or researcher is interested in benchmarking. This calls for a standard by which other programmes, processes, brands, points of sale or people can be compared. The **comparative scale** is ideal for such comparisons if the participants are familiar with the standard. In the Exhibit 12.11 example, the standard is the participant's previous mutual fund. The new fund is being assessed relative to it. The provision to compare yet other funds to the standard is not shown in the example but is nonetheless available to the researcher.

Some researchers treat the data produced by comparative scales as interval data since the

Paired-comparison data may be treated in several ways. If there is substantial consistency, we will find that if A is preferred to B, and B to C, then A will be consistently preferred to C. This condition of transitivity need not always be true but should occur most of the time. When it does, take the total number of preferences among the comparisons as the score for that stimulus.

Assume a union-bargaining committee is considering five major demand proposals. The committee would like to know how the union membership ranks these proposals. One option would be to ask a sample of the members to pair-compare the personnel suggestions. With a rough comparison of the total preferences for each option, it is apparent that B is the most popular.

| | Suggestion | | | | |
|---|---|---|---|---|---|
| | A | B | C | D | E |
| A | – | 164* | 138 | 50 | 70 |
| B | 36 | – | 54 | 14 | 30 |
| C | 62 | 146 | – | 32 | 50 |
| D | 150 | 186 | 168 | – | 118 |
| E | 130 | 170 | 150 | 82 | – |
| Total | 378 | 666 | 510 | 178 | 268 |
| Rank order | 3 | 1 | 2 | 5 | 4 |
| Mp | 0.478 | 0.766 | 0.610 | 0.278 | 0.368 |
| Zj | −0.060 | 0.730 | 0.280 | −0.590 | −0.340 |
| Rj | 0.530 | 1.320 | 0.870 | 0.000 | 0.250 |

Note: *interpret this cell, 164 members preferred suggestion B (column) to suggestion A (row).

Exhibit 12.12 Response patterns of 200 union members' paired comparisons on five suggestions for bargaining proposal priorities.

scoring reflects an interval between the standard and what is being compared. We would treat the rank or position of the item as ordinal data unless the linearity of the variables in question could be supported.

None of the ranking methods covered is particularly useful when there are many items. The method of **successive intervals** is sometimes used to sort the items (usually one per card) into piles or groups representing a succession of values. From the sort, an interval scale can then be developed.[34] This procedure is not used frequently and then only in unique studies.

## 12.7 Measurement scale construction

Earlier we discussed scales in terms of the techniques used to construct them. Of the five techniques examined, three are used frequently: the arbitrary approach, item analysis and factoring.

These are highlighted in this section along with a preview of multivariate scales (which is described in more detail in Chapter 19). Consensus and cumulative methods receive less attention because they are time-consuming to construct or have fewer management applications. They are mentioned briefly because of their influence on current methods.

## Arbitrary scaling

We design **arbitrary scales** by collecting several items that we believe are unambiguous and appropriate to a given topic. Some are chosen for inclusion in the instrument. To illustrate, consider a company image study.

We choose a sample of items that we believe are the components of company image. We might score each of these from 1 to 5, depending on the degree of favourableness reported. The results may be studied in several ways. Totals may be made by individual items, by company, by companies as places to work, for ecological concern, and so on. Totals for each company or for individuals may be calculated to determine how they compare to others. Based on a total for these four items, each company would receive from 4 to 20 points from each participant. These data may also be analysed from a participant-centred point of view. Thus, we might use the attitude scores of each individual to study differences among individuals.

Arbitrary scales are easy to develop, inexpensive, and can be designed to be highly specific. They provide useful information and are adequate if developed skilfully. There are also weaknesses, though. The design approach is subjective. The researcher's insight and ability offer the only assurance that the items chosen are a representative sample of the universe of content (the totality of what constitutes 'company image'). We have no evidence that participants will view all items with the same frame of reference. While arbitrary scales are often used, there has been a great effort to develop construction techniques that overcome some of their deficiencies. An early attempt was consensus scaling.

## Consensus scaling

**Consensus scaling** requires items to be selected by a panel of judges and then evaluated on:

- their relevance to the topic area
- their potential for ambiguity
- the level of attitude they represent.

A widely known form of this approach is the Thurstone **equal-appearing interval scale**. Also known as the Thurstone scale, this approach resulted in an interval rating scale for attitude measurement. Often, 50 or more judges evaluate a large number of statements expressing different degrees of favourableness towards an object. There is one statement per card. The judges sort each card into one of 11 piles representing their evaluation of the degree of favourableness that the statement expresses. The judge's agreement or disagreement with the statement is not involved. Of the 11 piles, three are identified to the judges by labels of 'favourable' and 'unfavourable' at the extremes, and 'neutral' at the midpoint. The eight intermediate piles are left unlabelled to create the impression of equal-appearing intervals between the three labelled positions.

# Diversity in Europe

In the future, companies and organizations will have to deal with internal and external environments that are very different from the ones they know. The continuous integration of the European Union (EU), together with growing globalization, will change the composition of companies' customers and employees significantly. In the past, most companies in Europe had a rather homogeneous work force, consisting mainly of nationals of the host country. As the work force in the EU becomes geographically more flexible and immigration to the EU from other parts of the world increases, more and more companies are facing dramatic shifts in the composition of their work forces. These changes require new approaches to human research management in order to facilitate adaptation to the increasing heterogeneity (diversity) of the work force.

In January 2000, Sweden's Minerva Foundation, together with teams from Denmark, Estonia, Italy, Portugal and Spain, initiated a project within the EU's educational programme known as 'Leonardo'. The project's purpose was to spread knowledge about the economic benefits of diversity and diversity management. In particular, the project intended to develop a training model for diversity management and to publish a guide detailing best practice in diversity management.

Part of the project was an anonymous web survey to assess management barriers to, and the benefits of, diversity. An extract from this questionnaire is reproduced below.

Where do you encounter diversity management barriers?

Company culture
☐    Many?
☐    Some
☐    Few
☐    Very few

Leadership
☐    Many?
☐    Some
☐    Few
☐    Very few

Internal politics
☐    Many?
☐    Some
☐    Few
☐    Very few

Team-building
☐    Many?
☐    Some
☐    Few
☐    Very few

▶ Where do you encounter diversity management benefits?
Recruitment of employees
- ☐   Many?
- ☐   Some
- ☐   Few
- ☐   Very few

New markets
- ☐   Many?
- ☐   Some
- ☐   Few
- ☐   Very few

Increasing creativity
- ☐   Many?
- ☐   Some
- ☐   Few
- ☐   Very few

Public image
- ☐   Many?

Some
- ☐   Few
- ☐   Very few

Flexibility
- ☐   Many?
- ☐   Some
- ☐   Few
- ☐   Very few

What do you think about how the project tried to assess the benefits and barriers of diversity management?

# References and further reading

**Diversity in Europe (http://www.diversityineurope/indexeng.html)**
**Managing Diversity (http://www.minerva.nu/managing_diversity_uk.html)**
**www.diversityineurope.com**
**www.minerva.nu**

This method of scale construction is rarely used in applied management research these days. Its cost, time and staff requirements make it impractical. The importance of this historic method, however, is its influence on the Likert and semantic differential scales.

## Item analysis scaling

**Item analysis scaling** is a procedure for evaluating an item based on how well it discriminates between those persons whose total score is high and those whose total score is low. The most popular scale using this approach is the summated or Likert scale.

Item analysis involves calculating the mean scores for each scale item among the low scorers and high scorers. The item means between the high-score group and the low-score group are then tested for significance by calculating t values. Finally, the 20 to 25 items that have the greatest t values (significant differences between means) are selected for inclusion in the final scale.[35]

Likert-type scales are relatively easy to construct compared to the equal-appearing interval scale.[36] The first step is to collect a large number of statements that meet two criteria.

1  Each statement is believed to be relevant to the attitude being studied.

2  Each is believed to reflect a favourable or unfavourable position on that attitude.

People similar to those who are going to be studied are asked to read each statement and to state the level of their agreement with it, using a five-point scale. A scale value of 1 might indicate a strongly unfavourable attitude; 5, a strongly favourable attitude (see Exhibit 12.9).

Each person's responses are then added to secure a total score. The next step is to array these total scores and select some portion representing the highest and lowest total scores: say, the top 25 per cent and the bottom 25 per cent. These two extreme groups represent people with the most favourable and least favourable attitudes towards the topic being studied. The extremes are the two criterion groups by which we evaluate individual statements. Through a comparative analysis of response patterns to each statement by members of these two groups, we learn which statements consistently correlate with low favourability and which correlate with high favourability attitudes.

This procedure is illustrated in Exhibit 12.13. In evaluating response patterns of the high and low groups to the statement 'I consider my job exciting', we secure the results shown. After finding the t values for each statement, we rank-order them and select those statements with the highest t values. As an approximate indicator of a statement's discrimination power, Edwards suggests using only those statements whose t value is 1.75 or greater, provided there are 25 or more subjects in each group.[37] To safeguard against response-set bias, we should word approximately one-half of the statements to be favourable and the other half to be unfavourable.

The Likert scale has many advantages that account for its popularity. It is easy and quick to construct. Each item that is included has met an empirical test for discriminating ability. Since participants answer each item, it is probably more reliable and it provides a greater volume of data than many other scales.

| Response Categories | Low Total Score Group | | | | High Total Score Group | | | |
|---|---|---|---|---|---|---|---|---|
| | $X$ | $f$ | $fX$ | $fX^2$ | $X$ | $f$ | $fX$ | $fX^2$ |
| Strongly agree | 5 | 3 | 15 | 75 | 5 | 22 | 110 | 550 |
| Agree | 4 | 4 | 16 | 64 | 4 | 30 | 120 | 480 |
| Undecided | 3 | 29 | 87 | 261 | 3 | 15 | 45 | 135 |
| Disagree | 2 | 22 | 44 | 88 | 2 | 4 | 8 | 16 |
| Strongly disagree | 1 | 15 | 15 | 15 | 1 | 2 | 2 | 2 |
| Total | | 73 | 177 | 503 | | 73 | 285 | 1183 |
| | | $n_L$ | $\Sigma X_L$ | $\Sigma X_L^2$ | $n_H$ | $\Sigma X_H$ | $\Sigma X_H^2$ | |

*Steps*

1 For the statement 'I consider my job exciting', we select the data from the bottom 25 per cent of the distribution (low total score group) and the top 25 per cent (high total score group). There are 73 people in each group. The remaining 50 per cent in the middle of the distribution are not considered for this analysis. For each of the response categories, the scale's value ($X$) is multiplied by the frequency or number of respondents ($f$) who chose that value. These values produce the product ($fX$). This number is then multiplied by X ($fX^2$). For example, there are three respondents in the low-score group who scored a 5 (strongly agreed with the statement): ($fX$) = 5 × 3 = 15; ($fX^2$) = 15 × 5 = 75.

2 The frequencies, products and squares are summed.

3 A mean score for each group is computed.

4 Deviation scores are computed, squared and summed as required for the formula.

5 The data are tested in a modified *t*-test that compares the high- and low-scoring groups for the item. Notice the mean scores in the numerator of the formula.

6 The calculated value is compared with a criterion, 1.75. If the calculated value (in this case, 8.92) is equal to or exceeds the criterion, the statement is said to be a good discriminator of the measured attitude. (If it is less than the criterion, we would consider it a poor discriminator of the target attitude and delete it from the measuring instrument.) We then select the next item and repeat the process.

*Exhibit 12.13* Evaluating a scale statement by item analysis.

## Cumulative scaling

Total scores on **cumulative scales** have the same meaning. Given a person's total score, it is possible to estimate which items were answered positively and which negatively. A pioneering scale of this type was the **scalogram**. Scalogram analysis is a procedure for determining whether a set of items forms a unidimensional scale.[38] A scale is unidimensional if the responses fall into a pattern in which endorsement of the item reflecting the extreme position also results in endorsing all items that are less extreme.

Assume we are surveying opinions regarding a new style of running shoe. We have developed a preference scale of four items as follows.

1  The Airsole is good looking.

2  I will insist on Airsole next time because it is great looking.

3  The appearance of Airsole is acceptable to me.

4  I prefer the Airsole style to other styles.

Participants indicate whether they agree or disagree with each item. If these items form a unidimensional scale, the response patterns will approach the ideal configuration as shown in Exhibit 12.14.

A score of 4 indicates that all statements are agreed upon and represents the most favourable attitude. Persons with a score of 3 should disagree with item 2 but agree with all others, and so on. According to scalogram theory, this pattern confirms that the universe of content (attitude towards the appearance of this running shoe) is scalable.

The scalogram and similar procedures for discovering underlying structure are useful for assessing behaviours that are highly structured, such as social distance, organizational hierarchies and evolutionary product stages.[39] Although used less often today, the scalogram retains potential for managerial applications.

## Factor scaling

Factor scales include a variety of techniques that have been developed to address two problems:

1  how to deal with a universe of content that is multidimensional

2  how to uncover underlying (latent) dimensions that have not been identified by exploratory research.

These techniques are designed to inter-correlate items so that their degree of interdependence may be detected. There are many approaches that the advanced student will want to explore, such as latent structure analysis (of which the scalogram is a special case), factor analysis, cluster

| Item | | | | |
| --- | --- | --- | --- | --- |
| I will insist on Airsole next time because it is great looking | I prefer the Airsole style to other styles | The Airsole is good looking | The appearance of Airsole is acceptable to me | Respondent score |
| 2 | 4 | 1 | 3 | |
| X | X | X | X | 4 |
| — | X | X | X | 3 |
| — | — | X | X | 2 |
| — | — | — | X | 1 |
| — | — | — | — | 0 |
| X = Agree | — = Disagree | | | |

*Exhibit 12.14*  Ideal scalogram response pattern.

analysis, and metric and non-metric multidimensional scaling. We limit the discussion in this section to the semantic differential (SD), which is based on factor analysis.[40]

Osgood and his associates developed the semantic differential method to measure the psychological meanings of an object to an individual.[41] They produced a long list of adjective pairs useful for attitude research. Searching *Roget's Thesaurus* for such adjectives, they located 289 pairs. These were reduced to 76 pairs that were formed into rating scales. They chose 20 concepts that evoked the psychological meanings they wished to probe. The concepts from this historical study illustrate the wide applicability of the technique to persons, abstract concepts (such as leadership), events, institutions and physical objects.[42]

By factor-analysing the data, they concluded that semantic space is multidimensional rather than unidimensional. Three factors contributed most to meaningful judgements by participants:

1  evaluation

2  potency

3  activity.

The evaluation dimension usually accounts for one-half to three-quarters of the extractable variance. (The evaluation dimension is the only dimension possessed by Likert scales.) Potency and activity are about equal, and together account for a little over one-quarter of the extractable variance. Occasionally, the potency and activity dimensions combine to form 'dynamism'. The results of the Thesaurus study are shown in Exhibit 12.15.

The SD scale should be adapted to each research problem. SD construction involves the following steps.

1  Select the concepts. The concepts are nouns, noun phrases or non-verbal stimuli such as visual sketches. Concepts are chosen by judgement and reflect the nature of the investigative question. Or in a study to evaluate multiple candidates for an executive position in an industry association, the concept might be a candidate, for example 'Darnell Williams'.

2  Select the original bipolar word pairs or pairs you adapt to your needs. If the traditional Osgood items are used, several criteria guide your selection. The first is the factor(s) composition.

   a  You need at least three bipolar pairs for each factor to use evaluation, potency and activity. Scores on these individual items should be averaged, by factor, to improve their test reliability.

   b  The scale must be relevant to the concepts being judged. Choose adjectives that allow connotative perceptions to be expressed. Irrelevant concept-scale pairings yield neutral midpoint values that convey little information.

   c  Scales should be stable across subjects and concepts. A pair such as 'large–small' may be interpreted by some to be denotative when judging a physical object such as a 'car but may be used connotatively in judging abstract concepts such as 'quality management'.

   d  Scales should be linear between polar opposites and pass through the origin. A pair that fails this test is 'rugged–delicate', which is non-linear on the evaluation dimension. When used separately, both adjectives have favourable meanings.[43]

| Evaluation (E) | Potency (P) | | Activity (A) |
|---|---|---|---|
| Good – bad | Hard – soft | | Active – passive |
| Positive – negative | Strong – weak | | Fast – slow |
| Optimistic – pessimistic | Heavy – light | | Hot – cold |
| Complete – incomplete | Masculine – feminine | | Excitable – calm |
| Timely – untimely | Severe – lenient | | Tenacious – yielding |
| *Sub-categories of Evaluation* | | | |
| Meek goodness | Dynamic goodness | Dependable goodness | Hedonistic goodness |
| Clean – dirty | Successful – unsuccessful | True – false | Pleasurable – painful |
| Kind – cruel | High – low | Reputable – disreputable | Beautiful – ugly |
| Sociable – unsociable | Meaningful – meaningless | Believing – sceptical | Sociable – unsociable |
| Light – dark | Important – unimportant | Wise – foolish | |
| Meaningful – meaningless | | | |
| Altruistic – egotistical | Progressive – regressive | Healthy – sick | |
| Grateful – ungrateful | | Clean – dirty | |
| Beautiful – ugly | | | |
| Harmonious – dissonant | | | |

**Exhibit 12.15** Results of the thesaurus study.

*Source*: adapted from Charles E. Osgood, G.J. Suci and P.H. Tannenbaum, *The Measurement of Meaning*. Urbana, IL: University of Illinois Press, 1957, Table 5, pp. 52 – 61.

Exhibit 12.16 shows the scale being used by a panel of corporate leaders to rate candidates for an industry leadership position. The selection of concepts in this case is simple: there are three candidates, plus a fourth – the ideal candidate.

The nature of the problem determines the selection of dimensions and bipolar pairs. Since the person who wins this position must influence business leaders, we decide to use all three factors. The candidate must deal with many people, often in a social setting; must have high integrity; and must take a leadership role in encouraging more progressive policies in the industry. The position will also involve a high degree of personal activity. Based on these requirements, we choose 10 scales to score the candidates from 7 to 1. The negative signs in the original scoring procedure (−3, −2, −1, 0, +1, +2, +3) were found to produce coding errors.

Exhibit 12.16 illustrates the scale used for the research. The letters along the left side, which show the relevant factor, would be omitted from the actual scale, as would the numerical values shown. Note also that the evaluation, potency and activity scales are mixed, and about half are reversed to minimize the halo effect. To analyse the results, the set of evaluation (E) values is averaged, as are those for the potency (P) and activity (A) dimensions.

The data are plotted in Exhibit 12.17. Here the adjective pairs are reordered so evaluation, potency and activity descriptors are grouped together with the ideal factor reflected by the left side of the scale. Profiles of the three candidates may be compared to each other and to the ideal.

Analyse (candidate) for current position:

| | | | | | | | | | | | | | | | |
|---|---|---|---|---|---|---|---|---|---|---|---|---|---|---|---|
| (E) | Sociable | (7): | : | ___ | : | ___ | : | ___ | : | ___ | : | ___ | : ___ | : (1) Unsociable |
| (P) | Weak | (1): | : | ___ | : | ___ | : | ___ | : | ___ | : | ___ | : ___ | : (7) Strong |
| (A) | Active | (7): | : | ___ | : | ___ | : | ___ | : | ___ | : | ___ | : ___ | : (1) Passive |
| (E) | Progressive | (7): | : | ___ | : | ___ | : | ___ | : | ___ | : | ___ | : ___ | : (1) Regressive |
| (P) | Yielding | (1): | : | ___ | : | ___ | : | ___ | : | ___ | : | ___ | : ___ | : (7) Tenacious |
| (A) | Slow | (1): | : | ___ | : | ___ | : | ___ | : | ___ | : | ___ | : ___ | : (7) Fast |
| (E) | True | (7): | : | ___ | : | ___ | : | ___ | : | ___ | : | ___ | : ___ | : (1) False |
| (P) | Heavy | (7): | : | ___ | : | ___ | : | ___ | : | ___ | : | ___ | : ___ | : (1) Light |
| (A) | Hot | (7): | : | ___ | : | ___ | : | ___ | : | ___ | : | ___ | : ___ | : (1) Cold |
| (E) | Unsuccessful | (1): | : | ___ | : | ___ | : | ___ | : | ___ | : | ___ | : ___ | : (7) Successful |

*Exhibit 12.16* SD scale for analysing candidates for an industry leadership position.

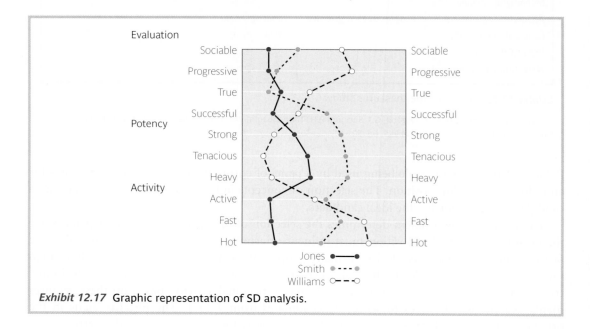

*Exhibit 12.17* Graphic representation of SD analysis.

## Adapting SD scales to the management question

One study explored a retail store image using 35 pairs of words or phrases classified into eight groups. These word pairs were especially created for the study. Excerpts from this scale are presented in Exhibit 12.18. Other categories of scale items were 'general characteristics of the company', 'physical characteristics of the store', 'prices charged by the store', 'store personnel', 'advertising by the store' and 'your friends and the store'. Since the scale pairs are associated closely with the characteristics of the store and its use, one could develop image profiles of various stores.

**Convenience of reaching the store from your location**

| | | | |
|---|---|---|---|
| Nearby | : —— : —— : —— : —— : —— : —— : —— : | Distant |
| Short time required to reach store | : —— : —— : —— : —— : —— : —— : —— : | Long time required to reach store |
| Difficult drive | : —— : —— : —— : —— : —— : —— : —— : | Easy drive |
| Difficult to find parking place | : —— : —— : —— : —— : —— : —— : —— : | Easy to find parking place |
| Convenient to other stores I shop | : —— : —— : —— : —— : —— : —— : —— : | Inconvenient to other stores I shop |

**Products offered**

| | | | |
|---|---|---|---|
| Wide selection of different kinds of product | : —— : —— : —— : —— : —— : —— : —— : | Limited selection of different kinds of product |
| Fully stocked | : —— : —— : —— : —— : —— : —— : —— : | Understocked |
| Undependable products | : —— : —— : —— : —— : —— : —— : —— : | Dependable products |
| High quality | : —— : —— : —— : —— : —— : —— : —— : | Low quality |
| Numerous brands | : —— : —— : —— : —— : —— : —— : —— : | Few brands |
| Unknown brands | : —— : —— : —— : —— : —— : —— : —— : | Well-known brands |

*Exhibit 12.18* Adapting SD scales for retail store image study 1.

*Source:* Robert F. Kelly and Ronald Stephenson, 'The semantic differential: an information source for designing retail patronage appeals', *Journal of Marketing* 31, October 1967, p. 45.

## Advanced scaling techniques

New construction approaches have removed many of the deficiencies of traditional scales. Some have evolved to handle specific management research applications. Most techniques mentioned in this section rely on complex computer algorithms and require an understanding of multivariate statistics. Students interested in further information on these topics should refer to the statistical examples in Chapter 18 and the references.

**Multidimensional scaling** (MDS) describes a collection of techniques that deal with property space in a more general manner than the semantic differential. With MDS, one can scale objects, people or both, in ways that provide a visual impression of the relationships among variables. The data-handling characteristics of MDS provide several options: ordinal input (with interval output), and fully metric (interval) and non-metric modes. The various techniques use proximities as input data. A **proximity** is an index of perceived similarity or dissimilarity between objects. The objects might be 20 nations (or 10 primary exports) that participants are asked to judge in pairs of possible combinations as to their similarity. By means of a computer program, the ranked or rated relationships are then represented as points on a map in multidimensional space.[44]

We may think of three types of attribute space, each representing a multidimensional map. First, in objective space a product can be positioned in terms of, say, its price, taste and brand image. Second, a person's perceptions may also be positioned in subjective space using similar dimensions. These maps do not always coincide, but they do provide information about perceptual disparities. Since the subjective maps vary over time, they also provide important trend data. Third, we can describe our preferences for the object's ideal attributes. All objects close to the ideal are more preferred than those further away. These various configurations are said to reflect the 'hidden structure' of the data and make complicated problems much easier to understand.

In Exhibit 12.19 two dimensions are plotted: price and taste. The high-sodium beers are closest to the ideal beer on the price dimension while the imported beers are farthest away.

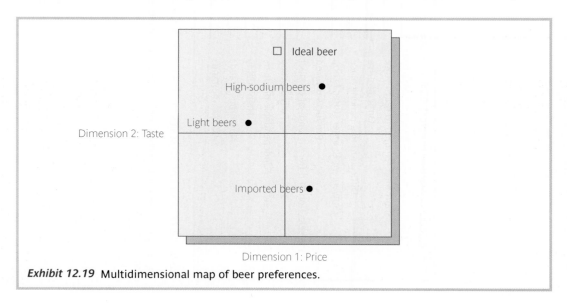

*Exhibit 12.19* Multidimensional map of beer preferences.

Another approach, representing a collection of techniques, is conjoint analysis. **Conjoint analysis** is used to measure complex decision-making that requires multi-attribute judgements. Its primary focus has been the explanation of consumer behaviour, with numerous applications in product development and marketing.[45]

When discovering and learning about products, consumers define a set of attributes or characteristics they use to compare competing brands or models in a product class. Using these attributes, they evaluate the product range and eliminate some brands. Then a final set of alternatives (including a non-purchase or delayed purchase decision) is developed. These evaluations can change if there is new information about additional competitors, corrections to attribute knowledge or further thoughts about the attribute. Algebraic theory can be used to model these cognitive processes and develop statistical approximations that reveal the rules the consumer follows in decision-making.[46]

For example, a consumer might be considering the purchase of a personal computer. Brand A has a fast processing speed and a high price. Brand B has a low price and a slower processor. The consumer's choice will be evidence of the utility of the processing-speed attribute. Simultaneously, other attributes are being evaluated – such as memory, portability, graphics support and user-friendliness.

Conjoint analysis can produce a scaled value for each attribute as well as a utility value for attributes that have levels (e.g. memory may have a range of 128 to more than 512 megabytes). Both ranking and rating inputs may be used to evaluate product attributes. Conjoint analysis is not restricted to marketing applications, nor should it be considered a single generalized technique (see Chapter 19).

Finally, advanced students who are interested in the above techniques may also wish to investigate magnitude estimation scaling.[47] Magnitude scales provide access to ratio measurement and open new alternatives to management problems previously addressed through ordinal scales alone. Rasch models also offer alternative approaches to a range of traditional measures, from dichotomous responses to Likert-type response formats.[48]

For a more in-depth insight into this topic please see Spotlight on Research 6 at the end of this chapter.

## Research Methods in Practice 12

### Measuring contracts and uncertainty

How to measure contracts? Previous research (see Exhibit 3.12 in Chapter 3) focused on one specific aspect of a contract, such as the contract duration or whether it was an oral or written contract. We were, however, interested in contracts as a whole, but how could we reduce the contracts often longer than 20 pages to one or a couple of simple numbers that could be used in statistical analyses.

We needed a yardstick to measure the contracts, but there was no such yardstick available so we had to develop one. Our main problem in developing this yardstick was the choice between having a widely usable but coarse stick and a fine stick with limited applicability. If the yardstick was too specific, it would not be suitable to measure every one of our contracts, but if it was too coarse we would not be able to detect smaller differences between the cooperations. Our first task was to think about what kind of dimension such a yardstick could have; looking at earlier studies suggested that possible options would be inches (to measure the thickness of a written contract) or a number of clauses. Also, the idea to measure contracts in inches is for its simplicity appealing. We settled for a measurement of clauses, as clauses are the natural sub-elements of a contract. The decision to measure contracts with clauses did not solve the problem entirely, because now we had to decide what counts for just one clause and what counts already for two clauses, because what in one contract was mentioned in three separate clauses was mentioned in one clause in another contract.

To solve this problem we developed a list of possible clauses in close cooperation with experts from the law faculty and company lawyers. Although theoretically a complete contract, that is a contract that covers everything, is impossible, we tried to create a quasi-complete contract. Thus, none of the contracts we investigated should contain a clause that is not mentioned in our quasi-complete contractual clauses list. Exhibit 12.20 provides an overview on which clauses we asked for in each cooperation and whether a clause serves as a commitment mitigating opportunism or whether a clause serves another function, such as solving coordination problems. We asked the respondents whether the respondent and the partner had agreed on the mentioned aspect and whether it was a written or oral agreement.

As we had split the clauses into different types, we measured the contracts onto related dimensions,

| Commitments mitigating opportunism | Other functions |
|---|---|
| • cost calculations<br>• sanction for late payment<br>• sanction for late delivery | • payment days<br>• delivery date<br>• cost changes<br>• cost determination<br>• liabilities<br>• arbitrage |
| • secrecy issue<br>• patents, licences, and so on brought into the cooperation<br>• allocation of patents, licences resulting from the cooperaton<br>• access to partner's plants<br>• 'escrow'-rules | |
| • contract termination<br>• contract prolongation<br>• exchange of employees<br>• provision of machinery<br>• buying obligations | • quality norms (ISO 9000)<br>• spare parts<br>• maintenance<br>• updating<br>• planning and objectives<br>• flexibility<br>• contact persons<br>• reporting<br>• partner assessment<br>• joint management |
| • exclusivity | • participation of third |

Exhibit 12.20 Overview of contractual clauses covered in the questionnaires.

both times by simply counting how many written clauses a contract contained. The first measure considered all clauses and the second measure considered only the opportunism mitigating clauses. Of course, aggregating the different clauses by simply summing them up is an ad hoc aggregation. One could also consider giving weights to certain clauses or to use even more complex forms of aggregation. More complex forms of aggregation are often, however, also ad hoc. Personally, I prefer simple forms of aggregation unless there are strong and convincing reasons for more complex forms of aggregation, that is if your aggregation is ad hoc keep it simple, if you have reasons you can make it more complex.

For the dissertation project, I did not use the information on which clauses the partners agreed orally. Oral agreement on clauses occurred very rarely and either together with a written agreement or referred to very specific clauses, for example on joint management or contact persons. However, it should be stated that the project on research and development (R&D) cooperation emphasized the formal governance structures and social embeddedness and it did not address informal management. One could, of course, use the data collected to explore in which cooperations oral agreements that are difficult to enforce are more or less likely.

If you compare how we developed a scale for contracting in the R&D project with what is written in the main text of this chapter, you will easily see that we did not fulfil many of the requirements mentioned there. For many abstract concepts, such as personality, and so on, scholars work with one or more established scales, but establishing a scale takes time. Research measuring contracts is still in an early phase and when the project took place just a few people had attempted to measure contracts at all. After we completed the project on R&D cooperations, we continued to explore and investigate issues of inter-firm cooperation. One issue we are interested in is whether contracts only serve the mitigation of opportunism as transaction cost theory suggests. In the R&D project, we have already stated that some clauses serve another purpose. Once you subscribe to the idea that a contract has different purposes, you need to concede that any scale on contracting should be multidimensional. But what are these dimensions and how could you empirically check that a contract is multidimensional?

# Summary

1 While people measure things casually in daily life, research measurement is more precise and controlled. In measurement, one settles for measuring properties of the objects rather than the objects themselves. An event is measured in terms of its duration. What happened during it, who was involved, where it occurred, and so on, are all properties of the event. To be more precise, what are measured are indicants of the properties. Thus, for duration, one measures the number of hours and minutes recorded. For what happened, one uses some system to classify the types of activity that occurred. Measurement typically uses some sort of scale to classify or quantify the data collected.

2 There are four scale types. In increasing order of power, these are nominal, ordinal, interval and ratio. Nominal scales classify without indicating order, distance or unique origin. Ordinal data show magnitude relationships of more than and less than but have no distance or unique origin. Interval scales have both order and distance but no unique origin. Ratio scales possess all these features.

3 Instruments may yield incorrect readings of an indicant for many reasons. These may be classified according to error sources: (i) the participant or subject, (ii) situational factors, (iii) the measurer, and (iv) the instrument.

4 Sound measurement must meet the tests of validity, reliability and practicality. Validity reveals the degree to which an instrument measures what it is supposed to measure to assist the researcher in solving the research problem. Three forms of validity are used to evaluate measurement scales. Content validity exists to the degree that a measure provides an adequate reflection of the topic under study. Its determination is primarily judgemental and intuitive. Criterion-related validity relates to our ability to predict some outcome or estimate the existence of some current condition. Construct validity is the most complex and abstract. A measure has construct validity to the degree that it conforms to predicted correlations of other theoretical propositions.

   A measure is reliable if it provides consistent results. Reliability is a partial contributor to validity, but a measurement tool may be reliable without being valid. Three forms of reliability are stability, equivalence and internal consistency. A measure has practical value for the research if it is economical, convenient and interpretable.

5 Scaling describes the procedures by which we assign numbers to measurements of opinions, attitudes and other concepts. Selection of a measurement scale to best meet our needs involves six decisions as follows.
   a Study objective: do we measure the characteristics of the participant or the stimulus object?
   b Response form: do we measure with a rating scale or a ranking scale?
   c Degree of preference: do we measure our preferences or make non-preference judgements?
   d Data properties: do we measure with nominal, ordinal, interval or ratio data?

   e  Number of dimensions: do we measure using a unidimensional or multidimensional scale?

   f  Scale construction: do we develop scales by arbitrary decision, consensus, item analysis, cumulative scaling or factor analysis?

   In this chapter, two classifications – the response form and scale construction techniques – were emphasized.

6  When using rating scales, one judges an object in absolute terms against certain specified criteria. Several scales were proposed: simple category; multiple-choice, single-response; multiple-choice, multiple-response; Likert scales; semantic differential; numerical scales; multiple rating lists; fixed sum scales; stapel scales; and graphic rating scales. When you use ranking methods, you make relative comparisons against other similar objects. Three well-known methods are the paired-comparison, forced ranking and the comparative scale.

7  Scaled measurement strategies are classified by the techniques used to construct them. Of the five techniques, three are used frequently: the arbitrary approach, item analysis and factoring. Consensus and cumulative methods receive less attention because they are time-consuming or have fewer business applications. Arbitrary scales are designed by the researcher's own subjective selection of items. These scales are simple to construct and have content validity only.

   In the consensus method, a panel is used to judge the relevance, ambiguity and attitude level of scale items. Those items that are judged best are then included in the final instrument. The Thurstone method of equal-appearing intervals is a historic consensus method that has given impetus for many current scales.

   With the item analysis approach, one develops many items believed to express either a favourable or an unfavourable attitude towards some general object. These items are then pre-tested to decide which ones discriminate between persons with high total scores and those with low total scores on the test. Those items that meet this discrimination test are included in the final instrument. The most successful Likert scales are developed using this approach.

   With the cumulative approach scales, it is possible to estimate how a participant has answered individual items by knowing the total score. The items are related to each other on a particular attitude dimension, so that if one agrees with a more extreme item, one will also agree with items representing less extreme views. The scalogram is the classic example.

   Factoring develops measurement questions through factor analysis or similar correlation techniques. It is particularly useful in uncovering latent attitude dimensions, and it approaches scaling through the concept of multidimensional attribute space. The semantic differential scale is an example.

   Other developments in scaling include multidimensional scaling and conjoint analysis. Each represents a family of related techniques with a variety of applications for handling complex judgements. Magnitude estimation and Rasch models provide an avenue for reconceptualizing traditional scaling techniques for greater efficiency and freedom from error.

## Discussion questions

## Terms in review

1 What can we measure about the four objects listed below? Be as specific as possible.
   a laundry detergent
   b employees
   c factory output
   d job satisfaction

2 What are the essential differences among nominal, ordinal, interval and ratio scales? How do these differences affect the statistical analysis techniques we can use?

3 What are the four major sources of measurement error? Illustrate by example how each of these might affect measurement results in a face-to-face interview situation.

4 Do you agree or disagree with the following statements? Explain.
   a Validity is more critical to measurement than reliability.
   b Content validity is the most difficult type of validity to determine.
   c A valid measurement is reliable, but a reliable measurement may not be valid.
   d Stability and equivalence are essentially the same thing.

5 Discuss the relative merits of and problems with:
   a rating and ranking scales
   b Likert and differential scales
   c unidimensional and multidimensional scales.

## Making research decisions

6 You have data from a corporation on the annual salary of each of its 200 employees.
   a Illustrate how the data can be presented as ratio, interval, ordinal and nominal data.
   b Describe the successive loss of information as the presentation changes from ratio to nominal.

7 Below are listed some objects of varying degrees of abstraction. Suggest properties of each of these objects that can be measured by ranking or rating scales:
   a store customers
   b voter attitudes
   c hardness of steel alloys
   d preference for a particular common stock
   e profitability of various divisions in a company.

8 You have been asked by the head of marketing to design an instrument by which your private, for-profit school can evaluate the quality and value of its various curricula and courses. How might you try to ensure that your instrument has:
   a stability
   b equivalence
   c internal consistency
   d content validity
   e predictive validity (f) construct validity?

9 A new employee at Michelin, you are asked to assume the management of the *Red Michelin Restaurant Guide*. Each restaurant striving to be included in the guide needs to be evaluated. Only a select

few restaurants may earn three-star status. What dimensions would you choose to measure to apply one to three stars in the *Red Michelin Restaurant Guide*?

10 You have been asked to develop an index of student morale at your school.
   a  What constructs or concepts might you employ?
   b  Choose several of the major concepts and specify their dimensions.
   c  Select observable indicators you might use to measure these dimensions.
   d  How would you compile these various dimensions into a single index?
   e  How would you judge the reliability and/or validity of these measurements?

11 Suppose your firm had planned a major research study. Two months before the study, the government resigned. It is the third government resignation in less than three years. This government, and all previous governments, were unable to obtain a majority of votes in the parliament for law initiatives reducing state expenditure on social welfare. In the meantime, the state's budget deficit is rising and exceeds 3 per cent of gross national product (GNP), a criterion set by the members of the Euro Zone. Given these recent developments, your superior decides to add a question to the study. The question must measure consumers' confidence that the economic system will be able to rebound in the next 12 months, and the subsequent effects (increased layoffs, higher unemployment, numerous firms failing to meet their sales and profit projections, lower holiday retail sales, war on terrorism). Draft a scale of each of the following types to measure that confidence level:
   a  fixed sum scale
   b  Likert-type summated scale
   c  semantic differential scale
   d  stapel scale
   e  forced ranking scale.

12 An investigative question in your employee satisfaction study seeks to assess employee 'job involvement'. Create a measurement question that uses the following scales:
   a  a graphic rating scale
   b  a multiple rating list.
   c  Which do you recommend and why?

13 You receive the results of a paired-comparison preference test of four soft drinks from a sample of 200 people. The results are as shown in the table below:

|            | Koak | Zip  | Pabze | Mr Peepers |
|------------|------|------|-------|------------|
| Koak       | –    | 50*  | 115   | 35         |
| Zip        | 150  | –    | 160   | 70         |
| Pabze      | 85   | 40   | –     | 45         |
| Mr Peepers | 165  | 130  | 155   | –          |

*reads as 50 people preferred Zip to Koak.

   a  How do these brands rank in overall preference in this sample?
   b  Develop an interval scale for these four brands.

14 One of the problems in developing rating scales is the choice of response terms to use. Below are samples of some widely used scaling codes. Do you see any problems with them?
   a  Yes _____ Depends _____ No _____
   b  Excellent _____ Good _____ Fair _____ Poor _____

   c　Excellent _____ Good _____ Average _____ Fair _____ Poor _____

   d　Strongly Approve _____ Approve _____ Uncertain _____ Disapprove _____Strongly Disapprove _____

15　You are working on a consumer perception study of four brands of bicycle. You will need to develop measurement questions and scales to accomplish the following tasks. Also be sure to explain which data levels (nominal, ordinal, interval, ratio) are appropriate and which quantitative techniques you will use.

   a　Prepare an overall assessment of all the brands.

   b　Provide a comparison of the brands for each of the following dimensions:

      i　styling

      ii　durability

      iii　gear quality

      iv　brand image.

16　Below is a Likert-type scale that might be used to evaluate your opinion of the educational pro-gramme you are in. There are five response categories: 'Strongly agree' (SA) via 'Neither agree nor disagree' (AND) to 'Strongly disagree' (SD). If 5 represents the most positive attitude, how would the different items be valued?

   a　This programme is not very challenging.
     SA AND SD

   b　The general level of teaching is good.
     SA AND SD

   c　I really think I am learning a lot from this programme.
     SA AND SD

   d　Students' suggestions are given little attention here.
     SA AND SD

   e　This programme does a good job of preparing one for a career.
     SA AND SD

   f　This programme is below my expectations.
     SA AND SD

Record your answers to the above items. In what two different ways could such responses be used? What would be the purpose of each?

# From concept to practice

17　Using Exhibits 12.8 and 12.2, match each question to its appropriate data type. For each data type not represented, develop a measurement question that would obtain that type of data.

18　Using the response strategies within Exhibit 12.10 or 12.11, which would be appropriate to, and add insight to, understanding the various indicants of student demand for the academic pro-gramme in which they are enrolled?

# Classroom discussion

19　The story of how business studies has attempted to explain organizational performance is a disap-pointing one. Although thousands of quantitative as well as qualitative studies have looked at the question of why certain firms perform better than others, we still know next to nothing about the reasons. Studies revealing that certain success factors, such as firm size, market share, R&D expenditure, and so on, enhance organizational performance are contradicted by other studies that find no evidence for this, or even a negative correlation between these factors and performance. The problem starts with the question 'What do we mean when we talk about organizational performance?' Brainstorm in the class about the meanings of the term 'organizational performance' and then discuss how the relationship between certain success factors and performance is affected by the different meanings attached to the term.

**20** In psychology, in particular, the development and validation of scales has become a commercial business. For example, several research institutes offer validated scales to measure emotional intelligence (EQ) and to use them you need to commission research according to them. Discuss the consequences of such commercial practice in terms of the advancement of knowledge, cross-checking of the quality of research studies, and so on.

**Online**
*Learning* **Centre**

## Get started with understanding statistical techniques!

When you have read this chapter, log on to the Online Learning Centre website at **www.mcgraw-hill.co.uk/textbooks/blumberg** to explore chapter-by-chapter test questions, additional case studies, a glossary and more online study tools for Business Research Methods.

# Notes

[1] Fred N. Kerlinger, *Foundations of Behavioral Research* (3rd edn.). New York: Holt, Rinehart & Winston, 1986, p. 396; S. Stevens, 'Measurement, statistics, and the schemapiric view', *Science* (August 1968), p. 384.

[2] W.S. Torgerson, *Theory and Method of Scaling*. New York: Wiley, 1958, p. 19.

[3] We assume the reader has had an introductory statistics course in which measures of central tendency such as arithmetic mean, median and mode have been treated. Similarly, we assume familiarity with measures of dispersion such as the standard deviation, range and interquartile range. For a brief review of these concepts, refer to the 'Descriptive statistics' section in Chapter 15 on the CD-Rom or see an introductory statistics text.

[4] While this might intuitively seem to be the case, consider that one might prefer a over b, b over c, yet c over a. These results cannot be scaled as ordinal data because there is apparently more than one dimension involved.

[5] L.L. Thurstone, *The Measurement of Values*. Chicago: University of Chicago Press, 1959.

[6] Parametric tests are appropriate when the measurement is interval or ratio, and when we can accept certain assumptions about the underlying distributions of the data with which we are

working. Non-parametric tests usually involve much weaker assumptions about measurement scales (nominal and ordinal), and the assumptions about the underlying distribution of the population are fewer and less restrictive. More on these tests is found in Chapters 16–18 and Appendix D.

[7] Sidney Siegel, *Nonparametric Statistics for the Behavioral Sciences*. New York: McGraw-Hill, 1956, p. 32.

[8] Norman A. Anderson, 'Scales and statistics: parametric and nonparametric', *Psychological Bulletin* 58(4), pp. 315–16.

[9] Kerlinger, *Foundations*, p. 403.

[10] See later in this chapter for a discussion of the differential scale.

[11] See Chapters 16 and 17 for a discussion of these procedures.

[12] The exception involves the creation of a dummy variable for use in a regression or discriminant equation. A non-metric variable is transformed into a metric variable through the assignment of a 0 or 1, and used in a predictive equation.

[13] Claire Selltiz, Lawrence S. Wrightsman and Stuart W. Cook, *Research Methods in Social Relations* (3rd edn.). New York: Holt, Rinehart & Winston, 1976, pp. 164–9.

[14] Robert L. Thorndike and Elizabeth Hagen, *Measurement and Evaluation in Psychology and Education* (3rd edn.). New York: Wiley, 1969, p. 5.

[15] Examples of other conceptualizations of validity are factorial validity, job-analytic validity, synthetic validity, rational validity and statistical conclusion validity.

[16] Thomas D. Cook and Donald T. Campbell, 'The design and conduct of quasi experiments and true experiments in field settings', in Marvin D. Dunnette (ed.), *Handbook of Industrial and Organizational Psychology*. Chicago: Rand McNally, 1976, p. 223.

[17] *Standards for Educational and Psychological Tests and Manuals*. Washington, DC: American Psychological Association, 1974, p. 26.

[18] Wayne F. Cascio, *Applied Psychology in Personnel Management*. Reston, VA: Reston Publishing, 1982, p. 149.

[19] Thorndike and Hagen, *Measurement and Evaluation*, p. 168.

[20] See, for example, Cascio, *Applied Psychology*, pp. 146–7; Edward G. Carmines and Richard A. Zeller, *Reliability and Validity Assessment*. Beverly Hills, CA: Sage, 1979, pp. 48–50.

[21] Emanuel J. Mason and William J. Bramble, *Understanding and Conducting Research*. New York: McGraw-Hill, 1989, pp. 260–3.

[22] Cascio, *Applied Psychology*, pp. 135–6.

[23] Mason and Bramble, *Understanding and Conducting Research*, p. 268.

[24] Thorndike and Hagen, *Measurement and Evaluation*, p. 199.

[25] Martin Patchen, *Some Questionnaire Measures of Employee Motivation and Morale*, Monograph No. 41. Ann Arbor: Institute for Social Research, University of Michigan, 1965, p. 17.

[26] Ibid., p. 25.

[27] Bernard S. Phillips, *Social Research Strategy and Tactics* (2nd edn.). New York: Macmillan, 1971, p. 205.

[28] For a discussion of various scale classifications, see W.S. Torgerson, *Theory and Methods of Scaling.* New York: Wiley, 1958, Chapter 3.

[29] E.A. Suchman and R.G. Francis, 'Scaling techniques in social research', in J.T. Doby (ed.), *An Introduction to Social Research.* Harrisburg, PA: Stackpole, 1954, pp. 126–9.

[30] A study of the historic research literature found that more than three-quarters of the attitude scales used were of the five-point type. An examination of more recent literature suggests that the five-point scale is still common but that there is a growing use of longer scales. For the historic study, see Daniel D. Day, 'Methods in attitude research', *American Sociological Review* 5 (1940), pp. 395–410. Single versus multiple-item scaling requirements are discussed in Jum C. Nunnally, *Psychometric Theory.* New York: McGraw-Hill, 1967, Chapter 14.

[31] This section is adapted from Pamela L. Alreck and Robert B. Settle, *The Survey Research Handbook.* Burr Ridge, IL: Irwin, 1995, Chapter 5.

[32] J.P. Guilford, *Psychometric Methods.* New York: McGraw-Hill, 1954, pp. 278–79.

[33] P.M. Synonds, 'Notes on rating', *Journal of Applied Psychology* 9 (1925), pp. 188–95.

[34] See L.L. Thurstone, 'A law of comparative judgment', *Psychological Review* 34 (1927), pp. 273–86.

[35] Guilford, *Psychometric Methods.*

[36] See Milton A. Saffir, 'A comparative study of scales constructed by three psychophysical methods', *Psychometrica* 11(3) (September 1937), pp. 179–98.

[37] Allen L. Edwards, *Techniques of Attitude Scale Construction.* New York: Appleton-Century-Crofts, 1957, pp. 152–4.

[38] One study reported that the construction of a Likert scale took only half the time required to construct a Thurstone scale. See L.L. Thurstone and K.K. Kenney, 'A comparison of the Thurstone and Likert techniques of attitude scale construction', *Journal of Applied Psychology* 30 (1946), pp. 72–83.

[39] Edwards, *Techniques*, p. 153.

[40] Louis Guttman, 'A basis for scaling qualitative data', *American Sociological Review* 9 (1944), pp. 139–50.

[41] John P. Robinson, 'Toward a more appropriate use of Guttman scaling', *Public Opinion Quarterly* 37 (Summer 1973), pp. 260–7.

[42] For more on the process of factor analysis, see Chapter 18.

[43] Charles E. Osgood, G.J. Suci and P.H. Tannenbaum, *The Measurement of Meaning.* Urbana, IL: University of Illinois Press, 1957.

[44] Ibid., p. 49. See also James G. Snider and Charles E. Osgood (eds.), *Semantic Differential Technique.* Chicago: Aldine, 1969.

[45] Ibid., p. 79.

[46] See, for example, Joseph B. Kruskal and Myron Wish, *Multidimensional Scaling.* Beverly Hills, CA: Sage, 1978; Paul Green and V.R. Rao, *Applied Multidimensional Scaling: A Comparison of Approaches and Algorithms.* New York: Holt, Rinehart & Winston, 1972; Paul E. Green and F.J. Carmone, *Multidimensional Scaling in Marketing Analysis.* Boston: Allyn & Bacon, 1970.

[47] See P. Cattin and D.R. Wittink, 'Commercial use of conjoint analysis: a survey', *Journal of Market-*

*ing* 46 (1982), pp. 44–53; Cattin and Wittink, 'Commercial use of conjoint analysis: an update', paper presented at the ORSA/TIMS Marketing Science Meetings, Richardson, TX, 12–15 March 1986.

[48] Jordan J. Louviere, *Analyzing Decision Making: Metric Conjoint Analysis*. Beverly Hills, CA: Sage, 1988, pp. 9–11.

[49] See, for example, Milton Lodge, *Magnitude Scaling: Quantitative Measurement of Opinions*. Beverly Hills, CA: Sage, 1981; Donald R. Cooper and Donald A. Clare, 'A magnitude estimation scale for human values', *Psychological Reports* 49 (1981).

[50] David Andrich, *Rasch Models for Measurement*. Beverly Hills, CA: Sage, 1988.

# Recommended further reading

Edwards, Allen L., *Techniques of Attitude Scale Construction*. New York: Irvington, 1979. Thorough discussion of basic unidimensional scaling techniques.

Embretson, Susan E. and Hershberger, Scott L., *The New Rules of Measurement*. Mahwah, NJ: Lawrence Erlbaum Associates, 1999. Bridges the gap between theoretical and practical measurement.

Guilford, J.P., *Psychometric Methods* (2nd edn.). New York: McGraw-Hill, 1954.

Kelley, D. Lynn, *Measurement Made Accessible: A Research Approach Using Qualitative, Quantitative, and TQM Methods*. Thousand Oaks, CA: Sage Publications, 1999. Sections on bias, reliability and validity are appropriate for this chapter.

Miller, Delbert C., *Handbook of Research Design and Social Measurement* (5th edn.). Thousand Oaks, CA: Sage, 1991. Presents a large number of existing sociometric scales and indexes as well as information on their characteristics, validity and sources.

Nunnally, J.C. and Bernstein, Ira, *Psychometric Theory* (3rd edn.). New York: McGraw-Hill, 1993. The classic text on psychometric theory.

Osgood, Charles E., Suci, George J. and Tannenbaum, Percy H., *The Measurement of Meaning*. Urbana, IL: University of Illinois Press, 1957. The basic reference on SD scaling.

Singh, Jagdip, 'Tackling measurement problems with item response theory: principles, characteristics and assessment, with an illustrative example', *Journal of Business Research* 57(2), 2004, pp. 184–208. This article introduces several new measurement models developed by psychometricians and discusses how these can be applied in a business research context.

Thorndike, Robert M., *Measurement and Evaluation in Psychology and Education* (6th edn.). Upper Saddle River, NJ: Prentice-Hall, 1996.

# Spotlight on research 5

## Measuring job satisfaction

Measuring the job satisfaction and motivation of employees is a recurring activity in many firms. Within the scientific literature you will find it easy to locate studies reporting such findings, as well as details of how exactly the researchers measured job satisfaction and motivation.

An early account of such a study is a piece of research conducted at five geographically separate units of the Tennessee Valley Authority (TVA), three divisions of an electronics company, and five departments of an appliance manufacturing company. The procedure for developing the measures was first to hold a number of informal interviews with supervisory and non-supervisory employees. From the knowledge acquired, the researchers constructed the questions. These were then pre-tested and revised twice on separate groups of TVA employees. Out of this process came the six-item questionnaire on 'Interest in Work Innovation', shown in Exhibit S5.1. This instrument and the others were completed by employees of the three companies.

The reliability of the Interest in Work Innovation Index was measured by a test-retest of individual questions. The retest was done one month after the first test. Correlating the test-retest scores question by question gave the following results (see the Pearson correlation coefficient in Chapter 17 for more information on how these correlation coefficients were computed).

| Question | r |
|---|---|
| Q1 | .72 |
| Q2 | .72 |
| Q3 | .64 |
| Q4 | .67 |
| Q5 | .54 |
| Q6 | .85 |

The researchers measured criterion-based validity by comparing worker scores on the six questions to ratings of the same workers by their supervisors. Supervisors were asked to 'think of specific instances where employees in their units had suggested new or better ways of doing the job'. They then ranked employees they personally knew on 'looking out for new ideas'.[49] The median correlation between the index scores and the supervisor ratings was about .35. At TVA, where there was an active suggestion system in operation, they also found that the index scores of those making suggestions were significantly higher than those not making suggestions.

Construct validity was evaluated by comparing scores on the Interest in Work Innovation Index to other job-related variables. Mean scores on the index were computed for 90 work groups at TVA. These means were then correlated with group scores on other variables that were hypothesized to relate to interest in innovation. The results are shown in Exhibit S5.2.

The researchers concluded that, 'The Index of Interest in Work Innovation, while a rough one, shows adequate reliability and sufficient evidence of validity to warrant its use in making rough distinctions among groups of people (or among units).'[50] In addition, they tested a short version of the index (items 1, 5 and 6) and found its validity to be almost equal to that of the longer form.

1   In your kind of work, if a person tries to change his or her usual way of doing things, how does it generally turn out?

(1) _____ Usually turns out worse; the tried and true methods work best in my work.

(3) _____ Usually doesn't.

(5) _____ Usually turns out better; our methods need improvement.

2   Some people prefer doing a job in pretty much the same way because this way they can count on always doing a good job. Others like to go out of their way in order to think up new ways of doing things. How is it with you on your job?

(1) _____ I always prefer doing things pretty much in the same way.

(2) _____ I mostly prefer doing things pretty much in the same way.

(4) _____ I mostly prefer doing things in new and different ways.

(5) _____ I always prefer doing things in new and different ways.

3   How often do you try out, on your own, a better or faster way of doing something on the job?

(5) _____ Once a week or more often.

(4) _____ Two or three times a month.

(3) _____ About once a month.

(2) _____ Every few months.

(1) _____ Rarely or never.

4   How often do you get chances to try out your own ideas on the job, either before or after checking with your supervisor?

(5) _____ Several times a week or more.

(4) _____ About once a week.

(3) _____ Several times a month.

(2) _____ About once a month.

(1) _____ Less than once a month.

5   In my kind of job, it's usually better to let my supervisor worry about new or better ways of doing things.

(1) _____ Strongly agree.

(2) _____ Mostly agree.

(4) _____ Mostly disagree.

(5) _____ Strongly disagree.

6   How many times in the past year have you suggested to your supervisor a different or better way of doing something on the job?

(1) _____ Never had occasion to do this during the past year.

(2) _____ Once or twice.

(3) _____ About three times.

(4) _____ About five times.

(5) _____ Six to ten times.

(6) More than ten times had occasion to do this during the past year.

*Exhibit S5.1*  Interest in work innovation index*.

*Note*: *Numbers in parentheses preceding each response category indicate the score assigned to each response.

*Source*: Martin Patchen, *Some Questionnaire Measures of Employee Motivation and Morale*, Monograph No. 41. Ann Arbor: Institute for Social Research, University of Michigan, 1965, pp. 15 – 16.

| Correlation | Variable Name |
|---|---|
| .44[‡] | Job difficulty |
| .39[‡] | Identification with own occupation |
| .29[‡] | Control over work methods |
| .28[‡] | Perceived opportunity for achievement |
| .19 | Feedback on performance |
| .13 | Control over goals in work |
| .06 | Need for achievement[§] |
| −.05 | Pressure from peers to do a good job |
| .36[‡] | General job motivation |
| .36[‡] | Willingness to disagree with supervisors |
| .12 | Acceptance of changes in work situation |
| .00 | Identification with TVA |
| .21[‖] | Overall satisfaction (with pay, promotion, supervisors and peers) |

*Notes*
\* The shorter three-item Index B was used for these correlations.
[†] Variables listed are all indexes; each index is composed of several specific questions.
[‡] $p<.01$, two-tailed t-test
[§] This is the Achievement Risk Preference Scale developed by P. O'Connor and
J.W. Atkinson (1960)
[‖] $p<.05$, two-tailed t-test

**Exhibit S5.2** Relation of scores on interest in work innovation index\* to scores on other job-related variables[†] for 90 work groups at TVA (Pearson product-moment correlation coefficient, *r*).

*Source*: Martin Patcher, *Some Questionnaire Measures of Employee Motivation and Morale*, Monograph No. 41, Ann Artor: Institute for Social Research, University of Michigan, 1965, p. 24.

Suppose you were asked to conduct a survey on job satisfaction and motivation for your firm's human resources department. One option would be to use questions from an earlier study. However, the head of the human resources department believes she needs a device tailored to the unique situation of the firm (a belief that is common among many managers and researchers). Such a belief can be costly and time-consuming. Reliability testing may be ignored and validity assessments may be confined to impressions about content. Typically, there is no comparable evidence from other studies by which to calibrate the findings but, currently, so many measures for job satisfaction exist that you should be able to find one that is suitable for your firm and you can even obtain those that are copyrighted from commercial sources.

# Chapter 13

# Fieldwork: Questionnaires and Responses

## Chapter contents

## LEARNING OBJECTIVES

When you have read this chapter, you should understand:

- ☑ the link forged by the management research question hierarchy between the management dilemma and the communication instrument

- ☑ the influence of communication method on instrument design

- ☑ how to construct good questions

- ☑ how question design issues influence instrument quality, reliability and validity

- ☑ sources of measurement questions

- ☑ the importance of pre-testing questions and instruments.

## 13.1 Developing the instrument design strategy

New researchers often want to draft questions immediately. They are reluctant to go through the preliminaries that make for successful surveys. Exhibit 13.1 is a suggested flowchart for instrument design. The procedures followed in developing an instrument vary from study to study, but the flowchart suggests three phases. Each phase is discussed in this chapter, starting with a review of the management research question hierarchy and its application to the study presented in the case study. The chapter concludes with a discussion of procedures for pre-testing the completed instrument.

## 13.2 The management research question hierarchy revisited: phase 1

The management research question hierarchy is the foundation of successful instrument development (see Exhibit 13.2). The process of moving from the general management or research dilemma to specific measurement questions goes through four question levels.

1 Dilemma question – the dilemma, stated in question form, that the manager or researcher wants to solve.

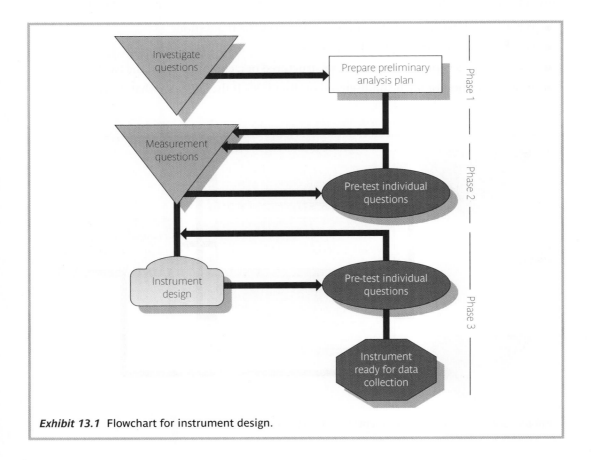

*Exhibit 13.1* Flowchart for instrument design.

**2** Research question(s) – the fact-based translation of the question the researcher must answer to contribute to the solution of the management question.

**3** Investigative questions – specific questions the researcher must answer to provide sufficient detail and coverage of the research question; within this level, there may be several questions as the researcher moves from the general to the specific.

**4** Measurement questions – questions participants must answer if the researcher is to gather the required information and resolve the management question.

Addressing the dilemma research question hierarchy is the first step in planning for the collection of data. Investigative questions are the core of the researcher's information needs. In many studies, an exploratory investigation helps the researcher understand all dimensions of the subject. In the Prince Corporation image study (see Chapter 10), many exploratory interviews were needed to ensure that all investigative topics were covered.

The case in this section reveals the thinking that leads to the final questionnaire; it also illustrates the direction of this chapter. Normally, once the researcher understands the connection between the investigative questions and the potential measurement questions, the next logical step is to plan a strategy for the survey. This requires the researcher to get down to the nitty-gritty of instrument design. The following are prominent among the strategic concerns.

- What type of data is needed to answer the management question?
- What communication approach will be used?
- Should the questions be structured, unstructured or a combination of the two?
- Should the questioning be undisguised or disguised? If the latter, to what degree?

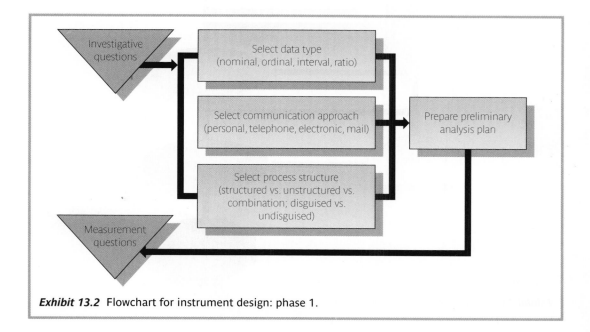

**Exhibit 13.2** Flowchart for instrument design: phase 1.

## Type of data

Data type determines the analytical procedures that are possible during data analysis. Chapter 6 discussed nominal, ordinal, interval and ratio data, and how the characteristics of each type influence the analysis (statistical choices and hypothesis testing). We now demonstrate how to code and extract the data from the instrument, and select appropriate descriptive measures or tests; the results will be analysed in Chapters 15–19.

## Communication approach

As discussed in Chapter 7, communication-based research may be conducted by personal interview, telephone, mail, computer or some combination of these. Decisions regarding which method to use, as well as where to interact with the participant (at home, at a neutral site, at the sponsor's place of business, etc.), will affect the design of the instrument. In personal interviewing and computer questioning, it is possible to use graphics and other questioning tools more easily than when questioning is done by mail or telephone. The differing delivery mechanisms result in different introductions, instructions, instrument layout and conclusions.

## Question structure

The degree of question and response structure must also be decided upon. Response strategy decisions (the type of question used) depend on the content and objectives of specific questions. Question wording is affected largely by the communication mode chosen and attempts to control bias. Questionnaires and interview schedules (**interview schedule** is an alternative term for the questionnaire used in an interview) can range from those that have a great deal of structure to those that are essentially unstructured. Both questionnaires and interview schedules contain three types of measurement question:

1 administrative questions
2 classification questions
3 target questions (structured or unstructured).

**Administrative questions** identify the participant, interviewer, interview location and conditions. These questions are rarely asked of the participant but are necessary if the researcher wishes to study patterns within the data and identify possible error sources. **Classification questions** are usually demographic variables that allow participants' answers to be grouped so that patterns are revealed and can be studied. **Target questions** address the investigative questions of a specific study. Target questions may be **structured questions** (they present the participants with a fixed set of choices, often called closed questions) or **unstructured questions** (they do not limit responses but do provide a frame of reference for participants' answers, sometimes referred to as open-ended questions).

The type of interview also affects question structure. In extremely unstructured interviews, the interviewer's task is to encourage the participant to talk in depth about a set of topics. The **in-depth interview** encourages participants to share as much information as possible in an unconstrained environment. The interviewer uses a minimum of prompts and guiding questions.

With more focused in-depth interviews, the researcher provides additional guidance by using a set of questions to promote discussion and elaboration by the participant. In these interviews, the researcher guides the topical direction and coverage. Whether the interview is focused or more in depth, the aim is to provide a relaxed environment in which the participant will be open to fully discuss topics. This kind of questioning is often used in exploratory research or where the investigator is dealing with complex topics that do not lend themselves to structured interviewing. If we were doing case research among various participants at a major event, a substantial portion of the questioning would be unique to each participant and would benefit from an unstructured approach.

Interviews with participants in **focus groups** are widely used in exploratory research. As noted in Chapter 4, the interviewer-moderator generally has a list of specific points he or she would like to see discussed, and these are used to prompt the group members. When the discussion stays within these bounds, the interviewer lets group members continue their interaction.

## Disguising objectives and sponsors

Another consideration in communication instrument design is whether the purpose of the study should be disguised. Some degree of disguise is often present in survey questions. A **disguised question** is designed to conceal the question's true purpose. The researcher will disguise the sponsor and the objective of a study if he or she believes that participants will respond differently than they would if both or either were known.

The accepted wisdom is that, often, we must disguise the study's objective or abandon the research. The decision about when to use disguised questioning may be made easier by identifying four situations where disguising the study objective is or is not an issue:

1  willingly shared, conscious-level information
2  reluctantly shared, conscious-level information
3  knowable, limitedly conscious-level information
4  subconscious-level information.

### *Willingly shared, conscious-level information*

When requesting this type of information, either disguised or undisguised questions may be used, but the situation rarely requires disguised techniques. For example: 'Have you attended the showing of a foreign-language film in the last six months?'

### *Reluctantly shared, conscious-level information*

When we ask for an opinion on some topic on which participants may hold a socially unacceptable view, we often use **projective techniques** (a disguised questioning method) because participants may not wish to reveal their true feelings or may give stereotypical answers. The researcher can encourage more accurate answers by phrasing the questions in a hypothetical way or by asking how 'people around here feel about this topic'. The assumption is that responses to these questions will indirectly reveal the participant's opinions.

### Knowable, limitedly conscious-level information

In some situations individuals know that they have a certain attitude but it is not clear to them why they hold that attitude. A classic example is a study of government bond-buying during the Second World War.[1] A survey sought reasons why, among people with equal ability to buy, some bought more war bonds than others. Frequent buyers had been personally solicited to buy bonds while most infrequent buyers had not received personal solicitation. No direct 'why' question to participants could have provided the answer to this question because participants did not know that they were receiving differing solicitation approaches.

### Subconscious-level information

Seeking insight into the basic motivations, underlying attitudes or consumption practices may or may not require disguised techniques. Projective techniques (such as sentence-completion tests, cartoon or balloon tests, and word-association tests) thoroughly disguise the study objective, but they are often difficult to interpret. For example: interview probes – 'Would you say, then, that the attitude you just expressed indicates you oppose or favour requiring adult drivers to declare their position on being an organ donor at the time of licence renewal?'

Another form of disguising refers to the sponsor, who either might prefer not to be revealed for strategic considerations or should not be revealed as knowing who sponsors the survey, might alter the response behaviour of the participants. An example of the first case, which is typical in commercial research, is that a firm thinking about entering a foreign market and conducting a country and market analysis often will prefer to remain anonymous as the study's sponsor to ensure that its future strategic plans are kept confidential. The latter case refers especially to sponsors who provoke strong associations with at least a proportion of the respondents, such as political parties or a company that has recently been the subject of a public scandal. In both cases the decision not to reveal the identity of the sponsor contains an ethical dimension, as knowledge of who is going to use the responses is part of the principal rights of the respondent (see also Chapter 3 on research ethics).

## Preliminary analysis plan

Researchers are concerned with adequate coverage of the topic and with securing the information in its most usable form. A good way to test how well a study plan meets these needs is to develop 'dummy' tables that display the data one expects to secure. This serves as a check on whether the planned measurement questions meet the data needs of the research question. It also helps the researcher determine the type of data needed for each question – a preliminary step to developing measurement questions for investigative questions.

# 13.3 Constructing and refining the measurement questions: phase 2

Drafting the questions begins once you develop a complete list of investigative questions and decide on the collection processes to be used. In phase 2 (see Exhibit 13.3) you draft specific

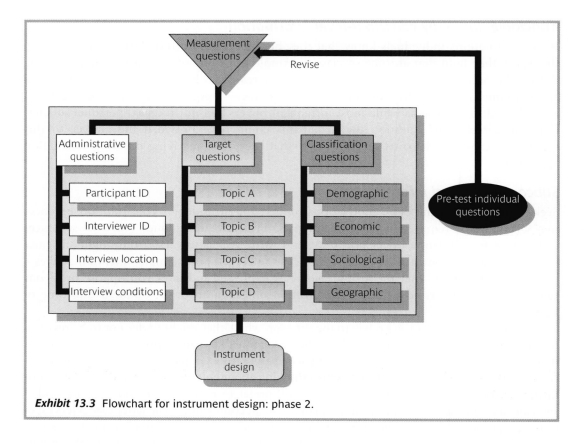

***Exhibit 13.3*** Flowchart for instrument design: phase 2.

measurement questions considering subject content, the wording of each question (influenced by the degree of disguise and the need to provide operational definitions for constructs and concepts), and response strategy (each producing a different level of data as necessary for your preliminary analysis plan). In phase 3 you must address topic and question sequencing. We will discuss these topics sequentially, although in practice the process is not orderly. For this discussion, we will assume that the questions are structured. The order, type and wording of the measurement questions, the introduction, the instructions, the transitions and the closure in a quality communication instrument should accomplish the following tasks.

## Encourage each participant to provide accurate responses

The proverb 'children and drunkards speak the truth' points at the danger that extensive cognitive processes intended to deliver more accurate answers might in fact disguise the 'truth'. A quick answer is often closer to what a respondent 'really' thinks and feels, than a well-elaborated one. For example, quick answers to the rating question 'How much do you like your boss?' will provide better responses than a thoroughly thought-through answer considering how your response to this question will affect the picture you give of your boss. Likewise, you have to know a priori what level of accuracy is sufficient for your study. For example, scholars at INSEAD were able to obtain a data set from an investment bank. This data set contains information on how each investment banker rated the support that they received from their fellow investment bankers, along with demographic information on the respondents. The bank, however, was reluctant to give accurate figures on the salary and bonuses each investment banker received, instead of precise figures, it 'only' provided a ranking of the investment banker's income on a 20-point scale without attaching real euro values to each scale. The researchers were very happy with this level of accuracy, because this ranking was sufficient for their purposes. Knowing the real values of income might even have depressed them, as investment bankers count their income in millions (salary levels beyond the reach and imagination of academics!).

## Encourage each participant to provide an adequate amount of information

This is a particular problem in unstructured interviews. While some respondents are very talkative, others are very limited in their answers. The skills of the interviewer are crucial to ensuring that participants deliver comparable information. Probing (i.e. repeating the answer to provoke additional responses) is one strategy used to encourage 'lazy' respondents to provide more information as well as to encourage talkative respondents to focus their extensive response accounts on the crucial points.

## Discourage each participant from refusing to answer specific questions

The chance of response refusal increases with the sensitivity of the question. Emphasizing that the answer of the respondent to a particular question is essential for the study, and that the answer is confidential, can increase the response to such questions. Acknowledging the sensitivity of the question in its introduction encourages participants to answer. For example, assume that you ask employees in a firm whether they have ever engaged in an affectional relationship with colleagues. An introduction to the question, stating that we know from previous studies that in every organization where people work together closely, professional relationships sometimes turn into affectional relationships, signals to the participant that these relationships are not unusual. Consequently, the respondent is more likely to provide an 'honest' account as the researcher has changed the frame of what is socially desirable.

## Discourage each participant from early discontinuation of participation

This applies mainly to mail questionnaires, because in telephone and personal interviews you have the chance to convince the participant to continue. The main point here is that participants enjoy answering your questions, that is they have the feeling that the questions relate to what they experience. Here follows a bad example. Recently one of the authors of this book received an online questionnaire investigating why academics choose to publish in certain journals:

> I started filling in my demographic details, an easy task. Then I was asked to select three journals in which I had published recently. Having answered this question I was confronted with a battery of questions investigating my reasons for choosing the particular journals for publishing, along with a general assessment of each journal. However, many questions asked did not even touch on the criteria I had used to assess or choose a journal (such as 'Please rate the scientific appearance of the journal's cover page on a 5-point scale'). Furthermore, answers to other questions required such complex comparative elaborations, that thinking about the answer simply took too long for an online mail questionnaire. After running through two-thirds of the questions for the first journal, and imagining that I would get the same questions for the other two journals I had mentioned, I soon decided to abandon the questionnaire, which resulted in the appearance of a pop-up window with the statement 'Unfortunately, you did not complete our questionnaire. Please click the button below, as we are interested very much in YOUR motives'. I just hit Alt-F4 to exit.

## Leave the participant with a positive attitude about survey participation

Introducing a survey with an emphasis on the importance of the participant's responses to the project, and closing it with an appreciation of the participant's willingness to cooperate are simple and easy ways to create a general positive attitude to the survey. In addition, it is often wise to include questions that are crucial to the investigation of the topic from the participant's perspective, even if they are not of any particular interest to you as a researcher. With this in mind, you could also include an open question at the end of the survey asking whether respondents want to add anything that they consider to be important.

## 13.4 Question content

Four questions, covering numerous issues, guide the instrument designer in selecting appropriate question content.

1 Should this question be asked?
2 Is the question of proper scope and coverage?
3 Can the participant adequately answer this question, as asked?
4 Will the participant willingly answer this question, as asked?

## Should this question be asked?
### Issue 1: Purposeful versus interesting

Questions that merely produce 'interesting information' cannot be justified on either economic or research grounds. Challenge each question's function. Does it contribute significant information towards answering the research question? Will its omission limit or prevent the thorough analysis of other data? Can we infer the answer from another question? Is the

# Earn a penny for taking surveys

Are you annoyed by telephone calls from marketing research agencies just as you sit down to dinner or to watch your favourite TV show? Telephone interviews have been an extremely popular way of conducting opinion polls and consumer research. Conducting a telephone survey is quite cheap and data-collection can be done in a very short time. Have you ever responded to a request for a telephone interview with asking for a small reward, say €4 for a 20-minute interview? Why not? By answering similar questionnaires online, you can earn these amounts.

*Ciao*! is one of Europe's largest consumer opinion websites, with about nine million customers from five European core markets as users. Once you have registered as a user you can earn a penny either by writing product reviews or by answering online questionnaires. Websites such as www.apennyearned.co.uk/surveyUK provide even more links to the sites of research agencies that will either pay you directly or enrol you in prize lotteries in return for answering questionnaires. Time is money. Why waste time doing a telephone interview when you can do a similar job and earn money?

What do you think of such online surveys from a researcher's point of view? Do you think that in the future people will still be willing to participate in non-paying telephone interviews and, if so, what kind of people?

## References and further reading

www.apennyearned.co.uk
www.ciao.com

information asked for available from other easily accessible and equally, or even more, reliable sources? A good question designer knows the value of learning more from fewer questions.

## Is the question of proper scope and coverage?
### Issue 2: Incomplete or unfocused

We can test this content issue by asking, 'Will this question reveal all we need to know?' We sometimes ask participants to reveal their motivations for particular behaviours or attitudes by asking them, 'Why?' This simple question is inadequate for probing the range of most causal relationships. When studying product-use behaviour, for example, direct two or three questions on product use to the heavy-use consumer and only one question to the light user.

Questions are also inadequate if they do not provide the information you need to interpret responses fully. If you ask about, say, the Prince Corporation's image as an employer (see Chapter 11), have you recognized that different groups of employees may have different reactions? Do you need to ask the same question about other companies so that you can evaluate relative attitudes?

### Issue 3: Multiple questions

Does the question request so much content that it should be broken into two or more questions (**multiple questions**)? While reducing the overall number of questions in a study is highly desirable, don't try to ask **double-barrelled questions** (two or more questions in one that the participant might need to answer differently in order to preserve the accuracy of the data). Here's a common example posed to menswear retailers: 'Are this year's shoe sales and gross profits higher than last year's?' Couldn't sales be higher with stagnant profits, or profits higher with level or lower sales? A less obvious multiple question is the question that we ask to identify a family's TV station preference. A better question would ask the station preference of each family member separately or, alternatively, screen for the member who most often controls channel selection on Monday evenings during prime time. Also, it's highly probable that no one station would serve as an individual's preferred station when we cover a wide range of times (8–11 p.m.). This reveals another problem: the imprecise question.

### Issue 4: Precision

To test a question for precision ask, 'Does the question ask precisely what we want and need to know?' We sometimes ask for a participant's income when we really want to know the family's total annual income before taxes in the past calendar year. We ask what a participant purchased 'last week' when we really want to know what he or she purchased in a 'typical seven-day period during the past 90 days'. In particular, if you ask about recurring events, it is wise either to keep the time period asked for short or to extend the answer possibilities from yes/no to a frequency estimate. For example, more precise alternatives to the question 'Did you visit a pub last year?' (which is very likely to be answered with a yes by the vast majority of the respondents) include: (i) 'Did you visit a pub in the last week?' and (ii) 'How often did you visit a pub in the last month?'

A second precision issue deals with common vocabulary between researcher and participant. To test your question for this problem ask, 'Do I need to offer operational definitions of concepts and constructs used in the question?' For example, in a survey among microbusinesses, the researchers also asked for some information regarding the financial structure of the business. Terms like equity capital are comprehensible to business students, managers, and so on, but many owners of a microbusiness do not really have any idea what equity capital is. This points to the need for operational definitions as part of question wording.

## Can the participant answer adequately?
### Issue 5: Time for thought

Although the question may address the topic, is it asked in such a way that the participant will be able to frame an answer, or is it reasonable to assume that the participant can determine the answer? This is also a question that drives sample design, but once the ideal sample unit is determined, researchers often assume that participants who fit the sample profile have all the answers, preferably on the tips of their tongues. To frame a response to some questions takes time and thought; such questions are best left to self-administered questionnaires. Another approach, especially useful for personal interviews is, when you make the appointment for the interview, to inform the participant of the kind of detailed information you will be asking about.

## Issue 6: Participation at the expense of accuracy

Participants typically want to cooperate in interviews; thus they assume giving any answer is more helpful than denying knowledge of a topic. Their desire to impress the interviewer may encourage them to give answers based on no information. A classic illustration of this problem occurred with the following question:[2] 'Which of the following statements most closely coincides with your opinion of the Metallic Metals Act?' The response pattern shows that 70 per cent of those interviewed had a fairly clear opinion of the Metallic Metals Act; however, there is no such act. Similarly, research has shown that on a question asking for a subjective assessment of the performance of individual cabinet members, a fantasy name (i.e. the name of a person who does not belong to the cabinet) usually receives quite moderate performance ratings. The participants apparently assume that if a question is asked they should provide an answer. Given reasonable-sounding choices, they will select one even though they know nothing about the topic.

In telephone interviews such questions are called screening questions, because they determine whether the person on the other end of the line is a qualified sample unit.

## Issue 7: Presumed knowledge

The question designer should consider the participants' information level when determining the content and appropriateness of a question. In some studies, the degree of participant expertise can be substantial, and simplified explanations are inappropriate and discourage participation. In asking the public about gross margins in menswear stores, we would want to be sure that the 'general public' participant understands the nature of 'gross margin'. If our sample unit were a merchant, explanations might not be needed. A high level of knowledge among our sample units, however, may not eliminate the need for operational definitions. Among merchants, gross margin per unit in dollars is commonly accepted as the difference between cost and selling price; but when offered as a percentage rather than a dollar figure, it can be calculated as a percentage of unit selling price or as a percentage of unit cost. A participant answering from the 'cost' frame of reference would calculate gross margin at 100 per cent; another participant, using the same dollars and the 'selling price' frame of reference, would calculate gross margin at 50 per cent. If a construct is involved and differing interpretations of a concept are feasible, operational definitions may still be needed.

## Issue 8: Recall and memory decay

The adequacy problem also occurs when you ask questions that overtax participants' recall ability. People cannot recall much that has happened in their past, unless it was dramatic. If the events surveyed are of incidental interest to participants, they will probably be unable to recall them correctly even a short time later. An unaided recall question, such as 'What radio programmes did you listen to last night?' might identify as few as 10 per cent of those individuals who actually listened to a programme.[3] Retrospectivity is another precision problem, and becomes more severe the longer the period between the occurrence of the behaviour and the time of the interview because participants find it harder to remember events the longer the time since their occurrence. For example, if you ask a representative sample of the population whether they have been unemployed in the last year or whether they are currently unemployed, this will yield higher unemployment rates for the latter question, as respondents tend to forget short periods of unemployment once they are employed again.

### *Issue 9: Balance (general versus specific)*

Answering adequacy also depends on the proper balance between generality and specificity. We often ask questions in terms too general and detached from participants' experiences. Asking for average annual consumption of a product may make an unrealistic demand for generalization on people who do not think in these terms. Why not ask how often the product was used last week or last month? Too often, participants are asked to recall individual use experiences over an extended time and to average them for us. This is asking participants to do the researcher's work and encourages substantial response errors. It may also contribute to a higher refusal rate and higher discontinuation rate.

There is a danger in being too narrow in the time frame applied to behaviour questions. We may ask about cinema attendance for the last seven days, although this is too short a time span on which to base attendance estimates. It may be better to ask about attendance, say, for the last 30 days. There are no firm rules about this generality–specificity problem. Developing the right level of generality depends on the subject, industry, setting and experience of the question designer.

### *Issue 10: Objectivity*

The ability of participants to answer adequately is also often distorted by questions whose content is biased by what is included or omitted. The question may explicitly mention only the positive or negative aspects of the topic or make unwarranted assumptions about the participant's position. Consider an experiment in which two different forms of a question were asked: 57 randomly chosen graduate business students answered version A, and 56 answered version B. Their responses are shown in Exhibit 13.4.

The probable cause of the difference in brand preference is that A is a **leading question**. It assumes and suggests that everyone has a favourite brand of ice-cream and will report it. Version B indicates that the participant need not have a favourite.

A deficiency of both versions is that about one participant in five misinterpreted the meaning of the term brand. This misinterpretation cannot be attributed to low education, low intelligence, lack of exposure to the topic, or quick or lazy reading of the question. The subjects were students who had taken at least one course in marketing in which branding was treated prominently. (Word-confusion difficulties are discussed in greater detail later in this chapter.)

## Will the participants answer willingly?

### *Issue 11: Sensitive information*

Even if participants have the information, they may be unwilling to give it. Some topics are considered too sensitive to discuss with strangers. These vary from person to person, but one study suggests that the most sensitive topics concern money matters and family life.[4] More than a quarter of those interviewed mentioned these as the topics about which they would be 'least willing to answer questions'. Participants of lower socio-economic status also included political matters in this 'least willing' list.

Participants may also be unwilling to give correct answers for ego reasons. Many exaggerate their incomes, the number of times they visit a museum, their social status and the amount of high-prestige literature they read. They also minimize their ages and the amount of low-prestige

| Response | Version A:<br>What is your favourite brand of ice cream?<br>_____<br>_____ | Version B:<br>Some people have a favourite brand of ice cream, while others do not have a favourite brand. In which group are you? (please tick)<br>● I have a favourite ice cream brand.<br>● I do not have a favourite ice-cream brand.<br>What is your favourite (if you have a favourite)?<br>_____<br>_____ |
|---|---|---|
| Named a favourite brand | 77% | 39% |
| Named a favourite flavour rather than a brand | 19% | 18% |
| Had no favourite brand | 4% | 43% |
| Total | 100% | 100% |
|  | n = 57 | n = 56 |

**Exhibit 13.4** Response effects depending on question format.

literature they read. Many participants are reluctant to try to give an adequate response. Often this will occur when they see the topic as irrelevant to their own interests or to their perception of the survey's purpose. They participate half-heartedly, often answer with 'don't know', give negative replies, refuse to be interviewed, or give stereotypical responses.

## Question wording

It is frustrating when people misunderstand a question that has been written painstakingly. This problem is partially due to the lack of a shared vocabulary. The difficulty of understanding long and complex sentences or involved phraseology aggravates the problem further. Our dilemma arises from the requirements of question design (the need to be explicit, to present alternatives and to explain meanings). All contribute to longer and more involved sentences.[5]

The difficulties caused by question wording exceed most other sources of distortion in surveys. They have led one social scientist to conclude:

> To many who worked in the Research Branch it soon became evident that error or bias attributable to sampling and to methods of questionnaire administration were relatively small as compared with other types of variations – especially variation attributable to different ways of wording questions.[6]

While it is impossible to say which wording of a question is best, we can point out several areas that cause participant confusion and measurement error. The diligent question designer will put a given question through many revisions before it satisfies the following criteria.[7]

- Is the question stated in terms of a shared vocabulary?
- Does the question contain vocabulary with a single meaning?
- Does the question contain unsupported or misleading assumptions?
- Does the question contain biased wording?
- Is the question personalized correctly?
- Are adequate alternatives presented within the question?

## Issue 12: Shared vocabulary

Because surveying is an exchange of ideas between interviewer and participant, each must understand what the other says, and this is possible only if the vocabulary used is common to both parties.[8] Two problems arise. First, the words must be simple enough to allow adequate communication with persons of limited education. This is dealt with by reducing the level of word difficulty to simple English words and phrases (more is said about this in Issue 4 on precision).

Technical language is the second issue. Even highly educated participants cannot answer questions stated in unfamiliar technical terms. Technical language also poses difficulties for interviewers. In one study of how corporation executives handled various financial problems, interviewers had to be conversant with technical financial terms. This necessity presented the researcher with two alternatives – hiring people knowledgeable in finance and teaching them interviewing skills or teaching financial concepts to experienced interviewers.[9]

This vocabulary problem also exists where similar or identical studies are conducted in different countries and multiple languages. In surveys conducted in multiple languages the problem of shared vocabulary becomes even more severe, as, for example, the connotation of the word 'friend' can be rather different. In some cultures people refer only to close friends as friends, while in other cultures even loose acquaintances are called 'friend'. In some African countries, you are even likely to be called a 'brother' or 'sister', meaning that you are considered a 'good friend'. At the other extreme, studies on relationships among colleagues show that Germans hardly ever have 'friends' at work, because they would call them 'good colleagues'. One widely used method in cross-country studies to mitigate translation problems is to define a research master language, for example English, and then ask a translator to translate the English questionnaires into the other language. The translated questionnaire is then handed to another translator with the request to translate it back into English. Comparing the master questionnaire with the backtranslated questionnaire will reveal the questions and words that are difficult to translate.

A great obstacle to effective question wording is choice of words. Questions to be asked of the public should be restricted to the 2000 most common words in the language used.[10] Even the use of simple words is not enough. Many words have vague references or meanings that must be gleaned from their context. In a repair study, technicians were asked, 'How many radio sets did you repair last month?' This question may seem unambiguous, but participants interpreted it in two ways. Some viewed it as a question of them alone; others interpreted 'you' more inclusively, as referring to the total output of the shop. There is also the possibility of misinterpreting 'last month', depending on the timing of the questioning. Using 'during the last 30 days' would be much more precise and unambiguous. Typical of the many problem words are any, could, would, should, fair, near, often, average and regular. One author recommends that after stating a question as precisely as possible, we should test each word against the following checklist.

- Does the chosen word mean what we intend?
- Does the word have multiple meanings? If so, does the context make the intended meaning clear?
- Does the chosen word have more than one pronunciation? Is there any word with similar pronunciation with which the chosen word might be confused?
- Is a simpler word or phrase suggested or possible?[11]

In the Prince Corporation study (see Chapter 11), what percentage of the population would understand the terms conglomerate or multinational company? We cause other problems when we use abstract concepts that have many overtones or emotional qualifications.[12] Without concrete referents, meanings are too vague for the researcher's needs. Examples of such words are business, government and society. Suppose we asked the question, 'How involved is business in the affairs of our society?' What is meant by 'involved'? What parts of 'society'? Is there such a thing as 'business' per se?

Shared vocabulary issues are addressed by using the following:

- simple rather than complex words
- interviewers with content knowledge
- commonly known, unambiguous words
- precise words.

## Issue 13: Unsupported assumptions

Unwarranted assumptions contribute to many problems of question wording. One national newspaper, the *National Chronicle*, conducted a study in an attempt to discover what readers would like to see in its redesigned lifestyle section. One notable question asked readers: 'Who selects your clothes? You or the man in your life?' In this age of educated, working, independent women, the question managed to offend a significant portion of the female readership. In addition, the *National Chronicle* discovered that many of its female readers were younger than researchers had originally assumed and the only man in their lives was their father, not the spousal or romantic relationship alluded to by the questions that followed. Once men reached this question, they assumed that the paper was interested in serving only the needs of its female readers. The unwarranted assumptions built into the questionnaire caused a significantly smaller response rate than expected and caused several of the answers to be uninterpretable.

## Issue 14: Frame of reference

Inherent in word meaning problems is also the matter of a frame of reference. Each of us understands concepts, words and expressions in light of our own experience. How many people are self-employed, for instance, differs considerably depending on the question one asks. If you ask the simple question, 'Are you currently self-employed?' you are likely to miss all self-employed people who are part-time self-employed alongside the paid job they hold. You would have erroneously assumed that there would be a common frame of reference between you and the participants on the meaning of self-employed. Unfortunately, many persons viewed themselves primarily or foremost as wage earners or students. They failed to report that they also earned some money from self-employed work. This difference in frame of reference results in a consistent underestimation of the number of people who are self-employed in a country.

Alternatively, you could replace this question with two questions, the first of which seeks a statement on the participant's major activity during the week. If the participant gives a non-self-employment classification, a second question is asked to determine if he or she has done any self-employed work for pay besides this major activity.

The frame of reference can be controlled in two ways. First, the interviewer may seek to learn the frame of reference used by the participant. When asking participants to evaluate their reasons for judging a labour contract offer, the interviewer must learn the frames of reference that they use. Is the contract offer being evaluated in terms of the specific offer, the failure of management to respond to other demands, the personalities involved or the personal economic pressures that have resulted from a long strike?

Second, it is useful to specify the frame of reference for the participant. In asking for an opinion about the new labour contract offer, the interviewer might specify that the question should be answered based on the participant's opinion of the size of the offer, the sincerity of management, or another frame of reference of interest.

## Issue 15: Biased wording

Bias is the distortion of responses in one direction. It can result from many of the problems already discussed, but word choice is often the major source. Obviously, words or phrases such as politically correct or fundamentalist must be used with great care. Strong adjectives can be particularly distorting. One alleged opinion survey concerned with the subject of preparation for death included the following question: 'Do you think that decent, low-cost funerals are sensible?' Who could be against anything that is decent or sensible? There is a question about whether this was a legitimate survey or a burial service sales campaign, but it shows how suggestive an adjective can be.

Members of parliament have been known to use surveys as a means of communicating with their constituencies. Questions are often worded, however, to imply the issue stance that the representative favours. In opinion surveys, in particular, questions are often phrased in a way that makes the outcome very predictable. A cruel example would be the following two-question sequences on the issue of whether a general speed limit should be introduced on German highways.

> **Sequence A:** Every year, thousands of people are killed in traffic accidents, which are often caused by driving too fast. Do you think that less speedy driving would reduce the number of fatal accidents on our streets? Would you support a parliament initiative to introduce a general speed limit on highways?

**Sequence B**: German car manufacturers have earned a worldwide reputation for the quality and technological advances of their cars, including many safety devices that have reduced the occurrence and severity of accidents. Do you think that the faster cars of today are safer than those of 10 years ago? Would you support a parliament initiative to introduce a general speed limit on highways?

A more subtle form of bias is that we know that respondents are more likely to agree with a question and answer it with a yes, especially if they do not have a strong opinion on the issue asked. For example, a recurring discussion in pubs and bars is whether the number of football teams in the national premier leagues, such as the Premier League in England, the Series A in Italy or the Bundesliga in Germany, should be decreased in order to reduce the number of matches. If you are in favour of such a reduction you should ask, 'Would you prefer a reduction of the number of teams in the premier league?' If you are against such a reduction you should ask, 'Do you think that the current number of teams in the premier league is the optimal amount?'

We can also strongly bias the participant by using prestigious names in a question. In a historic survey on whether the US war and navy departments should be combined into a single defence department, one survey said, 'General Eisenhower says the army and navy should be combined,' while the other version omitted his name. Given the first version (name included), 49 per cent of the participants approved of having one department; given the second version, only 29 per cent favoured one department.[13]

We also can bias response through the use of superlatives, slang expressions and fad words. These are best excluded unless they are critical to the objective of the question. Ethnic references should also be stated with care.

## Issue 16: Personalization

How personalized should a question be? Should we ask, 'What would you do about …?' Or should we ask, 'What would people with whom you work do about …?' The effect of personalization is shown in a classic example reported by Cantril.[14] A split test was made of a question concerning attitudes about the expansion of US armed forces in 1940:

Should the United States do any of the following at this time?
  **A**  Increase our armed forces further, even if it means more taxes.
  **B**  Increase our armed forces further, even if you have to pay a special tax.

Eight-eight per cent of those answering question A thought that the armed forces should be increased, while only 79 per cent of those answering question B favoured increasing the armed forces.

These and other examples show that personalizing questions changes responses, but it is not clear whether this change is for the better or the worse. We often cannot tell which method is superior. Perhaps the best that can be said is that when either form is acceptable, we should choose that which appears to present the issues more realistically. If there are doubts, then split survey versions should be used.

### Issue 17: Adequate alternatives

Have we adequately expressed the alternatives with regard to the point of the question? It is usually wise to express each alternative explicitly to avoid bias. This is illustrated well with a pair of questions that were asked of matched samples of participants (see Exhibit 13.5).[15]

Often the above issues are present simultaneously in a single question. Exhibit 13.6 reveals several questions drawn from actual mail surveys. We've identified the problem issues and suggest one solution for improvement. While the suggested improvement might not be the only possible solution, it does correct the issues identified. What other solutions could be applied to correct the problems identified?

## 13.5 Response strategy

A third major decision area in question design is the degree and form of structure imposed on the participant. The various response strategies offer options that include **unstructured response** (open-ended response, the free choice of words) and **structured response** (closed response, specified alternatives provided). Free responses, in turn, range from those in which the participants express themselves extensively to those in which participants' latitude is restricted by space, layout or instructions to choose one word or phrase, as in a 'fill-in' question. Closed responses are typically categorized as dichotomous, multiple-choice, checklist, rating or ranking response strategies.

### Situational determinants of response strategy choice

Several situational factors affect the decision of whether to use open-ended or closed questions.[16] The decision is also affected by the degree to which the following factors are known to the interviewer:

- objectives of the study
- participant's level of information about the topic
- degree to which participant has thought through the topic

| | Do you think most manufacturing companies that lay off workers during slack periods could arrange things to avoid layoffs and give steady work throughout the year? | Do you think most manufacturing companies that lay off workers in slack periods could avoid layoffs and provide steady work right through the year, or do you think layoffs are unavoidable? |
|---|---|---|
| Company could avoid layoffs | 63% | 35% |
| Company could not avoid layoffs | 22% | 41% |
| No opinion | 15% | 24% |

*Exhibit 13.5* Response effects depending on adequate alternatives.

| | Poor Measurement Question | Improved Measurement Question |
|---|---|---|
| **Problems:** Checklist appears to offer options that are neither exhaustive nor mutually exclusive. Also, it doesn't fully address the content needs of understanding why people choose a hotel when they travel for personal reasons versus business reasons.<br><br>**Solution:** Organize the alternatives. Create sub-sets within choices; use colour or shading to highlight sub-sets. For coding ease, expand the alternatives so the participant does not frequently choose 'Other'. | If your purpose for THIS hotel stay included personal pleasure, for what ONE purpose specifically?<br><br>☐ Visit friend/relative  ☐ Sightseeing<br>☐ Weekend escape  ☐ Family event<br>☐ Sporting event  ☐ Vacation<br>☐ Other: | Which reason BEST explains your purpose for THIS personal pleasure hotel stay?<br><br>☐ Dining ............ Was this for a ..... ☐ Sport-related event?<br>☐ Shopping ☐ Theatre, musical or other performance?<br>☐ Entertainment ☐ Museum or exhibit?<br>☐ Visit friend/relative ..... was this for a special event ----> ☐ Yes ☐ No<br>☐ Vacation ...was this primarily for .... ☐ Sightseeing? ☐ Weekend break?<br>☐ Other: |
| **Problems:** Double-barrelled question: no time frame for the behaviour; likely to experience memory decay. 'Frequently' is an undefined construct for eating behaviour, depending on the study's purpose. 'order' is not as powerful a concept for measurement as others (e.g. purchase, consume or eat).<br><br>**Solution:** Split the questions; expand the response alternatives; clearly define the construct you want to measure. | When you eat out, do you frequently order appetizers and dessert?<br><br>☐ Yes<br>☐ No | Considering your personal eating experiences away from home in the last 30 days, did you purchase an appetizer or dessert more than half the time?<br><br>More than half the time ☐  Less than half the time ☐<br><br>☐ Purchased an appetizer<br>☐ Purchased a dessert<br>☐ Purchased neither appetizers nor desserts |
| **Problems:** Non-specific time frame; likely to experience memory decay; non-specific screen (not asking what you really need to know to qualify a participant).<br><br>**Solution:** Replace 'ever' with a more appropriate time frame; screen for the desired behaviour. | Have you ever attended a college basketball game?<br><br>☐ Yes<br>☐ No | In the last six months, have you been a spectator at a basketball game played by college teams on a college campus?<br><br>☐ Yes<br>☐ No |
| **Problems:** Question faces serious memory decay as a coat may not be purchased each year; aren't asking if the coat was a personal purchase or for someone else; nor do you know the type of coat purchased; nor do you know whether the coat was purchased for full price or at a discount. | How much did you pay for the last coat you purchased? | Did you purchase a dress coat for your personal use in the last 60 days?<br><br>☐ Yes  ☐ No<br><br>Thinking of this dress coat, how much did you pay? (to the nearest euro) €_____.00<br>Was this coat purchase made at a discounted price?<br>☐ Yes  ☐ No |

*Exhibit 13.6* Reconstructing questions.

- ease with which participant communicates
- participant's motivation level to share information.

### Issue 18: Objective of the study

If the objective of the question is only to classify the participant on some stated point of view, then the closed question will serve well. Assume you are interested only in whether a participant approves of or disapproves of a certain corporate policy. A closed question will provide this answer. This response strategy ignores the full scope of the participant's opinion and its antecedents. If the objective is to explore a wider territory, then an open-ended question (free-response strategy) is preferable.

Open-ended questions are appropriate when the objective is to discover opinions and degrees of knowledge. They are also appropriate when the interviewer seeks sources of information, dates of events and suggestions, or when probes are used to secure more information. When the topic of a question is outside the participant's experience, the open-ended question may offer the better way to learn his or her level of information. Open-ended questions also help to uncover certainty of feelings and expressions of intensity, although well-designed closed questions can do the same.

Finally, it may be better to use open-ended questions when the interviewer does not have a clear idea of the participant's frame of reference or level of information. Such conditions are likely to occur in exploratory research or in pilot testing. Closed questions are better when there is a clear frame of reference, the participant's level of information is predictable, and the researcher believes that the participant understands the topic.

### Issue 19: Thoroughness of prior thought

If a participant has developed a clear opinion on the topic, a closed question will serve well. If an answer has not been thought out, an open-ended question may give the participant a chance to ponder a reply, then elaborate on and revise it.

### Issue 20: Communication skill

Open-ended questions require a stronger grasp of vocabulary and a greater ability to frame responses than do closed questions.

### Issue 21: Participant motivation

Experience has shown that closed questions typically require less motivation, and answering them is less threatening to participants. But the response alternatives sometimes suggest which answer is appropriate; for this reason, closed questions may be biased.

While the open-ended question offers many advantages, closed questions are generally preferable in large surveys. They reduce the variability of response, make fewer demands on interviewer skills, are less costly to administer, and are much easier to code and analyse. After adequate exploration and testing, we can often develop closed questions that will perform as effectively as open-ended questions in many situations. Experimental studies suggest that closed questions are equal or superior to open-ended questions in many more applications than is commonly believed.[17]

# Response strategies illustrated

The characteristics of participants, the nature of the topic(s) being studied, the type of data needed, and your analysis plan dictate the response strategy. Examples of the strategies described in this section are given in Exhibit 13.7.

## Free-response strategy

**Free-response questions**, also known as open-ended questions, ask the participant a question while the interviewer pauses for the answer (which is unaided), or the participant records his or her ideas in his or her own words in the space provided on a questionnaire.

## Dichotomous response strategy

A topic may present clearly dichotomous choices: something is a fact or it is not; a participant can either recall or not recall information; a participant attended or didn't attend an event. **Dichotomous questions** suggest opposing responses, but this is not always the case. One response may be so unlikely that it would be better to adopt the middle-ground alternative as one of the two choices. For example, if we ask participants whether they are underpaid or over-paid, we are not likely to get many selections of the latter choice. The better alternatives to present to the participant might be 'underpaid' and 'fairly paid'.

In many two-way questions, there are potential alternatives beyond the stated two alternat-ives. If the participant cannot accept either alternative in a dichotomous question, he or she may convert the question to a multiple-choice or rating question by writing in his or her desired alternative. For example, the participant may prefer an alternative such as 'don't know' to a yes/no question, or 'no opinion' when faced with a favour/oppose option. In other cases, when there are two opposing or complementary choices, the participant may prefer a qualified choice ('yes, if X doesn't occur', or 'sometimes yes and sometimes no', or 'about the same'). Thus, two-way questions may become multiple-choice or rating questions, and these additional responses should be reflected in your revised analysis plan. Dichotomous questions generate nominal data.

## Multiple-choice response strategy

**Multiple-choice questions** are appropriate where there are more than two alternatives or where we seek gradations of preference, interest or agreement; the latter situation also calls for **rating questions**. While such questions offer more than one alternative answer, they request the par-ticipant to make a single choice. Multiple-choice questions can be efficient, but they also present unique design problems.

Assume we ask whether work safety rules should be determined by (i) companies, (ii) employees, (iii) state government, or (iv) the European Commission. One type of problem occurs when one or more responses have not been anticipated. For example, the union has not been mentioned in the alternatives on work safety rules. Many participants might combine this alternative with 'employees', but others will view 'unions' as a distinct alternative. Exploration prior to drafting the measurement question attempts to identify the most likely choices.

A second problem occurs when the list of choices is not exhaustive. Participants may want

It should be obvious to most participants that at least three of these choices are not reasonable, given general knowledge about the population of the UK.

The order in which choices are given can also be a problem. Numbers are normally presented in order of magnitude. This practice introduces bias. The participant assumes that if there is a list of five numbers, the correct answer will lie somewhere in the middle of the group. Researchers are assumed to add a couple of incorrect numbers on each side of the correct one. To counteract this tendency to choose the central position, put the correct number at an extreme position more often when you design a multiple-choice question.

Order bias with non-numeric alternatives often leads the participant to choose the first alternative (primacy effect) or the last alternative (recency effect) over the middle ones. The explanation for this response behavior lies in the short- and long-term memory of our brains. The first answer choices can easily access our long-term memory, as it is not occupied then and the last answer choices are still present in the short-term memory. In personal face-to-face interviews you can partly control these effects by presenting cards with all answer choices supporting the respondents' memory. Nevertheless, research has shown that even using cards or written questionnaires suffer from these memory problems. Using the split-ballot technique allows you to identify this bias. To implement this strategy in face-to-face interviews, list the alternatives on a card to be handed to the participant when the question is asked. Cards with different choice orders can be alternated to ensure positional balance. You need, however, to understand that this technique does not solve the problem, because a random ordering of answer choices does not remove the bias but ensures that the bias is randomly distributed across the sample. Moreover, you can check whether respondents' answers depend on the position of the answer giving you an idea about the magnitude of the problem. A further good practice in designing such answer cards is leaving the choices unnumbered on the card so participants reply by giving the choice itself rather than its identifying number. It is recommended to use cards like this any time there are four or more choice alternatives. This saves the interviewer's reading time and ensures a more valid answer by keeping the full range of choices in front of the participant.

In most multiple-choice questions, there is also a problem of ensuring that the choices represent a unidimensional scale – that is, the alternatives to a given question should represent different aspects of the same conceptual dimension. In the college selection example, the list included features associated with a college that might be attractive to a student. This list, while not exhaustive, illustrated aspects of the concept 'college attractiveness factors within the control of the college'. The list did not mention other factors that might affect a school attendance decision. Parents and peer advice, local alumni efforts, and one's high school adviser may influence the decision, but these represent a different conceptual dimension of 'college attractiveness factors' – those not within the control of the college.

Multiple-choice questions usually generate nominal data. When the choices are numbers, this response structure will produce at least interval and sometimes ratio data. When the choices represent ordered numerical ranges (e.g. a question on family income) or a verbal rating scale (e.g. a question on how you prefer your steak prepared: well-done, medium-well, medium-rare or rare), the multiple-choice question generates ordinal data.

## Checklist response strategy

When you want a participant to give multiple responses to a single question, you will ask the question in one of three ways. If relative order is not important, the **checklist** is the logical choice. Questions like 'Which of the following factors encouraged you to apply to Lake University? (Check all that apply)' force the participant to exercise a dichotomous response (yes, encouraged; no, didn't encourage) to each factor presented. Of course you could have asked for the same information as a series of dichotomous selection questions, one for each individual factor, but that would have been time- and space-consuming. Checklists are more efficient. Checklists generate nominal data.

## Rating response strategy

Rating questions ask the participant to position each factor on a companion scale, either verbal, numeric or graphic. 'Each of the following factors has been shown to have some influence on a student's choice to apply to Lake University. Using your own experience, for each factor please tell us whether the factor was "strongly influential", "somewhat influential" or "not at all influential". Generally, rating-scale structures generate ordinal data; some carefully crafted scales generate interval data.

## Ranking strategy

When the relative order of alternatives is important, the **ranking question** is ideal. For example:

> Please rank-order your top three factors from the following list based on their influence in encouraging you to apply to Lake University. Use 1 to indicate the most encouraging factor, 2 the next most encouraging factor, and so on.

The checklist strategy would provide the three factors of influence, but we would have no way of knowing the importance that the participant places on each factor. Even in a personal interview, the order in which the factors are mentioned is not a guarantee of influence. Ranking as a response strategy solves this problem.

One concern surfaces with ranking activities. How many presented factors should be ranked? If you listed the 15 brands of potato chips sold in a given market, would you have the participant rank all 15 in order of preference? In most instances it is helpful to remind yourself that while participants may have been selected for a given study due to their experience or the likelihood that they can provide the desired information, this does not mean that they have knowledge of all conceivable aspects of an issue. It is always better to have participants rank only those elements with which they are familiar. If you want motivation to remain strong, avoid asking a participant to rank more than seven items, even if your list is longer. Ranking generates ordinal data.

All types of response strategy have their advantages and disadvantages. Several different strategies are often found in the same questionnaire, and the situational factors mentioned earlier are the major guides in this matter. There is a tendency, however, to use closed questions instead of the more flexible open-ended type. Exhibit 13.8 summarizes some important considerations in choosing between the various response strategies.

| Characteristics | Dichotomous | Multiple Choice | Checklist | Rating | Rank Ordering | Free Response |
|---|---|---|---|---|---|---|
| Type of data | Nominal | Nominal, ordinal or ratio | Nominal | Ordinal or interval | Ordinal | Nominal or ratio |
| Usual number of answer alternatives provided | 2 | 3 to 10 | 10 or fewer | 3 to 7 | 10 or fewer | None |
| Desired number of participant answers | 1 | 1 | 10 or fewer | 7 or fewer | 10 or fewer | 1 |
| Used to provide … | Classification | Classification, order or specific numerical estimate | Classification | Order or distance | Order | Classification (of idea), order or specific numerical estimate |

*Exhibit 13.8* Characteristics of response strategies.

# 13.6  Sources of existing questions

The tools of data-collection should be adapted to the problem, not the reverse. Thus, the focus of this chapter has been on crafting an instrument to answer specific investigative questions. But inventing and refining questions demands considerable time and effort. For some topics, a

| Author(s) | Title | Source |
|---|---|---|
| Philip E. Converse, Jean D. Dotson, Wendy J. Hoag and William H. McGee III (eds.) | *American Social Attitudes Data Sourcebook, 1947 – 1978* | Cambridge, MA: Harvard University Press, 1980 |
| Alec Gallup and George H. Gallup (eds.) | *The Gallup Poll Cumulative Index: Public Opinion, 1935 – 1997* | Wilmington, DE: Scholarly Resources Inc., 1999 |
| George H. Gallup Jr. (ed.) | *The Gallup Poll: Public Opinion 1998* | Wilmington, DE: 1999 |
| Elizabeth H. Hastings and Philip K. Hastings (eds.) | *Index to International Public Opinion 1986 – 1987* | Westport, CT: Greenwood Press, 1988 |
| Philip K. Hastings and Jessie C. Southwick (eds.) | *Survey Data for Trend Analysis: An Index to Repeated Questions in the US National Surveys Held by the Roper Public Opinion Research Center* | Storrs, CT: Roper Center for Public Opinion Research, Inc., 1974 |
| Elizabeth Martin, Diana McDuffee and Stanley Presser | *Sourcebook of Harris National Surveys: Repeated Questions 1963 – 1976* | Chapel Hill: Institute for Research in Social Science, University of North Carolina Press, 1981 |
| National Opinion Research Center | *General Social Surveys 1972 – 1985: Cumulative Code Book* | Chicago: NORC, 1985 |
| John P. Robinson, Robert Athanasiou and Kendra B. Head | *Measures of Occupational Attitudes and Occupational Characteristics* | Ann Arbor: Institute for Social Research, University of Michigan, 1968 |
| John P. Robinson, Philip R. Shaver and Lawrence S. Wrightsman | *Measures of Personality and Social-psychological Attitudes* | San Diego, CA: Academic Press, 1991 |

*Exhibit 13.9* Sources of questions.

careful review of the related literature and an examination of existing instrument sourcebooks can shorten this process.

A review of literature will reveal instruments used in similar studies that may be obtained by writing to the researchers or, if copyrighted, purchased through a clearing house. Many instruments are available through compilations and sourcebooks. While these tend to be oriented towards social science applications, they are a rich source of ideas for tailoring questions to meet a manager's needs. Several compilations are recommended and these are noted in Exhibit 13.9.[19]

Borrowing items from existing sources is not without risk. It is quite difficult to generalize the reliability and validity of selected items or portions of a questionnaire that have been taken out of the original context. Pre-testing is also warranted if it is necessary to report the reliability and validity of the instrument being constructed. Time and situation-specific fluctuations should be scrutinized. Remember that the original estimates are only as good as the sampling and testing procedures, and many researchers you borrow from may not have reported that information.

Language, phrasing and idiom can also pose problems. Questions tend to age and may not appear (or sound) as relevant to the participant as freshly worded ones would. Integrating existing and newly constructed questions is problematic. When adjacent questions are relied on to carry context in one questionnaire and then are not selected for the customized application, the newly selected question is left without necessary meaning.[20] Whether an instrument is constructed from scratch or adapted from the ideas of others, pre-testing is recommended.

# 13.7 Drafting and refining the instrument: phase 3

As depicted in Exhibit 13.10, phase 3 of instrument design – drafting and refinement – is a multistep process, as outlined below.

1 Develop the participant-screening process (personal or telephone interview), along with the introduction.
2 Arrange the measurement question sequence:
    a identify topic groups
    b establish a logical sequence for the question groups and questions within groups
    c develop transitions between these groups.
3 Prepare and insert instructions – for the interviewer or participant – including termination, skip directions and probes.
4 Create and insert a conclusion, including a survey disposition statement.
5 Pre-test specific questions and the instrument as a whole.

## Introduction and participant screening

The introduction must supply the sample unit with the motivation to participate in the study. It must reveal enough about the forthcoming questions, usually by revealing some or all the topics to be covered, for participants to judge their interest level and their ability to provide the

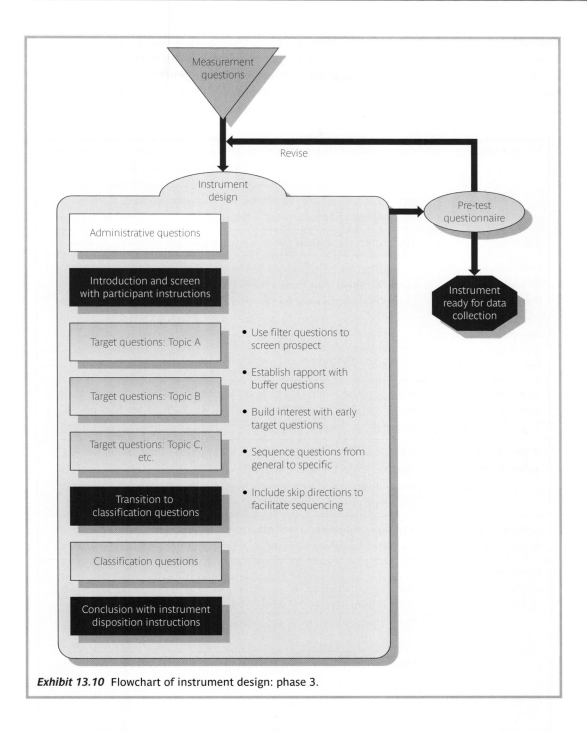

**Measurement questions**

Revise

**Instrument design**

Administrative questions

Introduction and screen with participant instructions

Target questions: Topic A

Target questions: Topic B

Target questions: Topic C, etc.

Transition to classification questions

Classification questions

Conclusion with instrument disposition instructions

- Use filter questions to screen prospect
- Establish rapport with buffer questions
- Build interest with early target questions
- Sequence questions from general to specific
- Include skip directions to facilitate sequencing

**Pre-test questionnaire**

**Instrument ready for data collection**

*Exhibit 13.10*  Flowchart of instrument design: phase 3.

desired information. In any communication study, the introduction also reveals the amount of time participation is likely to take. In a personal or telephone interview, the introduction usually contains a filter or **screen question** to determine if the potential participant has the knowledge or experience necessary to participate in the study. The introduction also reveals the identity of the research organization and/or sponsor (unless the study is disguised) and possibly

| | |
|---|---|
| Introduction | Good evening. May I speak with (name of participant)? Mr/Ms (last name of participant), I'm (your name) calling on behalf of the Alumni Network of Hull University. You have recently requested information concerning the Alumni Network. Could you take 10 minutes to tell us what you think about the activities employed by the Alumni Network? |
| Transition | The next set of questions asks about your career since you left university. |
| Instructions for … <br> (a) terminating (following a filter or screen question informing you that the participant never attended Hull University) | I am sorry, today we are only talking with individuals who attended Hull University, but thank you for speaking with me (pause for reply). Goodbye. |
| (b) participant discontinue | Would there be a time I could call back to complete the interview, which is more convenient for you? (Pause: record time.) We'll call you back then at (repeat day and time). Thank you for talking with me this evening. Goodbye. |
| (c) skip directions (between questions or group of questions) | 3. Did you ever participate in an activity organized by the Alumni Network or visit the annual Alumni Day at Hull University? <br> Yes, both (go to next question) Yes, visited Alumni Day (go to next question) Yes, visited other Alumni Activity (go to question 8) No (go to question 12) |
| (d) disposition Instructions | A postage-paid envelope was included with your survey. Please refold your completed survey and mail it to us in the postage-paid envelope. |
| Conclusion <br> (a) phone or personal interview | That's my last question. Your insights and the ideas of other valuable alumni will help us to improve the service and activities of the Alumni Network. Thank you for talking with us this evening (pause for participant reply). Good evening. |
| (b) Self-administered questionnaire (usually precedes the disposition instructions) | Thank you for sharing your ideas about the Alumni Network and its activities. Your insights will help us to serve you and other alumni better. |

*Exhibit 13.11* Example of components in communication instruments.

the objective of the study. At a minimum, a phone or personal interviewer will introduce him or herself to help establish critical rapport with the potential participant. Exhibit 13.11 provides an example introduction and other components of a telephone study of non-participants to a self-administered mail survey.

## Measurement question sequencing

Often the content of one question (called a **branched question**) assumes other questions have been asked and answered. The psychological order of the questions is also important; question sequence can encourage or discourage commitment and promote or hinder the development of researcher–participant rapport.

The design of survey questions is influenced by the need to relate each question to the others in the instrument. The basic principle used to guide sequence decisions is: the nature and needs of the participant must determine the sequence of questions and the organization of the interview schedule. Four guidelines are suggested to implement this principle.

1 The question process must quickly awaken interest and motivate the participant to participate in the interview. Place the more interesting topical target questions early on.

2 The participant should not be confronted by early requests for information that might be considered personal or ego threatening. Place questions that might influence the participant to discontinue or terminate the questioning process near the end.

3 The questioning process should begin with simple items and move to the more complex, and also from general items to the more specific. Place taxing and challenging questions later in the questioning process.

4 Changes in the frame of reference should be small and should be clearly pointed out. Use transition statements between the different topics of the target question set.

### Awaken interest and motivation

We awaken interest and stimulate motivation to participate by choosing or designing questions that are attention-getting and not controversial. If the questions have human-interest value, so much the better. It is possible that the early questions will contribute hard data to the major study objective, but their major task is to overcome the motivational barrier.

### Sensitive and ego-involving information

Regarding the introduction of sensitive information too early in the process, two forms of this error are common. Most studies need to ask for personal classification information about participants. Participants will normally provide these data, but the request should be made towards the end of the process. If made immediately, it often causes participants to feel threatened, dampening their interest and motivation to continue. It is also dangerous to ask any question at the start that is too personal. For example, participants in one survey were asked whether they suffered from insomnia. When the question was asked immediately after the interviewer's introductory remarks, about 12 per cent of those interviewed admitted to having insomnia. When a matched sample was asked the same question after two **buffer questions** (neutral questions designed chiefly to establish rapport with the participant), 23 per cent admitted suffering from insomnia.[21]

### Complex to simplistic

Deferring complex questions or simple questions that require much thought can help reduce the number of 'don't know' responses that are so prevalent early in interviews.

### General to specific

The procedure of moving from general to more specific questions is sometimes called the **funnel approach**. The objectives of this procedure are to learn the participant's frame of reference and to extract the full range of desired information while limiting the distortion effect of earlier questions on later ones. This process may be illustrated with the following series of questions.

1  How do you think this country is getting along in its relationship with other countries?
2  How do you think we are doing in our relationship with Israel?
3  Do you think we ought to be dealing with Israel differently than we are now?
4  (If yes) What should we be doing differently?
5  Some people say we should get tougher with Israel and others think that we are too tough as it is; how do you feel about it?[22]

The first question introduces the general subject and provides some insight into the participant's frame of reference. The second narrows the concern to a single country, while the third and fourth seek views on how the home country should deal with Israel. The fifth question illustrates a specific opinion area and would be asked only if this point of toughness had not been covered in earlier responses. Question 4 is an example of a branched question; the response to the previous question determines whether or not question 4 is asked of the participant.

There is also a risk of interaction whenever two or more questions are related. Question-order influence is especially problematic with self-administered questionnaires, because the participant is at liberty to refer back to questions previously answered. In an attempt to 'correctly align' two responses, accurate opinions and attitudes may be sacrificed. Exhibit 13.12 illustrates this problem by showing the percentages of respondents agreeing to two related questions depending on the question order.

Exhibit 13.12 shows that, apparently, some participants who first endorsed a salary reduction for the management board felt obliged to extend this consequence to all employees of the firm. Where the decision was first made against reducing employees' salaries, a percentage of participants felt constrained in agreeing to reduce management salaries.

### Question groups and transitions

The last question-sequencing guideline suggests arranging questions to minimize shifting in subject matter and frame of reference. Participants often interpret questions in the light of earlier questions and miss shifts of perspective or subject unless they are clearly stated. Participants fail to listen carefully and frequently jump to conclusions about the import of a given question before it is completely stated. Their answers are strongly influenced by their frame of reference. Any change in subject by the interviewer may not register with them unless it is made strong and obvious. Most questionnaires that cover a range of topics are divided into sections

| Questions | Percentage answering yes | |
| --- | --- | --- |
| | A asked first | B asked first |
| A. Should the fixed salary of the management board be reduced if the firm's performance has been poor in the previous year? | 55% | 48% |
| B. Should the wages and salaries of employees be reduced if the firm's performance has been poor in the previous year? | 28% | 17% |

Exhibit 13.12 An example of the effect of question-order influence.

with clearly defined transitions between sections to alert the participant to the change in frame of reference. Exhibit 13.12 provides a sample of a transition in a study of Hull University Alumni Network when measurement questions changed from personal questions to questions asking for an assessment of the Alumni Network.

## Instructions

Instructions to the interviewer or participant attempt to ensure that all participants are treated equally, thus avoiding building error into the results. Two principles form the foundation for good instructions: clarity and courtesy. Instruction language needs to be unfailingly simple and polite.

Instruction topics include the following.

- Termination of an unqualified participant – how to terminate an interview when the participant does not correctly answer the screen or filter questions.
- Termination of a discontinued interview – how to conclude an interview when the participant decides to discontinue.
- Skip directions – instructions for moving between topic sections of an instrument when movement is dependent on the answer to specific questions or when branched questions are used.
- Disposition instructions – telling the respondent to a self-administered instrument about the disposition of the completed questionnaire.

In a self-administered questionnaire, instructions must be contained within the survey instrument. Personal interviewer instructions are sometimes in a document that is separate from the questionnaire (a document thoroughly discussed during interviewer training) or are distinctly and clearly marked (highlighted, printed in coloured ink, or boxed on the computer screen) on the data-collection instrument itself. Sample instructions are presented in Exhibit 13.12.

## Conclusion

The role of the conclusion is to leave the participant with the impression that his or her involvement has been valuable. Subsequent researchers may need this individual to participate in new studies. If every interviewer or instrument expresses appreciation for participation, cooperation in subsequent studies is more likely. A sample conclusion is shown in Exhibit 13.12.

## Overcoming instrument problems

There is no substitute for a thorough understanding of question wording, question content and sequencing issues. However, the researcher can do several things to help improve survey results, among them:

- build rapport with the participant
- redesign the questioning process
- explore alternative response strategies
- use methods other than surveying to secure the data
- pre-test all the survey elements.

### *Build rapport with the participant*

Most information can be secured by direct undisguised questioning if rapport has been developed. Rapport is particularly useful in building participant interest in the project, and the more interest participants have, the more cooperation they will give. One can also overcome participant unwillingness by providing some material compensation for cooperation. This approach has been especially successful in mail surveys. Using an experimental design, Statistics Netherlands investigated the effects of different incentives on the response rate. The three modes were (i) no incentive, (ii) a prepaid telephone card (value: €5) was sent along with the questionnaire, and (iii) a prepaid telephone card (value: €5) was promised once the respondent had returned the questionnaire. The overall response rate was highest in mode 2 and, in particular, increased the response rate among younger men, who are notorious for being lazy respondents.

The assurance of confidentiality can also increase participants' motivation. One approach is to give discreet assurances, both by question wording and interviewer comments and actions, that all types of behaviour, attitudes and positions on controversial or sensitive subjects are acceptable and normal. Where you can say so truthfully, guarantee that participants' answers will be used only in combined statistical totals. If participants are convinced that their replies contribute to some important purpose, they are more likely to be candid, even about taboo topics.

### *Redesign the questioning process*

You can redesign the questioning process to improve the quality of answers by modifying the administrative process and the response strategy. We might show that confidentiality is indispensable to the administration of the survey by using a group administration of questionnaires, accompanied by a ballot-box collection procedure. Even in face-to-face interviews, the participant may fill in the part of the questionnaire containing sensitive information and then seal the entire instrument in an envelope. While this does not guarantee confidentiality, it does suggest it.

We can also develop appropriate questioning sequences that will gradually lead a participant from 'safe' questions to those that are more sensitive. As already noted in our discussion of disguised questions, indirect questioning (using projective techniques) is a widely used approach for securing opinions on sensitive topics. The participants are asked how 'other people' or 'people around here' feel about a topic. It is assumed that the participants will reply in terms of their own attitudes and experiences, but this outcome is hardly certain. Indirect questioning may give a good measure of the majority opinion on a topic but fail to reflect the views either of the participant or minority segments.

With certain topics, it is possible to secure answers by using a proxy code. When we seek family income classes, we can hand the participant a card with income brackets like these:

**A**   Under €25,000 per year

**B**   €25,000 to €49,999 per year

**C**   €50,000 to €74,999 per year

**D**   €75,000 and over per year

The participant is then asked to report the appropriate bracket as either A, B, C or D. For some reason, participants are more willing to provide such an obvious proxy measure than to verbalize actual monetary values.

### Explore alternative response strategies

At the original question drafting, try developing positive, negative and neutral versions of each type of question. This practice dramatizes the problems of bias, helping you to select question wording that minimizes such problems. Sometimes use an extreme version of a question rather than the expected one.

Minimize non-responses to particular questions by recognizing the sensitivity of certain topics. In a self-administered instrument, for example, asking a multiple-choice question about income or age, where incomes and ages are offered in ranges, is usually more successful than using a free-response question such as 'What is your age, please? _____'.

### Use methods other than surveying

Sometimes surveying will not secure the information needed. A classic example concerns a survey conducted to discover magazines read by participants. An unusually high rate was reported for prestigious magazines, and an unusually low rate was reported for tabloid magazines. The study was revised so that the subjects, instead of being interviewed, were asked to contribute their old magazines to a charity drive. The collection gave a more realistic estimate of readership of both types of magazine.[23] Another study on the use of similar unobtrusive measures cites many other types of research situation where unique techniques have been used to secure more valid information than was possible from a survey.[24]

### The value of pre-testing

The final step towards improving survey results is **pre-testing** (see Exhibits 12.4 and 12.12). There are abundant reasons for pre-testing individual questions, questionnaires and interview schedules. In this section we discuss several of these and raise questions to help you plan an effective test of your instrument. Most of what we know about pre-testing is prescriptive. According to contemporary authors,

> There are no general principles of good pre-testing, no systematization of practice, no consensus about expectations, and we rarely leave records for each other. How a pre-test was conducted, what investigators learned from it, how they redesigned their questionnaire on the basis of it – these matters are reported only sketchily in research reports, if at all.[25]

Nevertheless, conventional wisdom suggests that pre-testing is not only an established practice for discovering errors but is also useful for training the research team. Ironically, professionals who have participated in scores of studies are more likely to pre-test an instrument than a newly qualified researcher who is hurrying to complete a project. Revising questions five or more times is not unusual. Yet inexperienced researchers often underestimate the need to follow the design-test-revise process.

## Participant interest

An important purpose of pre-testing is to discover participants' reactions to the questions. If participants do not find the experience stimulating when an interviewer is physically present, how will they react on the telephone or in the self-administered mode? Pre-testing should help to discover where repetitiveness or redundancy is bothersome or what topics were not covered that the participant expected. An alert interviewer will look for questions or even sections that the participant perceives to be sensitive or threatening, or topics about which the participant knows nothing. Another valuable approach to testing questionnaires is to discuss them within focus groups (see Chapter 4 for a more detailed discussion on focus groups). A typical set-up for such a focus group would be to send out the questionnaire to the participants of the focus group discussion a week before the meeting, with the request to have a look at the question-naire. Then in the focus group discussion you would start by asking for the general impression the questionnaire made, and continue by running through each question and asking for com-ments from the focus group members. The participants in a focus group discussion need not be restricted to those who would fit the population for which the questionnaire is intended. For example, one of the authors discussed a CAPI questionnaire intended for people who recently started a business not only with new business starters, but also in focus groups consisting of other field experts, such as representatives from banks, the chamber of commerce and fellow researchers from other universities.

## Meaning

Questions that we borrow or adapt from the work of others carry an authoritativeness that may prompt us to avoid pre-testing them, but they are often most in need of examination. Are they still timely? Is the language relevant? Do they need context from adjacent questions? Newly con-structed questions should similarly be checked for meaningfulness to the participant. Does the question evoke the same meaning as that intended by the researcher? How different is the researcher's frame of reference from that of the average participant? Words and phrases that trigger a 'What do you mean?' response from the participant need to be singled out for further refinement.

## Question transformation

Participants do not necessarily process every word in the question and they may not share the same definitions of the terms they hear. When this happens, participants modify the question to make it fit their own frame of reference or simply change it so it makes sense to them. Probing is necessary to discover how participants have transformed a question when this is suspected.[26]

## Continuity and flow

In self-administered questionnaires, questions should read effortlessly and flow from one to another, and from one section to another. In personal and telephone interviews, the sound of the question and its transition must be fluid as well. A long set of questions with nine-point scales that worked well in a mail instrument would not be effective on the telephone unless you were to ask participants to visualize the scale as the touch keys on their telephone. Moreover, transitions that may appear redundant in a self-administered questionnaire may be exactly what needs to be heard in personal or telephone interviewing.

## Question sequence

Question arrangement can play a significant role in the success of the instrument. Many authorities recommend starting with stimulating questions and placing sensitive questions last. Since questions concerning income and family life are most likely to be refused, this is often good advice for building trust before getting into a refusal situation. However, interest-building questions need to be tested first to be sure that they are stimulating. And when background questions are asked earlier in the interview, some demographic information will be salvaged if the interview stops unexpectedly. Pre-testing with a large enough group permits some experimentation with question sequence.

## Skip instructions

In interviews and questionnaires, **skip patterns** and their contingency sequences may not work as envisioned on paper. Skip patterns are designed to route or sequence the response to another question contingent on the answer to the previous question (branched questions). Pre-testing in the field helps to identify problems with box-and-arrow schematics that the designers may not have thought of. By correcting them at the revision stage, we also avoid problems with flow and continuity. In general, you should minimize skip patterns in self-administered questionnaires, while telephone and personal interviews can contain more complex skip patterns if the interviewers are trained accordingly. Any form of computer-assisted interview also allows the use of more complex skipping. You need, however, to consider that the more complex the skip pattern, the more difficult it is even for the researcher to oversee the whole structure of the questionnaire, which may result in skipping certain questions that were not intended to be skipped. Thus, the more complex the skip patterns you use, the more pre-testing is needed to ensure that the computer or the interviewer carries out the skipping instructions correctly.

## Variability

With a small group of participants, pre-testing cannot provide definitive quantitative conclusions but will deliver an early warning about items that may not discriminate among participants or places where meaningful sub-grouping may occur in the final sample. With 25–100 participants in the pre-test group, statistical data on the proportion of participants answering yes or no or marking 'strongly agree' to 'strongly disagree' can supplement the qualitative information noted by the interviewers. This information is useful for sample size calculations and for getting preliminary indications of reliability problems with scaled questions.

## Length and timing

Most draft questionnaires or interview schedules suffer from lengthiness. By timing each question and section, the researcher is in a better position to make decisions about modifying or cutting material. In personal and telephone interviews, labour is a project expense. Thus, if the budget influences the final length of the questionnaire, an accurate estimate of elapsed time is essential. Videotaped or audiotaped pre-tests may also be used for this purpose. Their function in reducing errors in data recording is widely accepted.

# Pre-testing options

There are various ways that pre-testing can be used to refine an instrument. They range from informal reviews by colleagues to creating conditions similar to those of the final study.

## *Researcher pre-testing*

Designers typically test informally in the initial stages and build more structure into the tests along the way. Fellow instrument designers can do the first-level pre-test. Their many differences of opinion are likely to create numerous suggestions for improvement. Usually at least two or three drafts can be effectively developed by bringing research colleagues into the process.

## *Participant pre-testing*

Participant pre-tests require that the questionnaire be field-tested by sample participants or participant surrogates (individuals with characteristics and backgrounds similar to the desired participants).

Field pre-tests also involve distributing the test instrument exactly as the actual instrument will be distributed. Most studies use two or more pre-tests. National projects may use one trial to examine local reaction and another to check for regional differences. Although many researchers try to keep pre-test conditions and times close to what they expect for the actual study, personal interview and telephone limitations make it desirable to test in the evenings or at weekends in order to interview people who are not available for contact at other times.

Test mailings are useful, but it is often quicker to use a substitute procedure, in which you ask people you already know to test the questionnaire. For example, the survey we looked at elsewhere, among self-employed people, was pre-tested by young entrepreneurs, who were contacted at a local trade fair for young entrepreneurial talent. After these entrepreneurs had filled in the questionnaire, they were also invited to participate in a focus-group discussion to reflect on the questionnaire.

## *Collaborative pre-tests*

Different approaches taken by interviewers and the participants' awareness of those approaches affect the pre-test. If the researcher alerts participants to their involvement in a preliminary test of the questionnaire, the participants are essentially being enlisted as collaborators in the refinement process. Under these conditions, detailed probing of the parts of the question, including phrases and words, is appropriate. Because of the time required for probing and discussion, it is likely that only the most critical questions will be reviewed. The participant group may therefore need to be conscripted from colleagues and friends to secure the additional time and motivation needed to cover an entire questionnaire. If friends or associates are used, experience suggests that they introduce more bias than strangers, argue more about wording, and generally make it more difficult to accomplish other goals of pre-testing such as timing the length of questions or sections.[27]

Occasionally, a highly experienced researcher may improvise questions during a pre-test. When this occurs, it is essential to record the interview or take detailed notes so that the questionnaire may be reconstructed later. Ultimately, a team of interviewers would be required to follow the interview schedule's prearranged sequence of questions. Only experienced investigators should be free to depart from the interview schedule during a pre-test and explore participants' answers by adding probes.

## Non-collaborative pre-tests

When the researcher does not inform the participant that the activity is a pre-test, it is still possible to probe for reactions but without the cooperation and commitment of time provided by collaborators. The comprehensiveness of the effort also suffers because of flagging cooperation. The virtue of this approach is that the questionnaire can be tested under conditions approaching those of the final study. This realism is similarly useful for training interviewers.

## Research Methods in Practice 13

Replacing a research or management question with specific measurement questions is an exercise in analytical reasoning. This part of the case describes how a research question is translated into investigative questions, hypotheses and, finally, measurement questions. Recall that we derived the following research questions from the research problem 'contracting behaviour of firms in interfirm alliances'.

### Research questions

1 What determines the problem potential of a cooperation?
2 Does the problem potential of a cooperation influence contracting?
3 How does the problem potential affect contracting?

Which lead to the following:

### Investigative questions

1 We try to clarify what the 'problem potential' is.
  a What is dependency between the partners in this project?
  b How well can the firm monitor the partner?
  c What is the volume of the project?
  d What is the importance of the project?
2 We try to clarify what contracting is?
  a How extensive is the contract?
  b How much effort was spent on the negotiations?

3 We relate the different investigative questions as follows:
   a  Does the dependency between the partners affect the extensiveness of the contract?
   b  Does the dependency between the partners affect the time spent on negotiations?
   c  Does the monitoring capability of the firm affect the extensiveness of the contract?
   d  Does the monitoring capability of the firm affect the time spent on negotiations?
   e  Does the importance of the cooperation affect the extensiveness of the contract?
   f  Does the importance of the cooperation affect the time spent on negotiations?

## Measurement questions

For the study described above, managers of the research and development (R&D) cooperation were asked to fill in a self-administered questionnaire and to agree upon an interview of about an hour. The

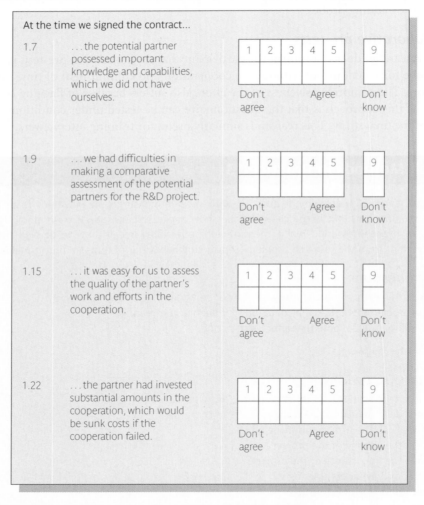

*Exhibit 13.13* Measurement questions (excerpt from questionnaire).

questionnaire was usually collected at the interview appointment. Exhibit 13.13 shows some excerpts from this questionnaire. The questions belonging to the first section (1.7, 1.8 . . . 1.25) were asked in the self-administered questionnaire. Question 3.1 was asked in the personal interview, and questions 9 and 10 were asked at the end of the interview. For this part of the interview we recommended that the respondent should have the written cooperation contract at hand.

Most of the different dimensions of the problem potential were measured in the first question section. The measurement questions, 1.7, 1.22 and 1.23, address the dependency of the partners and will provide the answers to the investigative question a1. Further, these measurement questions are used to answer investigative question c. Measurement questions 1.9 and 1.15 provide the answer for investigative question a2 and will also be used for investigative question d. Measurement question 3.1 answers investigative question a3 and the information is also needed for investigative question b. Finally,

| 1.23 | . . . we had invested substantial amounts in the cooperation, which would be sunk costs if the cooperation failed. | 1 2 3 4 5  9 — Don't agree / Agree / Don't know |
| 1.24 | . . . we knew that a termination of the cooperation would cause a decrease in the partner's sales. | 1 2 3 4 5  9 — Don't agree / Agree / Don't know |
| 1.25 | . . . we knew that a termination of the cooperation would cause a decrease in our sales. | 1 2 3 4 5  9 — Don't agree / Agree / Don't know |

3.1    How large were the following figures for this R&D project at the time we signed the contract?

(a) Your annual budget for the project: _____ NLG

(b) Your labour contribution (in man years) _____ (man years)

(c) Partner's annual budget for the project: _____ NLG

(d) Partner's labour contribution (in man years) _____ (man years)

6.1    Please recall the negotiations for this specific project. Compared to other projects how much time did you spend on the negotiations?

☐ [almost] none    ☐ not much    ☐ a fair amount    ☐ quite a lot    ☐ a lot

*Exhibit 13.13* Continued.

6.2     How long did the negotiations last?

_____ [please fill in the number of months]

6.5     Who in your company was involved in the negotiations of this project?
[name] [function]

1. you _____

2. _____    _____

3. _____    _____

4. _____    _____

5. _____    _____

6. _____    _____

...

9.1     Clauses concerning the contributions of the partner

[a]     Planning of the project

☐ written    ☐ no (please go on to 9.1.b)

☐ oral

☐ 'milestones' are established

☐ the project's progress is agreed on a couple of months in advance

☐ all steps are clearly laid down

[b]     Technical specifications

☐ written    ☐ no (please go on to 9.1.c)

☐ oral

Who decided on the specifications?

☐ you

☐ partner

☐ both

☐ specifications are fixed

☐ later adjustments are possible

☐ are decided upon depending on the course of the joint project

...

10.     Which aspects of the agreement were discussed during the negotiations?

Please tick a number for each aspect. The numbers have the following meaning:

1 – we did not discuss this aspect
2 – this aspect was mentioned briefly
3 – this aspect was discussed
4 – this aspect was discussed at length
5 – after discussing this aspect we still disagreed about it

**Exhibit 13.13** Continued.

1.  Clauses concerning the contributions of the partners

| 1 | 2 | 3 | 4 | 5 | | 9 |
|---|---|---|---|---|---|---|
|   |   |   |   |   | |   |

Don't agree      Agree      Don't know

2.  Clauses concerning the participation of third parties

| 1 | 2 | 3 | 4 | 5 | | 9 |
|---|---|---|---|---|---|---|
|   |   |   |   |   | |   |

Don't agree      Agree      Don't know

3.  Clauses concerning reporting, project coordination, communication and exchange of employees

| 1 | 2 | 3 | 4 | 5 | | 9 |
|---|---|---|---|---|---|---|
|   |   |   |   |   | |   |

Don't agree      Agree      Don't know

4.  Clauses concerning the termination of the project

| 1 | 2 | 3 | 4 | 5 | | 9 |
|---|---|---|---|---|---|---|
|   |   |   |   |   | |   |

Don't agree      Agree      Don't know

5.  Clauses concerning the calculation and payment of costs

| 1 | 2 | 3 | 4 | 5 | | 9 |
|---|---|---|---|---|---|---|
|   |   |   |   |   | |   |

Don't agree      Agree      Don't know

6.  Clauses concerning property rights (patents, licences, etc.)

| 1 | 2 | 3 | 4 | 5 | | 9 |
|---|---|---|---|---|---|---|
|   |   |   |   |   | |   |

Don't agree      Agree      Don't know

7.  Clauses concerning confidentiality and secrecy agreements

| 1 | 2 | 3 | 4 | 5 | | 9 |
|---|---|---|---|---|---|---|
|   |   |   |   |   | |   |

Don't agree      Agree      Don't know

*Exhibit 13.13* Continued.

measurement questions 1.24 and 1.25 address investigative question a4 and are part of the answer for the investigative question e.

The investigative questions b to e all have a second part. The extensiveness of the contract is measured by the measurement question 9 (the exhibit shows only two examples of the total of 33 questions). The measurement questions 6.1 and 6.2 inform us about the time spent on the negotiations, which is reflected in the second part of investigative questions b–e. Measurement question 6.5 points to a different perspective on the negotiation efforts, which can be measured in time, but also by the number of people involved weighted for their function. Measurement question 10 is, again, an alternative shorter measurement to the 33 sub-questions in question 9.

# Summary

1  The instrument design process starts with a comprehensive list of investigative questions drawn from the management research question hierarchy. Instrument design is a three-phase process with numerous issues within each phase: (phase 1) developing the instrument design strategy, (phase 2) constructing and refining the measurement questions, and (phase 3) drafting and refining the instrument.

2  Several choices must be made in designing a communication study instrument. Surveying can be a face-to-face interview, or it can be much less personal, using indirect media and self-administered questionnaires. The questioning process can be unstructured, as in in-depth interviewing, or the questions can be clearly structured. Responses may be unstructured and open-ended, or structured with the participant choosing from a list of possibilities. The degree to which the objectives and intent of the questions should be disguised must also be decided.

3  Instruments obtain three general classes of information. Target questions address the investigative questions and are the most important. Classification questions concern participant characteristics and allow participants' answers to be grouped for analysis. Administrative questions identify the participant, interviewer, and interview location and conditions.

4  Question construction involves three critical decision areas. These are (i) question content, (ii) question wording and (iii) response strategy. Question content should pass the following tests.
   - Should the question be asked?
   - Is it of proper scope?
   - Can and will the participant answer adequately?
   Question wording difficulties exceed most other sources of distortion in surveys. Retention of a question should be confirmed by answering the following questions.
   - Is the question stated in terms of a shared vocabulary?
   - Does the vocabulary have a single meaning?
   - Does the question contain misleading assumptions?
   - Is the wording biased?
   - Is it correctly personalized?
   - Are adequate alternatives presented?
   The study's objective and participant factors affect the decision as to whether to use open-ended or closed questions. Each response strategy generates a specific level of data, with available statistical procedures for each data type influencing the desired response strategy. Participant factors include level of information about the topic, degree to which the topic has been thought through, ease of communication, and motivation to share information. The decision is also affected by the interviewer's perception of participant factors.

   Both dichotomous response and multiple-choice questions are valuable but, on balance, the latter are preferred if only because few questions have just two possible answers. Checklist, rating and ranking strategies are also common.

5   Question sequence can drastically affect participant willingness to cooperate and the quality of responses. Generally, the sequence should begin with efforts to awaken the participant's interest in continuing the interview. Early questions should be simple rather than complex, easy rather than difficult, non-threatening and, obviously, germane to the announced objective of the study. Frame-of-reference changes should be minimal, and questions should be sequenced so that early questions do not distort replies to later ones.

6   Sources of questions for the construction of questionnaires include the literature on related research, and sourcebooks of scales and questionnaires. Borrowing items has attendant risks, such as time- and situation-specific problems, or reliability and validity. The incompatibility of language and idiom also needs to be considered.

7   Pre-testing the instrument is recommended to identify problems before the actual collection of data begins. Insights and ideas for refining instruments result from thoroughness in pre-testing. Effective revision is the result of determining participant interest, discovering if the questions have meaning for the participant, checking for participant modification of a question's intent, examining question continuity and flow, experimenting with question-sequencing patterns, evaluating skip instructions for the interviewers, collecting early warning data on item variability, and fixing the length and timing of the instrument.

## Discussion questions

### Terms in review

1   Distinguish between:
   a   direct and indirect questions
   b   open-ended and closed questions
   c   research, investigative and measurement questions
   d   alternative response strategies.
2   Why is the survey technique so popular? When is it not appropriate?
3   What special problems do open-ended questions have? How can these be minimized? In what situations are open-ended questions most useful?
4   Why might a researcher wish to disguise the objective of a study?
5   One of the major reasons why survey research may not be effective is that the survey instruments are less useful than they should be. What would you say are the four possible major faults of the survey instrument design?
6   Why is it desirable to pre-test survey instruments? What information can you secure from such a pre-test? How can you find the best wording for a question on a questionnaire?
7   One design problem in the development of survey instruments concerns the sequence of questions. What suggestions would you give to researchers designing their first questionnaire?
8   One of the major problems facing the designer of a survey instrument concerns the assumptions made. What are the major 'problem assumptions'?

# Making research decisions

**9** Below are six questions that might be found on questionnaires. Comment on each as to whether or not it is a good question. If it is not, explain why. (Assume that no lead-in or screening questions are required. Judge each question on its own merits.)

  **a** Do you read *National Geographic* magazine regularly?

  **b** What percentage of your time is spent asking for information from others in your organization?

  **c** When did you first start chewing gum?

  **d** How much discretionary buying power do you have each year?

  **e** Why did you decide to attend Hull University?

  **f** Do you think that the prime minister is doing a good job now?

**10** In a class project, students developed a brief self-administered questionnaire by which they might quickly evaluate a professor. One student submitted the following instrument. Evaluate the questions asked and the format of the instrument.

Professor Evaluation Form

**1** Overall, how would you rate this professor? _____ Good _____ Fair _____ Poor

**2** Does this professor:

  **a** have good class delivery? _____

  **b** know the subject? _____

  **c** have a positive attitude towards the subject? _____

  **d** grade fairly? _____

  **e** have a sense of humour? _____

  **f** use audio-visuals, case examples or other classroom aids? _____

  **g** return exams promptly? _____

**3** What is the professor's strongest point? _____

**4** What is the professor's weakest point? _____

**5** What kind of class does the professor teach? _____

**6** Is this course required? _____

**7** Would you take another course from this professor? _____

**11** Below is a copy of a covering letter and mail questionnaire received by a professor who is also a member of the national professional trainer association (NPTA). Please evaluate the usefulness and tone of the letter and the questions and format of the instrument.

Dear NPTA member,

In partial fulfilment of Master's degree work, I have chosen to do a descriptive study of the professional trainer in our country. Using the roster of the NPTA as a mailing list, your name came to me. I am enclosing a short questionnaire and a return envelope. I hope you will take a few minutes and fill out the questionnaire as soon as possible, as the sooner the information is returned to me, the better.

Sincerely,

Professor XYZ

QUESTIONNAIRE

Directions: please answer as briefly as possible

1  With what company did you enter the field of professional training?

   _____

2  How long have you been in the field of professional training?

   _____

3  How long have you been in the training department of the company where you are presently employed?

   _____

4  How long has the training department in your company been in existence?

   _____

5  Is the training department a subsidiary of another department? If so, what department?

   _____

6  For what functions (other than training) is your department responsible?

   _____

7  How many people, including yourself, are in the training department of your company (local plant or establishment)

   _____

8  What degrees do you hold and from what institutions?

   _____

   Major _____

   Minor _____

9  Why were you chosen for training? What special qualifications prompted your entry into training?

   _____

10 What experience would you consider necessary for an individual to enter into the field of training with your company? Include both educational requirements and actual experience.

   _____

## From concept to practice

12 Develop a flowchart for instrument design for your Master's thesis.
13 Develop a flowchart for instrument design for a study assessing the quality of lectures at your university.

## Classroom discussion

14 Take some questionnaires, which were conducted either for scientific or commercial purposes, to your next class session and discuss how they could be improved.
15 Discuss the problems of translating questionnaires to be used in cross-national studies.

## Online Learning Centre

### Get started with understanding statistical techniques!

When you have read this chapter, log on to the Online Learning Centre website at **www.mcgraw-hill.co.uk/textbooks/blumberg** to explore chapter-by-chapter test questions, additional case studies, a glossary and more online study tools for Business Research Methods.

## Notes

[1] Dorwin Cartwright, 'Some principles of mass persuasion', *Human Relations* 2, 1948, p. 266.

[2] Sam Gill, 'How do you stand on sin?' *Tide* (14 March 1947), p. 72.

[3] Unaided recall gives respondents no clues as to possible answers. Aided recall gives them a list of radio programmes that were played last night and then asks them which ones they heard. See Harper W. Boyd Jr. and Ralph Westfall, *Marketing Research* (3rd edn.). Homewood, IL: Irwin, 1972, p. 293.

[4] Gideon Sjoberg, 'A questionnaire on questionnaires', *Public Opinion Quarterly* 18 (Winter 1954), p. 425.

[5] More will be said on the problems of readability in Chapter 20.

[6] S.A. Stouffer et al., *Measurement and Prediction: Studies in Social Psychology in World War II*, Vol. 4. Princeton, NJ: Princeton University Press, 1950, p. 709.

[7] An excellent example of the question revision process is presented in Payne, *The Art of Asking Questions*, Princeton, NJ: Princeton University Press, 1951, pp. 214–25. This example illustrates that a relatively simple question can go through as many as 41 different versions before being judged satisfactory.

[8] Robert L. Kahn and Charles F. Cannell, *The Dynamics of Interviewing*. New York: Wiley, 1957, p. 108.

[9] Ibid., p. 110.

[10] Payne, *The Art of Asking Questions*, p. 140.

[11] Ibid., p. 141.

[12] Ibid., p. 149.

[13] National Opinion Research Center, Proceedings of the Central City Conference on Public Opinion Research. Denver, CO: University of Denver, 1946, p. 73.

[14] Hadley Cantril (ed.), *Gauging Public Opinion*. Princeton, NJ: Princeton University Press, 1944, p. 48.

[15] Payne, *The Art of Asking Questions*, pp. 7–8.

[16] Kahn and Cannell, *The Dynamics of Interviewing*, p. 132.

[17] Barbara Snell Dohrenwend, 'Some effects of open and closed questions on respondents' answers', *Human Organization* 24 (Summer 1965), pp. 175–84.

[18] Cantril, *Gauging Public Opinion*, p. 31.

[19] Jean M. Converse and Stanley Presser, *Survey Questions: Handcrafting the Standardized Questionnaire*. Beverly Hills, CA: Sage, 1986, pp. 50–1.

[20] Ibid., p. 51.

[21] Frederick J. Thumin, 'Watch for these unseen variables', *Journal of Marketing* 26 (July 1962), pp. 58–60.

[22] F. Cannell and Robert L. Kahn, 'The collection of data by interviewing', in *Research Methods in the Behavioral Sciences*, ed. Leon Festinger and Daniel Katz. New York: Holt, Rinehart & Winston, 1953, p. 349.

[23] Percival White, *Market Analysis*. New York: McGraw-Hill, 1921.

[24] Eugene J. Webb, Donald T. Campbell, Richard D. Schwartz and Lee Sechrest, *Unobtrusive Measures: Nonreactive Research in the Social Sciences*. Chicago: Rand McNally, 1966.

[25] Converse and Presser, *Survey Questions*, p. 52.

[26] W.R. Belson, *The Design and Understanding of Survey Questions*. Aldershot, England: Gower, 1981, pp. 76–86.

[27] The sections in this chapter on the methods and purposes of pre-testing have largely been adapted from Converse and Presser, *Survey Questions*, pp. 51–64; and Survey Research Center, *Interviewer's Manual* (rev. edn.). Ann Arbor: Institute for Social Research, University of Michigan, 1976, pp. 133–4. For an extended discussion of the phases of pre-testing, see Converse and Presser, *Survey Questions*, pp. 65–75.

# Recommended further reading

Converse, Jean M. and Presser, Stanley, *Survey Questions: Handcrafting the Standardized Questionnaire*. Beverly Hills, CA: Sage, 1986. A worthy successor to Stanley Payne's classic (see below). Advice on how to write survey questions based on professional experience and the experimental literature.

Deutskens, Elisabeth, de Ruyter, Ko, Wetzels, Martin and Oosterveld, Paul, 'Response rates and response quality of internet-based surveys: an experimental study', *Marketing Letters* 15(1), 2004, pp. 21–36. This article reports the results of a study on design effects on the response behaviour of people in Internet surveys.

Dillman, Don A., *Mail and Internet Surveys: The Tailored Design Method*. New York: Wiley, 1999. A contemporary treatment of Dillman's classic work.

Fink, Arlene and Kosecoff, Jaqueline, *How to Conduct Surveys: A Step-by-Step Guide*. Thousand Oaks, CA: Sage, 1998. Emphasis on computer-assisted and interactive surveys, and a good section on creating questions.

Foddy, William, *Constructing Questions for Interviews and Questionnaires: Theory and Practice in Social Research*. Cambridge: Cambridge University Press, 1994. This book provides clear theory-based guidelines on how questions should be formulated.

Kahn, Robert L. and Cannell, Charles F., *The Dynamics of Interviewing*. New York: Wiley, 1957. Chapters 5 and 6 cover questionnaire design.

Payne, Stanley L., *The Art of Asking Questions*. Princeton, NJ: Princeton University Press, 1951. An enjoyable book on the many problems encountered in developing useful survey questions. A classic resource.

Sudman, Seymour and Bradburn, Norman N., *Asking Questions: A Practical Guide to Questionnaire Design*. San Francisco: Jossey-Bass, 1982. This book covers the major issues in writing individual questions and constructing scales. The emphasis is on structured questions and interview schedules.

Chapter **14**

# Writing up and presenting research outcomes

## Chapter contents

## LEARNING OBJECTIVES

When you have read this chapter, you should understand:

☑ the link between presentation quality and perceived study quality

☑ that writing a research report requires you to consider its purpose, readership, circumstances/limitations and use

☑ that most statistical data are best presented in tables, charts or graphs.

# 14.1  The written research report

It may seem unscientific and even unfair, but a poor final report or presentation can destroy a study. Research technicians may appreciate the brilliance of badly reported content, but most readers will be influenced by the quality of the reporting. A main reason for this is that an argument that is presented well is more easily understood. If you want to transmit information, either orally or in writing, it is mainly your responsibility to ensure that the transmission between the sender (you) and the receiver (the people you want to address) does not suffer from disturbing 'noise'. This fact should prompt researchers to make a special effort to communicate clearly and fully.

The research report contains findings, analyses of findings, interpretations, conclusions and, sometimes, recommendations. The researcher is the expert on the topic and knows the specifics in a way no one else can. Because a research report is an authoritative one-way communication, it imposes a special obligation for maintaining objectivity. Even if your findings seem to point to an action, you should exercise restraint and caution when proposing that course.

Reports may be defined by their degree of formality/design and the audience. The formal report follows a well-delineated and relatively long format. This is in contrast to the informal or short report. Further, writing a report on the outcomes of a study for an academic audience, such as a thesis, a working paper or an article for an academic journal, requires additional considerations.

## Short reports

Short reports are appropriate when a problem is well defined, is of limited scope, and has a simple and straightforward methodology. Most informational, progress and interim reports are of this kind: a report on cost-of-living changes for upcoming labour negotiations or a report on the general socio-economic conditions of a country to which a firm is considering exporting.

Short reports are about five pages long. At the beginning, there should be a brief statement about the authorization for the study, the problem examined, and its breadth and depth. Next come the conclusions and recommendations, followed by the findings that support them. Section headings should be used.

A **letter of transmittal** is a vehicle to convey short reports. A five-page report may be produced to track sales on a quarterly basis. The report should be direct, make ample use of graphics to show trends, and refer the reader to the research department for further information. Detailed information on the research method would be omitted, although an overview could appear in an appendix. The purpose of this type of report is to distribute information quickly in an easy-to-use format. Short reports are also produced for clients with small, relatively inexpensive research projects.

The letter is a form of a short report. Its tone should be informal. The format follows that of any good business letter and should not exceed a few pages. A letter report is often written in personal style (using the words 'we', 'you', etc.), although this depends on the situation. Memorandum reports are another variety and follow the 'To, From, Subject' format.

The following suggestions may be helpful in writing short reports.

- Tell the reader why you are writing (it may be in response to a request).
- If the memo is in response to a request for information, remind the reader of the exact point raised, answer it, and follow with any necessary details.

- Write in an expository style with brevity and directness.
- If time permits, write the report today and leave it for review tomorrow before sending it.
- Attach detailed materials as appendices when needed.

## Long reports

Long reports are of two types: the technical or base report, and the management report. The choice of which approach to take depends on the audience and the researcher's objectives.

Many projects will require both types of report: a technical report, written for an audience of researchers, and a management report, written for the non-technically oriented manager or client. While some researchers try to write a single report that satisfies both needs, this complicates the task and is seldom satisfactory. The two types of audience have different technical training, interests and goals.

### *The management report*

Sometimes the client has no research background and is interested in results rather than in methodology. The major communication medium in this case is the **management report**. It is still helpful to have a technical report if the client later wishes to have a technical appraisal of the study.

Because the management report is designed for a non-technical audience, the researcher faces some special problems. Readers are less concerned with methodological details but more interested in learning quickly the major findings and conclusions. They want help in making decisions. Often the report is developed for a single person and needs to be written with that person's characteristics and needs in mind.

The style of the report should encourage rapid reading and quick comprehension of major findings, and it should prompt understanding of the implications and conclusions. The report tone is journalistic and must be accurate. Headlines and underlining for emphasis are helpful; pictures and graphs often replace tables. Sentences and paragraphs should be short and direct. Consider liberal use of white space and wide margins. It may be desirable to put a single finding on each page. It also helps to have a theme running through the report, and even graphic or animated characters designed to vary the presentation.

### *The technical report*

The **technical report** should include full documentation and detail. It will normally survive all working papers and original data files, so will become the major source document. It is the report that other researchers will want to see because it has the full story of what was done and how it was done.

While completeness is a goal, you must guard against including non-essential material. A good guide is that sufficient procedural information should be included to enable others to replicate the study. This includes sources of data, research procedures, sampling design, data-gathering instruments, index construction and data analysis methods. Most information should be attached in an appendix. A technical report should also include a full presentation and analysis of significant data. Conclusions and recommendations should be clearly related to specific findings.

# Online reporting

Medical Radar International (MRI), a Swedish research company, works exclusively in the pharmaceuticals field. It conducts its syndicated study – Radar Dynamics – on the use of pharmaceuticals by doctors across several European countries, by interviewing 150–300 physicians (depending on the size of the country) twice each year.

Using a variety of SPSS software products, including In2quest's In2data for database development, Quantum for fast data tabulation, and SmartViewer, MRI can report results quickly. With SmartViewer web server software, a pharmaceutical company participating in the syndicated study can view password-protected results from Medical Radar's own website, even customizing the data in tables that specifically suit its needs, while the underlying data are tamper-protected. Staffan Hallstram, systems manager at MRI, reports that web distribution is the 'ideal method' for distributing its syndicated research reports.

## References and further reading

'Medical Radar', SPSS, February 2002 (http://www.spss.com/spssatwork/template_view.cfm?Story_ID=24).

'Take action with organized, interactive analytic information', SPSS, February 2002 (http://www.spss.com/svws).

www.medicalradar.com

www.spss.com

### The academic report

If your study also has a scientific objective, the technical report comes close to offering what is needed in the writing of a working paper or even a contribution to a scientific journal. What distinguishes a technical report from a working paper or article in an academic journal is that the latter will have a substantial theoretical section. Usually, such a section will contain a review of the current academic literature on the issue (see also Chapter 5) and elaborated argumentation regarding the development of a new theory or the extension/adjustment of an existing theory. With respect to the section reporting the findings of a study, an academic report discusses the study's outcomes in light of the particular theory followed. Similarly, the conclusions also discuss the outcome in terms of its impact on theory development. Finally, writers of academic reports are more inclined to refer to the work of others and to acknowledge their contribution to the field, which results in much longer lists of references.

With regard to style, academic reports have their own language, and may tend to use particular words. For example, in academic writing the word 'significant(ly)' is used with the statistical definition of significance in mind, while in a management report the word might be used to denote importance, although no one has checked any test statistics. If you are writing a paper for publication in an academic journal, it is important to bear in mind that you will need to comply with the rules of the specific journal, which will either be available at the journal's website or from the editor. Such rules lay out how you must refer to the literature, whether you should use footnotes or endnotes, how tables and figures should be labelled and presented, and what writing style is preferred.

## 14.2  Research report components

Research reports, long and short, have a set of identifiable components. Usually headings and sub-headings divide the sections. Each report is individual: sections may be dropped or added, condensed or expanded to meet the needs of the audience. Exhibit 14.1 lists five types of report,

| Report modules | Short report | | Long report | | Academic report |
| --- | --- | --- | --- | --- | --- |
| | **Memo or letter** | **Short technical** | **Management** | **Technical** | |
| Prefatory information | | 1 | 1 | 1 | 1 |
| Letter of transmittal | | | ✓ | ✓ | ✓ |
| Title page | | ✓ | ✓ | ✓ | ✓ |
| Authorization statement | | ✓ | ✓ | ✓ | |
| Executive summary | | ✓ | ✓ | ✓ | ✓ (suitable for researchers) |
| Table of contents | | | ✓ | ✓ | |
| Introduction | 1 | 2 | 2 | 2 | 2 |
| Problem statement | ✓ | ✓ | ✓ | ✓ | ✓ |
| Research objectives | ✓ | ✓ | ✓ | ✓ | ✓ |
| Background | ✓ | ✓ | ✓ | ✓ | ✓ |
| Theoretical section | | | ✓ (briefly) | ✓ (briefly) | 3 |
| Literature review | | | | | ✓ |
| Theory development (deriving of hypotheses) | | | | | ✓ |
| Methodology | | ✓ (briefly) | ✓ (briefly) | 3 | 4 |
| Sampling design | | | | ✓ | ✓ |
| Research design | | | | ✓ | ✓ |
| Data-collection | | | | ✓ | ✓ |
| Data analysis | | | | ✓ | ✓ |
| Limitations | | ✓ | ✓ | ✓ | ✓ |
| Findings | | 3 | 4 | 4 | 5 |
| Conclusions | 2 | 4 | 3 | 5 | 6 |
| Appendices | | 5 | 5 | 6 | 7 |
| Bibliography | | | | 7 | 8 |

*Exhibit 14.1*  Research report sections and their order of inclusion.

the sections that are typically included, and the general order of presentation. Each of these formats can be modified to meet the needs of the audience.

The technical report and the academic report follow the flow of the research. The prefatory materials, such as a letter of authorization and a table of contents, are first in the technical report, but not contained in the academic one. An introduction covers the purpose of the study. An academic report continues with an elaborated theoretical section, while the technical report moves straight to a section on methodology. The findings are presented next, including tables and other graphics. The conclusions section includes recommendations. Finally, the appendices contain technical information, instruments, glossaries and references.

In contrast to the technical report, the management report is for the non-technical client. The reader has little time to absorb details and requires prompt exposure to the most critical findings; thus the report's sections are in an inverted order. After the prefatory and introductory sections, the conclusions are presented, along with accompanying recommendations. Individual findings are presented next, supporting the conclusions already made. The appendices present any necessary methodological details. The order of the management report allows clients to grasp the conclusions and recommendations quickly, without much reading. Then, if they wish to go further, they may read on into the findings. The management report should make liberal use of visual display.

The short technical report covers the same items as the long technical report but in an abbreviated form. The methodology is included as part of the introduction and takes no more than a few paragraphs. Most of the emphasis is placed on the findings and conclusions. A memo or letter format covers only the minimum: what the problem is and what the research conclusions are.

## The modules in detail

In the following, we describe the modules in detail with a special emphasis on writing a thesis or academic report.

## Prefatory items

Prefatory materials do not have a direct bearing on the research itself. Instead, they assist the reader in using the research report. Examples for such items in a thesis are a CD-Rom containing the data, transcripts, screenshots of used websites, and so on.

## Letter of transmittal

When the relationship between the researcher and the client is formal, a letter of transmittal should be included. This is appropriate when a report is for a specific client (e.g. the company president) and when it is generated for an outside organization. The letter should refer to the authorization for the project, and any specific instructions or limitations placed on the study. It should also state the purpose and scope of the study. For many internal projects and academic reports, it is not necessary to include a letter of transmittal.

## Title page

The title page should include four items: the title of the report, the date, and for whom and by whom it was prepared. The title should be brief but include the following three elements:

1 the variables included in the study

2 the type of relationship among the variables, and

3 the population to which the results may be applied.[1]

If including these three elements results in a very long title, a possible solution is to work with a sub-title, which is divided by a full stop or colon from the main title and often printed in a smaller font. For example: this applies particularly if in the final design of your report, the title reappears in the page heading; in such a case it is advisable to work with sub-titles. Superfluous phrases such as 'A report on …' and 'A discussion of …' add length to a title but little else. Single-word titles are also of little value. Exhibit 14.2 shows three acceptable ways to word report titles. It should be noted that most universities have formal requirements of what needs to be included in a thesis on the title page, and these should be checked with your university.

## Authorization letter

When the report is sent to a public organization, it is common to include a letter of authorization showing the authority for undertaking the research. This is especially true for reports conducted for federal and state governments and non-profit organizations. The letter not only shows who sponsored the research but also delineates the original request.

## Executive summary

An **executive summary** can serve two purposes. It may be a report in miniature – covering all the aspects in the body of the report, but in abbreviated form – or it may be a concise summary

| Descriptive study | The five-year demand outlook for plastic pipes in France |
| --- | --- |
| | Five-year demand outlook for plastic pipes. A study of the French market |
| Correlation study | The relationship between the value of the dollar in world markets and the national inflation rates in emerging markets |
| | Value of the dollar in world markets and national inflation rates. A correlational study in emerging markets |
| Causal study | The effect of various motivation methods on worker attitudes among British workers in the chemical industry |
| | The effect of various motivation methods on worker attitudes. An investigation among British workers in the chemical industry |

*Exhibit 14.2* Sample report titles.

of the major findings and conclusions, including recommendations. Two pages are generally sufficient for executive summaries. Write this section once the rest of the report is finished. It should not include new information but may require graphics to present a particular conclusion. Expect the summary to contain a high density of significant terms since it is repeating the highlights of the report. Academic reports are also accompanied by a summary, which briefly reflects the problem statement, the theoretical approach used, the research design and the main finding. A summary of an academic report is usually very short (i.e. less than half a page). Executive summaries are especially useful for a thesis that has been written with the support of any organization.

## Table of contents

As a rough guide, any report of several sections that totals more than six to ten pages should have a table of contents. If there are many tables, charts or other exhibits, these should also be listed after the table of contents in a separate table of illustrations/figures.

## Introduction

The introduction prepares the reader for the report by describing the parts of the project: the problem statement, research objectives and background material.[2] In most projects, the introduction can be taken from the research proposal with minor editing. A thesis' introduction needs to provide a rationale for the thesis, that is you need to tell the reader what the added value of your thesis is, and why it is worth reading. The introduction serves the following functions:

- introduce and develop the problem statement
- show the relevance of the problem statement
- provide and outline for the paper.

There are a couple of standard answers why a thesis is important. Suppose you write a thesis on telecommunication markets in some African countries. Here are a couple of rationale you might use:

*We do not know a lot about the topic.* Here, you need to show in the introduction that the main literature hardly covers the topic; there might be a lot of literature on telecommunication markets but not in Africa or there might be a lot of literature on markets in developing countries, but not telecommunication markets or other markets characterized by intensive technology and network effects. There is, however, one potential caveat to this answer, namely that others could argue the reason that we do not know a lot about the topic is that the topic is not interesting.

*Other people think that the problem is important.* Start with quoting a scholar, preferably a well-known one, claiming that more research on markets in developing nations is needed. Using the quote of a well-known scholar shows that you are not the only one who thinks that the problem is interesting, but the question is why should you research what other people believe and not what you like.

*My research problem affects a lot of people and can save money.* This rationale is convincing to most. For example, you could argue that telecommunication markets in all industrialized countries are saturated, but that developing countries still show remarkable growth rates, or you could argue that building up mobile telecommunication structures in developing countries is an important infrastructure investment that enable much larger parts of the population to engage in worldwide communication and thereby become part of a globalized world. However, the academic world views research studies that only focus on providing benefits in terms of money with some scepticism. If (consulting) firms or governments conduct such studies that is fine, but the scientific community expects something more than just a pecuniary motive; it expects that the study contributes to our understanding of the world, that is contributes to our theoretical knowledge.

*The research is theoretically important.* This rationale is the most respected in academics and although the chances that your thesis will be the founding stone of a new theory are small, a thesis should contribute to the knowledge. From a theoretical perspective, even the replication of an existing study can be a valuable contribution, if you conduct the study in a different country, industry, and so on. Thus, in our example case, you might argue that we are well aware of how the innovation of mobile telephones penetrated western markets, but we are not aware how this happens in developing nations. In other cases you might take an idea from a theoretical paper and explore it through a case study, that is you are the first to present some empirical evidence for the theory.

There are, of course, many other arguments to build up a rationale for your thesis, but the above are very often used and you should check whether you can use some of them eventually together with any other arguments you have in mind to build a rationale for your thesis.

## Problem statement and research objective

The problem statement contains the need for the research project and is usually represented in question form. Note that from a scientific perspective why-like questions are much more interesting than what-like questions, as the former really attempt to find an explanation for a mechanism, while answers to the latter are sufficient if they purely provide a descriptive account of the phenomena or situation. If you start with a why question, you can either attempt to check the validity of certain explanations (explanatory study) or you can attempt to find possible explanations (explorative study). Which type of study is more appropriate mainly depends on what is already known about a phenomenon and how complex the explanation is.

In quantitative studies, the research problem is often followed by some indication of the main hypotheses you want to test, that is when you start specifying the problem statement, you state what kind of explanation you are advancing. Whether you state them as real hypotheses or additional sub-questions does not matter; what matters is that you inform the reader in which direction you are heading, that is what kind of theories and explanations you will test. In qualitative studies, you often do not have main hypotheses, as you are still exploring and searching for suitable explanations. Nevertheless, even when you start a qualitative study you have some kind of expectations, which might turn out right or wrong, and it is important to inform the reader about these expectations.

If the problem you investigate is rather complex, that is it takes into account multiple possible explanations and/or multiple phenomena that are interrelated, it might be advisable to use a figure sketching the relations you are testing or exploring. Boiling a problem statement down to a simple figure also helps you to clearly state which variables or phenomena are of concern and how they are defined, how they are distinct from other variables or phenomena, and how they relate with other variables.

Finally, you briefly state your target group in this section. Thus, if you conduct a qualitative study, you could state that the study will be based on mobile telephone users in Ethiopia or you could state that it would be a comparison of the telecommunication markets in 25 African countries. In the case of a quantitative study, you could state that the exploration is based on a case study of how mobile telecommunication was introduced to a small village in the north of Ghana. Thus, you give the reader a first idea in which context you will examine the research question later on.

## Theoretical section

As mentioned earlier, this section distinguishes academic reports from all other types of report; it forms a substantial part of any scientific paper. The two typical elements of a theoretical section are the review of the current academic literature on the issue investigated and a substantial part covering the theory development presented in the report. The style of a theoretical section depends largely on what kind of study is presented. In theoretical studies, this section will provide a detailed description and argument for the theoretical model developed. In quantitative empirical studies, you will use this section either to introduce the formal mathematical model or to provide convincing arguments for the hypotheses you derive. In qualitative empirical studies, this section usually contains a very critical and extensive review of the literature, closing with convincing arguments concerning the points you will make later on.

There are three ways to look at the literature you collected.

1 You can read through it **to identify problems**. If a book or article makes a claim that seems inaccurate or too simplistic to you, you have detected a research problem, as you can now investigate whether a more complex or differentiated explanation would describe the phenomena better. For example, at the beginning of transaction cost theory, most studies argued that firms can choose to make or buy, that is they could either produce an input they needed themselves (hierarchy) or buy it on the market. However, this claim was inaccurate to the extent that firms also used other structures to govern the exchange, such as long-term contracting or alliances. A new branch of research investigating contracting and alliances was the response to the oversimplified view that interfirm transactions occur either via markets or with a hierarchy (the firm).

2 You can read through **to find arguments**. Suppose your research problem starts with the observation that the market leaders in the mobile telephone market has changed rather quickly in the last 20 years, while in other markets the number 1 firm remained stable for long periods. Microsoft has been the number 1 software company for more than two decades and General Motors the number 1 in cars for even more than two decades. But in mobile telecommunication, we observed that Motorola lost its number 1 position to Nokia, which, in turn, lost its to Samsung. What would explain that some markets are

more dynamic than others? Reading through articles you will find several explanations for the dynamic within markets. Likely arguments mentioned in the literature are technology shocks that restructure the industry, changes in consumer preferences, such as fashion waves that favour certain brands until the brand is so widely accepted that it gets 'uncool'.

3  You can read **to find evidence**. Previous literature is often used to support the claims that you made yourself. If you look through the literature to find such evidence it is important to distinguish, whether previous literature just also claims what you claim or whether they provide evidence, for their claim, that is they have qualitative or quantitative data that supports the claim. If previous studies present evidence supporting your claim, that is a start. It shows that at least one other person has similar thoughts but, of course, just one other person is not sufficient evidence to claim that your argument is valid.

Next to reviewing the literature, the development of your own theory is an important part of this section. Developing a theory is essentially based on good arguments. To check whether an argument you use is good and sound, you should ask the following five questions. You can also use these questions to check the quality of the arguments made by others.

1  What is the claim exactly? You need to be very precise on what your claim is. For example, the two following claims differ substantially: (i) large firms are more innovative than small firms; and (ii) large firms are more innovative than small firms in industries with a high research and development intensity. The first claim applies in general, while the second is restricted to specific industries.

2  What reasons support the claim? A viable reason for the second restricted claim would be that in an industry with high R&D expenditure it is costly to innovate, that is it means you need to invest large sums of money upfront before you introduce a new product. Only large firms with sufficient resources are able to finance such large up-front investments.

3  What is the evidence pointing to the reasons mentioned? Here you need to find studies that show a positive correlation between firm size and the number of new products or patents in R&D-intensive industries.

4  Are there alternative explanations for the evidence? With regard to the first question, we ask whether differences in financial resources really explain the relationship between firms' size and innovativeness. Alternative explanations could be that large firms are better able to attract good people and are more innovative even if you control for financial resources. Or large firms are more innovative, not because they have more resources, but because they have different resources that encourage them to combine different types of resource resulting in innovations. Especially in a world in which we too easily rely on facts, it is important to think about what the possible reasons are behind the facts and often we come to the conclusion that there are multiple reasons for the observation of a phenomenon.

5  Is there different evidence? The second question asks how valid the evidence is. Are there R&D-intensive industries where small firms are more innovative than large firms? Is the biotechnology sector a counter-example, that is an R&D-intensive sector in which small firms are more innovative? Although the provision of a counter-example does not allow us

to conclude that the opposite argument is true, each counter-example points at the limited range of an argument and it is up to you to show these range restrictions.

The better your argument withstands these five questions, the sounder it is. Sound arguments lead either to strong hypotheses or strong potential explanations in explorative studies and are the cornerstones of any good research study.

## Methodology

Management and short academic reports usually do not have a separate section on the methodology. However, for technical and academic reports, that is also for theses, the section on methodology is important. One important reason for being explicit on methodology is that this section is the only part in a thesis where you can show how much effort you have put in to the collection and analysis of the information. Approaching respondents, collecting information and editing the collected information often takes a substantial slice of the total time devoted to a thesis project. The methodological section or chapter is the place where you can show how thorough you have been on these issues.

1 *Sampling design or research participants*   The researcher explicitly defines the target population being studied and the sampling methods used. In quantitative studies this will include answers to the questions: What was the intended population? What did the population look like from the sample that was drawn? Was this a probability or non-probability sample? If probability, was it simple random or complex random? How were the elements selected? How was the size determined? How much confidence do we have, and how much error was allowed? If you report on a qualitative study, typical elements covered would be a thicker and more detailed description of where the research was conducted and would include answers to the questions: Which firm(s) or department(s) does the study address? Who provided the information? Thus, to summarize, you start a methodological section by describing whom you researched and how you approached the research participants. In a second step, it is wise to justify that the sample population or the case chosen is based on a wise selection. As it is impossible to research all people or all firms in the world, you usually address a particular country, industry or even firm. Give some arguments why it makes sense to investigate this particular country, industry or firm. What do they have in particular that makes them an interesting case or sample for your research problem? The reasons given here often link to the rationales of the whole research. For example, a specific country can be interesting to research if it has not yet been covered by previous research, or an industry is interesting to examine because you expect that the phenomena that interest you are particularly strong in this industry.

2 *Research design*   The coverage of the design must be adapted to the purpose. In an experimental study, the materials, tests, equipment, control conditions and other devices should be described. In descriptive or *ex-post facto* designs, it may be sufficient to cover the rationale for using one design instead of competing alternatives. Even with a sophisticated design, the strengths and weaknesses should be identified, and the instrumentation and materials discussed. Copies of materials, such as the used questionnaire, are placed in an appendix.

3 *Data-collection*   This part of the report describes the specifics of gathering the data. Its contents depend on the design selected. Survey work generally uses a team with field and central supervision. How many were involved? What was their training? How were they managed? When were the data collected? How much time did it take? What were the conditions in the field? How were irregularities handled? In an experiment, we would want to know about subject assignment to groups, the use of standardized procedures and protocols, the administration of tests or observational forms, manipulation of the variables, and so on. For a qualitative case study, you would extensively describe from which sources you obtained the information and by what means (e.g. interviews, observations, etc.). What kind of observation, if any, did you conduct? What kind of archival sources and documents did you look at? How long did it take to collect the information and who else was involved in collecting it?

4 *Measurements*   There is always a gap between the information you gathered and the concepts or variables that you used in the theoretical section; identity between these two is extremely rare. In the measurement sections, you describe how you transformed the information collected to the theoretical concepts and variables. For example, in a thesis based on a quantitative survey you describe which question you combined to generate a new variable reflecting the theoretical concept you are interested in and you also report any results from reliability and scaling tests. Studies employing a more qualitative methodology also need a measurement section that clarifies how you decided that the obtained qualitative information really indicates that a certain situation occurred or a certain behaviour happened. Has it been sufficient if a certain issue was mentioned just by one interviewee or had it to be mentioned by more than one, or has any information that was obtained from the interview been cross-checked with the information obtained from archival sources. Explaining how you assessed the information obtained, either quantitative or qualitative, is an important element in building up readers' confidence in the validity of your study.

## Data analysis

This section summarizes the methods used to analyse the data. It describes data handling, preliminary analysis, statistical tests, computer programs and other technical information. The rationale for the choice of analysis approaches should be clear. A brief commentary on assumptions and appropriateness of use should be presented.

## Findings

This is generally the longest section of the report. The objective is to explain the data rather than draw interpretations or conclusions. When quantitative data can be presented, this should be done as simply as possible with charts, graphics and tables.

The data need not include everything you have collected. The criterion for inclusion is, 'Is this material important to the reader's understanding of the problem and the findings?' However, make sure that you include findings unfavourable to your hypotheses as well as those that support them.

# Limitations

This topic is often handled with ambivalence. Some people wish to ignore the matter, feeling that mentioning limitations detracts from the impact of their study. This attitude is unprofessional and possibly unethical. Others seem to adopt a masochistic approach of detailing everything. The section should be a thoughtful presentation of significant methodology or implementation problems and the consequences these limitations might have for the validity of the outcomes. An even-handed approach is one of the hallmarks of an honest and competent investigator.

Some people put this section at the end of the report, but a good reason to put it before the conclusions is that you do not want to finish the report with a section pointing at the weaknesses of the research, rather you want to close your thesis or report with a statement on what the thesis or report contributes.

The main concern of any limitation is that it might bias your results, that is it might lead to the wrong results. Common limitations refer to the used sample, the used measurements and the used analysis techniques.

- Sample: If you use a specific sample, for example employees in information technology (IT) firms, your results might be biased because employees in IT firms earn above-average salaries, work in less hierarchical firms, and so on.
- Measurement: Your measurement might be flawed, because you only used a limited set of questions; it has not been validated in previous studies; you are unsure whether respondents from different countries understood the question in the same way; and you had to impute data, and so on.
- Analysis: You could not use more advanced analysis techniques because your sample size was not large enough to employ them.

A good way to discuss the limitations is to assess how much they could bias your results. You should note that not all biases work in your favour, that is the bias makes it more likely that you support a hypothesis. For example, if you use a specific sample, this usually means that the variance in the sample is smaller than in the larger population and smaller variance means that it is harder to obtain significant effects. Thus, such a bias does not make your results better, but the consequences of the bias are less severe, because the estimates you obtain are more likely to be an underestimation than an overestimation.

# Conclusions
## *Summary and conclusions*

The summary is a brief statement of the essential findings. Sectional summaries may be used if there are many specific findings. These may be combined into an overall summary. In simple descriptive research, a summary may complete the report, because conclusions and recommendations may not be required.

Findings state facts; conclusions represent inferences drawn from the findings. A writer is sometimes reluctant to make conclusions and thus leaves the task to the reader. Avoid this temptation when possible. As the researcher, you are the one best informed on the factors that critically influence the findings and conclusions. Especially in business research, conclusion can also take the form of recommendations. Thus, you answer the question of what companies can learn from the results of your study and what should they do in the light of your findings. In more academic papers the conclusions often end with recommendations for future studies that depart from where your study ended.

## Appendices

The appendices are the place for complex tables, statistical tests, supporting documents, copies of forms and questionnaires, detailed descriptions of methodology, instructions to fieldworkers, and other evidence important for later support. The reader who wishes to learn about the technical aspects of the study and to look at statistical breakdowns will want a complete appendix.

## Bibliography

The use of secondary data requires a bibliography. Proper citation styles and formats are unique to the purpose of the report. The instructor, programme, institution or client often specifies style requirements. The uniqueness of varying requirements makes detailed examples in this chapter impractical although the endnotes and references in this book provide one example. As cited in Chapter 2, on the research proposal, we recommend the *Publication Manual of the American Psychological Association*; Kate L. Turabian, *A Manual for Writers of Term Papers, Theses, and Dissertations*; and Joseph Gibaldi and Walter S. Achtert, *MLA Handbook for Writers of Research Papers*.

# 14.3  Writing the report

Students often pay inadequate attention to reporting their findings and conclusions. This is unfortunate. A well-presented study will often impress the reader more than a study with greater scientific quality but a weaker presentation. Report-writing skills are especially valuable to academic researchers and the junior executive or management trainee.

## Pre-writing concerns

Before writing, one should ask again, 'What is the purpose of this report?' Responding to this question is one way to crystallize the problem.

The second pre-writing question is, 'Who will read the report?' Thought should be given to the needs, temperament and biases of the audience. You should not distort facts to meet these needs and biases, but should consider them while developing the presentation. Knowing who will read the report may suggest its appropriate length. For management reports, the higher the report goes in an organization, the shorter it should be.

Another consideration is technical background – the gap in subject knowledge between the reader and the writer. The greater the gap, the more difficult it is to convey the full findings meaningfully and concisely. In academic writing, it is safe to assume that the reader's knowledge is very similar to the author's knowledge.

The third pre-writing question is, 'What are the circumstances and limitations under which you are writing?' Is the nature of the subject highly technical? Do you need statistics? Charts?

What is the importance of the topic? A crucial subject justifies more effort than a minor one. What should be the scope of the report? How much time is available? Deadlines often impose limitations on the report.

Finally, 'How will the report be used?' Try to visualize the reader using the report. How can the information be made more convenient? How much effort must be given to getting the attention and interest of the reader? Will the report be read by more than one person? If so, how many copies should be made? What will be the distribution of the report?

## The outline

Once the researcher has made the first analysis of the data, drawn tentative conclusions and completed statistical significance tests, it is time to develop an outline. A useful system employs the following organization structure using Roman numbers for the major headings, and letters and Arabic numbers for the different sub-levels. Others also use small Roman numbers (i, ii, iii, iv …) or even Greek letters ($\alpha$, $\beta$, $\gamma$, $\delta$ …) to add structure.

> I.  Major Topic Heading
> A.  Major sub-topic heading
> 1.  Sub-topic
> a.  Minor sub-topic
> (1) Further detail
> (a) Even further detail

The structure depth of your outline depends very much on the total length of the report. Short reports should not be structured deeper than the second level. In addition, you might choose not to use letter or number 'numbering' at the lower levels, but just different printing formats, such as bold, underlined or italic text. When choosing the depth of your outline structure, you should try to keep some balance in the depth. Thus, structuring your second section B deep down to the sixth level, while all other sections are structured much less deeply creates an unbalanced structure. Further, you should be aware that introducing a new lower level requires that you have at least two distinct aspects at this level. Thus, if you introduce a minor sub-topic – (a) – to your sub-topic – 1. – you also need a minor sub-topic (b).

Software for developing outlines and visually connecting ideas simplifies this once onerous task. Two styles of outlining are widely used: the topic outline and the sentence outline. In the **topic outline**, a key word/phrase is used. The assumption is that the writer knows its significance and will later remember the nature of the argument represented by that word or phrase or, alternatively, the outliner knows that a point should be made but is not yet sure how to make it.

The **sentence outline** expresses the essential thoughts associated with the specific topic. This approach leaves less development work for later writing, other than elaboration and explanation to improve readability. It has the obvious advantages of pushing the writer to make decisions on what to include and how to say it. It is probably the best outlining style for the inexperienced researcher because it divides the writing job into its two major components: what to say and how to say it.

Exhibit 14.3 gives an example of the type of detail found with each of these outlining formats.

| Topic outline | Sentence outline |
| --- | --- |
| I. Demand | I. Demand for refrigerators |
| A. How measured? | A. Measured in terms of factory shipments as reported by the EU trade commission |
| 1. Voluntary error | 1. Error is introduced into year-to-year comparisons because reporting is voluntary |
| 2. Shipping error | 2. A second factor is variations from month to month because of shipping and invoicing patterns |
| (a) Monthly variances | (a) Variations up to 30 per cent this year depend on whether shipments were measured by actual shipping date or invoice date |

*Exhibit 14.3*  Example of a structure.

## The bibliography

Long reports, particularly technical ones, require a bibliography. A bibliography documents the sources used by the writer. Although bibliographies may contain work used as a background or for further study, it is preferable to include only those sources used in preparing the report.

Bibliographic retrieval software allows researchers to locate and save references from online services and translate them into database records. Entries can be further searched, sorted, indexed and formatted into bibliographies of any style. Many retrieval programs are network compatible and connect to popular word processors. (Chapter 10 also mentions a recording system for converting source notes to footnotes and bibliographies.)

Style manuals provide guidelines on form, section and alphabetical arrangement, and annotation. Projects using many electronic sources may benefit from the comparison of APA and MLA citations in Exhibit 14.4.

## Writing the draft

Once the outline is complete, decisions can be made on the placement of graphics, tables and charts. Each should be matched to a particular section in the outline. It is helpful to make these decisions before your first draft. While graphics might be added later or tables changed into charts, it is helpful to make a first approximation of the graphics before beginning to write. Choices for reporting statistics will be reviewed later in this chapter.

Each writer uses different mechanisms for getting thoughts into written form. Some will write in longhand, relying on someone else to transcribe their prose into word-processed format. Others are happiest in front of a word processor, able to add, delete and move sections at will. Use whatever is the best approach for you.

Computer software packages check for spelling errors and provide a Thesaurus for looking up alternative ways of expressing a thought. A CD-ROM can call up the 20-volume *Oxford English Dictionary*, believed to be the greatest dictionary in any language. Currently, even some common word confusion ('there' for 'their', 'to' for 'too' or 'effect' for 'affect') will be found by standard spellcheckers, but there are some mistakes that they are unable to detect. Advanced programs will scrutinize your report for grammar, punctuation, capitalization, repeated words, transposed letters, homonyms, style problems and readability level. The style checker will reveal misused words and indicate awkward phrasing.

## *Readability*

Sensitive writers will consider the reading ability of their audience in order to achieve high readership levels. You can obtain high readership more easily if the topic interests the readers and is in their field of expertise. In addition, you can demonstrate the usefulness of your report by pointing out how it will help the readers. Finally, you can write at a level that is appropriate to the readers' reading abilities. To test writing for difficulty level, there are standard **readability indexes**. The Flesch Reading Ease Score gives a score between 0 and 100. The lower the score, the harder the material is to read. The Flesch–Kincaid Grade Level and Gunning's Fog Index both provide a score that corresponds with the grade level needed to easily read and understand a document. Although it is possible to calculate these indexes by hand, some software packages will do it automatically. The most sophisticated packages allow you to specify the preferred reading level. Words that are above that level are highlighted to allow you to choose an alternative.

Advocates of readability measurement do not claim that all written material should be at the simplest level possible. They argue only that the level should be appropriate for the audience. They point out that comic books score about 6 on the Gunning scale (that is, a person with a sixth-grade education should be able to read that material), while *Time* magazine usually scores about 10. Material that scores much above 12 becomes difficult for the public to read comfortably. Such measures obviously give only a rough idea of the true readability of a report, and good writing calls for a variety of other skills to enhance reading comprehension.

## *Comprehensibility*

Good writing varies with the writing objective. Research writing is designed to convey information of a precise nature. Avoid ambiguity, multiple meanings and allusions. Take care to choose the right words – words that convey thoughts accurately, clearly and efficiently. When concepts and constructs are used, they must be defined, either operationally or descriptively.

Words and sentences should be organized and edited carefully. Misplaced modifiers run rampant in carelessly written reports. Subordinate ideas mixed with major ideas make the report confusing to readers, forcing them to sort out what is important and what is secondary when this should have been done for them.

Finally, there is the matter of pace. Pace is defined as:

> The rate at which the printed page presents information to the reader … The proper pace in technical writing is one that enables the reader to keep his mind working just a fraction of a second behind his eye as he reads along. It logically would be slow when the information is complex or difficult to understand; fast when the information is straightforward and familiar. If the reader's mind lags behind his eye, the pace is too rapid; if his mind wanders ahead of his eye (or wants to) the pace is too slow.[3]

| Type | APA | MLA |
|---|---|---|
| Full-text sources from library resources (online and CD-ROM) | Last name of author, first initial. (Year, month, day.) Title. Journal [type of medium], volume (issue), paging if given or other indicator of length. Available: supplier/database name and number/identifier number, item or accession number [access date].<br><br>Crow, P. (1994). GATT shows progress in Congress. The Oil and Gas Journal [Online], 92(49), 32 (1p.). Available: Information Access/Expanded Academic Index ASAP/A15955498 [1996, 13 March]. | Last name of author, first initial. Journal [type of medium] volume(issue) (year): paging if given or other indicator of length. Available: supplier/database name and number/ identifier number, item or accession number [access date].*<br><br>Crow, P. 'GATT shows progress in The Oil and Gas Journal [Online] 92(49) (1994): 32–3. Online. Available: Information Access Company. Expanded Academic Index ASAP. 13 March 1996. |
| WWW sites: individual works with print equivalent | Last name of author/editor, first initial. (Year, month, day.) Title (Edition). [Type of medium]. Producer. Available: address or source/path/file [access date]. | Last name of author/editor, first name. Title of print version of work. Edition statement. Place of publication: publisher, date. Title of electronic work. Medium [Online]. Information supplier. Available protocol: http://www.address.goes. here. Access date [dy mo yr]. |
|  | Bartlett, J. (1995, March). Familiar quotations: Passages, phrases and proverbs traced to theirsources (9th edn.). [Online]. Columbia University. Available: http//www.columbia.edu/acis/bartleby/bartlett/ [1996, 19 March]. | Bartlett, J. Familiar Quotations: Passages, Phrases & Proverbs Traced to Their Sources in Ancient & Modern Literature. 9th edn. Boston: Little, Brown & Co., 1901. Familiar Quotations: Passages, Phrases & Proverbs Traced to Their Sources. Online. Columbia University. Available HTTP: http://www.columbia.edu/acis/bartleby/ bartlett. 19 March 1996. |
| WWW sites: parts of works | Last name of author/editor, first initial. (Year, month, day.) Title of article or document. In Title of Source (edition), [Online], volume (issue), paging or indicator of length. Available: address or source/path/file [access date]. | Last name of author, first name. 'Title of Article or Document. Newsletter, or Conference volume(issue number) (year) or date of publication: number of pages or pars. Medium [online]. Available protocol: http://www.address.goes. here. Access date [dy mo yr]. |

| | | |
|---|---|---|
| | Steinfield, C., Kraut, R. & Plummer, A. (1995). The impact of interorganizational networks on buyer–seller relationships. *Journal of Computer-mediated Communication* [Online], 1(3), 56 paragraphs. Available: http://shum.juji.ac.il/jcmc/vol1/issue3/steinfld.html [1996, April 22]. | Steinfield, C., Kraut, R. & Plummer, A. 'The Impact of Interorganizational Networks on Buyer-Seller Relationships. *Journal of Computer-mediated Communication* 1(3) (1995): 56 pars Online. Available HTTP: http://shum.juji.ac.il/jcmc/vol1/issue3/steinfld.html. 22 April 1996. |
| WWW sites: e-mail, listserv and discussion list messages | Last name of author, first initial (if known). 'Subject line from posting.' Message. Discussion list [online]. Available e-mail: LISTSERV@e-mail address [Access date]. | Last name of author, first name (if known). 'Discussion list message.' Date. Medium [online]. Discussion list. Available e-mail: LISTSERV @e-mail address. Access date. |
| | Wagner, K. (1996, 6 February). Re: Citing/evaluating web resources. NETLIBS [Online]. Available e-mail netlibs@qut.edu.au [1996, 7 February]. | Wagner, Kurt W. 'Re: Citing/evaluating web resources.' Available e-mail: netlibs@qut.edu.au 7 February 1996. |
| WWW sites: homepages | Last name of author/editor, first initial (if known). (Last update or copyright date). Home Page Title [Home page of ...]. Available: http//www. address. goes.here [Access date]. | |
| | House, P. (1997, 26 March – last update). The Smithsonian: America's treasure house for learning [Home Page of the Smithsonian Institution] [Online]. Available: http://www.si.edu/newstart.htm [1997 27 March]. | |

*Note:* *access date not needed if CD-ROM.
*Source:* adapted from *APA Guides for Citing Electronic Sources and Guidelines for Citing Electronic Sources.* MLA, Cedarville College Centennial Library, Cedarville, OH, 45314

*Exhibit 14.4* Citing electronic sources.

If the text is overcrowded with concepts, there is too much information per sentence. By contrast, sparse writing has too few significant ideas per sentence. Writers use a variety of methods to adjust the **pace** of their writing, as outlined below.

- Use ample white space and wide margins to create a positive psychological effect on the reader.
- Break large units of text into smaller units with headings and sub-headings to show organization of the topics.
- Relieve difficult text with visual aids when possible.
- Emphasize important material and de-emphasize secondary material through sentence construction and judicious use of italicizing, underlining, capitalization and parentheses.
- Choose words carefully, opting for the known and short rather than the unknown and long. Graduate students, in particular, seem to revel in using jargon, pompous constructions, and long or arcane words. Naturally, technical terms are appropriate, when they belong to the common jargon of the audience.
- Repeat and summarize critical and difficult ideas so readers have time to absorb them.
- Make strategic use of service words. These are words that 'do not represent objects or ideas, but show relationship. Transitional words, such as the conjunctions, are service words. So are phrases such as "on the other hand," "in summary," and "in contrast."'[4]

### Tone

Review the writing to ensure that the tone is appropriate. The reader can, and should, be referred to, but researchers should avoid referring to themselves. One author notes that the 'application of the "you" attitude … makes the message sound like it is written to the reader, not sent by the author. A message prepared for the reader conveys sincerity, personalization, warmth, and involvement on the part of the author.'[5] To accomplish this, remove negative phrasing and rewrite the thought positively. Do not change your recommendations or your findings to make them positive. Instead, review the phrasing. Which of the following sounds better?

1   End-users do not want the Information Systems Department telling them what software to buy.
2   End-users want more autonomy over their computer software choices.

The messages convey the same information, but the positive tone of the second message will not put readers from the Information Systems Department on the defensive.

### Final proof

It is helpful to put the draft away for a day before doing the final editing. Go to the beach, ride a bicycle in the park or go to the cinema – do anything that is unrelated to the research project. Then return to the report and read it with a critical eye. Does the writing flow smoothly? Are there transitions where they are needed? Is the organization apparent to the reader? Do the findings and conclusions adequately meet the problem statement and the research objectives? Are the tables and graphics displaying the proper information in an easy-to-read format? After assuring yourself that the draft is complete, write the executive summary.

## 14.4  Presentation considerations

The final consideration in the report-writing process is production. Reports can be printed on an ink-jet, laser, colour or other printer; or sent out for typesetting. Most student and small research reports are produced on a computer printer. The presentation of the report conveys to the readers the professional approach used throughout the project. Care should be taken to use compatible fonts throughout the entire report. The printer should produce consistent, easy-to-read letters on quality paper. When reports are photocopied for more than one reader, make sure that the copies are clean and have no black streaks or grey areas.

Overcrowding of text creates an appearance problem. Readers need the visual relief provided by ample white space. We define 'ample' as two and a half centimetres of white space at the top, bottom and right-hand margins. On the left side, the margin should be at least three centimetres to provide room for binding or punched holes. Even greater margins will often improve report appearance and help to highlight key points or sections. Overcrowding also occurs when the report contains page after page of large blocks of unbroken text. This produces an unpleasant psychological effect on readers because of its formidable appearance. Overcrowded text, however, may be avoided in the following ways.

- Use shorter paragraphs. As a rough guide, any paragraph longer than half a page is suspect. Remember that each paragraph should represent a distinct thought. But also be aware that a paragraph should be longer than one sentence.
- Indent parts of text that represent listings, long quotations or examples.
- Use headings and sub-headings to divide the report and its major sections into homogeneous topical parts.
- Use vertical listings of points (such as this list).

Inadequate labelling creates another physical problem. Each graph or table should contain enough information to be self-explanatory. Text headings and sub-headings also help with labelling. They function as signs for the audience, describing the organization of the report and indicating the progress of discussion. They also help readers to skim the material and to return easily to particular sections of the report.

## Presentation of statistics[6]

The presentation of statistics in research reports is a special challenge for writers. Four basic ways to present such data are in:

1  a text paragraph
2  semi-tabular form
3  tables
4  graphics.

### Text presentation

This is probably the most common method of presentation when there are only a few statistics. The writer can direct the reader's attention to certain numbers or comparisons and emphasize specific points. The drawback is that the statistics are submerged in the text, requiring the reader to scan the entire paragraph to extract the meaning. For example, the material in the paragraph below has a few simple comparisons but becomes more complicated when text and statistics are combined.

> A comparison of the three largest PC sellers in Europe shows that the position of the market leader, Compaq, was threatened in 1999. Its growth was just 4.0 per cent – although its market share remains 50 per cent larger than that of the second largest competitor, Fujitsu-Siemens, which sold 3.5 million units. This compares to sales growth for Fujitsu-Siemens of 19.5 per cent, and Dell with a sales increase of 16.3 per cent. In 1999 Fujitsu-Siemens reached a market share of 10.8 per cent, Compaq sold 5 million units for a market share of 15.6 per cent and Dell reached a market share of 9.2 per cent, selling 2.5 million units.

## Semi-tabular presentation

When there are just a few figures, they may be taken from the text and listed. Lists of quantitative comparisons are much easier to read and understand than embedded statistics. Exhibit 14.5 offers an example of semi-tabular presentation.

## Tabular presentation

Tables are generally superior to text for presenting statistics, although they should be accompanied by comments directing the reader's attention to important figures in the table. Tables facilitate quantitative comparisons and provide a concise, efficient way to present numerical data.

Tables are either general or summary in nature. General tables tend to be large, complex and detailed. They serve as the repository for the statistical findings of the study and are usually presented in the appendix of a research report. Summary tables contain only a few key pieces of data, closely related to a specific finding. To make them inviting to the reader (who might otherwise skip over them), the table designer should omit unimportant details and collapse multiple classifications into composite measures that may be substituted for the original data.

Any table should contain sufficient enough information to enable the reader to understand its contents. The title should explain the subject of the table, how the data are classified, the time period, or other related matters. A sub-title is sometimes included under the main title to

| | PC units sold 1999 (thousands) | Growth 1998–1999 (%) | Market share 1999 (%) |
|---|---|---|---|
| Compaq | 5000 | +4.0 | 15.6 |
| Fujitsu-Siemens | 3500 | +19.5 | 10.8 |
| Dell | 3500 | +16.3 | 9.2 |

Note: a comparison of the top three sellers in Europe in 1999 shows that Compaq still holds the largest market share, but that Fujitsu-Siemens and Dell are growing faster.

*Exhibit 14.5* Semi-tabular presentation.

explain something about the table; most often this is a statement of the measurement units in which the data are expressed. The contents of the columns should be clearly identified by the column heads, and what is written in the row labels should do the same for the rows. The body of the table contains the data, while the footnotes contain any necessary explanations. Footnotes should be identified by letters, or symbols such as asterisks (*), rather than by numbers, to avoid confusion with data values. Finally, there should be a source note if the data do not come from your original research. Exhibit 14.6 illustrates the various parts of a table.

| $CO_2$ – emission in Europe[a] | | | | |
|---|---|---|---|---|
| Country | Million tons 1990 | Million tons 1996[b] | Change in % | ← Title / Column heads |
| Germany[c] | 1014 | 910 | −10.3 | |
| UK[d] | 615 | 593 | −3.6 | |
| Italy | 442 | 448 | +1.4 | |
| France[e] | 392 | 399 | +1.8 | |
| Spain | 226 | 248 | +9.7 | |
| Netherlands | 161 | 185 | +14.9 | ← Body |
| Belgium | 116 | 129 | +11.2 | |
| Greece | 85 | 92 | +9.3 | |
| Finland[f] | 59 | 66 | +11.9 | |
| Sweden[f] | 55 | 63 | +14.5 | |
| EU total | 3372 | 3348 | −0.7 | |

Notes:
(a)  Including $CO_2$ emissions from uses other than fossil energy.
(b)  Latest available figures for all countries; due to the climate, the total $CO_2$ emission in the EU was larger in 1996 than in 1995, 1997 and 1998.
(c)  Decrease mainly in Eastern Germany.
(d)  Decrease due to switching from coal to gas for energy generation.
(e)  Relatively low due to the large share of nuclear energy.
(f)  Relatively low due to the large share of energy from water power.
Source: WUA, www.eea.eu.int

**Exhibit 14.6** Sample tabular findings.

## *Graphics*

Compared with tables, graphs show less information and often only approximate values. However, they are more often read and remembered than tables. Their great advantage is that they convey quantitative values and comparisons more readily than tables. With personal computer charting programs, you can easily turn a set of numbers into a chart or graph.

There are many different graphic forms. Exhibit 14.7 shows the most common ones and how they should be used. Statistical explanation charts such as boxplots, stem-and-leaf displays and histograms is discussed in Chapter 15. Line graphs, area, pie and bar charts, and pictographs and 3-D graphics receive additional attention here.

### Line graphs

**Line graphs** are used chiefly for time series and frequency distribution. There are several guidelines for designing a line graph.

- Put the time units or the independent variable on the horizontal axis.
- When showing more than one line, use different line types (solid, dashed, dotted, dash-dot) to enable the reader to distinguish between them easily.
- Try not to put more than four lines on one chart.
- Use a solid line for the primary data.

It is important to be aware of perceptual problems with line diagrams. The first is the use of a zero baseline. Since the length of the bar or distance above the baseline indicates the statistic, it is important that graphs give accurate visual impressions of values. A good way to achieve this is to include a zero baseline on the scale on which the curves are plotted. To set the base at some other value is to introduce a visual bias. This can be seen by comparing the visual impressions in Parts A and B of Exhibit 14.8. Both are accurate plots of the oil price in US$ per barrel between April 2003 and April 2004. In Part A, however, using the baseline of zero places the curve well up on the chart and gives a better perception of the relation between the absolute level of the oil price and the changes between two months. The graph in Part B, with a baseline at US$20, can easily give the impression that the increase was at a more rapid rate. When space or other reasons dictate using shortened scales, the zero base point should still be used but with a break in the scale as shown in Part C of Exhibit 14.8. This will warn the reader that the scale has been reduced.

The balance of size between vertical and horizontal scales also affects the reader's impression of the data. There is no single solution to this problem, but the results can be seen by comparing Parts B and C of Exhibit 14.8. In Part C, the horizontal scale is twice that in Part B. This changes the slope of the curve, creating a different perception of growth rate.

A third distortion with line diagrams occurs when relative and absolute changes among two or more sets of data are shown. In most charts, we use arithmetic scales where each space unit has identical value. This shows the absolute differences between variables, as in Part A of Exhibit 14.9, which presents the total wind energy production between 1986 and 1998 in the USA, Germany, Denmark and India. This is an arithmetically correct way to present these data; but if we are interested in rates of growth, the visual impressions from a semi-logarithmic scale are more accurate. A comparison of the line diagrams in Parts A and B of Exhibit 14.9 shows

**Column** Compares sizes and amounts of categories usually for the same time. Places categories on *X* axis and values on *Y* axis.

**Bar** Same as the column but positions categories on *Y* axis and values on *X* axis. Deviations, when used, distinguish positive from negative values.

**Stacked bar** In either bar or column shows how components contribute to the total of the category.

**Pie** Shows relationship of parts to the whole. Wedges are raw values of data.

**Stacked pie** Same as pie but diplays two or more data series.

**Multiple pie** Uses same data as stacked pie but plots separate pies for each column of data without stacking.

**Line** Compares values over time to show changes in trends.

**Filled line** Similar to line chart, but uses fill to highlight series.

**Area (surface)** Like line chart, compares changing values but emphasizes relative value of each series.

**Step** Compares discrete points on the value axis with vertical lines showing difference between points. Not for showing a trend.

**Scatter** Shows if relationship between variables follows a pattern. May be used with one variable at different times.

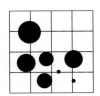

**Bubble** Used to introduce third variable (dots of different sizes). Axes could be sales, profits: bubbles are assets.

**Spider [and radar]** Radiating lines are categories; values are distances from centre (shows multiple variables, e.g. performance, ratings, progress).

**Polar** Shows relationship between a variable and angle measured in degrees (cyclical trends, pollution source vs. wind direction, etc.).

**Open hi lo close** Shows fluctuating values in a given period (hour, day) often used for investments.

**Boxplots** Displays distribution(s) and compares characteristics of shape.

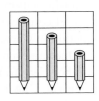

**Pictographic** Special chart that uses pictures or graphic elements in lieu of bars.

*Exhibit 14.7* Guide to graphs.

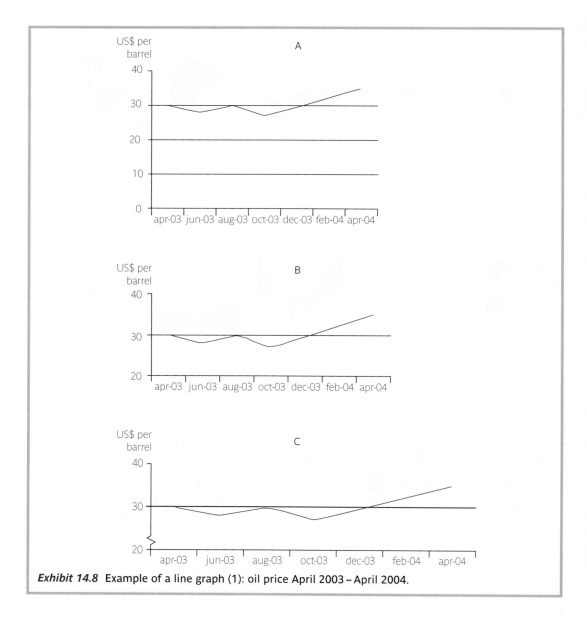

*Exhibit 14.8* Example of a line graph (1): oil price April 2003 – April 2004.

how much difference a semi-logarithmic scale makes. Each is valuable and each can be misleading. In Part A, notice that all countries have growing wind energy production and that in the 1980s wind energy production in Germany, Denmark and India was only a small portion of US wind energy production. One can even estimate what this proportion is. Part B gives an insight into growth rates that are not clear from the arithmetic scale. Part B shows that the growth in wind energy production in the USA is very moderate, Danish production increased substantially in the late 1980s, while German and Indian wind energy production grew mainly in the 1990s.

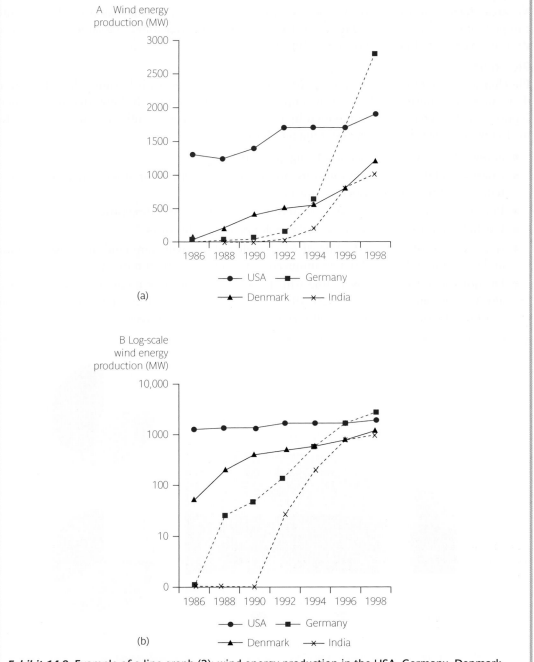

*Exhibit 14.9* Example of a line graph (2): wind energy production in the USA, Germany, Denmark and India, 1986–98 (MW).

## Area (stratum or surface) charts

An **area chart** is also used for a time series. Consisting of a line that has been divided into component parts, it is best used to show changes in patterns over time. The same rules apply to stratum charts as to line charts (see Exhibit 14.7).

## Pie charts

**Pie charts** are another form of area chart. They are often used with business data. However, they can easily mislead the reader or be improperly prepared. Research shows that readers' perceptions of the percentages represented by the pie slices are consistently inaccurate.[7] Consider the following suggestions when designing pie charts.

- Show 100 per cent of the subject being graphed.
- Always label the slices with 'call-outs' and with the percentage or amount that is represented. This allows you to dispense with a legend.
- Put the largest slice at 12 o'clock and move clockwise in descending order.
- Use light colours for large slices, darker colours for smaller slices.
- In a pie chart of black and white slices, a single red one will command the most attention and be memorable. Use it to communicate your most important message.[8]
- Do not show evolution over time with pie charts as the only medium. Since pie charts always represent 100 per cent, growth of the overall whole will not be recognized. If you must use a series of pie charts, complement them with an area chart.

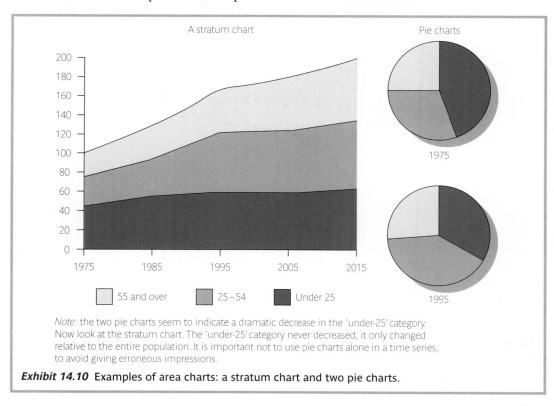

*Note:* the two pie charts seem to indicate a dramatic decrease in the 'under-25' category. Now look at the stratum chart. The 'under-25' category never decreased; it only changed relative to the entire population. It is important not to use pie charts alone in a time series, to avoid giving erroneous impressions.

**Exhibit 14.10** Examples of area charts: a stratum chart and two pie charts.

As shown in Exhibit 14.10, pie charts portray frequency data in interesting ways. In addition, they can be stacked to show relationships between two sets of data.

## Bar charts

**Bar charts** can be very effective if constructed properly. Use the horizontal axis to represent time, and the vertical axis to represent units or growth-related variables. Vertical bars are generally used for time series and for quantitative classifications. Horizontal bars are rarely used for time series, but mainly for nominal categories (e.g. European Union (EU) member countries). If neither variable is time related, either format can be used. A computer-charting program will generate charts quickly and easily. If you are preparing a bar chart by hand, leave space between the bars equal to at least half the width of a bar. An exception to this is the specialized chart – the histogram – where continuous data are grouped into intervals for a frequency distribution (see Chapter 15). A second exception is the multiple-variable chart, where more than one bar is located at a particular time segment. In this case, the space between the groups of bars is at least half the width of the group. Bar charts come in a variety of patterns. In Chapter 15, Exhibit 15.5 shows a standard vertical bar graph. Variations are illustrated in Exhibit 14.7.

## Pictographs and geographics

**Pictographs (geographics)** are used in popular magazines and newspapers because they are eye-catching and imaginative. Broad audience magazines and newspapers, such as *Business Week* and the *Daily Mirror*, are often guilty of taking this to the extreme, creating graphs that are incomprehensible. A pictograph uses pictorial symbols (an oil drum for barrels of oil, a wrench figure for numbers of workers, or a pine tree for amount of wood). The symbols represent data volume and are used instead of a bar in a bar-type chart. It is proper to stack same-size images to express more of a quantity and to show fractions of an image to show less. But altering the scale of the symbol produces problems. Since the pictures represent actual objects, doubling the size will increase the area of the symbol by four (and the volume by more). This misleads the reader into believing that the increase is larger than it really is. The exception is a graphic that is easily substituted for a bar, such as the pencils in Exhibit 14.7.

Geographic charts use (a portion of) the world's map, in pictorial form, to show differences in regions. They can be used for product production, per capita rates, demographics or any of a number of other geographically specific variables. The geographic chart in Exhibit 14.11 shows a map of Europe and the Russian Federation. Countries are shaded in different blue tones, representing the number of physicians per 100,000 inhabitants. The lighter the country appears, the fewer physicians it has per capita.

Stacked data sets produce variables of interest that can be aligned on a common geographical referent. The resulting pictorial display allows the user to drill through the layers and visualize the relationships. With better Windows-based software, and government agencies providing geocodes and reference points, geographic spatial displays like the image in Exhibit 14.11 are becoming a more common form of graphic.

## 3-D graphics

With current charting techniques, virtually all charts can now be made three-dimensional. Although **3-D graphics** add interest, they can also obscure data. Care must be used in selecting 3-D chart candidates (see Exhibit 14.12). Pie and bar charts achieve dimensionality simply by

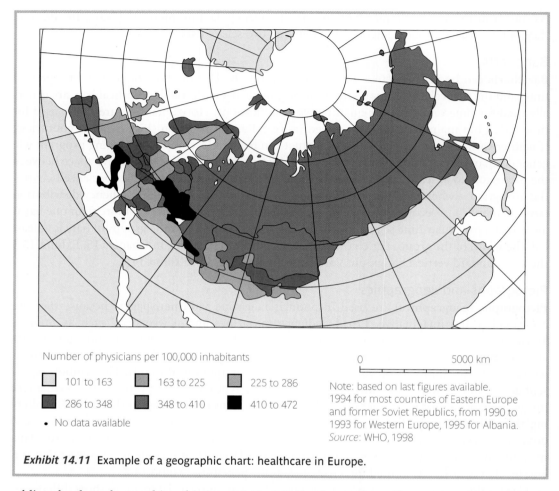

Number of physicians per 100,000 inhabitants

- ☐ 101 to 163
- ☐ 163 to 225
- ☐ 225 to 286
- ☐ 286 to 348
- ☐ 348 to 410
- ■ 410 to 472
- • No data available

0 ———————— 5000 km

Note: based on last figures available. 1994 for most countries of Eastern Europe and former Soviet Republics, from 1990 to 1993 for Western Europe, 1995 for Albania. *Source*: WHO, 1998

**Exhibit 14.11** Example of a geographic chart: healthcare in Europe.

adding depth to the graphics; this is not 3-D. A 3-D column chart allows you to compare three or more variables from the sample in one bar chart-type graph. If you want to display several quarters of sales results for the Hertz, Avis, Budget and National car-rental chains, you have 3-D data. But be careful about converting line charts to ribbon charts, and area charts to 3-D area charts.

Surface charts and 3-D scatter charts are helpful for displaying complex data patterns if the underlying distributions are multivariate. Otherwise, do not enter the third dimension unless your data are there.

# 14.5  Oral presentations

Researchers often present their findings orally. These presentations have some unique characteristics that distinguish them from most other kinds of public speaking: only a small group of people is involved; statistics normally constitute an important portion of the topic; the audience members are, in a business context, managers or, in an academic context, fellow

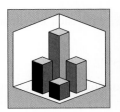

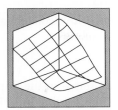
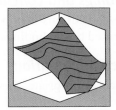

**3-D Column**
A variation on column charts, they compare variables to each other or over time. Axes: $X$ = categories $Y$ = series, $Z$ = values. Other variations include 3-D area charts and connect-the-dots scatter charts.

**3-D Ribbon** This example is a one-wall plot showing columns of data (series) as ribbons. One or more columns are used. Axes: $X$ = categories, $Y$ = series, $Z$ = values.

**3-D Wireframe**
A variation of a contour or response surface; suitable for changes in time and multivariate data. Axes: $X$ = categories, $Y$ = series, $Z$ = values.

**3-D Surface line**
Handles three columns of data and plots XYZ coordinates to show a response surface. Helpful for multivariate applications.

*Exhibit 14.12*  Examples of 3D charts.

researchers. Both usually have an interest in the topic, but they want to hear only the critical elements; speaking time will often be as short as 20 minutes but may run longer than an hour; and the presentation is normally followed by questions and discussion.

## Preparation

A successful presentation typically calls for a lengthy and complex body of information to be condensed. Since speaking rates should not exceed 100–150 words per minute, a 20-minute presentation limits you to about 2000 to 3000 words. If you are to communicate effectively under such conditions, you must plan carefully. Begin by asking two questions. First, how long should you plan to talk? Usually there is an indication of the acceptable presentation length. If the time is severely limited, then the need for topical priorities is obvious. This leads to the second question: What is the purpose of the presentation? Is it to raise concern about problems that have been uncovered? Is it to add to the knowledge of audience members? Is it to give them conclusions and recommendations for their decision-making? Questions such as these illustrate the general objectives of the report. Having answered these questions, you should develop a detailed outline of what you are going to say. Such an outline should contain the following major parts.

### Opening

A brief statement, probably not more than 10 per cent of the allotted time, sets the stage for the body of the report. The opening should be direct, grab attention and introduce the nature of the discussion that follows. It should explain the nature of the project, how it came about and what it attempted to do.

### Findings and conclusions

The conclusions may be stated immediately after the opening remarks, with each conclusion followed by the findings that support it.

### Recommendations

Where appropriate, these are stated in the third stage; each recommendation may be followed by references to the conclusions leading to it. Presented in this manner, they provide a natural climax to the report. At the end of the presentation, it may be appropriate to call for questions from the audience.

## Two further important planning decisions

Early in the planning stage you need to make two further decisions. The first concerns the type of audio-visuals (AVs) that will be used and the role they will play in the presentation. AV decisions are so important that they are often made before the briefing outline and text are developed.

Presenting your research findings using PowerPoint or other presentation software requires preparation similar to presenting with non-electronic **visual aids**. The researcher must still determine his or her style of presentation, the order of findings, and which findings will be presented graphically, in tabular format or verbally. As most visual aids are prepared using computer software, the key hyperlink files are already available. It might seem as though the presenter could bypass the costly printing of visual aids, which can be a time-consuming task. However, the electronic presenter must have a contingency plan for a malfunctioning computer. Colour transparencies are the low-tech back-up, but clearly don't allow the full range of possibilities that electronic hyperlinks afford. Having a second laptop and projection system, as well as multi-prong power cords and spare computer connection cords make up the usual high-tech insurance plan. The same general rule applied to all presentations is critical for electronic ones – practise, practise, practise – but a caveat is added: practise with your equipment so that movement between files and between hyperlinks and your PowerPoint control presentation seems effortless.

The second decision you must make as you plan for your presentation is what type it will be. Will it be memorized, read from your manuscript or given extemporaneously? Your reputation and the research effort should not be jeopardized by 'winging it'.

Memorization is a risky and time-consuming course to follow. Any memory slip during the presentation can be a catastrophe, and the delivery will sound stilted and distant. Memorization virtually precludes establishing rapport with the audience and adapting to their reactions while you speak. It produces a self- or speaker-centred approach and is not recommended.

Reading a manuscript is not advisable either, even though many professors seem to reward students who do so (perhaps because they themselves get away with it at professional meetings). The delivery sounds dull and lifeless because most people are not trained to read aloud and therefore do it badly. They become focused on the manuscript to the exclusion of the audience. This head-down preoccupation with the text is clearly inappropriate for management presentations.

The **extemporaneous presentation** is audience-centred and made from minimal notes or an outline. This mode permits the speaker to be natural, conversational and flexible. Clearly, it is the best choice for an organizational setting. Preparation consists of writing a draft along with a complete sentence outline and converting the main points to notes. In this way, you can try lines of argument, experiment with various ways of expressing thoughts, and develop phraseology. Along the way, the main points are fixed sequentially in your mind, and supporting connections are made.

Audiences accept notes, and their presence does wonders in allaying speaker fears. Even if you never use them, they are there for psychological support. Many speakers prefer to use A6 cards for their briefing notes because they hold more information and so require less shuffling than the smaller A7 size. Card contents vary widely, but here are some general guidelines for their design.

- Place title and preliminary remarks on the first card.
- Use each of the remaining cards to carry a major section of the presentation. The amount of detail depends on the need for precision and the speaker's desire for supporting information.
- Include key phrases, illustrations, statistics, dates and pronunciation guides for difficult words. Also include quotations and ideas that bear repeating.
- Along the margin, place instructions and cues, such as 'SLOW', 'FAST', 'EMPHASIZE', 'TRANSPARENCY A', 'TURN CHART' and 'GO BACK TO CHART 3'.

After the outline and the AV aids comes the final stage of preparation: the rehearsal. Rehearsal, a prerequisite to effective briefing, is too often overlooked, especially by inexperienced speakers. Giving a presentation is an artistic performance, and nothing improves it more than for the speaker to demonstrate mastery of the art. First rehearsal efforts should concentrate on those parts of the presentation that are awkward or poorly developed. After the problem areas have been worked out, there should be at least a few full-scale practice sessions under simulated presentation conditions. All parts should be timed and edited until the target time is met. A videotape recorder is an excellent diagnostic tool.

## Delivery

While the content of a report is the chief concern, the speaker's delivery is also important. A polished presentation adds to the receptiveness of the audience, but there is some danger that the presentation may overpower the message. Fortunately, the typical research audience knows why it is assembled, has a high level of interest and does not need to be entertained. Even so, the speaker faces a real challenge in communicating effectively. The delivery should be restrained. Demeanour, posture, dress and overall appearance should be appropriate to the occasion. Speed of speech, clarity of enunciation, pauses and gestures all play their part. Voice pitch, tone quality and inflections are proper subjects for concern. There is little time for anecdotes and other rapport-developing techniques, yet the speaker must grab and hold audience attention.

## Speaker problems

Inexperienced speakers have many difficulties in making presentations. They are often nervous at the start of a presentation and may even find breathing difficult. This is natural and should not be of undue concern. It may help to take a deep breath or two, holding each for a brief period before exhaling as fully as possible. This can be done inconspicuously on the way to the podium.

Several characteristics of inexperienced speakers may be summarized as questions. Even if you are an accomplished speaker, it is still helpful to review them as you watch a videotape of your presentation.

### Vocal characteristics

**a** Do you speak so softly that someone cannot hear you well? It is helpful to have someone at the back of the room who can signal if your voice is not carrying far enough. Another trick for people who tend to speak softly is to do some sound exercises before the presentation, like those that theatre actors do – for example, make a 'mmm' (humming) sound as hard as you can (i.e. so hard that your lips tremble).

**b** Do you speak too rapidly? Remind yourself to slow down. Make deliberate pauses before sentences. Speak words with precision without exaggerating. At the opposite end of the spectrum, some people talk too slowly, and this can make the audience restive.

**c** Do you vary volume, tone quality and rate of speaking? Any of these can be used successfully to add interest to the message and engage audience attention. Speakers should not let their words tail off as they complete a sentence.

**d** Do you use overworked pet phrases, repeated 'uhs', 'you know' and 'in other words'? It is hard to get rid of such phrases, because you use them unconsciously. Being aware of using pet phrases is an important first step in controlling them.

### Physical characteristics

**a** Do you rock back and forth, or roll or twist from side to side or lean too much on the lectern?

**b** Do you hitch or tug on your clothing, scratch, or fiddle with your loose change, keys, pencils or other devices?

**c** Do you stare into space? Lack of eye contact is particularly bothersome to listeners and is a common failing of inexperienced speakers. Many seem to choose a spot above the heads of the audience and continue to stare at this except when looking at their notes. Eye contact is important. Audience members need to feel that you are looking at them. It may be helpful to pick out three people in the audience (left, right and centre) and practise looking at them successively as you talk.

**d** Do you misuse visuals by fumbling, putting them on in the incorrect order or upside-down?

**e** Do you turn your back to the audience to read from visuals? Be aware that an overhead projector offers the opportunity to read directly from the transparency and you can be sure that there is no difference between the transparency and what is projected on the screen. If you use computer equipment to show a presentation on a screen, make sure that you have a good view of the computer screen from the point where you speak.

## Audio-visuals

Researchers can use a variety of AV media with good results. While there is a need for computer-assisted media in many business applications, they will be mentioned only briefly. Our emphasis is on visual aids that are relatively simple and inexpensive to make.

### Chalkboards and whiteboards

Chalkboards are flexible, inexpensive, and require little specific preparation. On the other hand, they are not novel and do not project a polished appearance. If you use a chalkboard, make sure that it is wiped clean before your presentation and does not appear dusty. Whiteboards, both portable and fixed, provide visual relief, particularly when coloured markers are used. Both

## Overcoming the jitters

The fear of public speaking ranks up there with the fear of death and/or public nudity. Whether you are a seasoned pro or this is your first speech, stage fright – the illogical fear of facing an audience – can be a paralysing emotion. How do you handle those times when your mind starts going blank and your stomach is turning? Patricia Fripp, an award-winning keynote speaker and speech coach, provides some answers. She suggests that you 'need to anticipate your speech mentally, physically and logistically'. Mental preparation is key and should be on a six-to-one ratio: invest three hours of preparation for a 30-minute speech. There is no substitute for rehearsal. Spend some time memorizing your opening and closing remarks – three or four sentences each. Although you may speak from notes, knowing your opening and closing remarks helps your fluency, allowing you to make the vital connection in rapport with your audience when you are likely to be most nervous.

Logistically, know the room. Go there as early as possible to get comfortable in the environment. Practise using the microphone and check the equipment. A quick review of your visual aids is also helpful. Then, during the presentation, you can focus on your audience and not be concerned with the environment.

The physical part of overcoming nervousness is varied and may be constrained by your setting. In a small-group setting, shake hands, exchange greetings and make eye contact with everybody beforehand. In a larger meeting, at least connect with the people in the front row. Do so sincerely and they'll be cheering for your success. They are not waiting for you to fail – they are far too worried about themselves – and they are there to listen to you. If possible, avoid sitting while you're waiting to speak. Find a position in the room where you can stand occasionally. The rear of the room gives you access to the bathroom and drinking fountain.

If your anxiety level is still high, then you need an outlet for your energy. Comedians and actors find that doing light exercises in their dressing rooms or in another private area can release excess energy. Fripp adds, 'Find a private spot, and wave your hands in the air. Relax your jaw, and shake your head from side to side. Then shake your legs one at a time. Physically shake the tension out of your body.' The object is to release enough nervous energy to calm your anxieties – without becoming so stress-free that you forget your purpose and audience.

## References and further reading

Patricia Fripp CSP CPAE, award-winning keynote speaker and speech coach, author of *Get What You Want!* and past president of the National Speakers Association. E-mail: PFripp@fripp.com, Tel: +1–800–634–3035, Website: http://www.fripp.com. www.fripp.com

varieties reduce speaking time while the speaker is writing. If you use either, write legibly or print, leave space between lines and do not talk to the board with your back to the audience. If you are in an unfamiliar room, it is best to arrive prepared with erasable markers (or chalk) and erasure materials. You should, however, note that chalkboards and whiteboards can be extremely helpful in a post-presentation discussion, when you are responding to questions.

## Handout materials

These are inexpensive but can have a professional appearance if prepared carefully. Handouts can include pictures and graphic materials that might otherwise be difficult to display. The disadvantages include the time needed to produce them and their distracting impact if not used properly. You may distribute them when the audience leaves, but a better use is to refer to them during your presentation. If you use them this way, do not hand them out until you are ready to refer to them.

## Flipcharts

You can show colour, pictures and large letters with these. They are easy and inexpensive to make; they can focus listener attention on a specific idea. If not well made, however, they can be distracting. Unless they are large, they should be restricted to small groups and to types of material that can be summarized in a few words.

## Overhead transparencies

These may be of different sizes, but the most common is about the same as an A4 page. They are easily made with colour markers or with a copy machine. Computer graphics can be plotted or printed directly on to transparencies for a more accurate and professional appearance. Multiple-colour and single-colour renditions are available. You can also show overlays and build-ups. In using transparencies, be sure that they are in the correct order and right side up when you place them on the projector.

## Slides

Most slides are 35 mm, but larger sizes are sometimes used. They are relatively inexpensive and colourful, and present a professional-looking image if done well, but they are, more and more, an expiring technology.

## Computer-drawn visuals

For transparencies and slides, the draw-and-paint programs available for personal computers provide the presenter with limitless options for illustrating his or her message. Stored visuals can be teamed with a device for projecting the computer output to a screen, or the briefer can use the software to create the image at the moment a question is asked or a demonstration is appropriate. Be careful that the technology does not distract from the purpose of the message.

## LCD projectors

In recent years, LCD projectors have become more and more popular and are widely available. The LCD projector is linked to a computer and projects what you see on the computer monitor on a large screen. The big advantage of LCD projectors is their ability to use multimedia. You can easily integrate photographs, audio and video clips, you can access any website on the Internet 'live', you can project classical PowerPoint® slides, but you could also show how you run any other software package. There are two cautions in using LCD projectors. First, if you connect your own laptop to a LCD projector, the general settings of the two may not be entirely compatible and you might see only a part of what you see on your computer on the screen. Of course fixing the problem is often possible, but the occurrence of a such a problem just minutes before the start of your presentation make even experienced computer users nervous. Instead of getting focused on your presentation, you focus on fixing the computer problem. Presentations with LCD projectors often use colours, but especially older LCD projectors sometimes distort colours, for example what appears orange on your laptop monitor appears yellow on the screen. This becomes a problem if you refer to an orange box, but the audience does not see it because it appears yellow.

The choice of visual aids is determined by your intended purpose, the size of the audience, meeting room conditions, time and budget constraints, and available equipment.

## Choosing visual aids

Visual aids serve the presenter of a research presentation in several ways. They make it possible to present materials that cannot otherwise be communicated effectively. Statistical relationships are difficult to describe verbally, but a picture or graph communicates well. How better to describe some object or material than to show or picture it?

Visual aids help the speaker to clarify major points. With visual reinforcement of a verbal statement, the speaker can stress the importance of points. In addition, the use of two channels of communication (hearing and sight) enhances the probability that the listener will understand and remember the message.

The continuity and memorability of the speaker's message are also improved with visual aids. Verbal information is so transient that any slight lapse of listener attention results in losing the information thread. The failure to fully comprehend a given point cannot be remedied by going back to hear it again, for the speaker has gone on. With a visual aid, however, there is more opportunity to review this point, relate it to earlier comments by the speaker and improve retention.

### Research Methods in Practice 14

How often have I sat at my desk and stared at the monitor's white screen not knowing how to start writing. I have accused the laptop of blocking the connection between my thoughts and the computer. I turned to the old way of writing and grabbed a pen and a notepad, but the notepad remained white as well. When I was again struggling to write the first word of a chapter, my office mate commented "*If you cannot write it down, you have not thought it through sufficiently. The writing is a further proof for the consistency and logic in your arguments.*"

There is a lot of truth in what my office mate said. It is easy to think through an argument, a little bit more difficult to talk about it and most difficult to write it down. Thus, if you cannot write down what you thought about, you might want to talk about it. Have you noticed during your studies that most scientific articles are co-authored and even single-authored articles express gratitude to other scholars in the acknowledgement section? One reason for co-authorships is that such alliances are often based on complementary assets; one is good in analysis and the other in the theory. But another important reason for co-authoring is that writing becomes easier if you have a well-informed sparring partner for your arguments. Discussions sharpen your arguments and reveal their strong and weak points.

Discussions form an important part in researchers' daily life. Some of the discussions are institutionalized by regular conferences and seminars in which scholars present their current work. But many discussions are not organized but simply occur during lunch, at the coffee machine or in the local pub. Discussions on my Ph.D. project were most fruitful if they were open, critical and at best constructive. Essential to every academic paper is that you make a point, that is you present a convincing idea by thorough reasoning complemented with evidence that support your idea. In the different studies presented here, the evidence took various forms. In the project on the trust experiments the reasoning was complemented with formal modelling from which hypotheses could be derived. The qualitative study on 'how cattle farmers settled conflicts?' relied on observations in Shasta county that fitted with the theoretical considerations put forward. The results of quantitative analysis formed the evidence in the study on R&D cooperations. All studies complemented the reasoning with evidence; whether the evidence provided was satisfactory is an open question worth discussing.

In the project on R&D cooperations we investigated how different characteristics of the transaction and the relation affects different components of cooperation management, namely the effort spend on negotiations, the contract and partner searching. Thus, we had a set of independent variables (transaction and relation characteristics) influencing a set of dependent variables (components of management), which could be described in a $2 \times 3$ matrix as shown in Exhibit 14.13.

A more dimensional structure asks for a decision regarding the structure of a thesis or a presentation. There are two options:

1　Structure it along the dependent variables. First discuss searching, then negotiations and then contracts.
2　Structure it along independent variables, that is by the theories employed. First you look at the effects of transaction characteristics and then at the relation characteristics, that is you look at transaction cost theory and then at theoretical considerations related to the social embeddedness.

In the Ph.D. thesis I started with introducing transaction cost theory and then argued that arguments on the social embeddedness add to transaction cost theory. Thus, in the introduction and the first part of the theory chapter I chose option 2. In the section that derived the hypotheses, however, I switched, and derived first the hypotheses explaining searching and then those explaining negotiations and contracts. Thus, I turned to option 1 and kept this structure for the analysis chapter as well. This structure emphasized that the main contribution of the thesis was that network theory (arguments on social embeddedness) adds to transaction cost theory. Then I switched the structure to show that network theory is a useful addition to transaction cost theory for different components of management (governance in terms of transaction cost theory). If I had wanted to emphasize that investigating the management of cooperations needs to go beyond understanding how firms contract and needs to include management activities before the actual contracting, such as partner search, it might have been advisable to use the option 1 for all chapters of the thesis.

|  | Searching | Negotiation | Contract |
|---|---|---|---|
| Transaction characteristic |  |  |  |
| Relation characteristics |  |  |  |

Exhibit 14.13　Structure of the research problem.

# Summary

1 A good-quality presentation of research findings can have an inordinate effect on a reader's or listener's perceptions of a study's quality. Recognition of this fact should prompt a researcher to make a special effort to communicate skilfully and clearly.

2 Research reports contain findings, analysis, interpretations, conclusions and sometimes recommendations. They may follow the short, informal format typical of memoranda and letters, or they may be longer and more complex. Long reports are of either an academic, technical or management type. In the former two, the problem is presented and followed by the findings, conclusions and recommendations. In the management report, the conclusions and recommendations precede the findings. The academic report addresses fellow researchers; the technical report is targeted at the technically trained reader; the management report is intended for the manager–client.

3 The writer of research reports should be guided by four questions.
   a What is the purpose of this report?
   b Who will read it?
   c What are the circumstances and limitations under which it is written?
   d How will the report be used?
   Reports should be clearly organized, physically inviting and easy to read. Writers can achieve these goals if they are careful with mechanical details, writing style and comprehensibility.

4 There is a special challenge in presenting statistical data. While some of this data may be incorporated in the text, most statistics should be placed in tables, charts or graphs. The choice of a table, chart or graph depends on the specific data and presentation purpose.

5 Oral presentations of research findings are common and should be developed with concern for the communication problems that are unique to such settings. Presentations are usually conducted under time constraints; good briefings require careful organization and preparation. Visual aids are a particularly important aspect of briefings but are too often ignored or treated inadequately.

   Whether written or oral, poor presentations do a grave injustice to what might otherwise be excellent research. Good presentations, on the other hand, add lustre to both the research and the reputation of the researcher.

## Discussion questions

### Terms in review

1 Distinguish between the following:
  a speaker-centred presentation and extemporaneous presentation
  b academic report, technical report and management report
  c topic outline and sentence outline.

### Making research decisions

2 What should you do about each of the following?
  a Putting information in a research report concerning the study's limitations
  b The size and complexity of tables in a research report
  c The physical presentation of a report
  d Pace in your writing.

3 What type of report would you suggest be written in each of the following cases?
  a The president of the company has asked for a study of the company's pension plan and its comparison to the plans of other firms in the industry.
  b You have been asked to write up a survey on the relationship between pay and satisfaction among paid employees of voluntary organizations, which you recently completed, for submission to the organization Studies Research.
  c Your division manager has asked you to prepare a forecast of cash requirements for the division for the next three months.
  d The European Commission has given you a grant to study the relationship between industrial accidents and departmental employee morale.

4 There are a number of graphic presentation forms. Which would you recommend to show each of the following? Why?
  a A comparison of changes in average annual per capita income for the UK, Germany and France from 1990 to 2000.
  b The percentage composition of average family expenditure patterns, by the major types of expenditures, for families whose heads of household are under age 35, compared with families whose heads of household are 55-plus.
  c A comparison of the change between 31 December 2001 and 31 December 2000 in the value of the common stock of the six largest European banks. How would you design a graphic representing not 6 firms, but all 50 firms of the EUROSTOXX index?

### From concept to practice

5 Outline a set of visual aids that you might use in an oral briefing on these topics.
  a How to write a research report.
  b The outlook for the economy over the next year.
  c The major analytical article in the latest issue of *Business Week*.

6 Conduct a search of websites that provide Internet presentations. Select one and critique its content, visuals and the presenter's skills.

7 Research reports often contain statistical materials of great importance that are presented poorly. Find examples of research reports, annual reports or government reports that illustrate this point and devise ways to improve their presentation.

## Classroom discussion

8 Discuss whether the proverb 'There is no accounting for taste' also holds for presentations. Would you enjoy multimedia elements, such as photographs, short video segments, music, or moving and blinking objects, in a research report presentation?

9 Discuss whether there is a trade-off between a research report that is understandable to a broad audience and the accuracy of the findings presented.

### Online
### *Learning* Centre

### Get started with understanding statistical techniques!

When you have read this chapter, log on to the Online Learning Centre website at *www.mcgraw-hill.co.uk/textbooks/blumberg* to explore chapter-by-chapter test questions, additional case studies, a glossary and more online study tools for Business Research Methods.

## Notes

[1] Paul E. Resta, *The Research Report*. New York: American Book Company, 1972, p. 5.

[2] John M. Penrose Jr., Robert W. Rasberry and Robert J. Myers, *Advanced Business Communication*. Boston: PWS–Kent Publishing, 1989, p. 185.

[3] Robert R. Rathbone, *Communicating Technical Information*. Reading, MA: Addison-Wesley, 1966, p. 64 (reprinted with permission).

[4] Ibid., p. 72.

[5] Penrose, Rasberry and Myers, *Advanced Business Communication*, p. 89.

[6] The material in this section draws on Stephen M. Kosslyn, *Elements of Graph Design*. San Francisco: W.H. Freeman, 1993; DeltaPoint, Inc., *DeltaGraph User's Guide* 4.0. Monterey, CA: DeltaPoint, Inc., 1996; Gene Zelazny, *Say it with Charts*. Homewood, IL: Business One Irwin, 1991; Jim Heid, 'Graphs that work', *MacWorld* (February 1994), pp. 155–6; and Penrose, Rasberry and Myers, *Advanced Business Communication*, Chapter 3.

[7] Marilyn Stoll, 'Charts other than pie are appealing to the eye', *PC Week*, 25 March 1986, pp. 138–9.

[8] Stephen M. Kosslyn and Christopher Chabris, 'The mind is not a camera, the brain is not a VCR', *Aldus Magazine* (September/October) 1993, p. 34.

## Recommended further reading

Booth, Wayne C., Colomb, Gregory G. and Williams, Joseph M., *The Craft of Research* (2nd edn.). Chicago: University of Chicago Press, 2003. A thorough guide on how to do research.

Campbell, Steve, *Statistics You Can't Trust*. Parker, CO: Think Twice Publishing, 2000. An enjoyable and entertaining approach to interpreting statistical charts and arguments.

Kosslyn, Stephen M., *Elements of Graph Design*. San Francisco: W.H. Freeman, 1993. Fundamentals of graph and chart construction.

Lesikar, Raymond V. and Flatley, Marie E., *Basic Business Communication* (10th edn.). New York: McGraw-Hill, 2004. Practical guidance for writing and presenting reports.

Strunk, William Jr., and White, E.B., *The Elements of Style*. New York: Macmillan, 1959. A classic on the problems of writing style.

Tufte, Edward R., *The Visual Display of Quantitative Information*. New Haven, CT: Graphics Press, 1992. The book that started the revolution against gaudy infographics.

Tufte, Edward R., *Visual Explanations: Images and Quantities, Evidence and Narrative*. New Haven, CT: Graphics Press, 1997. Uses the principle of 'the smallest effective difference' to display distinctions in data. Beautifully illustrated.

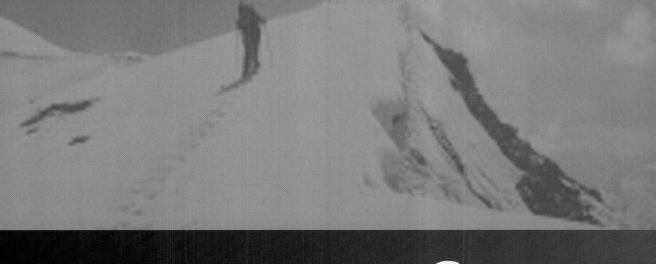

# Cases

## Part contents

# Case 1

# A GEM of a study

What government policies and initiatives are most likely to generate high levels of entrepreneurial activity? Which are positively correlated with the economic well-being of a country as measured by growth in gross domestic product (GDP) and job formation? Project directors of the Global Entrepreneurship Monitor (GEM), who define entrepreneurship as 'any attempt at new business or new venture creation, such as self-employment, a new business organization, or the expansion of an existing business, by an individual, a team of individuals, or an established business', suggest the following:

- promoting entrepreneurship, especially outside the most active age group (25–44), with specific programmes that support entrepreneurial activity
- facilitating the availability of resources to women so that they can participate in the entrepreneurial process
- committing to long-term, substantial post-secondary education, including training programmes designed to develop the skills required to start a business
- an emphasis on developing an individual's capacity to recognize and pursue new opportunities
- developing the capacity of a society to accommodate the higher levels of income disparity associated with entrepreneurial activity
- creating a culture that validates and promotes entrepreneurship throughout society.

Researchers at the Kauffman Center for Entrepreneurial Leadership (Babson College) and the London Business School revealed these propositions, based on a study designed to prove a causal relationship between factors that affect entrepreneurial opportunities and potential, to business dynamics and national economic growth and well-being. The research design compensated for a lack of control of extraneous variables by using data from 10 nations 'with diversity in framework conditions, entrepreneurial sectors, business dynamics and economic growth'. The longitudinal study proposed to prove or disprove a new conceptual model of cultural, economic, physical and political factors to predict economic growth (see Exhibit C1.1). Various data-collection methods were employed, including:

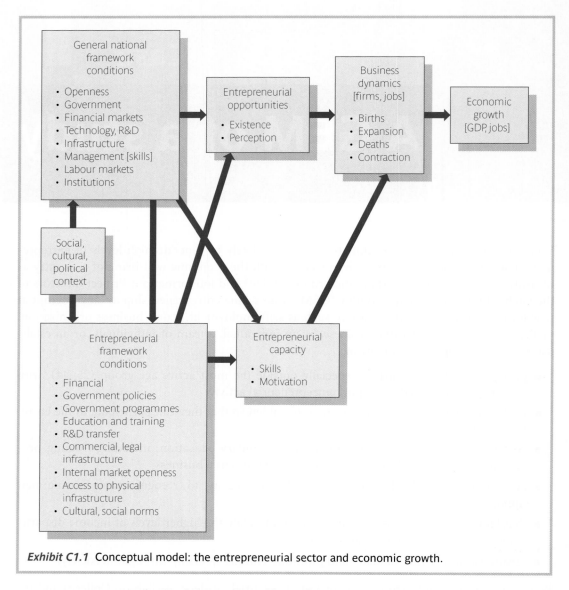

*Exhibit C1.1* Conceptual model: the entrepreneurial sector and economic growth.

- current, non-standardized data collected by each national research team
- two rounds of adult population surveys (1000 randomly selected adults per country) to measure entrepreneurial activity and attitude, completed and coordinated by an international market survey firm by phone – or face to face in Japan; Market Facts (Arlington, VA) did the first round of data-collection in June 1998 (Canada, Finland, Germany, the UK and the USA); Audience Selection, Ltd (London) conducted the second round in March 1999 from all 10 countries
- hour-long personal interviews with 4–39 experts (key informants) in each country
- detailed 12-page questionnaire completed by each key informant.

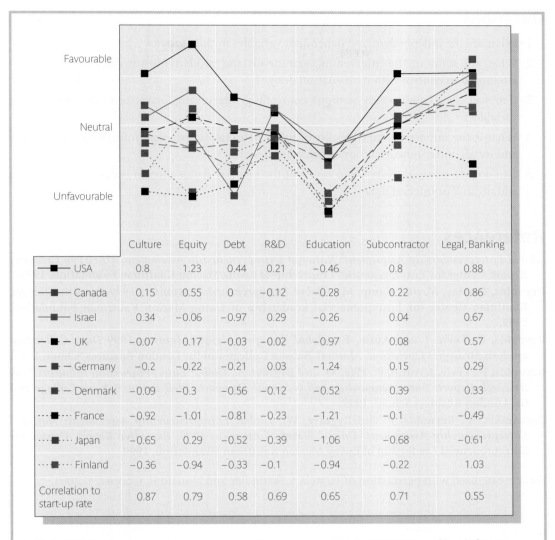

| | Culture | Equity | Debt | R&D | Education | Subcontractor | Legal, Banking |
|---|---|---|---|---|---|---|---|
| USA | 0.8 | 1.23 | 0.44 | 0.21 | −0.46 | 0.8 | 0.88 |
| Canada | 0.15 | 0.55 | 0 | −0.12 | −0.28 | 0.22 | 0.86 |
| Israel | 0.34 | −0.06 | −0.97 | 0.29 | −0.26 | 0.04 | 0.67 |
| UK | −0.07 | 0.17 | −0.03 | −0.02 | −0.97 | 0.08 | 0.57 |
| Germany | −0.2 | −0.22 | −0.21 | 0.03 | −1.24 | 0.15 | 0.29 |
| Denmark | −0.09 | −0.3 | −0.56 | −0.12 | −0.52 | 0.39 | 0.33 |
| France | −0.92 | −1.01 | −0.81 | −0.23 | −1.21 | −0.1 | −0.49 |
| Japan | −0.65 | 0.29 | −0.52 | −0.39 | −1.06 | −0.68 | −0.61 |
| Finland | −0.36 | −0.94 | −0.33 | −0.1 | −0.94 | −0.22 | 1.03 |
| Correlation to start-up rate | 0.87 | 0.79 | 0.58 | 0.69 | 0.65 | 0.71 | 0.55 |

*Exhibit C1.2* Entrepreneurial framework conditions: cross-national comparisons of key informant multi-item indexes.

The perception of opportunity (.79) and the two measures of entrepreneurial potential of the population – capacity (.64) and motivation (.93) – positively correlate with business start-up rates. And start-up rates positively correlate with growth in GDP (.60) and level of employment (.47). (See Exhibit C1.2.)

While many cross-sectional measures still remain in this ongoing study, study directors claim that, 'The support for the conceptual model is encouraging, although clearly not conclusive. GEM provides a robust framework within which national governments can evolve a set of effective policies for enhancing entrepreneurship.'

## Questions

1  What are the independent and dependent variables in this study?

2  What are some of the intervening, extraneous and moderating variables that the study attempted to control with its 10-nation design?

3  Can you do a causal study without controlling intervening, extraneous and moderating variables?

4  What is the impact on study results of using national experts (key informants) to identify and weigh entrepreneurial framework conditions?

5  Can you do a causal study when much of the primary data collected is descriptive opinion and ordinal or interval data?

## References

*Global Entrepreneurship Assessment: National Entrepreneurship Assessment, UK: 1999 Executive Report.* Center for Entrepreneurial Leadership of Ewing Marion Kauffman Foundation, 1999.

Reynolds, P., Hay, M. and Camp, M., *Global Entrepreneurship Monitor: 1999 Executive Report.* Kauffman Center for Entrepreneurial Leadership of Ewing Marion Kauffman Foundation, 1999.

Reynolds, P., Levie, J. and Autio, E., *Global Entrepreneurship Monitor: 1999 Data Collection-analysis Strategies Operations Manual.* Babson College and the London Business School, 1999.

Reynolds, P., Levie, J. Autio, E., Hay, M. and Bygrave B., *Global Entrepreneurship Monitor: 1999 Research Report: Entrepreneurship and National Economic Well-Being.* Babson College and the London Business School, 1999.

Zacharakis, A., Reynolds, P. and Bygrave, W., *Global Entrepreneurship Assessment: National Entrepreneurship Assessment, United States of America, 1999: Executive Report.* Center for Entrepreneurial Leadership of Ewing Marion Kauffman Foundation, 1999.

*Source*: case used with permission of Pamela S. Schindler and Donald R. Cooper, © 2001.

# Can this study be saved?

'What's troubling me is that you can't just pick a new random sample just because somebody didn't like the results of the first survey. Please tell me more about what's been done.' Your voice is clear and steady, trying to discover what's actually happened and, hopefully, to identify some useful information without the additional expense of a new survey.

'It's not that we didn't like the results of the first survey,' responded R.L. Steegmans, 'it's that only 54 per cent of the membership responded. We hadn't even looked at their planned spending when the decision [to sample again] was made. Since we had (naively) planned on receiving answers from nearly all of the 400 people initially selected, we chose 200 more at random and surveyed them too. That's the second sample.' At this point, sensing that there's more to the story, you simply respond, 'Uh-huh.' Sure enough, more follows …

'Then E.S. Eldredge had this great idea of following up on those who didn't respond. We sent them another whole questionnaire, together with a crisp dollar and a letter telling them how important their responses are to the planning of the industry. Worked pretty well. Then, of course, we had to follow up the second sample as well.'

'Let me see if I understand,' you reply. 'You have two samples: one of 400 people and one of 200. For each, you have the initial responses and follow-up responses. Is that it?'

'Well, yes, but there was also the pilot study – 12 people in offices downstairs and across the street. We'd kinda like to include them, average them, with the rest because we worked so hard on that at the start and it seems a shame to throw them away. But all we really want to know is average spending to within about a hundred euros.'

At this point, you feel that you have enough of the background information to evaluate the situation and to either recommend an estimate or an additional survey. Exhibit C2.1 offers additional details for the survey of the 8391 overall membership in order to determine planned spending over the next quarter.

| | Pilot study | First sample | Second sample | Both samples | All combined |
|---|---|---|---|---|---|
| *Initial mailing* | | | | | |
| Mailed | 12 | 400 | 200 | 600 | 612 |
| Responded | 12 | 216 | 120 | 336 | 348 |
| Average | €39,274.89 | 3,949.40 | 3,795.55 | 3,894.45 | 5,114.47 |
| Standard deviation | €9,061.91 | 849.26 | 868.39 | 858.02 | 6,716.42 |
| *Follow-up mailing* | | | | | |
| Mailed | 0 | 184 | 80 | 264 | 264 |
| Responded | 0 | 64 | 18 | 82 | 82 |
| Average | | €1,238.34 | 1,262.34 | 1,243.60 | 1,243.60 |
| Standard deviation | | €155.19 | 156.59 | 153.29 | 153.29 |
| *Initial and follow-up* | | | | | |
| Mailed | 12 | 400 | 200 | 600 | 612 |
| Responded | 12 | 280 | 138 | 418 | 430 |
| Average | €39,274.89 | 3,329.73 | 3,465.13 | 3,374.43 | 4,376.30 |
| Standard deviation | €9,061.91 | 1,364.45 | 1,179.50 | 1,306.42 | 6,229.77 |

**Exhibit C2.1** Methodology details.

## Questions

1  Was drawing a second sample a good idea? Explain.

2  Were the follow-up mailings a good idea? Explain.

3  Which of the results are useful? Are these data sufficient to solve the management dilemma or is further study needed?

*Source*: adapted from 'Can this survey be saved?' Used with permission of Andrew F. Siegel, *Practical Business Statistics*, 4th edn. (Irwin/McGraw-Hill, 2000), p. 298.

# Inquiring minds want to know – NOW!

Nordic Media, a publisher of such business magazines as *Industri Nyheter*, *Finans & Penge* and *Aksjebørs Uken*, was experiencing a decline in the use of publication reader service cards. This postcard-sized device features a series of numbers, with one number assigned to each advertisement appearing in the publication. Readers circle the advertiser's number to request product or service information by mail. Cards are used to track reader inquiries stimulated by advertising within the magazine. 'By 1998 there was a growing belief in many quarters that business publication advertising was generating fewer leads than in the past,' shares Bo Svenson, director of Nordic Research Services. 'Knowing whether or not this is true is complicated by the fact that many companies don't track the source of their leads.' This belief, however, could ultimately have led to lower advertising revenues if alternate methods of inquiry stimulation went untracked.

Nordic started its research by comparing inquiry response options offered within the September issues of 12 Nordic magazines, including *Industri Nyheter*. Advertisements were drawn from two years: 1992 (648 advertisements) and 1997 (690 advertisements). The average number of response options per advertisement was 3.3 in 1992, growing to 4.1 in 1997. More than half of 1997 advertisements offered freefone telephone and/or fax numbers. 'Two inquiry methods that are commonplace today, sending e-mail and visiting an advertiser's website, were virtually non-existent in 1992,' notes Svenson. Not a single 1992 advertisement invited readers to visit a website and just one listed an e-mail address. Website addresses were found in three of five (60.9 per cent) 1997 advertisements, with e-mail addresses provided in 17.7 per cent of advertisements. Today, many websites contain a 'contact us' feature that generates an e-mail message of inquiry. In 1997, advertisers were including their postal mailing address only 55.5 per cent of the time, compared with 69 per cent in 1992 advertisements.

Nordic pre-tested a reader-targeted mail questionnaire by telephone with a small sample drawn from its database of 1.7 million domestic subscribers. A second pre-test, by mail, involved 300 subscribers (see Exhibit C3.1). Nordic mailed the finalized study to 4000 managers, executives, engineers and purchasing agents selected from the Scandinavian Nordic database. The survey sample was constructed using stratified disproportionate random sampling with subscribers considered as belonging to one of 42 cells (seven industry groups by six job titles). A total of 710 completed questionnaires were received, with 676 of the respondents indicating that they were purchase decision-makers for their organization. Nordic analysed only the answers of these 676 buyers. Data were analysed by weighting responses in each cell by their percentage make-up in the overall population. The overall margin of error for the survey was $\pm 4$ per cent at the 95 per cent level of confidence. In-depth follow-up telephone interviews were conducted with 40 respondents to gain a deeper understanding of their behaviour and attitudes.

Almost every respondent (97.7 per cent) had contacted at least one advertiser during the past year. Newer methods of making inquiries – web visits, fax-on-demand or e-mail – were used by half (49.1 per cent) of the buyers surveyed. But a look ahead shows the true impact of information technology. Within the next five years, 73.7 per cent expect to respond to more advertisements by sending e-mails to the company. In addition, 72.2 per cent anticipate visiting an advertiser's website and 60 per cent expect to increase their use of fax-on-demand. Three out of five purchasing decision-makers have access to the Internet and 74.3 per cent of those without Internet service expect to have it within the next five years. Seven of ten (72.4 per cent) respondents plan to use the Internet to research potential suppliers, products or services during the next five years, compared to 33.1 per cent using it for that purpose during the past year.

Findings revealed that the need for fast response and the need for information on product availability and delivery are influenced by:

1 time pressures created by downsizing of the work force and demands for greater productivity
2 the fast pace of doing business
3 cost considerations.

Behaviour varied depending on immediacy of purpose. When buyers have an immediate need for a product or service, telephone contact is the inquiry method of choice. Of the respondents, 79.5 per cent reported that they had called a freefone number in the past year for an immediate need, while 66.1 per cent had called a local number and 64.7 per cent a long-distance number. When the need for a product or service is not immediate, buyers are more likely to use mail. Among respondents, 71.4 per cent reported that they had mailed a reader service card in the past year for a non-immediate need and 69.3 per cent had mailed a business-reply card to an advertiser.

'A new paradigm is emerging for industrial purchasing,' concludes Svenson. 'Buyers are working in real time. They want information more quickly and they want more information.'

Could we ask a favour of you?

We are conducting a survey of executives to help companies better understand and respond to your requests for information.

Your name has been selected as part of a relatively small sample, so your reply is vital to the accuracy of the study findings. All individual responses will remain completely confidential, with answers combined and presented in statistical form only.

We would be grateful if you could take a few minutes to respond to this survey.

An international postage-paid envelope is enclosed for your convenience.

We look forward to your reply!

Cordially,

Director of Research

P.S. To ensure a correct entry in the random draw for the hand-held colour TV, please make any necessary changes to your mailing label.

*Questionnaire for mail survey*

**1** Are you involved in specifying, recommending, purchasing or approving the purchase of any of the following for your organization? (Tick all that apply.)

☐ Construction/renovation work

☐ Equipment/machinery

☐ Maintenance/repair/operating supplies

☐ Production material/components

☐ Services

☐ Other

☐ Not involved in purchasing decisions

**2** During the past year, which of the following actions have you taken in response to an advertisement, to obtain information about potential suppliers/products/services for your organization? (Tick all that apply.) Please check the box in the last column if you have not taken the indicated action in the past year.

*Action taken during the past year*

|  | For an immediate product/ service | For a non-immediate product/ service | Did not do in the past year |
|---|---|---|---|
| **Faxed** |  |  |  |
| – Business reply card to company | ☐ | ☐ | ☐ |
| – Coupon from advertisement | ☐ | ☐ | ☐ |
| – Letter to company | ☐ | ☐ | ☐ |
| – Publication reader service card | ☐ | ☐ | ☐ |
| **Mailed** |  |  |  |
| – Business reply card to company | ☐ | ☐ | ☐ |
| – Coupon from advertisement | ☐ | ☐ | ☐ |
| – Letter to company | ☐ | ☐ | ☐ |

▶

– Publication reader service card   ☐   ☐   ☐

Sent e-mail to company

Telephoned company

– Local number   ☐   ☐   ☐
– Non-freefone long-distance number   ☐   ☐   ☐
– Freefone number   ☐   ☐   ☐

Used advertiser's fax-on-demand service   ☐   ☐   ☐

Visited the company's website   ☐   ☐   ☐

Other   ☐   ☐   ☐

**3** What are the three most useful types of information an advertiser can provide when responding to your inquiry? (Tick only three.)

☐ Ability to customize products/services    ☐ ISO/professional certification
☐ Availability/delivery    ☐ List of sales/service locations
☐ Complete company catalogue    ☐ Price list
☐ Short-form (condensed) catalogue    ☐ Product specifications
☐ Company experience/expertise    ☐ Quality/reliability
☐ Company financial strength/stability    ☐ Savings in time/money
☐ Customer/client list    ☐ Warranty/guarantee offered
☐ Customer service/technical support    ☐ Other (please specify):

_____

_____

**4 a** Please estimate the change over the past five years in your use of each of the following methods of obtaining information, in response to advertising, about potential suppliers/products/services for your organization. Check the box in the fourth column if you have not taken the indicated action in the past five years.

**b** Over the next five years, do you expect your use of each method of obtaining information to increase, decrease, or stay about the same?

| | Change over the past five years | | | | Expected change over the next five years | | |
| --- | --- | --- | --- | --- | --- | --- | --- |
| | Has increased | Has stayed the same | Has decreased | Haven't done in the past 5 years | Increase | Stay the same | Decrease |
| Faxed | | | | | | | |
| – Business-reply card to company | ☐ | ☐ | ☐ | ☐ | ☐ | ☐ | ☐ |
| – Coupon from advertisement | ☐ | ☐ | ☐ | ☐ | ☐ | ☐ | ☐ |
| – Letter to company | ☐ | ☐ | ☐ | ☐ | ☐ | ☐ | ☐ |
| – Publication reader service card | ☐ | ☐ | ☐ | ☐ | ☐ | ☐ | ☐ |

Mailed
- Business-reply card to company    ☐ ☐ ☐ ☐ ☐ ☐ ☐
- Coupon from advertisement    ☐ ☐ ☐ ☐ ☐ ☐ ☐
- Letter to company    ☐ ☐ ☐ ☐ ☐ ☐ ☐
- Publication reader service card    ☐ ☐ ☐ ☐ ☐ ☐ ☐

Sent e-mail to company    ☐ ☐ ☐ ☐ ☐ ☐ ☐

Telephoned company
- Local number    ☐ ☐ ☐ ☐ ☐ ☐ ☐
- Non-freefone (long-distance) number    ☐ ☐ ☐ ☐ ☐ ☐ ☐
- Freefone number    ☐ ☐ ☐ ☐ ☐ ☐ ☐

Used advertiser's fax-on-demand service    ☐ ☐ ☐ ☐ ☐ ☐ ☐

Visited the company's website    ☐ ☐ ☐ ☐ ☐ ☐ ☐

Other    ☐ ☐ ☐ ☐ ☐ ☐ ☐

**5 a** Overall, which one method of obtaining information about potential suppliers/products/services for your organization do you most prefer to use? (Tick only one.)

Faxing:
- ☐ Business-reply card to company
- ☐ Coupon from advertisement
- ☐ Letter to company
- ☐ Publication reader service card

Telephoning the company:
- ☐ Local number
- ☐ Non-freefone (long-distance) number
- ☐ Freefone (e.g. 0800) number
- ☐ Using company's fax-on-demand service
- ☐ Visiting the company's website
- ☐ Other (please specify:)

_____

_____

Mailing:
- ☐ Business-reply card to company
- ☐ Coupon from advertisement
- ☐ Letter to company
- ☐ Publication reader service card
- ☐ Sending e-mail to company

**b** Why do you prefer to use this method?

_____

_____

**6 a** Do you currently have access to the Internet? (Tick all that apply.)
- ☐ Yes, at work.
- ☐ Yes, at home/away from home.
- ☐ No current Internet access.

**b** If you don't currently have Internet access, do you expect to have access in the future?
- ☐ Yes, within the next year.
- ☐ Yes, in 1 – 5 years.
- ☐ No, not within next 5 years.

> **7 a** If you currently have Internet access, in which of the following ways have you used the Internet in your job during the past year?
>   **b** If you currently have or plan to have Internet access, how do you expect to use the Internet in your job in the next five years?

| | Use of Internet during the past year | Expected use of Internet during the next 5 years |
|---|---|---|
| Reading industry/professional newsgroup postings (e.g. bulletin boards) | ☐ | ☐ |
| Researching potential suppliers/products/ services for your organization | ☐ | ☐ |
| Obtaining technical information | ☐ | ☐ |
| Communicating by e-mail: | | |
| – With potential suppliers for your organization | ☐ | ☐ |
| – With other buyers about potential suppliers/products/services | ☐ | ☐ |
| Purchasing products or services for your organization | ☐ | ☐ |
| Other (please specify): | ☐ | ☐ |
| _____ | | |
| NO JOB-RELATED USE OF INTERNET | ☐ | ☐ |

*General Information*

**8** Are you male or female? ☐ Male? ☐ Female?

**9** What is your age? ☐ Under 30? ☐ 30–39? ☐ 40–49? ☐ 50 or older

**10** How many years have you been with your current organization? _____ years

**11** How many years have you been involved in the purchasing process at your organization? _____ years

*Exhibit C3.1* Cover letter and questionnaire for mail survey.

## Questions

1 Build the management research question hierarchy.
2 What ethical issues are relevant to this study?
3 Describe the sampling plan. Analyse its strengths and weaknesses.
4 Describe the research design. Analyse its strengths and weaknesses.
5 Critique the survey used for the study.
6 Prepare the survey for analysis. Set up the code sheet for this study. How will this study be set up to be tabulated by a statistical analysis program like SPSS?
7 Assume you are compiling your research report. How would you present the statistical

information within this case to the *Industri Nyheter* decision-maker, the manager who must decide whether or not to continue to publish reader service cards?

8   Assume you are compiling your research report. What are the limitations of this study?

9   Assume you are the decision-maker for *Industri Nyheter*. Given the declining value of the reader response card to subscribers, originally designed as a value-enhancing service to *Industri Nyheter* readers and advertisers alike, what further research might be suggested by the findings of this study? Or do you have sufficient information to stop the use of reader response cards in *Industri Nyheter*?

*Source*: instruments and data are adapted from a case used with permission of Pamela S. Schindler and Donald R. Cooper, © 2001.

# Highland Bank: teeing up a new strategic direction

Highland Bank Country Club (HBCC) started in 1954 as an employee benefit of Highland Bank (HB) but is now an open-membership club. This country club, located south of Edinburgh, hosts two 18-hole golf courses. The HB South course, a par 71 championship course of 6824 yards is located in heavily wooded rolling countryside. The 'Highland' style of the North course, a 6358-yard par 70 course, is considered challenging. Within a 30-minute radius of HBCC, the avid golfer will find eight other private golf and country clubs, as well as 29 public golf clubs and courses.

In 1997, after the purchase of Highland Bank by Anglia Finance (AF), AF provided a £3 million interest-free loan to raze the original clapboard-sided clubhouse and replace it with an all-brick colonial-style facility. Boasting both formal and informal, inside and outside eating facilities, as well as banquet and party rooms, the members voted that the new clubhouse would be totally smoke-free. The rich cherrywood panelling and the hunter-green and burgundy decor mellow the high-ceilinged interior spaces. Golf memberships are £12,000, with social (non-golf) memberships at £650 each. HB employees did not and do not pay membership fees to join. Additionally, each member must spend £100 per quarter in dining receipts and pay £150 (golf) or £100 (social) in annual dues.

Needing to attract new members to support the renovated facility after AF divested itself of HB, and given the growing age of its members, HBCC implemented an aggressive membership campaign in 1998. The goal was to bring golf memberships to 680 and attract as many social memberships as possible. After only moderate success, HBCC commissioned Dixon Group to assist with strategic planning.

Dixon specializes in providing research and strategic consulting to golf clubs and full-service golfing facilities. 'Golf club membership within the UK is perceived as a discretionary luxury of life. HB faces a similar situation to that found elsewhere in clubs around the country – an older satisfied membership, which sees no reason to change what they perceive to be a good thing,' shares Stuart Dixon, president of Dixon. 'With HB, we faced another problem. Because HB was once corporately owned, HB retirees and current employees saw membership as an entitlement, a right.'

After Dixon's 'First Impressions' visit (a free on-site assessment where a club specialist tours facilities, collects information on membership and operations, and discusses industry trends with strategic planning committees), HBCC's board hired Dixon to provide direction and assistance to HBCC's strategic planning committee. 'Historically, HBCC has a 7 per cent penetration rate among HB employees. HB's employee pool was becoming smaller, providing continuing downward pressure on HBCC membership,' explains Dixon. 'With membership segments of HB retirees (one-third of members) and current HB employees (another one-third of members) getting less numerous each year, only the segment comprised of non-HB affiliates provides an opportunity for growth. HBCC needs to become a stand-alone club to survive.'

Dixon conducted six focus groups at HBCC on 3–4 December 1998, involving 43 members, 7 non-members and 12 employees. Among younger members (under 46) and non-members in particular, a golf-only club was less attractive than the full-service array that some other area country clubs offered. A consistent theme was that members did not feel that they received the

| | % All Members | % Members under 46 |
|---|---|---|
| **Facility additions** | | |
| Swimming pool | 30 | 60 |
| Tennis courts | 22 | 36 |
| Health and fitness centre | 30 | 49 |
| Spa | 30 | 58 |
| **Activities** | | |
| For adults | 26 | 40 |
| For families | 23 | 53 |
| For children | 18 | 47 |
| **Current facility alterations** | | |
| Expanding bar/lounge | 41%<br>Important or very important | |
| Improving the driving range | 36%<br>Important or very important | |
| Improving short game practice area | 40%<br><br>Important or very important | |

*Exhibit C4.1* Importance of future facility additions to new strategic direction.

overall level of service at HBCC that they expected from a fine private country club, whether it be in terms of the dining operation or on the golf course. Staff members were frustrated that meeting the board's profit directive was often counterproductive to a high level of service. The HBCC board directed Dixon to conduct a membership study to explore the feasibility of adding additional facilities, including swimming and fitness facilities to attract younger adults and families with children (see Exhibit C4.1).

Dixon distributed mail surveys to 1650 members and their spouses in January 1999 (see Exhibit C4.2). A return rate of 57 per cent and 48 per cent, respectively, netted 886 usable surveys. Data were interpreted at ±3% (or ±0.1) at the 95 per cent confidence level. Due to Dixon's extensive consulting and research experience with golf facilities nationwide, it was able to compare HBCC's membership survey results with those of members of 80 other country clubs.

Overall, 72 per cent of HBCC members were either satisfied or very satisfied. This is slightly less than the 79 per cent satisfaction level for other clubs. Only 12 per cent were very satisfied, with other clubs averaging 21 per cent. The group with the highest dissatisfaction rate (19 per cent dissatisfied or very dissatisfied) was the key 55–64 age group, with the under-46 group generating 11 per cent dissatisfaction. While members currently saw the club as an 'Adult Golf and Dining Club' (63 per cent), many believed its future would need to incorporate facilities for children if the club were to remain competitive for new members. This was especially true for those members under age 46.

Most current members joined for golf (80 per cent either important or very important) or dining (77 per cent either important or very important). Most members were satisfied with golf (81 per cent either satisfied (29 per cent) or very satisfied (69 per cent)). However, level of satisfaction was lower with the over-65 group when it came to course layout (58 per cent very satisfied) and condition (77 per cent very satisfied). Fewer members were satisfied with dining (49 per cent either satisfied or very satisfied). However, even given some dissatisfaction, 61 per cent felt their membership was good value.

The 37th Hole, the casual dining facility, generated concerns about speed of service (27 per cent either dissatisfied or very dissatisfied), professionalism of waiting staff (19 per cent either dissatisfied or very dissatisfied) and menu variety (36 per cent either dissatisfied or very dissatisfied). The same concerns surfaced in the formal dining area, with menu variety and meal-to-meal consistency generating the highest dissatisfaction scores. It is very important for HBCC to provide casual adult dining (95 per cent either very important or important), but less so casual family dining (78 per cent), outdoor dining (69 per cent), formal dining (44 per cent), men's grill (37 per cent) and women's grill (22 per cent). Dining prices are seen as the same (65 per cent lunch, 48 per cent dinner) or higher (32 per cent lunch, 47 per cent dinner) than other clubs and restaurants frequented by members. Members overwhelmingly continue to endorse the no-smoking rule (97 per cent formal dining, 94 per cent 37th Hole, 83 per cent bar/lounge).

'Members think of HBCC as a golf club first, but the golf wasn't meeting expectations. Second, members see HBCC as a dining club, but the members were dissatisfied with the casual dining product and service,' says Dixon.

Survey results offered good and bad news. Additional facilities would not be attractions to most current members, but many members are interested in improving the current facilities. Fully 59 per cent, however, were unwilling to pay higher fees (including 43 per cent of those under age 46) to obtain the changes they found attractive.

Who answered the survey?

- [ ] 74% golf (single or family) and 24% social, with 2% corporate memberships
- [ ] 65% are (23%) or had been (42%) employed at HBCC
- [ ] 55% male, 45% female
- [ ] In each of four age groups:
  Under 46 (19%)
  46 – 55 (23%)
  56 – 65 (26%)
  66 or older (33%)
- [ ] 74% lived within seven miles of HBCC
- [ ] 42% had been members for 20 or more years
- [ ] 78% did not have children (under age 21) living at home
- [ ] 41% belonged to a swimming/tennis club (15%) or fitness facility (26%)
- [ ] 81% reside in the south of Edinburgh area all year round

INSTRUCTIONS

Please complete the questionnaire, answering all questions that pertain to your interests at the Club. If you do not participate in a particular Club activity and do not feel qualified to respond to the questions regarding that activity, please leave those questions blank or indicate 'No Opinion' and move on to the next question. *Note*: Space is provided at the end of the questionnaire for your written comments and suggestions.

Completed questionnaires should be mailed in the enclosed postage-paid envelope by the date printed on the cover letter directly to Dixon Group.

IMPORTANT: Completely fill in the ovals that correspond to your answers for each question with either a pen or a pencil. The surveys will be electronically scanned. Please do not make extra marks on the questionnaire except in the space provided for written responses at the end of the survey.

> Fill in your answers like this ●
> Not like ✓ or ✗ or ◎

**1** Please indicate your 'overall' satisfaction with HB Country Club:

| (5) Very satisfied | (4) Satisfied | (3) Neutral | (2) Dissatisfied | (1) Very dissatisfied |
|:---:|:---:|:---:|:---:|:---:|
| ○ | ○ | ○ | ○ | ○ |

2 Which of the following best represents what you feel (1) is currently and (2) should be the primary purpose of HB Country Club? (Please mark only one per column.)

|  | (1) Currently | (2) Should be |
|---|---|---|
| A *family*-oriented, full-service country club with activities for children | O | O |
| An *adult*-oriented, full-service country club with *limited* activities for children | O | O |
| A golf *and* dining club primarily for adults | O | O |
| A golf club primarily for adults | O | O |

3 Using a scale from '5' (Very Important) to '1' (Very unimportant), how important were each of the following to you in your decision to join HB Country Club?

|  | (5) Very important | (4) Important | (3) Neutral | (2) Unimportant | (1) Very unimportant |
|---|---|---|---|---|---|
| To meet new friends | O | O | O | O | O |
| Club location |  |  |  |  |  |
| – in relation to home | O | O | O | O | O |
| – in relation to work | O | O | O | O | O |
| Club social functions | O | O | O | O | O |
| Friends were/are members | O | O | O | O | O |
| Parents were/are members | O | O | O | O | O |

|  | (5) Very important | (4) Important | (3) Neutral | (2) Unimportant | (1) Very unimportant |
|---|---|---|---|---|---|
| Exclusivity of club's members | O | O | O | O | O |
| Affiliation with HB Corporation | O | O | O | O | O |
| Competitive initiation fee | O | O | O | O | O |
| Private parties/banquets | O | O | O | O | O |
| Reputation of Club | O | O | O | O | O |
| Dining | O | O | O | O | O |
| Golf | O | O | O | O | O |
| Availability of 36 holes of golf | O | O | O | O | O |
| 'Top 100' ranking of golf course | O | O | O | O | O |

**4** Please indicate your satisfaction with these characteristics of your Club's Board of Trustees, Committees and Management:

|  | (5) Very satisfied | (4) Satisfied | (3) Neutral | (2) Dissatisfied | (1) Very dissatisfied |
|---|---|---|---|---|---|
| **BOARD** | | | | | |
| Communication with the membership | O | O | O | O | O |
| Degree to which board is representative of membership | O | O | O | O | O |
| **COMMITTEES** | | | | | |
| Effectiveness of Club committees | O | O | O | O | O |
| **MANAGEMENT STAFF** | | | | | |
| Effectiveness of Club management | O | O | O | O | O |
| Responsiveness to member questions and suggestions | O | O | O | O | O |
| Overall level of service provided by Club's management and staff | O | O | O | O | O |

**5** Please indicate how important each of the following Club activities/services is to you and also how satisfied you are with each:

Rating scale: 5 = Very satisfied, 4 = Satisfied, 3 = Neutral, 2 = Dissatisfied, 1 = Very dissatisfied, N.O. = No opinion

Rating scale: 5 = Very important, 4 = Important, 3 = Neutral, 2 = Unimportant, 1 = Very unimportant, N.O. No opinion

|  | SATISFACTION | | | | | | IMPORTANCE | | | | | |
|---|---|---|---|---|---|---|---|---|---|---|---|---|
|  | 5 | 4 | 3 | 2 | 1 | N.O. | 5 | 4 | 3 | 2 | 1 | N.O. |
| Golf | O | O | O | O | O | O | O | O | O | O | O | O |
| Dining | O | O | O | O | O | O | O | O | O | O | O | O |
| Club social functions | O | O | O | O | O | O | O | O | O | O | O | O |
| Private parties | O | O | O | O | O | O | O | O | O | O | O | O |
| Children's activities | O | O | O | O | O | O | O | O | O | O | O | O |
| Family activities | O | O | O | O | O | O | O | O | O | O | O | O |

**6** Please respond to the following statement: 'I receive good value for the cost of my membership at HB Country Club'.

| (5) Strongly agree | (4) Agree | (3) Neutral | (2) Disagree | (1) Stongly disagree | No opinion |
|---|---|---|---|---|---|
| O | O | O | O | O | O |

**7** Please respond to the following statement: 'There are a sufficient number of social activities at the Club that appeal to my age and interest group.'

| (5) Strongly agree | (4) Agree | (3) Neutral | (2) Disagree | (1) Stongly disagree | No opinion |
|---|---|---|---|---|---|
| O | O | O | O | O | O |

**8** Do you have access to the Internet?

○ Yes          ○ No

Are you aware the Club has a website?

○ Yes          ○ No

Would you like e-mail notifications from the Club on a regular basis?

○ Yes          ○ No

**9** Please indicate your satisfaction with the following aspects of the Club's newsletter, *The Highlander*, and also Club communications in general.

| | (5) Very satisfied | (4) Satisfied | (3) Neutral | (2) Dissatisfied | (1) Very dissatisfied |
|---|---|---|---|---|---|
| *Newsletter content* | | | | | |
| Notification of upcoming events | ○ | ○ | ○ | ○ | ○ |
| Membership activities and stories | ○ | ○ | ○ | ○ | ○ |
| Club business (reports from board committees) | ○ | ○ | ○ | ○ | ○ |
| Newsletter appearance/format | ○ | ○ | ○ | ○ | ○ |
| Newsletter timeliness | ○ | ○ | ○ | ○ | ○ |
| Club communication in general | ○ | ○ | ○ | ○ | ○ |

## SECTION II. GOLF

IF YOU ARE NOT FAMILIAR WITH THE GOLF FACILITIES AND OPERATIONS, PLEASE SKIP TO THE NEXT SECTION OF THE QUESTIONNAIRE

**10** Please indicate your satisfaction with these aspects of the SOUTH and NORTH golf courses.

Rating scale: 5 = Very satisfied, 4 = Satisfied, 3 = Neutral, 2 = Dissatisfied, 1 = Very dissatisfied, N.O. = No opinion

| | SOUTH COURSE | | | | | | NORTH COURSE | | | | | |
|---|---|---|---|---|---|---|---|---|---|---|---|---|
| | 5 | 4 | 3 | 2 | 1 | N.O. | 5 | 4 | 3 | 2 | 1 | N.O. |
| Course layout | ○ | ○ | ○ | ○ | ○ | ○ | ○ | ○ | ○ | ○ | ○ | ○ |
| Overall course condition | ○ | ○ | ○ | ○ | ○ | ○ | ○ | ○ | ○ | ○ | ○ | ○ |
| Course landscaping (flowers and plantings) | ○ | ○ | ○ | ○ | ○ | ○ | ○ | ○ | ○ | ○ | ○ | ○ |
| Tee box conditions | ○ | ○ | ○ | ○ | ○ | ○ | ○ | ○ | ○ | ○ | ○ | ○ |
| Condition of fairways | ○ | ○ | ○ | ○ | ○ | ○ | ○ | ○ | ○ | ○ | ○ | ○ |
| Condition of greens | ○ | ○ | ○ | ○ | ○ | ○ | ○ | ○ | ○ | ○ | ○ | ○ |
| Condition of bunkers | ○ | ○ | ○ | ○ | ○ | ○ | ○ | ○ | ○ | ○ | ○ | ○ |

| | SOUTH COURSE | | | | | | NORTH COURSE | | | | | |
|---|---|---|---|---|---|---|---|---|---|---|---|---|
| | 5 | 4 | 3 | 2 | 1 | N.O. | 5 | 4 | 3 | 2 | 1 | N.O. |
| Irrigation | ○ | ○ | ○ | ○ | ○ | ○ | ○ | ○ | ○ | ○ | ○ | ○ |

| | (5) | (4) | (3) | (2) | (1) |
|---|---|---|---|---|---|
| Drainage | O O O O O | O O | O O O | O O | O |
| Condition of cart paths | O O O O O | O O | O O O | O O | O |
| Course rest rooms | O O O O O | O O | O O O | O O | O |
| Availability | O O O O O | O O | O O O | O O | O |
| Condition | O O O O O | O O | O O O | O O | O |
| Availability of drinking water | O O O O O | O O | O O O | O O | O |
| Beverage cart availability | O O O O O | O O | O O O | O O | O |

11 Please indicate your satisfaction with these aspects of the golf operations at the Club:

(*answer survey for question 11 on the following page*)

| | (5) Very satisfied | (4) Satisfied | (3) Neutral | (2) Dissatisfied | (1) Very dissatisfied |
|---|---|---|---|---|---|
| *Golf Pro Shop* | | | | | |
| Interior appearance | O | O | O | O | O |
| Pro Shop cleanliness | O | O | O | O | O |
| Merchandise selection | O | O | O | O | O |
| Pro Shop service | O | O | O | O | O |
| Pro Shop prices | O | O | O | O | O |
| Pro lessons | O | O | O | O | O |
| Bag drop service | O | O | O | O | O |
| Bag storage and club cleaning services | O | O | O | O | O |
| Cart services | O | O | O | O | O |
| Cart cleanliness | O | O | O | O | O |
| *Practice range* | | | | | |
| Condition | O | O | O | O | O |
| Size | O | O | O | O | O |
| Range ball condition | O | O | O | O | O |
| Speed of play | O | O | O | O | O |
| *Tournaments* | | | | | |
| Quality | O | O | O | O | O |
| Value for price | O | O | O | O | O |
| Format of tournaments | O | O | O | O | O |
| Adult golf programmes (i.e. leagues) | O | O | O | O | O |
| Junior golf programmes | O | O | O | O | O |
| Tee time reservation system | O | O | O | O | O |
| *Halfway House* | | | | | |
| Hours of operation | O | O | O | O | O |
| Service | O | O | O | O | O |
| Menu variety | O | O | O | O | O |

**12** How do you feel about the overall use of the golf course as it now exists at the club?

| | (5) Excessive | (4) Somewhat excessive | (3) Fine as is | (2) Not quite dissatisfied | (1) Not enough |
|---|---|---|---|---|---|
| Amount of time available for casual, open member play | O | O | O | O | O |
| Amount of time permitted for guest use | O | O | O | O | O |
| Amount of time available for junior play | O | O | O | O | O |
| Number of member-scheduled events/ tournaments | O | O | O | O | O |
| Number of non-member outings on Mondays | O | O | O | O | O |
| Number of non-member outings on days other than Mondays | O | O | O | O | O |

**13** Please respond to the following statement: 'If the Club had a caddy programme I would support the programme and use caddies on a regular basis when I play golf'.

| (5) Strongly agree | (4) Agree | (3) Neutral | (2) Disagree | (1) Stongly disagree | No opinion |
|---|---|---|---|---|---|
| O | O | O | O | O | O |

**14** Please indicate your satisfaction regarding the aspects of the dining in the 37th HOLE, the MEMBERS' DINING ROOM and for PRIVATE PARTIES:

Rating scale: 5 = Very satisfied, 4 = Satisfied, 3 = Neutral, 2 = Dissatisfied, 1 = Very dissatisfied, N.O. = No opinion

| | 37TH HOLE | | | | | | MEMBERS' DINNING ROOM | | | | | | PRIVATE PARTIES | | | | | |
|---|---|---|---|---|---|---|---|---|---|---|---|---|---|---|---|---|---|---|
| *Service:* | 5 | 4 | 3 | 2 | 1 | N.O. | 5 | 4 | 3 | 2 | 1 | N.O. | 5 | 4 | 3 | 2 | 1 | N.O. |
| Staff appearance | O | O | O | O | O | O | O | O | O | O | O | O | O | O | O | O | O | O |
| Speed of service | O | O | O | O | O | O | O | O | O | O | O | O | O | O | O | O | O | O |
| Friendliness of waiting staff | O | O | O | O | O | O | O | O | O | O | O | O | O | O | O | O | O | O |
| Professionalism/training of waiting staff | O | O | O | O | O | O | O | O | O | O | O | O | O | O | O | O | O | O |
| *Food:* | | | | | | | | | | | | | | | | | | |
| Quality-food well prepared | O | O | O | O | O | O | O | O | O | O | O | O | O | O | O | O | O | O |
| Food presentation (visually pleasing) | O | O | O | O | O | O | O | O | O | O | O | O | O | O | O | O | O | O |
| Meal-to-meal consistency | O | O | O | O | O | O | O | O | O | O | O | O | O | O | O | O | O | O |
| Menu variety | O | O | O | O | O | O | O | O | O | O | O | O | O | O | O | O | O | O |

| *Other:* | MEMBERS' | | | | | | | | | | | | | | | | | |
| --- | --- | --- | --- | --- | --- | --- | --- | --- | --- | --- | --- | --- | --- | --- | --- | --- | --- | --- |
| | 37TH HOLE | | | | | | DINNING ROOM | | | | | | PRIVATE PARTIES | | | | | |
| | 5 | 4 | 3 | 2 | 1 | N.O. | 5 | 4 | 3 | 2 | 1 | N.O. | 5 | 4 | 3 | 2 | 1 | N.O. |
| Ambience/decor of rooms | O | O | O | O | O | O | O | O | O | O | O | O | O | O | O | O | O | O |
| Wine list/selections | O | O | O | O | O | O | O | O | O | O | O | O | O | O | O | O | O | O |
| Value for money | O | O | O | O | O | O | O | O | O | O | O | O | O | O | O | O | O | O |
| Party planning assistance | O | O | O | O | O | O | O | O | O | O | O | O | O | O | O | O | O | O |
| Party follow-up by staff | O | O | O | O | O | O | O | O | O | O | O | O | O | O | O | O | O | O |

**15** How important is it for the Club to provide each of the following dining styles?

| | (5) Very important | (4) Important | (3) Neutral | (2) Unimportant | (1) Very unimportant |
| --- | --- | --- | --- | --- | --- |
| Casual adult dining | O | O | O | O | O |
| Casual family dining | O | O | O | O | O |
| Formal dining (coat and tie required) | O | O | O | O | O |
| Outdoor dining | O | O | O | O | O |
| Men's grill | O | O | O | O | O |
| Women's grill | O | O | O | O | O |

**16** How do the Club's prices compare to the prices charged for similar meals at other clubs and restaurants you visit regularly? Please compare similar dining experiences (i.e. dining in the 37th Hole should be compared to dining in a casual golf-type restaurant and dining at the Members' Dining Room should be compared to a more upscale type restaurant).

| *The Club's prices are:* | (5) Much lower | (4) Lower | (3) About the same | (2) Somewhat higher | (1) Much higher |
| --- | --- | --- | --- | --- | --- |
| Lunch | O | O | O | O | O |
| Dinner | O | O | O | O | O |
| Private parties | O | O | O | O | O |
| Social events | O | O | O | O | O |
| Wine | O | O | O | O | O |
| Cocktails | O | O | O | O | O |

**17** Please respond to the following statement: 'The Clubhouse should remain a totally nonsmoking facility'.

| (5) Strongly agree | (4) Agree | (3) Neutral | (2) Disagree | (1) Stongly disagree | No opinion |
| --- | --- | --- | --- | --- | --- |
| O | O | O | O | O | O |

SECTION IV: THE FUTURE

18  Listed below are examples of new facilities or additional services the Club may consider adding in the future. Using a scale from '5' (Very important) to '1' (Very unimportant), please indicate how important you feel each item is to the future of the Club.

| | (5) Very important | (4) Important | (3) Neutral | (2) Unimportant | (1) Very unimportant |
|---|---|---|---|---|---|
| Add a swimming pool | O | O | O | O | O |
| Add tennis courts | O | O | O | O | O |
| Add a health/fitness facility | O | O | O | O | O |
| Add paddle tennis courts | O | O | O | O | O |
| Add a bowling alley | O | O | O | O | O |
| Add spa facilities (sauna, steam room, jacuzzi, etc.) | O | O | O | O | O |
| Provide more social activities | O | O | O | O | O |
| Provide more family activities | O | O | O | O | O |
| Provide more children activities | O | O | O | O | O |
| Add a year-round driving range | O | O | O | O | O |

19  Listed below are examples of improvements to the existing Club facilities that may be considered in the future. Using a scale from '5' (very important) to '1' (Very unimportant), please indicate how important you feel each item is to the future of the Club.

| | (5) Very important | (4) Important | (3) Neutral | (2) Unimportant | (1) Very unimportant |
|---|---|---|---|---|---|
| Enlarge the bar/lounge | O | O | O | O | O |
| Enlarge the banquet room to better accommodate large functions such as weddings | O | O | O | O | O |
| Provide better pedestrian access | O | O | O | O | O |
| Improve the golf driving range | O | O | O | O | O |
| Improve the golf short game practice area | O | O | O | O | O |
| Modify the North Course where possible to make it more challenging | O | O | O | O | O |
| Modify the South Course where possible to make it more challenging | O | O | O | O | O |

**20 a** Please respond to the following statement: 'I would be willing to pay somewhat higher annual dues in order to make the Club more private and provide a higher level of service.'

> (5) Strongly agree   (4) Agree   (3) Neutral   (2) Disagree   (1) Stongly disagree   No opinion
>     O        O        O        O        O        O

**b** How much of an annual dues increase would you be willing to pay to make the Club more private and provide a higher level of service? (Please mark only one.)

- O Nothing
- O 5%
- O 10%
- O 15%
- O 20%
- O 30%
- O 40%
- O 50% or more

**21** At present, the Club allows non-member outings on the golf course on Mondays as well as other days of the week. These outings generate substantial revenue for the Club, which help to keep member dues lower than they would be without this revenue. However, these outings also reduce member access to the course, add wear and tear to the course, and limit the amount of time available for course maintenance.

Please respond to the following statements.

**a** 'The Club should eliminate outings on days of the week other than Mondays, and I would be willing to pay an additional €100 in annual dues for improved course access and to make up for this lost revenue.'

> (5) Strongly agree   (4) Agree   (3) Neutral   (2) Disagree   (1) Stongly disagree   No opinion
>     O        O        O        O        O        O

**b** 'The Club should eliminate half the outings on Mondays and all outings on days of the week other than Mondays and I would be willing to pay an additional €300 in annual dues for improved course access and to make up for this lost revenue.'

> (5) Strongly agree   (4) Agree   (3) Neutral   (2) Disagree   (1) Stongly disagree   No opinion
>     O        O        O        O        O        O

**c** 'The Club should eliminate all outings, both on Mondays and other days of the week, and I would be willing to pay an additional €500 in annual dues for improved course access and to make up for this lost revenue.'

> (5) Strongly agree   (4) Agree   (3) Neutral   (2) Disagree   (1) Stongly disagree   No opinion
>     O        O        O        O        O        O

**22** Please respond to the following statement: 'One of the golf courses should always be open for member play on Mondays.'

| (5) Strongly agree | (4) Agree | (3) Neutral | (2) Disagree | (1) Stongly disagree | No opinion |
| :---: | :---: | :---: | :---: | :---: | :---: |
| O | O | O | O | O | O |

**23** Some clubs include additional fees such as locker rental, bag storage, shoe-shine service and driving range in the annual or monthly dues. At HB Country Club, additional charges such as locker rental and shoe-shine service are optional services and fees and are billed as separate items.

Please respond to the following statement: 'Over the next few years HB Country Club should move in the direction of bundling all fees and charges (such as locker rental and shoe-shine service) into one dues amount to be paid annually.'

| (5) Strongly agree | (4) Agree | (3) Neutral | (2) Disagree | (1) Stongly disagree | No opinion |
| :---: | :---: | :---: | :---: | :---: | :---: |
| O | O | O | O | O | O |

## SECTION V: ABOUT YOU

**24** Your membership classification is (spouses of members – please mark the membership classification of your husband or wife):
- O  Family, Golf
- O  Single, Golf
- O  Corporate
- O  Non-resident
- O  Social

**25** Which of the following best describes your membership status?
- O  Current HB employee
- O  Retired or RIF'd HB employee
- O  Associate member

**26** What is your gender?
- O  Male
- O  Female

**27** What is your age category?
- O  Under 36
- O  36–45
- O  46–55
- O  56–65
- O  66–75
- O  Over 75

**28** How many miles is your home from the Club?
- O  0 to 3 miles
- O  4 to 7 miles
- O  8 to 15 miles
- O  More than 15 miles

**29** How many miles is your business from the Club?
- O  0 to 3 miles
- O  4 to 7 miles
- O  8 to 15 miles
- O  More than 15 miles

**30** When did you first become a member of HB Country Club?
- O  1970 or before
- O  1971–1980
- O  1981–1985
- O  1986–1990
- O  1991–1994
- O  1995–present

**31** Do you have any children age 21 or younger living in your home?
- O  Yes
- O  No

**32** What other types of club do you belong to in the south of Edinburgh area? (Please mark all that apply.)

- ○ Another Golf/Country Club
- ○ Swim/Tennis Club
- ○ City/Dining Club
- ○ Fraternal Club
- ○ Fitness/Health Club
- ○ None

**33** How much of the year do you reside in the south of Edinburgh area?

- ○ Year round
- ○ 9 to 11 months
- ○ 6 to 8 months
- ○ Less than 6 months

### WRITTEN COMMENTS AND SUGGESTIONS

*Please provide any comments and suggestions you may have regarding the FUTURE DIRECTION OF THE CLUB.*

*If you could improve EXISTING OPERATIONS OR SERVICES at the Club, what would you improve?*

*What do you feel HB Country Club needs to do to ATTRACT MORE MEMBERS?*

The Board of Trustees thanks you for helping us in the evaluation of your Club. Please send the survey back to the Dixon Group in the enclosed envelope.

Very truly yours,

Dixon Group

*Note*: *this survey has been reformatted from its original design to fit the specification of this text. neither the questions nor the essence of the design has been modified.

*Exhibit C4.2* HBCC Country Club membership survey*.

## Questions

1 Build the management research question hierarchy through the investigative questions stage. Then compare your list with the measurement questions asked.

2 Given the research question, how appropriate were the measurement questions?

3 Describe the sampling strategy. How appropriate were the various sampling design decisions?

4 What, if any, problems did you find with the questionnaire as a whole? Consider structure, directions, question order, question phrasing, appropriateness of response strategy chosen, and so on.

5 If you were Dixon Group, how would you present the findings of your study to the HBCC board? Explain the rationale for your chosen method.

6 Given the data presented in the case:

    a What would you recommend to the board of HBCC with respect to adding facilities like tennis courts, a swimming pool, a spa, a fitness centre and a year-round driving range?

    b What would you recommend to the board of HBCC with regard to adding or changing programming activities like social activities for adults, families with children and children?

    c What would you recommend with regard to changing current operations?

*Source*: instrument and data are adapted from a case used with permission of Pamela S. Schindler and Donald R. Cooper, © 2000.

# Ramada demonstrates its personal best

In 1996, the latest D.K. Shifflet survey of customer satisfaction in the hospitality industry showed mid-tier hotels continuing their downward trend in perceived customer service, reflected by more and more respondents giving ratings on customer service in the 7 or lower range on Shifflet's 10-point scale. While Ramada's satisfaction rates held steady, 'It was only a matter of time before we experienced the problem,' says Tim Pigsley, director of operations for Ramada Franchise Systems (RFS). Shifflet research highlighted three critical areas for study that could influence customer satisfaction: hiring (finding the best people to deliver Ramada's brand of exceptional service), training (giving employees the tools to deliver exceptional service) and motivation (providing the impetus for Ramada employees to deliver exceptional service).

Unlike some of its competitors, RFS is a totally franchised system. In such an environment, not only must headquarters contend with the variable human factor of all service operations, but, additionally, RFS must contend with differing 'exceptional service' standards among owners of the 900 or so Ramada properties. 'Due to the franchised system of property management, we needed each management team and each employee to be committed to the change – to buy in to any new programme – whatever shape it would take,' explains Pigsley.

## Research

'We wanted to learn and borrow from the best, so we started with Disney. In every study done, the Disney experience is the benchmark for exceptional customer service. And it has a reputation for hiring the best people.' Next, RFS approached Southwest Airlines. 'They have captured the essence of "fun" when air travel is seen as a commodity, a hassle. People disembarking Southwest planes have smiles on their faces,' says Pigsley. Next Ramada's fact-finders approached Carlson Hospitality, owners of restaurant TGI Friday's. 'We wanted to understand what Carlson did to generate its low employee turnover and high employee loyalty and commitment.'

Ramada's individual property owners do their own hiring. The process differs widely from property to property. Ramada called on research firm Predictive Index to identify characteristics that were indicative of self-motivated performers.

RFS also wanted direct, face-to-face employee input into the process of developing new programmes in hiring, training and motivation. 'But this was a daunting prospect with more than 31,000 employees, many of whom spoke a language other than English,' explains Pigsley. Twenty-four researchers spanned out to visit each of Ramada's 900 properties within a six-month period. 'To bring about change in corporate culture and mindset would take more than employees checking off boxes on a piece of paper,' claims Pigsley. So Ramada launched the research project more as it would the opening of a new hotel – a festive atmosphere, complete with food and comedic entertainment. Headquarters staff arrived at each property, usually spending the morning extracting issues and information from management. Then in an atmosphere evocative of a new hotel launch, employees were invited to share their ideas and concerns about the three initiatives. Employee suggestions and needs flowed as freely as the food and drink. The information-collection team recorded employee and management input on a detailed summary form generated for each property.

Research with employees revealed that the current training approach was considered boring and ineffective. Most training involved videotapes, developed internally or purchased, with new employees or groups of employees watching the videos. RFS's benchmarking research with the hospitality industry's stellar examples of exceptional customer satisfaction, however, demonstrated that training incorporating high employee involvement generates more knowledgeable employees, one of the critical elements of customers' perceptions of higher-quality customer service. In addition, training approaches that involve 'fun' are winners with all employees – no matter what position they fill – and are more likely to generate a positive employee attitude, a second critical element of exceptional customer service.

It was standard industry practice for employee motivation programmes to develop around a limited number of big-ticket rewards. Employees indicated that they had a hard time maintaining enthusiasm for a programme that took too much effort to achieve one or a limited number of rewards over a long time. RFS found that more numerous awards that directly affect their everyday lives motivate employees.

Before Ramada started on its programme of change, it knew it would need to document the programme's success, so it hired Unifocus to conduct in-depth guest surveys at every property as the Personal Best programme rolled out. Additionally, it continues to subscribe to Shifflet's syndicated research on customer satisfaction.

## Management decisions

When hiring, Ramada property managers now screen prospective employees for characteristics revealed by Predictive Index. RFS scrapped its traditional training, replacing it with interactive, CD-based, multimedia training. Self-paced learning now drives the lighthearted, 24-component training sequence. Property managers, who often do not hire large numbers of employees at any one time, are pleased with the more flexible approach and employees find the process more interesting.

The newly devised motivation programme focuses on rewarding employees, not only for exceptional performance reflected in customer letters and surveys, but also for supervisor and peer nominations, completion of training modules and continued self-directed efforts for personal development by employees. 'We had had grandiose ideas of awarding big-ticket items like airline tickets to the vacation of a lifetime, but after listening to employees, we substituted certificates for shoes at FootLocker, lunch at Macaroni Grill and free tanks of petrol. We literally have hundreds of reward partners in the Personal Best programme,' reveals Pigsley, 'all related to the way our 31,000 employees spend their personal time.'

By many standards the Personal Best initiative is a success.

- In the latest Shifflet service ratings, Ramada's scores in the 8–10 range (good to exceptional) were up 30.5 per cent and its scores in the 1–4 range (unacceptable to poor) were down 24 per cent.

- Employees are cashing in exceptional service points for a growing number of rewards each year.

- Personal Best is no longer just a human resources programme, but an overall strategic planning initiative. Employees' stories of exceptional customer service are prominently reflected in Ramada's advertising and RFS has committed US$8 million (€6.5 million) over the past three years to sharing these stories.

'Ramada's Personal Best hospitality advertising campaign (winner of the travel industry's most prestigious advertising award: HSMAI's Best of Show) is a reflection of our commitment to the employee of Ramada franchises,' says Steve Belmonte, president and chief executive officer (CEO) of RFS, Inc. One spot's closing line, 'At Ramada, we throw ourselves into our work', sums up the effort that Ramada is putting into customer satisfaction – an effort that won it the 1999 American Express 'Best Practice' award.

## Questions

1 Build the management research question hierarchy for Ramada.
2 Apply the research process model to the Ramada research initiative.
  a Explain the role and process of exploration in Ramada's research.
  b What role did secondary data play in the exploration phase of the research?
  c What steps and phases in the process model can you match to the Ramada research?
  d What research process decisions were made? (Remember to include research by outside suppliers.)
  e What sampling methodology was used? Why was this appropriate for this study?
  f Describe the research design, and discuss its strengths and weaknesses.
  g What role did property owners/managers play in the research design?
  h Why did Ramada choose to conduct the research in a non-traditional, party-like atmosphere? What are some advantages and disadvantages of such an approach?
3 How are the research findings reflected in the ultimate management decisions?

*Source*: this case was developed from interviews with and material provided by Tim Pigsley, director of operations for Ramada Franchise Systems. Used with permission of Pamela S. Schindler and Donald R. Cooper, © 2001.

# Women getting Equal in public services

In 1996 Floor Martens, Claire Mulder, Jennifer van Dijk and 22 others filed an official complaint to the ombudsman of their employer, the Dutch municipality Dijkstad, against the municipality and a department head of the social service unit, Bas Verhoeven, citing a rash of incidents. These included 'intimidation, retaliation and humiliation', as well as lack of fairness in terms of pay, denial of promotion, demotion due to maternity leave, unfairness in distribution of accounts, sexual harassment and discharge without cause. Initially Verhoeven was discharged, but when the plaintiffs did not drop their suit, he was reinstated as a department head in the public service unit.

In May 1998, the ombudsman advised a settlement. Part of the settlement was that the municipality agreed to conduct an independent study of the issues underlying the complaint. The ombudsman ordered a research project to be carried out by 'Equal, or another similar firm', one that understood the issues under investigation. 'Equal is a non-profit research and advisory organization working to advance women in business,' says project director Paulette van de Laar. 'There are no other firms that do exactly what we do, so we were the clear choice.'

Equal was hired, and directed the subsequent research project designed to accomplish the following five goals.

1 To assess employees' perceptions of their work environment.
2 To examine why employees seek careers in the financial services industry, why they stay and why they might leave.
3 To examine the connection between perceptions of the work environment and job satisfaction, job commitment and employees' intention to stay with their firms.
4 To determine what barriers women face in advancing within their firms.
5 To assess how employees balance the demands of work and personal life.

'Our prior research with women's issues provided several tested measurement questions that were suitable for use in this study,' explains van de Laar. Equal also conducted nine focus groups – two all-men, six all-women and one mixed-gender group – to add insight into developing other measurement questions, and to clarify numerous concepts and constructs. At no time during the research did the municipality influence the process.

Equal mailed the survey to approximately 2200 potential respondents: men and women employed in the public service. A second mailing was sent to the whole sample frame to increase the participation rate. A total of 838 (38 per cent) members of the sample responded, 482 women (57.5 per cent) and 356 men (42.5 per cent).

'Our prior research led us to believe that a gender gap would exist between men and women on some fundamental issues. So men's opinions were sought to give the women's opinions a context,' says van de Laar.

To measure job satisfaction, Equal used a multiple-item evaluation including current position satisfaction, satisfaction with employer, work schedule control, career advancement opportunities, opportunities for networking and mentoring, and compensation fairness. Only on 'opportunities to network with influential clients' and 'compensation fairness' did men and women differ significantly ($p < 05$). Women's greater dissatisfaction with these two constructs did not, however, significantly affect their overwhelmingly positive satisfaction with their current position and their employer (77 per cent and 74 per cent, respectively).

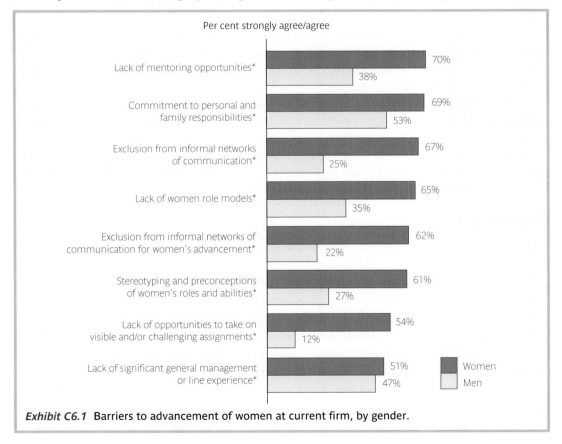

*Exhibit C6.1* **Barriers to advancement of women at current firm, by gender.**

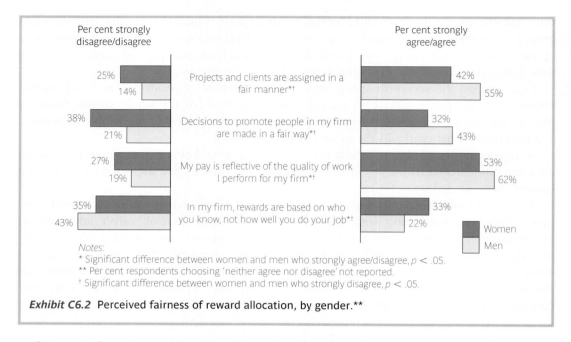

**Exhibit C6.2** Perceived fairness of reward allocation, by gender.**

'Because of our interest in advancing women in management, we were particularly interested in the factors that might lead a qualified woman to leave the profession,' says van de Laar. The executive summary of the findings noted that, 'Money appears to be a critical driver of intent to stay, both for men and women.'

To assess barriers to advancement, Equal used a multiple-item five-point scale exercise. As Exhibit C6.1 shows, women's perceptions were significantly different to men's for almost all these items.

As Exhibit C6.2 shows, on four elements used to assess fairness (assignment of clients, opportunities for promotion, pay for performance and rewards for performance), women again had significantly different perceptions compared to men ($p < .05$).

## Questions

1 Discuss the potential conflicts between researcher (Equal) and research user (Municipality Dijkstad).

2 What constructs and concepts are inherent in this study?

3 What are the ethical considerations in this study?

4 Speculate on how the researchers created operational definitions for the constructs.

5 Assume that the limited findings presented here are all the study covered. What would you recommend that Municipality Dijkstad include in a follow-up study?

6 Evaluate the data displays in Exhibits C6.1 and C6.2 as part of a research report. What recommendations, if any, would you make?

*Sources*: adapted from the case 'The catalyst for women in financial services' in Donald R. Cooper and Pamela S. Schindler, *Business Research Methods*, 8th edn., McGraw-Hill, 2003.

# Appendices

## Appendices contents

# Core business reference sources, printed and electronic

Printed reference sources are shown in italics, electronic sources in the regular font.

*101 Business Ratios: A Manager's Handbook of Definitions, Equations, and Computer Algorithms: How to Select, Compute, Present, and Understand Measures of Sales, Profit, Debt, Capital, Efficiency, Marketing, and Investment* (C. Sheldon Gates), McLane, 1993.
411 Stocks, http://www.411stocks.com/

**A**
ABI World, http://www.abiworld.org/
*Accountants' Handbook* (Carmichael, D.R., Steven B. Lilien and Martin Mellman, eds.), 6th edn., Wiley, 1996, 2 volumes.
*Accounting Desk Book: The Accountant's Everyday Instant Answer Book* (Tom Plank), 11th edn., Prentice-Hall, 2000.
*Accounting Handbook* (Joel G. Siegel and Jai K. Shim, eds.), 3rd edn., Barron's, 2000.
*Accounting Literature Index* (Jean Louise Heck *et al.*, eds.), 4th edn., McGraw-Hill, 1996.
*Accounting Research Directory: The Database of Accounting Literature*, 3rd edn., Wiener, 1994.
Accounting websites (compiled by the American Accounting Association) http://accounting.rutgers.edu/raw/aaa/links/accsites.htm
Ad*Access, http://scriptorium.lib.duke.edu/adaccess/
Advertising Age, http://www.adage.com/
Advertising Association, http://www.adassoc.org.uk

Advertising Research Foundation, http://www.arfsite.org/

Advertising Standards Authority, http://www.asa.org.uk

Advertising World (University of Texas), http://advertising.utexas.edu/world/

Advisory Conciliation and Arbitration Service, http://www.acas.org.uk

AFL-CIO, http://www.aflcio.org/

*Almanac of Business and Industrial Ratios*, Prentice-Hall, annual.

American Academy of Advertising, http://advertising.utexas.edu/aaa/

American Advertising Federation, http://www.aaf.org/

*American Almanac of Jobs and Salaries* (John W. Wright), 2000–2001 edn., Avon Books, 2000.

American Arbitration Association, http://www.adr.org/

American Association for Public Opinion Research, http://www.aapor.org/main.html

American Association of Individual Investors, http://www.aaii.com/

American Banker's Association, http://www.aba.com/default.htm

*American Banker's Banking Factbook*, American Banker, annual.

American Demographics, http://www.inside.com/default.asp?entity=AmericanDemo

American Enterprise Institute for Public Policy Research, http://www.aei.org/

American Finance Association, http://www.afajof.org/

American Institute of Certified Public Accountants, http://www.aicpa.org/

American League for Financial Institutions, http://www.alfi.org/

American Management Association, http://www.amanet.org/

American Marketing Association, http://www.marketingpower.com/

American Public Health Association, http://www.apha.org/

*American Salaries and Wages Survey: Statistical Data from More than 300 Government Business News Sources.* Gale, annual.

American Society for Public Administration, http://www.aspanet.org/

American Society for Training and Development, http://www.astd.org/

*American Statistics Index.* Congressional Information Service, monthly and annual.

American Stock Exchange, http://www.amex.com/

American Taxation Association, http://www.atasection.org/

Americans for Tax Reform, http://www.atr.org/

*Americans with Disabilities Act Handbook* (Henry H. Perritt, Jr.) 3rd edn., Wiley, 1997.

*AMEX Fact Book.* American Stock Exchange, annual.

AMEX Glossary, http://www.amex.com/reference/glossary.stm

Annual Report Gallery, A–Z link, http://www.reportgallery.com/

Annual Reports Online, http://www.zpub.com/sf/arl/arl_www.html

Association of Chartered Certified Accountants, http://accaglobal.com

Association of Consumer Research, http://www.acrweb.org/

AuditNet.org, http://www.auditnet.org/karlhome.htm

## B

Background Notes on Countries of the World, http://www.state.gov/www/background_notes/

Bank Administration Institute, http://www.bai.org/

Bank Marketing Association, http://www.aba.com/MarketingNetwork/default.htm

Barkley's Comprehensive Financial Glossary, http://www.oasismanagement.com/glossary/index.html

*Barron's Finance and Investment Handbook* (John Downes and Jordan Elliot Goodman, eds.) 5th edn., Barrons, 1998.

*Basic Business Library: Core Resources* (Bernard S. Schlessinger), 3rd edn., Oryx, 1995.

BBC world, country profiles (overview, facts, leaders, media), http://news.bbc.co.uk/2/hi/country_profiles/default.stm

*Biographical Dictionary of Management* (Morgan Nitzel, ed.), University of Chicago Press, 2001, 2 volumes.

*Blackwell Encyclopedia of Management* (Gary L. Cooper and Chris Argyris, eds.), Blackwell Business, 1997, 11 volumes.

Bloomberg.com, http://www.bloomberg.com/

*BNA's Human Resources Library.* Bureau of National Affairs, update varies with format.

*Book of the States.* Council of State Governments, annual.

*Brands and their Companies.* Gale, annual, 2 volumes.

British Household Panel Survey (BHPS), data deposited in UK archive, http://www.iser.essex.ac.uk/bhps

British Social Attitude Survey (BSA), data deposited in UK archive, http://www.natcen.ac.uk

Business Advisor, http://www.business.gov/busadv/index.cfm

*Business and Company Resource Center.* Gale Group, updated daily.

*Business Information Handbook* (D. Mort), Headland Press, 2000.

*Business Information: How to Find It, How to Use It* (Michael R. Lavin), 3rd edn., Oryx, 2001.

*Business Periodicals Database.* H.W. Wilson, updating varies with version.

*Business Plans Handbook: A Compilation of Actual Business Plans Developed by Small Businesses Throughout North America* (Erin Hoss, ed.), Gale, annual.

*Business Source.* EBSCOHost, updated daily.

*Business Statistics of the United States.* 7th edn., Bernan, 2002.

Business Zone, a library of research findings, http://www.businesszone.co.uk

## C

*Cabell's Directory of Publishing Opportunities in Accounting, Economics, and Finance*, 7th edn., Cabell, 1997 2 volumes.

*CCH Internet Tax Research Network*, http://tax.cch.com/ipnetwork

Census UK, www.census.ac.uk

Certified Financial Planner Board of Standards, http://www.cfp_board.org/

Chartered Institute of Management Accountants, http://www.cima.org.uk

Chartered Institute of Marketing (CMI), http://www.cim.co.uk

Chartered Institute of Personnel and Development, http://www.cipd.co.uk

Chicago Mercantile Exchange, http://www.cme.com/

CIA, world fact book, http://www.cia.gov/cia/publications/factbook

*CIFAR's Global Company Handbook.* Center for International Financial Analysis & Research, annual.

Citizens for a Sound Economy, http://www.cse.org/n_index.php

CNNfn (the financial network), http://www.cnnfn.com/

*Codification of Statements on Auditing Standards*, numbers 1 to 87. AICPA, 1999.

*Commercial Atlas and Marketing Guide.* Rand McNally, annual.

*Companies and their Brand Names.* Gale, annual, 2 volumes.

CompaniesOnline, http://www.companiesonline.com/

*Complete Guide to Human Resources and the Law* (Dana Shilling), Prentice Hall, 1998.

Confederation of British Industry (CBI), http://www.cbi.org.uk

Conference Board, http://www.conference_board.org/

Consumer Connection, http://www.aba.com/consumer+connection/default.htm

*Consumer Expenditure Survey.* US Bureau of Labor Statistics, annual, http://www.bls.gov/cex/

Corporate Information, http://www.corporateinformation.com/

Council of State Governments, http://www.statesnews.org/

Country Commercial Guides, http://www.state.gov/www/about_state/business/

CRB Commodity Year Book. Commodity Research Bureau, annual.

## D

*D&B Million Dollar Directory: America's Leading Public and Private Companies*, Dun & Bradstreet, annual, 5 volumes.

*Daily Stock Price Record: American Stock Exchange.* Standard & Poor's, quarterly.

*Daily Stock Price Record: NASDAQ.* Standard & Poor's, quarterly.

*Daily Stock Price Record: New York Stock Exchange.* Standard & Poor's, quarterly.

*Data Sources for Business and Market Analysis* (John V. Ganly), 4th edn., Scarecrow, 1994.

*Dictionary of Accounting Terms* (Joel G. Siegel and Jae K. Shim), 3rd edn., Barron's, 2000.

*Dictionary of Business and Management* (Jerry M. Rosenberg), 3rd edn., Wiley, 1993.

*Dictionary of Conflict Resolution* (Douglas H. Yarn, comp.), Jossey-Bass, 1999.

*Dictionary of International Business Terms* (John J. Capela and Stephen W. Hartman), Barron's Educational Series, 1996.

*Dictionary of Marketing and Advertising* (Jerry M. Rosenberg), Wiley, 1995.

*Dictionary of Marketing Terms* (Peter D. Bennett, ed.), 2nd edn., NTC Business Books, 1995.

Direct Marketing Association, http://www.the_dma.org/

*Direction of Trade Statistics Yearbook.* International Monetary Fund, annual.

*Directory of American Firms Operating in Foreign Countries.* Uniworld Business Publications, annual, 3 volumes.

*Directory of Corporate Affiliations.* National Register, annual, 5 volumes.

*Directory of Foreign Firms Operating in the United States*, 9th edn., Uniworld Business Publications, 1998.

*Directory of Marketing Information Companies Featuring the Best 100.* American Demographics, annual.

*Directory of Mutual Funds, Closed-end Funds, Unit Investment Trust Sponsors.* Investment Company Institute, annual.

*Dow Jones Averages,* 1885–1995 (Phyllis Pierce, ed.), Irwin Professional Pubs, 1996.

*Dun & Bradstreet/Gale Industry Reference Handbooks.* Gale, 1998.

*Dun & Bradstreet's Guide to Doing Business Around the World* (Terri Morrison *et al.*), Prentice Hall, 2001.

# E

*E-Commerce: The Complete Reference Guide* (Arthur H. Bell), Greenwood/Oryx, 2001.

Ecommerce-guide.com, http://ecommerce.internet.com

*Economic Indicators Handbook*, 6th edn., Gale, 2002.

*Economic Report of the President.* Office of the President of the USA, annual.

EDGAR Database of Corporate Information, http://www.sec.gov/edgarhp.htm

*EEOC Compliance Manual.* Bureau of National Affairs, looseleaf.

Election resources, Europe, http://electionresources.org/eurpe.html

*Elsevier's Dictionary of Financial Terms in English, German, Spanish, French, Italian, and Dutch* (Diana Phillips and Marie-Claude Bignaud, comp.), 2nd edn., rev. and enlarged, Elsevier, 1997.

*Elsevier's Banking Dictionary in Seven Languages* (Julio Ricci), 3rd edn., Elsevier, 1990.

*Employee Benefit Plans: A Glossary of Terms* (Mary Jo Brzezinski, ed.), 8th edn., International Foundation of Employee Benefit Plans, 1993.

Employee Benefits Research Institute, http://www.ebri.org/

Employment Survey (Great Britain), census of employment annual, www.statistics.gov.uk

*Encyclopedia of American Industries* (Scott Heil and Terrance W. Peck, eds.), 3rd edn., Gale, 2001, 2 volumes.

*Encyclopedia of Banking and Finance* (Glenn G. Munn and Charles J. Woelfel), 9th edn., St James Press, 1991.

*Encyclopedia of Business Information Sources*, 16th edn., Gale, 2000.

*Encyclopedia of Business* (Jane A. Malonis, ed.), 2nd edn., Gale, 2000, 2 volumes.

*Encyclopedia of Consumer Brands* (Janice Jorgensen, ed.), St James Press, 1994, 3 volumes.

*Encyclopedia of Emerging Industries*, 4th edn., Gale, 2001.

*Encyclopedia of Housing* (William van Vleit, ed.), Sage, 1998.

*Encyclopedia of Major Marketing Campaigns.* Gale, 2000.

*Encyclopedia of Management* (Marilyn M. Helms, ed.), 4th edn., Gale, 1999.

*Encyclopedia of Taxation and Tax Policy* (Joseph J. Cordes, Robert D. Ebel and Jane G. Gravelles, eds.), Urban Institute Press, 1999.

Entreworld: Resources for Entrepreneurs, http://www.entreworld.org/

*Eurojargon: A Dictionary of European Union Acronyms, Abbreviations, and Sobriquets* (Anne Ramsay, ed.), 6th edn., Dearborn, 2000.

Europe, Information on the European Union, http://www.europa.eu.int/

*Europa World Year Book.* Europa Publications, annual.

European Cities, network of 100 major cities in Europe, http://www.eurocities.org/frontend/front.html

European Industrial Relations Observatory Online (EIRONLINE), http://www.eiro.eurofound.ie

European Observatory on Heath Care Systems, http://www.euro.who/observatory.toppage

European Social Survey, http://www.europeansocialsurvey.org/

*EUROSTAT*, Statistical Office of the European Communities, http://europa.eu.int/comm/eurostat/Public/print-catalogue/EN?catalogue=Eurostat

Eurybase, database on educational systems in Europe, http://www.eurydice.org/Eurybase/frameset_eurybase.htm

*Exporters' Encyclopedia.* Dun & Bradstreet, annual.

## F

*F&S Index: United States.* Information Access Co., monthly and quarterly with annual cumulation online.

Fed in Print, http://www.frbsf.org/publications/fedinprint/index.html

Federal Register, http://www.access.gpo.gov/su_docs/aces/aces140.html

*Federal Tax Handbook.* Research Institute of America, annual.

Federation of Tax Administrators, http://www.taxadmin.org/

FedStats, http://www.fedstats.gov/

*Finance Literature Index* (Jean Louise Heck, ed.), 3rd edn., McGraw-Hill, 1992.

Financial Accounting Standards Board, http://www.rutgers.edu/Accounting/raw/fasb

*Financial Accounting Standards Board. Current Text, Accounting Standards as of June 1, 2002.* FASB, annual.

*Financial Accounting Standards Board. Original Pronouncements. Accounting Standards as of June 1, 2002.* Wiley, annual.

*Financial History of the United States* (Jerry W. Markham, ed.), Sharpe, 2002, 3 volumes.

*Financial Planning Association*, http://www.fpanet.org/

FINWeb, http://www.finweb.com/

*FIS/online.* Mergent FIS, updated weekly.

*Forbes* 200 Best Small Companies in America, http://www.forbes.com/200best/

*Fortune* 500, http://www.pathfinder.com/fortune/fortune500/

France, National Institute of Statistics, http://www.insee.fr

Free Management Library, http://www.mapnp.org/library

FT info, company information provided by the *Financial Times*, http://www.news.ft.com

FT interactive data, global security data, etc., provided by the *Financial Times*, http://www.ftinteractivedata.com

## G

*Geographic Reference Report.* ERI Economic Research Institute, annual.

Germany, Federal Statistics Office, http://www.destatis.de

Global Edge (MSU-CIBER International Business Resources on the WWW), http://globaledge.msu.edu/ibrd/ibrd.asp

Glossaries of Financial Terms (from the Federal Reserve Bank of Chicago), http://www.chicagofed.org/publications/glossary/index.cfm

Government Accounting Standards Board, http://raw.rutgers.edu/raw/gasb/welcome.htm

GPO Access, http://www.access.gpo.gov/su_docs/

Green Box Resources, http://www.indiana.edu/~libgpd/guides/green/home.html

*Guide to Country Information in International Governmental Organization Publications.* American Library Association, Government Documents Round Table, 1996.

Guide to Labor-oriented Internet Resources, http://www.lib.berkeley.edu/IIRL/iirlnet.html

*Guide to Libraries and Information Units in Government Departments and Other Organisations* (P. Dale), London: British Library, 1998.

*Guide to Official Statistics* (A. Corris, B. Yin and C. Ricketts), London: Stationery Books, 2000.

*Guide to Reference Books* (Robert Balay, ed.), 11th edn., American Library Assn, 1996.

## H

*Handbook of Common Stocks*. Mergent FIS, quarterly.

*Handbook of Interest and Annuity Tables* (Jack C. Estes), McGraw-Hill, 1976.

*Handbook of Loan Payment Tables* (Jack C. Estes), McGraw-Hill, 1976.

*Handbook of Mortgage-backed Securities* (Frank J. Fabozzi, ed.), 5th edn., McGraw-Hill, 2001.

*Handbook of NASDAQ Stocks*. Mergent FIS, quarterly.

*Handbook of Public Relations* (Robert L. Heath and Gabriel Vasquez, eds.), Sage, 2001.

*Handbook of State Government Administration* (John Gargan), Dekker, 2000.

*Handbook of Strategic Public Relations and Integrated Communications* (Clarke L. Caywood, ed.), McGraw-Hill, 1997.

*Handbook of US Labor Statistics: Employment, Earnings, Prices, Productivity, and Other Labor Data* (Eva E. Jacobs, ed.), 5th edn., Bernan, 2001.

*History of Accounting: An International Encyclopedia* (Michael Chatfield and Richard Vangermeersch, eds.), Garland, 1996.

*Hoover's Handbook of World Business*. Reference Press, annual.

Hoover's Online, http://www.hoovers.com/

*Household Spending: Who Spends How Much on What*, 4th edn., New Strategist Publications, 1997.

*Human Development Reports*, Report and Statistics 2004 (including country files), http://hdr.undp.org./statistics/

## I

IBE (International Bureau of Education), world data on education, www.ibe.unesco.org/International/Databanks/dba.htm

Inc. 500 Fastest Growing Companies in America, http://www.inc.com/500/home.html

Independent Community Bankers Association of America, http://www.ibaa.org/

*Index to Accounting and Auditing Technical Pronouncements as of July 1, 1994*. AICPA, annual.

*Index to Current Urban Documents*. Greenwood Press, monthly.

Industrial Relations Research Association, http://www.irra.uiuc.edu/

Industrial Society, http://www.indsoc.co.uk

InfoNation, http://www.un.org/Pubs/CyberSchoolBus/infonation/e_infonation.htm

Institute of Directors, http://www.iod.com

Institute of Financial Services, http://www.cib.org.uk

Institute of Management, http://www.inst-mgt.org.uk

Institute of Practitioners in Advertising (IPA), http://www.ipa.co.uk

*International Accounting and Auditing Standards as of October 1, 2001*. AICPA, annual.

International Accounting Standards Committee, http://www.iasc.org.uk/

*International Business Information: How to Find It, How to Use It* (Ruth A. Pagell and Michael Halperin), 2nd edn., Oryx, 1998.

International City/County Management Association, http://www.icma.org/

*International Directory of Company Histories* (Thomas Derdak, ed.), St James Press, 1988.

International Directory of Finance and Economics Professionals, http://welch.som.yale.edu/dir/

International Economics, http://www.mnsfld.edu/depts/lib/globecon.html

*International Encyclopedia of Business and Management*, 2nd edn., Thompson Learning, 2001.

*International Encyclopedia of Public Policy and Administration* (Jay M. Shafritz, ed.), Westview, 1998, 4 volumes.

*International Financial Statistics Yearbook.* International Monetary Fund, annual.

*International Guide to Accounting Journals* (J. David Spiceland and Surendra P. Agrawal, eds.), 2nd edn., Wiener, 1993.

International Labour Organization, http://www.ilo.org/

*International Marketing Data and Statistics.* Euromonitor, 2001.

*International Monetary Fund,* http://www.imf.org/

International Monetary Fund Competiveness Yearbook 2004, http://www01.imd.ch/wcy

International Reform Monitor on social, labour market and industrial relations policies, http://www.reformmonitor.org

International Telecommunication Union (ITU), http://www.itu.int/ITU-D/ict/statistics

*International Trade Statistics Yearbook.* United Nations, annual, 2 volumes.

Internet Public Library Business Associations, http://www.ipl.org/cgi_bin/ref/aon.out.pl?id=bus0000

Internet Resources for International Economics & Business, http://www.ship.edu/~business/

Investment Company Institute ('the mutual fund connection'), http://www.ici.org/

Ireland, Central Statistical Office (CSO) of Ireland, http://www.cso.ie

IRS Bulletin, http://www.irs.ustreas.gov/prod/bus_info/bullet.html

IRS Tax Terms, http://www.irs.ustreas.gov/prod/taxi/taxterms.html

*Irwin Investor's Handbook.* Irwin Professional Publications, annual.


**K**

Kipplinger's Global Investor, http://www.global_investor.com/

Knowledge@Wharton, http://knowledge.wharton.upenn.edu/


**L**

*Labor Arbitration Reports and Dispute Settlements.* Bureau of National Affairs, looseleaf.

*Labor Conflict in the United States: An Encyclopedia* (Ronald L. Filippelli, ed.), Garland, 1990.

Labor Research Association, http://www.lra_ny.com/

*Lexis-Nexis Academic Universe.* Lexis-Nexis, updated daily, http://web.lexis-nexis.com/universe/

*Libraries in the United Kingdom and Republic of Ireland.* Library Association, London: Library Association, 1997.

London Stock Exchange, http://www.londonstockexchange.com


**M**

*Major US Statistical Series* (Jean Stratford), American Library Association, 1992.

Mark Bernkopf's Central Banking Resource Center, http://www.patriot.net/users/bernkopf

*Market Share Reporter, an Annual Compilation of Reported Market Share: Data on Companies, Products, and Services.* Gale, annual.

*Marketing Information: A Professional Reference Guide* (Hiram C. Barksdale and Jac L. Goldstucker, eds.) 3rd edn. Georgia State University Business Press, 1995.

Marketing Research Association, http://www.mra_net.org/

Marketing Virtual Library (Knowthis.com), http://www.knowthis.com/

*Marketing: The Encyclopedic Dictionary* (David Mercer, ed.), Blackwell Business, 1999.

*Mergent Bond Record.* Financial Information Services, monthly and annual.

*Mergent Dividend Record.* Mergent FIS, weekly and annual.

*Mergent Unit Investment Trusts.* Mergent FIS, annual.

*Miller GAAP Guide: Restatement and Analysis of Current FASB Standards* (Jan R. Williams), CCH, annual.

MIMAS, UK data centre for higher education (e-journals and UK census), http://www.mimas.ac.uk

Money – Past, Present & Future – http://www.ex.ac.uk/~RDavies/arian/money.html

*Monthly Labor Review.* US Bureau of Labor Statistics, monthly.

*Moody's Handbook of Dividend Achievers.* Mergent FIS, annual.

Mortgage Bankers Association of America, http://www.mbaa.org/

MSU-CIBER International Business Resources on the WWW, http://globaledge.msu.edu/ibrd/ibrd.asp

*Multilingual Dictionary of Local Government and Business* (Clive Leo McNeir), Cassell, 1993. See also multilingual and bilingual dictionaries listed in the library's online catalogue.

*Municipal Year Book.* International City/County Management Association, annual.

*Mutual Fund Encyclopedia* (Gerald W. Perritt), 1993–1994 edn., Dearborn Financial Publishing, 1993.

Mutual Fund Fact Book, http://www.ici.org/facts_figures/factbook_toc.html

**N**

Nasdaq Stock Exchange, http://www.nasdaq.com

National Assembly of State Arts Agencies, http://www.nasaa_arts.org/

National Association of Counties, http://www.naco.org/

National Association of Credit Management, http://www.nacm.org/

National Association of Purchasing Management, http://www.icma.org/

National Association of Securities Dealers, http://www.nasd.com/

National Association of State Information Resource Executives, http://www.nasire.org/

National Association of Tax Practitioners, http://www.natptax.com/

National Center for State Courts, http://www.statesnews.org/

National Conference of State Legislatures, http://www.ncsl.org/

National Governors' Association, http://www.nga.org/

*National Labor Relations Board Decisions and Orders.* NLRB, irregular.

National League of Cities, http://www.nlc.org/

National Tax Association, http://ntanet.org

National Taxpayers Union, http://www.ntu.org/

*Nelson's Directory of Investment Research: The Financial Professional's Guide to the Research Marketplace.* Nelson Publications, annual.

Netherlands, Site of Statistics Netherlands with free downloads of statistical data, http://www.cbs.nl

*New Palgrave Dictionary of Economics and the Law* (Peter Newman, ed.), Macmillan, 1998, 3 volumes.

*New Palgrave Dictionary of Money and Finance* (Peter Newman, Murray Milgate and John Eatwell, eds.), Stockton, 1992, 3 volumes.

New York Stock Exchange, http://www.nyse.com/

*New York Stock Exchange Fact Book.* New York Stock Exchange, annual.

New York Stock Exchange Glossary of Financial Terms, http://www.nyse.com/

*North American Industry Classification System (NAICS).* US Office of Management and Budget, 1997.

Norway, Site of Statistics Norway, http://www.ssb.no

*NTC's Dictionary of Advertising* (Jack G. Wiechmann, ed.), 2nd edn., National Textbook Co., 1992.

## O

Occupational Employment Statistics. US Bureau of Labor Statistics website, http://stats.bls.gov/oes/

*Occupational Outlook Handbook.* US Bureau of Labor Statistics, annual.

OECD (Organization for Economic Co-operation and Development), http://www.oecd.org

OTC Bulletin Board, http://www.otcbb.com/dynamic/

*Other Markets Online* (from NASDAQ), http://dynamic.international.nasdaq.com/asp/globalmar-kets.asp?lang-eng

Overseas Private Investment Corp., http://www.opic.gov/

## P

Pacific Exchange, http://www.pacificex.com/

*PAIS International.* OCLC Public Affairs Information Service, updates vary with subscription.

*Portable MBA Desk Reference: An Essential Business Companion* (Paul A. Argenti), Wiley, 1994.

*Principal International Businesses: The World Marketing Directory.* Dun & Bradstreet, annual.

Public Record Office (UK), http://www.pro.gov.uk

Public Relations Society of America, http://www.prsa.org/

## Q

*Quarterly Financial Report for Manufacturing, Mining, and Trade Corporations.* US Department of Commerce, quarterly.

## R

*Rand McNally Commercial Atlas and Marketing Guide.* Rand McNally, annual.

*Reference Book of Corporate Managements.* Dun & Bradstreet, annual.

*Research on the Net* (K. McGuinness and T. Short), London: Old Bailey Press, 1998.

RIA OnPoint Federal Tax Service (available through Lexis-Nexis).

*RMA Annual Statement Studies, Including Comparative Historical Data and Other Sources of Composite Financial Data.* Robert Morris Associates, annual.

Robert Morris Associates, the Association of Lending and Credit Risk Professionals, http://www.rmahq.org/

*Roberts' Dictionary of Industrial Relations* (Harold S. Roberts), 4th edn., Bureau of National Affairs, 1994.

Rutgers Accounting Web, http://accounting.rutgers.edu/raw/

Rutgers University Libraries: Research and Reference Gateway: Business,

http://www.libraries.rutgers.edu/rul/rr_gateway/research_guides/busi/business.shtml

## S

*S&P Advantage.* Standard & Poor's, updated daily.

Sales and Marketing Management, http://www.salesandmarketing.com/

Scout Report, http://scout.cs.wisc.edu/

Securities Industry Association, http://www.sia.com/

*Sexual Harassment on the Job: What It Is and How to Stop It* (William Petrocelli and Barbara Kate Repa) 4th edn., Nolo Press, 1999.

SOSIG, Gateway to social science sites with statistical data, http://www.sosig.ac.uk

*Sources of Unofficial Statistics* (D. Mort and W. Wilkins), Aldershot: Gower, 2000.

Spireproject, overview on country profiles, http://spireproject.com/country.htm

*Standard & Poor's Bond Guide.* Standard & Poor's, monthly.

*Standard & Poor's Corporate Descriptions.* Standard & Poor's, semi-monthly, 6 volumes.

*Standard & Poor's CreditWeek.* Standard & Poor's, weekly.

*Standard & Poor's Dividend Record.* Standard & Poor's, quarterly.

*Standard & Poor's Industry Surveys.* Standard & Poor's, quarterly.

*Standard & Poor's Outlook.* Standard & Poor's, weekly.

*Standard & Poor's Register of Corporations, Directors, and Executives.* Standard & Poor's, annual.

*Standard Directory of Advertisers.* National Register, annual.

*Standard Industrial Classification (SIC) Manual.* US Office of Management and Budget, 1987.

STAT-USA/Internet, http://www.stat_usa.gov/

*Statesman's Year-book: The Essential Political and Economic Guide to All the Countries of the World.* St. Martin's Press, annual.

*Statistical Abstract of the United States.* US Bureau of the Census, annual.

*Statistical Abstract of the World* (Marlita A. Reddy, ed.), Gale, 1996.

*Still More Words of Wall Street* (Allan H. Pessin and Joseph A. Ross), Dow Jones-Irwin, 1990.

SuperPages.com, the *Yellow Pages* on the Web, http://www.bigyellow.com/

*Survey of Current Business.* US Bureau of Economic Analysis, monthly.

**T**

Tax Analysts: Tax Information Worldwide Online, http://www.tax.org/default.htm

Tax and Accounting Sites Directory, http://www.taxsites.com/

Tax Executives Institute, http://www.tei.org/

Tax Foundation, http://www.taxfoundation.org/

Taxpayer Information Publications, http://www.irs.ustreas.gov/prod/forms_pubs/pubs/index.htm

*The 100 Best Stocks to Own in the World* (Gene Walden), 4th edn., Dearborn Financial.

*The Ad Men and Women: A Biographical Dictionary of Advertising* (Edd Applegate, ed.), Greenwood, 1994.

*The International Business Dictionary and Reference* (Lewis A. Presner), Wiley, 1991.

*The New Illustrated Book of Development Definitions* (Harvey S. Moskowitz and Carl G. Lindbloom), Center for Urban Policy Research, 1993.

Thomas Register of American Manufacturers, http://www.thomasregister.com/index.html

Thomas: Legislative Information on the Internet, http://thomas.loc.gov/

*Thomson/Polk Bank Directory.* Thomson, semi-annual.

Trades Union Congress (TUC), http://www.tuc.org.uk

Transparency International, expertise on combating corruption, http://www.transparency.com

**U**

UK data archive, links to data archives worldwide, http://data-archive.ac.uk

UK Department of Trade and Industry, http://www.dti.gov.uk

UK Equities direct, guide to companies and trusts, http://www.hemscott.net

UK online, government information service, http://www.ukonline.gov.uk

UK Statistics, site of UK statistics, http://www.statistics.gov.uk

*Understanding American Business Jargon: A Dictionary* (W. Davis Folsom), Greenwood, 1997.

*Understanding the Census: A Guide for Marketers, Planners, Grant Writers, and Other Data Users* (Michael R. Lavin), library edn., Epoch Books, 1996.

UNESCO, statistics, http://www.uis.unsesco.org/en/stats/stats0.htm

*UN/ECE*, The Statistical Yearbook of the Economic Commission for Europe 2003: country profiles, http://www.unece.org/stats/trend/trend_h.htm

*Union Labor Report.* Bureau of National Affairs, looseleaf.

United Nations, official site, http://www.un.org

University of Michigan Documents Center, http://www.lib.umich.edu/govdocs/index.html

US Bureau of the Census, http://www.census.gov/

US Bureau of Labor Statistics, http://www.bls.gov/blshome.html

US Chamber of Commerce, http://www.uschamber.org/

US Conference of Mayors, http://www.usmayors.org/uscm/

US Congress House Banking and Financial Services Committee, http://www.house.gov/banking/

US Congress Joint Committee on Taxation, http://www.house.gov/jct/

US Congress Senate Banking, Housing, and Urban Affairs Committee, http://www.senate.gov/banking/

US Customs Service, http://www.customs.ustreas.gov/

US Department of Commerce, http://www.doc.gov/

US Department of Commerce, Office of Trade and Economic Analysis, http://www.ita.doc.gov/tradestats/

US Department of Labor, http://www.dol.gov/

US Department of the Treasury (includes the US Comptroller of the Currency), http://www.ustreas.gov/

US Employment and Training Administration, http://www.doleta.gov/

US Equal Employment Opportunity Commission, http://www.eeoc.gov/

US Federal Deposit Insurance Corp., http://www.fdic.gov/

US Federal Reserve System, http://www.federalreserve.gov/

US Internal Revenue Service, http://www.irs.gov/; http://www.irs.ustreas.gov/

US International Information Program, http://usinfo.state.gov/homepage.htm

US International Trade Administration, http://www.ita.doc.gov/

US International Trade Commission, http://www.usitc.gov/

US Justice Department, Tax Division, http://www.usdoj.gov/tax/

*US Master Tax Guide.* CCH, annual.

US National Credit Union Administration, http://www.ncua.gov/

US National Labor Relations Board, http://www.nlrb.gov/

US Securities and Exchange Commission, http://www.sec.gov/

US Small Business Administration, http://www.sbaonline.sba.gov/

US State & Local Gateway, http://www.statelocal.gov/

US Tax Court, http://www.ustaxcourt.gov/

US Trade Representative, http://www.ustr.gov/

US Treasury OTS Glossary of Thrift Terms, http://www.ots.treas.gov/glossary.html

## V

*Value Line Investment Survey.* Value Line, weekly, http://www.valueline.com/

Virtual International Business and Economics Sources (VIBES), http://libweb.uncc.edu/ref_bus/vibehome.htm

## W

*Wall Street Journal Index.* Dow Jones, monthly, http://public.wsj.com/home.html

*Wall Street Words: An Essential A to Z Guide for Today's Investor* (David L. Scott), rev. edn., Houghton Mifflin, 1997.

*Washington Post* Business Glossary, http://www.washingtonpost.com/wpdyn/business/specials/glossary/index.html

WorkIndex, http://workindex.com/

*World Directory of Marketing Information Sources*, 3rd edn., Euromonitor, 2001.

World Economic Forum, http://www.weforum.org

World Fact Book, http://www.odci.gov/cia/publications/factbook/index.html

World Health Organization (WHO), http://www.who.int

*World Market Share Reporter: A Compilation of Reported World Market Share Data and Rankings on Companies, Products, and Services* (Marlita A. Reddy and Robert S. Lazich), Gale, annual.

World Trade Organization, http://www.wto.org/; http://www.wto.org/ABI/Inform (Proquest Information and Learning, updated daily).

# Decision theory problem

The value of research information can be assessed by several means, one of which is decision theory. The example considered here concerns the case of a manager who is deciding on a change in production equipment. Research information will play a major role in this decision. The new equipment can be leased for five years and will replace several old machines that require constant attention in order to operate. The problem facing the manager is, 'Shall I lease the new machines with the attendant efficiencies, reduced labour and higher lease charges or shall I continue to use the old equipment?'

The decision situation has been prompted by news that the firm might secure several large orders from companies that have not previously been customers. With added volume, departmental profit contributions will increase substantially with the new equipment. For this decision, the manager adopts the decision variable 'average annual departmental profit contribution.'[1] The decision rule is, 'Choose that course of action that will provide the highest average annual contribution to departmental profits.'

Exhibit B.1 indicates the results of the evaluation of the two available actions. Under the conditions cited, it is obvious that course $A_1$ is preferred.

| Course of action | Average annual departmental profit contribution |
|---|---|
| $A_1$ – Lease new equipment | €20,000 |
| $A_2$ – Retain old equipment | €12,000 |

*Exhibit B.1* Payoff under conditions of certainty.

## Conditions of certainty

Exhibit B.1 presents the case with the assumption that the anticipated new business will materialize. It therefore represents, in decision theory terminology, *decision-making under conditions of certainty*. It is assumed that the payoffs are certain to occur if the particular action is chosen and the probability of the additional business being secured is 1.0.[2] The decision to choose action $A_1$ is obvious under these conditions with the given payoff data and decision rule.

## Conditions of uncertainty

In a more realistic situation, the outcome is less than certain. The new business may not materialize, and then the department might be left with costly excess capacity. The union may resist introduction of the new equipment because it replaces workers. The new equipment may not perform as anticipated. For these or other reasons, the decision-maker may be uncertain about the consequences (for instance that course $A_1$ will result in a €20,000 contribution).

Suppose the manager considers these other possible outcomes and concludes that the one serious uncertainty is that the new business may not be forthcoming. For purposes of simplicity, one of two conditions will exist in the future – either the new business will be secured as expected ($O_1$) or the new business will not materialize ($O_2$). In the first case, the expected payoffs would be the same as shown in Exhibit B.1; but if the new business is not secured, then the addition of the new equipment would give the department costly excess capacity, with fixed lease charges. The payoff table may now be revised as shown in Exhibit B.2.

Under these conditions, the original decision rule does not apply. That rule said, 'Choose that course of action that will provide the highest average annual contribution to departmental profits.' Under the conditions in Exhibit B.2, action $A_1$ would be better if the new business were secured, but $A_2$ would be the better choice if the new business were not secured. If the decision can be delayed until the new order question is resolved, the dilemma is escapable. However, because of lead times, the equipment decision may need to be made first.

When faced with two or more possible outcomes for each alternative, the manager can adopt one of two approaches. First, the likelihood that the company will receive the new business cannot be judged. Even so, a rational decision can be made by adopting an appropriate

| Course of action | Average annual departmental profit contribution | | |
| --- | --- | --- | --- |
| | New business ($O_1$) | No new business ($O_2$) | Expected monetary value |
| $A_1$ – Lease new equipment | €20,000 | €5000 | €14,000 |
| $A_2$ – Retain old equipment | €12,000 | €9000 | €10,800 |

*Exhibit B.2* Payoff under conditions of uncertainty.

decision rule – for example, 'Choose that course of action for which the minimum payoff is the highest.' This is known as the *maximum criterion* because it calls for maximizing the minimum payoff. In Exhibit B.2, the minimum payoff for alternative $A_1$ is shown as €5000, and the minimum payoff for $A_2$ is €9000. According to the *maximum rule*, the choice would be $A_2$ because it is the best of the worst outcomes. This decision is a 'cut your losses' strategy.

The second approach is to use subjective judgement to estimate the probability that either $O_1$ or $O_2$ will occur.[3] When the assumption was decision under certainty, only one event was possible (had a probability of 1.0). Now, however, with experience and information from other sources, there is a less-than-certain chance of the new business materializing, and this doubt should be part of the decision.

One might estimate that there is a 0.6 chance that the new business will be secured and a 0.4 chance that it will not. With this or any other set of similar probabilities, an overall evaluation of the two courses of action is possible. One approach is to calculate an *expected monetary value (EMV)* for each alternative.[4]

## The decision flow diagram

The decision problem already has been summarized in a payoff table, but further illustration in the form of a decision flow diagram (or decision tree) may be helpful. The decision tree for the equipment problem is shown in Exhibit B.3. The diagram may be seen as a sequential decision flow. At the square node on the left, the manager must choose between $A_1$ and $A_2$. After one of these actions, a chance event will occur – either the new business will be received by the company ($O_1$), or it will not be received ($O_2$). At the right extremity of the branches are listed the conditional payoffs that will occur for each combination of decision and chance event. On each 'chance branch' is placed the expected probability of that chance event occurring. Bear in mind that these are subjective probability estimates by the manager that express a degree of belief that such a chance event will occur.

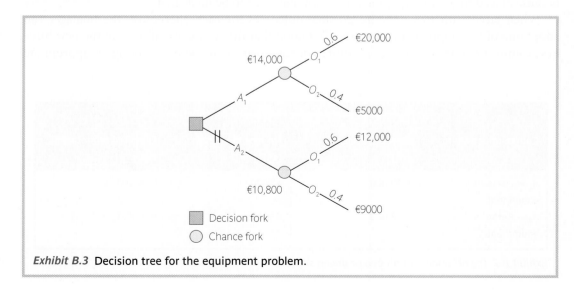

Exhibit B.3 Decision tree for the equipment problem.

Having set up this series of relationships, one calculates back from right to left on the diagram by an *averaging out and folding back* process. At each decision juncture, the path that yields the best alternative for the decision rule is selected. Here the EMV for $A_1$ averages out to €14,000, while the EMV for $A_2$ is €10,800. The double slash line on the $A_2$ branch indicates that it is the inferior alternative and should be dropped in favour of $A_1$.

## The contribution of research

Now the contribution of research can be assessed. Recall that the value of research may be judged as 'the difference between the results of decisions made with the information and the results of decisions that would be made without it.' In this example, the research need is to decide whether the new business will be secured. This is the uncertainty that, if known, would make a perfect forecast possible. Just how much is a perfect forecast worth in this case?

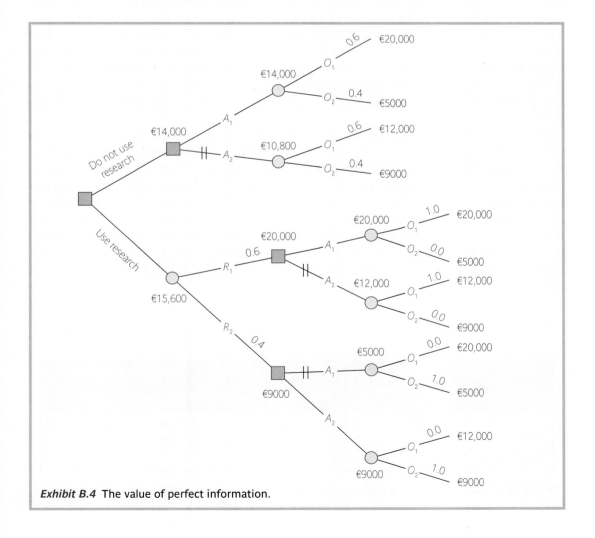

*Exhibit B.4* The value of perfect information.

Consider Exhibit B.3 once again. What would happen if the manager had information to accurately predict whether the new business orders would be secured? The choice would be $A_1$ if the research indicated that the orders would be received, and $A_2$ if the research indicated that the orders would not be received. However, at the decision point (before the research is undertaken), the best estimate is that there is a 0.6 chance that the research will indicate the $O_1$ condition and a 0.4 chance that the condition will be $O_2$. The decision flow implications of the use of research are illustrated in Exhibit B.4.

The decision sequence begins with the decision fork at the left. If the manager chooses to do research ($R$), the first chance fork is reached where one of two things will occur. Research indicates either that the orders will be received ($R_1$) or the orders will not be received ($R_2$). Before doing the research, the best estimate of the probability of $R_1$ taking place is the same as the estimate that $O_1$ will occur (0.6). Similarly, the best estimate that $R_2$ will occur is 0.4.

After the manager learns $R_1$ or $R_2$, there is a second decision fork: $A_1$ or $A_2$. After the $A_1$–$A_2$ decision, there is a second chance fork ($O_1$ or $O_2$) that indicates whether the orders were received. Note that the probabilities at $O_1$ and $O_2$ have now changed from 0.6 and 0.4, respectively, to 1.0 and 0.0, or to 0.0 and 1.0, depending on what was learned from the research. This change occurs because we have evaluated the effect of the research information on our original $O_1$ and $O_2$ probability estimates by calculating *posterior probabilities* (see Exhibit B.5). These are revisions of our prior probabilities that result from the assumed research findings. The posterior probabilities – for example, $P(O_1|R_i)$ and $P(O_2|R_i)$ – are calculated by using Bayes's theorem.[5]

The manager is now ready to average out and fold back the analysis from right to left to evaluate the research alternative. Clearly, if $R_1$ is found, $A_1$ will be chosen with its EMV of €20,000 over the $A_2$ alternative of €12,000. If $R_2$ is reported, then $A_2$ is more attractive. However, before the research, the probabilities of $R_1$ and $R_2$ being secured must be incorporated by a second averaging out. The result is an EMV of €15,600 for the research alternative versus an EMV of €14,000 for the no-research path. The conclusion, then, is as follows. Research that would enable the manager to make a perfect forecast regarding the potential new orders would be worth up to €1600. If the research costs more than €1600, decline to buy it because the net EMV of the research alternative would be less than the EMV of €14,000 of the no-research alternative.

| Research outcomes | State of nature | | Marginal probabilities | Posterior probabilities | |
|---|---|---|---|---|---|
| | $O_1$ | $O_2$ | | $P(O_1|R_i)$ | $P(O_2|R_i)$ |
| $R_1$ | 0.6 | 0.0 | 0.6 | 1.0 | 0.0 |
| $R_2$ | 0.0 | 0.4 | 0.4 | 0.0 | 1.0 |
| Marginal probabilities | 0.6 | | | | |

*Exhibit B.5* States of nature and posterior probabilities.

# Imperfect information

The analysis up to this point assumes that research on decision options will give a perfect prediction of the future states of nature, $O_1$ and $O_2$. Perfect prediction seldom occurs in practice. Sometimes research reveals one condition when later evidence shows something else to be true. Thus, we need to consider that the research in the machinery decision will provide less-than-perfect information and is, therefore, worth less than the €1600 calculated in Exhibit B.4.

Suppose the research in that example involves interviews with the customers' key personnel and some customers' executives. They might all answer our questions to the best of their ability but still predict imperfectly what will happen. Consequently, we might judge that the chances of their predictions being correct are no better than 3 to 1, or 0.75. If we accept that our research results may provide imperfect information in this manner, we need to factor this into our evaluation decision. We do this by averaging out and folding back again. The results are shown in Exhibits B.6 and B.7. The revised EMV, given research judged to be 75 per cent reliable, is €14,010. This revised EMV is only €10 higher than the €14,000 EMV using no research and would seem to be hardly worth consideration.

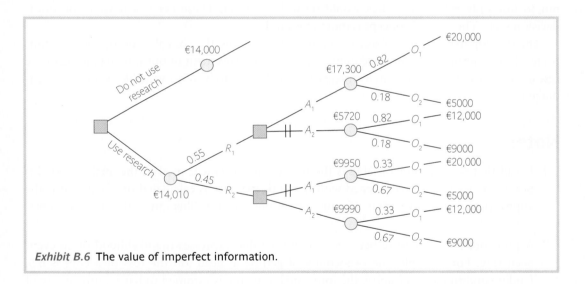

Exhibit B.6 The value of imperfect information.

| Research outcomes | State of nature | | | Posterior probabilities | |
|---|---|---|---|---|---|
| | $O_1$ | $O_2$ | Marginal probabilities | $P(O_1|R_i)$ | $P(O_2|R_i)$ |
| $R_1$ | 0.45 | 0.1 | 0.55 | 0.82 | 0.18 |
| $R_2$ | 0.15 | 0.3 | 0.45 | 0.33 | 0.67 |
| Marginal probabilities | 0.6 | 0.4 | | | |

Exhibit B.7 States of nature and posterior probabilities (complicated).

# Pragmatic complications

This discussion, while simplified, contains the basic concepts for finding the value of research. Practical difficulties complicate the use of these concepts. First, the situation with two events and two alternatives is artificial. Problems with more choices and events are common, and the chief complication is the increased number of calculations.

A more serious problem is posed by the measurement of outcomes. We have assumed we could assess the various actions in terms of an unambiguous euro (€) value, but often we cannot. It is difficult to place a euro value on outcomes related to morale or public image, for example.

An allied problem lies in the exclusive use of EMV as the criterion for decision-making. This is correct in an actuarial sense and implies that each decision-maker has a linear system of evaluation. In truth, we often use another evaluation system. The person who accepts EMV as a criterion sees that an even bet of €20 between two people on the toss of a fair coin is a fair bet. Many people, however, may not be willing to make such a bet because they fear the loss of €20 more than they value the gain of €20. They may need to be offered a chance, say, to win €20 but to lose only €10 before they would be willing to bet. These persons have a non-linear decision scale. The 'utility' concept is more relevant here.

The development of more precise methods of evaluating the contribution of research continues. In the meantime, continued emphasis on the improvement of our understanding of the researcher's task and the research process will make research more valuable when it is conducted.

# Notes

1 Recall that the decision variable is the unit of measurement used in the analysis. At this point, we need not be concerned with how this measure is calculated or whether it is the appropriate decision variable. Assume for purposes of this illustration that it is appropriate.

2 A probability is a measure between 1.0 and 0.0 that expresses the likelihood of an event occurring. For example, the probability of getting a 'head' on the toss of a coin is 0.5. Under conditions of certainty, the forecasted outcome is assumed to have a probability of 1.0 even though we might agree that we normally cannot know the future with certainty. In most forecasting where a specific amount is named, there is an implicit assumption of certainty.

3 Concepts of probability enter into three types of situation. In the classical situation, each possible outcome has a known chance of occurrence. For example, a coin tossed in the air has a 0.5 chance of landing heads up; a spade has a 0.25 chance of being drawn from a well-mixed deck of cards.

In the same type of situation, probabilities are thought of as 'relative frequencies'. Even if the probability is not known from the structure of the problem (as it is in the classical case), it can still be estimated if there is a body of empirical evidence. For example, experience may show that about 1 in 50 products produced is defective. From this statistic, one can estimate that there is a 0.02 chance that any given product will be defective.

If there is no direct empirical evidence, one can still assess probability on the basis of opinion, intuition and/or general experience. In such cases, uncertainty is expressed as a subjectively felt 'degree of confidence' or 'degree of belief' that a given event will occur. The discussions in this appendix are cases in point. For more information on probability concepts, see any modern statistics text.

4 One calculates an EMV for an alternative by weighting each conditional value (for example, €20,000 and €5,000 for $A_1$) by the estimated probability of the occurrence of the associated event (0.6 probability of the €20,000 being made).

$$\text{EMV} = P_1(\text{€20,000}) + (P_2(\text{€5000}) = 0.6(\text{€20,000}) + 0.4(\text{€5000}) = \text{€14,000}$$

5 Bayes' theorem with two states of nature is:

$$P(O_1|R_1) = \frac{P(R_1|O_1) \times P(O_1)}{P(R_j|O_1) \times P(O_1) + P(R_j|O_2) \times P(O_2)} = \frac{1.0 \times 1.6}{(1.0 \times 1.6) + (0.0 \times 0.4)} = 1.0$$

# Appendix C

# Sample student term project

Four members of a graduate research methods course formed a team to investigate career prospects in product management. Their stated research objectives were:

1 to provide an inventory of major European manufacturers that use the product management system
2 to gather descriptive data on the nature and degree of product management
3 to collect information on how product managers are recruited, selected and prepared for their responsibilities.

The research question was: 'What is the role and scope of product management in European manufacturing companies?' Since financial support from the student research fund was limited to Europe's top 1000 manufacturing companies, the students further defined manufacturers according to this criterion. Their investigative questions were as follows.

1 What is the incidence of use of the product manager system?
   a To what degree is it presently in use?
   b Has it been used in the past and discontinued?
   c Was it considered and not adopted?
   d What are future expectations regarding its use?
2 How are product managers recruited and selected?
3 What are the qualifications for employment as a product manager?
4 How does the product manager function in the company?
5 How can we classify the characteristics of individuals and companies to discern trends and differences?

The students selected a mail survey as their data-collection method. Their initial plan was to use a screening or qualifying question to establish which companies use product management.

1   What is your position in the company?

2   Is your company engaged primarily in industrial products, consumer products, or both?

3   Does your company use product managers (PMs)?

4   How many PMs does the company have?

5   How many products are assigned to one PM?

6   Would you please give or include a job description of your company's PM position?

7   How many brands does your company have?

8   Approximately what percentage of your company's brands have PMs?

9   What percentage of sales volume do the brands in question 8 account for as a whole?

10  How long have PMs been used in your company? If yes, why was it dropped?

11  Has a PM system been used and dropped in your company? If yes, why was it dropped?

12  Has a PM system ever been considered but never adopted in your company? If yes, why was it not adopted?

13  Are there any plans for the adoption of a PM system in the future?

14  What percentage of your PMs come *directly* from each of the following sources? Campuses, within the company, other companies, other (list).

15  If PMs come from within the company, what department, or departments, do they come from? Sales, marketing, production, advertising, other (list).

16  If PMs come from outside the company (other than campuses), what department or departments do they come from? PM, sales, marketing, production, advertising, other (list).

17  If PMs are recruited directly from campuses, what, if any, are the typical degrees required?

18  Rank on a scale from 1 to 5 the relative importance of each of the following qualifications for a PM (1 denotes the greatest importance): education, age, work experience, personality, creativity.

19  If PMs are recruited from within the company, what is the average age, length of work experience (with the company) and educational background?

20  If PMs are recruited from outside the company (not including campuses), what is the average age, length of work experience and educational background?

21  What functions (advertising, pricing, etc.) does the PM actually perform in day-to-day activities, and what percentage of time is spent on each?

22  Of those functions listed in question **21**, which, if any, does the PM have *final* authority over?

23  To whom does the PM report?

24  Does your company have a structured training programme for product management? If yes, please explain.

25  On the basis of which of the following is the PM evaluated? Market share, ROI, sales volume, profits, other (list).

26  What were the objectives of the company in instituting the PM concept?

27  How successful has the PM concept been in fulfilling the objectives set for it?

28  What were the characteristics of the PM concept that contributed to the fulfilment of these objectives?

29  What elements, if any, of the PM system did not adequately contribute to the fulfilment of the objectives?

30  What specific actions, if any, have been taken to deal with the inadequacies listed in question 29?

31  If your company is currently planning any broad revisions to the present PM programme, please describe.

*Exhibit C.1* Preliminary questionnaire, PM study: draft 1.

1 Does your company now use PMs? yes _____ no _____ (If no, please go to question 17).

2 Would you please send a copy of your job description?

3 How many PMs does your company have? _____

4 What percentage of your total sales is accounted for by PMs? _____ %

5 How long have PMs been used by your company? _____ years

6 What percentage of your personnel enters the product management programme from the following sources?

Campuses _____ %

Within the company _____ %

From elsewhere _____ %

7 If PMs come from within the company or elsewhere, what department(s) do they come from?

Sales _____ %

Marketing _____ %

Production _____ %

Advertising _____ %

Other product management programmes _____ %

Advertising agencies _____ %

Elsewhere _____ %

8 If PMs are recruited directly from campuses, please rank the following degrees from 1 to 6, with 1 being the most desirable, 2 the next most desirable, and so on.

BS _____

areas _____

AB _____

areas _____

BSBA (BBA) _____

areas _____

MA _____

areas _____

MBA _____

areas _____

Ph.D. _____

areas _____

9 Briefly state what you consider to be an appropriate profile of a PM recruited directly from the campus.

Age:

Work experience (length and type):

Personal traits (personality, creativity, aggressiveness, etc.):

Education:

10 What do you consider to be an appropriate profile for a PM recruited from within or from another company?

Age:

Work experience (length and type):

Personal traits (personality, creativity, aggressiveness, etc.):

Education:

11 To whom does the PM report?

_____

12 What percentage of his or her time does the PM spend in various functionary areas, such as production, advertising, pricing, etc.? Please list.

13 Please rank on a scale of 1 to 5 (1 is most important) the following criteria used in evaluating a PM.

_____ Market share

_____ Return on investment

_____ Sales volume

_____ Profits

_____ Other (please explain)

_____

14 Does the company have a structured training programme?

yes _____ no _____ If yes, please describe.

_____

15 What prompted your firm to initiate the PM system?

16 Is your company currently planning any future revisions to the PM system?

yes _____ no _____ If yes, please explain.

17 Is your company primarily engaged in

Industrial goods _____ %

Food products _____ %

Consumer package goods _____ %

Consumer durable goods _____ %

Automotive products _____ %

Other (list)

_____ _____ %

_____ _____ %

18 What is your company's total _ _____

If you answered yes to question 1, you have completed the questionnaire. If your answer was no, please answer question 19. Thank you for your cooperation.

19 Please tick which of the following best describes your PMs.

_____ Have never considered PMs.

_____ Have considered, but never adopted product management.

_____ Have used previously and discontinued.

_____ Presently considering adoption of the system in the future.

*Exhibit C.2* PM questionnaire: draft 2.

Lakeside University

GRADUATE SCHOOL OF BUSINESS ADMINISTRATION

[Inside Address]

Dear Sir,

We at the Lakeside University Business School are interested in learning more about the actual recruitment and use of product or brand managers (BMs). Our objective is to help expand the body of knowledge about this important area of marketing.

To do this, of course, means going to someone such as yourself who *knows*. Your help with the few questions on the attached pages will take only a few minutes and will make a real contribution to the accuracy and success of this study.

Your reply will be treated in strict confidence and will be available only to my research staff and me. Any publication will be only of statistical totals for groups of companies.

Your assistance will be greatly appreciated and will help us to know more about product management and to teach students about it in a more relevant and effective manner.

Sincerely,

William Urbandale

Professor of Marketing

---

We define a *PM* (also called a *BM*) as one who is responsible for the integration and planning of a broad range of marketing functions (pricing, distribution, and so forth) for a specific product, brand or homogeneous group of products. The position usually has limited or no line authority, especially over the sales force.

1 Please indicate which of the following best describes your company/division's use of product managers.

_____ We are currently using PMs.

_____ We have previously used PMs, but discontinued.

_____ We have considered the system, but never implemented it.

_____ Presently considering adoption of the system in the future.

_____ We have never considered PMs.

If you are currently using PMs, please continue. If you are not currently using PMs, you have completed the questionnaire. Thank you for your cooperation.

2 Will you be answering the following for:

_____ your company?

_____ your division?

3 How many PMs (include all levels such as group PM, PM, associate PM, and assistant PM) does your company/division employ? _____

4 How long have PMs been used by your company/division? _____ years

5 What percentage of your company/division total sales are accounted for by products controlled by PMs? _____ %

6 From the following, please indicate whether the position exists in your company/division. Then indicate the source from which the personnel at the various levels were obtained to fill that

position. If you have a similar position but with a different name, please indicate that position in the blank.

*(please tick)*

Major sources

Major sources

|  | Do you have? | | | Within company | | |
|---|---|---|---|---|---|---|
|  | Yes | No | Campuses | Other PM jobs | Other jobs | Other companies |
| Group PMs | ____ | ____ | ____ | ____ | ____ | ____ |
| PMs | ____ | ____ | ____ | ____ | ____ | ____ |
| Associate PMs | ____ | ____ | ____ | ____ | ____ | ____ |
| Assistant PMs | ____ | ____ | ____ | ____ | ____ | ____ |
| Other (specify) | ____ | ____ | ____ | ____ | ____ | ____ |

7  What is the typical age of your

Group PMs?        _____ years

PMs?        _____ years

Associate PMs?        _____ years

Assistant PMs?        _____ years

8  Of the following personal traits, please indicate their degree of importance in the evaluation of a candidate for a product management position.

*(please tick)*

|  | Not important | Desirable | Very desirable | Essential |
|---|---|---|---|---|
| Leadership | ____ | ____ | ____ | ____ |
| Creativity | ____ | ____ | ____ | ____ |
| Aggressiveness | ____ | ____ | ____ | ____ |
| Analytical ability | ____ | ____ | ____ | ____ |
| Communications skill | ____ | ____ | ____ | ____ |
| Ability to work with others | ____ | ____ | ____ | ____ |
| Other _____ | ____ | ____ | ____ | ____ |

9  If you recruit directly from campus, please indicate the importance of the following traits of a PM candidate.

*(please tick)*

|  | Not important | Desirable | Very desirable | Essential |
|---|---|---|---|---|
| Business experience | ____ | ____ | ____ | ____ |
| High grade-point average | ____ | ____ | ____ | ____ |
| Extra-curricular activities | ____ | ____ | ____ | ____ |
| MBA | ____ | ____ | ____ | ____ |
| Master's, technical | ____ | ____ | ____ | ____ |
| Bachelor's, business | ____ | ____ | ____ | ____ |
| Other (specify) _____ | ____ | ____ | ____ | ____ |

10  If you recruit into your PM group from other jobs (either from within your company or from other companies), please indicate the importance of the following experiences.
*(please tick)*

| Experience | Not important | Desirable | Very desirable | Essential |
|---|---|---|---|---|
| Sales | _____ | _____ | _____ | _____ |
| Other PM programmes | _____ | _____ | _____ | _____ |
| Other marketing positions | _____ | _____ | _____ | _____ |
| Production | _____ | _____ | _____ | _____ |
| Advertising agencies | _____ | _____ | _____ | _____ |
| Undergraduate degree | _____ | _____ | _____ | _____ |
| Graduate degree | _____ | _____ | _____ | _____ |
| Other (specify) _____ | _____ | _____ | _____ | _____ |

11  Please indicate the percentage of time a typical PM spends in the following activities:

Advertising _____ %
Pricing _____
Distribution _____
Packaging _____
Product development _____
Marketing research _____
Production liaison _____
Finance and budgeting _____
Other (specify) _____ _____
Other (specify) _____ _____
Total 100%

12  Please indicate which of the following criteria are used in evaluating PMs in your company/division.
a _____ Market share
_____ Return on investment
_____ Sales volume
Profits _____
_____ Other (please specify)
b Which one is most important? _____

13  Does your company/division have a structured training programme for PMs?
yes _____ no _____ (If yes, please describe.)
_____

14  Is your company/division currently planning any revision in its PM system?
yes _____ no _____ (If yes, please describe.)
_____
_____

15  Judging from your company's experience, what do you feel is the major problem facing the product management system?
_____
_____

---

**16** It would be most valuable to our studies if you could supply a sample job description of your PM positions.

Are such available?

_____ Yes, examples enclosed

_____ Yes, examples sent under separate cover

_____ Not available Thank you for your assistance.

**17** If you would like a summary of the results of this survey, please tick here. \_\_\_\_

Thank you for your assistance.

---

*Exhibit C.3* PM questionnaire: final draft.

The team members developed the following procedure for constructing their questionnaire. Having agreed on the investigative questions, each member attempted to write measurement questions aimed at tapping the essence of each investigative question. Each measurement question was written on an A5 card to facilitate comparisons, revisions, additions and deletions. At a meeting of the team, all questions were reviewed, duplicates were eliminated and a general winnowing occurred. The remaining 31 questions were included in questionnaire draft 1, shown in Exhibit C.1. In this first draft, there was no effort to place questions in sequence or to present them graphically as they would eventually be seen by respondents.

After some discussion, the team members concluded that the questionnaire would probably need to be three pages long. In addition, the covering letter would take up a page. They decided to use a printed covering letter and to incorporate it as the first page of the questionnaire. The combination would be printed on both sides of an A3 sheet of paper, folded in booklet form to A4 size.

Each team member was assigned the task of translating draft 1 into draft 2. In the new draft, the questions were in planned sequence, had response formats chosen, and had graphic arrangements selected. Individual drafts were submitted to a sub-committee of the team, which used them as the basis for developing questionnaire draft 2. This is shown in Exhibit C.2.

Draft 2 was reproduced and submitted to other members of the research class for critique. Comments and challenges were sought on (i) sources of confusion and vagueness; (ii) question value (What useful information does the question provide? Not provide?); (iii) appropriateness of the proposed response formats and suggestions for improvement; and (iv) gaps in question coverage.

After this critique, a second sub-committee revised the questionnaire. This resulted in questionnaire draft 3 (not presented here). The draft was again reviewed by the full team, and modest changes were made to produce draft 4.

By this time, the team members were eager to test the questionnaire with respondents. Arrangements were made to have several local corporate executives complete the questionnaire. Team members picked up the completed questionnaires, interviewed the executives about their answers, and secured any comments they had about the questions and the study. These experiences led to a revised draft, draft 5. This was repeated twice more with other executives, finally ending with draft 7, shown here as Exhibit C.3. The limitations of time and money led the team to depend on local product managers for testing rather than on a full-scale 'dress rehearsal' by mail. This decision limited the value of the pre-testing but was accepted as a limitation of a student project.

The survey was sent to the top 1000 manufacturing companies in the form described. Only one mailing was made because of time and money limitations. Usable returns numbered 492 at the cut-off point. Approximately 50 companies sent job descriptions of their product management positions.

# Non-parametric significance tests

This appendix contains additional non-parametric tests of hypotheses to augment those described in Chapter 16 (see Exhibit 16.7).

## One-sample case

### Kolmogorov – Smirnov test

This test is appropriate when the data are at least ordinal and the research situation calls for a comparison of an observed sample distribution with a theoretical distribution. Under these conditions, the Kolmogorov–Smirnov (KS) one-sample test is more powerful than the $X^2$ test and can be used for small samples when the $X^2$ test cannot. The KS is a test of goodness of fit in which we specify the *cumulative* frequency distribution that would occur under the theoretical distribution and compare it with the observed cumulative frequency distribution. The theoretical distribution represents our expectations under $H_0$. We determine the point of greatest divergence between the observed and theoretical distributions and identify this value as $D$ (maximum deviation). From a table of critical values for $D$, we determine whether such a large divergence is likely on the basis of random sampling variations from the theoretical distribution. The value for $D$ is calculated as follows:

$$D = maximum / F_O(X) - F_T(X) /$$

in which

$F_0(X)$ = The observed cumulative frequency distribution of a random sample of $n$ observations.

Where $X$ is any possible score, $F_0(X) = k/n$, where $k$ = the number of observations equal to or less than $X$.

$$F_T(X) = \text{The theoretical frequency distribution under } H_0.$$

We illustrate the KS test with an analysis of the results of the dining club study, in terms of various class levels. Take an equal number of interviews from each class, but secure unequal numbers of people interested in joining. Assume class levels are ordinal measurements. The testing process is as follows (see also Exhibit D.1).

## 1 NULL HYPOTHESIS

$H_0$: There is no difference among student classes as to their intention of joining the dining club.
$H_A$: There is a difference among students in various classes as to their intention of joining the dining club.

| | First-year student | Second-year student | Junior | Senior | Graduate |
|---|---|---|---|---|---|
| Number in each class | 5 | 9 | 11 | 16 | 19 |
| $F_0(X)$ | 5/60 | 14/60 | 25/60 | 41/60 | 60/60 |
| $F_T(X)$ | 12/60 | 24/60 | 36/60 | 48/60 | 60/60 |
| $\lvert F_0(X) - F_T(X)\rvert$ | 7/60 | 10/60 | 11/60 | 7/60 | 0 |
| $D = 11/60 = .183$ | | | | | |
| $n = 60$ | | | | | |

*Exhibit D.1* Testing process of Kolmogorov–Smirnov test.

## 2 STATISTICAL TEST

Choose the KS one-sample test because the data are ordinal measures and we are interested in comparing an observed distribution with a theoretical one.

## 3 SIGNIFICANCE LEVEL

$\alpha = .05$, $n = 60$.

## 4 CALCULATED VALUE

$D = \text{Maximum } \lvert F_0(X) - F_T(X)\rvert$.

## 5 CRITICAL TEST VALUE

We enter the table of critical values of $D$ in the KS one-sample test (see Appendix E, Exhibit E.5) and learn that with $\alpha = .05$ the critical value for $D$ is

$$D = \frac{1.36}{60} = .175$$

## 6 INTERPRET

The calculated value is greater than the critical value, indicating that we should reject the null hypothesis.

# Two-samples case

## Sign test

The sign test is used with matched pairs when the only information is the identification of the pair member that is larger or smaller, or has more or less of some characteristic. Under $H_0$, one would expect the number of cases in which $X_A > X_B$ to equal the number of pairs in which $X_B > X_A$. All ties are dropped from the analysis, and $n$ is adjusted to allow for these eliminated pairs. This test is based on the binomial expansion and has a good power efficiency for small samples.

## Wilcoxon-matched pairs test

When you can determine both *direction* and *magnitude* of difference between carefully matched pairs, use the Wilcoxon matched-pairs test. This test has excellent efficiency and can be more powerful than the *t*-test in cases where the latter is not particularly appropriate. The mechanics of calculation are also quite simple. Find the difference score ($d_i$) between each pair of values, and rank-order the differences from smallest to largest without regard to sign. The actual signs of each difference are then added to the rank values and the test statistic $T$ is calculated. $T$ is the sum of the ranks with the less frequent sign. Typical of such research situations might be a study where husband and wife are matched, where twins are used, where a given subject is used in a before/after study, or where the outputs of two similar machines are compared.

 Two types of tie may occur with this test. When two observations are equal, the $d$ score becomes zero, and we drop this pair of observations from the calculation. When two or more pairs have the same $d$ value, we average their rank positions. For example, if two pairs have a rank score of 1, we assign the rank of 1.5 to each and rank the next largest difference as third. When $n < 25$, use the table of critical values (see Appendix E, Exhibit E.4). When $n > 25$, the sampling distribution of $T$ is approximately normal with

$$Mean = \mu_T = \frac{n(n+1)}{4}$$

$$Standard\ deviation = \sigma_T \sqrt{\frac{n(n+1)}{(2n+1)}}$$

$$\text{The formula for the text is: } z = \frac{T - \mu_T}{\sigma_T}$$

Suppose you conduct an experiment on the effect of brand name on quality perception. Ten subjects are recruited and asked to taste and compare two samples of a product, one identified as a well-known drink and the other as a new product being tested. In truth, however, the samples are identical. The subjects are then asked to rate the two samples on a set of scale items judged to be ordinal. Test these results for significance by the usual procedure.

### 1 NULL HYPOTHESIS

$H_0$: There is no difference between the perceived qualities of the two samples.
$H_A$: There is a difference in the perceived quality of the two samples.

## 2 STATISTICAL TEST

The Wilcoxon matched-pairs test is used because the study is of related samples in which the differences can be ranked in magnitude.

## 3 SIGNIFICANCE LEVEL

$\alpha = .05$, with $n = 10$ pairs of comparisons minus any pairs with a $d$ of zero.

## 4 CALCULATED VALUE

$T$ equals the sum of the ranks with the less frequent sign. Assume we secure the following results:

| Pair | Branded | Unbranded | $d_i$ | Rank of $d_i$ | Rank with less frequent sign |
|------|---------|-----------|-------|---------------|------------------------------|
| 1 | 52 | 48 | 4 | 4 | |
| 2 | 37 | 32 | 5 | 5.5* | |
| 3 | 50 | 52 | −1 | −2 | 2 |
| 4 | 45 | 32 | 13 | 9 | |
| 5 | 56 | 59 | −3 | −3 | 3 |
| 6 | 51 | 50 | 1 | 1 | |
| 7 | 40 | 29 | 11 | 8 | |
| 8 | 59 | 54 | 5 | 5.5* | |
| 9 | 38 | 38 | 0 | * | |
| 10 | 40 | 32 | 8 | 7 | $T = 5$ |

*Note:* *there are two types of tie situation. We drop out the pair with the type of tie shown by pair 9. Pairs 2 and 8 have a tie in rank of difference. In this case, we average the ranks and assign the average value to each.

**Exhibit D.2** Results of Wilcoxon-matched pairs test.

## 5 CRITICAL TEST VALUE

Enter the table of critical values of $T$ with $n = 9$ (see Appendix E, Exhibit E.4) and find that the critical value with $\alpha = .05$ is 6. Note that with this test, the calculated value must be smaller than the critical value to reject the null hypothesis.

## 6 INTERPRET

Since the calculated value is less than the critical value, reject the null hypothesis.

# Kolmogorov – Smirnov (KS) two-samples test

When a researcher has two independent samples of ordinal data, the (KS) two-samples test is useful. Like the one-sample test, this two-samples test is concerned with the agreement between two cumulative distributions, but both represent sample values. If the two samples have been drawn from the same population, the cumulative distributions of the samples should be fairly close to each other, showing only random deviations from the population distribution. If the cumulative distributions show a large enough maximum deviation $D$ (defined by the formula below), it is evidence for rejecting the $H_0$. To secure the maximum deviation, one should use as many intervals as are available so as not to obscure the maximum cumulative difference.

$$D = \text{Maximum } |F_{N1}(X) - F_{N2}(X)| \text{ (two-tailed test)}$$

$$D = \text{Maximum } |F_{N1}(X) - F_{N2}(X)| \text{ (one-tailed test)}$$

$D$ is calculated in the same manner as before, but the table for critical values for the numerator of $D$, $K_D$ (two-samples case) is presented in Appendix E, Exhibit E.6 when $n_1 = n_2$ and is less than 40 observations. When $n_1$ and/or $n_2$ are larger than 40, $D$ from Appendix E, Exhibit E.7 should be used. With this larger sample, it is not necessary that $n_1 = n_2$.

Here we use a different sample from the smoking-accident study. (To make $n_1 = n_2$, we increased the sample size of no accidents to 34. Non-smokers with no accidents is 24.) Suppose the smoking classifications represent an ordinal scale, and you test these data with the KS two-samples test. Proceed as follows.

## 1 NULL HYPOTHESIS
$H_0$: There is no difference in on-the-job accident occurrences between smokers and non-smokers.
$H_A$: The more a person smokes, the more likely that person is to have an on-the-job accident.

## 2 STATISTICAL TEST
The KS two-samples test is used because it is assumed the data are ordinal.

## 3 SIGNIFICANCE LEVEL
$\alpha = .05$. $n_1 = n_2 = 34$.

## 4 CALCULATED VALUE
See the one-sample calculation (KS test) and compare with Exhibit D.3 below.

## 5 CRITICAL TEST VALUE
We enter Appendix E, Exhibit E.6 with $n = 34$ to find that $K_D = 11$ when $p = \leq.05$ for a one-tailed distribution.

## 6 INTERPRET
Since the critical value equals the largest calculated value, we reject the null hypothesis.

| | Heavy smoker | Moderate smoker | Non-smoker |
|---|---|---|---|
| $F_{n1}(X)$ | 12/34 | 21/34 | 34/34 |
| $F_{n2}(X)$ | 4/34 | 10/34 | 34/34 |
| $D_i = K_{Din}$ | 8/34 | 11/34 | 0 |

**Exhibit D.3** Results of Kolmogorov–Smirnov two-sample test.

## Mann – Whitney U test

This test is also used with two independent samples if the data are at least ordinal; it is an alternative to the *t*-test without the latter's limiting assumptions. When the larger of the two samples is 20 or less, there are special tables for interpreting *U*; when the larger sample exceeds 20, a normal curve approximation is used.

In calculating the *U* test, treat all observations in a combined fashion and rank them, algebraically, from smallest to largest. The largest negative score receives the lowest rank. In case of ties, assign the average rank as in other tests. With this test, you can also test samples that are unequal. After the ranking, the rank values for each sample are totalled. Compute the *U* statistic as follows:

$$U = n_1 n_2 + \frac{n_1(n_1 + 1)}{2} - R_1 \text{ or } U = n_1 n_2 + \frac{n_2(n_2 + 1)}{2} - R_2$$

in which

$n_1$ = Number in sample 1
$n_2$ = Number in sample 2
$R_1$ = Sum of ranks in sample 1

With this equation, you can secure two *U* values, one using $R_1$ and the second using $R_2$. For testing purposes, use the smaller *U*.

An example may help to clarify the *U* statistic calculation procedure. Let's consider the sales training example with the *t* distribution discussion. Recall that salespeople with training method A averaged higher sales than salespeople with training method B. While these data are ratio measures, one still might not want to accept the other assumptions that underlie the *t*-test. What kind of a result could be secured with the *U* test? While the *U* test is designed for ordinal data, it can be used with interval and ratio measurements.

### 1 NULL HYPOTHESIS

$H_0$: There is no difference in sales results produced by the two training methods.
$H_A$: Training method A produces sales results superior to the results of method B.

### 2 STATISTICAL TEST

The Mann–Whitney *U* test is chosen because the measurement is at least ordinal, and the assumptions under the parametric *t*-test are rejected.

### 3 SIGNIFICANCE LEVEL

We calculate Mann–Whitney *U* values as shown in Exhibit D.4.

$$\alpha = .05 \text{ (one-tailed test)}.$$

## 4 CALCULATED VALUE

| Sales per week per salesperson | | | |
|---|---|---|---|
| **Training method A** | **Rank** | **Training method B** | **Rank** |
| 1500 | 15 | 1340 | 10 |
| 1540 | 16 | 1300 | 8.5 |
| 1860 | 22 | 1620 | 18 |
| 1230 | 6 | 1070 | 3 |
| 1370 | 12 | 1210 | 5 |
| 1550 | 17 | 1170 | 4 |
| 1840 | 21 | 1770 | 20 |
| 1250 | 7 | 950 | 1 |
| 1300 | 8.5 | 1380 | 13 |
| 1350 | 11 | 1460 | 14 |
| 1710 | 19 | 1030 | 2 |
| | $R_1 = .154.5$ | | $R_2 = .98.5$ |
| $U = (11)(11) + \dfrac{11(11 + 1)}{2} - 154.5 = 32.5$ | | $U = (11)(11) + \dfrac{11(11 + 1)}{2} - 98.5 = 88.5$ | |

**Exhibit D.4** Process of Mann–Whitney $U$ test.

## 5 CRITICAL TEST VALUE
Enter Appendix E, Exhibit E.8 with $n_1 = n_2 = 11$, and find a critical value of 34 for $\alpha = 0.5$, one-tailed test. Note that with this test, the calculated value must be smaller than the critical value to reject the null hypothesis.

## 6 INTERPRET
Since the calculated value is smaller than the critical value (34 > 32.5), reject the null hypothesis and conclude that training method A is probably superior.

Thus, one would reject the null hypothesis at $\alpha = .05$ in a one-tailed test using either the $t$-test or the $U$ test. In this example, the $U$ test has approximately the same power as the parametric test.

When $n > 20$ in one of the samples, the sampling distribution of $U$ approaches the normal distribution with

$$Mean = \mu_U = \frac{n_1 n_2}{2}$$

$$Standard\ deviation = \sigma_U = \sqrt{\frac{(n_1)(n_2)(n_1 + n_2 + 1)}{12}}$$

$$And\ z = \frac{U - \mu_U}{\sigma_U}$$

## Other non-parametric tests

Other tests are appropriate under certain conditions when testing two independent samples. When the measurement is only nominal, the Fisher exact probability test may be used. When the data are at least ordinal, use the median and Wald–Wolfowitz runs tests.

## k-Samples case

You can use tests more powerful than $X_2$ with data that are at least ordinal in nature. One such test is an extension of the median test mentioned earlier. We illustrate here the application of a second ordinal measurement test known as the Kruskal–Wallis one-way analysis of variance.

## Kruskal – Wallis test

This is a generalized version of the Mann–Whitney test. With it we rank all scores in the entire pool of observations from smallest to largest. The rank sum of each sample is then calculated, with ties being distributed as in other examples. We then compute the value of $H$ as follows:

$$H = \frac{12}{N(N+1)} \sum_{j=1}^{k} \frac{T_j^2}{n_j} - 3(N+1)$$

where
$T_j$ = Sum of ranks in column $j$
$n_j$ = Number of cases in $j$th sample
$N = \alpha w_j$ = Total number of cases
$k$ = Number of samples

When there are a number of ties, it is recommended that a correct factor ($C$) be calculated and used to correct the $H$ value as follows:

$$C = 1 - \left\{ \frac{\sum_{j}^{G} (t_i^3 - t_j)}{} \right\}$$

where
$G$ = Number of sets of tied observations
$t_i$ = Number tied in any set $i$
$H' = H/C$

To secure the critical value for $H'$, use the table for the distribution of $X^2$ (see Appendix E, Exhibit E.3), and enter it with the value of $H'$ and $d.f. = k - 1$.

To illustrate the application of this test, use the price discount experiment problem. The data and calculations are shown in Exhibit D.5 and indicate that, by the Kruskal–Wallis test, one again barely fails to reject the null hypothesis with $\alpha = .05$.

| One eurocent | | Three eurocents | | Five eurocents | |
|---|---|---|---|---|---|
| $X_A$ | Rank | $X_B$ | Rank | $X_C$ | Rank |
| 6 | 1 | 8 | 5 | 9 | 8.5 |
| 7 | 2.5 | 9 | 8.5 | 9 | 8.5 |
| 8 | 5 | 8 | 5 | 11 | 14 |
| 7 | 2.5 | 10 | 11.5 | 10 | 11.5 |
| 9 | 8.5 | 11 | 14 | 14 | 18 |
| 11 | 14 | 13 | 16,5 | 13 | 16.5 |
| | $T_j = .33.5$ | | 60.5 | | 77.0 |

$T = 33.5 + 60.5 + 77$

$= .171$

$$H = \frac{12}{18(18+1)} \left\{ \frac{33.5^2 + 60.5^2 + 77^2}{6} \right\} - 3(18+1)$$

$$= \frac{12}{342} \left\{ \frac{1122.25 + 3660.25 + 5929}{6} \right\} - 57$$

$$= 0.0351 \left\{ \frac{10711.5}{6} \right\} - 57$$

$H = 5.66$

$$C = 1 - \left\{ \frac{3(2)^3 - 2] + 2(3)^3 - 3] + 4(4)^3 - 4]}{18^3 - 18} \right\}$$

$$= 1 - \frac{18 + 48 + 60}{5814}$$

$$= 0.978$$

$$H' = \frac{H}{C} = \frac{5.66}{0.978} = 5.79$$

$d.f. = k - 1 = 2$

$p = .05$

*Exhibit D.5* Kruskal–Wallis one-way analysis of variance (price differentials).

# Appendix E

# Selected statistical tables

## List of exhibits

| | | | | | Second Decimal Place in z | | | | | |
|------|--------|--------|--------|--------|--------|--------|--------|--------|--------|--------|
| z | 0.00 | 0.01 | 0.02 | 0.03 | 0.04 | 0.05 | 0.06 | 0.07 | 0.08 | 0.09 |
| 0.00 | 0.0000 | 0.0040 | 0.0080 | 0.0120 | 0.0160 | 0.0199 | 0.0239 | 0.0279 | 0.0319 | 0.0359 |
| 0.1 | 0.0398 | 0.0438 | 0.0478 | 0.0517 | 0.0557 | 0.0596 | 0.0636 | 0.0675 | 0.0714 | 0.0753 |
| 0.2 | 0.0793 | 0.0832 | 0.0871 | 0.0910 | 0.0948 | 0.0987 | 0.1026 | 0.1064 | 0.1103 | 0.1141 |
| 0.3 | 0.1179 | 0.1217 | 0.1255 | 0.1293 | 0.1331 | 0.1368 | 0.1406 | 0.1443 | 0.1480 | 0.1517 |
| 0.4 | 0.1554 | 0.1591 | 0.1628 | 0.1664 | 0.1700 | 0.1736 | 0.1772 | 0.1808 | 0.1844 | 0.1879 |
| 0.5 | 0.1915 | 0.1950 | 0.1985 | 0.2019 | 0.2054 | 0.2088 | 0.2123 | 0.2157 | 0.2190 | 0.2224 |
| 0.6 | 0.2257 | 0.2291 | 0.2324 | 0.2357 | 0.2389 | 0.2422 | 0.2454 | 0.2486 | 0.2517 | 0.2549 |
| 0.7 | 0.2580 | 0.2611 | 0.2642 | 0.2673 | 0.2704 | 0.2734 | 0.2764 | 0.2794 | 0.2823 | 0.2852 |
| 0.8 | 0.2881 | 0.2910 | 0.2939 | 0.2967 | 0.2995 | 0.3023 | 0.3051 | 0.3078 | 0.3106 | 0.3133 |
| 0.9 | 0.3159 | 0.3186 | 0.3212 | 0.3238 | 0.3264 | 0.3289 | 0.3315 | 0.3340 | 0.3365 | 0.3389 |
| 1.0 | 0.3413 | 0.3438 | 0.3461 | 0.3485 | 0.3508 | 0.3531 | 0.3554 | 0.3577 | 0.3599 | 0.3621 |
| 1.1 | 0.3643 | 0.3665 | 0.3686 | 0.3708 | 0.3729 | 0.3749 | 0.3770 | 0.3790 | 0.3810 | 0.3830 |
| 1.2 | 0.3849 | 0.3869 | 0.3888 | 0.3907 | 0.3925 | 0.3944 | 0.3962 | 0.3980 | 0.3997 | 0.4015 |
| 1.3 | 0.4032 | 0.4049 | 0.4066 | 0.4082 | 0.4099 | 0.4115 | 0.4131 | 0.4147 | 0.4162 | 0.4177 |
| 1.4 | 0.4192 | 0.4207 | 0.4222 | 0.4236 | 0.4251 | 0.4265 | 0.4279 | 0.4292 | 0.4306 | 0.4319 |
| 1.5 | 0.4332 | 0.4345 | 0.4357 | 0.4370 | 0.4382 | 0.4394 | 0.4406 | 0.4418 | 0.4429 | 0.4441 |
| 1.6 | 0.4452 | 0.4463 | 0.4474 | 0.4484 | 0.4495 | 0.4505 | 0.4515 | 0.4525 | 0.4535 | 0.4545 |
| 1.7 | 0.4554 | 0.4564 | 0.4573 | 0.4582 | 0.4591 | 0.4599 | 0.4608 | 0.4616 | 0.4625 | 0.4633 |
| 1.8 | 0.4641 | 0.4649 | 0.4656 | 0.4664 | 0.4671 | 0.4678 | 0.4686 | 0.4693 | 0.4699 | 0.4706 |
| 1.9 | 0.4713 | 0.4719 | 0.4726 | 0.4732 | 0.4738 | 0.4744 | 0.4750 | 0.4756 | 0.4761 | 0.4767 |
| 2.0 | 0.4772 | 0.4778 | 0.4783 | 0.4788 | 0.4793 | 0.4798 | 0.4803 | 0.4808 | 0.4812 | 0.4817 |
| 2.1 | 0.4821 | 0.4826 | 0.4830 | 0.4834 | 0.4838 | 0.4842 | 0.4846 | 0.4850 | 0.4854 | 0.4857 |
| 2.2 | 0.4861 | 0.4864 | 0.4868 | 0.4871 | 0.4875 | 0.4878 | 0.4881 | 0.4884 | 0.4887 | 0.4890 |
| 2.3 | 0.4893 | 0.4896 | 0.4898 | 0.4901 | 0.4904 | 0.4906 | 0.4909 | 0.4911 | 0.4913 | 0.4916 |
| 2.4 | 0.4918 | 0.4920 | 0.4922 | 0.4925 | 0.4927 | 0.4929 | 0.4931 | 0.4932 | 0.4934 | 0.4936 |
| 2.5 | 0.4938 | 0.4940 | 0.4941 | 0.4943 | 0.4945 | 0.4946 | 0.4948 | 0.4949 | 0.4951 | 0.4952 |
| 2.6 | 0.4953 | 0.4955 | 0.4956 | 0.4957 | 0.4959 | 0.4960 | 0.4961 | 0.4962 | 0.4963 | 0.4964 |
| 2.7 | 0.4965 | 0.4966 | 0.4967 | 0.4968 | 0.4969 | 0.4970 | 0.4971 | 0.4972 | 0.4973 | 0.4974 |
| 2.8 | 0.4974 | 0.4975 | 0.4976 | 0.4977 | 0.4977 | 0.4978 | 0.4979 | 0.4979 | 0.4980 | 0.4981 |
| 2.9 | 0.4981 | 0.4982 | 0.4982 | 0.4983 | 0.4984 | 0.4984 | 0.4985 | 0.4985 | 0.4986 | 0.4986 |
| 3.0 | 0.4987 | 0.4987 | 0.4987 | 0.4988 | 0.4988 | 0.4989 | 0.4989 | 0.4989 | 0.4990 | 0.4990 |
| 3.1 | 0.4990 | 0.4991 | 0.4991 | 0.4991 | 0.4992 | 0.4992 | 0.4992 | 0.4992 | 0.4993 | 0.4993 |
| 3.2 | 0.4993 | 0.4993 | 0.4994 | 0.4994 | 0.4994 | 0.4994 | 0.4994 | 0.4995 | 0.4995 | 0.4995 |
| 3.3 | 0.4995 | 0.4995 | 0.4995 | 0.4996 | 0.4996 | 0.4996 | 0.4996 | 0.4996 | 0.4996 | 0.4997 |
| 3.4 | 0.4997 | 0.4997 | 0.4997 | 0.4997 | 0.4997 | 0.4997 | 0.4997 | 0.4997 | 0.4997 | 0.4998 |
| 3.5 | 0.4998 | | | | | | | | | |
| 4.0 | 0.49997 | | | | | | | | | |
| 4.5 | 0.499997 | | | | | | | | | |
| 5.0 | 0.4999997 | | | | | | | | | |
| 6.0 | 0.499999999 | | | | | | | | | |

*Exhibit E.1* Areas of the standard normal distribution.

| | Level of significance for one-tailed test | | | | | |
|---|---|---|---|---|---|---|
| | 0.10 | 0.05 | 0.025 | 0.1 | .005 | .0005 |
| | Level of significance for two-tailed test | | | | | |
| d.f. | .20 | .10 | .05 | .02 | .01 | .001 |
| 1 | 3.078 | 6.314 | 12.706 | 31.821 | 63.657 | 636.619 |
| 2 | 1.886 | 2.920 | 4.303 | 6.965 | 9.925 | 31.598 |
| 3 | 1.638 | 2.353 | 3.182 | 4.541 | 5.841 | 12.941 |
| 4 | 1.533 | 2.132 | 2.776 | 3.747 | 4.604 | 8.610 |
| 5 | 1.476 | 2.015 | 2.571 | 3.365 | 4.032 | 6.859 |
| 6 | 1.440 | 1.943 | 2.447 | 3.143 | 3.707 | 5.959 |
| 7 | 1.415 | 1.895 | 2.365 | 2.998 | 3.499 | 5.405 |
| 8 | 1.397 | 1.860 | 2.306 | 2.896 | 3.355 | 5.041 |
| 9 | 1.383 | 1.833 | 2.262 | 2.821 | 3.250 | 4.781 |
| 10 | 1.372 | 1.812 | 2.228 | 2.764 | 3.169 | 4.587 |
| 11 | 1.363 | 1.796 | 2.201 | 2.718 | 3.106 | 4.437 |
| 12 | 1.356 | 1.782 | 2.179 | 2.681 | 3.055 | 4.318 |
| 13 | 1.350 | 1.771 | 2.160 | 2.650 | 3.012 | 4.221 |
| 14 | 1.345 | 1.761 | 2.145 | 2.624 | 2.977 | 4.140 |
| 15 | 1.341 | 1.753 | 2.131 | 2.602 | 2.947 | 4.073 |
| 16 | 1.337 | 1.746 | 2.120 | 2.583 | 2.921 | 4.015 |
| 17 | 1.333 | 1.740 | 2.110 | 2.567 | 2.898 | 3.965 |
| 18 | 1.330 | 1.734 | 2.101 | 2.552 | 2.878 | 3.922 |
| 19 | 1.328 | 1.729 | 2.093 | 2.539 | 2.861 | 2.883 |
| 20 | 1.325 | 1.725 | 2.086 | 2.528 | 2.845 | 3.850 |
| 21 | 1.323 | 1.721 | 2.080 | 2.518 | 2.831 | 3.819 |
| 22 | 1.321 | 1.717 | 2.074 | 2.508 | 2.819 | 3.792 |
| 23 | 1.319 | 1.714 | 2.069 | 2.500 | 2.807 | 3.767 |
| 24 | 1.318 | 1.711 | 2.064 | 2.492 | 2.797 | 3.745 |
| 25 | 1.316 | 1.708 | 2.060 | 2.485 | 2.787 | 3.725 |
| 26 | 1.315 | 1.706 | 2.056 | 2.479 | 2.779 | 3.707 |
| 27 | 1.314 | 1.703 | 2.052 | 2.473 | 2.771 | 3.690 |
| 28 | 1.313 | 1.701 | 2.048 | 2.467 | 2.763 | 3.674 |
| 29 | 1.311 | 1.699 | 2.045 | 2.462 | 2.756 | 3.659 |
| 30 | 1.310 | 1.697 | 2.042 | 2.457 | 2.750 | 3.646 |
| 40 | 1.303 | 1.684 | 2.021 | 2.423 | 2.704 | 3.551 |
| 60 | 1.296 | 1.671 | 2.000 | 2.390 | 2.660 | 3.460 |
| 120 | 1.289 | 1.658 | 1.980 | 2.358 | 2.617 | 3.373 |
| ∞ | 1.282 | 1.645 | 1.960 | 2.326 | 2.576 | 3.291 |

Source: adapted from Table III of R.A. Fisher and F. Yates, Statistical Tables for Biological, Agricultural, and Medical Research, 6th edn. Edinburgh: Oliver and Boyd Ltd., 1963, with the kind permission of the publisher

Exhibit E.2 Critical values of $t$ for given probability levels.

| | Probability under $H_0$ that $\chi^2 \geq$ chi-square | | | | |
|---|---|---|---|---|---|
| d.f. | .10 | .05 | .02 | .01 | .001 |
| 1 | 2.71 | 3.84 | 5.41 | 6.64 | 10.83 |
| 2 | 4.60 | 5.99 | 7.82 | 9.21 | 13.82 |
| 3 | 6.25 | 7.82 | 9.84 | 11.34 | 16.27 |
| 4 | 7.78 | 9.49 | 11.67 | 13.28 | 18.46 |
| 5 | 9.24 | 11.07 | 13.39 | 15.09 | 20.52 |
| 6 | 10.64 | 12.59 | 15.03 | 16.81 | 22.46 |
| 7 | 12.02 | 14.07 | 16.62 | 18.48 | 24.32 |
| 8 | 13.36 | 15.51 | 18.17 | 20.09 | 26.12 |
| 9 | 14.68 | 16.92 | 19.68 | 21.67 | 27.88 |
| 10 | 15.99 | 18.31 | 21.16 | 23.21 | 29.59 |
| 11 | 17.28 | 19.68 | 22.62 | 24.72 | 31.62 |
| 12 | 18.55 | 21.03 | 24.05 | 26.22 | 32.91 |
| 13 | 19.81 | 22.36 | 25.47 | 27.69 | 34.53 |
| 14 | 21.06 | 23.68 | 26.87 | 29.14 | 36.12 |
| 15 | 22.31 | 25.00 | 28.26 | 30.58 | 37.70 |
| 16 | 23.54 | 26.30 | 29.63 | 32.00 | 39.29 |
| 17 | 24.77 | 27.59 | 31.00 | 33.41 | 40.75 |
| 18 | 25.99 | 28.87 | 32.35 | 34.80 | 42.31 |
| 19 | 27.20 | 30.14 | 33.69 | 36.19 | 43.82 |
| 20 | 28.41 | 31.41 | 35.02 | 37.57 | 45.32 |
| 21 | 29.62 | 32.67 | 36.34 | 38.93 | 46.80 |
| 22 | 30.81 | 33.92 | 37.66 | 40.29 | 48.27 |
| 23 | 32.01 | 35.17 | 38.97 | 41.64 | 49.73 |
| 24 | 33.20 | 36.42 | 40.27 | 42.98 | 51.18 |
| 25 | 34.38 | 37.65 | 41.57 | 44.31 | 52.62 |
| 26 | 35.56 | 38.88 | 42.86 | 45.64 | 54.05 |
| 27 | 36.74 | 40.11 | 44.14 | 46.96 | 55.48 |
| 28 | 37.92 | 41.34 | 45.42 | 48.28 | 56.89 |
| 29 | 39.09 | 42.56 | 46.69 | 49.59 | 58.30 |
| 30 | 40.26 | 43.77 | 47.96 | 50.89 | 59.70 |

*Source*: adapted from Table IV of R.A. Fisher and F. Yates, *Statistical Tables for Biological, Agricultural, and Medical Research*, 6th edn. Edinburgh: Oliver and Boyd Ltd., 1963, with the kind permission of the publisher

*Exhibit E.3* Critical values of the chi-square distribution.

| | Level of significance for one-tailed test | | |
| --- | --- | --- | --- |
| $n$ | .025 | .01 | .005 |
| | Level of significance for two-tailed test | | |
| | .05 | .02 | .01 |
| 6 | 0 | – | – |
| 7 | 2 | 0 | – |
| 8 | 4 | 2 | 0 |
| 9 | 6 | 3 | 2 |
| 10 | 8 | 5 | 3 |
| 11 | 11 | 7 | 5 |
| 12 | 14 | 10 | 7 |
| 13 | 17 | 13 | 10 |
| 14 | 21 | 16 | 13 |
| 15 | 25 | 20 | 16 |
| 16 | 30 | 24 | 20 |
| 17 | 35 | 28 | 23 |
| 18 | 40 | 33 | 28 |
| 19 | 46 | 38 | 32 |
| 20 | 52 | 43 | 38 |
| 21 | 59 | 49 | 43 |
| 22 | 66 | 56 | 49 |
| 23 | 73 | 62 | 55 |
| 24 | 81 | 69 | 61 |
| 25 | 89 | 77 | 68 |

*Source*: adapted from Table 1 of F. Wilcoxon, *Some Rapid Approximate Statistical Procedures*. New York: American Cyanamid Company, 1949, p. 13, with the kind permission of the publisher

*Exhibit E.4* Critical values of $t$ in the Wilcoxon-matched pairs test.

| Sample size $n$ | Level of significance for D = maximum $\lvert F_o(X) - S_N(X) \rvert$ | | | | |
|---|---|---|---|---|---|
| | .20 | .15 | .10 | .05 | .01 |
| 1 | .900 | .925 | .950 | .975 | .995 |
| 2 | .684 | .726 | .776 | .842 | .929 |
| 3 | .565 | .597 | .642 | .708 | .828 |
| 4 | .494 | .525 | .564 | .624 | .733 |
| 5 | .446 | .474 | .510 | .565 | .669 |
| 6 | .410 | .436 | .470 | .521 | .618 |
| 7 | .381 | .405 | .438 | .486 | .577 |
| 8 | .358 | .381 | .411 | .457 | .543 |
| 9 | .339 | .360 | .388 | .432 | .514 |
| 10 | .322 | .342 | .368 | .410 | .490 |
| 11 | .307 | .326 | .352 | .391 | .468 |
| 12 | .295 | .313 | .338 | .375 | .450 |
| 13 | .284 | .302 | .325 | .361 | .433 |
| 14 | .274 | .292 | .314 | .349 | .418 |
| 15 | .266 | .283 | .304 | .338 | .404 |
| 16 | .258 | .274 | .295 | .328 | .392 |
| 17 | .250 | .266 | .286 | .318 | .381 |
| 18 | .244 | .259 | .278 | .309 | .371 |
| 19 | .237 | .252 | .272 | .301 | .263 |
| 20 | .231 | .246 | .264 | .294 | .356 |
| 25 | .21 | .22 | .24 | .27 | .32 |
| 30 | .19 | .20 | .22 | .24 | .29 |
| 35 | .18 | .19 | .21 | .23 | .27 |
| Over 35 | $\dfrac{1.07}{\sqrt{N}}$ | $\dfrac{1.14}{\sqrt{N}}$ | $\dfrac{1.22}{\sqrt{N}}$ | $\dfrac{1.36}{\sqrt{N}}$ | $\dfrac{1.63}{\sqrt{N}}$ |

*Source*: F.J. Massey, Jr., 'The Kolmogorov–Smirnov test for goodness of fit', *Journal of the American Statistical Association* 46, p. 70. Adapted with the kind permission of the publisher

*Exhibit E.5* Critical values of $d$ in the Kolmogorov–Smirnov one-sample test.

| | One-tailed test* | | Two-tailed test** | |
|---|---|---|---|---|
| $n$ | $\alpha = .05$ | $\alpha = .01$ | $\alpha = .05$ | $\alpha = .01$ |
| 3 | 3 | – | – | – |
| 4 | 4 | – | 4 | – |
| 5 | 4 | 5 | 5 | 5 |
| 6 | 5 | 6 | 5 | 6 |
| 7 | 5 | 6 | 6 | 6 |
| 8 | 5 | 6 | 6 | 7 |
| 9 | 6 | 7 | 6 | 7 |
| 10 | 6 | 7 | 7 | 8 |
| 11 | 6 | 8 | 7 | 8 |
| 12 | 6 | 8 | 7 | 8 |
| 13 | 7 | 8 | 7 | 9 |
| 14 | 7 | 8 | 8 | 9 |
| 15 | 7 | 9 | 8 | 9 |
| 16 | 7 | 9 | 8 | 10 |
| 17 | 8 | 9 | 8 | 10 |
| 18 | 8 | 10 | 9 | 10 |
| 19 | 8 | 10 | 9 | 10 |
| 20 | 8 | 10 | 9 | 11 |
| 21 | 8 | 10 | 9 | 11 |
| 22 | 9 | 11 | 9 | 11 |
| 23 | 9 | 11 | 10 | 11 |
| 24 | 9 | 11 | 10 | 12 |
| 25 | 9 | 11 | 10 | 12 |
| 26 | 9 | 11 | 10 | 12 |
| 27 | 9 | 12 | 10 | 12 |
| 28 | 10 | 12 | 11 | 13 |
| 29 | 10 | 12 | 11 | 13 |
| 30 | 10 | 12 | 11 | 13 |
| 35 | 11 | 13 | 12 | |
| 40 | 11 | 14 | 13 | |

*Source*: *abridged from I.A. Goodman, 'Kolmogorov-Smirnov tests for psychological research,' *Psychological Bulletin* 51 (1951), p. 167, copyright (1951) by the American Psychological Association. Reprinted with the kind permission of the publisher

**Derived from Table 1 of F.J. Massey, Jr., 'The distribution of the maximum deviation between two sample cumulative step functions', *Annals of Mathematical Statistics* 23 (1951), pp. 126–27, with the kind permission of the publisher.

*Exhibit E.6* Critical values of $K_D$ in the Kolmogorov–Smirnov two-samples test (small samples).

| Level of significance | Value of $D$ so large as to call for rejection of $H_0$ at the indicated level of significance, where $D = $ maximum $\lvert Sn_1(X) - S_2(X)\rvert$ | |
|---|---|---|
| .10 | 1.22 | $\sqrt{\dfrac{n_1 + n_2}{n_1 n_2}}$ |
| .05 | 1.36 | $\sqrt{\dfrac{n_1 + n_2}{n_1 n_2}}$ |
| .025 | 1.48 | $\sqrt{\dfrac{n_1 + n_2}{n_1 n_2}}$ |
| .01 | 1.63 | $\sqrt{\dfrac{n_1 + n_2}{n_1 n_2}}$ |
| .005 | 1.75 | $\sqrt{\dfrac{n_1 + n_2}{n_1 n_2}}$ |
| .001 | 1.95 | $\sqrt{\dfrac{n_1 + n_2}{n_1 n_2}}$ |

*Source*: adapted from N. Smirnov, 'Table for Estimating the goodness of fit of empirical distribution,' *Annals of Mathematical Statistics* 18 (1948), pp. 280–81, with the kind permission of the publisher

**Exhibit E.7**  Critical values of $D$ in the Kolmogorov–Smirnov two-samples test for large samples (two-tailed).

**Critical values for one-tailed test at α = .025 or a two-tailed test at α = .05**

| $n_1$\$n_2$ | 9 | 10 | 11 | 12 | 13 | 14 | 15 | 16 | 17 | 18 | 19 | 20 |
|---|---|---|---|---|---|---|---|---|---|---|---|---|
| 1 | | | | | | | | | | | | |
| 2 | 0 | 0 | 0 | 1 | 1 | 1 | 1 | 1 | 2 | 2 | 2 | 2 |
| 3 | 2 | 3 | 3 | 4 | 4 | 5 | 5 | 6 | 6 | 7 | 7 | 8 |
| 4 | 4 | 5 | 6 | 7 | 8 | 9 | 10 | 11 | 11 | 12 | 13 | 13 |
| 5 | 7 | 8 | 9 | 11 | 12 | 13 | 14 | 15 | 17 | 18 | 19 | 20 |
| 6 | 10 | 11 | 13 | 14 | 16 | 17 | 19 | 21 | 22 | 24 | 25 | 27 |
| 7 | 12 | 14 | 16 | 18 | 20 | 22 | 24 | 26 | 28 | 30 | 32 | 34 |
| 8 | 15 | 17 | 19 | 22 | 24 | 26 | 29 | 31 | 34 | 36 | 38 | 41 |
| 9 | 17 | 20 | 23 | 26 | 28 | 31 | 34 | 37 | 39 | 42 | 45 | 48 |
| 10 | 20 | 23 | 26 | 29 | 33 | 36 | 39 | 42 | 45 | 48 | 52 | 55 |
| 11 | 23 | 26 | 30 | 33 | 37 | 40 | 44 | 47 | 51 | 55 | 58 | 62 |
| 12 | 26 | 29 | 33 | 37 | 41 | 45 | 49 | 53 | 57 | 61 | 66 | 69 |
| 13 | 28 | 33 | 37 | 41 | 45 | 50 | 54 | 59 | 63 | 67 | 72 | 76 |
| 14 | 31 | 36 | 40 | 45 | 50 | 55 | 59 | 64 | 67 | 74 | 78 | 83 |
| 15 | 34 | 39 | 44 | 49 | 54 | 59 | 64 | 70 | 75 | 80 | 85 | 90 |
| 16 | 37 | 42 | 47 | 53 | 59 | 64 | 70 | 75 | 81 | 86 | 92 | 98 |
| 17 | 39 | 45 | 51 | 57 | 63 | 67 | 75 | 81 | 87 | 93 | 99 | 105 |
| 18 | 42 | 48 | 55 | 61 | 67 | 74 | 80 | 86 | 93 | 99 | 106 | 112 |
| 19 | 45 | 52 | 58 | 65 | 72 | 78 | 85 | 92 | 99 | 106 | 113 | 119 |
| 20 | 48 | 55 | 62 | 69 | 76 | 83 | 90 | 98 | 105 | 112 | 119 | 127 |

**Critical values for one-tailed test at α = .05 or a two-tailed test at α = .10**

| $n_1$\$n_2$ | 9 | 10 | 11 | 12 | 13 | 14 | 15 | 16 | 17 | 18 | 19 | 20 |
|---|---|---|---|---|---|---|---|---|---|---|---|---|
| 1 | | | | | | | | | | | 0 | 0 |
| 2 | 1 | 1 | 1 | 2 | 2 | 2 | 3 | 3 | 3 | 4 | 4 | 4 |
| 3 | 3 | 4 | 5 | 5 | 6 | 7 | 7 | 8 | 9 | 9 | 10 | 11 |
| 4 | 6 | 7 | 8 | 9 | 10 | 11 | 12 | 14 | 15 | 16 | 17 | 18 |
| 5 | 9 | 11 | 12 | 13 | 15 | 16 | 18 | 19 | 20 | 22 | 23 | 25 |
| 6 | 12 | 14 | 16 | 17 | 19 | 21 | 23 | 25 | 26 | 28 | 30 | 32 |
| 7 | 15 | 17 | 19 | 21 | 24 | 26 | 28 | 30 | 33 | 35 | 37 | 39 |
| 8 | 18 | 20 | 23 | 26 | 28 | 31 | 33 | 36 | 39 | 41 | 44 | 47 |
| 9 | 21 | 24 | 27 | 30 | 33 | 36 | 39 | 42 | 45 | 48 | 51 | 54 |
| 10 | 24 | 27 | 31 | 34 | 37 | 41 | 44 | 48 | 51 | 55 | 58 | 62 |
| 11 | 27 | 31 | 34 | 38 | 42 | 46 | 50 | 54 | 57 | 61 | 65 | 69 |
| 12 | 30 | 34 | 38 | 42 | 47 | 51 | 55 | 60 | 64 | 68 | 72 | 77 |
| 13 | 33 | 37 | 42 | 47 | 51 | 56 | 61 | 65 | 70 | 75 | 80 | 84 |
| 14 | 36 | 41 | 46 | 51 | 56 | 61 | 66 | 71 | 77 | 82 | 87 | 92 |
| 15 | 39 | 44 | 50 | 55 | 61 | 66 | 72 | 77 | 83 | 88 | 94 | 100 |
| 16 | 42 | 48 | 54 | 60 | 65 | 71 | 77 | 83 | 89 | 95 | 101 | 107 |
| 17 | 45 | 51 | 57 | 64 | 70 | 77 | 83 | 89 | 96 | 102 | 109 | 115 |
| 18 | 48 | 55 | 61 | 68 | 75 | 82 | 88 | 95 | 102 | 109 | 116 | 223 |
| 19 | 51 | 58 | 65 | 72 | 80 | 87 | 94 | 101 | 109 | 116 | 123 | 130 |
| 20 | 54 | 62 | 69 | 77 | 84 | 92 | 100 | 107 | 115 | 123 | 130 | 138 |

*Source*: abridged from D. Auble, 'Extended tables from the Mann-Whitney Statistic', *Bulletin of the Institute of Educational Research at Indiana University* 1, no. 2. Reprinted with kind permission of the publisher. For tables for other size samples consult this source

*Exhibit E.8* Partial table of critical values of $U$ in the Mann–Whitney test.

Degrees of freedom for denominator

| $n_2$ | 1 | 2 | 3 | 4 | 5 | 6 | 7 | 8 | 9 | 10 | 12 | 15 | 20 | 24 | 30 | 40 | 60 | 120 | $\infty$ |
|---|---|---|---|---|---|---|---|---|---|---|---|---|---|---|---|---|---|---|---|
| 1 | 161.4 | 199.5 | 215.7 | 224.6 | 230.2 | 234.0 | 236.8 | 238.9 | 240.5 | 241.9 | 243.9 | 245.9 | 248.0 | 249.1 | 250.1 | 251.1 | 252.2 | 253.3 | 243.3 |
| 2 | 18.51 | 19.00 | 19.16 | 19.25 | 19.30 | 19.33 | 19.35 | 19.37 | 19.38 | 19.40 | 19.41 | 19.43 | 19.45 | 19.45 | 19.46 | 19.47 | 19.48 | 19.49 | 19.50 |
| 3 | 10.13 | 9.55 | 9.28 | 9.12 | 9.01 | 8.94 | 8.89 | 8.85 | 8.81 | 8.79 | 8.74 | 8.70 | 8.66 | 8.64 | 8.62 | 8.59 | 8.57 | 8.55 | 8.53 |
| 4 | 7.71 | 6.94 | 6.59 | 6.39 | 6.26 | 6.16 | 6.09 | 6.04 | 6.00 | 5.96 | 5.91 | 5.86 | 5.80 | 5.77 | 5.75 | 5.72 | 5.69 | 5.66 | 5.63 |
| 5 | 6.61 | 5.79 | 5.41 | 5.19 | 5.05 | 4.95 | 4.88 | 4.82 | 4.77 | 4.74 | 4.68 | 4.62 | 4.56 | 4.53 | 4.50 | 4.46 | 4.43 | 4.40 | 4.36 |
| 6 | 5.99 | 5.14 | 5.76 | 4.53 | 4.39 | 4.28 | 4.21 | 4.15 | 4.10 | 4.06 | 4.00 | 3.94 | 3.87 | 3.84 | 3.81 | 3.77 | 3.74 | 3.70 | 3.67 |
| 7 | 5.59 | 4.74 | 4.35 | 4.12 | 3.97 | 3.87 | 3.79 | 3.73 | 3.68 | 3.64 | 3.57 | 3.51 | 3.44 | 3.41 | 3.38 | 3.34 | 3.30 | 3.27 | 3.23 |
| 8 | 5.32 | 4.46 | 4.07 | 3.84 | 3.69 | 3.58 | 3.50 | 3.44 | 3.39 | 3.35 | 3.28 | 3.22 | 3.15 | 3.12 | 3.08 | 3.04 | 3.01 | 2.97 | 2.93 |
| 9 | 5.12 | 4.26 | 3.86 | 3.63 | 3.48 | 3.37 | 3.29 | 3.23 | 3.18 | 3.14 | 3.07 | 3.01 | 2.94 | 2.90 | 2.86 | 2.83 | 2.79 | 2.75 | 2.71 |
| 10 | 4.96 | 4.10 | 3.71 | 3.48 | 3.33 | 3.22 | 3.14 | 3.07 | 3.02 | 2.98 | 2.91 | 2.85 | 2.77 | 2.74 | 2.70 | 2.66 | 2.62 | 2.58 | 2.54 |
| 11 | 4.84 | 3.98 | 3.59 | 3.36 | 3.20 | 3.09 | 3.01 | 2.95 | 2.90 | 2.85 | 2.79 | 2.72 | 2.65 | 2.61 | 2.57 | 2.53 | 2.49 | 2.45 | 2.40 |
| 12 | 4.75 | 3.89 | 3.49 | 3.26 | 3.11 | 3.00 | 2.91 | 2.85 | 2.80 | 2.75 | 2.69 | 2.62 | 2.54 | 2.51 | 2.47 | 2.43 | 2.38 | 2.34 | 2.30 |
| 13 | 4.67 | 3.81 | 3.41 | 3.18 | 3.03 | 2.92 | 2.83 | 2.77 | 2.71 | 2.67 | 2.60 | 2.53 | 2.46 | 2.42 | 2.38 | 2.34 | 2.30 | 2.25 | 2.21 |
| 14 | 4.60 | 3.74 | 3.34 | 3.11 | 2.96 | 2.85 | 2.76 | 2.70 | 2.65 | 2.60 | 2.53 | 2.46 | 2.39 | 2.35 | 2.31 | 2.27 | 2.22 | 2.18 | 2.13 |
| 15 | 4.54 | 3.68 | 3.29 | 3.06 | 2.90 | 2.79 | 2.71 | 2.64 | 2.59 | 2.54 | 2.48 | 2.40 | 2.33 | 2.29 | 2.25 | 2.20 | 2.16 | 2.11 | 2.07 |
| 16 | 4.49 | 3.63 | 3.24 | 3.01 | 2.85 | 2.74 | 266 | 2.59 | 2.54 | 2.49 | 2.42 | 2.35 | 2.28 | 2.24 | 2.19 | 2.15 | 2.11 | 2.06 | 2.01 |
| 17 | 4.45 | 3.59 | 3.20 | 2.96 | 2.81 | 2.70 | 2.61 | 2.55 | 2.49 | 2.45 | 2.38 | 2.31 | 2.23 | 2.19 | 2.15 | 2.10 | 2.06 | 2.01 | 1.96 |
| 18 | 4.41 | 3.35 | 3.16 | 2.93 | 2.77 | 2.66 | 2.58 | 2.51 | 2.46 | 2.41 | 2.34 | 2.27 | 2.19 | 2.15 | 2.11 | 2.06 | 2.02 | 1.97 | 1.92 |
| 19 | 4.38 | 3.52 | 3.13 | 2.90 | 2.74 | 26.3 | 2.54 | 2.48 | 2.42 | 2.38 | 2.31 | 2.23 | 2.16 | 2.11 | 2.07 | 2.03 | 1.98 | 1.93 | 1.88 |
| 20 | 4.35 | 3.49 | 3.10 | 2.87 | 2.71 | 2.60 | 2.51 | 2.45 | 2.39 | 2.35 | 2.28 | 2.20 | 2.12 | 2.08 | 2.04 | 1.99 | 1.95 | 1.90 | 1.84 |
| 21 | 4.32 | 3.47 | 3.07 | 2.84 | 2.68 | 2.57 | 2.49 | 2.42 | 2.37 | 2.32 | 2.25 | 2.18 | 2.10 | 2.05 | 2.01 | 1.96 | 1.92 | 1.87 | 1.81 |

0.5

F

0

| $n_2$ | 1 | 2 | 3 | 4 | 5 | 6 | 7 | 8 | 9 | 10 | 12 | 15 | 20 | 24 | 30 | 40 | 60 | 120 | ∞ |
|---|---|---|---|---|---|---|---|---|---|---|---|---|---|---|---|---|---|---|---|
| 22 | 4.30 | 3.44 | 3.05 | 2.82 | 2.66 | 2.55 | 2.46 | 2.40 | 2.34 | 2.30 | 2.23 | 2.15 | 2.07 | 2.03 | 1.98 | 1.94 | 1.89 | 1.84 | 1.78 |
| 23 | 4.28 | 3.42 | 3.03 | 2.80 | 2.64 | 2.53 | 2.44 | 2.37 | 2.32 | 2.27 | 2.20 | 2.13 | 2.05 | 2.01 | 1.96 | 1.91 | 1.86 | 1.81 | 1.76 |
| 24 | 4.26 | 3.40 | 3.01 | 2.78 | 2.62 | 2.51 | 2.42 | 2.36 | 2.30 | 2.25 | 2.18 | 2.11 | 2.03 | 1.98 | 1.94 | 1.89 | 1.84 | 1.79 | 1.73 |
| 25 | 4.24 | 3.39 | 2.99 | 2.76 | 2.60 | 2.49 | 2.40 | 2.34 | 2.28 | 2.24 | 2.16 | 2.09 | 2.01 | 1.96 | 1.92 | 1.87 | 1.82 | 1.77 | 1.71 |
| 26 | 4.23 | 3.37 | 2.98 | 2.74 | 2.59 | 2.47 | 2.39 | 2.32 | 2.27 | 2.22 | 2.15 | 2.07 | 1.99 | 1.95 | 1.90 | 1.85 | 1.80 | 1.75 | 1.69 |
| 27 | 4.21 | 3.35 | 2.96 | 2.73 | 2.57 | 2.46 | 2.37 | 2.31 | 2.25 | 2.20 | 2.13 | 2.06 | 1.97 | 1.93 | 1.88 | 1.84 | 1.79 | 1.73 | 1.67 |
| 28 | 4.20 | 3.34 | 2.95 | 2.71 | 2.56 | 2.45 | 2.36 | 2.29 | 2.24 | 2.19 | 2.12 | 2.04 | 1.96 | 1.91 | 1.87 | 1.82 | 1.77 | 1.71 | 1.65 |
| 29 | 4.18 | 3.33 | 2.93 | 2.70 | 2.55 | 2.43 | 2.35 | 2.28 | 2.22 | 2.18 | 2.10 | 2.03 | 1.94 | 1.90 | 1.85 | 1.81 | 1.75 | 1.70 | 1.64 |
| 30 | 4.17 | 3.32 | 2.92 | 2.69 | 2.53 | 2.42 | 2.33 | 2.27 | 2.21 | 2.16 | 2.09 | 2.01 | 1.93 | 1.89 | 1.84 | 1.79 | 1.74 | 1.68 | 1.62 |
| 40 | 4.08 | 3.23 | 2.84 | 2.61 | 2.45 | 2.34 | 2.25 | 2.18 | 2.12 | 2.08 | 2.00 | 1.92 | 1.84 | 1.79 | 1.74 | 1.69 | 1.64 | 1.58 | 1.51 |
| 60 | 4.00 | 3.15 | 2.76 | 2.53 | 2.37 | 2.25 | 2.17 | 2.10 | 2.04 | 1.99 | 1.92 | 1.84 | 1.75 | 1.70 | 1.65 | 1.59 | 1.53 | 1.47 | 1.39 |
| 120 | 3.92 | 3.07 | 2.68 | 2.45 | 2.29 | 2.17 | 2.09 | 2.02 | 1.96 | 1.91 | 1.83 | 1.75 | 1.66 | 1.61 | 1.55 | 1.50 | 1.43 | 1.35 | 1.25 |
| ∞ | 3.84 | 3.00 | 2.60 | 2.37 | 2.21 | 2.10 | 2.01 | 1.94 | 1.88 | 1.83 | 1.75 | 1.67 | 1.57 | 1.52 | 1.46 | 1.39 | 1.32 | 1.22 | 1.00 |

Source: reprinted by permission from *Statistical Methods* by George W. Snedecor and William G. Cochran, 6th edn., © 1967 by Iowa State University Press, Ames, Iowa

**Exhibit E.9** Critical values of the $F$ distribution for $\alpha = .05$.

| | | | | | | | | | |
|---|---|---|---|---|---|---|---|---|---|
| 97446 | 30328 | 05262 | 77371 | 13523 | 62057 | 44349 | 85884 | 94555 | 23288 |
| 15453 | 75591 | 60540 | 77137 | 09485 | 27632 | 05477 | 99154 | 78720 | 10323 |
| 69995 | 77086 | 55217 | 53721 | 85713 | 27854 | 41981 | 88981 | 90041 | 20878 |
| 69726 | 58696 | 27272 | 38148 | 52521 | 73807 | 29685 | 49152 | 20309 | 58734 |
| 23604 | 31948 | 16926 | 26360 | 76957 | 99925 | 86045 | 11617 | 32777 | 38670 |
| 13640 | 17233 | 58650 | 47819 | 24935 | 28670 | 33415 | 77202 | 92492 | 40290 |
| 90779 | 09199 | 51169 | 94892 | 34271 | 22068 | 13923 | 53535 | 56358 | 50258 |
| 71068 | 19459 | 32339 | 10124 | 13012 | 79706 | 07611 | 52600 | 83088 | 26829 |
| 55019 | 79001 | 34442 | 16335 | 06428 | 52873 | 65316 | 01480 | 72204 | 39494 |
| 20879 | 50235 | 17389 | 25260 | 34039 | 99967 | 48044 | 05067 | 69284 | 53867 |
| 00380 | 11595 | 49372 | 95214 | 98529 | 46593 | 77046 | 27176 | 39668 | 20566 |
| 68142 | 40800 | 20527 | 79212 | 14166 | 84948 | 11748 | 69540 | 84288 | 37211 |
| 42667 | 89566 | 20440 | 57230 | 35356 | 01884 | 79921 | 94772 | 29882 | 24695 |
| 07756 | 78430 | 45576 | 86596 | 56720 | 65529 | 44211 | 18447 | 53921 | 92722 |
| 45221 | 31130 | 44312 | 63534 | 47741 | 02465 | 50629 | 94983 | 05984 | 88375 |
| 20140 | 77481 | 61686 | 82836 | 41058 | 41331 | 04290 | 61212 | 60294 | 95954 |
| 54922 | 25436 | 33804 | 51907 | 73223 | 66423 | 68706 | 36589 | 45267 | 35327 |
| 48340 | 30832 | 72209 | 07644 | 52747 | 40751 | 06808 | 85349 | 18005 | 52323 |
| 23603 | 84387 | 20416 | 88084 | 33103 | 41511 | 59391 | 71600 | 35091 | 52722 |
| 12548 | 01033 | 22974 | 59596 | 92087 | 02116 | 63524 | 00627 | 41778 | 24392 |
| 15251 | 87584 | 12942 | 03771 | 91413 | 75652 | 19468 | 83889 | 98531 | 91529 |
| 65548 | 59670 | 57355 | 18874 | 63601 | 55111 | 07278 | 32560 | 40028 | 36079 |
| 48488 | 76170 | 46282 | 76427 | 41693 | 04506 | 80979 | 26654 | 62159 | 83017 |
| 02862 | 15665 | 62159 | 15159 | 69576 | 20328 | 68873 | 28152 | 66087 | 39405 |
| 67929 | 06754 | 45842 | 66365 | 80848 | 15262 | 55144 | 37816 | 08421 | 30071 |
| 73237 | 07607 | 31615 | 04892 | 50989 | 87347 | 14393 | 21165 | 68169 | 70788 |
| 13788 | 20327 | 07960 | 95917 | 75112 | 01398 | 26381 | 41377 | 33549 | 19754 |
| 43877 | 66485 | 40825 | 45923 | 74410 | 69693 | 76959 | 70973 | 26343 | 63781 |
| 14047 | 08369 | 56414 | 78533 | 76378 | 44204 | 71493 | 68861 | 31042 | 81873 |
| 88383 | 46755 | 51342 | 13505 | 55324 | 52950 | 22244 | 28028 | 73486 | 98797 |
| 29567 | 16379 | 41994 | 65947 | 58926 | 50953 | 09388 | 00405 | 29874 | 44954 |
| 20508 | 60995 | 41539 | 26396 | 99825 | 25652 | 28089 | 57224 | 35222 | 58922 |
| 64178 | 76768 | 75747 | 32854 | 32893 | 61152 | 58565 | 33128 | 33354 | 16056 |
| 26373 | 51147 | 90362 | 93309 | 13175 | 66385 | 57822 | 31138 | 12893 | 68607 |
| 10083 | 47656 | 59241 | 73630 | 99200 | 94672 | 59785 | 95449 | 99279 | 25488 |
| 11683 | 14347 | 04369 | 98719 | 75005 | 43633 | 24125 | 30532 | 54830 | 95387 |
| 56548 | 76293 | 50904 | 88579 | 24621 | 94291 | 56881 | 35062 | 48765 | 22078 |
| 35292 | 47291 | 82610 | 27777 | 43965 | 31802 | 98444 | 88929 | 54383 | 93141 |
| 51329 | 87645 | 51623 | 08971 | 50704 | 82395 | 33916 | 95859 | 99788 | 97885 |
| 51860 | 19180 | 39324 | 68483 | 78650 | 74750 | 64893 | 58042 | 82878 | 20619 |
| 23886 | 01257 | 07945 | 71175 | 31243 | 87167 | 42829 | 44601 | 08769 | 26417 |
| 80028 | 82310 | 43989 | 09242 | 15056 | 48250 | 04529 | 96941 | 48190 | 69644 |
| 83946 | 46858 | 09164 | 18858 | 12672 | 55190 | 02820 | 45861 | 29104 | 75386 |
| 00000 | 41586 | 25972 | 25356 | 54260 | 95691 | 99431 | 89903 | 22306 | 43863 |
| 90615 | 12848 | 23376 | 29458 | 48239 | 37628 | 59265 | 50152 | 30340 | 40713 |
| 42003 | 10738 | 55835 | 48218 | 23204 | 19188 | 13556 | 06610 | 77667 | 88068 |
| 86135 | 26174 | 07834 | 17007 | 97938 | 96728 | 15689 | 77544 | 89186 | 41252 |
| 54436 | 10828 | 41212 | 19836 | 89476 | 53685 | 28085 | 22878 | 71868 | 35048 |
| 14545 | 72034 | 32131 | 38783 | 58588 | 47499 | 50945 | 97045 | 42357 | 53536 |
| 43925 | 49879 | 13339 | 78773 | 95626 | 67119 | 93023 | 96832 | 09757 | 98545 |

Source: The Rand Corporation, *A Million Random Digits with 100,000 Normal Deviates*. Glencoe, IL: Free Press, 1955, p. 225

**Exhibit E.10** Random numbers.

# Index